Charlesworth & Morse Company Law

AUSTRALIA
The Law Book Company
Sydney

CANADA
The Carswell Company
Toronto, Ontario

INDIA
N.M. Tripathi Private Ltd.
Bombay

Eastern Law House (Private) Ltd.
Calcutta

M.P.P. House
Bangalore

Universal Book Traders
Delhi

ISRAEL
Steimatzky's Agency Ltd.
Tel Aviv

PAKISTAN
Pakistan Law House
Karachi

Charlesworth & Morse
Company Law

FOURTEENTH EDITION

by

GEOFFREY MORSE, LL.B.

Barrister, Herbert Smith Professor of Company Law at the University of Nottingham

SCOTTISH EDITOR

ENID A. MARSHALL, M.A., LL.B., Ph.D.

Solicitor, Reader in Business Law at the University of Stirling

ACCOUNTING EDITOR

RICHARD MORRIS, B.A., M.SC., F.C.A.

Head of Department of Accounting at the University of Liverpool

INSOLVENCY EDITOR

LETITIA CRABB, LL.B., LL.M.

Solicitor, Lecturer in Law at University College of Wales, Aberystwyth

LONDON
SWEET & MAXWELL/STEVENS
1991

First Edition	(1932)	By His Honour Judge Charlesworth
Second Edition	(1938)	,, ,, ,, ,,
Third Edition	(1940)	,, ,, ,, ,,
Fourth Edition	(1946)	,, ,, ,, ,,
Second Impression	(1947)	
Third Impression	(1948)	
Fifth Edition	(1949)	,, ,, ,, ,,
Second Impression revised	(1950)	,, ,, ,, ,,
Sixth Edition	(1954)	,, ,, ,, ,,
Second Impression revised	(1956)	
Seventh Edition	(1960)	By T. E. Cain
Second Impression	(1962)	
Eighth Edition	(1965)	,, ,, ,, ,,
Ninth Edition	(1968)	,, ,, ,, ,,
Tenth Edition	(1972)	,, ,, ,, ,,
Eleventh Edition	(1977)	,, ,, ,, ,,
Second Impression	(1980)	
Twelfth Edition	(1983)	By Geoffrey Morse
Thirteenth Edition	(1987)	,, ,, ,,
Fourteenth Edition	(1991)	,, ,, ,,

Published by Sweet & Maxwell Limited,
South Quay Plaza,
183 Marsh Wall, London E14 9FT
Laserset by P.B. Computer Typesetting,
Pickering, N. Yorks
Printed in Great Britain by
Richard Clay (The Chaucer Press) Ltd.,
Bungay, Suffolk

A CIP catalogue record
for this book is available
from the British Library

PREFACE

In the four years which have elapsed since the previous edition of this book a further four EC company law harmonisation directives have been implemented by the United Kingdom. The third and sixth directives relating to the mergers and divisions of public companies were implemented by regulations which added one section and a Schedule to the Companies Act 1985. The seventh and eighth directives concerning group accounts and auditors, however, provided the impetus for a substantial piece of legislation, the Companies Act 1989. In addition to the changes required by those directives that Act made many other changes, both major and minor, across a wide spectrum of the existing law. These vary from the implementation of various reports: the Prentice Report on *ultra vires*; the Diamond Report (registration of company charges); and parts of the Jenkins Committee Report, first published in 1962, to the correction of minor drafting errors and inconvenient judicial decisions. Other areas of change include the introduction of totally new concepts such as elective resolutions for private companies and new forms of existing concepts such as the definition of holding and subsidiary companies. The one saving grace is that the vast majority of these new provisions have been worked into the 1985 Act so that an amended version of that Act will in general suffice for study purposes.

The company law harmonisation programme of the Community will ensure that this legislative reform is to continue. Other directives have been finalised and will require implementation in the near future, whilst others are in the Community's legislative machinery awaiting finalisation. Some may well be implemented by regulations but others will lead to further Companies Acts which will no doubt give the Department of Trade and Industry an opportunity for more wide-ranging reform. Company law is therefore destined to continue to be a moving target and any attempt at a text must inevitably be a snapshot of the law at a particular moment in time. The dynamics of the subject do, however, provide one of its fascinations.

In addition to legislative reform, the courts both north and south of the border have also been active. The Insolvency Act 1986 has now produced its own case-load, especially in the areas of administration orders and administrative receivers, both new concepts in 1986. So too has the related area of the disqualification of directors following an insolvent liquidation, requiring the Court of Appeal to issue guidelines in an attempt to provide a consistent approach by the judges of the Chancery Division. Petitions under section 459 of the 1985 Act also continue to provide the law reports with a substantial amount of material and there have been important developments in the areas of derivative actions and the provision by a company of financial assistance for the acquisition of its shares. Company meetings have not been immune either. The City Panel has also kept up its momentum with two revised versions of the City Code on Take-overs and Mergers in 1988 and 1990.

These and many other changes to the law have been incorporated into this edition. This has caused the book to expand slightly even though I have reluctantly cut out some introductory material and, less reluctantly, several pages rendered redundant by the abolition for third parties of problems posed by corporate capacity. The new regime for corporate transactions has thus reduced Chapter 3 but increased Chapter 6. There are, however, no structural changes to the book in this edition.

Although not all the 1989 Act provisions are in force at the time of writing, the book has been written on the assumption that they will be. In particular the provisions as to the registration of company charges will not come into effect in 1991. Charlesworth remains, hopefully, an accurate and comprehensive guide to the complexities of company law, a subject which continues to confound lawyers both developing and developed, and which is a necessary part of the knowledge required by many other professions.

There is one new member of the editorial team, Letitia Crabb of University College Aberystwyth, who has undertaken the revision of Chapters 24 to 29 on corporate insolvency. She has amply demonstrated those abilities of analysis and application which are the essentials of a legal writer and I am grateful for all the help and expertise she has given me in the preparation of this edition. The other two members of the team have been involved before. Professor Richard Morris of Liverpool University was persuaded, despite the additional pressures on him of being a head of department, to continue his responsibility for Chapters 20 to 22 on accounts, auditors and dividends. An accounting expert who can make his subject intelligible to this lawyer at least is a valuable asset. Finally Dr Enid Marshall continues to keep the book in line with developments in Scotland. This was no easy task; for example, one of the sections of the 1989 Act applicable only to Scotland was redrafted in 1990. The impact of Scottish decisions on company law in England continues to grow and in several cases the Scots solution in conflicting areas has been the one to prevail. To both of them I extend my admiration and thanks.

I would also like to thank my colleagues, Diane Birch and Michael Bridge, for their help and advice on aspects of criminal law (for Chapter 19 on insider dealing) and credit security (for Chapter 23 on debentures), respectively. My secretary Christine Mason typed the many manuscript changes without protest at their illegibility and my family endured the usual vicissitudes of an author with well-practised forbearance. To each of them I owe a debt far greater than I can imagine. This edition was finally prepared despite the attention of two new additions to the family circle in the shape of two Burmese kittens who seemed to have some difficulty in appreciating the conditions required to produce a legal text. The responsibility for all errors and omissions is, however, mine alone. The law is stated as known to me on January 1, 1991.

Storth, Cumbria
January 1991 GEOFFREY MORSE

CONTENTS

TABLE OF CASES

TABLE OF STATUTES

TABLE OF STATUTORY INSTRUMENTS

TABLE OF RULES OF THE SUPREME COURT

REFERENCES TO CITY CODE ON TAKEOVERS AND MERGERS

Chapter 1

NATURE OF REGISTERED COMPANIES

THIS book is mostly concerned with registered companies, whether public or private, limited by shares.[1] The term "registered company" means a company incorporated or formed by registration under the Companies Acts. The major Act is the Companies Act 1985, which consolidated the various Acts passed between 1948 and 1983. Although this Act has itself been amended, principally by the Companies Act 1989, and in one area reconsolidated,[2] it may still be regarded as the principal Act and in this book, unless it is otherwise stated or the context otherwise requires references to sections and Schedules are to those of the Companies Act 1985 and references to the "Act" are to the Companies Act 1985. This approach is facilitated by the fact that most of the changes made by the 1989 Act were effected by the substitution of sections into the 1985 Act.

The Act provides[3] that for the purpose of the registration of companies under the Act there shall be offices (Companies Registration Offices in England and Scotland) at such places as the Secretary of State (for Trade and Industry) thinks fit, and that he may appoint such registrars, assistant registrars, clerks and servants as he thinks necessary for the registration of companies and may make regulations with respect to their duties.

Section 1(1) enables two or more persons associated for any lawful purpose to form an incorporated company with or without limited liability, by complying with the requirements of the Act in respect of registration. As is explained later in this chapter, the requirements are that certain

[1] In general terms commercial companies.
[2] This is the area of insolvency and liquidation generally.
[3] s.704.

documents be delivered to the appropriate Registrar of Companies and certain fees paid. Under section 10, for example, a memorandum of association and, usually, articles of association must be delivered to the Registrar, who must retain and register them.

The rest of this chapter attempts first of all to give a simple answer to the question "what is a registered company?" and then to trace briefly the history of the registered company. After that there is a note on the current legislation applicable to companies in particular, including the ever increasing influence of the European Community. Finally, the following topics are dealt with: the procedure to obtain the registration of a company; the effect of the registration of a company—this is that the company is a corporation with a legal existence separate from that of its members, who usually have limited personal liability; the liability of a registered company, *i.e.* of this separate artificial legal person; the management of registered companies; a registered company's securities—these are the shares and debentures which it issues; registered companies and partnerships contrasted—a partnership is not a corporation and the partners do not have limited liability.

WHAT IS A REGISTERED COMPANY?

A registered company, *i.e.* a company incorporated by registration under the Companies Acts, is regarded by the law as a person, just as a human being, Mr. Smith or Mr. Jones, is a person. This artificial or juristic person can own land and other property, enter into contracts, sue and be sued, have a bank account in its own name, owe money to others and be a creditor of other people and other companies, and employ people to work for it. The company's money and property belong to the company and not to the members or shareholders, although the members or shareholders may be said to own the company. Similarly, the company's debts are the debts of the company and the shareholders cannot be compelled to pay them, although if, for example, the company is being wound up and its assets do not realise a sum sufficient to pay its debts, a shareholder whose liability is limited by shares is liable to contribute to the assets up to the amount, if any, unpaid on his shares. A company, of course, can only act through human agents, and those who manage its business are called directors. The directors are agents of the company and transact business, etc., on behalf of the company. They may authorise other agents to act on the company's behalf, *e.g.* the company secretary. The Company will be bound by any transaction entered into on its behalf if the agent is acting within his authority. The company is also liable for torts[4] and crimes committed by its servants and agents within the scope of their employment or authority. This concept of the company as a corporation, *i.e.* a person separate and distinct from the other persons who are its members and directors, is the fundamental principle of company law.

A company must have members, otherwise it would never exist at all, and in the case of a company with a share capital these members are called shareholders (or, if the shares have been converted into stock, stockholders). The shareholder's position with regard to the company itself and to his fellow shareholders is regulated by the Act and by the memorandum and the articles of association, and also by the principle that controlling shareholders, *i.e.* those with sufficient votes to pass a resolution in general meeting, must act bona fide for the benefit of the company as a whole. The memorandum and articles vary considerably among different companies, but in every case the shareholder's position is that of the owner of one or more shares in the company, which shares usually carry a right of voting at general meetings, and, if profits are made, he may receive dividends on his shares. His shares are something which he has bought—perhaps from the company, or perhaps from somebody else—and something which he can sell or give away, either in his lifetime or by his will. The general rule is that he cannot get his money back from the company so long as the company is in existence, because his position is not that of a person who has lent money to the company or has deposited his money as with a bank or a building society—it is that of the owner of property, namely, his shares, which can only be turned into money if a buyer can be found to pay for them. Shares may be fully paid or partly paid. When the shares are only partly paid the shareholder can be compelled to pay them up fully if

[4] Or, in Scots law, delicts.

called upon by the company or, if the company is being wound up and its debts exceed its assets, by the liquidator. In any event it is the general policy of the Act to see that the issued share capital is maintained intact, except for losses in the way of business, so that it may be available to satisfy the company's debts. Accordingly, while the company is a going concern the general rule is that no part of the paid-up capital may be returned to the shareholders without the consent of the court, or by following strict procedures intended to protect creditors.

A company may be formed to acquire and carry on an existing business, which may or may not belong to the promoters, or to start some new business. However, a company is commonly formed as a private company to acquire the promoters' business. In this case a price is put on the business and paid by the issue to the promoters of shares credited as fully or partly paid in the company. Most of the price will be left owing to the promoters so that if the company is later wound up they will rank for repayment of it as unsecured creditors, otherwise if they take the whole price in the form of shares credited as fully paid they will rank for repayment of capital after the unsecured creditors. If a company is formed to acquire a business which does not belong to the promoters they may provide the necessary funds for the company by taking shares in the company for cash.

A company can also raise money by borrowing.[5] Persons who lend money to a company may be issued with debentures to show that they have lent money and are entitled to interest on their loans. Unlike shareholders, they are not members of the company and they have no right to vote at general meetings. Creditors may take a charge over the company's property by way of security for repayment of their debt. Such charges must be registered with the Registrar of Companies.

Shares in, and debentures of, public companies are extensively bought as an investment by people who want to derive an income from their capital but who are unable, for reasons of inclination, business, age, health or lack of opportunity, to take any part in the management of the company. To protect investors from dishonest or incompetent people who form

[5] Money borrowed by a company is sometimes called "loan capital." It should not be confused with "share capital": Chap. 9.

companies in which the investors are likely to lose their money, disclosure of such things as the company's past financial record and the benefits of being a director, is required in the document on the strength of which the public is invited to subscribe for shares or debentures of the company. Provision is also made for a company's accounts and the balance sheet and profit and loss account to be audited every year by auditors appointed by the shareholders and for the balance sheet and the profit and loss account and certain other documents to be circulated to every shareholder and debenture holder. With the exception of small companies and unlimited companies a copy of the balance sheet and the other documents must also be lodged with the Registrar of Companies.

The directors of a company, who are usually appointed by the members at their annual general meeting, have wide powers to manage the company's business conferred upon them by the articles. The members cannot control the exercise of these powers, although they can, *e.g.* alter the articles. The directors owe certain duties of good faith and care to the company.

The Acts have increasingly required disclosure by companies, their directors and substantial shareholders of many financial and other particulars. Usually this will be to the Registrar who will keep the information on the company's file. Such information is then available to anyone who makes a search of that file and is seen as one of the prices of incorporation. There is no constructive notice of such information, however.

A registered company is capable of perpetual succession but it may become insolvent or it may decide to retire from business. In such a case it is wound up, *i.e.* it is put, or it goes, into liquidation, and a person, called a liquidator, is appointed to wind up its affairs. He sells the company's property and pays as much of its debts as he can do out of the proceeds of sale. If there is a surplus, he distributes it among the shareholders. When the liquidation is completed the company is dissolved and ceases to exist.

THE DEVELOPMENT OF MODERN COMPANY LAW

The modern commercial company, incorporated by registration under the Act, is the result of the fusion of two different legal principles. A registered company, like a statutory company or a chartered company, is a "corporation,"[6] *i.e.* in the eyes of the law it is a person, capable of perpetual succession and quite distinct from the natural persons who are its members at any given moment.[7] However, the expression "company" is not confined to a corporation but includes a partnership, which is not a corporation but, at least in the case of an English partnership,[8] is merely the relationship between the individual partners. The present-day registered company represents the fusion of the principle of incorporation with that of partnership.

At common law the Crown has always had the right of granting charters of incorporation.[9] Non-trading companies, such as the Law Society and the Institute of Chartered Accountants, are the kind of company now incorporated by charter but trading companies have in the past been formed in this way. The right was first used for creating commercial corporations at the end of the sixteenth and the beginning of the seventeenth centuries, when such companies as the Levant Company, the East India Company, the Hudson's Bay Company, and the notorious South Sea Company (afterwards incorporated by special Act of Parliament), were incorporated. As these corporations were legal entities quite distinct from their members, it followed that at common law the members were not liable for the debts of the corporation, and, indeed, the Crown had no power to incorporate persons so as to make them liable for the debts of the corporation.[10] In a partnership, on the other hand, the partners were always liable for all the debts of the firm and their liability was unlimited.

In England trading companies were originally regulated companies, that is, companies in which each member traded with his own stock subject to the rules of the company, but towards the end of the seventeenth century the joint-stock company emerged,[11] and this is the form of the company in common use today. In a joint-stock company, the company

[6] s.13(3), *post,* p. 24.
[7] *Salomon* v. *Salomon & Co. Ltd.* [1897] A.C. 22, *post,* p. 25.
[8] A Scottish partnership, although not a corporation, is a legal person distinct from the partners of whom it is composed: Partnership Act 1890, s.4(2).
[9] A chartered company is sometimes referred to as "a common law corporation."
[10] *Per* Lindley L.J. in *Elve* v. *Boyton* [1891] 1 Ch. 501 at p. 507 (C.A.).
[11] Holdsworth, *History of English Law,* Vol. 8, pp. 206–222.

trades as a single person with a stock which is jointly contributed by its members. Such companies could only be formed by special Act of Parliament or by charter but, as the advantages of the joint-stock form of trading became better known, these methods proved too expensive and dilatory to meet the growing commercial needs of the nation. Accordingly there grew up a new type of company based upon contract. This contract took the form of an elaborate deed of settlement containing provisions regulating the relations of the members among themselves and providing for the transfer of shares. A body formed in this way was only a partnership in the eyes of the law and the liability of the members was unlimited. This type of unincorporated company fell into disfavour with the legislature, largely owing to the activities of fraudulent promoters and unscrupulous share dealers, and in 1720 the Bubble Act was passed to deal with it. Unfortunately, that Act had the effect of suppressing unincorporated companies without satisfying the want which had given rise to their existence, so that "joint-stock" enterprises had to wait till the middle of the nineteenth century before incorporation "for any lawful purpose" could be obtained by the simple process of registration, and personal liability be limited by "one magic word."[12]

The origins of company law in Scotland were distinct from those in England, although regulated companies and joint-stock companies did exist from at least the later years of the seventeenth century. The common law of Scotland sanctioned formation of companies with transferable shares and under the management of directors, and recognised such companies as having a personality separate from that of their members.[13] In Scotland common law companies constituted under contracts of co-partnery corresponded to the English deed of settlement companies. The 1720 Bubble Act extended to Scotland but, because of the common law companies, probably had no legal effect there.[14]

[12] Carr, *Select Charters of Trading Companies,* Selden Society, Vol. 28, p. xx.

[13] The decision in *Stevenson & Co.* v. *Macnair and others* (1757) M. 14,560 and 14,667; 5 Brown's supp. 340 suggests that Scottish courts might even, under continental influence, have developed a principle of limited liability in relation to these companies.

[14] An Act of 1825 (6 Geo. 4 c. 131) mentioned with approval the practice which had prevailed in Scotland of forming joint-stock companies with transferable shares.

In 1825, by the Bubble Companies, etc., Act, the 1720 Bubble Act was repealed and the Crown was empowered in grants of future charters to provide that the members of the corporation should be personally liable for the debts of the corporation to such extent as the Crown should think proper. This was the beginning of "limited liability." By the Chartered Companies Act 1837 the Crown was empowered to grant letters patent, *i.e.* to grant the advantages of incorporation *without* granting a charter, to a body of persons associated together for trading purposes. The persons in question had to register a deed of partnership dividing the capital into shares and providing for transfers, and satisfy the other requirements of the Act; limited liability was then granted to them. The association to which the letters patent were granted did not become a body corporate and the grant of limited liability was an advantage to which they would otherwise not have been entitled.

By the Joint Stock Companies Registration, etc., Act 1844 provision was made in England for the incorporation of companies by registration without the necessity of obtaining a Royal Charter or a special Act of Parliament. The peculiarity of this statute was, however, that, instead of allowing the usual common law consequences of incorporation to follow, it proceeded on the lines of the Chartered Companies Act 1837 and merely gave a corporate existence to a body which it still evidently regarded as a partnership, because it imposed much the same liability on the members for the debts of the company as they would have had for the debts of a partnership. This Act also made it compulsory to register as companies all partnerships with more than 25[15] members. Liability limited by shares, *i.e.* where a member's liability is limited to the amount, if any, unpaid on his shares, was introduced in the case of registered companies by the Limited Liability Act 1855, and the Joint Stock Companies Act 1856 substituted two documents, the memorandum of association and articles of association, for the deed of settlement.

In Scotland the registered company was not introduced until the Act of 1856: neither the 1844 Act nor the 1855 Act applied to Scotland.

[15] The maximum number of members for a partnership is now 20, except in the case of certain professional firms: s.716 *post*, p. 36.

The Companies Act 1862 repealed and consolidated the previous Acts. It also established liability limited by guarantee and, in general, prohibited any alteration in the objects clause[16] of the memorandum of association. This prohibition remained until the Companies (Memorandum of Association) Act 1890 enabled the objects to be altered for some purposes with the leave of the court, after a special resolution[17] had been passed by the members in general meeting. The Companies Act 1867 contained a power to reduce share capital. The Directors' Liability Act 1890 introduced the principle of the liability of the directors to pay compensation to persons who have been induced to take shares on the strength of false statements in a prospectus. The Companies Act 1900 contained the first provisions relating to the contents of prospectuses, the compulsory audit of the company's accounts and the registration of charges with the Registrar. Modern company law was taking shape.

The Companies Act 1907 made provision for the private (as opposed to the public) company, *i.e.* a company which is prohibited from inviting the public to subscribe for its shares or debentures.[18] The Companies (Consolidation) Act 1908 consolidated the 1862 Act with the various Acts amending it, and this was followed by the Companies Act 1929. The Companies Act 1948, which came into operation on July 1, 1948, introduced the exempt private company, *i.e.* the "family" private company (as opposed to a private company which was, *e.g.*, a subsidiary of a public company) and called an exempt private company because it was the only kind of private company which was exempt from the necessity of making its balance sheet and profit and loss account public.[19]

The 1948 Act also made far-reaching changes in the law relating to company accounts. As the Cohen Report[20] (on which the 1948 Act was based) said, "The history of company legislation shows the increasing importance attached to publicity in connection with accounts. The Act of 1862 contained no

[16] Dealt with *post*, p. 71.
[17] *Post*, p. 72.
[18] *Post*, p. 45.
[19] This proved to be open to abuse and the exempt private company was abolished in 1967.
[20] (1945) Cmd. 6659, para. 96.

compulsory provisions with regard to audit or accounts, though Table A[21] to that Act did include certain clauses dealing with both matters. In 1879 provision was made for the audit of the accounts of banking companies, but it was not until 1900 that any such provision was made generally applicable. It was only on July 1, 1908, when the Companies Act 1907 came into force, that provision was made for including a statement in the form of a balance sheet in the annual return to the Registrar of Companies, and that provision exempted private companies from this requirement." The Companies Act 1929 required a balance sheet and a profit and loss account to be laid before the company every year, while the present Acts set out in great detail the contents of those accounts, with stringent provisions for their audit. The 1948 Act also for the first time required the auditor of a public or a private company to have a professional qualification.[22]

A number of the recommendations contained in the Jenkins Report[23] were given effect in the 1967 Act which amended the 1948 Act in a number of respects. The status of exempt private company was abolished—the definition of such a company in the 1948 Act was devised to save the small family business from disclosing its affairs to the public but many exempt private companies were not small in membership or in capital or in the extent of their undertakings. There were important new provisions in connection with a company's acounts. For example, a subsidiary company's accounts were required to disclose the name of its ultimate holding company, all accounts were required to give particulars of the directors' emoluments and of the salaries of employees earning more than £10,000 a year and the turnover for the year had to be stated. Other important new provisions were: (1) The provisions in connection with the directors' report. For example, the principal activities of the company and its subsidiaries during the year were required to be stated. The idea was to ensure that shareholders

[21] A model set of articles of association.

[22] For a fuller treatment of the history of company law, see Gower, *Modern Company Law* (4th ed. 1979), Chaps. 2 and 3.

[23] (1962) Cmnd. 1749. This is still the latest report covering the whole of company law. It has never been implemented in full or dealt with in any consistent manner although certain of its recommendations were implemented by the 1989 Act after a gap of 27 years.

were kept more fully informed of the company's activities. (2) The provisions penalising the dealing by directors, their spouses or children, in certain options to buy or sell shares or debentures of the company or associated companies quoted on a stock exchange, and for securing the disclosure of certain material facts concerning directors. (3) The provisions for securing the disclosure of a person's beneficial ownership of 10 per cent. or more of the shares in the company carrying unrestricted voting rights. Part III of the 1967 Act gave the Department of Trade wide powers to compel companies to produce books and papers for inspection. Many of these provisions have since been amended or replaced but the principles thereby established remain.

1972 saw the European Communities Act, section 9 of which related solely to company law since the U.K. was obliged on accession to comply with an existing EC Directive of 1968 on the harmonisation of company law.[24] This section's principal change was to modify the law relating to *ultra vires* and the problems of agency in relation to companies.[25] In Scotland, the Companies (Floating Charges and Receivers) (Scotland) Act 1972 modified the law of Scotland in relation to floating charges and made provision for the appointment of receivers.

The Companies Act 1976 enacted, amongst other things, some but not all of the clauses and schedules of the abortive Companies Bill 1973. The 1976 Act amended the law relating to the filing of company accounts and the keeping of accounting records. It provided for the disqualification of persons taking part in the management of companies if they were persistently in default in complying with the requirements to deliver documents to the Registrar. The Act also made new provision with respect to the qualifications, appointment, resignation and powers of auditors. It also required a statement of the first directors and secretary and of the intended situation of the registered office to be delivered to the Registrar on an application for registration of a company, and provided for the regulation of the names of oversea companies.

[24] The impact of EC Directives on company law is one of the modern features of the law. See p. 16, *post*.

[25] This worked along the lines of the Jenkins Committee recommendations in para. 42 of the Report. It proved to be defective in many ways, however, and was rewritten by the 1989 Act.

The Companies Act 1980 was inspired by an EC Directive of 1976 regulating the control of public companies. It provided for the first time a major distinction between public and private companies, including minimum financial requirements for the former. It also contained new provisions relating to the issuing of shares and the payment for them. Payment of dividends became the subject of statutory rules. Tighter restrictions on directors were imposed following the many "unacceptable faces of capitalism" which manifested themselves in the 1970s. Insider dealing,[26] one of the most obvious of those, became a criminal offence.

The 1981 Companies Act was likewise prompted by an EC Directive, this time of 1978, on company accounts. It provided a new format for accounts and for the public disclosure of them. In addition, however, new rules for company names, the purchase and redemption by a company of its own shares and for more stringent disclosure of shareholdings were included. Various other reforms were also appended. The technical nature of much of this recent legislation was so complex that mistakes were made. One particularly embarrassing one, the accidental prohibition of many employee share and pension trusts had to be corrected, in haste, by the Companies (Beneficial Interests) Act 1983.

The 1985 Consolidation and after

In 1981 proposals were made for a consolidation of the various Acts from 1948 onwards. There were two joint Reports of the Law Commission and the Law Commission for Scotland[27] which recommended many technical amendments to the existing law in order to assist consolidation. These amendments were effected by the Companies Acts (Pre-Consolidation Amendments) Order 1984[28] and the Companies Acts (Pre-Consolidation Amendments) (No. 2) Order 1984[29] which, by virtue of section 116 of the Companies Act 1981, only took effect on the consolidation itself coming into force. After consultation it was decided to produce a single main Act, the Companies Act 1985,

[26] See Chap. 19.
[27] (1983) Cmnd. 9114, (1984) Cmnd. 9272.
[28] S.I. 1984 No. 134.
[29] S.I. 1984 No. 1169.

with 747 sections and 25 Schedules (up to seven separate Acts had been canvassed) with three small satellite Acts. The 1981 Act provisions relating to the use of business names by all traders, including companies, were separated into the Business Names Act 1985, and those of the 1980 Act relating to insider dealing were also hived off into a separate Act, the Company Securities (Insider Dealing) Act 1985, since those rules apply to securities other than those belonging to companies. The fourth Act, the Companies Consolidation (Consequential Provisions) Act 1985, deals with transitional matters, savings provisions, repeals and consequential amendments to other Acts. In one area, however, it was not consequential: section 28 repealed, rather than consolidated, the existing provisions on cost book companies.

Whilst the consolidation was proceeding through Parliament the Companies (Accounts and Audit) Regulations 1984 and the Companies (Share Premium Account) Regulations 1984 were passed and had to be taken into account. The resulting consolidation, taking into account the various amendments referred to above and the need to harmonise legislative styles and phrases over a 30 year period, was by no means a "scissors and paste" consolidation. In the main it used short subsections and many of the pre-existing sections were divided. It was a triumph of draftsmanship in what was then the largest consolidation ever undertaken. By way of departure from previous practice, Tables A to F, the model forms of memorandum and articles etc., are now contained in separate regulations, the Companies (Tables A to F) Regulations 1985,[30] rather than in a schedule to the Act. Table A itself was redrafted for this purpose. The whole consolidation came into effect on July 1, 1985.

But it proved to be a short lived oasis of calm as a unified source of company legislation. Two more EC Directives, the third (on mergers)[31] and the sixth (on divisions),[32] were implemented by the Companies (Mergers and Divisions) Regulations 1987,[33] which added a new section (427A) and Schedule (15A) to the 1985 Act in the area of schemes of

[30] S.I. 1985 No. 805.
[31] Dir. 78/855/EEC, O.J. 1978 L295.
[32] Dir. 82/891/EEC O.J. 1982 L378.
[33] S.I. 1987 No. 1991.

arrangement.[34] More importantly, the Insolvency Act 1985, implementing some of the recommendations of the Cork Committee (Insolvency Law and Practice—Report of the Review Committee)[35] repealed many of the sections of the 1985 Act relating to liquidation and other aspects of corporate insolvency and replaced them with several new concepts, *e.g.* administration orders, as well as making several amendments to the rules governing insolvent liquidations. The Act was based on a White Paper,[36] itself based on the Cork Report. The resulting *pot pourri* of legislation on corporate liquidation and insolvency was itself consolidated into the Insolvency Act 1986, apart from the provisions relating to directors' disqualification which were consolidated into the Company Directors Disqualification Act 1986. The result is that some of the 1948 Act winding up provisions were consolidated in 1985, amended in that year and re-consolidated in 1986.

In addition the reform of the law governing the investment industry, prompted by a report by Professor Gower commissioned by the Department of Trade and Industry, was suggested by a White Paper, "Financial Services in the United Kingdom: A New Framework for Investor Protection"[37] and implemented by the Financial Services Act 1986. Whilst this Act is largely concerned with regulating the City and the investment industry generally it has had a double impact on company law. The first is indirect in that company securities are investments for this purpose and those who deal in them are, therefore, subject to the Act's new regulatory system. The second is direct. The Financial Services Act provided new rules for the public issue of shares whether listed on the Stock Exchange or otherwise. It also recast the provisions in the Companies Act 1985 relating to the compulsory acquisition of shares on a take-over and amended the rules relating to insider dealing in the Company Securities (Insider Dealing) Act 1985. The Financial Services Act thus repealed many of the 1985 Act sections relating to the public issue of shares and the Stock Exchange (Listing) Regulations 1984.[38] (The latter were passed to implement yet

[34] See Chap. 30, *post*.
[35] (1982) Cmnd. 8558.
[36] (1984) Cmnd. 9175.
[37] (1985) Cmnd. 9432.
[38] S.I. 1984 No. 716.

another set of EC directives, on listing particulars, the admission of securities to listing and the continuing disclosure of information by listed companies.[39] These lay alongside the 1985 Act provisions in a totally obscure manner and may usefully be consigned to history).

The most recent substantial changes have been made by the Companies Act 1989 which was occasioned by the need to implement two further EC directives, the seventh on group accounts (Dir.83/349/EEC, O.J. 1983 L 193) and the eighth on the qualification of auditors (Dr.84/253/EEC, O.J. 1984 L 126). Opportunity was taken, however, to amend and extend the 1985 Act provisions relating to investigations (together with investigations under the Insolvency Act 1986 and the Financial Services Act 1986), the registration of charges (following part of the Diamond Report, published early in 1989), the doctrine of *ultra vires* and application of the agency law to corporate transactions and in several other largely unrelated areas. The latter include the introduction of written and elective resolutions for private companies, a re-casting of the 1985 Act on the appointment and removal of auditors, new enabling provisions for the registrar to adapt his procedures to modern technology, the abolition of the need for a corporate seal, amendments to the share disclosure rules, changes to the consequences of a change of address of the registered office, directors' indemnity policies, annual returns, a new definition of holding and subsidary companies and the abolition of the constructive notice doctrine in relation to matters held on the company's file. The 1989 Act also implemented many other changes, some of which were recommended by the Jenkins Committee in 1962. It also made several amendments to other Acts, most importantly to the Financial Services Act 1986. Most of the 1989 Act changes were effected by adding, substituting or amending sections in the earlier Acts. One important feature of the 1989 Act is, however, that many of its changes are to be amplified by subsequent regulations to be made by the Secretary of State (for Trade and Industry). It follows that some of its effects may be felt for many years to come.

[39] Dir. 80/390/EEC, O.J. 1980, L100; Dir. 79/279/EEC O.J. 1979 L66; Dir. 82/121/EEC, O.J. 1982 L48.

To sum up, current company law can be found partly in the 1985 Act and its three satellite Acts, as amended and substituted by three major Acts (the Insolvency Act 1985, the Financial Services Act 1986 and the Companies Act 1989), partly in the Insolvency Act 1986, which contains both the 1985 Companies Act and Insolvency Act 1985 provisions on corporate insolvency and liquidations, partly in the Company Directors Disqualification Act 1986, partly in the Financial Services Act 1986 and partly in the extant provisions of the Companies Act 1989. Nor can it be supposed that this is the end. Pressure for reform continues—a short note on the EC company law harmonisation programme follows shortly.

No attempt, however, has been made to codify company law, *i.e.* to reduce to a code all the statute law and common law on the topic. Unlike Acts such as the Partnership Act 1890 the various major Companies Acts have generally simply consolidated provisions previously in several other Acts. Consequently a significant part of company law is still comprised of decided cases. The 1980, 1981, 1986 and 1989 legislation on the other hand contain many technical and complex provisions replacing case-law decisions, often of long standing. This trend, from cases to statutes, is now firmly established and likely to continue in the future. The legislation, unlike case-law, applies in general to both England and Scotland.

One final development has been the emergence of self-regulating bodies such as the City Panel on Take-overs and Mergers. The City Panel operates a code without the force of law but of great significance in certain areas such as the acquisition of shares and take-overs in the public company sphere. The City Panel has not, however, been assimilated into the general self-regulatory system of control of the investment industry under the Financial Services Act 1986 which is considered in outline only in this book.

Measures of the European Community

There are a number of measures of the European Community aimed at the harmonisation of the company laws of the Member States. In general this programme consists of a series of directives issued under Article 58 of the European Treaty. These prescribe common standards for areas of company law which require Member States to amend their law, if necessary, to comply with them. The First Directive of the EC Council of Ministers was given effect to in the United Kingdom by the European Communities Act 1972, now sections 35 and 35A of the Act, which among other things, modified the *ultra vires* doctrine and is dealt with in a number of places in the text. The Second and Fourth Directives on capital and accounts were implemented by the 1980 and 1981 Companies Acts. The Third and Sixth Directives on mergers and divisions were implemented by regulations and the Seventh and Eighth on group accounts and auditors by the 1989 Act. In addition to the company directives the Prospectus, Stock Exchange and Continuing Disclosure Directives were implemented initially by the Stock Exchange (Listing) Regulations 1984 and subsequently by the Financial Services Act 1986. But there are others in the pipeline, some in draft form, others awaiting implementation. Even without domestic pressures these will ensure a continuation of company law reform for the duration of the United Kingdom's membership of the EC. In fact the modern pattern of legislation is that reform is directive led and that Companies Acts require a directive to be implemented for their initiation.

The following are currently on the pending list:

Draft Fifth Directive on the Structure and Management of Public Companies; Draft Ninth Directive on Groups; Draft Tenth Directive on International Mergers; Eleventh Directive on Branches in other Member States; Twelfth Directive on single member companies; and the Draft Thirteenth Directive on take-over bids. There are other agreed directives on prospectuses for unlisted securities, disclosure of significant shareholdings and insider dealing.

Some of these will require implementation in the next few years, others, those still in draft form, will take longer. For example the Eleventh Directive on branches and the Twelfth Directive on single member companies must be implemented by January 1, 1992. The width and scope of these directives give some indication of future law reform in the UK.

Two further EC inspired developments are not, however, part of the harmonisation programme as such. They are both aimed at establishing cross-frontier entities which may operate throughout the Community—they will not have a purely national existence. These are the European Economic Interest Grouping (in existence since July 1989) and the proposed European Company.

The European Economic Interest Grouping

This new entity, an E.E.I.G., was created by an EC regulation (*i.e.* a document which has direct legislative effect in the UK unlike a directive which must in general terms be implemented by the U.K. Parliament to be effective), Council Regulation 2173/85,[40] as supplemented by the European Economic Grouping Regulations 1989.[41] The intention is to allow the creation of a separate legal entity for cross-border co-operation between businesses in different Member States. These may or may not be companies. Formation is by contract, registered with the registrar of companies. This contract must include the objects of the E.E.I.G.—since making profits in its own right is not allowed, these must require the E.E.I.G. to enhance the activities of its members, *e.g.* by joint research or development. The members of the E.E.I.G. will have unlimited liability for its debts, no public investment is allowed and the maximum number of employees is limited to 500. An E.E.I.G. can be formed in any Member State and is subject to some aspects of the national law in which it is registered, *e.g.* as to the use of name, certain winding up rules etc. UK law must equally recognise an E.E.I.G. registered in another Member State.

Proposed statute for a European Company

There is a proposal for a regulation establishing a new cross-border entity to be known as the European Company.[42] This is not a new idea, being originally suggested in 1970, but interest in it has been revived within the Community. In essence it will be formed by the merger of two or more public companies of different EC nationality, and would be subject to a new range of EC company law, although it would still remain subject to national law in certain areas. The relevant national law would

[40] O.J. 1985 L199/1.
[41] S.I. 1989 No. 638.
[42] O.J. 1989 C 263/41.

be that of the country in which it was registered. There are different views as to the need for such a transnational company and as to the contents of the supranational EC law to which it should be subject, *e.g.* as to the contentious issue of employee participation. If this proposal is implemented, however, it will provide a parallel but not identical system of company law to UK domestic company law, available in practice to all public companies.

Procedure to Obtain Registration of a Company

To obtain the registration of a company certain documents must be delivered to the appropriate Registrar of Companies and certain fees must be paid. If the registered office is to be situate in England or in Wales,[43] the appropriate registrar is the Registrar of Companies for England,[44] and his address is now Companies Registration Office, Crown Way, Maindy, Cardiff, CF4 3UZ.[45] If the registered office is to be situate in Scotland[46] the appropriate registrar is the Registrar of Companies for Scotland[47] and his address is Companies Registration Office, Exchequer Chambers, 102 George Street, Edinburgh EH2 3DJ.

Documents which must be delivered to the Registrar

The following documents must be delivered to the Registrar of Companies:

(1) A memorandum of association[48] stating, *inter alia,* the objects of the company and if, as is common, the company is a limited company with a share capital, the amount of share capital with which the company proposes to be registered and its division into shares of

[43] See *post*, p. 65.
[44] s.10.
[45] The main part of the Companies Registration Office is now in Cardiff. There are microfilm reading room facilities in London at Companies House, 55–71 City Road, London, EC1Y 1BB.
[46] *Post*, p. 65.
[47] s.10.
[48] s.10. The memorandum is dealt with in Chap. 3.

a fixed amount,[49] *e.g.* £10,000 divided into 10,000 shares of a nominal amount of £1 each. If the company is a public company this figure must be not less than the authorised minimum,[50] currently £50,000.[51]

(2) Usually, printed articles of association[52] providing for such matters as the transfer of shares in the company, the holding of general meetings, *i.e.* meetings of the members or shareholders, the directors' powers of management and the extent to which they can delegate their powers to a managing director, and the payment of dividends.

(3) If the memorandum states that the registered office is to be situated in Wales and the memorandum and articles are in Welsh, a certified translation in English.[53]

(4) A statement in the prescribed form of the names of the intended first director or directors, and first secretary or joint secretaries, and the particulars specified in Schedule 1.[54] Such statement must be signed by or on behalf of the subscribers of the memorandum and must contain a consent to act signed by each of the persons named in it. Where the memorandum is delivered for registration by an agent for the subscribers, such statement must specify that fact and the name and address of that person.[55] The statement must also specify the intended situation of the company's registered office.[56]

(5) A statutory declaration, by a solicitor engaged in the formation of the company or by a person named as director or secretary of the company in the statement delivered under (4) *ante*, of compliance with the requirements of the Acts in respect of registration.[57]

[49] s.2.
[50] s.11.
[51] s.118.
[52] s.7. Articles are dealt with in Chap. 4.
[53] s.21.
[54] *Post*, pp. 362, 428.
[55] s.10(4).
[56] s.10(6).
[57] s.12(3).

(6) A statement of capital (Form PUC1), unless the company is to have no share capital.

For the purpose of ensuring that documents delivered to the Registrar are of standard size, durable and easily legible, the Secretary of State may prescribe such requirements as he considers appropriate. If a document delivered to the Registrar does not, in his opinion, comply with such requirements, he may serve a notice on the person or persons by whom the document was required to be delivered, whereupon, for the purposes of any enactment which enables a penalty to be imposed in respect of an omission to deliver a document to the Registrar, the duty to deliver is not discharged but the person subject to the duty has 14 days after the date of service of the notice in which to discharge it.[58]

The Registrar may, if he thinks fit, accept, under any provision of the Companies Acts requiring a document to be delivered to him, such material in a non-legible, *i.e.* electronic, form.[59]

The duty of the Registrar on receiving the above-mentioned documents is to examine them to see whether the statutory requirements have been complied with, but in exercising his duty he has no power to hold a judicial inquiry on evidence.[60] Among the statutory requirements to be observed are:

(1) That the memorandum is signed by at least two persons, and, if the memorandum is accompanied by articles, that the articles are signed by the same persons.[61]

(2) That the company is being formed for a lawful purpose.[62]

If the company is being formed for a purpose prohibited by law, *e.g.* for the sale of tickets in a lottery illegal in the United Kingdom, such as the Irish Sweep,[63] the Registrar will decline to register it.

[58] s.706.
[59] s.707.
[60] *R.* v. *Registrar of Companies, ex p. Bowen* [1914] 3 K.B. 1161.
[61] ss.1(1), 2, 7 *post*, pp. 55, 86.
[62] s.1(1).
[63] *R.* v. *Registrar of Companies, ex p. More* [1931] 2 K.B. 197 (C.A.).

(3) That the other requirements of the Act, *e.g.* as to the contents of the memorandum and articles, are complied with.[64]
(4) That the proposed name is not one which is absolutely, or conditionally, prohibited.[65]
(5) That the memorandum and articles are in the statutory form.[66]

Any person may inspect a copy[67] of the documents or other material kept by the Registrar relative to individual companies on payment of a fee, and may require a copy or extract of them on payment of the current fee. Such copies may be furnished in an electronic form.[68]

Registration fees

Section 708 empowers the Secretary of State, by regulations made by statutory instrument, to require payment to the Registrar of such fees as may be specified in the regulations in respect of the performance by the Registrar of such functions under the Companies Acts as may be specified, including the receipt by him of any notice or other document which the Acts require to be given or delivered to him.

CERTIFICATE OF INCORPORATION

On the registration of a company the Registrar gives a certificate, either authenticated by a seal prepared under section 704(4) or under his hand, that the company is incorporated, in the case of a limited company that it is limited and, if it is a public company, that the company is a public company: section 13.[69] The certificate of incorporation, which may be described as the company's birth certificate, is in the following form for private companies.[70]

[64] ss.1(1), 2, 7, 11; *post*, pp. 54, 55, 85, 86.
[65] s.26, *post*, p. 57.
[66] ss.3, 8, *post*, pp. 55, 85.
[67] s.709.
[68] s.710A.
[69] Until 1981 a seal was compulsory—s.99 of the 1981 Act allowed for the simpler procedure.
[70] Public companies would have a different name and the additional declaration that it is a public limited company.

CERTIFICATE OF INCORPORATION

I HEREBY CERTIFY that , Limited, is this day Incorporated under the Companies Act 1985, and that the Company is Limited.
Given under my hand at Cardiff this day of .

Section 711(1)(*a*) requires the Registrar to publish in the appropriate *Gazette*[71] notice of the issue of a certificate of incorporation.

Section 13(7) provides that the certificate is conclusive evidence that all the requirements of the Act in respect of registration and of matters precedent and incidental thereto have been complied with, and that the association is a company authorised to be registered and duly registered. If the certificate states that the company is a public company it is conclusive evidence that it is such a company.

It is thought that the subsection means that it cannot be argued that a company is not validly incorporated, *e.g.* because the memorandum of association was not subscribed by two persons except where a statutory provision as to substance invalidates the registration.[72] In *Cotman* v. *Brougham*[73] Lord Wrenbury criticised[74] "the pernicious practice of registering memoranda of association which, under the clause relating to objects,[75] contain paragraph after paragraph not specifying or delimiting the proposed trade or purpose, but confusing power with purpose and indicating every class of act which the corporation is to have power to do." He went on to say: "Such a memorandum is not, I think, a compliance with the Act" but that if the Registrar registers the memorandum the court "must assume that all requirements in respect of matters precedent and incidental to registration have been complied with and confine [itself] to the construction of the document." The certificate of

[71] This amounts to official notification. The appropriate Gazette is either the London or the Edinburgh Gazette depending upon the company's residence.

[72] *Per* Megarry J. in *Gaiman* v. *National Association for Mental Health* [1971] Ch. 317, at p. 329. See also *R.* v. *Registrar of Companies, ex parte Central Bank of India* [1986] BCLC 465 as to judicial review of the registrar's powers in another context.

[73] [1918] A.C. 514.

[74] At p. 523. The "pernicious practice" referred to is now of historical interest only. See p. 73, *post*.

[75] *Post*, p. 70.

incorporation has also been held to be conclusive as to the date of incorporation.[76] The reason for this section is that once a company is registered and has begun business and entered into contracts it would be disastrous if any person could allege that the company was not duly registered.[77]

The certificate will not, however, be conclusive if a trade union should be registered as a company[78]—the registration of a trade union under the Companies Acts is void by statute.[79] Again, the certificate is not conclusive as to the legality of a company's objects—proceedings may be brought to have the registration cancelled where objects are illegal.[80]

The Registrar will allocate each registered company a registered number, *i.e.* a sequence of letters and numbers, which must be disclosed on all its business letters and order forms.[81]

Effect of Registration of a Company

From the date of incorporation mentioned in the certificate of incorporation, the subscribers of the memorandum, together with such other persons as may from time to time become members of the company, form a body corporate by the name contained in the memorandum, capable forthwith of exercising all the functions of an incorporated company, but with such liability on the part of the members to contribute to the assets of the company as is mentioned in the Act: section 13(3).

The registered company is a body corporate, *i.e.* a legal person separate and distinct from its members.

S. had for many years carried on business as a boot manufacturer. His business was solvent when it was converted into a company, *i.e.* a company limited by shares was formed, the subscribers to the

[76] *Jubilee Cotton Mills Ltd.* v. *Lewis* [1924] A.C. 958, where it was also held that "From the date of incorporation" in s.[13(3)] included any portion of the day on which the company was incorporated.

[77] *Per* Lord Cairns in *Peel's Case* (1867) L.R. 2 Ch.App. 674, at p. 682.

[78] *British Association of Glass Bottle Manufacturers Ltd.* v. *Nettlefold* (1911) 27 T.L.R. 527.

[79] Trade Union Act 1871, s.5; Companies Act 1948, s.459(9); Companies Consolidation (Consequential Provisions) Act 1985, s.31(9).

[80] *Per* Lord Parker of Waddington in *Bowman* v. *Secular Society Ltd.* [1917] A.C. 406, at p. 439.

[81] ss.705; 351(1)(*a*).

memorandum of which were S. and his wife, daughter and four sons (for one share each), and the business was sold to the company at a price of £39,000. The terms of sale were approved by all the shareholders. £9,000 was paid in cash. £20,000 fully paid shares of £1 each were allotted to S. so that S.'s wife and children held one share each and S. held 20,001 shares. S. left the rest of the price on loan to the company and for this sum of £10,000 he was given debentures secured by a charge on the company's assets. It seems that the directors were S. and his sons and that S. was appointed managing director. After a depression the company went into liquidation. The assets were sufficient to satisfy the debentures, but the unsecured creditors, with debts amounting to £7,000, received nothing. *Held,* that the proceedings were not contrary to the true intent and meaning of the Companies Act; that the company was duly registered and was not a mere "alias" or agent of or trustee for the vendor; that he was not liable to indemnify the company against creditors' claims; that there was no fraud upon creditors (or shareholders); that the company (or the liquidator) was not entitled to rescission of the contract of purchase: *Salomon* v. *Salomon & Co. Ltd.* [1897] A.C. 22.[82]

"The company is at law a different person altogether from the subscribers to the memorandum; and, though it may be that after incorporation the business is precisely the same as it was before, and the same persons are managers, and the same hands receive the profits, the company is not in law the agent of the subscribers or trustee for them. Nor are the subscribers as members liable, in any shape or form, except to the extent and in the manner provided by the Act": *per* Lord Macnaghten at p. 51.

One effect of this is that the property of the company belongs to the company itself and not to the individual members, so that even the largest shareholder has no insurable interest in the property of the company.[83] The managing director, even if he owns all the shares except one, cannot lawfully pay cheques to the company into his own banking acount or draw cheques for his own purposes upon the company's banking account,[84] and

[82] Although *Salomon's* case is now generally accepted in Scots law, the Scottish courts were, about the same time and independently of that authority, giving effect to the same principle, *e.g. Henderson* v. *Stubbs' Ltd.* (1894) 22 R. 51, *Grierson, Oldham & Co. Ltd.* v. *Forbes, Maxwell & Co. Ltd.* (1895) 22 R. 812 and *John Wilson & Son Ltd.* v. *Inland Revenue* (1895) 23 R. 18.

[83] *Macaura* v. *Northern Assurance Co. Ltd.* [1925] A.C. 619. In Canada however, it has been held that a *sole* shareholder has an insurable interest in the company's property; *Kosmopolous* v. *Constitution Insurance Co. of Canada* (1984) 149 D.L.R. (3d) 77.

[84] *A. L. Underwood Ltd.* v. *Bank of Liverpool & Martins Ltd.* [1924] 1 K.B. 775 (C.A.); *cf. Thompson* v. *Barke and Company* (*Caterers*) Ltd., 1975 S.L.T. 67 (O.H.) (Company's cheques used to repay loan made to director held *ultra vires*).

two sole shareholder/directors can be convicted of theft from "their" company.[85]

This principle of the independent corporate existence of a registered company is of the greatest importance in company law. As we shall see, it is this which mainly distinguishes a registered company from a partnership, which is the relation which subsists between persons carrying on a business in common with a view of profit. A partnership is not a corporation but, at least in the case of an English partnership,[86] is only a description of the relationship between the partners, *i.e.* a partnership has no legal existence but is merely the association of two or more persons carrying on business together. The property of the firm belongs to the partners and the firm's debts are the debts of the partners, *i.e.* the partners are personally liable for the firm's debts, whereas in a registered company the assets and liabilities are those of the corporation and not of the members.

This separation of the corporation and its members so that the members are not liable for the company's debts was reaffirmed by the House of Lords in *J. H. Rayner (Mincing Lane) Ltd.* v. *Department of Trade and Industry*.[87] This case arose out of the collapse of the International Tin Council in 1985 which left it owing millions of pounds to a number of metal traders and banks. The Council had been formed by several states and the Council's creditors sought to recover its debts from those member states. The House of Lords first decided that the Council was a corporate body with its own separate legal personality distinct from its members and it followed therefore that only the Council and not its members could be liable for the debts. Under English law only the party to a contract can be liable on that contract and the only contracting party here was the Council. It would be for Parliament to provide otherwise in any given case.[88]

Lord Oliver expressed the decision thus:

[85] *Att.-Gen's Reference (No. 2 of 1982)* [1984] Q.B. 624; *R.* v. *Phillipou* (1989) 5 BCC 33.

[86] A Scottish partnership or firm has a separate legal existence and is not merely the association of two or more persons. The property of the firm belongs to the firm, and the firm's debts are primarily those of the firm, although each partner may ultimately be made personally liable for the firm's debts.

[87] [1989] 3 W.L.R. 969 (H.L.).

[88] See, *e.g.* n. 86, above.

"Once given the existence of the I.T.C. as a separate legal person and given that it was the contracting party in the transactions upon which the appellants claim . . . there is no room for any further inquiry as to what type of legal person the contracting party is. The person who can enforce contracts and the persons against whom they can be enforced in English law are the parties to the contract and in identifying the parties to the contract there are no gradations of legal personality."[89]

The liability of a member of a company limited by shares to contribute to the company's assets (for the purpose of enabling its debts to be paid) is limited to the amount, if any, unpaid on his shares.[90] Thus if he has taken one thousand shares of £1 each in the company and the shares are fully paid up he is normally under no further liability to contribute to the assets. In the case of a partnership every partner is jointly liable with the other partners for all the firm's debts.[91]

A registered company is capable forthwith of exercising all the functions of an incorporated company, *e.g.* it can hold land and other property, and it can sue and be sued. If the company is a public company it cannot commence business until the requirements of section 117 have been complied with.[92]

The veil of incorporation

It was established in *Salomon* v. *Salomon & Co. Ltd., ante,* that a registered company is a legal person separate from its members. This principle may be referred to as "the veil of incorporation." In general, the law will not go behind the separate personality of the company to the members, so that, *e.g.* in *Macaura* v. *Northern Assurance Co. Ltd., ante,* it was held that the largest shareholder had no insurable interest in the property of the company. Similarly an employee cannot bring an action for unfair dismissal against the majority shareholder of a company which employed him.[93] However, there are exceptions

[89] [1989] 3 W.L.R. 969 at 1010.
[90] s.1(2).
[91] Further differences between registered companies and partnerships are dealt with later in this chapter.
[92] *Post*, p. 171.
[93] *Schouls* v. *Canadian Meat Processing Corp*. (1984) 147 D.L.R. (3d) 81.

to the principle in *Salomon's* case where the veil is lifted and the law disregards the corporate entity and pays regard instead to the economic realities behind the legal façade. In these exceptional cases "the law either goes behind the corporate personality to the individual members, or ignores the separate personality of each company in favour of the economic entity constituted by a group of associated concerns."[94]

Instances of the veil being lifted may be classified into those expressly provided by statute and those under judicial interpretation where the facts have been rather unusual.[95]

One example of a case where "the veil is lifted" by statute is where a company carries on business for more than six months with less than the statutory minimum of members (two), in which event every person who is a member during any part of the time that business is so carried on after the end of the six-month period and who knows that business is being so carried on, is jointly and severally liable for all the company's debts contracted during such time and may be severally sued therefor (s.24, intended to ensure that the number of members does not fall below the statutory minimum). This is exceptional because the general rule is that the company's debts cannot be enforced against the members.

Again, where an officer of a company signs, on behalf of the company, a bill of exchange, promissory note, cheque or order for money or goods in which the company's name is not mentioned, the officer is personally liable to the holder of the bill of exchange, etc., for the amount thereof unless it is paid by the company (s.349(4)).[96]

At common law there are several examples. Thus, a company registered in England is an alien enemy if its agents or the persons in *de facto* control of its affairs are alien enemies, and in determining whether alien enemies have such control, the number of alien enemy shareholders and the value of their holdings are material.[97] Another example is that in cases such as *Re Express Engineering Works Ltd.*[98] and the other cases dealt

[94] Gower, *Modern Company Law*, 4th ed., 1979, p. 112.

[95] See also Ruthven, *Lifting the Veil of Incorporation in Scotland*, 1969 Juridical Review, p. 1.

[96] *Post*, p. 61.

[97] *Daimler Co. Ltd.* v. *Continental Tyre etc. Ltd.* [1916] 2 A.C. 307.

[98] [1920] 1 Ch. 466 (C.A.), *post*, p. 321.

with on pages 321, 343, the decision of all the shareholders was held to be the decision of the company, *e.g.* something less formal than a resolution, even a special resolution, duly passed at a general meeting was regarded as the act of the company. Further, it was held in *Re Bugle Press Ltd.*[99] that if A Ltd. makes an offer for the shares in B Ltd. and in substance A Ltd. is the same as the majority shareholding in B Ltd., A Ltd. will not be able to invoke section 429[1] and compel the minority shareholders in B Ltd. to sell their shares to A Ltd. In these circumstances the law goes behind the corporate personality of A Ltd. to the individual members. The court will not allow that section to be invoked for an improper purpose.

Several examples arise from cases involving company fraud. Lord Denning M.R. was prepared to lift the veil in *Wallersteiner* v. *Moir*[2]—he said that in that case the plaintiff was also in breach of what is now section 330 (which in general prohibits a company making a loan to a director) because the company of which he was a director made a loan to another company which was his puppet, so that the loan should be treated as made to him. Recently the Court of Appeal lifted the veil when a defendant in a company fraud case took elaborate steps to conceal his assets by a complex network of companies and trusts. The court allowed the veil to be lifted in order to establish exactly what he owned and where it was located. They stated that this could be done in the interests of justice irrespective of the legal efficacy of the corporate structure provided he either substantially or effectively controlled the company concerned. The network of companies had been set up in an attempt to confuse and conceal.[3]

The case of *Gilford Motor Co. Ltd.* v. *Horne*[4] shows that the courts will not allow a company to be used as a device to mask the carrying on of a business by a former employee of another person and to enable the former employee to break a valid covenant in restraint of trade contained in the contract under which he was formerly employed. In that case the employee covenanted that after the termination of the employment he

[99] [1961] Ch. 270 (C.A.), *post*, p. 874.
[1] Chap. 31, *post*.
[2] [1974] 1 W.L.R. 991 (C.A.).
[3] *Re A Company* [1985] BCLC 333 (C.A.).
[4] [1933] Ch. 935 (C.A.).

would not solicit his employer's customers. Soon after the termination of his employment he formed a company of which the two directors and shareholders were his wife and one other person and which sent out circulars to customers of his former employer. An injunction was granted against the ex-employee and the company. The *Gilford* case was followed in *Jones* v. *Lipman*[5] where, having agreed to sell land to the plaintiff, the defendant sold and transferred the land to a company controlled by him. It was held that the company was the creature of the defendant, a mask to avoid recognition by the eye of equity, and therefore specific performance could not be resisted by the defendant. Specific performance was also granted against the company.

Although in *Salomon's* case, *ante,* it was held that the company was not a mere agent for Salomon, in *Smith, Stone & Knight Ltd.* v. *Birmingham Corporation*[6] a subsidiary company which was carrying on the parent company's business was held to be the agent of the parent shareholder. Conversely, in *Wm. Cory & Son Ltd.* v. *Dorman Long & Co. Ltd.*[7] the parent company was held to be the agent of the subsidiary.

In two recent cases the question has arisen whether a subsidiary could be regarded as a single entity with its parent company in order to enable the group to claim compensation for disturbance on a compulsory purchase. In *D.H.N. Food Distributors Ltd.* v. *Tower Hamlets London Borough Council*[8] the Court of Appeal in England allowed the claim on the basis that D.H.N. was in a position to control its subsidiaries in every respect. The House of Lords in the Scottish case of *Woolfson* v. *Strathclyde Regional Council*[9] distinguished the *D.H.N.* case on its facts but also doubted whether it was a correct application of the general principle that the veil should only be pierced where special circumstances exist indicating that it is a mere façade concealing the true facts. In *City of Glasgow District Council* v. *Hamlet Textiles Ltd.*,[10] the Scottish Court of Session allowed inquiry as to the true ownership of property in Glasgow where

[5] [1962] 1 W.L.R. 832.
[6] [1939] 4 All E.R. 116.
[7] [1936] 2 All E.R. 386 (C.A.).
[8] [1976] 1 W.L.R. 852 (C.A.).
[9] 1978 S.C. (H.L.) 90; 1977 S.C. 84.
[10] 1986 S.L.T. 415.

the formal title was held by an English wholly-owned subsidiary of a Scottish company and whose sole function was the holding of that formal title.

The approach taken by the House of Lords in the *Woolfson* case (above) has since been applied, however, in England in *National Dock Labour Board* v. *Pinn & Wheeler Ltd.*[11] The judge refused to regard three related companies as being a single entity for the purposes of a demarcation dispute. Only where there was a mere façade concealing the true facts would the corporate veil be pierced. In this case the companies had been retained for good commercial reasons.

LIABILITY OF REGISTERED COMPANIES

One consequence of the concept of a company's separate personality is that it can be liable for breaches of contract, torts (in Scots law, delicts), crimes etc. But for obvious reasons it can only act through human agents or employees, so that, as a general principle, a company can only be liable either where a principal would be liable for the acts of an agent or an employer liable for the acts of an employee. In Chapter 6 the concept of agency, which is central to an understanding of company commercial transactions, is discussed but sometimes the law only imposes obligations or affords benefits to those who ctually do the act and since a company cannot physically do anything there can be a problem assimilating companies into the general law. The answer is that in certain circumstances the acts and mind of the governing body of the company are regarded as the acts and mind of the company—thus, for example, if they intend to defraud, so does the company. Sometimes known as the *alter ego* doctrine this is the antithesis of the doctrine of separate corporate personality.

The doctrine was first laid down by the House of Lords in *Lennards Carrying Co.* v. *Asiatic Petroleum*[12] where the major shareholder's negligence in navigating the company's ship was held to be the negligence of the company for the purposes of assessing liability. Viscount Haldane L.C. said: "For if Mr.

[11] (1989) 5 BCC 75. See also *Adams* v. *Cape Industries plc* [1990] BCC 786.
[12] [1915] A.C. 705 (H.L.).

Lennard was the directing mind of the company, then his action must, unless a corporation is not to be liable at all, have been an action which was the action of the company itself.[13] This doctrine has been applied to both tort and criminal law but for some years it remained unclear as to exactly whose acts and intentions could be attributed to the company. In *Bolton (Engineering) Co. Ltd.* v. *Graham & Son*,[14] Lord Denning drew a distinction between the acts of those directors and managers who control what the company actually does and the acts of mere servants who simply carry out the course of action prescribed by those in control.

The leading case is now *Tesco Supermarkets Ltd.* v. *Nattrass*,[15] where the supermarket chain was prosecuted under section 11(2) of the Trade Descriptions Act 1968 for carrying an incorrect advertisement as to the availability of a brand of washing powder at a reduced price. Their defence was that provided by section 24(1) of the 1968 Act, *i.e.* that the commission of the offence was due to the act or default of another person and that they had taken all reasonable care etc. to avoid the commission of the offence. The relevant question was whether the manager of the particular branch, who had failed to check the stock, was "another person" for this purpose, or whether his default was that of the company. The House of Lords held that he was "another person"; a branch manager of his type was not sufficienly senior to be the *alter ego* of the company. Such an *ego* would be found amongst the directors, managers, secretary or other officers of the company, or someone to whom they had delegated control and management, with full discretionary powers, of some sections of the company's business.

On the other hand the *alter ego* doctrine does not apply to misappropriations *from* the company by those in control of its affairs. Such misappropriations are not the act of the company, however, as there is no consensus between the controller and the company.[16]

[13] *Ibid.* p. 717.
[14] [1957] 1 Q.B. 159 (C.A.).
[15] [1972] 2 All E.R. 127 (H.L.). As to the position in Scotland, see *Purcell Meats (Scotland) Ltd.* v. *McLeod*, 1987 S.L.T. 528.
[16] *Stephens* v. *T. Pittas Ltd.* [1983] S.T.C. 376; *Att-Gen.'s Reference (No. 2 of 1982)* [1984] Q.B. 624; *R.* v. *Phillipou* (1989) 5 BCC 33.

The doctrine has been applied to decide the procedural question of discovery of documents, *i.e.* to determine whether a company and an individual can be regarded as one person so that a document held by the company can be said to be in the possession of the individual. In *Re Tecnion Investments Ltd.*[17] the Court of Appeal held that the company would only be the *alter ego* of the individual for this purpose if it was under his unfettered control. It was not enough to show that he was the dominant figure in running the company's business.

REGISTERED COMPANIES AND PARTNERSHIPS CONTRASTED

Advantages of a registered company

A registered company has many advantages over a partnership, which is defined in the Partnership Act 1890[18] as the relationship which subsists between persons carrying on a business in common with a view of profit, and which is not, *e.g.* the relation between members of a company registered under the Companies Acts or incorporated by or in pursuance of any other Act of Parliament or Royal Charter. A registered company has the same advantages over an individual trader. These advantages include the following:

(1) A registered company is a corporation,[19] *i.e.* a separate legal person distinct from the members, whereas an English partnership is merely the aggregate of the partners (although a Scottish partnership has one of the attributes of a corporation in that it is "a legal person distinct from the partners of whom it is composed").[20] Consequently:

(*a*) The debts and contracts of a registered company are those of the company and not those of the members, whereas in the case of an English firm every partner is jointly and severally liable with the other

[17] [1985] BCLC 434 (C.A.). *Dallas* v. *Dallas* (1960) 24 D.L.R. (2d) 746.
[18] s.1. See generally on partnerships Burgess and Morse, *Partnership Law in England and Scotland* (1980). Morse, *Introduction to Partnership Law* (1986).
[19] s.13(3); *Salomon* v. *Salomon & Co. Ltd.* [1897] A.C. 22, *ante*, p. 24.
[20] Partnership Act 1980, s.4(2).

partners for all the firm's debts and obligations incurred while he is a partner.[21] (In Scotland the firm's debts are those of the firm but, if the firm fails to pay, each individual partner may be made liable. Again, the firm's contracts are those of the firm but the individual partners may be made liable for them.)

(*b*) Unless it is wound up a registered company continues in existence[22] so that it is not affected by the death, bankruptcy, mental disorder or retirement of any of its members. In the case of a partnership, on the other hand, on the death or bankruptcy of a partner, subject to any agreement between the partners the partnership is dissolved as regards all the partners.[23] In practice the share of a partner who dies or retires has to be found out of the business or provided for by the other partners, and this may cause serious financial embarrassment to the firm.

(*c*) The property of a registered company belongs to and is vested in the company, so that there is no change in the ownership of, or in the formal title to, the property on a change in the ownership of shares in the company. In an English partnership, the property belongs to the partners and is vested in them. Consequently there are changes in the ownership of, and in the formal title to, the firm's property from time to time on the death or retirement of a partner or trustee. (In a Scottish partnership, while the partnership property belongs to the firm as a separate *persona,* the formal title to that property may be, and in the case of heritable property must be, in the names of the partners or of other persons in trust for the firm.)

(*d*) A registered company can contract with its members and can sue and be sued on such contracts. In England a partner cannot contract with the firm. (In

[21] *Ibid*. s.9.
[22] See *ante*, p. 5.
[23] Partnership Act 1890, s.33(1). As to dissolution by the court in the event of the mental disorder of a partner, see 1890 Act, s.35, and Mental Health Act 1959, s.103 (the latter is not applicable to Scotland). As to dissolution by notice by a retiring partner, see 1980 Act, s.32.

Scotland, by virtue of the firm's separate personality, a partner can contract with the firm and can sue and be sued on such contracts.)

(*e*) Each partner is normally an agent for the firm for the purpose of the business of the partnership[24] and, subject to any agreement to the contrary between the parties, may take part in the management of the partnership business.[25] The members of a registered company as such are not its agents and have no power to manage its affairs—the directors are agents, *i.e.* they have the powers given to them by the articles.

(*f*) Subject to any restrictions in the articles, which there may be in the articles of a private company,[26] shares in a registered company can be transferred or mortgaged[27] without the consent of the other shareholders. Subject to any agreement to the contrary, a person cannot be introduced as a partner without the consent of all the existing partners[28] and if in England a partner charges his share of the partnership for his separate debt the other partners normally have the option to dissolve the partnership.[29]

(2) The liability of a member of a registered company to contribute to its assets may be, and usually is, limited, *e.g.* limited, in the case of a company limited by shares, to the amount unpaid on his shares[30] (although the person controlling a private company may have to give a personal guarantee of the company's bank overdraft) but the members of a partnership are jointly (and in Scotland severally also) liable for all the debts of the firm.[31] This advantage can be secured in a partnership by a person's being a limited partner in a limited partnership formed under the Limited Partnerships Act 1907, but few such partnerships have

[24] Partnership Act 1890, s.5.
[25] *Ibid.* s.24(5).
[26] These have not been compulsory for private companies since 1980.
[27] In Scots law "transferred in security."
[28] Partnership Act 1890, s.24(7).
[29] *Ibid.* s.33(2) (not applicable to Scotland: see s.23(5)).
[30] s.1.
[31] Partnership Act 1890, s.9, *ante*.

been formed, owing to the superior advantages of the private limited company.

(3) There is no limit to the number of members of a company, but, except in the case of, *e.g.*, certain partnerships of practising professional men such as solicitors, a partnership with more than 20 members for the purpose of carrying on any business which has for its object the acquisition of gain is prohibited.[32]

(4) A registered company has greater facilities for borrowing than a partnership, *e.g.* the company may borrow on debentures.[33]

(5) Floating charges can be created by a registered company but not by a partnership.[34]

Advantages of a partnership

A partnership or an individual trader has certain advantages over a registered company (although these are normally outweighed by the advantages of the latter over the former):

(1) There are fewer formalities to be observed, and therefore there is less publicity and less expense involved in forming a partnership, *e.g.* there is no need to be registered, or to file a memorandum and articles, with the Registrar, and therefore there are no registration fees, and legal costs are less. A partnership agreement may be oral or even inferred from conduct.

(2) There are fewer formalities and therefore less publicity and less expense in running a partnership, *e.g.* returns do not have to be delivered to a Registrar.

(3) A partnership's accounts are never open to public inspection. Except in the case of certain unlimited[35] and small companies,[36] those of a registered company are, as are the other documents which any registered company must lodge with the Registrar.[37]

[32] s.716.
[33] *Post*, Chap. 23.
[34] *Post*, Chap. 23.
[35] *Post*, p. 41.
[36] *Post*, Chap. 20.
[37] s.426.

(4) A partnership is not subject to the rules in connection with raising and maintenance of share capital, to which a registered company which is not an unlimited company is subject.[38]

(5) A partnership can make any arrangement with creditors that the partners think fit. A registered company can make only those authorised either by the Act or the Insolvency Act 1986.[39]

[38] *Post*, Chap. 9.

[39] 1985 Act, s.425; Insolvency Act 1986, ss.1, 165, 167.

Chapter 2

CLASSIFICATION OF REGISTERED COMPANIES

THIS chapter deals first with the two main legal classifications of registered companies. The first classifies registered companies as being limited by shares, limited by guarantee or unlimited. The second classifies them as being either public companies or private companies. (Any limited company with a share capital may be either a public or a private company.) Secondly, something is said of holding companies and subsidiary companies, which in turn defines the concept of a group.

COMPANIES LIMITED BY SHARES, COMPANIES LIMITED BY GUARANTEE AND UNLIMITED COMPANIES

A registered company may be—

(1) a company limited by shares, in which case the liability of a member to contribute to the company's assets is limited to the amount, if any, unpaid on his shares; or

(2) a company limited by guarantee, in which case the liability of a member is limited to the amount which he has undertaken to contribute *in the event of its being wound up*; or

(3) an unlimited company, in which case the liability of a member is unlimited: section 1(2).[1]

The vast majority of registered companies are companies limited by shares. Such companies must have a share capital,

[1] This section provides the statutory rules for the liability of the members of a company for its debts. The common law position is that there is otherwise no liability at all: see *J. H. Rayner* (*Mincing Lane*) v. *D.T.I.* [1989] 3 W.L.R. 969 (H.L.), p. 26, *ante*.

whereas unlimited companies may or may not have a share capital. Companies limited by guarantee cannot have a share capital if they were formed after December 22, 1980 and are instead supported by subscriptions or fees paid by the members: section 1(4).

Companies limited by guarantee

A company limited by guarantee is a registered company in which the liability of members is limited to such amount as they respectively undertake to contribute to the assets of the company in the event of its being wound up: section 1(2)(*b*). The members are not required to contribute whilst the company is a going concern. The memorandum of a company limited by guarantee, in addition to containing the clauses normally contained in a memorandum,[2] must state that each member undertakes to contribute to the assets of the company in the event of its being wound up while he is a member, or within one year after he ceases to be a member, for payment of its debts contracted before he ceases to be a member, and of the costs of winding up, and for adjustment of the rights of the contributories, such sum as may be required, not exceeding a specified amount: section 2(4). The sum specified in Table C, *post*, is £100. Whatever the amount of the guarantee specified in the memorandum, it cannot be increased or reduced.

The amounts which the members have agreed to contribute in a winding up cannot be mortgaged or charged by the company whilst it is a going concern.[3] They are not assets of the company whilst it is a going concern.

Prior to the 1980 Act a company limited by guarantee could be formed either with or without a share capital, but was usually formed without a share capital, in which event money to acquire such things as premises may be raised by loans from the members. Since the 1980 Act no such company can be formed with, or acquire, a share capital: section 1(4). The majority of companies limited by guarantee[4] are formed to incorporate

[2] *Post*, p. 54.
[3] *Re Irish Club* [1906] W.N. 127 *Robertson* v. *British Linen Co.* (1890) 18 R., 1225 (O.H.), approved *obiter* in *Lloyd's Bank Ltd.* v. *Morrison & Son*, 1927 S.C. 571.
[4] *Post*, p. 59.

professional, trade and research associations, or clubs supported by annual subscriptions. Many will be able to take advantage of section 304 and omit the word "Limited" from their names.

Every company limited by guarantee is obliged to register articles of association with the memorandum: section 7. If the company has no share capital, the memorandum and articles must be in the form set out in Table C, or as near thereto as circumstances admit: sections 3 and 8. Table C is a model form of memorandum and articles for such a company and is set out in the Companies (Tables A to F) Regulations 1985.

An article of a company limited by guarantee with no share capital is not invalid just because it is not contained in Table C. Section 8 is concerned with the form of the articles of such a company and the word "form" here does not embrace contents. Provided that the draftsman of such articles follows the general form of Table C he is free to add, subtract or vary as the needs of the case suggest.[5]

Every provision in the memorandum or articles of a company limited by guarantee and not having a share capital, or in any resolution of the company, purporting to give any person a right to participate in the divisible profits of the company otherwise than as a member is void, and every provision in the memorandum or articles, or in any resolution, purporting to divide the undertaking of the company into shares or interests is treated as a provision for share capital notwithstanding that the nominal amount or number of the shares or interests is not specified: section 15. The object of this section is to prevent the registration of companies with shares of no par value.[6]

Because of the strict régime applied to public companies few companies limited by guarantee can be registered as such companies. In practice they will be private companies.[7]

Companies limited by guarantee must, like other companies, file an annual return as required by section 363. The form of the return will depend upon whether or not it has a share capital.[8]

If the company has no share capital, an extraordinary general meeting of the company can be requisitioned by the members

[5] *Gaiman* v. *National Association for Mental Health* [1971] Ch. 317.

[6] Companies of the kind involved in *Malleson* v. *General Mineral Patents Syndicate Ltd.* [1894] 3 Ch. 538.

[7] *Post*, p. 45.

[8] *Post*, p. 256.

having at least one-tenth of the voting rights. If the company has a share capital, members holding at least one-tenth of the paid-up capital carrying the right to vote can requisition a meeting: section 368.

Apart from what has been said in this chapter, most of what is said elsewhere in this work applies to companies limited by guarantee as it does to companies limited by shares.

Unlimited companies

A company may be registered as an unlimited company, in which case there is no limit on the members' liability to contribute to the assets: section 1(1)(*c*). In the years immediately preceding 1967 comparatively few such companies were formed, although they are the oldest class of registered company, but the exemption from publication of accounts[9] given by the 1967 Act, made them more popular. Similar exemptions, are now applicable to all small private companies.[10]

The memorandum and articles of an unlimited company with a share caital must be in the form set out in Table E, or as near thereto as circumstances admit: sections 3 and 8. Table E is a model form of memorandum and articles set out in the Companies (Tables A to F) Regulations 1985. The company is obliged to register articles with the memorandum: section 7(1). The articles must state, if the company is to have a share capital, the amount of the share capital: section 7(2). There is no requirement that the division of the share capital into shares of a fixed amount be stated. The name will not, of course, include the word "Limited," and there will be no limitation of liability clause in the memorandum.

Since 1980 unlimited companies cannot be public companies: section 1(3).

In certain cases an unlimited company is exempted from the requirements to deliver accounts to the Registrar.[11] It must, however, deliver an annual return as required by section 363.[12]

An unlimited company is exceptional in that its members may be associated on the terms that they may withdraw in the mode

[9] *Post*, Chap. 20.
[10] *Ibid*.
[11] *Post*, Chap. 20.
[12] *Post*, p. 256.

pointed out by the memorandum and articles, so as to be free from liability in the event of a winding up,[13] and it seems that such a company may validly provide by its memorandum and articles for a return of capital to its members, *i.e.* without the consent of the court. Similarly an unlimited company may purchase its own shares if its constituent documents authorise it to do so.[14]

Re-registration of unlimited company as limited private company

Section 51 provides that an unlimited company (not registered by virtue of section 49, *post*) may be re-registered as a private company limited either by shares or by guarantee if a special resolution to that effect and complying with the requirements set out below is passed, and the application for re-registration is in the prescribed form, signed by a director or the secretary and lodged with the Registrar, together with certain documents, not earlier than the day on which the copy of the resolution filed under section 380 is received by him.

The resolution—

(1) must state the manner in which the liability of members is to be limited and the share capital if the company is to be limited by shares;

(2) must provide for the appropriate alterations in and additions to the memorandum and articles according to whether the company is to be limited by shares or by guarantee and so with or without a share capital.

The documents which must also be lodged are printed copies of the memorandum and articles as altered.

The Registrar must issue an appropriate certificate of incorporation, whereupon the status of the company is changed and the alterations in and additions to the memorandum and articles take effect. Such a certificate is conclusive evidence of compliance with the requirements of the section with respect to re-registration and of re-registration.[15]

[13] *Re Borough Commercial and Building Socy.* [1893] 2 Ch. 242.

[14] See, *e.g. Nelson Mitchell* v. *City of Glasgow Bank* (1879) 6 R. (H.L.) 66; (1878) 6 R. 420. See Chap. 10, *post*.

[15] s.52. As to the meaning of conclusive evidence see p. 23, *ante*.

Section 124 (power of unlimited company with a share capital to provide for reserve liability on re-registration as limited) applies to a re-registration under section 51.

In the winding up of a company re-registered under section 51—

(1) notwithstanding section 74(2)(*a*) of the Insolvency Act 1986,[16] a past member who was a member at the time of re-registration is, where the winding up commences within three years after the re-registration, liable to contribute to the assets of the company in respect of its debts and liabilities contracted before re-registration;

(2) where no persons who were members at the time of re-registration are existing members, a person who was then a present or past member is, subject to section 74(2)(*a*) and (1) of the 1986 Act, *ante*, but notwithstanding section 74(2)(*c*),[17] liable to contribute as above even though the existing members have satisfied the contributions required of them;

(3) notwithstanding section 74(2)(*d*)[18] and (*e*) of the 1986 Act, there is no limit on the amount which a person who, at the time of re-registration, was a past or present member is liable to contribute as above: section 77 of the 1986 Act.

Re-registration of unlimited company as a public company

No unlimited company can be a public company: section 1(3). Since such a company is therefore a private company, conversion of an unlimited company to a public company requires two steps. First, the acquisition of limited liability and a share capital and second, the acquisition of public company status. Both steps may be achieved in one process under sections 43 to 48. The procedure for re-registration of a private company as a public company is modified to include the appropriate requirements for the acquisition of limited liability;

[16] *Post*, p. 806.
[17] *Post*, p. 809.
[18] *Post*, p. 808.

i.e. a special resolution similar to that required by section 51: section 48. Following a pre-consolidation amendment[19] it is no longer possible to re-register a company which has already been re-registered as an unlimited company as a public company under section 43.[20]

The Registrar must issue a certificate stating that the company has been incorporated as a company limited by shares and is a public company. Such a certificate is conclusive evidence of the fact that it is a public company: sections 47, 48(3).

Re-registration of limited company as unlimited

Section 49 enables a limited private company (not registered in pursuance of section 51, *ante*) to be re-registered as unlimited with the unanimous consent of its members. The application for re-registration must be in the prescribed form, signed by a director or the secretary and lodged with the Registrar together with certain documents. A public company cannot be re-registered as an unlimited company—it must attain private company status first; nor can a company which has previously been re-registered or unlimited: section 49(3).

The application must set out the appropriate alterations in and additions to the memorandum and, if articles have been registered,[21] the articles according to whether or not the company is to have a share caital. If articles have not been registered the application must have annexed to it, and request the registration of, appropriate printed articles.

The following documents must be lodged with the application—

(1) the prescribed form of assent to the company's being registered as unlimited *subscribed by or on behalf of all the members* (a subscription by the personal representative of a dead member is deemed to be by him and the trustee in bankruptcy of a member is deemed a member to the exclusion of the member himself);

[19] The Companies Acts (Pre-Consolidation Amendments) Order 1984, para. 39.
[20] s.43(1). See *post*, p. 49.
[21] *Post*, p. 86.

(2) a statutory declaration by the directors that the subscribers constitute the whole membership and, if any member has not subscribed himself, that they have taken all reasonable steps to satisfy themselves that the person who subscribed on his behalf was lawfully empowered to do so;
(3) a printed copy of the memorandum incorporating the alterations therein;
(4) if articles have been registered, a printed copy thereof incorporating the alterations to them.

The Registrar must issue an appropriate certificate of incorporation, which will be conclusive evidence of proper re-registration: section 50.[22]

In a winding up a person who, when the application for re-registration was lodged, was a past member and did not thereafter again become a member, is not liable to contribute more than he would have been liable to contribute had there been no re-registration: section 78 of the Insolvency Act 1986.

PUBLIC AND PRIVATE COMPANIES

A registered limited company may be a public company or a private company.

By section 1(3) a public company is a limited company with a share capital which has a memorandum stating that it is a public company and which has been registered or re-registered as such.

A company which is not a public company is a private company. Thus the private company is the residual class of companies, without any special requirements. This is a complete reversal of the position prior to 1980 whereby all companies were public companies unless their articles contained three restrictions: *viz.* as to the transferability of shares, the number of members, and invitations to the public to invest in the company: 1948 Act, s.28, repealed by the 1980 Act. The reason for this change was the necessity to define more clearly the public company category so that the United Kingdom's obligations under the Second EC Directive (control of the

[22] For the meaning of conclusive evidence see p. 23, *ante*.

finances of public companies) and subsequent directives could be applied only to such companies.

There are three requirements for the registration of a company as a public company:

(1) it must state that it is a public company both in its memorandum and by its name. There must be a clause to that effect in the memorandum[23] and its name must end with the words "public limited company" (frequently abbreviated to "plc").[24] A private company uses the traditional "Limited" or "Ltd" at the end of its name;
(2) the memorandum must be in the form specified in Table F of the Companies (Tables A to F) Regulations 1985[25];
(3) the company must have an authorised capital figure (the amount of shares it may issue to the public) of at least the *authorised minimum*, currently £50,000[26]: section 11.

There are substantial differences in the capital requirements as applied to public and private companies. In particular a public company cannot commence business or exercise any borrowing powers unless it has actually allotted shares up to the authorised minimum and has received at least one quarter of that amount: sections 101 and 117.[27]

Private companies are no longer required to restrict the transferability of their shares, although they are perfectly at liberty to do so, *e.g.* to preserve family control of a company; nor need they limit their membership to 50. A private company cannot issue or cause to be issued any advertisement offering any of its securities to the public. However, by regulations the Secretary of State may allow advertisements of a private character as between the issuer and the recipients, advertisements dealing with investments only incidentally, or those issued only to investors expert enough to understand any risks

[23] s.1(3).
[24] *Post*, p. 56.
[25] s.3.
[26] s.118.
[27] *Post*, p. 171.

involved: Financial Services Act 1986, section 170.[28] Contravention of this provision will be regarded as a breach of the conduct of business rules made under that Act, and so have civil consequences. It will also constitute a criminal offence: Financial Services Act 1986, section 171. To use the Stock Exchange, a company must be a public company.

The minimum number of members for both public and private companies is two[29] but a public company must still have at least two directors whereas a private company need only have one director: section 282. Thus one recommendation of the Jenkins Committee has been implemented whilst another in the same paragraph (para. 31, Cmnd 1749) has not. A private company needs no minimum capital either for registration or the commencement of business.

Disadvantages of a private company

The effective embargo on access to the capital markets preserved by section 170 of the Financial Services Act 1986 may be regarded as the only disadvantage of a private company as compared with a public company.

Advantages of a private company

A private company has a number of advantages over a public company. There advantages include the following:

(1) A private company need not issue subsequent issues of shares by way of a rights issue: section 89.[30]

(2) A private company does not need an authorised minimum capital either for registration or to commence business under sections 11 and 117. It may commence business (and make binding contracts and exercise its borrowing powers) immediately on incorporation.[31]

[28] The Secretary of State has power to extend these categories by delegated legislation.

[29] The EC proposal for a single member company will, however, amend this position.

[30] *Post*, p. 165.

[31] *Post*, p. 171.

(3) A private company is not subject to the majority of the provisions relating to the payment for shares. This enables a private company to issue shares in return for assets other than cash without lengthy and complex valuations: sections 101–116.[32]

(4) A private company need not convene an extraordinary general meeting in the event of a serious loss of capital: section 142.[33]

(5) A private company may give itself wider charges on its own shares to recover debts owed to it by its members. Public companies are restricted in this respect: section 150.[34]

(6) A private company need not make provision for unrealised capital losses when distributing a dividend: section 264.[35]

(7) Directors of private companies are much less restricted in their financial dealings with their company and need disclose far less information about such arrangements in the accounts: sections 330–344.[36]

(8) The company secretary does not need to be specially qualified or experienced: section 286.[37]

(9) Private companies may be excused from publication of some or all of their accounts, depending on their size: sections 247–251.[38]

(10) Private companies may provide financial assistance for the purchase of their own shares by following the statutory procedure: sections 155–158.[39]

(11) Private companies may purchase or redeem their own shares out of capital: sections 170–177.[40]

(12) There is no obligation to disclose the true ownership of private company shares, however substantial the holding: sections 198–211.[41]

[32] *Post*, p. 176.
[33] *Post*, p. 204.
[34] *Post*, pp. 307, 311.
[35] *Post*, Chap 22.
[36] *Post*, p. 387.
[37] *Post*, p. 424.
[38] *Post*, Chap. 20.
[39] *Post*, Chap. 11.
[40] *Post*, Chap. 10.
[41] *Post*, p. 246.

(13) Private companies can use the written resolution procedure instead of holding a formal meeting.[42]

(14) Private companies may by passing elective resolutions dispense with the need to comply with certain internal requirements of the Act.[43]

Other differences between a private company and a public company are:

(1) At a general meeting of a private company a motion for the appointment of two or more directors may be made by a single resolution: section 292.[44]

(2) A proxy can speak at a meeting of a private company: section 372.[45]

Re-registration of a private company as a public company

A private company[46] may be re-registered as a public company if it complies with the three conditions set out in sections 43 to 47.

(1) It must pass a special resolution that it be so re-registered and that its memorandum and articles be amended accordingly (*e.g.* to provide for a change of name).

(2) It must send an application in the prescribed form signed by a director or secretary of the company to the Registrar together with a printed copy of the amended memorandum and articles, a copy of the latest balance sheet and an unqualified report by the auditors on that balance sheet, a copy of another report by the auditors that the company's net assets are not less than its capital as stated in that balance sheet, and a declaration of compliance by a director or secretary and that the company's position *vis-à-vis* its net assets is unchanged since the last balance sheet.

(3) It must comply with the necessary financial criteria both for a public company to be able to commence business[47] and as

[42] *Post*, p. 343.
[43] *Post*, p. 340.
[44] *Post*, p. 348.
[45] *Post*, p. 333.
[46] Other than one without a share capital or one that has previously been re-registered as a private company.
[47] *Post*, p. 171.

to the payment for shares in public companies.[48] This applies equally to shares issued since the last balance sheet and before the application; in particular it must have the *authorised minimum* capital.

If the Registrar is satisfied he must issue a certificate of incorporation stating that the company is a public company. This is conclusive evidence that the company is a public company and that all the procedures as to re-registration have been complied with.[49]

Re-registration of a public company as a private company

A public company may be re-registered as a private company if it complies with the conditions in sections 53 to 55.

(1) It must pass a special resolution that it be so re-registered and that its memorandum and articles be amended accordingly (*e.g.* to remove the statement in the memorandum that it is a public company).

(2) It must send an application in the prescribed form signed by a director or secretary of the company to the Registrar together with a printed copy of the amended memorandum and articles.

(3) 28 days must have elapsed from the passing of the resolution and, either, no application has been brought under section 54 to have the resolution set aside, or the court has confirmed the resolution despite such an application. A minority action may be brought for the cancellation of the resolution to re-register by, either, the holders of five per cent. or more of the issued share capital or any class of capital, or not less than 50 members, within 28 days of the passing of the resolution. No-one who voted for the resolution can make such an application. The court has extensive powers on hearing such an application including confirming or cancelling the resolution, adjourning the proceedings for an arrangement to be made, altering the memorandum and articles, and, if necessary, providing for the purchase by the company of the

[48] *Post*, p. 176.
[49] For the meaning of "conclusive evidence" see p. 23, *ante*.

shares of the dissentient members. This is one of several minority protection sections which occur throughout the Act.

If the Registrar is satisfied he must issue a certificate of incorporation "appropriate to a company that is not a public company." This is conclusive evidence that the requirements as to re-registration have been complied with and that the company is a private company.[50]

Re-registration of public companies by law

If a public company reduces its capital under section 135[51] so that its allotted share capital is less than the *authorised minimum* the court is empowered to order that the company be re-registered as a private company and that its memorandum and articles be amended accordingly. In such a case no special resolution is necessary and no application by a minority is possible: section 139.

Holding and Subsidiary Companies

It is sometimes important to know whether a registered company is a subsidiary or a holding company. One reason is that section 23[52] generally prevents a subsidiary from being a member of its holding company. Another reason is that the financial assistance regulations apply as between holding and subsidiary companies.[53] The meaning of the terms "subsidiary" and "holding company" is given in sections 736 and 736A and it is convenient to deal with those definitions here.

Sections 736 and 736A were introduced by the 1989 Act to provide a redefinition of holding and subsidiary companies for company law purposes. The 1989 Act introduced another, additional definition of a group purely for the purposes of the group accounting requirements introduced by that Act, as

[50] For the meaning of conclusive evidence, see p. 23, *ante*.
[51] *Post*, Chap. 9.
[52] *Post*, p. 237.
[53] *Post*, Chap. 11.

required by the 7th EC directive.[54] The need to redefine the general concept of a group of companies was made more imperative by the planned programme of EC legislation specifically aimed at groups.

Under section 736 there are three ways of establishing that a company (B) is a subsidiary of another company (A):

(i) where A holds a majority of the voting rights in B (this may be called *voting control*);
(ii) where A is a member of B and can appoint or dismiss a majority of its directors (this may be called *director control*);
(iii) where A is a member of B and controls alone or under an agreement with others a majority of the voting rights in B (this may be called *contract control*).

If C is a subsidiary of B and B is a subsidiary of A, then C is also regarded as being a subsidiary of A.

A wholly-owned subsidiary is one whose shares are all owned by one company, its wholly-owned subsidiaries and their and its nominees.

Section 736A expands upon this basic framework. When calculating the voting rights (for voting control or contract control) it is the rights attached to the shares which count. For the purposes of calculating a majority of the board (for director control) it is the majority of the voting rights on the board on all, or substantially all, matters which must be taken into account and not a numerical majority. A company is deemed to be able to control the appointment or dismissal of the director of another company if either that director's appointment follows necessarily from his appointment as a director of the first company or the directorship is held by the first company itself. Rights to appoint or dismiss a director which require another's consent do not count unless there is no-one else who has those rights under the new criteria.

The final aspect of the definition is to discover which *rights*, either as to voting or as to the appointment or dismissal of directors, should be attributed to whom for the purpose of establishing any of the three methods of control. The following rules will apply:

[54] *Post*, Chap. 21.

(a) rights which are applicable at all times will count. Restricted rights, *i.e.* ones which only apply in certain circumstances, will only count if they are in fact exercisable at the relevant time. On the other hand a general right which is in a temporary abeyance will still count;
(b) fiduciary rights (*i.e.* held only as a trustee) do not count against the trustee;
(c) nominee rights (*i.e.* those exercisable only on instructions or with consent) are to be attributed to the beneficial owner;
(d) where shares are mortgaged, the rights attached to those shares count as those of the lender and not the borrower only if, apart from normal creditor protection rights, they are exercisable only by or with the lender's, or the lender's subsidiaries', instructions;
(e) the rights of a subsidiary count as those of its holding company and rules (c) and (d) above must not be read as applying to the contrary;
(f) any voting rights held by a company in itself must be discounted when making the calculation; and
(g) rights held under (b)–(f) are cumulative if necessary.

The above, complex definition may be amended subsequently by regulations made by the Secretary of State under section 736B of the Act.

Lastly, it should be noted that section 736(3) also provides that in the section the expression "company" includes any body corporate and that section 740 provides that a reference in the Act to a body corporate is to be construed as including a company incorporated outside Great Britain but as not including a Scottish firm. Thus many companies registered in Great Britain either have subsidiaries registered abroad or are themselves subsidiaries of an overseas parent company. These are part of the so-called multinational companies. In one case an employee of a British subsidiary was refused permission to sue the foreign parent company in America. The fact that greater damages are available in that country makes an action there very desirable from the injured person's point of view.[55]

[55] *Smith, Kline & French Laboratories Ltd.* v. *Bloch* [1983] 1 W.L.R. 370 (C.A.).

Chapter 3

MEMORANDUM OF ASSOCIATION

EVERY registered company must have a memorandum of association, which is the registered company's charter.[1] In general the memorandum regulates the company's external affairs, whilst the articles regulate its internal affairs. The purpose of the memorandum is to enable persons who invest in or deal with the company to ascertain what its name is, whether it is a public company, whether it is an English or a Scottish company, what its objects are, whether the liability of its members is limited and what share capital it is authorised to issue. The memorandum may contain other matters apart from those just referred to. It must contain an association clause and also be properly subscribed. The provisions of the memorandum can be altered in certain specified cases.

Section 2 provides that the memorandum of every company must state:

(1) The name of the company.[2]
(2) Whether the registered office of the company is to be situated in England, Wales or Scotland.
(3) The objects of the company.
(4) That the liability of the members is limited, if the company is limited by shares or by guarantee.
(5) In the case of a limited company having a share capital, the amount of share capital with which the company proposes to be registered and the division thereof into shares of a fixed amount.

[1] See *per* Lord. Cairns, L.C., in *Ashbury Railway Carriage Co. Ltd.* v. *Riche* (1875) L.R. 7 H.L. 653, at pp. 667, 668.
[2] See p. 55, *post*.

Section 1(3) provides that the memorandum of a public company must state, in addition, the fact that the company is a public company.

In the case of a company limited by guarantee the memorandum must also state that each member undertakes to contribute to the assets of the company in the event of its being wound up while he is a member, or within one year after he ceases to be a member, such amount as may be required, not exceeding a specified amount.

Where the memorandum states that the registered office is to be in Wales, the memorandum and the articles may be in Welsh but, if they are, they must be accompanied by a certified translation into English: section 21.

Subscription of the memorandum

The memorandum must state the desire of the subscribers to be formed into a company and the agreement of each to take a specified number of shares in the company. Two or more persons, must subscribe their names to the memorandum: section 1(1). The form of a memorandum of association of a private company must be that set out in Table B, and, for a public company, that set out in Table F, of the Companies (Tables A to F) Regulations 1985 or as near thereto as circumstances admit: section 3.

No subscriber may take less than one share and each subscriber must write opposite to his name the number of shares he takes and each subscriber must sign the memorandum in the presence of at least one witness, who must attest the signature: section 2.

The Name

The memorandum must state the name of the company: section 2. The general rule is that any name may be selected. However, a company cannot be registered by a name which is prohibited, either absolutely or conditionally: section 26.[3] Further, the last

[3] *Post*, p. 57.

word of the name of a private limited company must be the word "Limited" (section 25(2)), unless the company is able to comply with the criteria in section 30 and dispenses with the word. The last words of a public company must be "public limited company" (section 25(1)).[4] Where the memorandum of a limited company states that its registered office is to be in Wales, the last word of the name of the company may be "Cyfyngedig" if the company is a private company, or "Cwmni cyfyngedig cyhoeddus" if it is a public company. In all cases the appropriate abbreviations may be used: section 27. These are Ltd., plc, cyf, and ccc, respectively. In selecting a name, it is not necessary to use the word "Company," and the modern tendency is to omit it. A short name is an obvious practical convenience.

The word "Limited" is a misnomer. The company's liability for its own debts is not limited, but it is the members of the company who are not liable for the company's debts (except to the limited extent provided by section 24),[5] because the company is a legal entity separate and distinct from its shareholders. The important thing about the name is that it should show to others that the company is a body corporate, and not a mere unincorporated partnership. It is too late now to reserve the word "Company" for the exclusive use of incorporated companies, because that is in common use by persons who are not incorporated, *e.g* by partnerships. The American term "Incorporated" expresses the true idea, and that or some synonymous word is to be preferred to "Limited."

The use of the word "Limited" or "Cyfyngedig," or any contraction or imitation of it, as the last word of the name under which any person carries on business without being incorporated with limited liability, is prohibited: section 34. It has been held that a solicitor who enters an appearance for such a person, and uses the word "Limited" as describing his client, will be personally liable for the costs.[6] Similarly the use of the words "Public limited company" or its Welsh equivalent or any abbreviation of it by any person who is not a public limited company is an offence: section 33.

[4] *Post*, p. 57.
[5] *Ante*, p. 28.
[6] *Simmons* v. *Liberal Opinion Ltd.* [1911] 1 K.B. 966 (C.A.).

Prohibited and controlled names

Section 26(1) provides five grounds upon which the registration of a name or change of name is absolutely prohibited.

(1) A name including "limited," "unlimited" or "public limited company," or their Welsh equivalents otherwise than at the end of the name;
(2) A name including any abbreviation of those words otherwise than at the end of the name;
(3) A name which is *the same as* a name appearing in the index of registered names kept by the Registrar;
(4) A name, the use of which would, in the opinion of the Secretary of State, constitute a criminal offence;
(5) A name which in the opinion of the Secretary of State is offensive.

The important prohibition is (3)—a name which is *the same as* one already on the index of registered names kept by the Registrar under section 714. This includes the names of all registered companies, limited partnerships and industrial and provident societies, and so registration of a company name confers a partial monopoly of the use of that name. The onus of checking the index is on those who wish to register the name. There is no control on registration of names similar or "too like" those already on the index but such a name may be compulsorily altered within one year of registration under section 28—so called "post registration control."[7] When deciding whether one name is *the same as* another for this purpose minor differences are to be disregarded under section 26(3). Accents, type and case of letters and the word "the" if it is the first word of the name, are examples of such minor differences.

Section 26(2) provides for the controlled use of certain words and expressions either on the registration of a company or a change of name. The use of any name which in the opinion of the Secretary of State would be likely to give the impression that the company is connected in any way with Her Majesty's Government or with any local authority or includes any name or

[7] *Post*, p. 63.

expression specified in the appropriate regulations cannot be registered without his consent. The appropriate regulations are The Company and Business Names Regulations 1981.[8] These regulations specify 79 separate words or expressions which require consent before use. These include "Abortion," "Building Society," 'Chamber of Commerce," "Duke," "English," "Health Visitor," "Insurance," "National," "Royal," "Stock Exchange," "Trade Union," "Trust," and "Windsor."

When a company wishes to use such an expression it must request the "relevant body," if one is specified, to indicate whether (and if so why) it has any objections to the proposal. Relevant bodies include the Home Office and the Scottish Home and Health Department. The reply of the relevant body must be sent to the Registrar by the applicant when registration or the change of name is applied for; section 29. The Secretary of State will then make his decision.

Since similar names can be registered there is a possibility of passing-off actions being brought against registered companies, even though such names can be compulsorily changed within one year of registration.[9] Under the general law, the court has jurisdiction to grant an injunction[10] to restrain a company from using a trade name colourably resembling that of the plaintiff if the defendant's trade name, though innocently adopted, is calculated, *i.e.* likely,[11] to deceive, either by diverting customers from the plaintiff to the defendant or by occasioning confusion between the two business, *e.g.* by suggesting that the defendant's business is in some way connected with that of the plaintiff.

In *Ewing* v. *Buttercup Margarine Co. Ltd.*,[12] the plaintiff, who carried on business under the trade name of the Buttercup Dairy Company, was held entitled to restrain a newly registered company from carrying on business under the name of the Buttercup Margarine Company Ltd. on the ground that the public might reasonably think that the registered company was connected with his business.

[8] S.I. 1981/1685. See also the Company and Business Names (Amendement) Regulations 1982 (S.I. 1982 No. 1653).
[9] *Post*, p. 63.
[10] The Scottish equivalent is interdict.
[11] *Per* Earl of Halsbury L.C. in *The N. Cheshire and Manchester Brewery Co. Ltd.* v. *The Manchester Brewery Co. Ltd.* [1899] A.C. at p. 84.
[12] [1917] 2 Ch. 1 (C.A.).

However, if the company's business is or will be different from that of the complaining party, confusion is not likely to arise, and an injunction will not be granted.[13]

A company having a word in ordinary use as part of its name cannot prevent another company from using the same word.

So, Aerators Ltd. were unable to prevent the registration of Automatic Aerators Patents, Ltd. because the word "aerator" was a word in common use in the English language and Aerators Ltd. had no monopoly of it: *Aerators Ltd.* v. *Tollitt* [1902] 2 Ch. 319.

Exemption from using the word "Limited"

Under section 30 a private company limited by guarantee has a right to exclude the word "Limited" from the end of its name if certain criteria are met and certified, Prior to the 1981 Act such exemption was available to all private companies if they were so licensed by the Department of Trade. Such licensed companies continue to enjoy their exemption under the present section.

The present criteria are that the company is to be formed for the promotion of commerce, art, science, education, religion, charity or any profession and anything incidental or conducive to any of those objects; that by its memorandum or articles it must apply its income solely for the promotion of those objects, prohibit the payment of dividends to its members, and require all its surplus assets on a winding up to be transferred to a similar body rather than to its members.[14] A statutory declaration either by the solicitor engaged in the formation, or a director or secretary of the company, that the company is one to which the section applies will suffice to obtain the exemption: section 30(4), (5).

There is an absolute ban on any alterations of such a company's memorandum or articles so as to breach the criteria—there are fines in default: section 31(1), (5). Any purported alteration will thus be void. If there is a breach of

[13] *Dunlop Pneumatic Tyre Co. Ltd.* v. *Dunlop Motor Co. Ltd.*, 1907 S.C.(H.L.) 15, where the respondents carried on a motor-repairing company; similarly an interdict was refused in *The Scottish Union and National Insurance Co.* v. *The Scottish National Insurance Co. Ltd.*, 1909 S.C. 318.

[14] This requirement was always insisted on by the Department under the previous system.

any of the criteria without any such change the Secretary of State can require the addition of the word "Limited" to the company's name and a resolution of the directors to that effect will suffice for the change of name: section 31(2). Such a company cannot again acquire the exemption without the express approval of the Secretary of State: section 31(3).

Any company which obtains exemption under section 30 is relieved of the necessity of (1) having "Limited" as part of its name, (2) publishing its name,[15] and (3) sending lists of members to the Registrar,[16] although section 351 requires the fact that it is a limited company to be mentioned in its business letters and order forms.

Associations taking advantage of this exemption are typically chambers of commerce, schools and colleges, research associations, learned societies, professional qualifying bodies and charitable bodies doing social work.

Publication of name by company

The Act provides that every company must:

(1) paint or affix its name on the outside of every office or place in which its business is carried on, in a conspicuous position, in letters easily legible: section 348;
(2) mention its name in legible characters in all business letters of the company and in all notices and other official publications, and in all bills of exchange, promissory notes, endorsements, cheques and orders for money or goods, bills or parcels, invoices, receipts and letters of credit: section 349[17];
(3) engrave its name in legible characters on its seal, if it has one: section 350.

An exception is that by section 30(7) a company entitled to dispense with the word "Limited" as part of its name[18] is excepted from the provisions of the Act relating to the

[15] Under ss.348, 349, 350, *post*.
[16] Under s.363, *post*.
[17] There are additional requirements for charitable companies: Charities Act 1960, s.30(*c*).
[18] *Ante*, p. 59.

publishing of its name, although as noted above, section 351 requires the fact that it is a limited company to be mentioned in legible characters in all its business letters and order forms.

Where the name of a limited company ends with "Cyfyngedig," or "Cwmni cyfyngedig cyhoeddus" the fact that the company is a limited company must be stated in English and in legible characters—

(a) in all prospectuses, bill-heads, letter paper, notices and other official publications of the company;
(b) in a notice conspicuously displayed in every place in which the company's business is carried on: section 351(3).

Fines are imposed on the company and its officers for non-compliance with the above requirements.

Further, if an officer of the company or any person on its behalf, signs or authorises to be signed on behalf of the company any bill of exchange, cheque or order for money or goods in which the company's name is not correctly mentioned,[19] he is liable to a fine and, in addition, he is personally liable to the holder of the bill of exchange, cheque or order, for its amount, unless it is paid by the company: section 349(4). Such personal liability is a secondary liability, arising only if the company itself fails to pay, *e.g.* because of liquidation.

The courts have long established that liability under section 349(4) will be imposed upon such an officer when the words "limited" or "plc" are not included on the face of the bill or cheque.[20] The original intention was that third parties should not be misled into thinking that they were dealing with an unlimited organisation when they were dealing with a limited company. There need be no element of deceit involved, however, and the courts will not order rectification of the cheque simply on the basis that "everybody was aware of what the situation was." Rectification cannot be used by an individual simply to avoid a statutory liability.[21]

[19] Abbreviation of 'Company' to 'Co' is not a breach of the section, however: *Banque de l'Indochine et de Suez S.A.* v. *Euroseas Finance Co. Ltd.* [1981] 3 All E.R.

[20] *Penrose* v. *Martyr* (1858) 120 E.R. 595, *Atkin* v. *Wardle* (1889) 5 T.L.R., 734, *British Airways Board* v. *Parish* [1979] 2 Lloyds Rep. 361 (C.A.).

[21] *Blum* v. *O.C.P. Repartition SA* (1988) 4 BCC 771 (C.A.); *Rafsanjan Pistachio Producers Co-operative* v. *Reiss* [1990] BCC 730.

In one case, *Durham Fancy Goods Ltd.* v. *Michael Jackson (Fancy Goods) Ltd.*,[22] where the third party had prepared and specified the form of acceptance of the bill which it required and which misdescribed the company's name as "M. Jackson (Fancy Goods) Ltd," the court refused to allow the third party to enforce the personal liability of the officer who signed the bill on the basis of estoppel. The authority of this decision has since been doubted[23] and it has been distinguished in subsequent cases where the third party had not actually prepared the bill or cheque involved,[24] and more recently where although the third party had prepared the bill it had not *prescribed* the form of wording, but had simply put forward bills which it used for the officer to accept in the proper form.[25]

If the name of the company appears on the face of the bill it need not appear on the acceptance.

A bill was drawn on "J. & T.H. Wallis Ltd.," and accepted "James Wallis, Thomas Wallis, Henry Bowles, Secty." *Held*, (1) the correct name of the company was mentioned in the bill as required by the Companies Act, (2) the abbreviation "Ltd." might be used for the word "Limited," (3) the individuals who had signed the acceptance were not liable on the bill: *Stacey & Co. Ltd.* v. *Wallis* (1912) 28 T.L.R. 209.

An officer cannot be liable for authorising a signature, as distinct from the signature itself, unless he authorises the making of the order etc. on an incorrectly named document.

A company, Lee International (Footwear) Ltd., ordered several moccasins from the plaintiffs on an old order form which gave the company's former name. The order was signed by one director. The other director, being unaware of the fact that an old order form was being used, was held not to be liable under the section *John Wilkes (Footwear) Ltd.* v. *Lee International (Footwear) Ltd.* [1985] BCLC 444.

What amounts to a signature may vary according to the context, It is possible that a signature in the company's name alone will suffice, but there must be an individual affixation of

[22] [1968] 2 Q.B. 839.
[23] *Blum* v. *O.C.P. Repartition SA*, *ante*.
[24] *Barber & Nicholls* v. *R & G Associates (London)* Ltd. (1982) 132 NLJ 1076.
[25] *Linholst & Co. A/S* v. *Fowler* (1988) 4 BCC 776 (C.A.).

that name in confirmation of the order concerned by the officer for him to authorise that signature and so be liable under the section. Merely authorising the filling up of a form with an incorrect name printed on it will not suffice.[26]

Change of name

Companies may change their registered names voluntarily or under compulsion. The latter gives the Department of Trade and Industry control over names similar to those already registered even though they cannot prevent registration of such names.

(1) A company may change its name at any time by a special resolution which takes effect from the issue of a new certificate of incorporation by the Registrar: section 28(1). Such a change of name is subject to the same restrictions as are applicable to the choice of name for a new company registering a name for the first time.[27] The only exception to this freedom to change a name applies where it is proposed to remove the word "limited from a company's name and there had been a direction of the Secretary of State to the contrary.[28]

(2) If a name has been registered which is *the same as* one already on the index of registered names or one that ought to have appeared on the index at the time of registration or is in the opinion of the Secretary of State *too like* any such name, the name must be changed on the direction of the Secretary of State: section 28(2). Such a direction must be given within 12 months of the original registration and must be complied with within such period is specified.

Names are *the same as* existing ones as defined by section 26(3).[29] The Registrar has published notes for guidance as to what will be considered *too like* names, *e.g.* phonetically identical names or where two names have a distinctive element in common, or where because of a similarity of the name and operations of two companies there is likely to be some confusion. These are not conclusive criteria however.

[26] *Oshkosh B'Gosh Incorporated* v. *Dan Marbel Incorporated Ltd.* (1988) 4 BCC 795.
[27] *Ante*, p. 55.
[28] s.31(3). See *ante*, p. 59.
[29] See note 27, above.

(3) When a company has applied to have a controlled name or expression as part of is name it will furnish information to the relevant body and the Department in order to obtain permission under section 26(2)[30] If misleading information has been given or undertakings or assurances have not been fulfilled the Secretary of State may by direction require the company to change its name: section 28(3). Such a direction may be given up to five years from the original registration and must be complied with within such period as is specified.

(4) If the Secretary of State considers that a name gives a misleading indication of the nature of the company's activities so as to be likely to cause harm to the public, they may direct a change. A direction must normally be complied with within six weeks. Within three weeks the company may apply to the court to have the direction set aside: section 32. Failure to comply with any direction renders the company liable to fines.

When a company changes it name a new certificate of incorporation will be issued by the Registrar (sections 28(6), 32(5)) and the new name takes effect from the date of issue of the new certificate.[31]

A change of name does not affect any rights or obligations of the company or any legal proceedings by or against the company: sections 28(7), 32(6).

Business names

If a company which has a place of business in Great Britain, whether or not incorporated here, carries on business in Great Britain under a business name which does not consist of its corporate name without any addition other than one which indicates that the business is being carried on in succession to the former owner, it becomes subject to the Business Names Act 1985.

The first consequence of this is that the company's business name may not without permission of the Secretary of State

[30] *Ante*, p. 57.

[31] The old name continues until then. See *Shackleford, Ford & Co. Ltd.* v. *Dangerfield* (1868) L.R. 3 C.P. 407. In *Lin Pac Containers (Scotland) Ltd.* v. *Kelly*, 1982 S.L.T. 50 (O.H.), a contract entered into in the new name was held valid even though the new certificate was issued three days later.

include any of the words or expressions subject to control on registration of corporate name; *i.e.* those within section 26(2) and its regulations: Business Names Act, section 2. An identical procedure to obtain permission must be followed: Business Names Act, section 3. There is a 12 month period of grace where a business has been transferred to a company which then uses the previous permitted business name.

The second consequence is that a company using a business name distinct from its corporate name must disclose its corporate name and an address for the service of any document on all its business letters, written orders for goods or services, invoices and receipts, and written demands for payment arising in the course of the business, and display a statutory notice of such particulars in each of its business premises (to which either its customers or suppliers have access). Further it must supply such particulars to anyone who asks for them and with whom anything is done or discussed in the course of the business. This must be done by giving him notice "immediately" on request; Business Names Act, section 4.

In default of these obligations the company and its officers may be liable to fines. In addition, failure to comply with the disclosure provisions is subject to some civil consequences under section 5 of the Business Names Act 1985. If a company seeks to enforce any action arising out of a contract made at a time when it was in breach of the disclosure obligations, the court must dismiss the action if the other party can show that he either has a course of action against the company which he was unable to pursue because of the breach or has suffered some financial loss in respect of that contract by reason of the company's breach. The section however has no application either to proceedings brought by such a company on counter-claim or to the right of set-off if it is sued by the other party.

The Registered Office

A company must at all times have a registered office to which communications and notices may be addressed: section 287(1). The memorandum must state whether the registered office is to be in England, Wales or Scotland: section 2(1). The actual address of the registered office need not be set out in the memorandum, but notice of the address must be given to the

Registrar in the statement which, under section 10, *ante*,[32] must be delivered for registration with the memorandum. That address is thus the initial address on incorporation of the company: section 287(2).

The statement as to the registered office in the memorandum fixes the company's nationality and domicile, *e.g.* if the memorandum states that the office is to be in England the company is an English company with British nationality and an English domicile. A corporation is domiciled where it is incorporated and cannot change this domicile,[33] except by Act of Parliament, and the law of a corporation's domicile governs all questions of its status, *e.g.* is it duly incorporated, what are its powers, has it been dissolved? The nationality of a corporation, seldom relevant in private international law, also depends on the place of incorporation.

The reason for requiring a company to have a registered office is that, since the company has a legal existence but does not have a physical existence, it is necessary to know where the company can be found, where the communications and notices may be addressed and where documents can be served on it. A company need not, and very frequently does not, carry on its business at its registered office. There is nothing, for example, to prevent a company with a registered office in England from carrying on its business abroad.

A document can be served on a company by leaving it at or sending it by post to the registered office of the company: section 725(1). It is not necessary to send it by registered post.[34]

If a company registered in Scotland carries on business in England, the process of any court in England can be served at the principal place of the company's business in England, a copy being posted at the same time to the registered office: section 725(2), (3).

Section 351 requires every company to mention its place of registration and registered number, and the address of its registered office, in legible characters on all its business letters and order forms. A company which fails to comply with the subsection, or an officer of a company or other person on its

[32] p. 19.
[33] *Gasque* v. *I.R.C.* [1940] 2 K.B. 80.
[34] *T.O. Supplies (London) Ltd.* v. *Jerry Creighton Ltd.* [1952] 1 K.B. 42.

behalf who issues or authorises the issue of a letter or form which does not comply, is liable to a fine. The phrase "order forms" means forms which the company makes available for other persons to order goods or services from the company and includes, *e.g.* coupons in newspapers which the public fill in asking for goods to be supplied.

Change of address of the registered office

A company may change the address of its registered office on giving proper notice to the registrar. The new address takes effect on the entry of that address on the register but the company has 14 days after giving due notice in which to use the new address and to transfer the registers, etc., required to be kept there before it commits any offences for using the wrong address, etc. This is because the company will not be able to discover the actual date of registration without making a specific search of the register: section 287(3)(4)(5).

Persons dealing with the company may, on the other hand, validly serve any document on the company at the old address within 14 days of the registration of the new address: section 287(4). This is because the new address will in practice appear on the company's registered file a few days after registration.

If a company is unavoidably unable to keep its registers, etc., at its registered office in circumstances in which it was impracticable to give the registrar prior notice, the company and its officers will not be liable if it can show that it resumed performance of that duty at other premises as soon as practicable and notified the registrar of that new address within 14 days of doing so: section 287(6)(7).

Section 711 provides that the Registrar must publish in the *Gazette* notice of the receipt by him of notice of a change in the situation of a company's registered office; *i.e.* he must officially notify it. The point being that section 42 provides that a company cannot then rely against other persons (as regards service of any document on the company) on any change in the situation of the company's registered office if either it was not officially notified (under s.711) at the material time and is not shown by the company to have been known at that time to the person concerned, or if the material time is less than 16 days after official notification and it is shown that the person concerned was unavoidably prevented from knowing of the event at that time.[35]

Items which must be kept at the registered office

The following must be kept at the registered office of a company:

(1) The register of members and, if the company has one, the index of members, unless the register is made up at another office of the company, when they may be kept at that office, or is made up by an agent, when they may be kept at the agent's office: sections 352–354.

(2) The minute books of general meetings: section 383.

(3) The register of interests in the notifiable percentage (three per cent. at present) or more of the shares carrying unrestricted voting rights and, if there is one, the index of names, unless the register of directors' interests is not kept at the registered office, when it must be kept where the register of directors' interests is kept: sections 211, 213.

(4) The register of directors and secretaries: section 288.

(5) The register of directors' interests in shares in, or debentures of, the company or associated companies, together with, if the company has one, the index of names in the register, unless the register of members is not kept at its registered office, when they may be kept where the register of members is kept: section 324.

(6) A copy of each director's contract of service or a memorandum thereof, unless kept where the register of members is kept or kept at the company's principal place of business: section 318.

(7) If the company has one, the register of debenture holders, unless the register is made up at another office, when it may be kept where it is made up, or is made up by an agent, when it may be kept at the agent's office: section 190.

[35] On the other hand official notification does not constitute notice of such an change to anyone: *Official Custodian of Charities* v. *Parway Estates* [1985] Ch. 151 (C.A.).

(8) A copy of every instrument creating or evidencing any charge requiring registration under Part XII of the Act.

(9) The company's register of charges affecting property of the company: section 411.

(10) Any proposed contract or option for an off-market purchase by a company of its own shares, for 15 days prior to the resolution to approve it: sections 164, 165.

(11) Any proposed release by a company of its rights under an off-market purchase contract or option to purchase its own shares: section 167.

(12) Any contract for the purchase by a company of its own shares approved by the company must be kept at the registered office for 10 years from the purchase of the shares or the determination of the contract: section 169.

(13) The requisite statutory declaration of solvency and auditors' report where a private company intends to purchase or redeem its own shares out of capital: section 175.

In general these documents must be kept open for inspection by members without fee for such periods as the Secretary of State may prescribe by regulations. Those regulations will also apply to other rights of inspection and as to the permitted copying of information: section 723A. The minute books are open only to the inspection of members who may also request copies on payment of the prescribed fee. The register of debenture holders is also open to the inspection of creditors without fee. Copies of instruments creating a charge and the register of charges are also open to the inspection of creditors without fee: section 412. Any person may require the company to provide him with a copy of an instrument or entry in the register on payment of a fee. The register of members, the register of directors and secretaries, the register of directors' interests, the register of debenture holders, the register of charges, and, subject to exceptions, the register of interests in three per cent. of the shares, are open to the public on payment of the prescribed fee. The register of directors' interests must also be produced at the annual general meeting and remain open and accessible during the meeting to any person attending.

The Objects

The memorandum must state the objects of the company: section 2. As Lord Parker of Waddington said in *Cotman* v. *Brougham*,[36] the statement of the objects in the memorandum was originally intended to serve a double purpose:

(1) to protect the subscribers who learn from it the purposes to which their money can be applied[37];
(2) to protect persons dealing with the company, who can discover from it[38] the extent of the company's powers.

At common law, a corporation has the same legal capacity as a human being[39] but, in order to protect the shareholders and those who deal with the company, the courts evolved the *ultra vires* doctrine to the effect that since a registered company is an artificial person incorporated by Parliament for the objects stated in the memorandum, it has power only to carry out such objects together with anything incidental thereto. Anything done which is outside the scope of the objects clause was therefore *ultra vires* and void. The result of this doctrine was that objects clauses became very lengthy because companies took all the objects they could conceivably require and the original short form envisaged by the model memorandum in the Companies (Tables A to F) Regulations was rarely used. Nevertheless the *ultra vires* doctrine continually caused unnecessary hardship for innocent third parties and introduced extreme complexity into the law. An additional "protection" for shareholders and third parties was provided by the original rule that the objects clause could not be altered except by a special Act of Parliament or a reconstruction. Later, the objects could be altered but only for specified purposes, initially with the court's consent.

The first EC directive required a change in the law of *ultra vires* and this was implemented by section 9(1) of the European

[36] [1918] A.C. 514 at p. 520. See also *per* Lord Wrenbury at pp. 522, 523.

[37] A member can require the company to send him a copy of the memorandum on payment of a fee: s.19.

[38] They can inspect the memorandum and the other documents kept by the Registrar: s.709.

[39] *Case of Sutton's Hospital* (1612) 10 Co.Rep. 23a; Blackstone Comm. 1, 593; *University of Glasgow* v. *Faculty of Physicians and Surgeons* (1834) 13 S. 9; (1835) 2 S. & M. 275; (1837) 15 S. 736; (1840) 1 Rob. 397.

Communities Act 1972 which became section 35 of the Companies Act 1985. That section proved to have serious defects, however, and in 1985 Dr. Prentice, of Oxford University, was commissioned by the DTI to write a report on the *ultra vires* rule. This report led to major reforms by sections 108 to 112 of the 1989 Act. These reforms have effectively abolished the *ultra vires* rule so far as third parties are concerned, allowed for a catch-all short-form objects clause, given companies a general power of alteration of all such clauses, and limited even their internal effects. Most of the old law has been swept away and readers are referred to the previous edition of this work for a detailed analysis of the *ultra vires* rule, etc., prior to 1991. In this edition only a summary of the pre-1991 position is given.

Form and alteration of the objects clause

Companies are still required to have an objects clause: section 2(1)(*c*). As the result of the legacy of the *ultra vires* doctrine contemporary objects clauses are, as stated above, usually very long and have general clauses at the end, *e.g.* that every object is a separate main object[40] or that the company may do, in addition to the objects listed, anything which the directors consider can be carried on in conjunction with its other objects.[41] Such clauses, developed in response to the court's attempts to limit long objects clauses by discovering main objects and winding up a company for failure of that main object, are perfectly valid.

The first change in the law relating to the objects clause introduced by the 1989 Act is contained in section 3A of the 1985 Act.[42] This section relates to the form of the objects clause and provides that where the memorandum states that the object of the company is to carry on business as a general commercial company, that company is deemed to be able to carry on any trade or business whatsoever and have the power to do anything which is incidental or conducive to the conduct of any trade or business by it. This new short form of objects clause is therefore

[40] See, *e.g.* *Cotman* v. *Brougham* [1918] A.C. 514.
[41] See, *e.g.* *Bell Houses Ltd.* v. *City Wall Properties Ltd.* [1966] 2 Q.B. 656.
[42] Introduced by s.110(1) C.A. 1989.

available to any commercial company and if used will considerably shorten company memoranda. It is not clear, however, whether companies may adopt the wording of section 3A as part of a wider objects clause and still retain the benefit of that section. The section speaks only of *the* object of the company being set out as stated and not of one of the objects, etc.

The 1989 Act also substantially changed the power of a company to alter its objects. New section 4 of the 1985 Act[43] allows a company to alter its objects clause by a special resolution at any time and for any reason. Previously any alteration had to be for a specified purpose. The important point to note, however, is that any such change must be effected by a special resolution. This has consequences for the effects of the objects clause both on third parties[44] and internally on the directors and shareholders.[45]

The new general right of alteration remains, however, subject to section 5 of the 1985 Act. That section provides that certain dissentients may, within 21 days after the passing of the special resolution, apply to the court for an alteration of the objects to be cancelled, and then the alteration is of no effect unless it is confirmed by the court. The application for cancellation can be made by the holders of not less than 15 per cent. in nominal value of the company's issued share capital or any class thereof or, if the company is not limited by shares, not less than 15 per cent. of the members. An application cannot be made by a person who consented to or voted for the alteration.

Section 5 also provides that on an application for cancellation the court may confirm the alteration of objects wholly or in part and on such terms as it thinks fit, and may adjourn the proceedings to enable an arrangement to be made for the purchase, other than by the company of the interests of dissentient members. Alternative the court may provide for the purchase of the dissentient members' shares by the company or make any alterations to the memorandum or articles of the company. Such alterations have the same effect as ones duly authorised by the company. If the court orders that no specified

[43] Substituted by s.110(2) C.A. 1989.
[44] *Post*, p. 73.
[45] *Post*, p. 77.

or general alterations be made to the memorandum or articles this overrides any power in the Act to the contrary.[46]

Section 5 is thus a "minority section," *i.e.* a section designed to prevent the minority of the members of the company being oppressed by the majority. Even though the special resolution altering the objects was passed by the appropriate majority, the alteration requires confirmation by the court if a dissentient minority of members applies to the court.

A company exempt from using the word "Limited" at the end of its name cannot alter its objects so as to take them outside the conditions for such exemption: section 31.

When the objects are altered, a printed copy of the special resolution, or a copy in some other form approved by him, must be delivered to the Registrar within 15 days: section 380; and, if no application is made for cancellation of the alteration, section 6 requires that a printed copy of the memorandum as altered must be delivered to the Registrar between 21 and 36 days after the date of the resolution. If an application for cancellation is made to the court, the company must forthwith give notice in the prescribed form thereof to the Registrar and, on the alteration being cancelled or confirmed, an office copy of the court order must be delivered within 15 days. In the case of confirmation, a printed copy of the memorandum as altered must also be delivered: section 6(1).

If a company is a charitable company, however, it cannot alter its objects clause under section 4 without the prior written consent of the Charity Commissioners. This consent must be sent to the Registrar with the printed copy of the altered memorandum under section 6(1): Charities Act 1960, section 30A.[47]

Effect of the objects clause on corporate transactions—corporate capacity

As has been explained above the objects clause by virtue of the doctrine of *ultra vires* severely restricted the capacity of a company to make contracts, donations, etc. Any act which was

[46] *Post*, Chap. 18.

[47] Introduced by s.111 CA 1989. The Charities Act 1960 also contains restrictions on the effect of any change in the objects clause.

outside the objects clause was *ultra vires* and void. A company could not be sued on any such act[48] and probably could not enforce it.[49] A company was, however, allowed to do things which were reasonably incidental to its stated objects.[50] Above all an *ultra vires* act could not be ratified even by all the members.[51] A further restriction on third parties was that they were deemed to have constructive notice of the contents of the objects clause. An example of the potential injustice caused by a combination of these restrictions is *Re Jon Beauforte Ltd.*[52]

> A company, authorised by its memorandum to carry on business as costumiers and gown makers, started the business of making veneered panels. This was *ultra vires*. They ordered and received coke for this business from coke merchants. Correspondence showed that the coke suppliers had actual notice that the coke was required for the business of veneered panel manufacturers, and since they had constructive notice of the objects clause that this was an *ultra vires* activity. *Held*, they could not prove for their debts in the company's liquidation. Nor in practice could they recover the coke, which legally remained theirs, since it had been consumed.

It would have been different if the coke merchant had not known that the coke was to be used for an *ultra vires* purpose because he could have assumed that it was for an *intra vires* business.

The *ultra vires* doctrine therefore proved to be both unduly restrictive on shareholders and a trap for unwary third parties. In 1986, however, its operation was restricted by the Court of Appeal in *Rolled Steel Products Ltd.* v. *British Steel Corporation*,[53] so that it only applied to the capacity of the company strictly construed. Earlier cases had decided that a company had no capacity to exercise any of its powers, *e.g.* to borrow or lend money, otherwise than for the authorised objects of the company. This approach was rejected in the *Rolled Steel* case. If the company has a power in its objects clause, *e.g* to give

48 *Ashbury Railway Carriage Co. Ltd.* v. *Riche* (1875) L.R. 7 H.L. 653.
49 *Bell Houses Ltd.* v. *City Wall Properties Ltd.*, *ante*; *Cabaret Holdings Ltd.* v. *Meeance Sports & Radio Club Inc.* [1982] N.Z.L.R. 673.
50 *A.G.* v. *Great Eastern Railway Co.* (1880) 5 App.Cas. 473.
51 See note 48, above.
52 [1953] Ch. 131.
53 [1986] Ch. 246 (C.A.). See also *James Finlay Corporation Ltd.* v. *R. & R.S. Mearns*, 1988 S.L.T. 302 (O.H.).

guarantees, then it has the capacity to give a guarantee for any purpose. Questions as to the validity of the guarantee do not depend upon the company's capacity but the authority of the company's agents to bind the company to such a transaction. This also raises questions as to the fiduciary duties of the directors and the liability of third parties as constructive trustees. None of those questions, however, go to the capacity of the company and so the common law doctrine of *ultra vires* was finally refined so that a transaction or act would only be void if it was not capable of falling within the terms of the objects clause either as an object or as a power. Defects such as lack of authority of the agents and breaches of fiduciary duties of directors, etc., are ratifiable by a company if it has the necessary capacity.

It is important to note that the objects clause is important in relation to corporate transactions outside the area of corporate capacity because it could limit the authority of the company's agents. Questions of agency are dealt with in Chapter 6, *post*. In this chapter we are concerned only with the company's own capacity.

Statutory amendments to the ultra vires doctrine

Section 9(1) of the European Communities Act 1972, which became section 35 of the 1985 Act, provided that in favour of a person dealing with a company in good faith any transaction decided upon by the directors was deemed to be within the capacity of the company. Good faith was presumed in the absence of evidence to the contrary and the third party was not bound to enquire as to the company's capacity (thus reversing the concept of constructive notice). This section proved to be defective in several areas—it did not protect the company, it was limited to dealings and so arguably not to gratuitous transactions,[54] it required a transaction decided on by the directors (all of them?) and finally no definition was provided of good faith. In *International Sales & Agencies Ltd.* v. *Marcus*[55] it was suggested that good faith would be destroyed if the third party had actual knowledge that the transaction was *ultra vires*

[54] See, *e.g. Re Halt Garage (1964) Ltd.* [1982] 3 All E.R. 1016, 1024, *per* Oliver J.

[55] [1982] 3 All E.R. 551.

or could not in all the circumstances have been unaware of the *ultra vires* nature of the transaction. It was also suggested that a decision by a sole director or managing director would suffice if the full board had properly delegated the appropriate powers to him.[56]

As a result of the general dissatisfaction with the *ultra vires* concept and the perceived inadequacies of section 35, the 1989 Act made sweeping changes in this area. Section 108 of the 1989 Act substituted a new section 35 into the 1985 Act. Section 35(1) now reads:

> "The validity of an act done by a company shall not be called into question on the ground of lack of capacity by reason of anything in the company's memorandum."

This subsection effectively abolishes the *ultra vires* doctrine insofar as it affects the capacity of the company. It is actually framed so as to exclude any limits on corporate capacity in the whole memorandum but for practical purposes this will mean the objects clause.[57] Unlike its predecessor the new section 35 applies to all acts and for all purposes whatever the status of the third party.[58] However, it only applies to an act done by a company. It begs the question therefore as to whether those acting on the company's behalf have the power to bind the company to the act in question; *i.e.* have they the authority to act on the company's behalf so that it is an act of the company. The fact that the company has the necessary capacity is therefore only the first element in deciding whether the company is bound by an act. All these and other issues relating to corporate transactions and third parties are discussed in Chapter 6. One consequence is, however, that the company will now always have the ability to ratify any act which is contrary to its objects clause. Since such a ratification would amount to a *de facto* alteration of the objects clause it must be effected by a special resolution (new section 35(3), *post*) in the same way as any actual alteration of the clause under section 4.

[56] Agreement by all the directors individually would also suffice: *T.C.B. Ltd.* v. *Gray* [1987] Ch. 458.

[57] It is possible that the capital clause could be infringed by a corporate transaction.

[58] In any event the third party no longer has any constructive notice of the memorandum: s.711A C.A. 1985. See Chap. 6, below.

Section 35 is subject to limitations in the case of charitable companies. In such cases any act which is contrary to the objects clause of the company will only be valid in favour of a purchaser who does not know that the act is outside the memorandum or someone who does not know that the company is a charity. Subsequent purchasers of property without actual notice of the relevant circumstances affecting a transaction's validity are in any event protected: Charities Act 1960, section 30B.[59] Since charitable companies are now required to state their charitable status on all correspondence and other business documents, it is unlikely that the second category will be relevant.[60]

Section 35 is also subject to section 322A of the Companies Act 1985 where the third party is a director of the company concerned. That section is dealt with in Chapter 6, *post*.

Effect of the objects clause on shareholders' rights and directors' duties

A company's objects clause has, in addition to its effects on corporate transactions *vis-à-vis* third parties, always fulfilled a role in the internal aspects of company law. The memorandum binds the company and its members to the same extent as if they had been signed and sealed by each member, and contained covenants on the part of each member to observe all the provisions of the memorandum, especially the objects clause: section 14(1). The effect of this section is that generally there is a contract between the company and its members that the memorandum will be complied with.[61] One consequence of this is that any member has a personal right to seek an injunction to prevent the commission of any act which is outside the objects clause,[62] *i.e.* the investor is entitled to see that the objects for which he invested are adhered to. Since this is a personal right no question of a derivative action arises.[63]

[59] Introduced by s.111 C.A. 1989.
[60] Charities Act 1960, s.36C, introduced by s.111 C.A. 1989.
[61] Section 14 also applies to the articles of association. For a detailed analysis of this contract and its effects see p. 87, *post*, where what is said applies equally to the memorandum.
[62] *Colman* v. *Eastern Counties Railway* (1846) 10 Beav. 1.
[63] *Post*, p. 435.

The 1989 Act reforms expressly preserve this right to seek an injunction but it is now subject to two major limitations, one express and one implied.

New section 35(2) of the 1985 Act provides:

> "A member of a company may bring proceedings to restrain the doing of an act which but for subsection (1) would be beyond the company's capacity; but no such proceedings shall lie in respect of an act to be done in fulfilment of a legal obligation arising from a previous act of the company."

Thus there can be no right to an injunction if the company is legally bound to the act complained of, *i.e.* if the third party can rely on the validity of the act. In deciding that, the new rules as to corporate capacity (set out above) and corporate agency (see Chapter 6, *post*) will operate. It follows that if the directors have effectively bound the company to an act outside its objects clause no action for an injunction will lie. Since, in practice, members will probably only discover the existence of the act or transaction after it has been concluded, it is unlikely, as the result of section 35(2), that they will be able to prevent it happening by an injunction.

The second, implied, limitation on the granting of injunctions stems from the fact that the objects clause is now freely alterable by a special resolution under section 4 and any action outside the object clause can be ratified by such a resolution under section 35(3). Since an injunction is a discretionary remedy it is unlikely that one would be granted if either of the above were imminent or likely. One alternative possibility for an aggrieved minority shareholder may be to petition under section 459 of the Act on the basis of unfairly prejudicial conduct, but he would need to show in that case that acting outside the objects clause was in breach of his legitimate expectations.[64] Alternatively such a shareholder could petition under section 122(*g*) of the Insolvency Act 1986 for a winding up on the just and equitable ground.[65]

There remains, however, a second internal consequence of the objects clause. The directors, acting in the exercise of their powers, are under a duty to act both within the limits of the

[64] *Post*, p. 457.
[65] *Post*, p. 449.

objects clause and bona fide for the benefit of the company.[66] These duties are owed to the company and not to individual members *per se* so the rules as to derivative actions will apply and in general only the company may enforce them. In this connection section 35(3) provides that, notwithstanding the new rules as to corporate capacity:

> "It remains the duty of the directors to observe any limitations on their powers flowing from the company's memorandum."

Since the duties of the directors are owed to the company, the company may ratify such a breach and accordingly section 35(3) allows ratification of any act which would otherwise be contrary to the limitations imposed by the memorandum by a special resolution. However, such ratification is not to affect the liability of the directions, *e.g.* to make good any losses incurred as the result of the act, unless there is a separate resolution to that effect. Special resolutions are required since such ratification will amount to a *de facto* alteration of the objects clause.

If the directors act in breach of their duties in this respect, other persons involved in the breach may well become liable to the company as constructive trustees, if they have the requisite knowledge of the situation. Again the company may only excuse their liability by a special resolution: section 35(3).[67]

THE LIMITATION OF LIABILITY

Whether the liability of the members is limited by shares or by guarantee it is enough if the memorandum merely states that the liability of the members is limited: section 2(3).

Even though a company is exempted under section 30 from using the word "Limited" as part of its name, the memorandum must contain a statement that the liability of the members is limited.

We saw earlier that under section 24[68] a member who knows that the company is carrying on business with less that the statutory minimum of members may become severally liable for its debts and may be sued therefor, *i.e* not only does he lose the

[66] See generally, Chap. 15, *post*.
[67] The position of such third parties is discussed in Chapter 6, *post*.
[68] *Ante*, p. 28.

privilege of limited liability but the veil of incorporation is lifted and he can be sued by the creditors of the company.

It has been noted that a private limited company may be re-registered as unlimited and an unlimited company may be re-registered as limited.[69]

The Share Capital

In the case of a limited company with a share capital, section 2 provides that the memorandum must state the amount of share capital with which the company proposes to be registered and its division into shares of a fixed amount, *e.g.* one hundred thousand pounds divided into one hundred thousand shares of one pound each. This capital, called the "nominal capital" or the "authorised capital," is that which the company is authorised to raise by the issue of shares. This figure is, however, purely nominal. It is important only in that it represents the aggregate amount of shares which the company may issue. The actual or issued capital will depend on how many shares are issued. The stated amount of each share is called its nominal amount or par value. Today it is usual to have shares of a nominal amount of £1 or less each because of their marketability.[70]

It is perfectly legal to have an authorised capital expressed in more than one currency, *e.g.* £3m and 3m US dollars. There is no requirement to state the culmulative total. Similarly, individual shares can be expressed in any currency, although only one currency per share is allowed. The shares will still be of a fixed amount for the purposes of the Act, even though they may fluctuate in value due to the exchange rates.[71]

A public company, however, cannot be registered unless its memorandum has an authorised capital figure of not less than the *authorised minimum*: section 11. This is currently £50,000, (section 118), which is a low figure in practical terms. It is thought that this minimum amount must be expressed in sterling only. Other financial requirements must be met by public

[69] *Ante*, Chap. 2.

[70] The 1985 Tables B and F use the figure of £1. The former Table B used the figure of £200.

[71] *Re Scandinavian Bank Group plc* [1988] Ch. 87. There are in fact several multi-currency companies on the register.

companies before they commence business.[72] The present requirement merely relates to the shares it *may* issue.

The shares into which the nominal capital is divided may be divided into classes, *e.g* preference and ordinary shares, but it is usual to do this in the articles rather than in the memorandum.[73]

The nominal capital may be increased, if the articles authorise it, by an ordinary resolution under section 121.[74] Again, if the articles authorise it, capital can be reduced by a special resolution and the confirmation of the court under section 135.[75] No special provision need be made for these purposes in the memorandum.

Changes in the description of shares on decimalisation, from say, 5s. to 25p was not a change in the fixed amount of the share within section 2(5) and therefore were not an alteration of a condition of the memorandum so that no formalities were required by virtue of the Act.[76]

OTHER CLAUSES

The matters set out *supra* must be stated in the memorandum: section 2. The contents of the memorandum, however, are not restricted to these and may include any other provisions which the framers desire to insert. Sometimes the memorandum contains provisions dealing with the rights attaching to particular classes of shares such as preference shares, *e.g.* dividend and voting rights and the right to participate in the assets of a winding up. When this is so, the articles cannot be referred to for the purposes of ascertaining the rights of the shareholders, unless there is some ambiguity to be explained or some omission to be supplemented.

A company had ordinary and preference shares. The memorandum provided that the holders of the preference shares should have "a preferential right in the distribution of the assets of the company in the event of a winding up or otherwise." The articles provided that on a

[72] *Post*, p. 171.
[73] See *Andrews* v. *Gas Meter Co.* [1897] Ch. 361 (C.A.).
[74] *Post*, p. 186.
[75] *Post*, p. 192.
[76] *Re Harris & Sheldon Group Ltd.* [1971] 1 W.L.R. 899.

winding up the surplus assets after repayment of the whole of the paid-up capital should be divided between all the members in proportion to the capital paid up on their shares, both preference and ordinary. *Held*, (1) the rights conferred by the memorandum on the preference shareholders were exhaustive; (2) they were limited to a preference in the the distribution of the assets, and gave no right to participate in the surplus assets in a winding up or otherwise; and (3) the articles could not be referred to for the purpose of construing the memorandum: *Re Duncan Gilmour & Co. Ltd.* [1952] 2 All E.R. 871.[77]

However, the rights of the holders of particular classes of shares are now usually contained in the articles.

THE ASSOCIATION CLAUSE AND SUBSCRIPTION

The association clause is the clause by which the subscribers to the memorandum (at least two: section 1) declare that they desire to be formed into a company in pursuance of the memorandum and agree to take the number of shares set opposite their respective names. The subscription contains their names, addresses and descriptions and the number of shares which each subscribes for. The subscribers must take at least one share each. Each subscriber must write opposite his name the number of shares he takes and must sign in the presence of at least one witness. The signatures must be attested but one witness may attest all or both signatures: section 2. The Registrar requires the date of execution to be given.

It is usual for each subscriber to sign the memorandum for one share only. This is because the subscriber may by contract be bound to take up a definite number of shares in the company, and if he has signed the memorandum for that number he might be bound to take twice the number he intended, once under his contract, and again under the memorandum.

The subscribers need not be independent persons. They may be nominees, or one of two subscribers may be a trustee, of the one share for which he subscribes, for the other subscriber to

[77] *Cf. Liquidator of the Milford Haven Fishing Co. Ltd.* v. *Jones* (1895) 22 R. 577. Contrast, however, the Scottish cases which are authority for reading the memorandum and articles together as contemporaneous documents: *Oban, etc., Distilleries Ltd., Petitioners* (1903) 5 F. 1140, followed in *Marshall, Fleming & Co., Petitioners*, 1938 S.C. 873 (O.H.).

whom all the rest of the shares issued are allotted,[78] *i.e.* a "one-man" company is legal.

A minor[79] may sign the memorandum because, the contract being voidable and not void, any subsequent avoidance by him will not invalidate the registration.[80]

Another, existing, company may sign the memorandum. So can a person who is a partner in a firm, but an English firm cannot.

ALTERATION OF THE MEMORANDUM GENERALLY

A company may alter its memorandum of association only in the cases, in the mode and to the extent for which express provision is made in the Act: section 2(7). It has been seen that the name, objects and share capital clauses may be altered under section 28, section 4, and sections 121 and 135 of the Act respectively, *ante*. In addition, by section 17, subject to the provisions of sections 16 and 459, *infra*, any condition in the memorandum which could have been in the articles (*i.e.* not such things as the name, the objects or the share capital, which must be in the memorandum) can be altered by special resolution, unless the memorandum itself provides for or prohibits the alteration of the condition, or it relates to class rights, *i.e.* the special rights of any class of members.

Since provisions concerning class rights are the only important provisions which may be in either the memorandum or the articles, and they cannot be altered under section 17 if they are in the memorandum, it follows that the section is unimportant in practice. Further, as was stated earlier, class rights are normally contained in the articles. The methods of varying class rights are explained later.[81]

Section 17 contains the same provisions as to application to the court for cancellation of an alteration as sections 5 and 6,[82] except that there is no equivalent of section 6(4).

Section 16 provides that neither the memorandum nor the articles can be altered so as to require a member to take up

[78] See *Salomon* v. *Salomon & Co. Ltd.* [1897] A.C. 22.
[79] *i.e.* a person under the age of 18: see *post*, p. 233.
[80] *Re Laxon & Co.* (*No.* 2) [1892] 3 Ch. 555. And see s.13, *ante*, p. 22.
[81] *Post*, Chap. 12.
[82] *Ante*, p. 71.

more shares, or in any way increase his liability to contribute to the share capital or otherwise pay money to the company, unless he consents in writing. Section 16 is, therefore, a "minority section," *i.e.* a section intended to prevent the minority of the members being oppressed by the majority.[83] Under section 459 the court can make an order to relieve any part of the members who are being unfairly prejudiced and such an order may alter the memorandum or the articles, in which event the company cannot make a further alteration, inconsistent with the order, without the leave of the court: section 461(3).[84]

Any document making or evidencing an alteration in the memorandum or articles, and any copy of the memorandum or articles as altered, must be in the same language as the memorandum and articles originally registered[85] and, if that language is Welsh, must be accompanied by a certified translation into Engligh: section 27.

Section 351 provides that where a company is required to send to the Registrar any document making or evidencing an alteration in the company's memorandum or articles (other than a special resolution under section 4) the company must send with it a printed copy of the memorandum or articles as altered.

Section 711 requires the Registrar to publish in the *Gazette* notice of the receipt by him of any document making or evidencing an alteration in the memorandum or articles of a company. Section 42 provides that a company cannot rely against other persons on any alteration to the memorandum or articles if it had not been officially notified (under section 711) at the material time and is not shown by the company to have been known at that time to the person concerned, or if the material time is less than 16 days after official notification and it is shown that the person concerned was unavoidably prevented from knowing of the event at that time.[86]

[83] *Post*, Chap. 18.
[84] *Ibid.*
[85] *Ante*, p. 19.
[86] Official notification does not, however, constitute notice to anyone: *Official Custodian of Charities* v. *Parway Estates Ltd.* [1985] Ch. 151 (C.A.).

Chapter 4

ARTICLES OF ASSOCIATION

WHEREAS the memorandum is the company's charter, indicating its nationality, the nature of its business and its capital, the articles of association are the regulations for the internal arrangements and the management of the company. The articles deal with the issue of shares, transfer of shares, alteration of share capital, general meetings, voting rights, directors (including their appointment and powers), managing director, secretary, dividends, accounts, audit of accounts, winding up and various other matters which will be referred to later.

Re Duncan Gilmour, *ante*,[1] shows that, as between the memorandum and the articles, the memorandum is the dominant instrument so that in so far as their provisions conflict, the memorandum prevails, although, apart from matters which by statute must be in the memorandum, reference may be made to the articles to explain an ambiguity in the memorandum or to supplement it where it is silent.[2]

Section 7 provides that articles *may*, in the case of a company limited by shares, and *must* in the case of a company limited by guarantee[3] or an unlimited company,[3] be registered with the memorandum.

Table A in the Companies (Tables A to F) Regulations 1985 is a model form of articles for a public company limited by shares. Any company limited by shares however may (1) adopt Table A in full, (2) adopt Table A subject to modifications, or (3) register its own articles and exclude Table A: section 8(1).

In the case of a company limited by shares, if articles are not registered, or, if articles are registered, in so far as they do not

[1] p. 81.
[2] In *Liquidator of The Humboldt Redwood Co. Ltd.* v. *Coats*, 1908 S.C. 751, the memorandum was silent on the point and so the articles governed.
[3] Chap. 2.

modify or exclude Table A, Table A will automatically be the company's articles: section 8(2).

Tables C, D and E provide model articles for guarantee and unlimited companies which must be adopted by those companies. Section 8A[4] allows the Secretary of State to provide by regulations for Table G, a model form of articles for a partnership company[5]; *i.e.* a company limited by shares whose shares are intended to be held to a substantial extent by or on behalf of its employees.[6] Such companies may adopt part or all of Table G as their articles. This section was introduced to assist in employee buy-outs.

A private company should register its own articles adopting all or any of the regulations in Table A as are appropriate. Minimum requirements for the articles of a private company were abolished in 1980,[7] although it may still be thought desirable to indicate whether and how the transfer of shares is restricted.[8]

Articles must—

(1) be printed (typewriting is not admissible);
(2) be divided into paragraphs numbered consecutively;
(3) be signed by each subscriber to the memorandum of association in the presence of at least one witness, who must attest the signature. Such attestation is sufficient in Scotland as well as in England: section 7(3).

If the memorandum states that the registered office is to be situated in Wales, the memorandum and articles to be delivered for registration under section 10 may be in Welsh but, if they are, they must be accompanied by a certified translation into English: section 21.

The articles (and the memorandum) form a contract between the company and each member and between the members. The articles can be altered by special resolution.

[4] Introduced by s.128 C.A. 1989.
[5] This is an unusual use of the term and should not be confused with the judicial use of that term in connection with just and equitable winding up: see Chap. 18, *post.*
[6] This does not necessarily require a majority of such shareholders.
[7] s.28 of the 1948 Act was repealed by the 1980 Act.
[8] This was formerly one of the minimum requirements for forming a private company.

Effect of memorandum and articles

Subject to the provisions of the Act, the memorandum and articles, when registered, bind the company and the members as if they had been signed and sealed by each member, and contained covenants on the part of each member to observe their provisions: section 14. The result is:

(1) The articles (and the memorandum) form a contract binding the members to the company. Presumably the rule in *Foss* v. *Harbottle*, *infra* applies, *i.e.* an action to enforce the contract must be brought in the name of the company, except where a personal right is infringed.

The articles provided for the reference of differences between the company and any of the members to arbitration. H., a shareholder, brought an action against the company in connection with a dispute as to his expulsion from the company, *i.e.* a dispute between the company and him in his capacity as a member. *Held*, the company was entitled to have the action stayed, as the articles constituted a contract between the company and it members in respect of their ordinary rights as members: *Hickman* v. *Kent or Romney Marsh Sheep-Breeders' Assocn.* [1915] 1 Ch. 881.[9]

" ... articles regulating the rights and obligations of the members generally as such do create rights and obligations between them and the company respectively": *per* Astbury J. at p. 900.

A dispute as to a director's right to inspect the company's books, and accounts, including minutes of board meetings, *i.e.* a dispute between the company and the director in his capacity as director, is not within the terms of articles like those in *Hickman's* case *supra* even though the director is also a member. The plaintiff sued for *inter alia*, a declaration in a representative capacity as a shareholder. It was then claimed that a director had received remuneration to which he was not entitled. He asked for a stay but was refused it: *Beattie* v. *E. & F. Beattie Ltd.* [1938] Ch. 708 (C.A.).

(2) Although section 14 does *not* provide that the memorandum and articles shall bind the company and the members as if they had been signed and sealed *by the company*, and contained covenants *on the part of*

[9] An article prohibiting any member from taking legal proceedings against his company is contrary to public policy and not binding: *St. Johnstone Football Club Ltd.* v. *Scottish Football Assocn. Ltd.*, 1965 S.L.T. 171 (O.H.).

the company to observe their provisions, the articles constitute a contract binding the company to members.

A company declared a dividend and passed a resolution to pay it by giving to the shareholders debenture bonds bearing interest and redeemable at par, by an annual drawing, over 30 years. The articles empowered the company to declare a dividend "to be paid" to the shareholders. *Held* the words "to be paid" meant paid in cash, and a shareholder could restrain the company from acting on the resolution on the ground that it contravened the articles: *Wood* v. *Odessa Waterworks Co.* (1889) 42 Ch.D. 636.

On the other hand the fact that the articles are not so executed by the company limits the time for enforcing such a contract against the company to six years and not the 12 years allowed for contracts under seal: *Re Compania de Electricidad de la Provincia de Buenos Aires Ltd.* [1978] 3 All E.R. 668; *post.*

The courts will imply two terms into this contract insofar as it relates to the powers of the directors: (a) they must be exercised in good faith and in the interests of the company; and (b) they must be exercised fairly as between different shareholders (which does not mean identically).[10]

(3) Members are only bound by and entitled on the above mentioned contract *qua* members, *i.e.* in their capacity as members: *Beattie* v. *E. & F. Beattie Ltd.*, *ante*; *Eley* v. *Positive Life Assurance Co. Ltd.*, *post.*

(4) The articles (and the memorandum) constitute a contract between each individual member and every other member but in most cases the court will not enforce the contract as between individual members,[11] it is enforceable only through the company or, if the company is being wound up, the liquidator.

"It is quite true that ... there is no contract in terms between the individual members of the company; but the articles ... regulate their

[10] *Mutual Life Insurance Co. of New York* v. *The Rank Organisation Ltd.* [1985] BCLC 11.

[11] *Per* Farwell L.J. in *Salmon* v. *Quin and Axtens Ltd.* [1909] 1 Ch. 311 (C.A.) at p. 318.

rights *inter se*. Such rights can only be enforced by or against a member through the company, or through the liquidator representing the company; but ... no member has, as between himself and another member, any right beyond that which the contract with the company gives": *per* Lord Herschell in *Welton* v. *Saffery* [1897] A.C. 299 at p. 315.

It seems that it is the rule in *Foss* v. *Harbottle*[12] which prevents an individual member enforcing the contract. However, the rule is irrelevant where the articles give a member a personal right. In such a case the contract is directly enforceable by one member against another *without* the aid of the company.

Articles of a private company provided that if a member intending to transfer his shares should inform the directors, the *directors* "will take the said shares equally between them at a fair value." *Held*, the articles bound the defendant directors to buy the plaintiff's shares and related to the relationship between the plaintiff as a member and the defendants, not as directors, but as members of the company,[13] and it was not necessary for the company to be a party to the action: *Rayfield* v. *Hands* [1960] Ch. 1.

(5) The provisions of the articles and the memorandum do not constitute a contract binding the company or any member to an outsider,[14] *i.e.* a person who is not a member of the company,[15] or to a member in a capacity other than that of member, *e.g.* that of solicitor, promoter or director of the company.[16]

This is on the general principle that a person not a party to a contract has neither rights nor liabilities under it.

The articles provided that E. should be the solicitor to the company. He was employed as such for a time but subsequently the company ceased to employ him. *Held*, E. was not entitled to damages for breach of contract against the company. The articles did not create a contract

[12] *Post*, Chap. 18.
[13] As is usual, the directors had shares in the company and so were members.
[14] See *per* Astbury J. In *Hickman's* case at p. 900.
[15] A Scots illustration is *National Bank of Scotland Glasgow Nominees Ltd.* v. *Adamson*, 1932 S.L.T. 492 (O.H.); see also *Scottish Fishermen's Organisation Ltd.* v. *McLean*, 1980 S.L.T. (Sh. Ct.) 76.
[16] See note 15, above.

between E. and the company: *Eley* v. *Positive Life Assurance Co. Ltd.* (1876) 1 Ex.D. 88 (C.A.).[17]

However, if a director takes office on the footing of an article providing for remuneration for the director, although the article is not in itself a contract between the company and the director, its terms may be implied into the contract between the company and the director.

An article provided that the remuneration of the directors should be the annual sum of £1,000. The directors were employed and accepted office on the footing of the article. For some time the directors, who were also members, acted as directors but were not paid. The company went into liquidation. *Held*, the article was embodied in the contract between the company and the directors and they were entitled to recover the arrears of remuneration: *Re New British Iron Co.* [1898] 1 Ch. 324.

(6) Because of the words "Subject to the provisions of this Act" in section 14, the contract constituted by the memorandum and articles can be varied to the extent that those documents can be altered in accordance with the provisions of the Act. The extent to which the memorandum may be altered has been dealt with already.[18] It will be seen shortly that, subject to a number of restrictions, the company may alter the articles by special resolution.

Alteration of articles

Subject to the provisions of the Act and to the conditions in its memorandum, a company may by special resolution alter or add to its articles. An alteration or addition so made is as valid and can be altered in the same way as if originally contained in the articles: section 9. Thus a provision in the articles purporting to deprive the company of its power to alter them is void,[19] *e.g.*

[17] A comparable Scottish case is *Muirhead* v. *Forth etc. Steamboat Mutual Insce. Assocn.* (1893) 21 R. (H.L.); (1893) 20 R. 442.
[18] *Ante*, p. 83.
[19] *Malleson* v. *National Insurance Corporation* [1894] 1 Ch. 200.

a provision that no alteration of the articles shall be effective without the consent of X, or that on a proposed alteration only the shares of those opposed shall have a vote.[20]

(1) By section 9 the power to alter articles is subject to the provisions of the Act, *e.g.*, sections 16, 459[21] and 127.[22]

If, as is common, special rights are attached to a class of shares by the articles then the "modification of rights clause" which is either express or implied by the Act[23] (which provides for alteration of the class rights only with the consent of a specified proportion or the sanction of a specified resolution of the shareholders of the class), ensures that those class rights can only be altered with such consent or sanction.[24] Further, by section 127 dissentient holders of not less than 15 per cent. of the issued shares of the class may, within 21 days after the consent was given, apply to the court to have the variation cancelled.[25] This restriction on the alteration of the articles has been held in one case to apply not only to rights actually attached to a specific class of shares, *e.g.* preference shares, but also to rights given by the articles to certain members in their capacity as members. This means that a group of shareholders can enjoy the protection of the variation of class rights procedure if they *qua* shareholders enjoy different rights, *e.g.* of pre-emption of other shares, even though the shares they own are in no way distinguished from other shares; *i.e.* if their class rights attach to them as shareholders and not specifically to the shares themselves.[26]

(2) A company's power to alter its articles is subject to the conditions in the memorandum: section 9. Consequently an alteration of articles must not conflict with the memorandum.

[20] *Per* Russell L.J. in *Bushell* v. *Faith* [1969] 2 Ch. 438 (C.A.) at p. 448.
[21] *Post*, Chap. 18.
[22] *Post*, p. 268.
[23] *Post*, p. 265.
[24] *Post*, p. 269.
[25] See note 23, above.
[26] *Cumbrian Newspapers Group Ltd.* v. *Cumberland and Westmorland Herald Newspaper & Printing Co. Ltd.* [1987] Ch 1.

(3) Under the general law the power to alter articles must be exercised bona fide for the benefit of the company as a whole.

Articles gave the company a lien on partly paid shares for all debts and liabilities of a member to the company. Z., on his death, owed money to the company (arrears of calls on partly paid shares), and was the only holder of fully paid shares. The articles were altered so as to give the company a lien on fully paid shares. *Held*, the alteration was valid and, as from the date of the alteration, gave the company a lien on Z.'s fully paid shares in respect of the debts contracted before the date of the alteration: *Allen* v. *Gold Reefs of West Africa Ltd.* [1900] 1 Ch. 656 (C.A.).[27]

The power conferred on companies to alter articles "must, like all other powers, be exercised subject to those general principles of law and equity which are applicable to all powers conferred on majorities and enabling them to bind minorities. It must be exercised, not only in the manner required by law, but also bona fide for the benefit of the company as a whole, and it must not be exceeded. These conditions are always implied, and are seldom, if ever expressed": *Per* Lord Lindley M.R. at p. 671. "The fact that Zuccani's executors were the only persons practically affected at the time by the alterations made in the articles excites suspicion as to the bona fides of the company. But, although the executors were the only persons who were actually affected at the time, that was because Zuccani was the only holder of paid-up shares who at the time was in arrear of calls. The altered articles applied to all holders of fully paid shares, and made no distinction between them. The directors cannot be charged with bad faith": *Per* Lord Lindley M.R. at p. 675.[28] "Further, I may say that the alteration of the articles giving the extended lien was, in my opinion, in no true sense retrospective. The lien given was not made to take effect before the date of the alteration. It operated only from and after that date": *Per* Romer L.J. at p. 682.

It is for the shareholders, and not for the court to say whether an alteration of articles is for the benefit of the company, unless no reasonable man could so regard it.

The articles provided that S. and four others should be permanent directors of the company, unless they should become disqualified by any one of six specified events. None of the six events had occurred.

[27] *Cf. Liquidator of W. & A. M'Arthur Ltd.* v. *Gulf Line Ltd.*, 1909 S.C. 732. For comments on Allen's case, see *Moir* v. *Thomas Duff & Co. Ltd.* (1900) 2 F. 1265.

[28] On this point see also *Mutual Life Insurance Co. of New York* v. *The Rank Organisation* [1985] BCLC 11.

S. on 22 occasions within 12 months failed to account for the company's money he had received, and the articles were accordingly altered by adding a seventh event disqualifying a director, namely, a request in writing signed by all the other directors that he should resign. Such a request was made to S., who was also a shareholder. *Held*, the contract, if any, between the plaintiff and the company contained in the original articles was subject to the statutory power of alteration, and the alteration was bona fide for the benefit of the company as a whole and valid: *Shuttleworth* v. *Cox Bros. & Co.* (*Maidenhead*) *Ltd.* [1927] 2 K.B. 9 (C.A.).

"Then the first thing to be considered is whether, in formulating the test I have mentioned, Lindley M.R. [In *Allen's* case *supra*] had in mind two separate and distinct matters; first, bona fides, the state of mind of the persons whose act is complained of, and secondly, whether the alteration is for the benefit of the company, apart altogether from the state of mind of those who procured it. In my opinion this view of the test has been negatived by this Court in *Sidebottom's* case.[29] So the test is whether the alteration of the articles was in the opinion of the shareholders for the benefit of the company. By what criterion is the Court to ascertain the opinion of the shareholders upon this question? The alteration may be so oppressive as to cast suspicion on the honesty of the persons responsible for it, or so extravagant that no reasonable men could really consider it for the benefit of the company": *Per* Bankes L.J. at p. 18. See also *per* Scrutton L.J. at p. 23.

The expression "bona fide for the benefit of the company as a whole" means that the shareholder must proceed upon what, in his honest opinion, is for the benefit of the company as a whole. The phrase "the company as a whole" does not mean the company as a commercial entity, distinct from the corporators; it means the corporators as a general body. It may be asked whether what is proposed is, in the honest opinion of those who voted in its favour, for the benefit of an individual hypothetical member. Looking at the converse, an alteration of articles is liable to be impeached if its effect is to discriminate between the majority shareholders and the minority so as to give the former an advantage of which the latter are deprived. It is not necessary that persons voting for an alteration of articles should dissociate themselves altogether from their own prospects.[30]

The articles of a private company prohibited a transfer of shares to a non-member so long as another member was willing to buy them at a

[29] *Infra*.

[30] *Per* Lord Evershed M.R. in *Greenhalgh* v. *Arderne Cinemas* [1951] Ch. 286 (C.A.) at p. 291.

fair value. The holder of the majority of the shares wished to transfer them to a non-member, so the articles were altered so as to permit a transfer to any person with the sanction of an ordinary resolution. *Held* the alteration was bona fide and valid, although thereby the minority lost their rights of pre-emption: *Greenhalgh* v. *Arderne Cinemas Ltd.* [1951] Ch. 286 (C.A.).[31]

It has been said that the phrase "corporators as a general body" means both present and future members of the company.[32]

If an alteration of articles is bona fide for the benefit of the company, it is immaterial that it prejudices a minority of the members.

A private company, in which the directors held a majority of the shares, altered its articles so as to give the directors power to require any shareholder who competed with the company's business to transfer his shares, at their fair value to nominees of the directors. S., who had a minority of the shares and was in competition with the company, brought an action for a declaration that the special resolution was invalid. *Held*, (1) as a power to expel a shareholder by buying him out was valid in the case of original articles it could be introduced in altered articles, provided that the alteration was made bona fide for the benefit of the company as a whole; (2) the alteration was so made and was valid: *Sidebottom* v. *Kershaw, Leese & Co.* [1920] 1 Ch. 154 (C.A.).[33]

"I think . . . that it is for the benefit of the company that they should not be obliged to have amongst them as members persons who are competing with them in business and who may get knowledge from their membership which would enable them to compete better": *Per* Lord Sterndale M.R. at p. 166.

The principles of natural justice are not applicable in this field.[34]

It has been held that the members of a company, acting in accordance with the Act and the constitution of the company, and subject to any necessary consent on the part of the class affected, can alter the relative voting powers attached by the

[31] *Cf. Crumpton* v. *Morrine Hall Pty. Ltd.* [1965] N.S.W.R. 240.
[32] *Per* Megarry J. in *Gaiman* v. *National Association of Mental Health* [1971] 1 Ch. 317 at p. 330.
[33] See also *Crookston* v. *Lindsay, Crookston & Co. Ltd.*, 1922 S.L.T. 62 (O.H.).
[34] *Per* Megarry J. in *Gaiman's case, ante*, at p. 335.

articles to various classes of shares, provided that the special resolution is passed in good faith for the benefit of the company as a whole.

The issued capital of S. Ltd. comprised 400,000 management shares, which under the articles carried eight votes each, and 3,600,000 ordinary shares. On the acquisition by S. Ltd. of the shares in B. Ltd. in consideration of the issue of 8,400,000 ordinary shares in S. Ltd., the articles were altered so as to double the votes carried by management shares in order to ensure continuity of management. The special resolution was passed by a large majority at an extraordinary general meeting of the company. The holders of management shares, directors of S. Ltd., did not vote in respect of these shares or their ordinary shares. Nor did they vote at a separate class meeting of the ordinary shareholders which sanctioned the special resolution. *Held*, the alteration was valid: *Rights and Issues Investment Trust Ltd.* v.*Stylo Shoes Ltd.* [1965] Ch. 250.[35]

However, it has been said, in an Australian case, that the benefit of the company as a whole is an impossible test where the question is simply one as to the relative rights of different classes of shareholders. In this event there must be no fraud or oppression of the minority.[36]

The onus of showing that the power to alter articles has not been properly exercised is on the party complaining.[37]

If, in a rare case, an alteration is not for the benefit of the company as a whole, or its effect is to discriminate between the majority of the shareholders and the minority shareholders, so as to give the former an advantage of which the latter are deprived, the court will restrain the company from making it or acting on it.

In the New South Wales case of *Australian Fixed Trusts Pty. Ltd.* v. *Clyde Industries Ltd.* (1959) S.R. (N.S.W.) 33 the A. Co held, as trustee for the holders of units in a unit trust about 300,000 of the 2,000,000 ordinary shares issued by the C. Co. C. Co. proposed to alter its articles so as to provide that a member holding ordinary shares as trustee for the holders of units in a unit trust should not vote in respect of the shares without the direction of the majority of the holders of the

[35] A comparable Scottish case is *Caledonian Insurance Co.* v. *Scottish American Invest. Co. Ltd.*, 1951 S.L.T. 23 (O.H.).

[36] *Peter's American Delicacy Co. Ltd.* v. *Heath* (1939) 61 C.L.R. 457 (High Court of Australia), *per* Latham C.J. at p. 481 and Rich J. at p. 495.

[37] *Per* Latham C.J. in *Peters'* case *supra*, at p. 482.

units. *Held*, the alteration would be invalid. Its effect was to discriminate between the majority of the shareholders and the minority. No reasonable man could decide that it was for the benefit of the company as a whole.

In the absence of a prohibition in the memorandum the articles can be altered so as to authorise the issue of preference shares taking priority over existing shares although no power to issue preference shares is conferred by the memorandum or the original articles.[38]

(4) An alteration of articles in breach of a contract to which the company is a party is valid but the other party is entitled to damages. If a person enters into an arrangement which can only take effect by the continuance of an existing state of circumstances, he is under an obligation to do nothing to put an end to that state of circumstances.[39]

S., a director of B. Co., was properly appointed managing director for 10 years by a contract outside the articles. The articles provided that the managing director, *subject to his contract with the company*, was subject to the same provisions as to removal as the other directors, and that if he ceased to be a director, he should *ipso facto* cease to be managing director. The articles also provided that the company could remove a director before the expiration of this period of office. Later, F. Co. acquired the shares in B. Co. and the articles were altered so as to empower F. Co. to remove any director of B. Co. Before the expiration of 10 years F. Co removed S. from the board of directors of B. Co. and he thereby ceased to be managing director. *Held*, it was an implied term of the contract that B. Co. would not remove S. as director during the term of 10 years and B. Co. was liable to S. for breach of contract: *Southern Foundries* (1926) *Ltd.* v. *Shirlaw* [1940] A.C. 701.[40]

"A company cannot be precluded from altering its articles thereby giving itself power to act upon the provisions of the altered articles—but so to act may nevertheless be a breach of contract if it is contrary to a stipulation in a contract validly made before the alteration": *per* Lord Porter at p. 740.

[38] *Andrews* v. *Gas Meter Co.* [1897] 1 Ch. 361 (C.A.).

[39] *Per* Lords Atkin and Porter in the *Southern Foundries* case at pp. 717 and 741 respectively. See also *per* Scott J. in *Cumbrian Newspaper Group Ltd.* v. *Cumberland and Wesmorland Herald etc.*, *ante*.

[40] See also *Shindler* v. *Northern Raincoat Co. Ltd.* [1960] 1 W.L.R. 1038, *post*, p. 392, and *Carrier Australasia Ltd.* v. *Hunt* (1939) 61 C.L.R. 534, *post*, p. 391.

Note what was said earlier of sections 18, 42 and 711 and an alteration of articles.[41]

Any document making or evidencing an alteration in the company's memorandum or articles and a copy of the memorandum or articles as altered must be in the same language as the memorandum and articles originally registered and, if that language is Welsh, must be accompanied by a certified translation into English: section 21.

Inspection of articles

A company is required to furnish a copy of its memorandum (embodying any alterations) and of its articles to its members on request, on payment of not more than five pence a copy: sections 19, 20.

Any person, whether a member of the company or not, may inspect a copy of the memorandum and articles of association of any company at the office of the Registrar of Companies. He may also have a copy or extract of them: section 709, 710A.

Rectification of articles

The court has not inherent jurisdiction to rectify thearticles, even if it is proved that they were not in accordance with the intention of the original signatories.[42]

[41] p. 84.

[42] *Scott* v. *Frank F. Scott (London) Ltd.* [1940] Ch. 794 (C.A.).

Chapter 5

PROMOTERS

BEFORE a company can be formed there must be some persons who have an intention to form a company, and who take the necessary steps to carry that intention into operation. Such persons are called "promoters." Promoters stand in a fiduciary position towards the company and, as a result, they owe certain duties.

MEANING OF TERM "PROMOTER"

The term promoter was originally defined in the Act by reference to the preparation of a prospectus only for the purposes of liability for a misstatement in a prospectus. That part of the Act was repealed by the Financial Services Act 1986 which uses the term "promoter" but does not define it.[1] However, a promoter has been described, for example, as "one who undertakes to form a company with reference to a given project and to set it going, and who takes the necessary steps to accomplish that purpose."[2]

A company may have several promoters and, as is shown by cases such as the *Leeds Theatres* case, *post*, one existing company may promote another new company.

Persons who give instructions for the preparation and registration of the memorandum and articles of association are promoters. So, too, are persons who obtain the directors (very often a promoter is himself a prospective director), issue a prospectus, negotiate underwriting contracts or a contract for the purchase of property by the company, or procure capital.

[1] F.S.A. 1986 s.150(6). The former definition was in s.67 of the 1985 Act.
[2] *Per* Cockburn C.J. in *Twycross* v. *Grant* (1877) 2 C.P.D. 469 (C.A.) at p. 541.

A person may become a promoter after the company is incorporated, *e.g.* by issuing a prospectus or preparing listing particulars, or by procuring capital to enable the company to carry out a preliminary agreement. Whether a person is actually a promoter and, if so, the date when he became one and whether he is still one, are questions of fact.

A person who has taken no active part in the formation of a company and the raising of the necessary share capital but has left it to others to get up the company on the understanding that he will profit from the operation is a promoter.[3]

Anyone who acts merely as the servant or agent of a promoter is not himself a promoter. A solicitor, therefore, who merely does the legal work necessary to the formation of a company is not a promoter.[4]

At one time the business of a company promoter was almost a separate business in itself but this is not so today. Further, the increasingly strict provisions of successive Companies Acts, culminating in the Financial Services Act 1986, in relation to the issue and contents of listing particulars or a prospectus have almost eliminated the fraudulent company promoter.

POSITION AND DUTIES OF PROMOTERS

A promoter is not an agent for the company which he is forming because a company cannot have an agent before it comes into existence.[5] Furthermore, he is usually not treated as a trustee for the future company.[6] However, from the moment he acts with the company in mind, a promoter stands in a fiduciary position[7] towards the company and therefore he must not make any secret profit out of the promotion, *e.g.* a profit on

[3] See *per* Lindley J. in *Emma Silver Mining Co. Ltd.* v. *Lewis* (1879) 4 C.P.D. 396 at p. 408, and *Tracy* v. *Mandalay Pty. Ltd.* (1952–53) 88 C.L.R. 215.

[4] *Re Great Wheal Polgooth Ltd.* (1883) 53 L.J.Ch. 42.

[5] *Kelner* v. *Baxter* (1866) L.R. 2 C.P. 174, *post*, p. 106; *Tinnevelly Sugar Refining Co. Ltd.* v. *Mirrlees, Watson & Yaryan Co. Ltd.* (1894) 21 R. 1009.

[6] *Omnium Electric Palaces Ltd.* v. *Baines* [1914] 1 Ch. 332, *post*; *Edinburgh Northern Tramways Co.* v. *Mann* (1896) 23 R. 1056, *post*.

[7] *Henderson* v. *The Huntington Copper etc. Co. Ltd.* (1877) 5 R. (H.L.) 1; (1877) 4 R. 294; the fiduciary relationship was regarded as arising from agency rather than from trust in *Edinburgh Northern Tramways Co.* v. *Mann* (1896) 23 R. 1056.

a sale of property to the company. These liabilities are independent of any liability for misstatements etc. in listing particulars or a prospectus (see Chap. 7).

A promoter must disclose a profit which he is making out of the promotion to either—

(1) an *independent* board of directors[8]; or
(2) the existing and intended shareholders, *e.g.* by making disclosure in a prospectus.[9]

> "I do not say that an owner of property may not promote and form a joint stock company, and then sell his property to it, but I do say that if he does he is bound to take care that he sells it to the company through the medium of a board of directors who can and do exercise an independent and intelligent judgment on the transaction."[10]

The requirement of an independent board of directors is one which, in most cases, cannot be complied with, as the promoters, or some of them, are usually the first directors of the company. In the formation of a private company, the promoter usually sells his business to a company, of which he is managing director, and in which he is the largest shareholder, but, nevertheless, the transaction cannot be impeached on the ground that there is no independent board of directors.[11]

> "After *Salomon's Case* I think it is impossible to hold that it is the duty of the promoters of a company to provide it with an independent board of directors, if the real truth is disclosed to those who are induced by the promoters to join the company."[12]

If there no disclosure to an independent board, there must be *full* disclosure of the profit made by the promoters to the existing and intended shareholders, either in a prospectus or in some other way.

[8] *Erlanger* v. *New Sombrero Phosphate Co.* (1878) 3 App.Cas. 1218 (P.C.), *post*; *Tracy* v. *Mandalay Pty. Ltd.*, *ante.*
[9] *Lagunas Nitrate Co.* v. *Lagunas Syndicate* [1899] 2 Ch. 392 (C.A.); *Scottish Pacific Coast Mining Co. Ltd.* v. *Falkner, Bell & Co.* (1888) 15 R. 290.
[10] *Per* Lord Cairns L.C. in *Erlanger's* case, above, at p. 1236.
[11] *Salomon* v. *Salomon & Co. Ltd.* [1897] A.C. 22, *ante*, p. 24.
[12] *Per* Lindley M.R. in the *Lagunas* case, above, at p. 426.

" 'Disclosure' is not the most appropriate word to use when a person who plays many parts announces to himself in one character what he has done and is doing in another."[13]

If a person buys property with the intention of reselling it to a company which he is forming, he is not presumed to acquire that property as trustee for the company and if, as a matter of fact, he intends to acquire it as a promoter, it is quite legal for him to resell to the company at a profit, provided that he discloses the profit.[14] If he intends to acquire as a trustee, he will have to hand over the property to the company at the price paid by him.

Remedies for breach of duty

If a promoter fails to make full disclosure of a profit made by him out of the promotion the following remedies may be open to the company. Since the promoter's duties are owed to the company the rule in *Foss* v. *Harbottle*[15] is relevant to their enforcement.

(1) Where the promoter has, *e.g.* sold his own property to the company, the company may rescind the contract and recover the purchase-money paid.

A syndicate, of which E. was the head, purchased an island in the West Indies said to contain valuable mines of phosphates for £55,000. E. formed a company to buy this island, and a contract was made between X., a nominee of the syndicate, and the company for its purchase at £110,000. *Held*, as there had been no disclosure by the promoters of the profit they were making, the company was entitled to rescind the contract and recover the purchase-money from E. and the other members of the syndicate: *Erlanger* v. *New Sombrero Phosphate Co.* (1878) 3 App.Cas. 1218 (P.C.).

The right of rescission may be lost in a number of ways. For example, it will be lost if the parties cannot be restored to their

[13] *Per* Lord Macnaghten in *Gluckstein* v. *Barnes* [1900] A.C. 240, *post*, at p. 249.
[14] *Omnium Electric Palaces Ltd.* v. *Baines* [1914] 1 Ch. 332 (C.A.).
[15] *Post*, Chap. 18.

original positions, as where the property has been worked so that its character has been altered.[16] However, even if restitution is strictly not possible, rescission may be allowed if restitution is substantially possible. The right to rescind will also be lost if third parties have acquired rights for value, by mortgage or otherwise, under the contract.[17]

(2) The company may compel the promoter to account for any profit he has made.

Intending to buy property and to form a company and resell the property to the company or another purchaser, a syndicate of four persons bought charges on the property at a discount. They afterwards bought the property for £140,000, formed a company of which they were the first directors and resold the property to the company for £180,000. As a result of this, they made a profit of £40,000 on the property and one of £20,000 on the charges which were paid off in full with the £140,000 received for the property. A prospectus was issued, disclosing the profit of £40,000 but not that of £20,000. It appears that rescission had become impossible. *Held*, the £20,000 was a secret profit made by the syndicate as promoters of the company and they were bound to pay it to the company: *Gluckstein* v. *Barnes* [1900] A.C. 240.

(3) The company may sue the promoter for damages for breach of his fiduciary duty.

The F. Co. contracted to purchase two music-halls for £24,000 and had the property conveyed to its nominee, R., intending to sell it to the T. Co. when formed. The F. Co. then promoted the T. Co. and agreed to sell the music-halls to it for £75,000 and directed R. to convey them. The board of directors of T. Co. was not an independent board. A prospectus was issued to the public by the T. Co., giving R. as the vendor, and not disclosing the interest of F. Co. or the profit it was making. *Held*, the prospectus should have disclosed that F. Co. was the real vendor and the amount of profit it was making. For breach of their fiduciary duty to those invited to take shares the promoters were liable in damages to the company and the measure of damages was the promoters' profit: *Re Leeds and Hanley Theatres of Varieties Ltd.* [1902] 2 Ch. 809 (C.A.).

Where promoters sell their own property to the company, the company cannot affirm the contract and at the same time ask

[16] As in *Lagunas Nitrate Co.* v. *Lagunas Syndicate* [1899] 2 Ch. 392 (C.A.).

[17] As in *Re Leeds and Hanley Theatres of Varieties Ltd.* [1902] 2 Ch. 809, *post*, where the mortgagee of the property had sold it.

for an account of profits or for damages as this would be, in effect, asking the court to vary the contract of sale and order the defendants to sell their assets at a lower price.[18]

Apart from the remedies mentioned above, if a promoter fails to disclose a profit made by him out of the promotion other remedies may be available to the company. The company may be able to recover damages for fraud against the promoter[19] or, perhaps, damages for negligent misrepresentation.[20] And note section 212 of the Insolvency Act 1986 *post*.[21]

If a promoter, even though he has not sold property to the company, makes a secret profit out of the promotion of the company, he must account for that profit to the company.[22] He is, however, only bound to account for the profit he has made, that is, after deducting all legitimate expenses, *e.g.* surveyors' and solicitors' charges, and printing costs, incurred in the formation of the company.[23]

Payment for Promotion Services

A promoter has no right against the company to payment for his promotion services in the absence of an express contract with the company. In England such a contract will normally have to be under seal since the company cannot make a valid contract before incorporation and when the contract can be made the consideration by the promoter will normally be past. In the absence of such a contract he cannot even recover from the company payments he has made in connection with the formation of the company.

[18] *Re Cape Breton Co.* (1885) 29 Ch.D. 795 (C.A.); *Jacobus Marler Estates Ltd.* v. *Evatt* [1971] A.C.793 (P.C.) and cases such as *Esso Petroleum Co. Ltd.* v. *Marler* (1913) 85 L.J.P.C. 167n., *per* Lord Parker; *Tracy* v. *Mandalay Pty. Ltd.* (1952–3) 88 C.L.R. 215, *per* the High Court of Australia at p. 239.

[19] *Per* Romer L.J. in the *Leeds* case, *supra*.

[20] Under the principle in *Hedley Byrne Ltd.* v. *Heller & Partners* [1964] A.C. 645, *Mutual Life and Citizens' Assurance Co. Ltd.* v. *Evatt* [1971] A.C. 793 (P.C.) and cases such as *Esso Petroleum Co.Ltd.* v. *Mardon* [1975] 2 W.L.R. 147 or under the Misrepresentation Act 1967, s.2(1), *post*, p. 150.

[21] p. 419.

[22] *Henderson* v. *The Huntington Copper etc. Co. Ltd.* (1877) 5 R. (H.L.) 1; (1877) 4 R. 294; *Mann* v. *Edinburgh Northern Tramways Co.* (1892) 20 R. (H.L.) 7; (1891) 18 R. 1140.

[23] *Lydney and Wigpool Iron Ore Co.* v. *Bird* (1886) 33 Ch.D. 85 (C.A.).

A syndicate promoted a company and paid £416 2s. in respect of registration fees and *ad valorem* stamp duty incidental to the formation of the company. The company shortly afterward went into liquidation. *Held*, the syndicate were not entitled to prove for the payments they had made: *Clinton's Claim* [1908] 2 Ch. 515 (C.A.).

The rule that consideration must not be past is not of Scots law, and the promoter of a Scottish company might be entitled to found on a suitably worded provision in the memorandum or articles to the effect of recovering from the company payments made by him in connection with the formation of the company.[24] The success of a promoter's claim against the company seems to depend on his establishing that the relevant provision creates a *jus quaesitum tertio* in his favour. Where such a right is established, a promoter is entitled to remuneration for professional services rendered.[25] If no such right is established, neither promoters nor experts employed by them have a right to remuneration from the new company; such experts have no claim except against the persons who employed them, namely the promoters.[26]

Any amount or benefit paid or given within the two preceding years, or intended to be paid or given, to a promoter must normally be disclosed in a prospectus or listing particulars.[27]

SUSPENSION OF PROMOTERS

A person who has been convicted on indictment of any offence in connection with the promotion or formation of a company may have an order made against him by the court that he shall not, without leave of the court, be a director, liquidator, receiver or take part in the management of a company for a period of up to 15 years: Company Directors Disqualification Act 1986, section 2.[28]

[24] *Scott* v. *Money Order Co. etc. Ltd.* (1870) 42 Sc. Jur. 212.
[25] See, *e.g. Edinburgh Northern Tramways Co.* v. *Mann* (1896) 23 R. 1056.
[26] *Per* Lord M'Laren in *J. M. & J. H. Robertson* v. *Beatson, M'Leod & Co. Ltd.*, 1908 S.C. 921 at p. 928.
[27] F.S.A. 1986, ss.144, 162. See Chap. 7, *post*.
[28] *Post*, p. 352.

Chapter 6

CORPORATE TRANSACTIONS

THIS chapter deals, first, with contracts and other transactions made on behalf of a company before it is formed, and secondly, with those made after the company has been formed. Since a company is an artificial person it cannot physically enter into a transaction but must always do so either through a human agent or in writing under its common seal. This chapter is therefore also concerned with the impact of company law on the rules of agency as to the making of such transactions and the law relating to contracts under seal involving companies.

CONTRACTS MADE BEFORE INCORPORATION OF COMPANY

Effect on company

If, before the formation of a company, some person purports to make a contract on its behalf, or as trustee for it, *e.g.* a contract for the sale of property to the company, the contract, or "preliminary agreement" as it is sometimes called, is not binding on the company when it is formed, even if the company takes the benefit of the contract. Before incorporation the company lacks capacity to make the contract[1] and an agent cannot contract on behalf of a principal who is not in existence.[2]

Solicitors, on the instructions of persons who afterwards become directors of the company, prepared the memorandum and articles of

[1] "If somebody does not exist they cannot contract," *per* Harman J. in *Rover International Ltd.* v. *Cannon Film Sales Ltd.* [1987] 1 W.L.R. 1597, at p. 1599.

[2] This does not apply to a company which contracts in a new name prior to the change of name becoming operative. Such a company is at all times in existence: *Oshkosh B'Gosh Incorporated Ltd.* v. *Dan Marbel Inc. Ltd.* (1988) 4 BCC 795; *Vic Spence Associates* v. *Balchin*, 1990 S.L.T. 10 (O.H.).

association of the company, and paid the registration fees. *Held*, the company was not liable to pay their costs: *Re English and Colonial Produce Co. Ltd.* [1906] 2 Ch. 435 (C.A.).

"There is no binding authority for the proposition that a company, because it has taken the benefit of work done under a contract entered into before the formation of the company, can be made liable in equity under that contract": *per* Vaugham Williams L.J. at p. 442.[3]

Conversely, a company cannot, after incorporation, enforce a contract made in its name before incorporation, or sue for damages for breach of such a contract.

N. Co. agreed with a person acting on behalf of a future company, P. Co., that N. Co. would grant a mining lease to P. Co. P. Co. discovered coal whereupon N. Co. refused to grant the lease. *Held*, P. Co. could not compel N. Co. to grant the lease: *Natal Land etc. Co. Ltd.* v. *Pauline Colliery Syndicate Ltd.* [1904] A.C. 120 (P.C.).[4]

D., acting on behalf of a future company, T. Co., entered into a contract with M. Co. for the supply by the latter of certain machinery for a refinery. When T. Co. was registered it alleged that the machinery supplied was defective. *Held*, T. Co. could not sue M. Co. for damages: *Tinnevelly Sugar Refining Co. Ltd.* v. *Mirrlees, Watson & Yaryan Co. Ltd.* (1894) 21 R. 1009.

Further, such a contract cannot be ratified by the company after it is incorporated—the company was not a principal with contractual capacity at the time when the contract was made—although, as is explained later, the contract may be novated.[5]

The Gravesend Royal Alexandra Hotel Company Ltd. was being formed to buy an hotel from K. At a time when all concerned knew that the company had not been formed, a written contract was made "on behalf of" the proposed company by A, B and C for the purchase

[3] For Scots law *cf.* Lord President Dunedin in *Welsh & Forbes* v. *Johnston* (1906) 8 F. 453 at p. 457, and Lord M'Laren in *J. M. & J. H. Robertson* v. *Beatson, M'Leod & Co. Ltd.*, 1908 S.C. 921 at p. 928 *ante*, p. 104. See also *F. J. Neale (Glasgow) Ltd.* v. *Vickery*, 1971 S.L.T. (Sh. Ct.) 88.

[4] *Molleson and Grigor* v. *Fraser's Trustees* (1881) 8 R. 630 is a Scottish authority.

[5] *Kelner* v. *Baxter*, below; *Tinnevelly* case, above. See also *Cumming* v. *Quartzag Ltd.*, 1980 S.C. 276, in which, following the *Tinnevelly* case, the Court of Session held that an agreement made on behalf of a company to be incorporated could not give rise to a *jus quaesitum tertio* in favour of the company when incorporated; Hector L. MacQueen, *Promoters' Contracts, Agency and the Jus Quaesitum Tertio*, 1982 S.L.T. (News) 257.

of £900 worth of wine from K. The company was formed, and the wine handed over to it and consumed, but before payment was made the company went into liquidation. *Held*, A, B and C were personally liable on the contract, and no ratification could release them from their liability: *Kelner* v. *Baxter* (1866) L.R. 2 C.P. 174.

"Where a contract is signed by one who professes to be signing 'as agent,' but who has no principal existing at the time, and the contract would be altogether inoperative unless binding on the person who signed it, he is bound thereby; and a stranger cannot by a subsequent ratification relieve him from that responsibility": *per* Erle C.J. at p. 183.

This situation cannot be remedied by the operation of the doctrine of estoppel by convention. That requires an assumption of fact, *i.e.* that the company would be bound, by both parties to a contract prior to the "agreement." Since the company was not then in existence it could make no such assumptions.[6]

The Jenkins Report recommended[7] that a company should be enabled unilaterally to adopt, *i.e.* to ratify, contracts which purport to be made on its behalf or in its name prior to incorporation; until the company does so adopt such contracts, the persons who purported to act for the company should be entitled to sue and be liable to be sued thereon.

It appears that unilateral adoption (ratification) of such contracts by the company has been prevented by section 36C[8] *infra*, although a novation, *post*, has not. The question of individual liability has however been adopted by that section.

Effect on individuals

Under the general law, if an individual contracts as "agent"[9] or trustee for a future company, whether there is a contract between him and the other person involved depends upon what a reasonable man would think the parties intended. If they have expressed themselves in writing the question is one of construction of the written terms for the judge. If orally, the question is one of fact.[10]

[6] *Rover International Ltd.* v. *Cannon Film Sales Ltd.* [1987] 1 W.L.R. 1597.
[7] Para. 54.
[8] See *post*, p. 125. The suggestion was taken up in Singapore. See *Cosmic Insurance Corporaton Ltd.* v. *Khoo Chiang Poh* (1981) 13 N.L.J. 286 (P.C.).
[9] Strictly, one cannot be agent for a principal not yet in existence.
[10] *Per* Fullagar J. in *Summergreene* v. *Parker* (1950) 80 C.L.R. 304, at p. 324.

In *Kelner* v. *Baxter*, above, it was intended that A, B and C should contract personally. In the *Newborne* case, the intention was that the future company should contract.

Tinned ham was sold to S. Ltd. The contract was "We have this day sold to you ... (Signed) Leopold Newborne (London) Ltd." The signature was typed and underneath was written "Leopold Newborne." The market price of ham fell and S. Ltd. refused to take delivery. When an action was brought it was found that Leopold Newborne (London) Ltd. had not been incorporated at the time of the contract and Leopold Newborne tried to enforce the contract in his own name. *Held*, neither Leopold Newborne (London) Ltd. nor Leopold Newborne could enforce the contract. It was not a case of an agent undertaking to do certain things himself as agent for somebody else. It was a contract in which a company purported to sell. Leopold Newborne did not purport to contract as principal or agent—the contract purported to be made by Leopold Newborne (London) Ltd., on whose behalf it was signed by a future director. "This company was not in existence and ... the signature on that document, and indeed, the document itself ... is a complete nullity": *Newborne* v. *Sensolid* (*Great Britain*) *Ltd.* [1954] 1 Q.B. 45.

The position of the individual was, however, changed substantially by section 9(2) of the European Communities Act 1972, which became section 36(4) of the 1985 Act. That section was repealed by the 1989 Act and replaced by section 36C of the 1985 Act.[11] The latest section retains, however, the same concepts as its predecessor.

Section 36C(1) provides:

"A contract which purports to be made by or on behalf of a company at a time when the company has not been formed has effect, subject to any agreement to the contrary, as one made with the person purporting to act for the company or as agent for it, and he is personally liable on the contract accordingly."[12]

This means that in circumstances like those in *Newborne's* case, *ante*, today, unless there is an agreement to the contrary, there will be a contract between the individual who acts for the company and the other person involved. Presumably such individual will be entitled to sue on the contract as well as being

[11] Introduced by s.130(4) C.A. 1989. This implements the second part of the Jenkins Committee's recommendation. See above.

[12] Subs. 36C(2) extends this liability to deeds in England and obligations in Scotland.

liable to be sued on it. The words "subject to any agreement to the contrary" allow for the case where there is a novation.

In *Phonogram Ltd.* v. *Lane* [1981] 3 All E.R. 182, the Court of Appeal considered the effect of old section 36(4) which was identical in all relevant respects to section 36C. They held that it rendered the individual "agent" liable even though the company was not at the time in the course of formation.[13] Further a contract can be "purported" to be made by a company even though both parties to the contract knew that the company had not then been formed.

They also considered that signing the contract as an agent, or as in the *Newborne* case, *ante*, would not amount to an agreement to the contrary so as to avoid personal liability. Lord Denning M.R. considered that only a clear exclusion of personal liability would suffice.[14]

In *Rover International Ltd.* v. *Cannon Film Sales Ltd.*,[15] the court held that the former section 36(4) did not apply to companies incorporated outside the UK contracting in the UK so that the individual concerned was not liable. The judge also suggested that in any event there might have been a contrary intention since the individual could not have performed the contract himself due to foreign exchange control restrictions. Under section 130(6) of the 1989 Act the Secretary of State has power to apply section 36C to companies incorporated outside Great Britain by regulation.

New contract after incorporation—novation

Of course, a company may, after incorporation enter into a new contract with the other party to the same effect as a contract made on its behalf before incorporation, in which event there is a novation, *i.e.* the old contract is discharged and replaced by the new. Such a new contract may be inferred from the acts of the parties after incorporation.

J. had agreed with W., acting on behalf of a company about to be formed, to sell certain property to the company, After the company's

[13] A contrary argument based on the French text of the Directive implemented by the 1972 Act was rejected.
[14] Thus in effect overruling *Newborne's* case.
[15] [1987] 1 W.L.R. 1597.

incorporation, the directors resolved to adopt the agreement, and to accept J.'s offer to take part of the purchase-money in debentures instead of cash. *Held*, a contract was entered into by the company with J. to the effect of the previous agreement as subsequently modified: *Howard* v. *Patent Ivory Mfg. Co.* (1888) 38 Ch.D. 156.[16]

However, such a new contract will not be inferred if the acts of the company after incorporation are due to the mistaken belief that it is bound by the contract made before incorporation.

A contract was made between W. and D., who was acting on behalf of an intended company, for the grant of a lease to the company. The company, on its formation, entered on the land the subject of the lease and began to erect buildings on it but did not make any fresh agreement with respect to the lease. *Held*, the agreement, being made before the formation of the company, was not binding on the company, and was incapable of ratification; and the acts of the company were done in the erroneous belief that the agreement was binding on the company and not evidence of a fresh agreement between W. and the company: *Re Northumberland Avenue Hotel Co.* (1886) 33 Ch.D. 16 (C.A.).

Modern practice

Agreements to sell property to a company about to be formed are not now, as a rule, made with a person expressed to be acting on behalf of or as trustee for the company, because of the liability incurred by such person, and the absence of liability incurred by the company unless there is a novation. Although the other party will not be bound before the company is formed, the modern practice is for the promoters[17] to have prepared, before the company is incorporated, a draft agreement to which the company is expressed to be a party, and for the agreement to be executed by the other party and on behalf of the company after incorporation, pursuant to a clause in the company's memorandum to that effect. If, as is common, a company is being formed to acquire the promoters' business,[18] it does not matter that the promoters are not bound.

[16] *Cf. James Young & Sons Ltd. and Liquidator* v. *Gowans* (*James Young & Sons' Trustee*) (1902) 10 S.L.T. 85 (O.H.).
[17] *Ante*, Chap. 5.
[18] *Ante*, p. 96.

CONTRACTS MADE PRIOR TO COMMENCEMENT OF BUSINESS

Any contract made by a public company after it is incorporated but before it is entitled to commence business[19] is nevertheless valid, but in such cases if the company fails to comply with its obligations within 21 days of being asked to do so the directors are liable to compensate the other party for any loss or damage consequent on its inability to commence business: section 117(8).

FORM OF CONTRACTS

A company may make contracts either in writing under its common seal or by an agent acting within his authority on the company's behalf: section 36.[20] The rules as to the form of contracts for companies are the same as those for individuals, *e.g.* as to whether the contract needs to be in writing or under seal or can be made orally.

Execution of documents—England and Wales

A company may execute any document by affixing its common seal in accordance with the articles (see below). However, a company is not required to have a common seal and whether it has one or not it may execute a document in such a way that it will have the same effect as one made under the seal: section 36A.[21] That section provides that any document signed by a director and the company secretary or by two directors, and expressed, in either case, to be executed by the company (by any form of words) will be treated as if the seal had been affixed.

Further, if they intend the document to be a deed and that is made clear on the face of the document, it will take effect as a deed upon delivery. Such delivery will also be execution of the deed unless a contrary intention is proved.[22]

[19] See *post*, p. 171.
[20] As substituted by s.130(1) C.A. 1989.
[21] Introduced by s.130(2) C.A. 1989. This section only applies to England and Wales.
[22] Similar provisions apply to deeds executed by individuals: see s.1 of the Law of Property (Miscellaneous Amendments) Act 1989.

To protect third parties acting in good faith for valuable consideration,[23] a document which *purports* to be signed by a director and secretary or two directors will be as valid as if it was signed by actual directors and/or the actual secretary provided the other conditions are fulfilled. Thus third parties need not investigate the validity of the appointment of those signing the document.[24]

Execution of documents—Scotland

Under Scots law a document is validly executed by a company if it is signed on behalf of the company by a director or the secretary or by a person authorised to sign the document on its behalf, except that where authentication is required a document is validly executed by a company, and is probative, if it is subscribed on behalf of the company by —

(a) two of the directors;
(b) a director and the secretary; or
(c) two persons authorised to subscribe the document on behalf of the company.

The document need not be witnessed or sealed with the company's common seal (which a company is no longer required to have): section 36B as substituted by the Law Reform (Miscellaneous Provisions) (Scotland) Act 1990.

Use of the seal

Table A, article 101 provides: "The seal shall only be used by the authority of the directors or of a committee of directors authorised by the directors. The directors may determine who shall sign any instrument to which the seal is affixed and unless otherwise so determined it shall be signed by a director and by the secretary or by a second director."

A company which continues to have a common seal and whose objects comprise the transaction of business in foreign

[23] Including lessees and mortgagees.
[24] This is similar to the general protection given to conveyancers generally in s.74 Law of Property Act 1925.

countries may, if authorised by its articles, have for use in any place outside the United Kingdom, an official seal. The official seal must be a facsimile of the company's common seal, with the addition on its face of the name of every place where it is to be used: section 39.

Section 40 allows a company which continues to have a common seal to have an official seal for use for sealing securities issued by the company and for sealing documents creating or evidencing securities issued by the company. This official seal must be a facsimile of the common seal of the company with the addition on its face of the word "Securities."

A document requiring *authentication* by a company is sufficiently authenticated by the signature of a director, secretary or other authorised officer, and need not be under seal: section 41.

Bills of exchange

Bills of exchange and promissory notes can be drawn, accepted or indorsed on behalf of a company by any person acting under the company's authority: section 37. Officers who sign their own names without making it clear that they are signing on behalf of the company may incur personal liability.[25] But when a director signs the modern form of company cheque with the company name and account number printed on it, he has been held to be signing only as an agent and is not personally liable on the cheque, even though he has not expressly signed on behalf of the company or as its agent.[26]

TRANSACTIONS BY AGENCY

Unless a company contracts in writing using its common seal, or the equivalent procedures discussed in the previous section, it can only enter into a transaction through the medium of agency, *i.e.* by a transaction made by an agent acting on behalf of the company who either has authority to bind the company to that transaction at the time or whose actions are subsequently validly

[25] *Brebner* v. *Henderson*, 1925 S.C. 643; contrast *McLean* v. *Stuart and Others*, 1970 S.L.T. (Notes) 77 (O.H.).
[26] *Bondina Ltd.* v. *Rollaway Shower Blinds* [1986] 1 W.L.R. 517 (C.A.).

ratified by the company. In general, therefore, the central question is whether the agent has the requisite authority to bind the company (his principal), and in this respect companies are in many ways no different from individuals—the ordinary rules of agency apply as to establishing authority. But companies are artificial persons with a constitution laid down by the memorandum and articles. We have already seen, in Chapter 3, that the objects clause in the memorandum used to restrict the capacity of the company itself to enter into transactions which were outside that clause and a company clearly cannot authorise an agent to do what it itself had no capacity to effect. Section 35 of the Act (substituted by the 1989 Act) has removed any such constitutional restrictions based solely on corporate capacity[27] but the memorandum and articles may equally restrict the authority of a company's agents to act on its behalf. In such a case any person dealing with the company would not be able to rely on an agent having authority if the transaction was contrary to the company's constitution, *e.g.* if it was contrary to a restriction in either the memorandum or articles.

Limitations under the company's constitution—the position prior to 1990

The effect of company law on the general law of agency therefore has been that even if an agent is otherwise acting within his authority to bind the company, a third party will not be able to enforce the transaction if the agent was acting contrary to the company's constitution. Since a third party was deemed to have constructive notice of all the company's registered documents, including the memorandum and articles, he could not rely on the agent having authority where the act was contrary to such documents. This doctrine was, however, subject to an exception, known as the rule in *Royal British Bank* v. *Turquand*[28] whereby if an agent was acting apparently consistently with the company's constitution, the third party was not affected by any internal irregularity, *e.g.* the lack of a directors' resolution required under the articles to authorise the transaction, since he could not have discovered whether such a

[27] *Ante*, p. 75.
[28] (1856) 6 El. & Bl. 327.

resolution had or had not been passed. Third parties did not have constructive notice of matters not on the register.[29] Only actual notice of the irregularity would affect him.[30]

This situation was substantially changed, however, in 1972 by section 9(1) of the European Communities Act 1972, which became section 35 of the 1985 Act. That section, which attempted to remove the limits on corporate capacity,[31] also restricted the effect of limitations on the authority of the company's agents arising from the company's constitution. It suffered from serious defects, however, which have already been noted in Chapter 3, and was repealed by the 1989 Act. That Act substituted a new section 35 and added new sections 35A and 35B into the 1985 Act. These new sections apply as to the effects of the company's constitution on the authority of a company's agents as from 1991 onwards. For a detailed discussion of the position prior to 1991, readers are referred to the previous edition of this work.

Limitations under the company's constitution—the position from 1991

We have already seen in Chapter 3 that, from 1991 onwards, nothing in a company's memorandum can affect the capacity of a company to enter into a transaction, following the new section 35, and further that no one has constructive notice of any entry on the company's register, *e.g.* of the memorandum and articles, by virtue of section 711A. In addition, new section 35A removes any constitutional limitations on the powers of the directors and others to act on behalf of the company so far as bona fide third parties are concerned, whilst preserving the existing internal rights of members to control the directors if they do act contrary to the company's constitution. The position is slightly different for charitable companies and substantially different if the third party is himself a director of the company concerned (see below).

[29] Thus whether or not an ordinary resolution had been passed would not matter since there is no requirement to register an ordinary resolution, whereas the lack of a required special resolution authorising the deal would destroy the agent's authority—special resolutions must be registered.
[30] But see p. 116, *post.*
[31] *Ante*, p. 74.

Section 35A(1) provides that:

"In favour of a person dealing with a company in good faith, the power of the board of directors to bind the company, or authorise others to do so, shall be deemed to be free of any limitation under the company's constitution."

This therefore removes any restrictions imposed upon the authority of the directors, either to act themselves or to empower others to act, by the company's constitution if the third party is dealing in good faith. If section 35A(1) applies then the sole question is whether the agent was acting within his authority apart from the company's constitution. What amounts to authority is considered below.

It is necessary to analyse section 35A(1). First, the section only applies in favour of a third party and not the company. This is a distinction more apparent than real, however, since the company may always ratify any agent's acts, unless they are illegal, and then enforce the transaction. Such ratification will need to be by special resolution only if the transaction is contrary either to a provision in the memorandum or articles since a special resolution would be required to alter such a provision.[32] Second, that person must be "dealing with a company." Section 35(2)(*a*) provides that anyone who is a party to any transaction[33] or other act to which the company is a party is dealing with that company.[34] The use of the words "transaction" and "act" seem to indicate that gratuitous acts will be included.

Thirdly, the person dealing with a company must be acting in good faith. Section 35A(2)(*b*) provides that bad faith is not to be assumed simply because the third party knew that the act was contrary to the directors' powers under the constitution. This was intended to reverse the judicial interpretation of the

[32] Under ss.4 and 9 respectively. S.35(3) makes the position clear with respect to the memorandum, but it must equally apply to the articles. Ratification of a breach of the articles cannot be by anything less than a special resolution which must be registered.

[33] See *T.C.B. Ltd.* v. *Gray* [1986] Ch. 621 for the court's views as to what constitutes a transaction in this context.

[34] This clarifies earlier judicial statements on a similar phrase in the former section 35, see, *e.g. International Sales and Agencies Ltd.* v. *Marcus* [1982] 3 All E.R. 551, *Re Halt Garage* (1982) *Ltd.* [1982] 3 All E.R. 1016, *International Factors* (*N.I.*) *Ltd.* v. *Streeve Construction Ltd.* [1984] N.I.J.B.

phrase in the previous section 35 that good faith would be defeated if the third party actually knew or could not in all the circumstances have been unaware of the defect.[35] Something more than knowledge is now required, presumably understanding, although it is unclear whether this is to be subjectively or objectively tested. What was intended no doubt was a distinction between notice and knowledge, with only the latter counting, as it does for liability under constructive trusts.[36] The wording of the section is such however, that a third party may on the one hand be able to plead the validity of the transaction against the company under section 35A on the basis that, although he has objective knowledge of the defect, that is not enough to defeat a presumption of good faith, whilst on the other hand he may be liable to the company as a constructive trustee under the knowing receipt category because he has such knowledge and not simply notice of the defect.

The position of the third party with respect to good faith is further strengthened by section 35A(2)(*c*) which requires a presumption of good faith until the contrary is proved, and section 35B which provides that the third party is not bound to enquire whether a transaction[37] is either contrary to the memorandum or is subject to any constitutional limitations on the powers of the directors.

In favour of such a third party, the powers of the directors to bind the company or authorise others to do so are to be free of any limitations under the company's constitution. A company's constitution includes its memorandum and articles and under section 35A(3) any resolution of the company or of a class of shareholders and any shareholder agreement.[38] The freedom given by section 35(A)(1) thus applies to any acts of the directors as a whole or of any agent to whom they have delegated the transaction expressly or impliedly. The section is not intended to extend the authority of an agent, simply to

[35] *International Sales and Agencies Ltd.* v. *Marcus* (*supra*), approved in *International Factors* (*N.I.*) *Ltd.* v. *Streeve Construction Ltd.* (*supra*).

[36] *Re Montague's S.T.* [1987] Ch. 264. For the liability of third parties as constructive trustees, see *Hanbury and Maudsley, Modern Equity* (13th ed., 1989), pp. 288 *et seq.*

[37] But not in this case an act.

[38] All but special resolutions were covered by the rule in *Turquand's* case (see note 28, above) which is still valid, in any event.

remove fetters if he would otherwise have authority to bind the company. It is possible, however, that in one respect at least it has extended the ordinary rules of agency.[39]

If the third party is not acting in good faith, the company may always ratify the transaction either by an ordinary resolution, or by a special resolution if the defect relates to the memorandum or articles.[40]

Directors as third parties

The general rule, discussed above, that if the third party dealing with the company is in good faith no restrictions imposed upon the company's directors by the company's constitution will affect him, is modified where that third party is himself a director of that company or of its holding company.[41] In such a case if the board exceed any limitation on their powers under the company's constitution then the transaction[42] is voidable at the instance of the company whether or not the director is dealing in good faith: section 322A(1)(2).[43] The transaction remains valid, however, until it is avoided by the company, unless it is void for some other reason (*e.g.* if it is illegal under the Act): section 322A(4).

The company will lose the right to rescind (avoid) the transaction in any of the following circumstances:

(i) restitution of property supplied is no longer possible;
(ii) the company is indemnified against any loss or damage arising from the transaction;
(iii) bona fide purchasers without actual notice of the defect have acquired rights which would be affected by the avoidance, *e.g.* if the subject matter has been deposited as security with a bank; or
(iv) the transaction is ratified by the company either by an ordinary or special resolution[44] as necessary.

[39] See p. 121, *post*.
[40] See note 32, above.
[41] The modification also applies to persons connected with such a director or an associated company of such a director, as defined in s.346.
[42] Defined so as to include any "act."
[43] Introduced by s.109 C.A. 1989.
[44] A special resolution will be needed if the defect arises from limitations in the memorandum or articles. See note 32, above.

It is important to remember that to be valid the transaction does not need to be ratified in this way, it is valid unless avoided by the company. The right to rescind or avoid a transaction may be limited under the general law, *e.g.* by undue delay.

Where there are two (or more) persons dealing with a company, one of whom is a director and the other is neither a director nor connected with one, and where that second person is dealing in good faith then he may continue to rely on the protection given by section 35A, above, although the director will be subject to section 322A. To avoid the difficult situation of a transaction which is valid for one person under section 35A but voidable against another (the director) under section 322A, either the third party or the company may apply to the court to settle the matter. The court may then affirm the transaction as a whole, set it aside on just terms or sever it: section 322A(6)(7).

Finally, section 322A provides that whether or not the transaction is avoided the director who deals with the company and any director of the company who authorised the transactions must account to the company for any gain arising from the transaction and indemnify the company against any loss. The company may, however, waive this right by the appropriate resolution.

Charitable companies

Section 35A only applies in favour of a person dealing with a charitable company if that person either both gives full consideration in money or money's worth and does not know that the transaction is contrary to the company's constitution, or is unaware at the time that he is dealing with a charitable company: Charities Act 1960, section 30B.[45] The burden of proof is on the persons alleging the requisite knowledge.[46] Bona fide purchasers who subsequently acquire property without actual notice of any defect under the company's constitution

[45] Introduced by s.111 C.A. 1989. This section only applies in England and Wales. For the position in Scotland, see s.112 C.A. 1989. Since charitable companies must disclose their status on all letters, etc., the second type of third party is unlikely to occur very often. See s.30C Charities Act 1960.

[46] s.30B(3) Charities Act 1960.

relating to the original transaction are, however, protected by that section.[47]

The other major difference to the ordinary regime if the company is a charitable company is that the ratification of any act which is contrary to the objects clause[48] or of any transaction where a director has been dealing with his company (under section 322A, above) will be ineffective unless it has the prior written consent of the Charity Commissioners: Charities Act 1960, section 30(*b*)(4).

Internal consequences

Just as with the memorandum, any limitations on the powers of the directors, etc., contained in the company's constitution remain binding on the directors as a limitation on their powers and a contractual right for the members.[49] The liberalisation of the effects of such limitations on third parties under section 35A does not affect any right of the members to petition for an injunction preventing any breach of their powers by the directors or the liability of the directors and other for such breaches: section 35A(4)(5). No injunction can be granted, however, if the company is already legally obliged to carry out the transactions. This is identical to the equivalent provision in section 35 and what has been said on that section applies equally here.[50]

Agency—persons acting in good faith

If the outsider is dealing with the company in good faith, as defined in section 35A, *ante*, he will be able to enforce any contract made by an agent on the company's behalf if that agent was acting within his authority, irrespective of any limitations on his powers under the company's constitution. If the outsider is not acting in good faith, the position is different.[51] An agent may bind his principal (in this case the company) if he has acted within his actual, implied or apparent authority.

[47] Similar rules apply to any third party wishing to take advantage.
[48] See p. 76, *ante*.
[49] See the discussion at p. 77, *ante*.
[50] *Ante*, p. 78.
[51] *Post*, p. 125.

As to actual authority, an individual director may be specifically authorised by the board of directors to make a particular contract on behalf of the company.[52] In *Rolled Steel Products (Holdings) Ltd.* v. *B.S.C.*[53] Slade L.J. stated that the directors had no actual authority to exercise any express or implied power of the company other than for the purposes of the company as set out in the memorandum; although if the shareholders unanimously consented this might not be so. Browne-Wilkinson L.J. expressed no opinion on this point and it would seem that on agency principles a simple majority will suffice to give the directors such actual authority. Whether the directors are then acting in breach of their fiduciary duties is a separate question which does not *per se* affect the outsider.[54]

As to implied authority, a director may, under a power in the articles, be appointed to an office, *e.g.* that of managing director, which carries with it authority to make certain contracts on behalf of the company.[55] However, the question of implication does not stop there and authority may be implied from the conduct of the parties and the circumstances of the case.[56] A person with actual authority to obtain quotations of prices has no implied authority to communicate acceptance of such quotes where no decision to purchase has been made by his principal—at most such a person may have apparent authority.[57]

A company is also bound by the acts of an agent acting within his apparent authority[58] where he lacks actual authority

[52] Or a board of directors may pass a resolution authorising two of their number to sign cheques: *per* Lord Denning M.R. in *Hely-Hutchinson* v. *Brayhead Ltd.* [1968] 1 Q.B. 549 (C.A.) at p. 583.

[53] [1986] Ch. 246 (C.A.).

[54] *Post*, Chap. 15.

[55] *Per* Willmer L.J. in *Freeman & Lockyer* v. *Buckhurst Park Properties (Mangal) Ltd.* [1964] 2 Q.B. 480 (C.A.) at pp. 488, 489. Diplock L.J. agreed. And see *Paterson's Trustees* v. *Caledonian Heritable Security Co. Ltd.* (1885) 13 R. 369 (manager borrowed money for purposes of company, and used money to purchase heritable property the title to which was taken in his own name).

[56] As in *Hely-Hutchinson's* case, *ante.*

[57] *Crabtree-Vickers Pty. Ltd.* v. *Australia Direct Mail Advertising Co. Pty. Ltd.* (1976) 50 A.L.J.R. 203, following the *Freeman & Lockyer* case and *Turquand's* case.

[58] *Panorama Developments (Guildford) Ltd.* v. *Fidelis Furnishing Fabrics Ltd.* [1971] 2 Q.B. 711 (C.A.), *post*, p. 426, where the secretary had apparent authority to hire cars on behalf of the company.

(although actual authority and apparent authority are not mutually exclusive and generally co-exist). Thus an outsider may be protected where an individual director acts on behalf of the company without actual authority but with apparent authority, which apparent authority may arise from a representation that he has authority made by the board of directors or such a representation contained in the company's public documents. In *Rolled Steel Products (Holdings) Ltd.* v. *B.S.C.*,[59] Slade L.J. thought that the directors would have such authority in relation to any transaction which falls within the company's express or implied powers.

In such a case the company will be bound if the other party can prove—

(1) that he was induced to make the contract by the agent being held out as occupying a certain position in the company;
(2) that the representation, which is usually by conduct, was made by the persons with actual authority to manage the company, generally or in respect of the matters to which the contract relates, who are usually the board of directors[60]; and
(3) that the contract was either one which a person in the position which the agent was held out as occupying would usually have actual authority to make or one which the company had by its conduct as a whole represented that he had authority to make.[61]

Condition (2), *ante*, is due to the fact that the principal, the company, is not a natural person. It follows from the condition that the outsider cannot as a rule[62] rely on the agent's own representation that he has authority.[63]

R., the chairman of the directors of the defendant company, B. Ltd., acted as its *de facto* managing director. The board knew of and

[59] [1986] Ch. 246.
[60] But occasionally the shareholders: *Mahony* v. *East Holyford Mining Co.* (1875) L.R. 7 H.L. 869, *post*.
[61] *Ebeed* v. *Soplex Wholesale Supplies Ltd.* [1985] BCLC 404 (C.A.). Usually these will be the same.
[62] See the *Crabtree-Vickers* case, *ante*.
[63] *Per* Diplock L.J. in the *Freeman & Lockyer* case, *ante*, at p. 505 and Lord Pearson in the *Hely-Hutchinson* case, *ante*, at p. 593.

acquiesced in that and the articles of B. Ltd. empowered the board to appoint a managing director. H. was the chairman and managing director of a public company, P. Ltd., which needed financial assistance. B. Ltd. was prepared to help and accordingly in January, 1965. B. Ltd. bought shares in P. Ltd. from H. for £100,000 and proposed to inject £150,000 into P. Ltd. H. became a director of B. Ltd. but never saw its memorandum and articles and did not attend board meetings until May 19, 1965. After that meeting R. and H. agreed that H. would put more money into P. Ltd. if B. Ltd. would secure his position. R., on behalf of B. Ltd., signed letters to H. in which B. Ltd. purported to indemnify H. against loss on his guarantee of a bank loan of £50,000 to P. Ltd. and to guarantee a loan by H. to P. Ltd. H. then advanced £45,000 to P. Ltd. When P. Ltd. went into liquidation H. had to honour his guarantee and he claimed the £50,000 and the £45,000 from B. Ltd. B. Ltd. denied liability and said that R. had no authority to sign the letters (and that the contracts were unenforceable for non-disclosure of H.'s interest in accordance with s.317). *Held*, that on the facts R. had actual authority implied from the conduct of the parties and the circumstances of the case to enter into the contracts with H. (and that it was too late to avoid them for non-disclosure of H.'s interest as required by the articles): *Hely-Hutchinson* v. *Brayhead Ltd.* [1968] 1 Q.B. 549 (C.A.),[64] applying the *Freeman & Lockyer* case, below.

The articles of a company formed to purchase and resell an estate empowered the directors to appoint one of their body managing director. K., a director, was never appointed managing director but, to the knowledge of the board, he acted as such. On behalf of the company he instructed architects to do certain work in connection with the estate. *Held*, the company was bound by the contract and liable for the architects' fees. K. had apparent authority because he had been held out by the board as managing director and, therefore, as having authority to do what a managing director would usually be authorised to do on behalf of the company, and his act was within the usual authority of a managing director. Accordingly, the plaintiffs could assume that he had been properly appointed: *Freeman & Lockyer* v. *Buckhurst Park Properties* (*Mangal*) *Ltd.* [1964] 2 Q.B. 480 (C.A.).[65]

The persons who signed the articles of a company, and who under the articles were entitled to appoint directors, treated some of

[64] And see *post*, p. 408. A corresponding Scots case is *Allison* v. *Scotia Motor etc. Co. Ltd.* (1906) 14 S.L.T. 9 (O.H.), where a *de facto* managing director engaged a works manager of the company for a period of five years.

[65] Applying *Biggerstaff* v. *Rowatt's Wharf Ltd.* [1896] 2 Ch. 93 (C.A.) and *British Thomson-Houston Co.* v. *Federated European Bank Ltd.* [1932] 2 K.B. 176 (C.A.) See also *Clay Hill Brick Co. Ltd.* v. *Rawlings* [1938] 4 All E.R. 100; *Rhodian River Shipping Co. S.A.* v. *Halla Maritime Corp.* [1984] BCLC 139.

themselves as directors although there was no proper appointment. The articles provided that cheques should be signed as directed by the board. The person acting as secretary informed the company's bank that the "board" had resolved that cheques should be signed by two of three named directors and countersigned by the secretary. The bank acted on the communication and honoured cheques so signed. *Held*, the bank was entitled to honour the cheques and was not liable to refund the money paid. The rule in *Turquand's* case applied; *Mahony* v. *East Holyford Mining Co.* (1875) L.R. 7 H.L. 869.

The requirement appears to be that the representation was made by a person with "actual" authority to manage the business. Thus if the representation is made by someone with no such authority the outsider cannot rely on it.

A sales representative, with the title of "unit manager," purported to bind his company to repay sums advanced by the bank to another company. He had no actual or apparent authority to do so. The bank sought confirmation from the company's "general manager" of its City branch. He confirmed the "unit manager's" authority, but he himself had no authority to make loans. *Held*, the bank could no rely on the general manager's statements as to the unit manager's authority: *British Bank of the Middle East* v. *Sun Life Assurance of Canada (U.K.) Ltd.* [1983] BCLC 78 (H.L.).[66]

Where the outsider relies on a representation by the board of directors it is of course not necessary that he should actually have inspected the company's public documents but where he is seeking to rely on a representation in the public documents it is essential that he inspected them. A party seeking to set up an estoppel (or, in Scots law, a personal bar) must show that he relied on the representation which he alleges, be it a representation in words or a representation by conduct.

A director purported to make, on behalf of the company, an agreement whereby an outsider was to sell on commission goods imported by the company and to retain the proceeds as security for a debt due from another company. The outsider had not inspected the

[66] *Quaere* the effect of the wording of section 35A on this situation? Now the power of the director to authorise others to act on behalf of the company is free of any limitation under the company's constitution. Does this allow any representation to bind the company in such situations?

company's public documents and did not know of the power of delegation contained in the articles. Further, the agreement was so unusual as to put the outsider upon inquiry to ascertain whether the director had authority in fact. *Held*, the company was not bound: *Houghton & Co.* v. *Nothard, Lowe and Wills Ltd.*, [1927] 1 K.B. 246 (C.A.); affirmed on other grounds [1928] A.C. 1.

R. Co., by their principal director, A., purported to enter into an oral contract with B., who was a director of and purported to act for P. Co. but had no actual authority. The alleged contract was that the two companies should finance the sale of a telephone directory holder produced by a third company. R. Co. claimed repayment of money paid by them to B. as agent for P. Co. in pursuance of the contract. R. Co. alleged that P. Co. were estopped from denying B.'s authority because the P. Co.'s articles provided that the directors could delegate their powers to a committee of one or more directors. However, A. had not inspected the articles until after the action began (and even if A. had inspected the articles a single director would not normally have authority to act for the company). *Held*, because A. had not inspected the articles when the contract was made, they could not be relied on as conferring ostensible or apparent authority on B., and the action failed: *Rama Corporation Ltd.* v. *Proved Tin, etc., Ltd.* [1952] 2 Q.B. 147.

Agency—persons acting otherwise than in good faith

If the third party is not acting in good faith he cannot rely on section 35A and will by definition have knowledge of the express limitation in the company's constitution. Unless the transaction is ratified therefore the company will not be bound. In addition, the rule in *Turquand's* case has never applied in four situations, which in effect provide that an outsider acting in bad faith will be bound by internal irregularities as well. In such cases even if the agent is otherwise acting within his implied or apparent authority the outsider will be bound by the irregularity and the company will not be liable.

The rule in *Turquand's* case does not apply, *i.e.* the company is not bound and the outsider is not protected, in the following cases:—

(1) Where the outsider knows of the irregularity or lack of actual authority.

Under the articles the directors had power to borrow up to £1,000 on behalf of the company without the consent of a general meeting and to borrow further money with such consent. The directors themselves lent £3,500 to the company without such consent, and took debentures.

Held, the company was liable, and the debentures were valid, only to the extent of £1,000: *Howard* v. *Patent Ivory Manufacturing Co.* (1888) 38 Ch.D. 156.

(2) Where the outsider purported to act as a director in the transaction, *i.e.* to act for and on behalf of the company in the transaction. On the other hand, if a director, acting in his private capacity, contracts with his company, acting by another director, the former director is not automatically to be treated as having constructive knowledge of any defect in the latter's authority, so as to exclude the rule.[67]

C., whose appointment as director had ceased, and S., who had never been appointed a director, purported to hold a board meeting and appoint M. a director. Then all three purported to allot shares to M. *Held*, the invalid appointment of M. and allotment to him were not validated by what are now section 285 and Table A, article 92, *post*, because there was no appointment of C. and S. as directors after C.'s appointment had expired. Further, the rule in *Royal British Bank* v. *Turquand* did not apply to the allotment since M. purported to act as a director in the transaction: *Morris* v. *Kanssen* [1946] A.C. 459.

(3) Where there are suspicious circumstances putting the outsider on inquiry.

The sole director of and main shareholder in a company paid cheques, drawn in favour of the company, into his own account. *Held*, the bank was put upon inquiry and not entitled to rely on his ostensible authority, and could not rely on the rule: *A. L. Underwood Ltd.* v. *Bank of Liverpool & Martins* [1924] 1 K.B. 775 (C.A.).[68]

The articles of a company carrying on business as forwarding agents empowered the directors to determine who should have authority to draw bills of exchange on the company's behalf. C., the company's Manchester manager, drew bills on the company's behalf in favour of K., who took them, believing C. to be authorised to draw them. C. had no such authority, and it was unusual for a branch manager to have such authority. *Held*, the company was not liable to the holders on the bills because (1) K. did not know of the power of delegation in the articles and therefore could not rely on its supposed exercise; (2) the bills were forgeries; (3) even if K. had known of the power of delegation, he was not entitled to assume that a branch manager had

[67] *Hely-Hutchinson* v. *Brayhead Ltd.* [1968] 1 Q.B. 549 (Roskill J.).

[68] Followed in *Rolled Steel Products* (*Holdings*) *Ltd.* v. *B.S.C.* [1986] Ch. 246 (C.A.).

ostensible authority to draw bills on behalf of his company: *Kreditbank Cassel GmbH* v. *Schenkers Ltd.* [1927] 1 K.B. 826 (C.A.).

(4) Where a document is forged so as to purport to be the company's document, unless, perhaps, it is held out as genuine by an officer of the company acting within the scope of his authority.[69]

Validity of acts of directors—procedural defects in appointment

Where there is a defect in the appointment of a director who has acted for the company, the outsider may be protected by section 285 and an article like Table A, article 92. The section provides that the acts of a director or manager are valid notwithstanding any defect that may afterwards be discovered in his appointment or qualification. Table A, article 92, provides that all acts done by any meeting of the directors or of a committee of directors or by any person acting as a director shall, notwithstanding that it be afterwards discovered that there was some defect in the appointment of any such director or person acting as aforesaid, or that they or any of them were disqualified, be as valid as if every such person had been duly appointed and was qualified and had continued to be a director.

The effect of these provisions is to validate the acts of a director who has not been validly appointed because there was some procedural slip or irregularity in his appointment. Thus, an outsider dealing with the company, *or a member*, is entitled to assume that a person who appears to be a duly appointed and qualified director is so in fact.

The articles included an article like Table A, article 92. T., N. and S., *de facto* directors, made a call, payment of which was resisted by some shareholders on the ground that T., N. and S. were not *de jure* directors. For example, unknown to his co-directors, N. had vacated office by parting with his qualification shares, although he later acquired a share qualification and continued to act as a director. *Held*, the article operated not only as between the company and outsiders but also as between the company and its members, and covered the irregularities alleged, so that the call was valid: *Dawson* v. *African Consolidated Land etc. Co.* [1898] 1 Ch. 6 (C.A.).

[69] *Ruben* v. *Great Fingall Consolidated* [1906] A.C. 439, *post*, p. 276, particularly *per* Lord Loreburn L.C. at p. 443.

It is immaterial that it is clear from the company's public documents that a director is not duly qualified to act.[70]

The provisions do not validate acts where there has been no appointment at all.[71] Thus they have no effect on substantive rather than procedural defects. So they cannot validate acts which could not have been done even by a properly qualified director. In *Craven-Ellis* v. *Canons Ltd.*,[72] for example, what is now section 285 did not empower improperly qualified directors to do what properly qualified directors could not do, namely, appoint an improperly qualified director as managing director.

[70] *Per* Farwell J. in *British Asbestos Co. Ltd.* v. *Boyd* [1903] 2 Ch. 439 at p. 444. In this case a director vacated office on becoming secretary.

[71] *Morris* v. *Kanssen* [1946] A.C. 459, *ante*, p. 126, applied in *Grant* v. *John Grant & Sons Pty. Ltd.* (1950) 82 C.L.R. 1.

[72] [1936] 2 K.B. 403 (C.A.), *post*, p. 393.

Chapter 7

PUBLIC OFFERS OF SHARES

THE division of companies into public and private companies is based on economic criteria, *i.e.* a minimum capital requirement for public companies,[1] and it is clear that the law envisages that public companies are those which intend to seek finance from the investing public, since private companies are in general forbidden to raise capital in that way.[2] The most common way for companies to raise public finance is to issue shares or debentures to the public[3] and the 1985 Act contained provisions which controlled the document which a company was required to issue if it wished to invite the public to buy its shares. This document was referred to as a prospectus. The 1985 Act until recently not only controlled the issue, publication and contents of a prospectus but also provided a remedy for any mistatements contained therein.

In practice, however, companies who wished to have their shares, or other securities, quoted on the Stock Exchange have always had, in addition to legal constraints, to comply with the Stock Exchange's own rules—the Admission of Securities to Listing, which were more stringent than those in the Companies Act. The advantage of a Stock Exchange listing is that the shares are freely marketable—which in turn enhances their initial value to an outside investor. Until 1984 listing on the Stock Exchange was not regulated by law, but three European Community directives, which were implemented in that year, brought about significant changes. These directives were the Admissions Directive,[4] which covered the conditions for admission to a stock exchange listing, the Listing Particulars

[1] *Ante*, p. 45.
[2] See ss.143(3) and 170(1) of the Financial Services Act 1986.
[3] The methods available are set out *post*, p. 143.
[4] Dir. 79/279/EEC.

Directive,[5] which set out the requirements for drawing up, scrutiny and distribution of listing particulars to be published as a pre-requisite for admission, and the Interim Reports Directive,[6] which required information to be published on a regular basis by listed companies.

These directives were implemented in the UK by the Stock Exchange (Listing) Regulations 1984,[7] which directly incorporated the text of the three directives. The result of these regulations was to produce two sets of rules: the Companies Act provisions which applied to prospectuses where no listing was required and the Listing Regulations, together with certain of the Companies Act provisions, which applied to listed securities. The result was not entirely a happy one and many problems of construction arose.[8]

With the introduction of a new legal regulation for the investment industry by the Financial Services Act 1986 both of those existing provisions, the Companies Act prospectus rules and the Listing Regulations, were repealed and replaced by Parts IV and V of the 1986 Act. Shares and debentures are investments for the purposes of that Act[9] and the issue of shares to the public is clearly an important aspect of investment law. The general framework of investment law laid down by the Financial Services Act 1986 is dealt with in Chapter 19 below.

The new provisions were intended, in part, to implement the three EEC directives and so they adopted different rules for listed and unlisted securities. Part IV of the Act relates to listed securities and Part V to unlisted securities (since the latter are not subject to the directives).

None of these provisions apply to private companies. Section 143(3) of the Financial Services Act 1986 prevents any private company from applying for a stock exchange listing, and section 170 prohibits any such company from advertising its shares for sale, save in a few exceptional cases.[10]

[5] Dir. 80/390/EEC.
[6] Dir. 82/121/EEC.
[7] S.I. 1984/716.
[8] See Professor Robert Pennington: *Stock Exchange Listing—the new requirements*, Butterworths, 1985.
[9] F.S.A. 1986, Sched. 1, paras. 1 and 2.
[10] These exceptions are to be laid down by an order made by the Secretary of State. They apply in general to purely private issues or where the issue is addressed only to a specialist market: F.S.A. 1986 s.170(2), (3), as substituted by s.199 C.A. 1989.

It is now appropriate to consider the two regimes separately.

In the remainder of this chapter all references to sections are to sections of the Financial Services Act 1986 unless otherwise stated.

OFFICIAL LISTING OF SECURITIES

Scope of the provisions

Section 142(1) provides that no investments can be admitted to the Official List of the Stock Exchange, *i.e.* quoted, unless Part IV of the Act is complied with. Investments for this purpose include shares, debentures, instruments entitling the holders to subscribe for shares and certificates which represent property rights or contractual rights in shares.[11]

The competent authority

The Act envisages that, following the directives, the legal requirements of an admission to listing are to be under the control, not of the Department of Trade and Industry, but of the "competent authority." Section 142(6) specifies the latter as the Council of the Stock Exchange, although the Council may act through any of its committees, sub-committees, officers or employees: section 142(8). In practice the Stock Exchange operates in this area through its quotations department. In matters outside the scope of the Act the Stock Exchange remains free to act as it pleases.[12] The Act does allow the Secretary of State to change the competent authority either at the request of the Stock Exchange or on his own initiative.[13]

Following the directives, the Act also delegates the rule-making power for these purposes to the Stock Exchange.[14] Rules made by the Stock Exchange under this power are known

[11] s.142(2), (3), Sched. 1, paras. 1, 2, 4 and 5.
[12] s.142(9).
[13] s.157.
[14] This mirrors the general delegation of rule-making in other areas of the Act as a whole to a non-statutory body, see Chap. 19, *post*.

as the listing rules. Such rules must either be made by the Council itself or confirmed by them within 28 days if they are made by a committee or sub-committee: section 142(6), (8).

The listing rules

The Council of the Stock Exchange may make listing rules for the purpose of any of the matters dealt with below. Section 155 allows the rules to prescribe fees payable to the Stock Exchange. The rules must be in writing, printed and made available to the public and there are provisions for ensuring that the rules can be properly admitted as evidence in legal proceedings: section 156(3), (4), (8).

It is a defence to any action for contravention of any of the listing rules to show that at the time of the breach the particular rule had not been made available to the public. However, a certificate signed by the authorised officer of the Stock Exchange that the rule was so available is prima facie evidence of that fact: section 156(5), (6).[15]

The listing rules may make different provisions for different cases and allow the Stock Exchange to take powers to dispense with or modify their application in particular cases or circumstances: section 156(1), (2).

Applications and admissions to listing

Applications for listing are governed by the listing rules except that all such applications require the consent of the issuer of the securities[16] and it is provided that no private company may so apply: section 143.

No securities may be admitted to listing (*i.e.* quoted) unless the listing rules and any other requirements of the Stock Exchange are complied with: section 144(1). Section 144(2) provides that one of the requirements of the listing rules in this respect will be the approval by the Stock Exchange of "listing particulars" and the publication of these particulars or some other document. This is to comply with the EEC directives.

[15] Such a certificate is deemed to have been duly signed unless the contrary is proved: s.156(7).

[16] If the securities are certificates representing shares, the relevant consent is that of the issuer of the shares: s.142(7).

Once securities have been admitted to the Official List of the Stock Exchange, their admission cannot be challenged on the ground that any requirement or condition for their admission has not been complied with: section 144(6).

Listing particulars—publication and advertisements

Listing particulars are the "prospectus" required by the Stock Exchange. Their publication is as laid down in the listing rules, but section 154 provides that where an application for listing has been made and listing particulars either have been or are to be published, no advertisement or any other information relating to that application, as specified by the listing rules[17] shall be issued in connection with that application, unless the Stock Exchange has either seen and approved its contents or authorised publication without such approval. Any breach is a criminal offence, although there is a defence for someone who whilst acting in the ordinary course of non-investment business[18] can prove that he believed on reasonable grounds that its issue had been approved or authorised.

Where the advertisement or other document has been so approved or authorised for publication neither the publisher nor the person responsible for the listing particulars shall be liable under any civil remedy or to the rescission or repudiation of any subsequent agreement by reason of any misstatement or omission if the document and the listing particulars, taken together, would not be likely to mislead persons of the kind likely to consider the acquisition of the securities in question: section 154(5).[19]

Listing particulars—content

The listing rules specify the content of the listing particulars: section 144(2)(*a*). However, section 146 imposes a general duty of disclosure in addition to that required by the rules. The listing particulars must disclose all the information with respect to the assets and liabilities, financial position, profits and losses, and prospects of the issuer of the securities, and the rights

[17] Thus the Stock Exchange itself can specify the information it requires to see.
[18] *i.e.* not within Part II of Sched. 2 to the Act.
[19] s.154(5) was amended by s.197 C.A. 1989. See also *post*, pp. 144 *et seq.*

attaching to those securities as an investor and his professional advisers would reasonably require in order to make an informed assessment.

This general duty of disclosure is limited by the section to the information which the persons responsible for the listing particulars either knew about or could reasonably have discovered by making enquiries: section 146(2).

The section also lays down four criteria to assist in determining the information to be supplied under this general duty of disclosure. These are designed to cover the various forms of offer available in the market and are: (i) the nature of the securities and the issuer; (ii) the nature of the prospective buyers (*e.g.* the general public or professional investment managers); (iii) that professional advisers which may reasonably be expected to have been consulted will have professional knowledge of certain matters; and (iv) any information provided by the interim reports required of listed companies or under any other statutory provision or that required by recognised exchanges (including the Stock Exchange) to determine the value of the securities: section 146(3).

The Stock Exchange may grant an exemption from the general duty of disclosure for any information if disclosure of that information would be contrary to the public interest, seriously detrimental to the issuer of the securities, or, in the case of certain specialised debt securities, unnecessary for the potential specialised market: section 148(1). The Secretary of State or the Treasury may certify that the disclosure of information would not be in the public interest: section 148(3). Information detrimental to the issuer must still be published, however, if non-disclosure would be likely to mislead a potential buyer as to any knowledge which would be essential for him to have in order to make an informed decision: section 148(2).

In addition the Stock Exchange can under the listing rules dispense with or modify the content of the listing particulars as required by the rules: section 156(2).

Refusal to list

The Stock Exchange may refuse an application even if made in due form if the admission to listing would be detrimental to the interests of investors by reason of any matter relating to the issuer: section 144(3)(*a*). An alternative ground for refusal is failure to comply with the listing requirements in another EEC country in respect of securities quoted there: section 144(3)(*b*). Any such decision should be notified to the applicant within six months although if no such notification is made the Stock Exchange is assumed to have rejected the application: section 144(4), (5).

Disclosure of information

Information which the Stock Exchange receives in connection with an application for listing must not be disclosed without the consent of the supplier and/or the subject of that information: section 179(5). However this is subject to 18 exceptions set out in section 180. These include legal proceedings and other official investigative functions of various officials.

Discontinuance and suspension of listings

The Stock Exchange may discontinue a listing of securities in accordance with the listing rules if there are special circumstances which preclude normal regular dealings in the securities.[20] Alternatively a listing may be temporarily suspended, also in accordance with the listing rules: section 145.

Supplementary listing particulars

In two cases the issuer of the securities must, under the listing rules, submit supplementary listing particulars to the Stock Exchange for its approval and if they are approved must publish them.

These cases are where, in the time between the submission of the original listing particulars and the commencement of dealings on the Stock Exchange:

[20] *i.e.* where there is a false market in the shares, *e.g.* in a take-over bid—see Chap. 31, *post*.

(i) there is a significant change in any matter which was required to be disclosed in the listing particulars, either under the rules or the general duty of disclosure; or

(ii) a significant new matter arises which would have had to have been disclosed if it had arisen at the time of application.

If the issuer is unaware of the change or new matter he is under no duty to submit supplementary listing particulars. However, any person responsible for the listing particulars (as defined in section 152 below) who is aware of such a matter is under a duty to notify the issuer of it: section 147. Failure to comply with these requirements renders the appropriate person liable to compensate any person who has acquired the securities and suffered loss as a result: section 150(3).[21]

Registration of listing particulars

The listing particulars must be registered with the registrar on or before the date of publication. A statement that a copy has been delivered to him must appear in the particulars. There is a criminal sanction in default: section 149.

Continuing obligations

The listing rules require certain continuing obligations of issuers of listed securities. These relate to half-yearly disclosures of certain matters. Contravention can be made public. The Stock Exchange itself may publish any such information if the issuer fails to do so: section 153.

Misrepresentation and omissions

Civil and criminal liability for misrepresentations and omissions in listing and supplementary particulars are dealt with later in this chapter.[22]

[21] See *post*, p. 145.
[22] *Post*, p. 144.

OFFERS OF UNLISTED SECURITIES

Scope of the provisions

Part V of the Financial Services Act 1986 is designed to control the public advertisement of shares and other securities for which an official listing on the Stock Exchange is not being sought. Parts IV and V are therefore mutually exclusive. The former rules relating to prospectuses in the Companies Act 1985 were repealed by the 1986 Act. The investments concerned are shares and debentures issued by companies, any warranty entitling the holder to such shares or debentures and certificates representing shares or debentures: section 158(1)–(3).[23]

The 1985 Act prospectus provisions applied to any offer made to the public. Case law on those provisions produced a wide variety of meanings of that concept. In *Nash* v. *Lynde*[24] it was suggested that in certain cases an offer to one person could be construed as an offer to the public whereas in *Government Stocks etc.* v. *Christopher*[25] a document issued to the shareholders of another company as part of a take-over offer was held not to be part of an offer to the public and so not a prospectus. Since the content, publication and liabilities connected with a prospectus were strictly regulated the distinction was an important one in practice.

Part V of the 1986 Act has rejected that definition and instead applies to all advertisements offering securities except those which are specifically exempted by the Act.

Advertisements offering securities

An advertisement offers securities (and so attracts the provisions of the Act) if:

(a) it invites a person to enter into an agreement for or with a view to subscribing for or otherwise acquiring or underwriting[26] any securities; or

[23] See also Sched. 1, paras. (1), (2), (4), (5).
[24] [1929] A.C. 158.
[25] [1956] 1 W.L.R. 237.
[26] The process of underwriting is explained later, *post*, p. 160.

(b) it contains information calculated to lead directly or indirectly to a person entering into such an agreement: section 158(4).

Offers of securities on admission to an approved exchange

Part V applies in different ways to advertisements involving securities which are to be admitted to dealings on an approved exchange and to other offers. An approved exchange is a recognised investment exchange (*i.e.* one designated as such by the Secretary of State under section 207) which has been approved for this purpose by the Secretary of State: section 158(6).

Prospectus requirement

No advertisement offering securities can be made on the occasion of their admission to dealings on an approved exchange unless either a prospectus has been submitted to and approved by the exchange and delivered to the appropriate registrar,[27] or the advertisement is so worded that no agreement can be made as a result of it until a prospectus has been so submitted: section 159(1). This requirement is subject to the following exceptions and exemptions.

Exceptions to the need for a prospectus

There are five exceptions to the need to register a prospectus:

(1) *Previous prospectus issued within twelve months* (s.159(2)). Where a prospectus dealing with the securities has been registered in the previous twelve months and the approved exchange certifies that potential investors will have sufficient information from that earlier prospectus and any other published information, no further prospectus is required.

(2) *Securities listed or to be listed on the stock exchange* (s.161(1)). If the offer under the advertisement is conditional on the securities being listed or if they have been so listed in the previous twelve months and the exchange certifies that there is

[27] The appropriate registrar is that of the country where the company has its registered office: s.158(5).

sufficient information available to investors already, no prospectus is required. Instead Part IV of the Act will apply.

(3) *Advertisements consisting of a registered prospectus or limited in content* (s.161(2)). No further prospectus is required if the advertisement is of a type specified in section 58(2) of the Act. These are advertisements by the issuer inviting subscriptions for cash which consist of a prospectus already registered under section 159 or which contains only the name and address of the issuer, the nature, number, nominal value and price of the investments, a statement that a prospectus is or will be available and instructions for obtaining a copy.

(4) *Securities already dealt with on the exchange* (s.161(3)). If the issuer of the securities has other securities being dealt with on the exchange no prospectus is required if the exchange certifies that, having regard to other published information as to the current value of those securities, the nature of the securities and the circumstances of the issue, potential investors will have sufficient information.

(5) *Overseas securities* (s.161(4)). The Secretary of State may by order exempt securities subject to an equivalent regime applicable to an overseas exchange.

(6) *Advertisements exempted by order of the Secretary of State* (s.160A). See p. 140, *post*.

Other offers of securities

Where no dealings on an approved exchange are sought section 160 applies. This includes all "primary" and "secondary" offers except those specifically exempted, *e.g.* those of a private character.

Primary and secondary offers—prospectus requirement

No advertisement offering securities which amounts to a primary or secondary offer can be made unless a prospectus has been delivered to the registrar or no agreement can be entered into as a result of the advertisement until such delivery section 160(1).

A *primary offer* is an advertisement (not connected with an approved exchange) directly or indirectly inviting persons to subscribe for or to underwrite the securities involved: section 160(2).

A *secondary offer* is an advertisement (not connected with an approved exchange) directly or indirectly inviting persons to acquire the securities involved (*i.e.* not direct from the issuer). In such a case the offeror must either have acquired the securities from the issuer with a view to making such an offer, or have acquired them otherwise than from the issuer with a view to making an offer, provided that they have never been dealt with on an exchange or held by a person purely as an investment, or be a controller of the issuer who is acting with the issuer's consent in making the offer: section 160(3).

Secondary offers are in fact much more common and are known as "offers for sale" and are dealt with below. For this purpose an offeror is presumed to have acquired the securities with a view to making an offer if he makes it either within six months of the issue of the securities or before he has paid the issuer: section 160(4).

Exceptions to the need for registration of a prospectus

There are six exceptions and exemptions to the requirement of the registration of a prospectus under section 160:

(1) *Prospectus issued in previous six months* (s.160(5)). If a previous prospectus has been delivered for registration in the previous six months by either a primary or secondary offeror, a secondary offer does not need a prospectus.

(2) *Exemptions by order of the Secretary of State* (s.160A).[28] An order by the Secretary of State may exempt offers in the following categories:

(a) advertisements appearing to him to be of a private character, *e.g.* by reason of a connection between the owner and the potential investors. This is a central area in the new regime and may not include take-over

[28] This section which applies equally to section 159 was introduced by s.198 C.A. 1989.

documents formerly exempt under the Companies Act criteria;

(b) advertisements dealing with investments only incidentally;

(c) advertisements issued only to expert investors who can understand the risks involved;

(d) any other class of advertisement as he thinks fit; and

(e) any advertisement "issued in whatever circumstances" in relation to securities normally dealt in by experts.

Such orders can specify other requirements which are to be complied with: section 160A(3).

(3) *Securities listed or to be listed on the stock exchange* (s.161(1)).

(4) *Advertisements consisting of a registered prospectus or limited in content* (s.161(2)).

(5) *Securities already dealt with on an approved exchange* (s.161(3)).

(6) *Overseas securities* (s.161(4)). Exceptions (3)–(6) are identical to those outlined in relation to those offers connected with an approved exchange and have been discussed above.

Form and content of a prospectus

The provisions relating to the form and content of a prospectus are similar to those relating to listing particulars for listed shares.[29] There are detailed requirements set out in the prospectus rules, issued in this case, however, by the Secretary of State and not the Stock Exchange. Compliance with overseas requirements are treated as compliance with the rules in certain circumstances: section 162.

There is also a general duty of disclosure which corresponds to that applicable to listing particulars in section 146, above. Section 163 thus requires disclosure of all information with respect to the assets and liabilities, financial position, profits and losses, prospects of the issuer and the rights attaching to the securities as a person or his professional advisers would

[29] *Ante*, p. 132.

reasonably require for the purpose of making an informed assessment. This duty is limited to the knowledge (actual or constructive) of the persons responsible for the prospectus and the criteria for ascertaining the information to be disclosed under this duty are the same as for those for listing particulars. The reader is referred to the discussion on section 146 above.[30] Section 165 provides similar exemptions from disclosure to those relating to quoted securities in section 148, *ante*.

Supplementary prospectus

Section 164 requires the registration of a supplementary prospectus in exactly the same circumstances as a section 147 applies to supplementary listing particulars,[31] *i.e.* to note a significant change or where a significant new matter has arisen which affects the original prospectus and the disclosure requirements.

Private companies

In general private companies are forbidden to issue any advertisements offering their securities. However, it may be permitted to do so if the advertisement falls within one of the categories of offers similar to those exempted by the Secretary of State from the prospectus requirements by section 160A, *i.e.* those of a private character, of an incidental nature or aimed at a specialist market. Such permission will be by an order which may specify additional requirements for such companies; section 170(2)–(4).

Contravention of Part V

A person who fails to register a prospectus or issues an advertisement in breach of sections 159 or 160 is, if he is a person authorised to deal in investments,[32] deemed to have breached either the rules of his self-regulatory organisation or recognised professional body or those laid down by the Secretary of State, as appropriate. The effect of this is that he

[30] *Ante*, p. 133.
[31] *Ante*, p. 134.
[32] Under Part I of the F.S.A. 1986. See Chap. 19, *post*.

may lose his authority to deal and be liable for damages to anyone who suffers loss. An unauthorised person acting in breach is guilty of a criminal offence: section 171.

If the breach relates to a private company issuing an advertisement, an authorised person will be deemed to have broken the investment rules applicable to him. Any such person will also be guilty of an offence.[33] In addition any agreement entered into will be voidable at the option of the purchaser who may recover any money etc. paid with interest, unless the court orders otherwise on grounds that the advertisement was largely irrelevant or the terms of the agreement, etc., were fair in all the circumstances: section 171.

Misrepresentations and omissions

Civil and criminal liability for misrepresentations and omissions in a prospectus and a supplementary prospectus are dealt with later in this chapter.[34]

DIRECT INVITATIONS, OFFERS FOR SALE, PLACINGS

Shares or debentures may be offered to the public by means of—

(1) a direct invitation to the public; or
(2) an offer for sale; or
(3) a "placing."

We shall see that placing securities directly with financial institutions can be unfair in that it favours the big investor and deprives the small one of the opportunity to acquire securities at bargain prices (although it must be remembered that The Stock Exchange requires a substantial percentage of a placing to be offered to the market). An offer for sale to the public is fairer. On the other hand, placing is simpler, quicker and cheaper than an offer for sale. Underwriting is unnecessary, advertising is reduced to a minimum and a large number of prospectuses need not be printed.

[33] There is a defence for a person who is not carrying on an investment business and who reasonably believed that the advertisement was authorised.
[34] *Post*, p. 144.

Offers for sale

An offer for sale is the usual way in which shares or debentures are offered to the public. It occurs when an issuing house (either a specialised concern or a department of a merchant bank) subscribes for an issue of shares or debentures and then invites the public or purchase from it at a higher price.

Where it is difficult to fix the issue price of the shares or debentures being offered to the public, because it is uncertain what the public response to the offer will be, an offer for sale by tender may be made. In this event, a minimum price is fixed and the issue price is determined by the prices tendered in the applications. Thus, where 250,000 ordinary 25p shares are offered, a minimum price of 80p a share may be fixed. The prices tendered may range from 80p to £2 and the shares may all be sold at 87p. The object is to ensure that the company receives what the shares are worth to the public, and to defeat stags who, by taking shares and then immediately selling them at a higher price, would otherwise receive the difference between the issue price of a share and its worth to the public.

Placings

An issue of shares or debentures may be placed in one of two ways. An issuing house may subscribe for the issue and then invite its clients (*e.g.* insurance companies and pension funds) to purchase from it at a higher price.

Alternatively, an issuing house or stockbrokers or a bank may, without subscribing, act as agents for the company and invite their clients to take from the company. In this case the agents will be paid a commission called "brokerage" for their services.

Misrepresentations and Omissions in Listing Particulars or Prospectus

Statutory right to compensation

Sections 150 to 152 of the Financial Services Act provide a statutory remedy for misrepresentations and omissions in listing particulars and supplementary listing particulars. An almost identical remedy for a prospectus and supplementary prospectus is provided by sections 166 to 168. *In the following text it can be assumed that the wording applies equally to a prospectus as to listing particulars* (*or supplementary prospectus and supplementary listing particulars as appropriate*) *unless the contrary is stated.*

This remedy is available in addition to other common law and statutory remedies which are set out below[35]: sections 150(4), 166(4).

There are two basic heads of liability, followed by seven defences, and finally the Act details those deemed to be responsible for the listing particulars/prospectus who can be sued for compensation.

Heads of liability

(a) Any person responsible for listing particulars or supplementary listing particulars (as defined below) *shall be liable* to compensate anyone who has acquired relevant securities (or an interest therein) and has suffered loss as a result of any untrue or misleading statement in the particulars or the omission of anything required to be included by virtue of the general duty of disclosure under sections 146(1) (or section 163(1) as appropriate)[36] or the duty to publish particulars of any significant new matter or change under section 147 (or section 164 as appropriate)[37]: sections 150(1), 166(1).

Omission of any matter required by the rules to be included, even in the negative, is to be regarded as a statement that there is no such matter for this purpose: section 150(2), 166(2).

The plaintiff need only prove a misstatement or omission and loss as a result to establish liability. Once established it is for the defendant to establish a defence. There must be causation, however, between the misstatement/omission and the loss. Unlike the predecessor of these sections, section 67 of the Companies Act 1985, there is no need to show that the securities were acquired "on the faith of the prospectus." Subsequent purchasers may therefore be able to claim if they

[35] *Post*, p. 149.
[36] *Ante*, pp. 132, 141.
[37] *Ante*, pp. 134, 141.

acquire their shares within a reasonable time.[38] Section 67 only applied to those acquiring their shares under the offer.

(b) Anyone who fails to issue supplementary listing particulars when required to do so or is otherwise in breach of section 147 (or section 164 as appropriate)[39] is liable to compensate any person who has acquired those securities (or an interest in them) and suffered loss as a result of the failure.

Section 150(6) provides that no-one, whether as promoter or otherwise, is to be liable for failing to disclose any information which he would not be required to disclose or would be exempt from disclosing in listing particulars. This exemption extends to any civil liability and to any action for rescission or repudiation of any subsequent agreement, by words introduced by section 197 of the Companies Act 1989. These words do not lie easily with section 150(4) which provides that the section cannot affect any liability outside that section. The main effect will be to ensure that information which has been withheld under section 148 (*e.g.* on public interest grounds) and which then makes the information given misleading, will not give rise to civil liability. There is no equivalent provision in section 166 relating to a prospectus.[40]

Exemptions from liability

There are six defences available to anyone who has been sued for compensation under sections 150 or 166. The first four are applicable to the general liability (a) above, the next to both that liability and the specific liability for failing to submit supplementary listing particulars, and the sixth to the latter liability only.

(1) *Reasonable Belief* (ss.151(1), 167(1)). It is a defence to show that the defendant, having made reasonable enquiries, believed at the time when the particulars were submitted (or the prospectus sent for registration as appropriate) either that the statement was true and not misleading or that the omission was a proper one, provided that he can also show one of four

[38] The defence, under section 151(1)(*c*) and (*d*) and 167(1)(*c*) and (*d*) would otherwise be irrelevant. See *post*, p. 147.
[39] See note 37.
[40] *Ante*, p. 145.

additional facts: (i) that he still held the belief when the securities were acquired; (ii) that they were acquired before he could bring the matter to the attention of potential investors; (iii) that before they were acquired he had taken all reasonable steps to bring a correction to the attention of potential investors; of (iv) that he held that belief until dealings commenced (in the case of listing particulars) and (in both cases) that the securities were so acquired after such a lapse of time that he ought fairly to be excused.

(2) *Expert's Statements* (ss.151(2), 167(2)). Where the offending statement is made by or on the authority of an expert with his consent, the defendant (other than the expert) will be excused if he can show reasonable belief in the expert's competence and consent to the statement's inclusion in that form and context. This belief must be held at the time when the particulars were submitted and maintained until the securities have been acquired, unless either they were acquired before he could reasonably bring the matter to potential investors' attention, or he took reasonable steps before they were acquired to bring a correction to the attention of potential investors, or that he continued in that belief until after dealings were commenced on the Stock Exchange or approved exchange and the securities were acquired after such a lapse of time that he ought in the circumstances to be excused. (Where no dealings on an exchange are involved that part of the requirement will not apply.)

(3) *Reasonable Steps to Correct Defect* (ss.151(3), 167(3). If the defendant takes reasonable steps to bring a correction or a defect in an expert's competence or consent to the attention of potential investors before the securities were acquired there is no liability. This defence is complementary to (1) and (2) above.

(4) *Official Statements and Documents* (ss.151(4), 167(4)). There is no liability for any loss resulting from the accurate and fair reproduction of a statement by official persons or contained in an official document.

(5) *Plaintiff's Knowledge* (ss.151(5), 167(5)). If the defendant can prove that the person suffering the loss acquired the securities "with knowledge" of the misrepresentation or omission in listing particulars or a prospectus or of any change

or new matter giving rise to the obligation to publish supplementary particulars or prospectus, he will not be liable under the appropriate head of liability. In practice such knowledge would probably destroy the causation between the statement and the loss so that no liability would arise.

(6) *Reasonable Belief and Supplementary Listing Particulars/ Prospectus* (ss.151(6), 167(6)). Reasonable belief that the change or new matter was not such as to call for supplementary listing particulars is a defence to liability under head (b) above.

Persons responsible for the particulars/prospectus

Section 152(1) details five groups of persons who are deemed to be responsible for the listing or supplementary listing particulars and so liable for misrepresentations and omissions. Section 168(1) contains a similar test for those responsible for a prospectus or supplementary prospectus. The five groups are:

(a) the issuer of the securities involved;
(b) the directors of the issuer;
(c) anyone who is named, and has authorised himself to be named in the document as a director of the issuer or as having agreed to become a director at some future time;
(d) those who accept and are stated as having accepted responsibility for all or any part of the document; and
(e) anyone else who has authorised the contents of all or part of the document.

Those liable under (d) or (e) are only so liable for those parts of the document which they have accepted responsibility for or authorised: sections 152(3), 168(3).

For a prospectus only, section 168(2) provides that no-one is to be held liable under categories (a)–(c) unless he has made or authorised the offer to which the prospectus relates. This applies particularly to secondary offers.

If the issuer becomes liable to pay compensation no account is to be taken of that liability in deciding the amount due or to be due for those shares. This is because it would otherwise affect the principle of capital maintenance: sections 152(9), 168(8).

The basic principle is that all directors of the issuer are responsible for the particulars and liable as such under paragraph (b) above. This liability extends to those who have authorised themselves to be described either as a director or as having agreed to become a director in the particulars under paragraph (c) above. These directors may, of course, rely on the defences under section 151 or 167 but sections 152(2) and 168(2) provide an exemption from liability for those in category (b) and sections 152(5) and 168(5) provide two further exemptions for those in categories (b) and (c).

Sections 152(2) and 168(2) provide that no director under category (b) is to be regarded as being responsible if the document was issued without his knowledge or consent provided that when he became aware of its publication he gave reasonable public notice of that fact. Such notice must be given "forthwith."

The second exemption, available to those under (b) or (c) above, applies to directors of issuers of specialised international debt securities which is a specialist market: section 152(5)(6). The third is of more general application. Liability under category (b) above can be excluded in advance by any director who is certified by the Stock Exchange as being exempted by reason of his having an interest, or any other circumstances, which makes it inappropriate for him to be responsible for the particulars: section 152(5). Under section 168(5) similar exemption is available to a director who can obtain such a certificate from an approved exchange.

Measurement of liability

It was held in respect of the predecessor of these sections that the measure of compensation available was the same as for damages for fraud.[41]

Other civil liability

Since a company is liable for the misrepresentations of its directors and other agents acting within the scope of their authority, a person induced to subscribe for shares or debentures by a misrepresentation in a prospectus or listing

[41] *Clark* v. *Urquhart* [1930] A.C. 28; *Davidson* v. *Hamilton* (1904) 12 S.L.T. 353 (O.H.).

particulars may have other remedies under the general law against the individual or the individuals responsible, *e.g.* promoters, directors or experts.[42] The remedy may be available under the general law or it may be statutory. It should be remembered that persons protected under sections 150(6)[43] and 154(5)[44] are protected from all civil liability, including actions for rescission or repudiation of a subsequent agreement, if those sections apply.

The main remedy against the *company* is rescission[45] of the contract of allotment, with or without an action for damages. At common law it was held that a shareholder cannot recover damages for fraud against the company without rescission, because that would be inconsistent with the contract between him and the other shareholders.[46] The same was true of a claim for damages, *e.g.* for breach of contract, which a shareholder *qua* shareholder may seek to enforce against the company.[47] These prohibitions were removed by section 111A of the Act,[48] and there is nothing in principle to prevent such actions now. Damages in lieu of rescission may be recovered in England and Wales under the Misrepresentation Act 1967, s.2(2), which states that where a person has entered into a contract after a misrepresentation made to him *otherwise than fraudulently*, and he would be entitled to rescind, then if rescission is claimed the court may award damages in lieu of rescission, if of opinion that it would be equitable to do so. Damages for *negligent* misrepresentation may be recovered from the company under section 2(1) of the Misrepresentation Act, which provides that where a person has entered into a contract after a misrepresentation made to him by another party thereto and as a result has

[42] As in *Frankenburg* v. *Great Horseless Carriage Co.* [1900] 1 Q.B. 504 (C.A.).
[43] *Ante*, p. 146.
[44] *Ante*, p. 133.
[45] The representee may elect to repudiate the contract, and legal proceedings are not essential, in the event of misrepresentation. However, if, as is usual, he wishes to recover money or property transferred by him under the contract he may have to initiate proceedings for rescission.
[46] *Houldsworth* v. *City of Glasgow Bank* (1880) 7 R. (H.L.) 53; (1880) 5 App.Cas. 317, where it was too late to rescind since the company had gone into liquidation. See also *Western Bank* v. *Addie* (1867) 5 M. (H.L.) 80.
[47] *Re Dividend Fund Incorporated* (*In Liquidation*) [1974] V.R. 451, where an unlimited company failed to repurchase shares in accordance with the articles and the shareholder had to pay calls in a liquidation.
[48] Introduced by s.131 C.A. 1989.

suffered loss, then the representor is liable in damages unless he proves that on reasonable grounds he believed up to the time when the contract was made that the representation was true. A similar provision to section 2(1) applies to Scotland under section 10(1) of the Law Reform (Miscellaneous Provisions) (Scotland) Act 1985.

One non-statutory remedy against the *individuals* responsible is damages for fraud.[49]

It may also be possible to claim damages for negligent misrepresentation under the principle in *Hedley Byrne & Co. Ltd.* v. *Heller & Partners Ltd.*,[50] which is that a negligent, although honest, misrepresentation, spoken or written, may give rise to an action for damages for financial loss caused thereby. The law implies a duty of care where one party seeks information or advice from another party, trusts the other to exercise due care, it is reasonable for him to do so, the other knows or ought to known that reliance is being placed on his skill or judgment or ability to make careful inquiry and he does not expressly disclaim responsibility for his representation. In *Mutual Life and Citizens' Assurance Co. Ltd.* v. *Evatt*[51] the Privy Council advised that the party from whom information or advice is sought must carry on the business of giving advice or in some other way he must have let it be know that he claims to possess the necessary skill and competence to do so and is prepared to exercise the necessary diligence to give reliable advice.

The restrictive nature of this liability was affirmed by the House of Lords in *Caparo Industries plc* v. *Dickman*,[52] where their Lordships stressed that the defendant's liability was limited to those whom he knew would receive the statement and would rely upon it for the purposes of a particular transaction. Thus reliance for another purpose, *e.g.* a subsequent purchase on the market, will not suffice for liability on a prospectus issued in respect of original purchases only.[53]

[49] *Post*, p. 156.
[50] [1964] A.C. 465.
[51] [1971] A.C. 793 (P.C.).
[52] [1990] 2 W.L.R. 358.
[53] *Al-Nahib Investments (Jersey) Ltd.* v. *Longcroft*, [1990] BCC 517. See also *Morgan Crucible Co.* v. *Hill Samuel Bank Ltd., The Independent*, July 27, 1990.

Rescission of the contract of allotment

In order to obtain rescission of a contract of allotment on the ground that it was induced by misrepresentation, the allottee must prove (1) a material false statement of fact, (2) which induced him to subscribe.[54]

(1) There must be a material false statement of fact.

A prospectus stated: "a large number of gentlemen in the trade and others have become shareholders." When the register of members was made up there were 55 shareholders, of whom 10 or 12 were connected with the trade. *Held*, there was not a sufficiently material misrepresentation to entitle a person who had taken shares on the faith of the prospectus to have his name deleted from the register: *City of Edinburgh Brewery Co. Ltd.* v. *Gibson's Trustee* (1869) 7 M. 886.

A statement of fact must be distinguished from a statement of opinion.[55] A statement that the property of the company is worth a certain sum of money, or that the profits are expected to reach a certain figure, is only opinion and gives no right to rescission except where it can be shown that the maker of the statement did not hold the opinion. Statements, on the other hand, that "the surplus assets, as appear by the last balance sheet, amount to upwards of £10,000"[56] that £200,000 of share capital has been subscribed,[57] and that certain persons have agreed to be directors,[58] are all material statements of fact and, if false, will give rise to a right to rescission.

Where the facts are not equally well known to both sides a statement of opinion by one who should know the facts often implies a statement of fact, *i.e.* that there are reasonable grounds for his opinion, and if it can be proved that he could not as a reasonable man honestly have had the opinion, there is

[54] The right to rescind is qualified by ss.150(6) and 154(5) F.S.A. 1986. See pp. 133 and 146, *ante*.

[55] *Liverpool Palace of Varieties Ltd.* v. *Miller* (1896) 4 S.L.T. 153 (O.H.).

[56] *Re London and Staffordshire Fire Insurance Co.* (1883) 24 Ch.D. 149.

[57] *Arnison* v. *Smith* (1889) 41 Ch.D. 348 (C.A.), where the share capital had only been allotted *as* fully paid up. But see *Akerhielm* v. *De Mare* [1959] A.C. 789 (P.C.), *post*, p. 156.

[58] *Re Scottish Petroleum Co.* (1883) 23 Ch.D. 413 (C.A.); *Blakiston* v. *London and Scottish Banking etc. Corpn. Ltd.* (1894) 21 R. 417; contrast *Chambers* v. *Edinburgh etc. Aerated Bread Co. Ltd.* (1891) 18 R. 1039.

misrepresentation of fact.[59] Again, a statement of intention does not amount to a representation of fact unless it can be proved that the alleged intention never existed.[60]

If a prospectus refers to a report which contains inaccurate statements of fact, the contract can be rescinded if the company has vouched for the accuracy of the report, but otherwise it cannot. Thus, if the company employs an accountant to go through the books and make a report, and then sets out the report in a prospectus, it will not be liable for any inaccuracy in the report.[61] But if the company makes statements of its own, although they are expressed to be based upon a report, it will be liable for an inaccuracy unless in clear and unambiguous terms it has warned intending applicants that it does not vouch for the accuracy of the report, or of any statement based on it.

A company issued a prospectus inviting subscriptions for the purpose of buying a rubber estate in Peru. The prospectus contained extracts from the report of an expert on the spot, which gave the number of matured rubber trees on the estate, and other information. The report was false. *Held*, the accuracy of the report was prima facie the basis of the contract and, therefore, if the company did not intend to contract on that basis, it should have dissociated itself from the report in clear and unambiguous terms, and warned the public that it did not vouch for the accuracy of the report. As there was no such warning the contracts to take shares could be rescinded: *Re Pacaya Rubber and Produce Co. Ltd.* [1914] 1 Ch. 542.[62]

An *innocent* misrepresentation is a sufficient ground for rescission. It is not necessary to prove knowledge of the untruth of the statement.[63]

Non-disclosure of a material fact amounts to misrepresentation if the omission makes what is stated misleading. It has been said[64] that "It is not that the omission of material facts is an

[59] *Per* Bowen L.J. in *Smith* v. *Land, etc., Corpn.* (1884) 28 Ch.D. 7 (C.A.) at p. 15.

[60] *Edgington* v. *Fitzmaurice* (1885) 29 Ch.D. 459 (C.A.).

[61] *Bentley & Co.* v. *Black* (1893) 9 T.L.R. 580 (C.A.).

[62] An earlier Scottish case which went to the House of Lords is *Mair* v. *Rio Grande Rubber Estates Ltd.*, 1913 S.C. (H.L.) 74.

[63] *Per* Lord Shaw of Dunfermline in *Mair* v. *Rio Grande Rubber Estates Ltd.*, 1913 S.C. (H.L.) 74 at p. 81.

[64] *Per* Rigby L.J. in *McKeown* v. *Boudard Peveril Gear Co. Ltd.* (1896) 74 L.T. 712 at p. 713.

independent ground for rescission, but the omission must be of such a nature as to make the statement actually made misleading." In other words, at least in English law, a contract of allotment is not a true contract *uberrimae fidei*,[65] *i.e.* a contract in which all material facts must be disclosed, although, as has been seen, the Financial Services Act usually requires a number of particulars to be disclosed in listing particulars or a prospectus.[66]

A prospectus described a piece of land as "eminently suitable" for greyhound racing. The land in question was, however, affected by a town planning resolution, with the result that, unless the local authority's consent was obtained before any buildings were erected, the company would not be entitled to any compensation in the event of the removal of the buildings under the town planning scheme. The local authority refused its consent. *Held*, the omission to disclose the facts set out above rendered the description of the land as "eminently suitable" misleading, and persons who had subscribed for shares on the strength of the prospectus were entitled to rescind their contracts: *Coles* v. *White City* (*Manchester*) *Greyhound Assn. Ltd.* (1929) 45 T.L.R. 230 (C.A.).

(2) The allottee must have been induced to subscribe by the false statement.

Whether or not an allottee was induced to subscribe by reason of the misrepresentation is a question of fact depending on the circumstances of each case. It is not sufficient that the prospectus has been widely advertised in the locality if there is proof that the applicant relied, not on the prospectus, but on independent advice.[67] He is entitled to rely upon the prospectus, and is not bound to verify the statements it contains. Where, therefore, a prospectus simply gave the dates of and parties to contracts and stated where they could be inspected, without indicating that they were material contracts, the omission of the applicant to inspect them did not fix him with notice of their contents.[68]

[65] And see *per* Lord Watson in *Aaron's Reefs Ltd.* v. *Twiss* [1896] A.C. 273 at p. 287. There is no definitive authority as to the common law of Scotland on the point and, in view of the statutory provisions, it is now unlikely that there will be.

[66] *Ante*, pp. 133, 141.

[67] *M'Morland's Trustees* v. *Fraser* (1896) 24 R. 65.

[68] Aaron's Reefs Ltd. v. *Twiss* [1896] A.C. 273.

The false statement need not have been the decisive inducing cause of the contract. It is enough that it was one of the contributory causes.[69]

Rescission enables the allottee to recover what he paid for the shares or debentures, plus interest.[70]

The right to rescind is lost—

(1) If, after discovering the misrepresentation, the allottee does an act which shows that he elects to retain the shares and so affirms the contract; for example, he attends and votes at general meetings,[71] receives dividends,[72] or attempt to sell the shares.[73]

(2) If he fails to act within a reasonable time of discovering the true facts.

The right to rescind must be exercised promptly if the company is a going concern, and even a delay of a fortnight has been held to be too long in such a case.[74] When a shareholder was put on inquiry in June, but took no steps to make any investigation until November, his delay prevented him from rescinding the contract.[75]

(3) If restitution is impossible[76] *e.g.* because he sells the shares.

(4) If the company goes into liquidation.[77]

Events leading up to liquidation may have the same effect, *e.g.* where an unlimited banking company stops payment,[78] or calls a meeting to consider winding up.[79]

[69] *Edgington* v. *Fitzmaurice* (1885) 29 Ch.D. 459 (C.A.).

[70] *Cf.* the damages available for actions in tort, *post*, p. 156.

[71] *Sharpley* v. *South and East Coast Ry. Co.* (1876) 2 Ch.D. 663 (C.A.).

[72] Scholey v. *Central Ry. of Venezuela* (1868) L.R. 9 Eq. 266n.

[73] *Ex p. Briggs* (1866) L.R. 1 Eq. 483.

[74] See *Re Scottish Petroleum Co.* (1883) 23 Ch.D. 413 (C.A.).

[75] *Re Christineville Rubber Estates Ltd.* [1911] W.N. 216; *cf. Caledonian Debenture Co. Ltd.* v. *Bernard* (1898) 5 S.L.T. 392 (O.H.). See also Lord President Inglis in *City of Edinburgh Brewery Co. Ltd.* v. *Gibson's Trustee* (1869) 7 M. 886 at p. 891.

[76] *Western Bank* v. *Addie* (1867) 5 M. (H.L.) 80.

[77] *Oakes* v. *Turquand* (1867) L.R. 2 (H.L.) 325; *Western Bank* v. *Addie*, *ante*; *Houldsworth* v. *City of Glasgow Bank* (1880) 7 R. (H.L.) 53; (1879) 6 R. 1164.

[78] *Myles* v. *City of Glasgow Bank* (1879) 6 R. 718.

[79] *Alexander Mitchell* v. *City of Glasgow Bank* (1879) 6 R. (H.L.) 60; (1878) 6 R. 439.

Damages for fraud

Fraud is difficult to prove. Nevertheless, promoters, directors, experts or the persons making an offer for sale, are liable for fraud if it can be shown that they signed, or authorised the issue of, a prospectus or listing particulars containing a false statement which they did not honestly believe to be true[80] with the intention that another person should act upon it, and that he acted on it to his detriment. The test is subjective, *i.e.* did they honestly believe the statement to be true according to its meaning as understood *by them*, albeit erroneously, when it was made?[81] If they cannot be proved to have made a false representation knowingly, or without belief in its truth, or recklessly, careless whether it be true or false, they may have to pay compensation under the statutory provisions, *ante*, the predecessor of which[82] was first enacted as a result of the decision in *Derry* v. *Peek*.[83]

A tramway company by a special Act had power to move trams by animal power and, with the consent of the Board of Trade, by steam power. A prospectus was issued by the directors stating that the company, under its special Act, had the right to use steam power instead of horses. P. subscribed for shares on the strength of this statement. The Board of Trade afterwards refused its consent, and the company was wound up. P. sued the directors for damages for fraud. *Held*, the directors were not liable, the statement as to steam power having been made in the honest belief that it was true: *Derry* v. *Peek* (1889) 14 App.Cas. 337.

In *Akerhielm* v. *De Mare* [1959] A.C. 789 (P.C.), the representation that capital had been "subscribed in Denmark" was inapt to include shares allotted as fully paid to Kenya residents for services rendered in Denmark in connection with the formulation of the company. The representor was not liable for fraud because he honestly believed the representation to be true *in the sense in which he understood it*.

The measure of damages for fraud is prima facie the difference between the actual value of the shares at the time of

[80] *Per* Lord Herschell in *Derry* v. *Peek* (1889) 14 App.Cas. 337 at p. 374.
[81] *Akerhielm* v. *De Mare* [1959] A.C. 789 (P.C.), *post*.
[82] Directors' Liability Act 1890.
[83] The explanation of fraud given in that case was referred to with approval in the Scottish case of *Boyd & Forrest* v. *Glasgow etc. Rlwy. Co.*, 1912 S.C. (H.L.) 93. See also *Lees* v. *Tod* (1882) 9 R. 807.

allotment and the sum paid for them.[84] The plaintiff recovers for all the actual damage directly flowing from the fraudulent misrepresentation.[85] It is not an action for breach of contract and therefore no damages in respect of prospective gains can be recovered.

Criminal liability

The Larceny Act 1861, s.84, provided that a director, manager or public officer of a body corporate who made a written statement, which he knew to be false in any material particular, with intent to deceive or defraud any member, shareholder or creditor, or with intent to induce any person to become a shareholder, or to entrust or advance any property to the company, or to enter into any security for its benefit, was liable to seven years' imprisonment.

A statement was false within section 84 if in its context it conveyed a misleading impression although it was literally correct.

Section 84 did not apply to Scotland.

A prospectus contained a statement which was true, that the company had paid dividends every year between 1921 and 1927. The result was that the prospectus gave the impression that the company had made trading profits during the years in question. However, during each of those years the company had incurred substantial trading losses and was only able to pay the specified dividends by the introduction into the accounts of non-recurring items, earned in the abnormal war period, such as repayments of excess profits duty, adjustment of income tax reserves and the like. No disclosure was made of these trading losses. *Held*, the prospectus was false, because it put before intending investors figures which apparently disclosed the existing position of the company, but in fact hid it, and K., a director who knew that it was false was guilty of an offence under the Larceny Act, s.84: *R.* v. *Kyslant* [1932] 1 K.B. 442 (C.C.A.).

Section 84 of the Larceny Act was repealed and replaced by section 19 of the Theft Act 1968 but the wording of section 19 is different. It provides that an officer of a body corporate or

[84] *McConnel* v. *Wright* [1903] 1 Ch. 546 (C.A.); *Davidson* v. *Tulloch* (1860) 3 Macq. 783; 22 D. (H.L.) 7.

[85] *Doyle* v. *Olby* (*Ironmongers*) Ltd. [1969] 2 Q.B. 158 (C.A.).

unincorporated association (or a person purporting to act as such) who, with intent to deceive members or creditors about its affairs, publishes or concurs in publishing a written statement or account which to his knowledge is or may be misleading, false or deceptive in a material particular, is liable to seven years' imprisonment. A person who has entered into a security for the benefit of a body corporate is treated as a creditor of it. In particular, the words "or with intent to induce any person to become a shareholder" do not appear in section 19. This provision of the Theft Act does not apply in Scotland.

In addition to this specific offence a person issuing a false prospectus or listing particulars may commit an offence under section 47 of the Financial Services Act 1986.

Under that section it is an offence for a person either to make a statement, promise or forecast which he knows to be misleading, false or deceptive, or if he dishonestly conceals any material facts, or if he recklessly makes (dishonestly or otherwise) a statement, promise or forecast which is misleading, false or deceptive if that statement etc. is for the purpose of inducing another to enter into any investment agreement.

It is also an offence for a person to do any act or engage in any course of conduct which creates a false or misleading impression as to the market in or value of any investments if that for the purpose of inducing a person to subscribe or refrain from subscribing investments unless he can show that he reasonably believed that he would not create such an impression.

The maximum sentence is seven years' imprisonment.

In practice those involved in issuing listing particulars or prospectuses will be subject to the much wider system of regulation laid down by the Financial Services Act 1986. This regulation is set out in Chapter 19, *post*.

Commissions and Discounts

In order to procure capital a company frequently desires to pay a commission or discount to a person introducing capital.

Section 97(1) of the Companies Act 1985 allows a company to pay a commission to a person in consideration of his subscribing or agreeing to subscribe, absolutely or conditionally, or procuring or agreeing to procure subscriptions, for *shares* in the company if, in addition to complying with any conditions in rules made by the Secretary of State under section 169 of the Financial Services Act 1986 (*ante*):

(1) the payment is authorised by the articles (authority in the memorandum is insufficient[86]);
(2) the commission does not exceed either (*a*) any limit imposed by such rules or, if there are no such limits, 10 per cent. of the price at which the shares are issued, or (*b*) the amount or rate authorised by the articles, whichever is the less.

This subsection applies as well to private as to public companies.[87] It enables a company to pay underwriting commission or brokerage, which commissions are dealt with in detail later.[88]

Section 98 of the 1985 Act provides that, except as allowed by subsection (1), no company shall apply any of its shares or capital money, either directly or indirectly, in payment of any commission, discount or allowance to any person in consideration of his subscribing or agreeing to subscribe, whether absolutely or conditionally, or procuring or agreeing to procure subscriptions, absolute or conditional, for any *shares* in the company, whether the shares or money be applied by being added to the purchase money of any property acquired by the company or to the contract price of any work to be done for the company, or the money be paid out of the nominal purchase money or contract price, or otherwise.

An agreement to pay commission in contravention of section 98 is invalid.

The company agreed to pay A. a commission of 10 per cent. on any sum accepted by the company on A.'s introduction. No statement in prescribed form, as required by section 53, was registered with the Registrar. A. was the means of introducing £4,600 to the company, and was paid £200 on account. A. sued for £260, the balance of commission. *Held*, A. was not entitled to recover, as the commission was unlawful, but the company could not recover the £200 already paid to A.: *Andreae* v. *Zinc Mines of Great Britain Ltd.* [1918] 2 K.B. 454.

[86] *Re Republic of Bolivia Exploration Syndicate Ltd.* [1914] 1 Ch. 139.
[87] *Dominion of Canada General Trading Syndicate* v. *Brigstocke* [1911] 2 K.B. 648.
[88] pp. 160, 163.

An agreement by a company to apply some of its shares partly for underwriting services and partly for other services is caught by section 98, *ante*, and the whole agreement is invalid.[89]

If shares are allotted at par to persons who are given an option to subscribe for further shares at par within a certain time, an allotment of such further shares at par is not subject to the provisions of section 98 of the 1985 Act, even though the market value of the shares has risen to a premium, because it does not involve the payment of a commission or discount.[90]

UNDERWRITING

Before an issue of shares is made to the public, it is usual to insure the success of the issue by having it underwritten. Underwriting means "agreeing to take so many shares, more or less in number, as are specified in the underwriting letter if the public do not subscribe for them."[91] Another definition is, an agreement "to take up by way of subscription in a new company or new issue a certain number of share if and so far as not applied for by the public.[92] An underwriter does not guarantee that the public will take up the shares; he agrees with the company to subscribe for them himself on the happening of an event, *i.e.* the failure of the public to subscribe them fully. The underwriter may be, for example, a broker, a bank or an issuing house.

The consideration for underwriting usually takes the form of an underwriting commission which the underwriter receives whether or not the public take up all the shares underwritten. The commission may be in the form of shares or it may be a payment out of the money derived from the issue of shares underwritten. Again, it is thought that it may be a payment out of the company's profits, if the company has profits in hand and they have not been capitalised. In any case, section 97 of the 1985 Act, above must be complied with.

[89] *Banking Service Corporation Ltd.* v. *Toronto Finance Corporation Ltd.* [1928] A.C. 333 (P.C.).

[90] *Hilder* v. *Dexter* [1902] A.C. 474; *cf. Cameron* v. *Glenmorangie Distillery Co. Ltd.* (1896) 23 R. 1092.

[91] *Per* Lindley L.J. in *Re Licensed Victuallers' Mutual Trading Association* (1889) 42 Ch.D. 1 (C.A.), at p. 7.

[92] *Per* Lord Tomlin in *Australian Investment Trust Ltd.* v. *Strand and Pitt Street Properties Ltd.* [1932] A.C. 735 (P.C.) at p. 745.

An underwriting contract may take the form of an agreement expressed to be made between the underwriter and the company, not necessarily signed by the underwriter,[93] or an offer may be made by letter from the underwriter which requires an acceptance on the part of the company and notice of acceptance given to the underwriter to make it a contract.[94]

In underwriting contracts the underwriter usually irrevocably appoints some person—frequently a director—to apply in his name for the shares he may have to take up. In such a case the authority being, according to English law, coupled with an interest, cannot be revoked by the underwriter.[95]

The underwriting contract being made before the listing particulars or prospectus is issued, it is usual to enter into it on the basis of a draft document, and to provide that the contract is to be binding notwithstanding any variations between the draft and the final version. If, however, there is a material variation between the draft and the final documents, the underwriter will not be bound, in spite of such a clause.[96]

Liability on an underwriting contract passes to the executors of the underwriter, if he dies, as the contract is not one involving personal skill on the part of the underwriter.[97]

Sub-underwriting

It is a common practice for underwriters to relieve themselves from some of their risk by entering into sub-underwriting contracts. In such cases a sub-underwriter, in return for a commission, becomes bound to take and pay for his proportion of the shares sub-underwritten which are not allotted to the public.

By the nature of a sub-underwriting contract the sub-underwriter authorises the underwriter to apply for shares on his behalf if the public do not apply for them and he cannot revoke the authority so given, whether or not the sub-underwriting

[93] *Curror's Trustee* v. *Caledonian Heritable Security Co. Ltd.* (1880) 7 R. 479.
[94] *Consort Deep Level Gold Mines Ltd.* [1897] 1 Ch. 575 (C.A.).
[95] *Carmichael's Case* [1896] 2 Ch. 643 (C.A.); *cf. Premier Briquette Co. Ltd.* v. *Gray*, 1922 S.C. 329.
[96] *Warner International, etc. Co. Ltd.* v. *Kilburn, Brown & Co.* (1914) 84 L.J.K.B. 365 (C.A.).
[97] *Warner Engineering Co. Ltd.* v. *Brennan* (1913) 30 T.L.R. 191; *Curror's* case, *ante*.

letter contains a formal grant of authority to the underwriter. The authority is coupled with an interest.[98]

In a sub-underwriting contract the personality of the sub-underwriter is of importance, and therefore an undisclosed principal cannot sue on such a contract made on his behalf by an agent.

X underwrote shares in a company on the basis of a draft prospectus and Y sub-underwrote some of those shares on the same basis. Y was agent for C., but this was not disclosed to X or the company. The public response to the issue was insufficient and shares were allotted to Y, who renounced in favour of C., who was entered on the register. The prospectus contained misrepresentations and, on learning of this, C. applied for his name to be removed from the register and for repayment of his money. *Held*, C. was not entitled to rescission because (1) the contract between Y and the company was of such a class that Y must be treated as a principal and not as agent for C., and (2) the contract between the company and C. through the entry of C.'s name on the register was not entered into on the basis of the prospectus, the function of the prospectus having been fulfilled before that contract was made: *Collins* v. *Associated Greyhound Racecourses Ltd.* [1930] 1 Ch. 1 (C.A.).

Underwriting debentures

The provisions of section 98 of the 1985 Act do not apply to the underwriting of debentures, as there is nothing to prevent the issue of debentures at a discount.[99]

Brokerage

Brokerage is a payment made to an issuing house or brokers in return for their placing shares or debentures without subscribing.[1] It differs from underwriting commission in that it is a payment made to a person for placing shares or debentures without involving him in any risk of having to take them. Section 98(3) of the Companies Act 1985 provides that nothing in the section affects the power of any company to pay such brokerage as was previously lawful. It was previously held in

[98] *Re Olympic etc. Reinsurance Co. Ltd.* [1920] 2 Ch. 341 (C.A.); *cf. Premier Briquette Co. Ltd.* v. *Gray*, 1922 S.C. 329.
[99] *Post*, p. 181.
[1] *Ante*, p. 144.

Metropolitan Coal Consumers' Association v. *Scrimgeour*[2] that brokerage of a reasonable amount payable in the ordinary course of business was legal. In that case the brokerage was two and a half per cent. but a usual brokerage is one quarter per cent. Authority to pay brokerage must be contained in the articles, and need not be given in the memorandum.[3]

A payment is brokerage only if it is paid to "stockbrokers, bankers and the like, who exhibit prospectuses and send them to their customers, and by whose mediation the customers are induced to subscribe."[4] The person to whom it is paid must be one who, in some way, carries on the business of a broker. A payment, therefore, to a lady of a percentage on the amount of capital which she induced third parties to subscribe for shares in a company—such a transaction being an isolated one, and not in the ordinary course of the lady's business—was held not to be brokerage.[5]

[2] [1895] 2 Q.B. 604 (C.A.).
[3] See *per* Lindley L.J. [1895] 2 Q.B. 604 at p. 607.
[4] *Per* Bailhache J. in *Andreae* v. *Zinc Mines of Great Britain Ltd.* [1918] 2 K.B. 454, at p. 458.
[5] *Andreae* v. *Zinc Mines of Great Britain Ltd.*

Chapter 8

ALLOTMENT AND COMMENCEMENT OF BUSINESS

THIS chapter deals first with the powers of the directors and the company to allot shares, then with the contract of allotment under which shares are allotted by a company to a person who has applied for them, certain statutory restrictions on allotment by a public company, and the return which the company usually must deliver to the Registrar after it has allotted shares. Finally, the chapter deals with certain statutory restrictions on the commencement of business by a public company.

Power to allot shares

Prior to the 1980 Act directors generally had the power to issue shares up to the limit of the authorised capital.[1] This led to several abuses by directors issuing shares to their allies in order to forestall take-over bids.[2] Under what is now section 80 of the 1985 Act, however, the directors of any company may not issue shares, or any right to acquire shares, without express authority being given either in the articles or by a resolution in general meeting.

Such authority may be given for a specific allotment or generally and must state the maximum amount of the shares which may be issued. Even if the authority is given by the articles it cannot last for more than five years, and, in any case, it can be varied, revoked or renewed by an ordinary resolution.

[1] *Ante*, p. 80.
[2] See, *e.g.* *Hogg* v. *Cramphorn* [1967] Ch. 254; *Bamford* v. *Bamford* [1970] Ch. 212; *post*, p. 400.

Thus the articles may actually be altered, on this one occasion, by an ordinary resolution.[3] A copy of any resolution either conferring, revoking, varying or renewing the authority must, however, be registered with the Registrar as if it were a special resolution, under section 380,[4] and notice of it must be put in the appropriate Gazette under section 711.[5]

A private company may by elective resolution[6] decide that section 80A shall apply. In such a case the directors can be given either an indefinite authority to allot shares or one for any fixed period, rather than for the five year maximum period. The only restrictions are that the authority must state the maximum amount of shares which may be allotted under it and, if it is for a fixed period, the date on which it is to expire. Such authority may still be varied or revoked by an ordinary resolution. If the election itself is revoked (by an ordinary resolution) then the authority under section 80A will be construed as one for five years only. Thus for example if it has been in existence for six years it will cease immediately.

Nothing in section 80 affects the validity of any allotment, but any director who knowingly and wilfully contravenes it may be prosecuted and fined. It has no application to employee share schemes.[7]

Pre-emption rights

The 1980 Act introduced further restrictions on the issue of ordinary, "equity," shares by companies for cash other than those subject to employee share schemes.[7] This basic restriction is, however, subject to wide exemptions.

Under what is now section 89 of the 1985 Act ordinary shares issued for cash must first be offered to existing,[8] ordinary shareholders in proportion to the nominal value of their existing holdings. The articles may go further and provide for such pre-emption rights to apply within each class of ordinary shares.

[3] *Cf.* s.9; *ante*, p. 90.
[4] *Post*, p. 341.
[5] *Post*, p. 341.
[6] Elective resolutions must be unanimous. See p. 340, *post*.
[7] *Post*, p. 272.
[8] Including those who held shares 28 days before the offer made.

Such rights are not given by the Act to the holders of preference shares or shares to be paid for, in whole or in part, otherwise than by cash. Any offer must be open for 21 days.[9] Any shares not taken up on the *pro rata* basis must then be offered to the ordinary shareholders generally.

Any contravention of the statutory or other pre-emption rights renders the company and any officer in default liable to compensate any existing shareholders who have suffered a loss as a result.

Private companies may exclude the effects of section 89 by a provision to that effect in their articles: section 91. In addition, both public and private companies may qualify or exclude pre-emption rights if their directors have the authority to issue shares under section 80.[10] If the directors have a general authority to issue shares under that section the company, either by its articles, or by a special resolution, may vary or exclude section 89 altogether. On the other hand, if the directors only have authority to make a specific allotment, section 89 can only be modified or excluded by a special resolution recommended by the directors and supported by a circular sent out with the notices of the meeting, setting out the directors' reasons for making the recommendation, the amount to be paid to the company on the allotment, and the directors' justification for that amount. Directors who issue a misleading, false or deceptive circular in support of such a resolution may be convicted and fined or imprisoned. The exclusion or modification of pre-emption rights in this way may be renewed or revoked by a special resolution: section 95.[11]

AGREEMENT FOR ALLOTMENT

The ordinary law of contract, which usually requires an offer and an acceptance if there is to be an agreement, applies to agreements to take shares in a company. Where a prospectus or listing particulars are issued by the company, otherwise than on

[9] s.90.

[10] *Ante*, p. 164.

[11] This procedure is modified by Sched. 15A, para. 3 if the written resolution procedure is used by a private company (see *post*, p. 343). The circular must be sent to each member prior to his signature.

a rights issue, the document is not an offer—it is merely an invitation to the public to make offers. An offer is made by the applicant in sending a form of application for shares to the company and it is accepted by the allotment of shares to the applicant. Under normal articles the power to allot shares is vested in the board of directors.

An acceptance must be unconditional[12] and correspond with the terms of the offer. If, therefore, the application was for 100 shares and only 25 were allotted, the allotment would be a counter-offer and the applicant could refuse to take any shares. An issue may be over-subscribed, and the company unable to make an allotment in full to every applicant; in order to obviate this difficulty the form of the application invariably runs, "I agree to accept such shares or any smaller number that may be allotted to me."

To constitute a binding contract, an acceptance must be communicated to the offeror.[13] If the parties must have contemplated that the post might be used to communicate acceptance, the posting of a letter of allotment is sufficient communication to the applicant.

G. applied for shares in the H. company. A letter of allotment was posted, but never reached G. *Held*, G. was a shareholder in the company: *Household Fire Insurance Co.* v. *Grant* (1879) 4 Ex.D. 216 (C.A.).[14]

Communication, however, may be made in any way which shows the applicant that the company has accepted his offer,[15] *e.g.* by a letter demanding payment of an instalment on the shares,[16] or by receipt of a notice calling a general meeting and notification given orally by the secretary that shares have been allotted.[17] The applicant must, however, have *agreed* to take

[12] *Liquidator of the Consolidated Copper Co. etc. Ltd.* v. *Peddie* (1877) 5 R. 393.
[13] See *Entores Ltd.* v. *Miles Far East Corporation* [1955] 2 Q.B. 327 (C.A.).
[14] Doubted in Scotland: *Mason* v. *Benhar Coal Co. Ltd.* (1882) 9 R. 883, *per* Lord Shand at p. 890.
[15] *Chapman* v. *Sulphite Pulp Co. Ltd.* (1892) 19 R. 837.
[16] *Forget* v. *Cement Products Co. of Canada* [1916] W.N. 259 (P.C.).
[17] *Chapman* v. *Sulphite Pulp Co. Ltd.* (1892) 19 R. 837; see also *Curror's Trustee* v. *Caledonian Heritable Security Co. Ltd.* (1880) 7 R. 479 and *Nelson* v. *Fraser* (1906) 14 S.L.T. 513 (O.H.).

shares and not merely have expressed a "willingness" to take them,[18] the sending to a person who has not so agreed of notices of meetings and of letters making calls on the shares does not of itself make the recipient a shareholder.[19]

An offer can be revoked at any time before acceptance is communicated.

H. applied for shares in a company. Shares were allotted to him, and the letter of allotment sent to the *company's* agent to deliver by hand to H. Before the letter was delivered. H. withdrew his application. *Held*, H. was not a shareholder in the company: *Re National Savings Bank Association* (1867) L.R. 4 Eq. 9.

To be effective, revocation of an offer must be communicated to the offeree. Thus notice of the revocation of an application must reach the company before the letter of allotment is posted.[20] If the revocation is communicated by post it is not effective until the letter is received by the company.

An offer lapses if it is not accepted within the time prescribed or, if none is prescribed, within a reasonable time. Thus an allotment must be made within a reasonable time after the application, otherwise the applicaton will lapse and the applicant will be entitled to refuse to take the shares.

On June 8 M. offered to take shares in the R. company. He heard nothing until November 23, when he received a letter of acceptance. M. refused to take the shares, *Held*, M. was entitled to refuse, as his offer had lapsed: *Ramsgate Victoria Hotel Co. Ltd.* v. *Montefiore* (1866) L.R. 1 Ex. 109.

An offer is also terminated by the failure of a condition subject to which it was made. Thus if an application for shares is conditional, *e.g.* on the applicant having a contract to supply goods to the company,[21] or on all capital being subscribed,[22]

[18] *Mason* v. *Benhar Coal Co. Ltd.* (1882) 9 R. 883.

[19] *Goldie* v. *Torrance* (1882) 10 R. 174; and see *Liquidator of the Florida etc. Co. Ltd.* v. *Bayley* (1890) 17 R. 525.

[20] *Byrne* v. *Van Tienhoven* (1880) 5 C.P.D. 344; *Thomson* v. *James* (1855) 18 D. 1.

[21] *Shackelford's Case* (1866) L.R. 1 Ch.App. 567.

[22] *Swedish Match Co. Ltd.* v. *Seivwright* (1889) 16 R. 989.

and the condition is not fulfilled when shares are allotted to him, the applicant is under no liability to take the shares.

A conditional application must be distinguished from an application for shares coupled with a collateral agreement, *e.g.* where £10 shares are to be paid up to the extent of £1.50 in cash on allotment, that the balance is to be set-off against goods to be supplied to the company by the allottee. In the latter case, when shares are allotted the applicant becomes a shareholder with the right merely of suing the company on the collateral agreement.[23]

Restrictions on Allotment

Sections 84, 85, 88 and 101 contain restrictions on allotment by *public* companies. In addition, where an offer for unlisted securities has been made the terms and implementation of the offer are governed by rules to be made under section 169 of the Financial Services Act 1986.

Section 84 provides that no allotment can be made unless either the capital is subscribed for in full or the offer states that if it is not so subscribed the allotment will nevertheless take place subject to any specified conditions.

If any of the above conditions are not satisfied within 40 days of the first issue of the prospectus, all money received must be forthwith returned to the applicants without interest. If it is not returned within 48 days of the issue of the prospectus, the directors are jointly and severally liable to repay it with interest at five per cent. per annum. A director is not liable, however, if he proves that the default in repayment was not due to any misconduct or negligence on his part.

A sum is for the purposes of this section, deemed to have been paid to and received by the company if a cheque for the sum has been received in good faith by the company and the directors have no reason to suspect that it will not be paid.

Any condition requiring an applicant to waive compliance with any of these requirements is void.

[23] *Elkington's Case* (1867) L.R. 2 Ch.App. 511; *cf. Liquidator of the Pelican etc. Insurance Co. Ltd.* v. *Bruce* (1904) 11 S.L.T. 658 (O.H.), and see opinions in *National House etc. Investment Co. Ltd.* v. *Watson*, 1908 S.C. 888.

No allotment unless minimum payment paid up

Under section 101 no share may be allotted unless one quarter of the nominal value and the whole of any premium on the share has been paid up. In breach the share will be regarded as having been so paid up but the allottee and any subsequent holder will be liable to pay that amount together with interest. A bona fide purchaser without actual notice of the breach is not liable nor any successor to such a person. In addition the court may grant relief under section 113. Contravention by the company and any officer in default is a criminal offence; section 114.

Effect of irregular allotment

When an allotment is made which does not satisfy the provisions of section 84, *ante*, section 85 gives the applicant two remedies, one against the company and the other against the directors.

As against the *company*, the allotment is *voidable* by the allottee within one month after allotment, even if the company is being wound up. Legal proceedings need not be taken within a month. Notice of avoidance within the month, followed by prompt legal proceedings after the month, is sufficient.[24]

As against the *directors*, the allottee can sue such of them as have knowingly contravened or authorised the contravention of the provisions for any loss, damages or costs he may have sustained or incurred thereby. Any such proceedings against directors must be brought within two years after allotment. The company has a similar remedy against the directors for any loss, damages or costs sustained or incurred by it.

Offers of unlisted securities following registration of a prospectus

Section 169 of the Financial Services Act 1986 authorises the Secretary of State to make rules regulating the terms upon which unlisted securities may be offered by advertisement and to provide that potential offerees are treated equally and fairly.

[24] Re *National Motor Mail-Coach Co. Ltd.* [1908] 2 Ch. 228.

In particular these rules apply to the priority between applicants and for the payment of commission.

RETURN AS TO ALLOTMENTS

Section 88 provides that whenever a limited company with a share capital makes any allotment of its *shares*, it must, within a month, deliver to the Registrar—

(1) A return of the allotments (on Form PUC 2), stating the number and nominal amount of the shares, the names, addresses and descriptions of the allottees and the amount paid or payable on each share, whether on account of the nominal value of the share or by way of premium.

(2) In the case of shares allotted *otherwise than for cash*, a contract constituting the title of the allottee to the allotment, together with any contract of sale or for services or other consideration for the allotment, and a return (on Form PUC 3) stating the number and nominal amount of shares so allotted, the extent to which they are to be treated as paid up, and the consideration for the allotment.

RESTRICTIONS ON COMMENCEMENT OF BUSINESS

A private company can commence business, exercise any borrowing power[25] which it has and make binding contracts immediately on incorporation.

By section 117 a public company must do none of these things until it has either obtained a certificate from the Registrar that it may do so or is re-registered as a private company.

To obtain a certificate under this section the company must make a declaration to the Registrar in the prescribed form signed by a director or secretary of the company:

(1) Stating that the nominal value of the company's *allotted* share capital is not less than the authorised minimum (£50,000)[26];

[25] *Post*, Chap. 23.
[26] s.118.

(2) Disclosing the amount of such allotted share capital actually paid up at that time (at least 25 per cent. of the nominal value and the whole of any premium is necessary)[27];

(3) Stating the amount, or estimated amount, of the preliminary expenses of the company and the persons by whom any of those expenses have been paid or are payable; and

(4) Detailing any amount or benefit paid or given or intended to be paid or given to any promoter of the company, and the consideration for the payment or benefit.

This declaration may be accepted by the Registrar as sufficient evidence of the matters stated therein.

If the registrar issues a certificate under this section it is conclusive evidence that the company is entitled to do business and exercise any borrowing powers.

If a public company enters into a transaction without a certificate under section 117, the transaction remains valid, but if the company fails to comply with any obligations under it within 21 days of being called upon to do so, the directors are liable to indemnify the other party for any loss suffered as a result. In addition, the company and any officer in default will be guilty of a criminal offence.

Finally, if more than a year after the incorporation of a public company it has not been issued with a section 117 certificate, the Secretary of State may petition the court for the company to be wound up under section 122 of the Insolvency Act 1986.[28]

[27] s.101, *post*, p. 177.
[28] *Post*, p. 743.

Chapter 9

SHARE CAPITAL

THE more important topics dealt with in this chapter are the rules that share capital must be raised and, once raised, must be maintained, and the consequent need to control the reduction of share capital. The associated topics of the purchase and redemption by a company of its own shares and the giving of financial assistance by a company for the acquistion of its own shares are dealt with in the following two chapters.

MEANING OF "CAPITAL"

The word "capital" used in connection with a company has several different meanings; thus it may mean the nominal or authorised share capital, the issued share capital, the paid-up share capital or the reserve share capital of the company.

The *nominal* or *authorised capital* is merely the amount of share capital which the company is authorised to issue. As we have seen,[1] in the case of a limited company the amount of potential share capital with which it proposes to be registered, and the division thereof into shares of a fixed amount, must be set out in the memorandum of association, but this amount may be increased or reduced as explained later.[2] The amount of the company's nominal capital depends on its business requirements, actual or potential. It must be remembered that public companies must have at least £50,000 authorised capital; sections 11 and 118.

[1] *Ante*, p. 80.
[2] *Post*, pp. 186, 192.

The *issued* or *allotted capital* is that part of the company's nominal capital which has been issued to the shareholders. The company is not bound to issue all its capital at once, although a public company must issue at least £50,000 nominal value of shares before it may commence business (section 117), and frequently when the nominal capital is increased the extent of the increase is not limited to the company's requirements at the time but covers its probable requirements in the future. In such a case, further issues of capital are made as they are needed. Such issues are made by the directors if properly authorised under the Act.[3]

The *paid-up capital* is that part of the issued capital which has been paid up by the shareholders. The company may, for example, have a nominal capital of £500,000 divided into 500,000 shares of a nominal amount of £1 each, of which £400,000 is issued, *i.e.* 400,000 of the shares have been issued, and only £100,000 is paid up, *i.e.* the company has so far required only 25p. to be paid up on each share. The *uncalled capital* is the remainder of the issued capital and can be called up at any time by the company from the shareholders in accordance with the provisions of the articles. Section 101 requires public companies to call up at least one quarter of the nominal value of a share and all the premium on allotment.

The *reserve capital*, or reserve liability, is that part of the uncalled capital which a limited company has by special resolution determined shall not be called up except in the event and for the purposes of the company's being wound up and which cannot otherwise be called up: section 120. This capital is not under the control of the directors and cannot be reconverted into ordinary uncalled capital, or charged by the company, *e.g.* as security for debentures.[4] It is available only for the creditors on the winding up of the company, although it will be seen that it can be reduced with the consent of the court under section 135.[5] Reserve capital must be distinguished from capital reserves, a capital redemption reserve, revenue reserves, and a reserve or a general reserve, all of which will be dealt with later.[6]

[3] *Ante*, p. 164.
[4] *Re Mayfair Property Co.* [1898] 2 Ch. 28 (C.A.).
[5] *Re Midland Rlwy. Carriage Co.* (1907) 23 T.L.R. 661.
[6] *Post*, Chap. 22.

Section 351 provides that if, in the case of a company having a share capital, there is on the stationary used for any business letters, or on the order forms of the company, a reference to the amount of the share capital, the reference must be to paid-up share capital.

The paid-up share capital includes the nominal value of the shares paid-up and any premium on such shares.[7] For example if 10,000 £1 shares are sold for £2 each the paid up capital will be £20,000. This will however be expressed as £10,000 share capital and £10,000 share premium account in the balance sheet.

Raising of Share Capital

The issued share capital of a company is the fund to which creditors of the company can look for payment of their debts, and so, to protect the creditors, it has been held that the issued share capital must be raised. This means that shares can be treated as paid up only to the extent of the amount actually received by the company in cash or in kind, and must not be issued at a discount, *i.e.* must not be issued as fully paid for a consideration less than payment or the promise of payment of the nominal amount of each share,[8] although the company may not require payment in full of the nominal amount on allotment. The rule that the share capital must be raised is intended to ensure that money or assets equal in amount or value to the paid-up capital on paper is or are received by the company. Certain sections of the Act, *e.g.* section 98, which generally prohibits the payment of commissions and discounts out of a company's shares or capital money,[9] and section 23, which provides that a subsidiary company generally may not be a member of its holding company,[10] also have the effect of ensuring that the capital is raised. The provisions relating to payment for share capital are also intended to strengthen this rule.[11] It will be seen, however, that the sections 151–157[12]

[7] *Post*, p. 182.
[8] *Ooregum Gold Mining Co.* v. *Roper* [1892[A.C. 125, codified by s.100, *post*, p. 181.
[9] *Ante*, Chap. 8.
[10] *Post*, p. 237.
[11] *Post*, p. 176.
[12] *Post*, Chap. 11.

allow companies considerable scope to assist in the acquisition of their own shares and may prove to be a negative factor in ensuring the adequate raising of capital. Of course, the rule is no protection to creditors where a company does not make a substantial issue of share capital.

There are certain exceptions to the rule that the share capital must be raised. These exceptions are:

(1) where shares are issued by a private company for an over-valued non-monetary consideration, as in *Re Wragg Ltd.*[13];
(2) where a company pays a commission under section 97 to a person who agrees to subscribe, or to procure subscriptions, for shares in the company.[14]

The rule does not apply to an unlimited company.[15]

Consideration for Allotment

The general rule has always been that an allottee must pay for his shares in full.[16] Under section 99(1) shares are only treated as paid up to the extent that the company has received money or money's worth (including goodwill and know-how) in return for them. This does not apply to bonus shares.[17] Section 99(2) further prohibits a public company from accepting an undertaking by any person to do work or perform services in return for shares. Such an undertaking may nevertheless be enforced by the company (section 115), and the holder of shares issued in return for such undertaking becomes liable to pay any shortfall in the value for the shares (section 99(3)).

Any subsequent holder of shares not regarded as fully paid up as a result of a breach of section 99, may be liable for the amount due, unless he is either a bona fide purchaser of the

[13] [1897] 1 Ch. 796 (C.A.), *post*, p. 180; *cf. Waterhouse* v. *Jamieson* (1870) 8 M. (H.L.) 88 and *Penang Foundry Co. Ltd.* v. *Gardiner*, 1913 S.C. 1203 (O.H.).
[14] *Ante*, Chap. 8.
[15] See *Nelson Mitchell* v. *City of Glasgow Bank* (1879) 6 R. (H.L.) 66; (1878) 6 R. 420, *ante*, p. 41.
[16] *Ooregum Gold Mining Co. of India Ltd.* v. *Roper* [1892] A.C. 125, *post*, p. 181; *Klenck* v. *East India Co. etc. Ltd.* (1888) 16 R. 271.
[17] *Post*, Chap. 22.

shares without actual notice of the defect, or an immediate or subsequent transferee from such a person (section 112). The court may grant relief in appropriate circumstances, (section 113). Contravention of section 99 by a company and any officer in default is a criminal offence (section 114).

Under section 101 public companies are further prevented from alloting shares unless at least one quarter of the nominal value and the whole of any premium has actually been paid. This is a restriction on allotment and has been dealt with in chapter 8.

Shares taken by any subscriber to the memorandum of a public company in pursuance of an undertaking of his in the memorandum must be paid up in cash (section 106).

Payment of non-cash consideration—public companies

Section 102 prohibits a public company from accepting as consideration for shares any undertaking, *e.g.* to transfer property, which is to be or may be performed more than five years after the date of the allotment. Any variation of a valid undertaking (*i.e.* within five years) taking it outside the five year period is void. Any allotment in contravention of this requirement, or a failure by the purchaser to fulfil a valid undertaking within the contract period, renders the allottee liable to pay the company the amount owed on the shares, together with interest. Any subsequent holder of the shares is also liable subject to the bona fide purchaser exemption noted above.[18]

Section 103 provides that a public company may not allot shares for any non-cash consideration unless a report on the value of the consideration had been made by an independant person qualified to be an auditor of the company. His report must be sent to the company within six months prior to the allotment and to the proposed allottee. He may accept another's valuation if it is reasonable to do so, provided that that person is also independent and appears to be qualified and such facts are disclosed in the report. The company's auditor may be so used: section 108.

[18] *Ante*, p. 176.

The report must state the amount payable on the shares, a description of the consideration and the valuation methods used, the date of valuation and the extent to which the shares are to be treated as paid up by the consideration and in cash. It must be filed with the Registrar: section 111.

In making his report the expert may require from the officers of the company such information and explanation as he thinks necessary to enable him to carry out the valuation or to make the report. False, misleading or deceptive statements made in this context constitute criminal offences: section 110.

There is a general exemption for shares issued generally to shareholders in another company on a take-over or merger with the other company: section 103(5). Such issues are, however, subject to the extra-statutory rules on take-overs: see Chapter 31, *post*.

In default of such a report the allottee will be liable to pay any amount owed on the shares if either he did not receive a copy of the report or he knew or ought to have known of the breach: section 103(6). Subsequent holders may also be liable subject to the bona fide purchaser exemption. Relief may again be given by the court if it is just and equitable to do so, taking into account the actual amount received for the shares and other liabilities of the allottee under the contract: section 113.[19] Contravention by the company and any officer in default is a criminal offence: section 114.

These provisions only apply if the shares are issued "otherwise than for cash." Issues for cash are defined in section 738(2) so as to include payment by a cheque received by the company in good faith, or the release of liability of the company for a defined sum (*i.e.* a set-off)[20] or an undertaking to pay cash at a future date. This may be thought to cover a multitude of sins although it does not include the assignment of a debt.[21]

It is convenient to note here that similar provisions apply, by virtue of sections 104 and 109, to the acquisitions by public companies of non-cash assets from any subscriber of the memorandum, within two years of the issue of the certificate

[19] See, *e.g. Re Ossory Estates plc* (1988) 4 BCC 460. In *Re Bradford Investments plc* [1990] BCC 740 the failure to obtain a report led to the shareholders losing their right to vote under the articles.
[20] Thus preserving the decision in *Spargo's Case* (1873) L.R. 8 Ch.App. 407.
[21] *Systems Control plc* v. *Munro Corporate* [1990] BCC 386.

entitling it to commence business, if the consideration to be given by the company is not less than 10 per cent. of the nominal value of the company's issued shares at that time.[22]

Payment of non-cash consideration—private companies

Shares may, with the consent of the company, be paid for otherwise than in cash, *e.g.* by the transfer of property to the company or by the rendering of services to the company. Sections 102–112 do not apply to private companies, but where shares are allotted as fully or partly paid up otherwise than in cash, a contract constituting the title of the allottee to the allotment together with any contract of sale, or for services or other consideration for the allotment, or, if such a contract is not in writing, particulars of the contract, must, with the return as to allotments, be delivered to the Registrar, usually within a month after the allotment: section 88.[23] Default renders the officers of the company liable to penalties but does not make the allotment void.

Registration under section 88 does not make a "contract" binding on the company if there is no consideration for it, and past consideration is no consideration.[24]

A private company decided to turn itself into a public company. Before doing so it resolved so allot £6,000 of fully paid shares to the existing directors and shareholders, and a contract was made agreeing to allot the shares in consideration of their past services and expenses in forming the company and establishing the business. The contract was registered and the shares were allotted. The company afterwards went into liquidation. *Held*, the director and shareholders were liable to pay for the shares, as there was no consideration in money or money's worth for the allotment, past services being no consideration: *Re Eddystone Marine Insurance Co.* [1893] 3 Ch. 9 (C.A.).

An agreement by a private company to allot shares in consideration of services to be performed in the future also renders the allottee liable to pay for the shares.[25] "It is not open

[22] *Ante*, p. 173.
[23] *Ante*, p. 171.
[24] The doctrine of consideration is not part of Scots law; *cf.* however, *Liquidator of the Pelican etc. Insurance Co. Ltd.* v. *Bruce* (1904) 11 S.L.T. 658 (O.H.).
[25] *National House etc. Investment Co. Ltd.* v. *Watson*, 1908 S.C. 888.

to a company to agree with the holder or proposed holder of its shares to replace the statutory liability by a special contract sounding in damages only."[26] However, a private company may agree to pay a fixed sum immediately for services to be performed in the future, *e.g.* for the erection of a building, and to satisfy that debt by the allotment of shares.[27]

If there is a contract for the acceptance by a private company of specified property or services of substantial value in payment for shares, the court will not, whilst the contract stands, inquire into the adequacy of the consideration, as it is for the parties to make their own bargain.

The goodwill, stock-in-trade and property of a business was sold to a company for £46,000, of which £20,000 was to be paid in fully paid shares. The stock-in-trade was shown in the company's books at a figure £11,000 less than the sum allocated to it in the agreement. On the company's going into liquidation, a misfeasance summons was taken out to obtain payment for the shares. *Held*, since the agreement could not be impeached, the adequacy of the consideration could not be gone into: *Re Wragg Ltd.* [1897] 1 Ch. 796 (C.A.).

"Where a company, in good faith, issues shares as fully paid-up in consideration of property transferred or services rendered, the Court will not inquire into the value of that which was accepted by the Company as an equivalent of money": *per* Lord Stormonth Darling (Ordinary) in *Brownlie and Others, Petitioners* (1898) 6 S.L.T. 249 (O.H.) at p. 251.

Where the contract is fraudulent or shows on the face of it that the consideraton is illusory, the allottee is liable to pay for the shares.

G. agreed to sell a concession to a company which agreed to allot him as fully paid 400 shares forthwith and also one-fifth of any future increase of capital. *Held*, the agreement was good so far as it obliged the company to allot one-fifth of any future increase of capital but void so far as it relieved G. from paying for the shares. It was apparent that the value of the concession bore no relation to the amount of the shares: *Hong Kong and China Gas Co. Ltd.* v. *Glen* [1914] 1 Ch. 527.

"If the agreement were that the property to be purchased should be valued, and that against this property shares should be issued as fully paid to an extent exceeding the amount of the valuation by one-third, the arrangement would . . . be bad as to this excess of one-third. It

[26] *Per* Parker J. in *Gardner* v. *Iredale* [1912] 1 Ch. 700, at p. 716.
[27] *Gardner* v. *Iredale*, above.

would to this extent be apparent on the face of the contract that the attempted discharge of a part of the liability was illusory": *per* Sargant J., at p. 539.

When shares are issued in pursuance of a contract registered under section 88, and the allottee also subscribes the memorandum for the same number of shares, care should be taken to see that the agreement makes it clear that the shares for which the memorandum is signed are the same as those referred to in the agreement, otherwise both lots of shares will have to be paid for.[28] To prevent this from happening, it is usual for the allottee under the agreement not to subscribe the memorandum.

Issue of Shares at a Discount

The general rule has always been that shares must *not* be issued at a discount, *i.e.* must not be issued as fully paid for a consideration less than the nominal amount. This is now expressly stated in section 100. The shareholder must pay the full nominal value of his shares, whether he pays in cash or in kind, together with interest on the discount. Any subsequent holder of the shares may also be held liable for the discount unless he is a bona fide purchaser for value without actual notice of the discount issue or a subsequent transferee of the shares from such a person. The court may grant relief in appropriate circumstances under section 113. Contravention of section 100 is a criminal offence by the company and any officer in default (section 114). The general principle was first established in England by the House of Lords in 1892.

The market value of the £1 ordinary shares of a company was 2s. 6d. The company thereupon issued preference shares of £1 each with 15s. credited as paid, leaving a liabilty of only 5s. a share. A contract to this effect was registered under what is now s.52. *Held*, the issue was *ultra vires*, and allottees were liable to pay for the shares in full: *Ooregum Gold Mining Co. of India Ltd.* v. *Roper* [1892] A.C. 125.[29]

"The dominant and cardinal principle of [the Companies] Acts is that the investor shall purchase immunity from liability beyond a certain

[28] *Fothergill's Case* (1873) L.R. 8 Ch. App. 270.

[29] An earlier Scottish case to the same effect is *Klenck* v. *East India Co. etc. Ltd.* (1888) 16 R. 271, where the memorandum contained a power to issue shares at a discount.

limit, on the terms that there shall be and remain a liability up to that limit": *per* Lord Macnaghten at p. 145.

The share capital of a company must be raised. This means that money or assets equal to the paid-up capital must be recieved by the company or, in other words, that shares can be treated as paid up only to the extent of the amount actually received by the company in cash or in kind. The idea is to protect creditors of the company.[30]

There is no issue at discount where shares are issued at par, *e.g.* after the exercise of an option to take them up at par, even though they could otherwise be issued at premium,[31] or where shares are issued at lesser premium than that at which they might have been paid.[32]

There is nothing to prevent debentures being issued at a discount. However, in the case of convertible debentures, if the debentures are issued at a discount, with a right to exchange them for fully paid shares equal in nominal amount to the par value of the debentures, the right has been held void as being a right to an issue of shares at discount.[33] The right will be valid if it is to fully paid shares equal in nominal amount to the issue price of the debentures—the shares will then not be issued at a discount.

The general rule is subject to the following exceptions:

(1) There is in effect a discount when shares are issued by a private company for an overvalued non-monetary consideration, as in *Re Wragg Ltd.*, *ante.*[34]

(2) Similarly where, under section 97, *ante*,[35] commission is paid to a person who agrees to subscribe, or to procure subscriptions, for shares in a company.

ISSUE OF SHARES AT A PREMIUM

Where a company's issued shares have a market value greater than the amount paid up on them, when further shares are

[30] See *ante*, p. 175.
[31] *Hilder* v. *Dexter* [1902] A.C. 474, *ante*, p. 160.
[32] *Cameron* v. *Glenmorangie Distillery Co. Ltd.* (1986) 23 R. 1092.
[33] *Mosely* v. *Koffyfontien Mines Ltd.* [1904] 2 Ch. 108 (C.A.).
[34] p. 180.
[35] p. 158.

being issued the company may require applicants to agree to pay more than the nominal amount of the new shares, *i.e.* to pay a premium.

A company may, without any special power in its articles, issue its shares at a premium, *i.e.›* for a consideration in cash or in kind which exceeds the nominal amount of the shares, although there is no law which obliges a company to issue its shares above par because they are saleable at a premium in the market.[36] However, by section 130, where shares are issued at a premium, whether for cash or otherwise, a sum equal to the aggregate amount or value of the premiums must be transferred to the "share premium account."

As will be seen later, section 130 extends the principle that the share capital of a company must be maintained[37] to a share premium account, because the section goes on to provide that the provisions of the Act relating to reduction of capital apply to this account, *i.e.* it cannot be reduced without leave of the court except where it is applied in—

(1) paying up unissued shares of the company to be issued to members as fully paid bonus shares[38]; or
(2) writing off (*a*) the preliminary expenses, or (*b*) the expenses of, or the commission paid or discount allowed on, an issue of shares or debentures of the company; or
(3) providing for the premium payable by the company on the redemption of debentures.[39]

In addition, by virtue of section 171 the share premium account may be used by private companies to pay off any premium on a redemption or purchase by such companies of their own shares.[40]

The object of the provision relating to the share premium account is to prevent dividends being paid out of premiums

[36] *Per* Lord Davey in *Hilder* v. *Dexter* [1902] A.C. 474, at p. 480, *Cameron's* case, *ante*.
[37] *Re Moorgate Mercantile Holdings Ltd.* [1980] 1 All E.R. *Post*, p. 194.
[38] Other ways in which bonus shares can be paid for are dealt with *post*, Chap. 22.
[39] *Post*, Chap. 23.
[40] *Post*, Chap. 10.

received on an issue of shares.[41]; When, therefore, any part of the share premium account is otherwise distributed among the shareholders it is to be treated as if the company were reducing its capital by repaying paid-up share capital.[42] Although share premiums are regarded as capital, it is not capital belonging to any individual shareholder. The shareholder paying the premium has no dividend rights in respect of it and has no right to repayment of it in a winding up.

The amount of the share premium account must be specified in the balance sheet: Schedule 4.

The issue of shares at premium accentuates the unreality of the nominal or par value of a share. The capital in the share premium account is an anomalous form of capital because it is capital on which no dividend is paid, which is not attributable to the ownership of any class of shares, which is not part of the company's nominal capital, and which the ordinary investor does not realise is part of the company's actual capital.

Share Premium Account and Issues Other Than for Cash

Shares can be issued at a premium not only for cash but also for consideration other than cash. If, in the latter case, the value of the consideration received, *e.g.* of land, exceeds the nominal value of the shares issued there is an issue of shares at a premium and section 130 applies.

In two cases this principle was applied where a company acquired shares in another company by virtue of an exchange of shares, *e.g.* on a merger or take-over, and the value of the shares acquired exceeded the value of the shares issued. The excess had to be transferred to the share premium account, with the result that the pre-acquisition profits of the acquired company, reflected in the value of its shares, were frozen and could not be distributed as dividends by the acquiring company: *Shearer* v. *Bercain* [1980] 3 All E.R. 295: *Head* (*Henry*) *& Co. Ltd.* v. *Ropner Holdings Ltd.* [1952] Ch. 124. Until the 1980

[41] As in *Drown* v. *Gaumont-British Picture Corporation Ltd.* [1937] Ch. 402, where there was a trading loss in one year but a dividend was paid out of the reserve fund, part of which consisted of premium on issues of shares.

[42] *Re Duff's Settlements* [1951] Ch. 923 (C.A.).

decision, however, this principle was regarded as fallacious by many lawyers and accountants, with the result that few such transfers to share premium accounts has been made. Following the 1980 decision, the Act provides two forms of relief from the obligations of section 130 in certain defined circumstances.[43] The basic rule, however, remains valid in other circumstances.

Merger relief

Where the issuing company acquires a 90 per cent. holding in another company by way of a share for share exchange no transfer to the share premium account need be made: section 131. In fact this is a wide relief as it applies whether or not the issuing company owned any shares in the other company, *e.g*, it applies to a company owning 60 per cent. of the shares of a subsidiary acquiring another 30 per cent. There is no obligation in such cases to disclose any "premiums" in the balance sheet. It also applies if the consideration provided by the acquired company is a cancellation of its issued shares rather than an issue—a frequent practice in schemes of reconstruction.

Group reconstruction relief

Where a wholly-owned subsidiary aquires a shareholding (not necessarily 100 per cent.) in a fellow subsidiary (not necessarily wholly-owned) in return for an allotment of its own shares or other non-cash assets to its holding company or another of its wholly-owned subsidiaries, relief from section 130 is available: section 132.[44] Only the lower of the cost or book value to the issuing company of the acquired shares need be taken into account.

[43] These reliefs can be extended or varied by subsequent regualtions: s.134. In fact this has been done with respect to the second relief—see *post*. A general amnesty for pre-February 1981 mergers can be found in s.12 of the Companies Consolidation (Consequential Provisions) Act 1985.

[44] The present form of this relief originates from the Companies (Share Premium Account) Regulations 1984 (S.I. 1984 No. 2007), which substituted the new section into the 1981 Act and so the 1985 Act. The original form of the relief, which operated until December 1984 can be found in Sched. 25 to the 1985 Act.

Where both sections 131 and 132 could apply only the latter relief can be claimed.[45]

ALTERATION OF SHARE CAPITAL

Section 121 provides that a limited company with a share capital, if so authorised by its articles, may alter the conditions of its memorandum relating to share capital by—

(1) increasing its share capital by new shares; or
(2) consolidating and dividing all or any of its share capital into shares of larger amount than its existing shares; or
(3) converting all or any of its paid-up shares into stock, or reconverting stock into paid-up shares of any denomination; or
(4) subdividing all or any of its shares into shares of smaller amount than is fixed by the memorandum; or
(5) cancelling shares which have not been taken or agreed to be taken by any person. (This is called "diminution of capital" and it should not be confused with reduction of capital which will be explained later[46]).

All these powers require for their exercise a resolution of the company in general meeting.

Increase of capital

Every increase of capital, *i.e.* nominal capital, must be effected by the company in general meeting: section 121. If the articles authorise the increase of capital, whether an ordinary or a special resolution is required depends on the articles.

Table A, regulation 32, provides: "The company may be by ordinary resolution—(a) increase its share capital by new shares of such amount as the resolution prescribes; ... "

If the articles do not give authority to increase capital, the articles must be altered by special resolution so that they do

[45] For this effect on group accounts see Chap. 22, *post*.
[46] s.121(5). See *post*, p. 192.

give authority but the one special resolution can both authorise and effect an increase.[47]

The notice convening the meeting must specify the amount of the proposed increase.[48] Within 15 days after the passing of the resolution effecting the increase, a notice in the prescribed form of the amount of the increase must be filed with the Registrar. A printed copy of the resolution effecting the increase, or a copy in some other form approved by him, must also be filed with the Registrar (section 123).

The conditions on which the new shares are held are set out in the terms of issue. The articles usually provide that they shall be subject to the same provisions with reference to the payment of calls, lien, transfer, transmission, forfeiture, and otherwise as the shares in the original capital.

Consolidation of shares

This takes place when several shares are consolidated into one, *e.g.* when twenty 5p. shares are consolidated into one £1 share. Consolidation is effected in the same way as an increase of capital under section 121, *i.e.* if the articles authorise consolidation, the resolution specified in the articles must be passed. If the articles are silent, a special resolution to give authority and to effect the consolidation is necessary. Table A, regulation 32(*b*), requires an ordinary resolution. Notice must be given to the Registrar within a month of the consolidation (section 122).

Conversion of shares into stock

The difference between stock and shares was described by Lord Hatherley as follows: "Shares in a company, as shares, cannot be bought in small fractions of any amount, fractions of less than a pound,[49] but the consolidated stock of a company can be bought just in the same way as the stock of the public debt can be bought, split up in as many portions as you like,

[47] *Campbell's Case* (1873) I.R. 9 Ch.App. 1.
[48] *MacConnell* v. *E. Prill & Co. Ltd.* [1916] 2 Ch. 57.
[49] This only refers to the shares of the particular company under discussion. The nominal value of shares may be less than a pound.

and subdivided into as small fractions as you please." He also referred to stock as "simply a set of shares put together in a bundle."[50]

A company *cannot issue stock directly* but can only convert shares into stock under section 121, although there seems to be no reason for this rule today. The conversion can only be made if the shares are fully paid. The conversion of shares into stock (or a reconversion of stock into shares) is effected in the same way as an increase of capital under section 121. Notice must be given to the Registrar within a month (section 122).

Although in theory stock can be transferred in fractional amounts, in practice the articles usually confer on the directors power to fix the minimum amount transferable.

When shares are converted into stock the register of members must show the amount of stock held by each member: section 352. Stock certificates similar in form to share certificates must be issued except that stock warrants transferable by delivery may be issued if the articles so provide.[51] When shares have been converted into stock the annual return must state the amount of stock held by each member: section 364a(8).

The advantage of converting shares into stock was that the work caused by the fact that each share had a seperate number was obviated. However, this advantage is now minimised by the proviso to section 182(2), under which shares need not have a distinguishing number.[52] In practise stock is now rare and Table A no longer contains any reference to it.

Subdivision of shares

This is the division of shares into shares of smaller amount, *e.g.* the division of one £1 share into 20 5p. shares, and it is often resorted to for the purpose of improving the marketability of expensive shares. Subdivision is effected in the same way as an increase of capital: section 121. Table A, regulation 32c, requires an ordinary resolution. If the shares are not fully paid up, the proportion between the amount paid and the amount unpaid on each reduced share must be the same as it was in the

[50] In *Morrice* v. *Aylmer* (1875) L.R. 7 H.L. 717 at pp. 724, 725.
[51] *Pilkington* v. *United Railways of The Havana etc. Warehouses Ltd.* [1930] 2 Ch. 108.
[52] *Post*, p. 258.

case of the share from which the reduced share is derived (section 121(3)). The subdivision of shares must be registered with the Registrar within a month (section 122).

Cancellation of unissued shares

A company can cancel shares which have not been taken or agreed to be taken[53] by any person, and *diminish* the amount of its nominal share capital by the amount of the shares so cancelled. This is not to be deemed a reduction of share capital (section 121(5)). Cancellation is effected in the same way as an increase of capital: section 121. Table A, regulation 32d, requires an ordinary resolution. Notice of cancellation must be registered with the Registrar within a month (section 122).

Effect of an alteration of share capital on an option to purchase shares

When a company has issued options to take up its shares and that company then chooses to alter its share capital under section 121, such an alteration may affect the option holders' rights. An increase of capital or a sub-division of shares may dilute the option rights since there will simply be more potential shares and thus the option will relate to a proportionately smaller percentage of the total. On the other hand, a consolidation of shares can result in a proportionate increase in the amount of share capital represented by an option when it is exercised. It is common therefore to include an express term in the option contract to meet such situations, *e.g.* for the terms of the option to be adjusted either by agreement or, failing that, as certified by a third party, say a nominated accountant. If there are no such express terms, however, the courts will allow the original option terms to stand despite the alteration, at least if this will benefit the option holder.

In *Forsayth Oil & Gas NL* v. *Livia Pty. Ltd.* [1985] BCLC 378 (P.C.) options has been issued for shares at $ Aus 1 nominal value. The

[53] Where a person offers to take unissued shares but that has not been accepted, there is no agreement to take shares for this purpose: *Re Swindon Town Football Co. Ltd.* [1990] BCLC 467.

company then wrote down its capital form $1 to 0.025 cents and then consolidated every ten shares into one share, with nominal value of 25 cents. The Privy Council held that in the absence of any express term the option holders' rights has not been modified by this consolidation.

Maintenance of Share Capital

It is a fundamental principle of company law that the share capital must be maintained. It has been said that "a company cannot, without the leave of the court or the adoption of a special procedure, return its capital to its shareholders. It follows that a transaction which amounts to an unauthorised return of capital is ultra vires and cannot be validated by shareholder ratification or approval."[54] This is not affected by section 35 of the Act since it is not derived from the company's memorandum.[55] Capital may be lost as a result of ordinary business risks and, as we shall see, it may be returned to the shareholders with the consent of the court under section 135, but otherwise, subject to the certain carefully controlled exceptions,[56] it must be maintained since it is the fund to which creditors of the company look for payment of their debts.[57]

The principle that the share capital of a company must be maintained boils down to this—paid up share capital must not be returned to its members and their liability in respect of capital not paid up on shares must not be reduced.

The principle has the following consequences:—

(1) A company generally must not purchase its own shares unless it follows the strict procedures laid down by the Act. In any event it must not be a member of itself.[58]

(2) A subsidiary company generally must not be a member of its holding company and any allotment or transfer of shares in a holding company to its subsidiary is void; section 23.[59]

[54] *Per* Hoffman J. in *Aveling Barford Ltd.* v. *Perion Ltd.* [1989] 1 W.L.R. 360 at p. 364.

[55] See Chap. 3, *ante*.

[56] See Chaps. 10 and 11, *post*.

[57] See, *e.g. Jenkins* v. *Harbour View Courts Ltd.* [1966] N.Z.L.R. 1 (C.A.), *post*, p. 203.

[58] *Post*, Chap. 10.

[59] *Post*, p. 236.

(3) It is generally unlawful for a company to give any kind of financial assistance for the acquisition by any person of its own shares or those of its holding company. There are however wide exceptions to this rule: sections 151–158.[60]

(4) Dividends must not be paid to the shareholders except out of distributable profits as defined by the Act, *i.e.* in general not out of capital.[61]

(5) Where a public company suffers a serious loss of capital, *i.e.* of more than half the subscribed capital, a meeting of the company must be called to discuss the issue.[62]

There are certain exceptions to the principle:—

(1) A company may reduce its share capital with the consent of the court under section 135, *post.*[63]

(2) A company may purchase or redeem its shares under the Act.[64]

(3) A company may purchase its own shares under a court order made either under section 459 to relieve an unfairly prejudiced minority[65] or section 54 to relieve a minority on the conversion of a public company to a private company.

(4) Capital may be returned to the members, after the company's debts have been paid, in a winding up.

Other apparent exceptions are forfeiture of shares and surrender to avoid a forfeiture, although here the amount paid on the shares remains with the company when the shareholder unable to pay a call is relieved of liability for future calls, and the shares revert to the company, bear no dividend and must either be reissued or cancelled.[66]

[60] *Post*, Chap. 11.
[61] *Post*, Chap. 22.
[62] *Post*, p. 204.
[63] p. 192.
[64] *Post*, Chap. 10.
[65] *Post*, Chap. 18.
[66] *Per* Lord Herschell at p. 417, and Lord Watson at p. 424, in *Trevor* v. *Whitworth*, *supra.*

Finally, the principle as to maintenance of share capital has been extended:—

(1) By section 170, to a capital redemption reserve set up when redeemable shares are redeemed or other shares purchased by the company out of profits.[67]
(2) By section 130, to a share premium account.[68]

A company limited by guarantee and not having a share capital is subject to the principle of raising and maintenance of capital as far as the guarantee fund is concerned. The principle as applied to such a company is stricter than as applied to the company limited by shares, since in the latter type of company the principle does not prevent the creation of security over called or uncalled capital.[69]

The principle does not apply to an unlimited company.[70]

Reduction of Capital

The share capital of the company must be subscribed in money or money's worth. This capital may be lost or diminished according to the fluctuations of the business, but otherwise, subject to the Act,[71] it generally cannot be reduced without the sanction of the court. The object of requiring this sanction is threefold—(1) to protect persons dealing with the company, so that the fund available for satisfying their claims shall not be diminished except by ordinary business risks; (2) to ensure that the reduction is equitable as between the various classes of shareholders in the company; (3) to protect the interests of the public.[72]

[67] *Post*, p. 213.
[68] *Ante*, p. 182.
[69] *Robertson* v. *British Linen Co.* (1890) 18 R. 1225 (O.H.); approved *obiter* in *Lloyds Bank Ltd.* v. *Morrison & Son*, 1927 S.C. 571.
[70] *Nelson Mitchell* v. *City of Glasgow Bank* (1879) 6 R. (H.L.) 66; (1878) 6 R. 420.
[71] See Chaps. 11 and 12, *post*.
[72] *Per* Lord Watson in *Trevor* v. *Whitworth* (1887) 12 App.Cas 409, at p. 423; *per* Lord Macnaghten in *British and American Finance Corporation Ltd.* v. *Couper* [1894] A.C. 399 at p. 411.

Reduction procedure

Section 135 provides that, subject to the confirmation by the court, a limited company with a share capital may, if authorised by its articles, by *special* resolution, reduce its share capital and, if and so far as is necessary, alter its memorandum by reducing the amount of its share capital and of its shares.

"The court," in relation to a company, means the court with jurisdiction to wind up the company: section 744. The courts with jurisdiction to wind up a company are set out in sections 117 and 120 of the Insolvency Act 1986 and will be dealt with later.[73] The application for confirmation is by petition: R.S.C., O: 102, r. 5 (England); R.C. 190 (Scotland).[74]

Power to reduce must be given in the articles; power in the memorandum is not effective.[75] The power must be a specific power to reduce.[76]

Table A, regulation 34, provides: "subject to the provisions of the Act, the company may by special resolution reduce its share capital, any capital redemption reserve fund and any share premium account in any way."

If the articles do not authorise the reduction of capital, *two* special resolutions—one to alter the articles so as to give authority and the other to effect the reduction—will be necessary, in addition to the consent of the court.[77]

The court cannot condone a reduction which has been carried out without its prior approval.[78] The resolution must be in the

[73] *Post*, Chap. 27.

[74] In Scotland the petition is presented to the Inner House of the Court of Session and, as a rule, a remit is made by the court to a "reporter" (a man of business, usually a soliciter of standing) who scrutinises the proposed reduction and draws the attention of the court to any doubtful points; the court may dispense with a remit to a "reporter," as in *Fowlers (Aberdeen) Ltd., Petitioners*, 1928 S.C. 186, and *Scottish Stamping etc. Co. Ltd., Petitioners*, 1928 S.C. 484, but only on sufficient cause being shown for departure from the ordinary practice: *J. Hay & Sons Ltd., Petitioners*, 1928 S.C. 622.

[75] *Re Dexine Rubber Co.* [1903] W.N. 82.

[76] *John Avery & Co. Ltd., Petitioners* (1890) 17 R. 1101.

[77] *Re Patent Invert Sugar Co.* (1885) 31 Ch.D. 166 (C.A.); *Oregon Mortgage Co. Ltd., Petitioners*, 1910 S.C. 964.

[78] *Alexander Henderson Ltd., Petitioners*, 1967 S.L.T. (Notes) 17.

correct form and comply with the requirements of section 378 as to the exact notice required.[79] In *Re Barry Artist Ltd.* [1985] B.C.L.C. 283, the court exceptionally allowed a written resolution signed by all the members authorising the reduction to suffice instead of a special resolution, but confirmed that it would not be prepared to do so in any similar case in the future. Reductions must also comply with the company's articles.[80]

Stock[81] may be reduced without being first converted into shares.[82] Reserve liability, *i.e.* capital which can only be called up on a winding up of the company, may also be reduced.[83]

Cases of reduction

The power to reduce capital given by section 135 is general, *i.e.* if the proper procedure is adopted a company can reduce its share capital in any case. However, the section specifies three particular cases of reduction—

(1) the extinction or reduction on shares in respect of capital not paid up;
(2) with or without the extinction or reduction of liability on shares, the cancellation of paid-up share capital which is lost or unrepresented by available assets;
(3) with or without the extinction or reduction of liability on shares, the payment off of any paid-up share capital which is in excess of the wants of the company.

For example, if a company has more than enough capital, it may reduce the nominal amount of shares by repaying paid-up capital, as where fully paid shares of a nominal amount of £5

[79] *Re Moorgate Mercantile Holdings Ltd.*, (1980) 1 All E.R. 40. However, if the error in the circular is so insignificant that no one would be prejudiced by its correction the court will allow the reduction to proceed: *Re Williams Systems plc* (1987) BCLC 67. See also *Re European Homes Products plc* (1988) 4 BCC 779.

[80] But see *Re M.B. Group plc* (1989) 5 BCC 684.

[81] *Ante*, pp. 187–188.

[82] *Re House Property and Investment Co.* [1912] W.N. 10; *cf. Doloi Tea Co. Ltd., Petitioners*, 1961 S.L.T. 168.

[83] *Re Midland Rlwy. Carriage Co.* (1907) 23 T.L.R. 661.

each are reduced to £2 fully paid shares and £3 is paid back on each share. This would reduce the company's nominal, issued and paid-up capital and, so far as the nominal capital and the nominal account of the shares are concerned, alter the memorandum. In one case 10 per cent. of the capital was returned on the footing that the amount returned could be called up again.[84]

A return of capital may be at a premium.

A reduction of capital involved repaying the capital paid-up on each of the company's preference shares of 10s. each plus a premium of 5s. per share. The court confirmed the reduction: *Re Saltdean Estate Co. Ltd.* [1968] 1 W.L.R. 1844.

A reduction may involve the company paying off part of its share capital not with money but by transferring to the shareholders shares of another company.[85] Alternatively it can be used to create a reserve out of the share premium account arising on an acquisition which will then be available to set off against that "surplus" on consolidated account.[86]

Moneys withdrawn from the capital and set free by the reduction can be employed in the purchase of the company's own shares which it is intended to extinguish.[86]

The reduction procedure cannot be used as a device to raise new capital to replace capital which has disappeared, *e.g.* by the conversion of £1 fully paid shares into £1 shares with only 75p. paid, thus imposing an additional liability on shareholders.[87] On the other hand it can be used as a method of varying the type of capital. In such cases the reduction resolution will be contingent on the corresponding increase of capital taking place. This practice was approved in *Re TIP-Europe Ltd.*[88] provided the increase has taken place prior to the court's approval being given.

[84] *Scottish Vulcanite Co. Ltd, Petitioners* (1894) 21 R. 752; *cf. William Brown Sons & Co. Ltd., Petitioners*, 1931 S.C. 701, and *Stevensons, Anderson & Co. Ltd., Petitioners*, 1951 S.C. 346.

[85] *Westburn Sugar Refineries Ltd., Petitioners*, 1951 S.C. (H.L.) 57; [1951] A.C. 625.

[86] *Per* Lord Macnaghten in *British and American Finance Corporation* v. *Couper* [1894] A.C. 399 at p. 414.

[87] See s.16 and also *W. Morrison & Co. Ltd., Petitioners* (1892) 19 R. 1049.

[88] (1987) 3 BCC 647. See also *Re M.B. Group plc* (1989) 5 BCC 684.

Questions for the court on reduction

Subject to the discretion conferred on the court by section 135 and the statutory provisions for the protection of creditors, *post*, the question whether there should be a reduction of capital and, if so, how it should be effected, is a domestic question for the prescribed majority of the shareholders to decide.[89] The court should sanction a reduction unless what is proposed to be done is unfair or inequitable in the interests of (1) the creditors, (2) the shareholders and (3) the public who may have dealings with the company or may invest in its securities.[90] When creditors are not concerned (because the reduction does not involve the diminution of any liability in respect of unpaid capital or the payment to any shareholder of any paid-up capital) the questions to be considered by the court are:

(1) ought the court to refuse its sanctions to the reduction out of regard to the interest of those members of the public who may be induced to take shares in the company?
(2) is the reduction fair and equitable as between the different classes of shareholders?[91]

In considering what is fair as between different classes of shareholders, the court proceeds upon the basis that a reduction is a sort of anticipation to a limited extent of what would take place in a winding up, *i.e.* the various classes of shareholders[92] have the rights which they would have in a liquidation. Accordingly, if capital is lost, the loss should, prima facie, fall upon all the shareholders equally if their rights in respect of capital are equal. If, therefore, preference shareholders are only preferential as to dividend and not as to capital, a reduction of capital should be borne rateably by the preference and the

[89] *British and American Finance Corpn.* v. *Couper* [1894] A.C. 399. See Lord President Inglis in *Hoggan* v. *Tharsis Sulpher etc. Co. Ltd.* (1882) 9 R. 1191 at p. 1212.
[90] *Westburn Sugar Refineries Ltd.*, *Petitioners*, 1951 S.C. (H.L.) 57; [1951] A.C. 625.
[91] *Poole* v. *National Bank Of China Ltd.* [1907] A.C. 229. See Lord Parker of Waddington in *Caldwell & Co. Ltd.* v. *Caldwell*, 1916 S.C. (H.L.) 120 at p. 121.
[92] See p. 259, *post*.

ordinary shareholders.[93] On the other hand, if on a winding up the preference shareholders are entitled to preference as to capital, the ordinary shares should normally bear the loss first.[94]

If, under the memorandum and articles, preference shareholders have no priority as to capital and no voting power but are merely entitled to a fixed cumulative preference dividend on the amount paid up on their shares, a rateable reduction on all the shares, preference and ordinary, cancelling lost paid-up capital, though diminishing the preference dividend, is not an alteration of the rights of the preference shareholders so as to require their sanction under an ordinary modification of rights clause: *Re Mackenzie & Co. Ltd.* [1916] 2 Ch. 450.

When liability on shares is being extinguished or reduced, the proper capital to reduce in the first instance, is the unpaid capital (if any).[95]

Reductions due to over capitalisation

When capital is being returned as surplus to the company's requirements, it should normally[96] be returned first to the class of shareholders with priority as to capital in a winding up,[97] at any rate where preference shares are not entitled to participate in surplus assets.[98]

A coal company with a capital of £400,000, half of which was in ordinary shares and half on 6 per cent. preference shares, had a surplus of capital as a result of nationalisation. A special resolution was passed reducing the capital by paying off the preference shares. By the articles, the preference shareholders in the event of a winding up has a right to priority of repayment of capital *but no further right to participate in the surplus assets*. *Held*, the reduction should be

[93] *Bannatyne* v. *Direct Spanish Telegraph Co.* (1886) 34 Ch.D. 287 (C.A.).

[94] *Re Floating Dock Co. of St. Thomas Ltd.* [1895] 1 Ch. 691. For exceptional circumstances where a different scheme of reduction was held just and equitable see *Balmenach-Glenlivet Distillery Ltd.* v. *Croall* (1906) 8 F. 1135.

[95] *Per* Lord President Inglis in *Hoggan* v. *Tharsis Sulpher etc. Co. Ltd.* (1882) 9 R. 1191 at p. 1211.

[96] But not always: see *William Dixon Ltd., Petitioners*, 1948 S.C. 511.

[97] *Wilsons and Clyde Coal Co. Ltd.* v. *Scottish Insurance Corporation Ltd.*, 1949 S.C. (H.L.) 90; 1948 S.C. 360; *Prudential Assurance Co. Ltd.* v. *Chatterley-Whitfield Collieries Ltd.* [1949] A.C. 512.

[98] *Per* Lord Greene M.R. in the *Prudential* case, *supra*, in the Court of Appeal [1948] 2 All E.R. 593 at pp. 596, 600.

confirmed as fair and equitable, the preference shareholders having no right to a continuance of their rate of dividend during the life of the company if the company desired and had the means to pay them off. The preference shareholders were being treated in accordance with their rights and it was immaterial that the elimination of their shares extinguished any hopes which they had of obtaining some additional advantage as a result of regulations to be made under the Coal Industry Nationalisation Act 1946, s.25: *Prudential Assurance Co. Ltd.* v. *Chatterley-Whitfield Collieries Ltd.* [1949] A.C. 512.

It is not necessary for the company to show by how much its capital is surplus to its requirements. "Public policy" is not a ground for the court's refusing to confirm a reduction which is otherwise unobjectionable, *e.g.* reduction may be confirmed although the motive for it may have been avoidance of the consequences of possible future nationalisation,[99] or minimisation of tax liability.[1]

A modification of rights clause in the articles has no application to a cancellation of shares on a reduction of capital which is in accord with the rights attached to the shares under the articles.[2]

If a modification of rights clause in the articles provides that the special rights of the holders of any class of shares can be modified with the sanction of a specified majority of the shareholders of that class, a reduction modifying such rights which is so sanctioned will be approved unless it is unfair or has been sanctioned by the influence of some improper or extraneous consideration.[3] The burden of proving that the reduction is unfair lies on those who oppose it.[4] (If the proper sanction is not obtained the burden of proving that the reduction is fair lies on those in favour).[5]

In one case, where there were special circumstances, a reduction involving a variation of class rights was confirmed

[99] See note 90, *ante*.

[1] *David Bell Ltd., Petitioners*, 1954 S.C. 33.

[2] *Re Saltdean Estate Co. Ltd.* [1968] 1 W.L.R. 1844; *House of Fraser* v. *A.C.G.E. Investments Ltd.* [1987] A.C. 387; 1987 S.L.T. 421 (H.L.); *cf. Re Old Silkstone Collieries Ltd.* [1954] Ch. 169 (C.A.).

[3] *Re Welshbach Incandescent Gas Light Co. Ltd.* [1904] Ch. 87 (C.A.). A scheme of arrangement is not necessary: *Oban and Aultmore-Glenlivet Distilleries Ltd., Petitioners* (1903) 5 F. 1140, and *Marshall, Fleming & Co. Ltd., Petitioners*, 1938 S.C. 873 (O.H.).

[4] *Carruth* v. *I.C.I. Ltd.* 1937) A.C. 707.

[5] *Re Holders Investment Trust Ltd.* [1971] 1 W.L.R. 583, *post*, p. 268.

although no class meeting of the class of shareholders (the preference shareholders) had been held—no one objected, there was no prospect of liquidation (when the preference shareholders had the right to participate in surplus assets after repayment of capital), and the preference shareholders received more, than they would have received by selling.[6]

When one part of a class of equity shareholders is treated differently from another, the usual practice is to proceed by scheme of arrangement under section 425, under which the interests of the minority are better protected.[7]

Reductions due to loss of capital

In England, where reduction is sought on the ground that capital has been lost or is not represented by available assets, evidence of the loss or that the available assets do not represent the capital must be given.[8] A reduction may be confirmed where capital has been lost but it is still represented by available assets.

A company had built up a reserve fund. It had incurred a loss arising from the depreciation in the value of its public-houses below the amount stated in the balance sheet, and it proposed to reduce its capital by apportioning the loss between its capital account and the reserve. *Held*, the loss ought to be rateably apportioned between the capital account and the reserve, and the company was not bound to apply the whole of its reserve to wipe out the loss: *Re Hoare & Co. Ltd.* [1904] 2 Ch. 208 (C.A.).

Capital is not lost unless it is permanently lost.[9] If the evidence is therefore that the loss might not be permanent the courts will not allow a reduction unless the company gives an undertaking to protect the creditors in the event of the loss being made good. In one case[10] the judge required an undertaking to place any sums recovered in respect of the loss

[6] *Re William Jones & Sons Ltd.* [1969] 1 W.L.R. 146.

[7] *Re Robert Stephen Holdings Ltd.* [1968] 1 W.L.R. 522.

[8] *Per* Lord Parker of Waddington in *Caldwell & Co. Ltd.* v. *Caldwell*, 1916 S.C. (H.L.) 120 at p. 121. Scottish courts dispense with such evidence where there is no reason to suspect the bona fides of the parties: *Caldwell's* case.

[9] *Re Haematite Steel Co.* [1901] 2 Ch. 746 at 749 *per* Romer L.J.; *Re Welsbach Incandescent Gas Light Co. Ltd.* [1904] 1 Ch. 87.

[10] *Re Jupiter House Investments* (*Cambridge*) *Ltd.* [1985] 1 W.L.R. 975.

(by way of compensation) to be put into capital reserve so that it could not be distributed as dividend. But in a subsequent case[11] Nourse J. refused to accept that such an undertaking must always require a reserve to be set aside indefinitely to safeguard the interests of future creditors and shareholders. The undertaking in most cases need only safeguard the interests of creditors at the time of the reduction.

Creditors' rights to object to reduction

If a proposed reduction of share capital involves either (1) diminution of liability in respect of unpaid share capital, or (2) payment to any shareholder of any paid-up capital,[12] and (3) in any other case where the court so directs, creditors who, if the company were being wound up, would be able to prove against it, are entitled to object to the reduction. For this purpose the court must settle a list of creditors, with the nature and amount of their claims, and may publish notices fixing a day by which creditors not entered on the list are to claim to be entered. Such of the creditors as do not consent to the reduction must be paid off or the company must secure payment of their claims by appropriating such amount as the court directs: section 136. In special circumstances the court may dispense with these requirements: section 136(6). The court might dispense with the requirements where the company has sufficient cash, trustee securities and good sundry debtors[13] to more than cover any capital to be returned to shareholders and the company's debts, or if the discharge of the debts is guaranteed to the court's satisfaction, or if a simultaneous increase in capital results in the paid-up capital being the same as it was before the reduction.[14]

Before dispensing with a list of creditors under section 136(6) the court must be satisfied that no creditor who might be entitled to object to the reduction would be prejudiced by it.

[11] *Re Grosvenor Press plc* [1985] 1 W.L.R. 980.

[12] Replacement of preference shares with loan stock, which became a common practice for the purposes of reducing liability to corporation tax, counts as such payment, although the loan stock does not fall to be repaid by the company until a future date: *Lawrie & Symington Ltd., Petitioners*, 1969 S.L.T. 221.

[13] *Anderson, Brown & Co. Ltd., Petitioners*, 1965 S.C. 81.

[14] *New Duff House Sanitarium, Petitioners*, 1931 S.L.T. 337 (O.H.); *cf. Cadzow Coal Co. Ltd., Petitioners*, 1931 S.C. 272.

A company had sufficient cash resources to cover paid-up capital being paid to preference shareholders and its liabilities but not rents prospectively payable in respect of long leases during the residues of the terms or ten years, whichever was less, and so a direction extending to the lessors could not be given under section 67(3): *Re Lucania Temperance Billiard Halls* (*London*) *Ltd.* [1966] Ch. 98.[15]

In cases not within (1) and (2) above, the creditors have, prima facie, no right to object to the proposed reduction of capital, because no asset out of which their claims could be satisfied is being given up or returned to the shareholders.

A company has a paid-up share capital of £1,000,000, and had also issued £1,000,000 debentures secured by a trust deed constituting a floating charge. In 1904 losses to the extent of £800,000 were incurred and no dividends has since been paid, any profits being applied in reduction of the deficiency. By 1917 the deficiency had been reduced to £640,000, and the company proposed to reduce its capital to £360,000 by writing off the lost capital. The latest balance sheet showed assets worth £1,500,000. The debenture holders objected. *Held*, as the reduction involved no diminution of unpaid capital or repayment to shareholders of paid-up capital, creditors were not entitled to object unless a strong case was made out, and the debenture holders had not made out any such case: *Re Meux's Brewery Co. Ltd.* [1919] Ch. 28.

The object of reducing capital, where capital has been lost or is not represented by available assets, is to enable the accounts to present a realistic picture of the company's financial position, which may permit the company to pay dividends. To safeguard the creditor's in the case of an application by a company to write off capital not lost or unrepresented by available assets, thereby setting free capital which might be distributed among the shareholders, the court is empowered by section 136 to give effect to a creditor's objection "in any other case."

Order for reduction; Minute of reduction

Confirmation by the court must precede the actual reduction of capital.[16]

[15] *Cf. Palace Billiard Rooms Ltd.* v. *City etc. Trust Corpn.*, 1912 S.C. 5.
[16] *Alexander Henderson Ltd.*, *Petitioners*, 1967 S.L.T. (Notes) 17.

On making an order confirming the reduction, the court may direct:

(1) for special reasons, that the company add the words "and reduced" to its name for a specified time.
(2) that the reasons for reduction and the causes leading to the reduction be published, with a view to giving proper information to the public (section 137).

These powers are rarely used today and the Jenkins Report recommended their repeal.[17]

Section 138 provides that the order for reduction must be produced in the Registrar, and a copy of the order and a minute approved by the court showing the amount of the share capital, the number of shares into which it is divided, the amount of each share and the amount, if any, deemed to be paid up on each share, must be registered with him. The Registrar then grants a certificate of registration, which is conclusive evidence of the reduction and that all the requirements of the Act with respect to reduction have been compiled with—even if it is afterwards discovered that the special resolution for a reduction was not properly passed,[18] or that there was no power in the articles to reduce capital.[19] The reduction takes effect as from the date of registration. By section 380,[20] a copy of the special resolution must be forwarded to the Registrar within 15 days.

Reduction without the consent of the court

There are a number of cases in which, despite section 135, capital can be reduced without the consent of the court. Three such cases are:

(1) where, under power in the articles, shares are forfeited by the company for non-payment of a call or an instalment[21]— and in this rare case, as was stated earlier,[22] the forfeited shares may be re-issued, in which event there is no permanent reduction.

[17] Paras. 159, 187.
[18] *Ladies' Dress Association* v. *Pullbrook* [1900] 2 Q.B. 276 (C.A.).
[19] *Re Walker and Smith Ltd.* [1903] W.N. 82.
[20] *Post*, p. 341.
[21] *Post*, p. 307.
[22] p. 191.

(2) where, under power in the articles, shares are surrendered to the company to avoid a forfeiture—in this rare case, too, the shares may be re-issued.[23]

(3) where a private company redeems or purchases its own shares out of capital under section 170. In this case there are stringent requirements for the protection of creditors.[24]

There are, however, cases in which at first sight there appears to be a reduction without consent but there is no reduction for the purposes of the Act, *e.g.*—

(1) where shares are redeemed or purchased otherwise than out of capital under sections 159 and 162[25]—there is no real reduction, whether the shares are redeemed out of profits (because of the provisions with regard to the capital redemption reserve) or out of the proceeds of a fresh issue of shares (because the fresh capital will replace the redeemed capital);

(2) where unissued shares are cancelled under section 121[26]—there is no real reduction because the issued capital is not reduced.

An example of an improper reduction of capital is the New Zealand case of *Jenkins* v. *Harbour View Courts Ltd.*[27] where the articles provided that each A class share should confer on the holder a right to occupy a flat in a block owned by the company on the terms of a lease in the schedule. The aggregate annual rentals were not to exceed the sum necessary to provide for rates, insurance and other outgoings as well as management and maintenance of the block. The plaintiff took 3,580 ordinary shares of £1 each and one A class share for which he paid £3,580. Since substantially the block was to be made the subject of leases for 99 years to shareholders for no rent in the form of landlord's reward to the company, this was held to be just as much an illegal return of capital to shareholders as if, from a fund of money, a substantial part was distributed among them. It made no difference that the plaintiff by a different transaction might for the same expenditure have purchased a valid lease of her flat if the agreement between the

[23] *Post*, p. 310.
[24] *Post*, p. 214.
[25] *Post*, p. 212.
[26] *Ante*, p. 188.
[27] [1966] N.Z.L.R. 1 (C.A.).

company and the shareholders had been for the "purchase" and allotment of one share followed by a purchase for £3,580 of the lease.

As to the liability of the officers responsible and of the shareholders concerned in the event of an illegal reduction of capital, see what is said later[28] as to the effect of paying dividends out of non-distributable profits.

Reduction below authorised minimum capital

Where the court confirms a reduction of capital of a public company which has the effect of bringing the nominal value of the company's allotted share capital below the authorised minimum capital[29] this will only be registered (and so will only be effective) if the company is first re-registered as private company: section 139.

To ease this process the court may authorise the company to re-register as a private company under section 53[30] without passing a special resolution and will also specify the necessary alterations to the company's memorandum and the articles. In practice many public companies prohibit any reduction of capital below the authorised minimum in their articles.[31]

Serious Loss of Capital

Following the EC Second Directive,[32] under section 142 the directors of a *public* company are obliged to call an extraordinary meeting of the company within 28 days from the earliest date on which any director knew that the company had suffered a serious loss of capital.

A serious loss of capital occurs where the net assets of the company are half or less of the amount of the company's called up share capital. In other words if it has lost half or more of its called up share capital.

The meeting must be fixed for a date not later than 56 days from when the obligation arose. It is to consider whether any,

[28] Chap. 22.
[29] £50,000: s.118.
[30] *Ante*, p. 50.
[31] But see *Re M.B. Group plc* (1989) 5 BCC 684.
[32] Art. 17.

and if so what, measures should be taken to deal with the situation. Directors who knowingly and wilfully authorise or permit a failure to convene such a meeting are liable on conviction to a fine.

There is some ambiguity as to what may actually be discussed. Section 142(3) provides that the meeting may not be used to discuss anything "which could not have been considered at that meeting apart from this section." Does this include a resolution to dismiss or censure the directors? Such a resolution may fall within the ambit of the section.

Chapter 10

THE ACQUISITION AND REDEMPTION BY A COMPANY OF ITS OWN SHARES

TRADITIONALLY companies have not been able to acquire their own shares. To do so was said to be a reduction of capital and the creation of a possible false market in those shares.[1] Companies were, however, able to issue redeemable preference shares under section 58 of the 1948 Act; *i.e.* preference shares which were expressly redeemable at a future date. The 1981 Act replaced that narrow power with a general power to issue redeemable shares of any type and gave companies the additional power for the first time to purchase their own shares.

This chapter is mainly concerned with these powers of purchase and redemption; covering a company's ability to do so, the mechanisms involved, the funds available and the capital consequences of so doing. The powers were part of a "package" designed to assist small companies in finding outside investors who might wish to be able to withdraw such investment at will. To this end it will be seen that private companies may in some cases fund the acquisition or redemption out of capital. The effect is that subject to certain procedures and authority all shares are now potentially redeemable either by the terms of their issue or by subsequent agreement.

ACQUISITIONS—THE GENERAL RULE

Section 143 prohibits a company from acquiring its own shares. However, this does not apply in the following cases:

[1] See *Trevor* v. *Whitworth* (1887) 12 App.Cas. 409; *General Property etc. Co. Ltd.* v. *Matheson's Trustees* (1888) 16 R. 282.

(i) gifts of shares to the company[2];
(ii) acquisitions on a reduction of capital under section 135[3];
(iii) the redemption or purchase of its shares under the Act[4];
(iv) purchases authorised by the court under sections 54,[5] 461[6] or 5[7];
(v) the forfeiture of shares or acceptance of any shares surrendered in lieu for failure to pay for them.[8]

Shares acquired under (ii) and (iv) must be cancelled at once on acquisition. Shares acquired under (iii) are dealt with below. In the case of (i) and (v) section 146 provides that the shares must be disposed of or cancelled within three years and that in the meantime the company may not vote with them.

Acquisitions by nominees

Section 144 provides that if a person subscribes for shares in a company or buys them for a third party partly-paid up, apparently in his own name, but in reality as a nominee for the company, he is to be regarded as the full owner of the shares to the exclusion of the company. He thus becomes personally liable for the amount owed on the shares. If he fails to pay within 21 days of being asked to do so the other subscribers, or the directors, whichever is appropriate, will be liable to pay, subject to a defence that they acted honestly and reasonably and ought fairly to be excused.

Section 145, however, provides that the company retains the ownership of such shares in two cases:

(i) if a public company provides financial assistance for the purchase of such shares. This topic is dealt with in the following chapter. Here we are only concerned

[2] Following *Re Castiglione's W.T.* [1958] Ch. 549; *cf. Gill* v. *Arizona Copper Co. Ltd.* (1900) 2 F. 843.
[3] *Ante*, p. 192.
[4] *Post*, p. 209.
[5] *Ante*, p. 50.
[6] *Post*, p. 464.
[7] *Ante*, p. 72.
[8] *Post*, p. 307.

with assistance given to a nominee. Such shares must be cancelled or disposed of within one year under section 146;

(ii) where the company is a trustee only of the shares and has no beneficial interest in them. Thus a company acting as a trustee may accept shares issued by itself in the name of a nominee on behalf of a trust fund. Beneficial interests for this purpose do not include certain residentual interests commonly found in trust deeds, corporate pension funds or employee share schemes, as defined in Schedule 2.

Of course the company retains the beneficial ownership of shares to which section 144 does not apply—*e.g.* fully paid up shares acquired from a third party.

Consequences of an acquisition

Apart from purchases and redemptions under the Act, shares acquired by a company or its nominee must be treated as follows:

(i) shares acquired by the company as gifts, or by forfeiture or surrender for non-payment of calls, shares acquired by a nominee without financial assistance from the company and in which the company has a beneficial interest (*e.g.* gifts of fully paid up shares to a company's nominee)—disposal or cancellation of the shares within three years: section 146;

(ii) shares acquired by a nominee of a public company with financial assistance from the company—disposal or cancellation of the shares within one year: section 146. Cancellation may be achieved by a resolution of the directors reducing the capital by the nominal amount of the shares acquired without complying with section 135: section 147. If necessary a public company must apply to be re-registered as a private company.[9]

[9] *i.e.* because it ceases to comply with the authorised minimum capital under s.118.

Redemption and Purchase of Shares

Redeemable shares

Section 159 allows companies to issue redeemable shares of any class, *i.e.* shares which are specifically redeemable under the terms of their issue.

To issue redeemable shares a company must have power to do so by its articles. No company may issue only redeemable shares[10] but one non-redeemable share will technically be enough. Shares issued under section 159 may be issued either as redeemable at a fixed date or event, or as redeemable at the option of the company or the shareholder; but any shares redeemed must be fully paid up at the date of redemption—there must be no incidental reduction of capital, and the terms of redemption must provide for payment on redemption.

Apart from those basic requirements, the terms and conditions of redemption are to be as specified in the company's articles. However, section 159A restricts both the date and amount of the redemption of the shares. First, the date or dates of redemption must either be fixed by the articles or delegated by the articles to the directors (and in that case fixed before issue). The articles must also set out any other redemption triggers. Secondly, the amount payable on redemption must be as set out in the article either specifically or by a formula which does not allow for any element of personal discretion or opinion.

When redeemable shares are redeemed they must be cancelled at once and the issued share capital figure reduced accordingly. A company must not be a member of itself: section 160(4). There is no option, as in section 146 noted above, for their re-issue within a limited time.

Replacement issues of shares can be made prior to the redemption without any increase in the authorised capital figure being necessary, so that if the new issue would take the nominal capital temporarily above the authorised figure, section 121 will not apply: section 160(5).[11]

[10] Nor can a company purchase its own shares if that would leave only redeemable shares in existence: s.162. See below.

[11] *Ante*, p. 186.

The funds available for redemption of shares are discussed below.

Purchase by a company of its own shares

Section 162 allows companies to purchase their own shares by following one of three procedures contained in sections 164 to 166 of the Act. This totally new power to purchase must be included in the articles—it can include the purchase of redeemable shares, *e.g.* if the date for redemption has not been reached. There is nothing in the Act which either allows or prohibits the *compulsory* purchase by a company of its own shares. It is doubtful whether a majority of the shareholders can be given this power because of the doctrine of a fraud on the minority[12] but the point remains open *vis-á-vis* the company itself.

Subject to the rule that a company cannot buy itself out completely or leave only redeemable shares, the power in the articles can be framed as desired.

The funds available to a company for the purchase of its own shares are dealt with below.[13] The power to purchase its own shares can only be implemented however by one of the following three procedures:

Off-market purchases. A purchase of unquoted shares,[14] *i.e.* in general, those of private companies, is governed by section 164. Such a purchase requires a special resolution of the company authorising it to make the contract to purchase (*N.B.* not the purchase itself). In the unlikely event of a public company buying its own unquoted shares such approval must then be limited to a contract made within a period of no more than 18 months from the granting of approval.

Such authority to contract may be varied, renewed or revoked by a special resolution.

[12] *Brown* v. *British Abrasive Wheel Co.* [1919] 2 Ch. 290; *Dafen Tinplate Co. Ltd.* v. *Llanelly Steel Co.* [1920] 2 Ch. 124; *cf. Sidebottom* v. *Kershaw, Leese and Co.* [1920] 1 Ch. 154.

[13] *Post*, p. 212.

[14] *i.e.* shares which are not traded on a recognised investment exchange within the meaning of the F.S.A. 1986: s.163.

The proposed contract, or a memorandum of its terms must be available for inspection for at least 15 days ending with the date of the meeting at the company's registered office and at the meeting itself.[15] The name of the proposed vendor(s) must be made clear. That is because such vendors may not vote with the shares concerned on the resolution if such a vote would affect the result. In such circumstances failure to abstain with those votes will invalidate the resolution.[16] The vendor(s) can however vote with any other shares owned and can demand a poll[17] to exercise them.

Any variation of the contract itself, as distinct from the authority to enter into it, must be authorised in the same way as the original contract except that both contracts must be available for inspection.

It has been decided in Scotland that a contract to purchase shares which has not complied with the statutory requirements for approval cannot be enforced.[18]

Contingent purchase contracts. Companies may purchase options to acquire their own shares under the terms of section 165. The procedure involved is that for an off-market purchase, *i.e.* a special resolution authorising each such option. Such a procedure means that listed companies cannot purchase traded options to acquire their own listed shares so as to speculate against the value of such shares.

Market purchases. Public companies may, however, purchase their quoted shares under the procedure laid down by section 166. In essence the company needs the prior approval of an ordinary resolution[19] for the purchase of a number of shares within a specified price band and within a specified time, not greater than 18 months. The maximum and minimum figures in the price band may be settled by reference to a formula.

[15] The documents must be sent to each member prior to his signature if the written resolution procedure is being used: Sched. 15A para. 5, see *post*, p. 343.

[16] In the case of a written resolution the vendor's signature is irrelevant provided all the other shareholders sign the resolution: Sched. 15A para. 5. See p. 346, *post*.

[17] *Post*, p. 332.

[18] *Western* v. *Rigblast Holdings Ltd.*, 1989 G.W.D. 23–950 (Sh.Ct.).

[19] This resolution must, however, be registered as if it was a special resolution.

The need for a general rather than a specific authority to purchase is dictated by the Stock Exchange rules on trading. It is difficult to see, however, why only an ordinary resolution should be required.

The Stock Exchange has its own rules covering such purchases.

Disclosure of purchases

Under section 169 details of all purchases must be registered within 28 days. A purchase may be effected by a surrender of shares so that no transfer document will be necessary.

All contracts of purchase or options to purchase must also be kept at the company's registered office for 10 years from the date of completion of the purchase or expiry of the options, as appropriate. These must be open to inspection. Option contracts need only be registered if activated.

Assignment and release of a company's rights to purchase

Under section 167 any assignment by a company of its rights under a contract to purchase its own shares is totally prohibited. Companies are not allowed to speculate against their own share price by buying and selling rights to purchase.

Companies with rights under an off-market purchase or option, however, may release such rights if such a release is approved by a special resolution. The vendor shareholders are, however, prohibited from voting with those shares if it would affect the result.

Funds available for redemption or purchase

The rules relating to the funding of a redemption or purchase or a company's own shares are the same. They are set out in sections 160(1) and (2).

The nominal value of the redeemed or purchased shares may be paid for either out of the company's distributable profits[20] or

[20] *Post*, Chap. 22.

the proceeds of a specific fresh issue of shares made for the purpose. In the event there will be no reduction of capital—in the latter case a fresh amount of capital will replace that used.

The premium of any such shares may, however, only be paid for out of distributable profits unless the shares themselves were originally issued at a premium. In that case the proceeds of a fresh issue may be used up to the amount of the company's share premium account at the time. In effect the share premium account may be used to fund the purchase or redemption and then be replaced by a fresh issue of shares.

Under section 168 any payment to acquire an option to purchase shares, or to obtain any variation or release from a contract to purchase, as distinct from the purchase itself, must be found from distributable profits.

In so far as the company uses distributable profits for such payments the funds available for dividends[21] are thereby reduced: section 274. Further, in such a case an amount equal to the amount of profits used must be transferred on the company's balance sheet to a fund known as the *capital redemption reserve*: section 170. This is a capital fund to which the rules relating to reduction of capital apply. The object of this section is to prevent the balance sheet showing a paper profit which might be distributed by way of dividend. The profit would otherwise arise through the current assets being reduced by the amount necessary to redeem or purchase the shares, an the share capital and the revenue reserves being reduced.

Failure by a company to redeem or purchase its own shares

If a company has issued redeemable shares under section 159 and fails to redeem them, or agrees to purchase its own shares and fails to honour that agreement, the shareholder has a right of action for breach of contract under section 178.

However, the shareholder is prevented by that section from suing for damages for breach of contract and specific performance will only be granted if the company is able to fulfil its obligations out of distributable profits.

If the company goes into liquidation after the obligation to redeem or purchase has arisen the shares are regarded as being

[21] *Post*, Chap. 22.

cancelled on the liquidation but the vendor/shareholder may prove (apply for) any loss suffered as a creditor in the liquidation unless the company could not have fulfilled its obligations out of distributable profits at any time between the date of redemption or purchase and the date of liquidation. Such a vendor/shareholder is a deferred creditor[22] and, as such, will be paid after all the other creditors but before the shareholders.

Redemption or Purchase of Shares out of Capital

Sections 171 to 177 allow private companies to purchase or redeem their own shares out of capital. These sections do not increase the powers of redemption or purchase themselves—sections 159 to 166 must first be complied with[23]—but they extend the funds available beyond distributable profits and proceeds of a fresh issue of shares. In essence, if those funds prove to be insufficient, *private* companies may resort to "capital."

"Capital" in this context is any fund other than distributable profits and the proceeds of a fresh issue, whether or not it is technically capital for the rules relating to reduction of capital etc.[24] Thus undistributable profits[25] may be used. Section 171 however, makes it clear that private companies must first utilise distributable profits before resorting to "capital."

To use the power a private company must have authority to do so in its articles. Secondly there must be a shortfall in the funds available to all companies (distributable profits and issue proceeds). In reality this means distributable profits as there is no obligation to make a special issue of shares to provide any proceeds: section 171.

To ascertain whether there is a genuine shortfall the company must calculate its available distributable profits under section 263[26] by reference to accounts drawn up at any date within the three months immediately preceding the date on which the

[22] *Post*, Chap. 29.
[23] *Ante*, p. 209.
[24] *Ante*, p. 192.
[25] *e.g.* the revaluation reserve.
[26] *Post*, Chap. 22.

directors make the required declaration of solvency, which initiates the procedure.[27] The accounts must enable a reasonable judgment to be made: section 172. The shortfall between available profits and the amount needed for purchase or redemption is known as the *permissible capital payment* (P.C.P.).

If the P.C.P. and the proceeds of any issue used for the redemption or purchase are together less than the nominal value of the shares redeemed or purchased the remainder must have come from distributable profits. In that case section 171(4) provides that an equivalent amount to those profits must be transferred to the *capital redemption reserve* as in the general funding power and for the same reasons.[28]

However if the P.C.P. and the proceeds of any issue used for the redemption or purchase amount to more than the nominal value of the shares redeemed or purchased, part of those capital funds must have been used to cover the redemption or purchase of the premium of those shares. In such a case section 171(5) provides that the excess must be deducted either from the capital redemption reserve, the share premium account, share capital figure or unrealised profits of the company. If such profits are subsequently realised they cannot then be used for dividends.

Exercise of the power

Section 173 makes it unlawful for a company to use its *permissible capital payment* (P.C.P.) unless the procedure laid down in that section is followed. This procedure is in addition to that required for the approval of the purchase; it is to approve the redemption or purchase *out of capital.*

Just as a specific off-market purchase requires the prior authority of a special resolution so does the use of capital. However in this case it must be preceeded not by details of the contract but by a statutory declaration of solvency by the directors. This declaration must relate both to the company's immediate ability to pay its debts after using its P.C.P. and its ability to do so for the following year, taking into account the

[27] *Ante*, p. 214.
[28] *Ante*, p. 213.

company's resources and the directors' management intentions.[29] It must be accompanied by an auditor's report that the P.C.P. has been properly ascertained and that the declaration of solvency itself is not unreasonable: section 173.

That declaration must be followed on the same day or within one week by the necessary special resolution.[30] After it has been passed no payment can be made for five weeks. (This is to enable any objection to the payment to be made to the court—see below). The resolution must then be implemented within two further weeks: section 174.

The proposed vendor will invalidate the resolution if he votes with the shares in question in such a way as to affect the result.[31]

The requirement of a special resolution will put the shareholders on notice as to what is intended. But since this involves "capital," the company's creditors need to know. It will affect their guarantee fund. Accordingly section 175 requires the company to place a notice both in the London or Edinburgh Gazette as appropriate[32] and in a national newspaper.[33] The latter can, theoretically, be avoided by giving a notice to each creditor of the company.

The notice must state that the resolution has been passed and what its effect is. It must also specify the P.C.P. and the date of the resolution and state first that the statutory declaration of solvency and auditors' report are available for inspection at the company's registered office and second that a creditor may apply to the court, within five weeks of the date of the resolution, to have the resolution set aside.

The declaration of solvency and the auditors' report must be available both for shareholders at the meeting, and subsequently, for either shareholders and creditors at the registered office during the five week holding period: section 174. Further

[29] A similar procedure applies to the rules allowing financial assistance to be given by private companies for the purchase by others of these shares. See Chap. 13, *post*.

[30] The written resolution procedure may be used (*post*, p. 343). In such a case the documents must be supplied to each member prior to his signature of the resolution: Sched. 15A, para. 6.

[31] If the resolution is a written resolution the signature, or otherwise, of the vendor is irrelevant: Sched. 15A, para. 6.

[32] Depending on the location of the company's registered office.

[33] In England and Wales, or Scotland as appropriate.

they must be registered with the registrar by the first notice date—*i.e.* the date of publication in the Gazettte or the newspaper, whichever is earlier.

Objections by members and creditors

Under section 176 a single member who did not vote for the special resolution authorising the use of capital, or any creditor[34] may petition the court to have the resolution set aside within five weeks of the date of the resolution. For a creditor the effective time limit may be four weeks since the advertisements putting him on notice can be put in up to a week after the resolution.

On such a petition the court has all the powers available to it as on a petition to prevent a public company re-registering as a private company under section 54.[35] Thus it may order a compulsory purchase of the shareholder's shares by the company, alter the company's constitution, cancel, amend or confirm the resolution or impose new time scales for its implementation: section 177.

If either there are no objections, or the court overrides them, the P.C.P. may be used by the company for the purchase or redemption as appropriate.

Liability of shareholders and directors

Where a private company which has made a payment out of capital under section 173 for the purchase or redemption of its own shares is wound up as being unable to pay its debts, within one year of the payments being made, section 76 of the Insolvency Act 1986 applies.

In such a case the recipient of the payment, known as the relevant payment, and any director who signed the statutory declaration of solvency without having reasonable grounds for doing so, are liable to repay the amount of the relevant payment up to the amount needed to cover the company's insolvency.

[34] There appears to be no minimum debt required.
[35] *Ante*, p. 50.

This liability is linked to the amount of the relevant payments needed to cover the company's outstanding debts. Liability is joint and several so that any of the recipients or directors may be sued for the whole amount leaving him to recover a contribution from the others.

By way of protection anyone who might be liable to make payment under this section may petition to wind up the company on the grounds of its insolvency or on the just and equitable ground under section 122(1)(*f*) or (*g*) of the Insolvency Act 1986.[36]

[36] *Post*, Chap. 27.

Chapter 11

FINANCIAL ASSISTANCE BY A COMPANY FOR THE PURCHASE OF ITS OWN SHARES

UNDER section 54 of the 1948 Act it was unlawful for a company to give any person financial assistance for the purchase of, or subscription for, its own shares or those of its holding company. The intention was to prevent avoidance of the rule prohibiting a company from being a member of itself and the creation of a false market in that company's shares—*i.e.* by artificially stimulating demand for the shares at a time when the share price may be particularly important, *e.g.* in a takeover situation.

Section 54 of the 1948 Act was repealed by the 1981 Act and replaced by what are now sections 151 to 158 of the 1985 Act. Section 151 re-enacts the basic prohibition in a much modified form and applies to all companies. Section 153 contains many exceptions to that prohibition. Private companies are, however, allowed to give such assistance generally, subject to safeguards for creditors and minority shareholders, under sections 154 to 158.

The basic prohibitions

Section 151 applies two basic prohibitions on the giving of financial assistance—one when the assistance precedes the acquisition and the other when it follows it. In both cases a breach is a criminal offence, both for the company and any officer in default, which can lead to a term of imprisonment, or a fine, or both.[1] There are differences from the original 1948

[1] Originally under section 54 of the 1948 Act the only sanction was a £100 fine. For the civil consequences see below.

prohibition brought about by the apparently very wide scope of the earlier section.

(1) *Financial assistance given before or at the time of the acquisition.* It is unlawful[2] for a company to give financial assistance[3] directly or indirectly for the purpose of an acquisition or proposed acquisition by any person of its own shares or those of its holding company, either before or at the same time as the acquisition took place: section 151(1).

Thus assistance may be direct or indirect. It applies to all acquisitions of shares so that it includes all transfers of shares. The most important phrase is that the assistance must be given *for the purpose* of an acquisition, etc. This is an attempt to narrow the scope of the section and is important to remember when the exceptions are considered below.

(2) *Financial assistance given after the acquisition.* It is also unlawful for a company to give financial assistance[4] directly or indirectly for the purposes of reducing or discharging any liability incurred by any person for the purpose of an acquisition of that company's own shares or those of its holding company, provided that the acquisition took place prior to the assistance being given: section 151(2).

Again the important phrases concern the word *purpose.* This liability must be incurred by the acquiror or another for the purpose of the acquisition, and the financial assistance given by the company to the person who has incurred that liability must be for the purpose of reducing or discharging that liability.

For this prohibition a person incurs a liability if he changes his financial position by making any agreement of any type: section 152(3)(*a*). That liability is reduced or discharged by the company if the financial assistance is given wholly or party *for the purpose of* restoring that person's financial position to what it was before the acquisition took place: section 152(3)(*b*).

Financial assistance for the purposes of both these prohibitions is very wide. It is defined in section 152(1) and clearly includes direct financing by the company and the more common indirect financing whereby a take-over bidder purchases the

[2] Subject to the exceptions set out below.
[3] *Infra.*
[4] *Infra.*

shares of a cash-filled company by means of a loan and then uses the assets of the company to repay the loan.[5] Guarantees, provision of security to cover a loan,[6] gifts, any form of credit are also included—in fact anything which reduces the net assets of a company to a material extent.

In *Carney* v. *Herbert* [1985] A.C. 301 (P.C.), the Privy Council decided that the fact that shares in a company were purchased by means of a cheque drawn on that company's account did not constitute evidence of financial assistance for the purposes of the equivalent New South Wales provisions. There were a number of ways that such a transaction could have been effected without breaching the section. It was also held that the release of the two vendor/directors from liability on their loan account with the company and a proportionate reduction in the purchase price of the shares did not amount to financial assistance, since the reduction was more than offset by a credit balance in the purchaser/director's loan account. Since that could be reduced to the extent of the release it would leave the company in an identical position to that prior to the transactions. The definition of financial assistance in section 152(1) now includes assistance given by waiver or release—the court in this case seems to have been prepared to adopt the best construction so as to validate the transaction.

The purpose exceptions

One of the reasons for the revision of the rule on financial assistance in 1981 was the judgment of the Court of Appeal in *Belmont Finance Corporation* v. *Williams Furniture Ltd.* (*No.* 2).[7] The case was concerned with the situation whereby a company enters into a commercial transaction, *e.g.* buying goods from X, and, at the same time, X uses the proceeds of sale to buy shares in the company. Buckley L.J. said[8] that in such a case if the company genuinely needed those goods there might be no breach of section 54 of the 1948 Act. On the other hand if the company made the purchases solely to provide X

[5] See, *e.g. Selangor United Rubber Estates Ltd.* v. *Cradock* (*No.* 3) [1968] 1 W.L.R. 1555; *Wallersteiner* v. *Moir* [1974] 1 W.L.R. 991.

[6] *Carney* v. *Herbert* [1985] A.C. 301 (P.C.).

[7] [1980] 1 All E.R. 393,

[8] [1980] 1 All E.R. 393, 402.

with the means to buy its shares then there was a breach, even if the company paid a fair price for the goods. More difficult is the middle case, *i.e.* when the company enters into the transaction genuinely in its own commercial interests but it is done partly to put X in funds to buy shares in that company. The Court of Appeal left that point open.[9]

It was also decided that financial assistance could be given in breach of section 54 of the 1948 Act if it was made not to the purchaser but to the vendor of the shares *e.g.* when the company made a payment to the owner of some of its shares which persuaded him to sell them to a purchaser, even when the purchaser then paid the full price for them.[10]

As a result of these and other cases two new exceptions were introduced by the 1981 Act. They can be found in section 153(1) in relation to financial assistance given before or at the same time as the acquisition and section 153(2) for post-acquisition assistance. However both contain the same two exceptions based on the purpose for which the assistance was given.

(1) *Where the principal purpose of giving the financial assistance was not for the purpose of the acquisition*[11] *and was given in good faith in the interests of the company.* The exception was designed to protect groups of companies with relevance to the post-acquisition assistance prohibition. For example where, following the acquisition of a new subsidiary company, the acquiring company has to charge the assets of that subsidiary to comply with a prior debenture which requires all the assets of the group to be charged on security. In such a case the security would not be given for the principal purpose of reducing a liability incurred for the purpose of acquiring the subsidiary.

(2) *Where even if the principal purpose of giving the financial assistance*[11] *was for the acquisition of shares it was an incidental part of some larger purpose and was given in good faith in the interests of the company.* This exception was also defined with with reference to post-acquisition financial assistance within a group of companies. For example, when a subsidiary company

[9] See now the test as stated in *Charterhouse Investment Trust Ltd.* v. *Tempest Diesels Ltd.*, [1986] BCLC 1.

[10] *Armour Hick Northern Ltd.* v. *Whitehouse* [1980] 3 All E.R. 833.

[11] Or reducing a liability as appropriate.

provides funds to its parent company some years after it has been acquired to effect a more efficient deployment of assets within the group, the proviso may relieve the parent company of indebtedness incurred for the purpose of acquiring the subsidiary but if the larger purpose can be established it will be exempt.

These two purpose exceptions contain an inherent difficulty. They could be interpreted very widely so that if there is any overall scheme, *e.g.* a take-over bid, which involves financial assistance being given for the purpose of the acquisition of shares, the overall scheme will serve as the principal or larger purpose for the exceptions to apply, even though the narrow purpose of giving the assistance was the acquisition (the latter is necessary for the prohibition to apply in the first place). On the other hand if the purpose of giving the assistance is the acquisition of shares (as above, the starting point) how can the giving of that assistance (as distinct from the acquisition of the shares) ever be part of a larger or principal purpose? In either event what is meant by good faith in this context?

Two recent decisions have provided some answers to these difficulties.

In *Brady* v. *Brady*,[12] a group of private companies, which ran two businesses, was controlled by two brothers who quarrelled with a resulting deadlock. The proposed solution was a division of the businesses between them, but one was more valuable than the other. To equalize the division, a complex series of transactions followed, one of which involved the transfer of a large proportion of one company's assets to pay off loan stock which had been issued as the purchase price of that company's shares. This was clearly a breach of section 151. The question arose as to whether the transaction could be saved under either of the purpose exceptions. The Court of Appeal was prepared to allow that the division of the group was a larger purpose of which the giving of the financial assistance was but an incidental part, but refused to apply the exception on the grounds that it was not given in good faith in the interests of the company, apparently on the basis that in the context of financial assistance the company includes the creditors as well as the shareholders, and the former had never been taken into consideration.

[12] [1989] A.C. 755 (H.C.); [1988] BCLC 20 (C.A.).

The House of Lords reversed the Court of Appeal on that point. Without deciding whether the interests of the creditors had to be considered, since at all times the group was solvent so that the creditors were not at risk and, in other respects, since the division of the group had prevented deadlock and expensive winding up petitions, it was in the interests of the company.

But on the main issue, the House decided that the assistance had not been given either as subsidiary to a principal purpose or incidental to a larger purpose. The key, according to Lord Oliver, was to distinguish between motive and purpose. The reason or motive was the division of the group but the only purpose of the assistance was to allow the shares to be acquired. "Larger" is not the same as "more important" nor is "reason" the same as "purpose." Thus the House of Lords has come down on the restrictive interpretation of the purpose exceptions. Indeed, since the financial assistance must be given for the purpose of the acquisition for a potential breach of section 151 to occur, how can the purpose exceptions ever apply on Lord Oliver's analysis?

This decision was followed, although on different reasoning, by Morrit J. in *Plaut* v. *Steiner*,[13] a case based on similar facts except that the company giving the assistance became insolvent as a result. With regard to the principal purpose exception the judge decided that the financial assistance was principally designed to make the division of the group equally attractive to both parties and not to effect the division itself. It followed that the principal purpose of the assistance was not to divide the group. As to the larger purpose exception, the judge decided that the division of the business and the acquisition of the shares were so interlinked that both "purposes" were equally large so that neither could be said to be incidental to the other. This does not accord with Lord Oliver's analysis of reason (the division) and purpose (the acquisition) in *Brady* v. *Brady*. If correct it means that a large purpose is neither a principal purpose nor a larger purpose.

Without commenting on the criteria to be adopted in ascertaining whether the assistance was given in good faith in the interests of the company, Morritt J. also decided that where the assisting company becomes insolvent as the resolution of the

[13] (1989) 5 BCC 352.

assistance being given, it can hardly be regarded as being given in the interests of the company.

Authorised transaction exceptions

Section 153(3) sets out nine specific transactions permitted under company law which are not to be subject to the prohibition. These are as follows:

(i) the distribution of lawful dividends.[14] The rules relating to the funds available for dividends are considered strong enough to protect companies. One of the old abuses was to extract unusually large dividends from a company to repay a loan used by the borrower to gain control of the company.
(ii) distributions made in the course of a winding-up[15];
(iii) the allotment of bonus shares[16];
(iv) anything done under a court order section 425[17];
(v) anything done under an arrangement between a company and its creditors under section 1 of the Insolvency Act 1986[18];
(vi) anything done under an arrangement made in pursuance of section 110 of the Insolvency Act 1986[19];
(vii) any reduction of capital confirmed by the court under section 137[20];
(viii) a redemption of shares under section 159[21];
(ix) a purchase of its own shares by a company under sections 162–178[21];

Loans and employee share scheme exceptions

The following three exceptions were, in general, available in the former section 54. They are only available to public

[14] *Post*, Chap. 22.
[15] *Post*, Chap. 29.
[16] *Post*, Chap. 22.
[17] *Post*, Chap. 30.
[18] *Post*, Chap. 24.
[19] *Post*, Chap. 30.
[20] *Ante*, p. 192.
[21] *Ante*, p. 209.

companies if the book value of the net assets is not reduced as a result, or, if it is, the assistance is paid out of distributable profits[22]: section 154.

(1) *Lending as part of the ordinary course of business.* If the lending of the money is in the company's course of business *and* the loan itself is within the ordinary course of that business section 151 does not apply. Banks may use this exception but an unusual loan will not qualify for exception[23]: section 153(4)(*a*).

(2) *Employee share schemes.* There is no prohibition on the provision of financial assistance by a company for the purposes of an employees' share scheme[24] if it is given in good faith in the interests of the company: section 153(4)(*b*). This exception was widened by the 1989 Act to allow companies, for example, to guarantee loans made to such schemes. Before, assistance was limited to the provision of money for the acquisition of such share. The good faith criteria was added, however, and as we have seen this is by no means easy to define in such a context.[25] Directors can be included. This exception also applies to the provision of assistance by the company or another company in the same group to allow beneficiaries under a scheme and their families to trade between themselves: section 153(4)(*bb*)(5).

(3) *Loans to employees to purchase shares.* A company may lend money to those employed in good faith by the company in order for them to purchase shares in that company or its holding company for their own benefit. It does not apply to directors: section 153(4)(*c*).

Validity of the transaction

Section 151, like its predecessor, creates only a criminal offence. What then is the validity of a loan or the provision of any security given to cover a loan which is in breach of the section? The judges have provided an answer.

[22] *Post*, Chap. 22.
[23] *Steen* v. *Law* [1964] A.C. 287. A loan deliberately made by a bank with the purpose of an acquisition in mind is unlikely to be regarded as a usual loan.
[24] Defined in s. 743.
[25] *Ante*, p. 224.

Any security given to provide financial assistance is void.[26] It cannot be enforced by the lender. So is any guarantee supporting the invalid agreement.[27] In most of the cases the action has simply sought to enforce the security but in other cases the wider issue as to the validity of the whole agreement to buy the shares has been considered.

In *South Western Mineral Water Co.* v. *Ashmore*[28] Cross J. suggested that the agreement might be saved if the parties proceed with the acquisition of the shares in a manner dissociating the purchase from the invalid security—*e.g.* by the seller/lender waiving his rights in the security or by the buyer paying the price at once. In the absence of this, however, the whole agreement was in his opinion void. In *Lawlor* v. *Gray*,[29] however, the controller of a company agreed to sell his shares. The agreement could have been carried out in many ways but the controller chose one which was in breach of the financial assistance rules. The court allowed the purchaser to enforce the agreement.

In *Carney* v. *Herbert*[30] the Privy Council decided that if the unlawful elements in the transaction could be severed from the overall transactions and their elimination would leave the sale of the shares unchanged, the remainder of the agreement could be enforced. Only the unlawful elements would be void. The fact that the vendor might have refused to enter into the transaction unless the unlawful elements had been included was *not* a relevant factor in determining their severability. The effect of this is to allow a contract of sale to be enforced where there is no damage to the company.

H, A and J were directors of A Ltd. and of its subsidiary N Ltd. C was the fourth director of these companies and he decided to buy the shares of the other directors. They agreed to sell their shares to I Ltd., a company controlled by C, the purchase price to be payable in three instalments by I Ltd. C guaranteed I Ltd.'s payments, which were also secured by mortgages executed over N Ltd.'s property. I Ltd. failed to

[26] *Selango United Rubber Estates Ltd.* v. *Cradock* (*No.* 3) [1968] 1 W.L.R. 1555; *Heald* v. *O'Connor* [1971] 1 W.L.R. 497; *Carney* v. *Herbert* [1985] A.C. 301 (P.C.); *cf. Victor Battery Co. Ltd.* v. *Curry's Ltd.* [1946] Ch. 242.

[27] *Heald* v. *O'Connor* [1971] 1 W.L.R. 497.

[28] [1967] 1 W.L.R. 1110.

[29] [1984] 3 All E.R. 345.

[30] [1985] A.C. 301 (P.C.). See also *Motor & General Insurance Co. Ltd.* v. *Gobin* (1987) 3 BCC 61.

pay for the shares and H, A and J sued C on his guarantee. C alleged that the whole transaction was void for unlawful financial assistance. The Privy Council held that the only unlawful financial assistance was the mortgage over N Ltd.'s property and that this could be severed so as to leave the sale and guarantee intact and enforceable: *Carney* v. *Herbert* [1985] A.C. 301 (P.C.).

Liability of those participating in the breach

It has been held that section 54 of the 1948 Act was passed to protect the company from having its assets misused and not merely to protect its creditors[31] and this must also apply to section 151. Thus any director who is knowingly a party to a breach of this section will be in breach of duty to the company and liable to repay the loss.[32]

In addition anyone who receives the funds of the company so misapplied is liable to it as a constructive trustee if he knew or ought to have known of the breach. Anyone who assists in the breach is also liable but only if he actually knew of the breach or was deliberately blind to it.[33]

It appears from the *Belmont* case that the company may also recover in the tort of conspiracy if it can prove: (1) that the conspirators combined to participate in a common agreement with a common purpose; (2) that the combination was to carry out an unlawful purpose; *i.e.* the provision of financial assistance contrary to section 151; (3) that the company suffered damages as a consequence. Damage must be proved.

General exemption for private companies

Private companies may obtain complete exemption from the prohibitions regarding the provision of financial assistance for the acquisition of their own shares provided that they comply with a set procedure and timetable under sections 154 to 158. This general exemption is in addition to the exceptions already mentioned which are applicable to all companies. It is not available, however, for the acquisition of shares in a holding company unless that is itself a private company: section 155.

[31] *Wallersteiner* v. *Moir* [1974] 1 W.L.R. 991, 1014, *per* Lord Denning M.R.

[32] *Belmont Finance Corp.* v. *Williams Furniture Ltd.* (*No.* 2) [1980] 1 All E.R. 393; *Wallersteiner* v. *Moir*, above; *Karak Rubber Co.* v. *Burden* (*No.* 2) [1972] 1 W.L.R. 602.

[33] *Belmont Finance Corp.* v. *Williams Furnituree Ltd.*, above.

A general restriction on the use of this exemption is that the assistance must either leave the book value net assets of the company untouched or be made out of distributable profits, section 155(2). The idea is to protect creditors by ensuring that only funds available under section 263 for distribution as dividend are used.[34] That section, however, does not require companies to make provision for unrealised losses, so section 155(6) requires the directors to make a statutory declaration of the company's solvency prior to giving the assistance. If the shares to be acquired are in the company's holding company the directors of that company must also make a declaration.

Statutory declaration. Section 156 prescribes the form of the declaration. First, it must be set out the assistance to be given, the business of the company and the identity of the recipient. Secondly the directors must state that *in their opinion* the company will be able to pay its debts both immediately after giving the assistance and as they fall due during the following year.[35]

Attached to the declaration must be an auditors' report to the effect that they are not aware of anything to indicate that the opinion of the directors is unreasonable.

Special resolution. To protect shareholders rather than creditors the financial assistance must be approved by a special resolution of each of the companies (holding, subsidiary) involved: section 155(4).

The statutory declaration and auditors' report must be available at the meeting at which the special resolution is passed. The meeting must take place on the same day as, or within one week of, the date on which the declaration is made.[36] The declaration, auditors' report and resolution must be registered with the Registrar within 15 days of the passing of the resolution: section 157.

[34] *Post*, Chap. 22. For the effect on profits available for dividend see s.274, *ante*, p. 213.

[35] If it is intended to wind up the company during this time the declaration must state that the company will be able to pay its debts within 12 months of the winding up.

[36] If the written resolution procedure (*post*, p. 343) is used then the relevant documents must be sent to each member prior to his signature: Sched. 15A para. 4.

After passing the resolution the company may not act upon it for four weeks unless all the members voted in favour. This allows a dissenting minority to petition the court to have the resolution set aside (see below). If more than one company is involved the period runs from the date of the last resolution to be passed: section 157.

Assuming that there are no minority shareholder objections the company must then implement the authority within eight weeks of the making of the declaration of solvency. In general therefore companies will have between three and four weeks to implement the authority after the four week delay, depending on how soon the resolution followed the declaration: section 158.

Minority protection. Holders of at least 10 per cent. of the nominal share capital or any class, who did not vote for the authorising resolution, may apply to the court to have the resolution set aside. Such applications must be made within 28 days of the passing of the resolution—which corresponds to the waiting period for the company: section 157(2).

The court has wide powers on such an application—those which are available to it on a petition under section 54[37] to prevent the re-registration of a public company as a private one. One of these powers is to order that the minority be bought out. The court may otherwise cancel, confirm or vary the resolution. Whilst the petition is being considered the resolution cannot be implemented unless the court orders otherwise: s.158(3).

The existence of this exemption procedure persuaded the House of Lords in *Brady* v. *Brady*,[38] to allow the company to adopt the procedure and so rectify the illegality. This was not done in *Plaut* v. *Steiner*[39] since the company was insolvent.

[37] *Ante*, p. 50.
[38] [1989] A.C. 755 (H.L.), *ante*, p. 223.
[39] (1989) 5 BCC 352; *ante*, p. 224.

Chapter 12

MEMBERSHIP

THIS chapter is concerned with the members of a company, *i.e.* in the case of a company limited by shares, the shareholders. In addition to the ways in which a person can become a member and the persons who can become members, the following topics are dealt with: the register of members which every company must keep, disclosure of substantial shareholdings in public companies, and the annual return which every company must make to the Registrar.

WAYS OF BECOMING A MEMBER

The members of a company consist of:

(1) The subscribers of the memorandum.[1] These are deemed to have agreed to become members, and on the registration of the company they must be entered as members in its register of members: section 22.
(2) Directors who have signed and delivered to the Registrar an undertaking to take and pay for their qualification shares.[2]
(3) All other persons who have agreed to become members of the company *and* whose names are entered in the register of members: section 22.

Subscribers of the memorandum

A subscriber of the memorandum becomes a member on registration of the company, and an entry in the register of members is not necessary to make him a member of the company. It is the duty of the directors to enter his name at

[1] *Ante*, pp. 55, 82.
[2] *Post*, p. 361.

once in the register, but their failure to do this will not enable him to escape liability for calls on the shares for which he has signed the memorandum.[3]

The subscribers to the memorandum of a company limited by shares are liable, by virtue of their subscription, to pay up the full amount of their shares, in cash if it is a public company,[4] as and when called up. Until the commencement of winding up the times and amounts of payment depend, apart from express agreement between the company and the signatories, on the articles.[5]

A subscriber's obligation to take the shares for which he has subscribed is not satisfied by the (later) allotment of shares credited as fully paid and to which someone else is entitled.

M. signed the memorandum for five shares. The company had agreed to allot paid up shares to C., as the purchase price of property sold to the company, and C. directed the company to allot five of these shares to M. This was done and the company was afterwards wound up. *Held*, M. was liable to pay for the five shares for which he had signed the memorandum: *Migotti's Case* (1867) L.R. 4 Eq. 238.

If, however, the entire share capital has been allotted to others, the subscriber is under no liability to take shares.[6]

A subscriber of the memorandum cannot rescind the contract to take shares on the ground of a misrepresentation made by a promoter, because (*a*) the company could not appoint an agent before it came into existence and it is therefore not liable for the promoter's acts, and (*b*) by signing the memorandum the subscriber became bound, on the registration of the company, not only as between himself and the company, but also as between himself and the other persons who should become members on the footing that the contract existed.[7]

Non-cash assets supplied by a subscriber to a public company in return for consideration from the company may require a valuation report from an independent valuer.[8]

[3] *Evans's Case* (1867) L.R. 2 Ch.App. 427.
[4] s.106.
[5] *Per* Lindley M.R. in *Alexander* v. *Automatic Telephone Co.* [1900] 2 Ch. 56 (C.A.) at p. 63.
[6] *Mackley's Case* (1875) 1 Ch.D. 247.
[7] *Lord Lurgan's Case* [1902] 1 Ch. 707.
[8] *Ante*, p. 177.

In Scotland, specific implement is available as a remedy to enforce an undertaking to subscribe for shares.[9]

Other members

A person, other than those mentioned above, who has agreed to become a member of the company does not actually become one until his name is entered in the register of members. Section 22 "makes the placing of the name of a shareholder on the register a condition precedent to membership."[10] Registration is essential for membership. A member agrees to become a member, however, if he consents to do so even though there is no contract between him and the company that he should be entered on the register: *Re Nuneaton Borough A.F.C. Ltd.* [1989] BCLC 454.

Such a person may take an allotment of his shares direct from the company,[11] or may purchase shares from an existing member,[12] or he may succeed to shares on the death or bankruptcy of a member.[13]

WHO CAN BE MEMBERS

Minors

In English law a minor, *i.e.* a person under the age of 18,[14] may be a member unless this is forbidden by the articles. However, a minor's contract to take shares is voidable by him before or within a reasonable time after he attains the age of 18. If he avoids he cannot recover the money paid for the shares unless there has been a total failure of the consideration for which the money was paid.

S., an infant,[15] agreed to take 500 £1 shares from a company, and paid 10s. on each share. She received no dividend on the shares. While

[9] *Beardmore & Co.* v. *Barry*, 1928 S.C. 101; affirmed 1928 S.C. (H.L.) 47.
[10] *Per* Fry L.J. in *Nicol's Case* (1885) 29 Ch.D. 421 (C.A.), at p. 447; *per* Lord Deas in *Macdonald* v. *City of Glasgow Bank* (1879) 6 R. 621 at p. 633.
[11] *Ante*, p. 166.
[12] *Post*, p. 276.
[13] *Post*, p. 294.
[14] Family Law Reform Act 1969, s.1.
[15] The age of majority was formerly 21 and persons under that age were called "infants."

still an infant she repudiated the shares, and brought an action (a) for a declaration that she was entitled to avoid the contract, and (b) to recover the money she had paid. *Held*, (a) S. was entitled to rescind and so was not liable for future calls, but (b) there was no total failure of consideration and S. could not recover money already paid because she had got the thing for which the money was paid, a thing of value: *Steinberg* v. *Scala* (*Leeds*) *Ltd.* [1923] 2 Ch. 452 (C.A.).

If the company is wound up the minor member loses his right to avoid unless the liquidator agrees.[16]

Scots law divides persons who are under the age of majority[17] into pupils (boys under 14 and girls under 12) and minors (young persons over the age of pupillarity but under the age of majority). A pupil has no capacity to be a member himself but his "tutor" (father or mother[18] or other guardian) may be a member on the pupil's behalf.[19] A minor may become a member, but only with the consent of his "curator" (father or mother[18] or other guardian) if he has one; a minor who has no curator may become a member on his own initiative. However, whether a minor has a curator or not, his contract to take shares may be "reduced" (set aside) up to the end of the *quadriennium utile i.e.* the four-year period after he attains majority) on proof of "lesion" (*i.e.* considerable loss to the minor's estate, the contract not being a fair and reasonable one at the time when it was entered into).[20] Lesion is more easily proved in the case of a minor who has no curator than in the case of a minor who transacted with his curator's consent.

Personal representatives

Ownership of the shares of a deceased member is transmitted to his executors[21] or administrators. They must produce to the company the grant of probate of the will, or of letters of administration of the estate, or, in Scotland, of confirmation and, notwithstanding anything in the articles, such document

[16] *Symons' Case* (1870) L.R. 5 Ch. 298.
[17] 18 since January 1, 1970: Age of Majority (Scotland) Act 1969.
[18] Law Reform (Parent and Child) (Scotland) Act 1986.
[19] See *Inland Revenue* v. *Wilson*, 1928 S.C. (H.L.) 42; 1927 S.C. 733.
[20] *Hill* v. *City of Glasgow Bank* (1879) 7 R. 68.
[21] In Scots law the term "executors" is used whether there is a will or not, and "confirmation" is the equivalent of both probate and letters of administration.

must be accepted by the company as sufficient evidence of the grant: section 187. Production to the company does *not*, however, make the representatives members of the company.[22] The deceased member's estate is the member for some purposes, such as an article providing that on an increase of capital the new shares are to be divided among the existing members in proportion to their existing shareholdings.[23] However, the deceased member is not a member within the meaning of a section such as section 24,[24] which is concerned with reduction of the number of members below the legal minimum.

The personal representatives are liable for calls[25] on partly paid shares only to the extent of the deceased's assets in their hands, and if in England the personal representatives make default in paying calls, the company can obtain an order for administration of the estate of the deceased member: section 81 of the Insolvency Act 1986.

The personal representatives are entitled to transfer the shares without being registered as members (s.183(3)),[26] and to receive all dividends, bonuses or other benefits from the shares, but the articles usually prevent them from voting at general meetings.

> Table A, regulation 31, provides: "A person becoming entitled to a share in consequence of the death or bankruptcy of a member shall have the rights to which he would be entitled if he were the holder of the share, except that he shall not, before being registered as the holder of the share, be entitled in respect of it to attend or vote at any meeting of the company or at any separate meeting of the holders of any class of shares in the company."

Personal representatives may, however, be entitled to be given notice of general meetings, even though they have no right to attend and vote at the meetings. Table A, regulation 38, gives them a right to be given notice of general meetings.

[22] *Macdonald* v. *City of Glasgow Bank* (1879) 6 R. 621.
[23] *Per* Lord Herschell in *James* v. *Buena Ventura Nitrate Grounds Syndicate Ltd.* [1896] 1 Ch. 456 (C.A.), at p. 464.
[24] *Ante*, p. 28 See *Re Bowling & Welby's Contract* [1895] 1 Ch. 663 (C.A.).
[25] *Post*, p. 300.
[26] See also *Buchan* v. *City of Glasgow Bank* (1879) 6 R. (H.L.) 44; (1879) 6 R. 567.

Personal representatives are entitled, if they so choose and there is no contrary provision in the articles, to be registered as members.[27] The articles may give the directors, the same power to decline to register personal representatives as members as the directors would have had in the case of a transfer by the deceased shareholder before his death.[28]

If personal representatives are registered as members, they become personally liable for calls, although they have a right of indemnity against the deceased's estate.[29]

Trustees in bankruptcy

A bankrupt may be a member of a company, although the beneficial interest in his shares will be vested in his trustee in bankruptcy as from the time when he is adjudged bankrupt.[30] Unless the articles provide to the contrary, a shareholder does not cease to be a member of the company on becoming bankrupt. Accordingly, as long as he is on the register he is entitled to exercise any vote conferred by his shares at the meetings of the company, even though the articles provide—as does regulation 38 of Table A—that notice of meetings is to be sent to the trustee in bankruptcy and not to the bankrupt.[31] The bankrupt must vote in accordance with the directions of the trustee.

A minority action[32] may be brought by a bankrupt shareholder who is on the register of members.[33]

Other companies

1. A company may, if authorised by its memorandum, take shares in and be a member of another company. It attends

[27] *Edwards* v. *Ransomes and Rapier Ltd.* [1930] W.N. 180.

[28] See, *e.g.* *Shepherd's Trustees* v. *Shepherd*, 1950 S.C. (H.L.) 60. See also *post*, p. 300.

[29] *Per* Cotton L.J. in *Duff's Executors' Case* (1886) 32 Ch.D. 301 (C.A.), at p. 309.

[30] Insolvency Act 1986, s.306. In Scots law, a debtor's estate vests as at the date of sequestration in the permanent trustee: Bankruptcy (Scotland) Act 1985, s.31.

[31] *Morgan* v. *Gray* [1953] Ch. 83.

[32] *Post*, Chap. 18.

[33] *Birch* v. *Sullivan* [1957] 1 W.L.R. 1247.

meetings of the other by a representative authorised by resolution of its directors: section 375.[34]

2. A company may in certain circumstances purchase or acquire its own shares. Under the Act companies may redeem or purchase their own shares but they must cancel the shares so acquired. It cannot be a member of itself as this would amount to a false statement of its capital. Companies may also forfeit or accept the surrender of their shares. This topic has been covered in Chapter 10.

3. For the same reason that a company cannot be a member of itself, section 23[35] provides that, subject to certain exceptions, a subsidiary company[36] cannot be a member of its holding company[36] and any allotment or transfer of shares in a holding company to its subsidiary is void.[37] This prohibition cannot be evaded by having a nominee for the subsidiary. There are exceptions where the subsidiary is concerned (a) as a personal representative, or (b) as a trustee, unless the holding company or a subsidiary of it is beneficially interested under the trust otherwise than by way of security for the purposes of a transaction entered into in the ordinary course of a business which includes the lending of money.

For example, as regards (a), Y, who holds shares in X Bank Ltd., appoints its subsidiary, X Bank (Executor & Trustee) Ltd., as his executor and on Y's death the subsidiary is registered in respect of the shares.

As to (b), Y transfers his shares to the subsidiary on trust for a beneficiary, Z, who borrows money from X Bank Ltd. and secures repayment by mortgaging his interest in the shares to X Bank Ltd.

The definition of beneficial interest for this purpose excludes those detailed in Schedule 2. These are minor and residual interests under company pension and employee share schemes. Otherwise a subsidiary's pension fund could not invest in its parent company.

[34] *Post*, p. 336.
[35] This section was redrafted and expanded by s.129 C.A. 1989.
[36] *Ante*, p. 51.
[37] In Scotland this does not prevent a company from arresting its subsidiary's shares to found jurisdiction, at least where the shares are marketable: *Stenhouse London Ltd.* v. *Allwright*, 1972 S.L.T. 255.

Another exception applies where the subsidiary is a market maker for the purposes of the Financial Services Act 1986.[38] In such cases the subsidiary may hold shares in its holding company for the purpose of market-making only.

Finally, where a company becomes a subsidiary of a company in which it already holds shares, it is allowed both to retain those shares and to accept subsequent bonus shares[39] provided it is not allowed to vote with any of them.

Issuing houses and brokers

A person who has only agreed to place[40] shares does not agree to become a member of the company, and should not be put on the register of members. His failure to perform his contract may make him liable in damages, but he is not liable for calls.[41] If, however, a person agrees to take shares himself for the purpose of placing them by the execution of transfers, his name is properly put on the register.[42]

Register of Members

Section 352 provides that every company must keep a register of its members containing:

(1) the names and addresses of the members, and, if the company has a share capital, a statement of the shares held by each member, distinguishing each share by its number[43] so long as it has one and by its class if there is more than one class of shares, and the amount paid or agreed to be considered as paid on the shares of each member. If the company has converted shares into stock, the register must show the amount of stock held by each member. In any other case where the company has more than one class of members the

[38] See Chap. 19, *post*.
[39] *Ante*, p. 51.
[40] *Ante*, p. 143.
[41] *Gorrissen's Case* (1873) L.R. 8 Ch.App. 507.
[42] *Miln* v. *North British Fresh Fish etc. Co. Ltd.* (1887) 15 R. 21.
[43] *Post*, p. 258.

register must show the class to which each member belongs.[44]

(2) the date at which each person was entered in the register as a member;

(3) the date at which any person ceased to be a member.

Default renders the company and every officer in default liable to a fine.

A guarantee company which does not have a share capital must disclose the particulars of any class of membership not stated in its memorandum, articles or by a special or extraordinary resolution, to the Registrar.[45]

The register may be kept by making entries in a bound book or by recording the required information in any other manner, including a computer, so long as adequate precautions are taken to guard against falsification: sections 722 and 723. Any entry relating to a former member may be removed from the register after 20 years from the date on which he ceased to be a member: section 352(6).

A company with more than 50 members must, unless the register of members constitutes an index, keep an index (which may be a card index) of the names of its members, and must alter the index within 14 days after any alteration in the register. The index must be kept at the same place as the register and must contain sufficient information to enable the account of each member in the register to be readily found: section 354.

The register of members is prima facie evidence of any matters directed by the Act to be inserted in it: section 361.

Inspection of register

The register is to be kept at the company's registered office, but if the register is made up at another office of the company, it may be kept there, and if it is made up by an agent, it may be kept at his office. If the company is registered in England, the register must not be kept outside England, and if the company is registered in Scotland, the register must not be kept outside

[44] This applies therefore to guarantee companies without a share capital. It was added by 1981 Act, s.101 and reverses the decision in *Re Performing Right Society Ltd.* [1978] 3 All E.R. 972 (C.A.).

[45] s.129.

Scotland. When the register has not always been kept at the registered office, notice must be given to the Registrar of the place where it is kept: section 353.

The Jenkins Report[46] recommended that these flexible provisions in section 353 should apply to the other statutory books such as the minutes of general meetings, the register of directors, copies of instruments creating charges registrable under section 395 and the company's own register of charges.

The register and index are to be open to the inspection of any member without charge, and of any other person on payment of the appropriate charge.[47] Within 10 days after being required to do so, the company is bound to furnish, either to a member or to any other person, a copy of any part of the register on payment of the appropriate charge[47]: section 356. A person inspecting the register has no right to take extracts from or make copies of the register.[48] The right of inspection terminates on the company going into liquidation.[49]

There is no obligation on the company to disclose under section 356 anything other than what is on the register. It need not disclose a part of the register which can only be defined by reference to something which is not on the register, *e.g.* those members over a certain age.[50]

The company may, on giving notice by advertisement in some newspaper circulating in the district in which its registered office is situate, close the register for any time or times not exceeding 30 days in each year: section 358. This is to enable the company to prepare a list of members entitled to payment of a dividend.

Importance of register

The importance of the register as a public representation of who the members are and what their liability is has often been emphasised in Scottish cases,[51] and a company has no power to

[46] Para. 470.

[47] This is the amount prescribed by the Secretary of State by regulations made under s.723A. These also fix the hours of availability for inspection.

[48] *Re Balaghat Co.* [1901] 2 K.B. 665.

[49] *Re Kent Coalfields Syndicate Ltd.* [1898] 1 Q.B. 754 (C.A.).

[50] *Re Performing Right Society Ltd.* [1978] 3 All E.R. 972 (C.A.).

[51] *e.g. per* Lord Curriehill in *Liquidator of the Garpel etc. Co. Ltd.* v. *Andrew* (1866) 4 M. 617 at p. 623.

create a right of pledge or lien over the register, since that would deprive the public of their statutory right of access and inspection.[52] The register and not the share certificate is the document of title to shares, the share certificate being merely an acknowledgment on the part of the company that the name of the person mentioned in it is duly recorded in the register.[53]

Any liability incurred by a company as the result of making or deleting an entry in its register, or failing to do either, cannot be enforced against it more than 20 years after the date of first default: section 352(7). This is a final limitation provision; earlier ones may well apply.

Power of court to rectify register

Section 359 gives the court a discretion to rectify the register of members in two cases, namely—

(1) if the name of any person is, without sufficient cause, entered in or omitted from the register;
(2) if default is made or unnecessary delay takes place in entering on the register the fact of any person having ceased to be a member.

Application to the court for rectification may be made by the person aggrieved, or any member of the company, or the company. The application is made in a summary way—by originating summons or originating motion in England: R.S.C., O. 102, r. 3, and by petition in Scotland: R.C. 189.

The court may order rectification of the register by deleting a reference to some only of the registered shareholder's shares. It need not delete his name entirely. Thus when an existing shareholder was registered as the holder of an additional number of shares issued in breach of the then Exchange Control Regulations the court deleted the reference to those shares only: *Re Transatlantic Life Assurance Co. Ltd.* [1979] 3 All E.R. 357.

There is no *Foss* v. *Harbottle*[54] complication—even a single member may apply to the court.

[52] *Liquidator of the Garpel etc. Co. Ltd.* v. *Andrew* (1866) 4 M. 617.
[53] *Per* Lord Sands in *Inland Revenue* v. *Wilson*, 1928 S.C. (H.L.) 42; 1927 S.C. 733 at p. 737.
[54] *Post*, Chap. 18.

The court may order not only rectification of the register but also payment by the company of any damages sustained by any party aggrieved. However, the applicant must show for subsection (1) that he was improperly entered in or omitted from the register. If the true complaint is that he was never allotted any shares at all and if instead they were validly allotted to a third party, the applicant will only be entitled to an action for damages for breach of contract. The applicant has never been entitled to be on the register and so has no remedy under section 359.[55]

If an order is made in the case of a company required to send a list of members to the Registrar[56] notice of the rectification must be given to the Registrar: section 359(4).

The period of two months specified in section 183(5) for giving a transferee of shares notice of the company's refusal to register the transfer is the outside limit after which there is normally unnecessary delay.[57]

An order for rectification may be made even if the company is being wound up.

B, a transferee of shares in a company, sent in his transfer for registration but, by mistake, registration of the transfer was omitted. The company then went into liquidation with a view to reconstruction and B, thinking that he was on the register of members, served the liquidator with notice of dissent to the scheme. The liquidator disregarded the notice on the ground that B was not a member. *Held*, there was such "default or unnecessary delay" in registration as entitled B to rectification of the register: *Re Sussex Brick Co.* [1904] 1 Ch. 598 (C.A.).[58]

Section 359 does not exhaust the court's power to order rectification and does not prevent the court from altering the register in cases other than those specified. Accordingly where shares were registered in the names of two joint holders, and under the articles the first alone could vote and if the first was ill or absent the second could not vote or be appointed a proxy, an order was made to have the holding split into two holdings

[55] *Re BTR plc* (1988) 4 BCC 45.
[56] See *post*.
[57] *Re Swaledale Cleaners Ltd.* [1968] 1 W.L.R. 1710 (C.A.), *post*, p. 283.
[58] See also *Stocker* v. *Liqdrs. of the Coustonholm Paper Mills Co. Ltd.* (1891) 19 R. 17; *Barbor* v. *Middleton*, 1988 S.L.T. 288 (O.H.) (petitioner declared never to have been a member).

with the names of the shareholders in different orders.[59] Rectification is, however, always a discretionary remedy and not one available as of right.[60]

Trusts not to be entered on register in England

Section 360 provides that no notice of any trust shall be entered on the register, or be received by the Registrar, in the case of companies registered in England (which, for this purpose, includes Wales). This means that, subject as below, the company is entitled to treat every person on the register of members as the beneficial owner of shares, even if in fact he holds them on trust for another, *i.e.* the company need not take notice of equitable interests in shares. If, therefore, the company registers a transfer of the shares held by a person as trustee, it is under no liability to the beneficiaries even if the sale was a breach of trust and in fraud of the beneficiaries.

X's shares were, on his death, registered in the name of his executors. They subsequently transferred the shares to Y in breach of the terms of X's will, and the transfer was registered by the company. The company had a copy of the will in its possession, and its president was one of X's executors. *Held*, the company did not act wrongfully, as it was only bound to satisfy itself from the will that the executors were executors, and was not concerned with the disposition by X of his property: *Simpson* v. *Molson's Bank* [1895] A.C. 270.

A further result is that the company is not a trustee for persons claiming the shares under equitable titles. For example, if A, the owner of shares, makes an equitable mortgage of his shares by depositing his share certificate and a blank transfer with B as security for a debt and afterwards makes another equitable mortgage of the same shares by depositing another blank transfer of them with C as security for another debt, saying that he has lost his share certificate, C cannot by giving notice to the company affect the company with notice of his interest in the shares or gain any priority over B.[61] As will be

[59] *Burns* v. *Siemens Brothers Dynamo Works Ltd.* [1919] 1 Ch. 225.
[60] *Re Piccadilly Radio plc* [1989] BCLC 683.
[61] *Société Générale de Paris* v. *Walker* (1885) 11 App.Cas. 20.

seen later,[62] the proper way to protect the interest of a beneficiary in shares is to serve a stop notice. As a rule, if a company receives notice of an equitable claim it should allow the person giving the notice to apply for a restraining order, if he makes a request to that effect, before registering a transfer to his prejudice.[63]

The articles frequently deal with notice of trusts, as does Table A, regulation 5:

"Except as required by law, no person shall be recognised . . . as holding any share upon any trust, and (except as otherwise provided by the articles or by law) the company shall not be bound by or recognise any interest in any share except an absolute right to the entirety thereof in the holder."

It is doubtful whether this adds anything to the effect of section 360, although the section deals only with entries on the register while the article is not limited to entries on the register.[64]

A trustee of shares who is entered on the register is entitled to exercise any vote conferred by the shares although he may be bound to vote in accordance with the directions of the beneficiary. The trustee is personally liable to the company for any calls or other obligations attaching to the shares but is entitled to an indemnity from the beneficiary, not only out of the trust property but to the full extent of his indebtedness in respect of the shares.[65] The company cannot put the beneficiary on the list of contributories but it can, through the trustee, enforce the trustee's right to an indemnity.[66]

A purchase of shares in the name of a nominee, even if a minor or a man of straw, is legal. In such a case the company cannot go behind the nominee to the beneficial owner.

M. and G., a firm of stockbrokers, bought shares which were registered in the name of L., their clerk. L. was an infant. On the

[62] *Post*, p. 297.
[63] *Per* Lindley L.J. in *Société Générale de Paris* v. *Tramways Union Co.* (1884) 14 Q.B.D. 424 (C.A.) at p. 453.
[64] See *post*, p. 297.
[65] *Hardoon* v. *Belilios* [1901] A.C. 118 (P.C.).
[66] *Per* James L.J. in *Re European Society Arbitration Acts* (1878) 8 Ch.D. 679 (C.A.) at p. 708.

company's going into liquidation, the liquidator applied that M. and G.'s names might be substituted for that of L. in the register of members and the list of contributories. *Held*, the application failed, as there was no contractual relation between the company and M. and G.: *Re National Bank of Wales Ltd.* [1907] 1 Ch. 582.

If a person applies for shares in a fictitious name, or in the name of a person who has never agreed to accept the shares, rectification of the register can be obtained so as to place the name of the real owner upon the register.[67]

Trusts may be entered on register in Scotland

It has always been competent for companies registered in Scotland to enter notices of trusts on their registers.[68]

Entry of a notice of trust does *not* have the effect of limiting the liability of the trustees to the amount of the trust estate in their hands.[69]

The legal position of trustees is distinct from that of executors.[70]

On the assumption of a new trustee by deed of assumption his name may be entered on the register without any transfer being executed, and the trustee will then be a member and liable as such.[71] A trustee who duly resigns his office by minute registered in the Books of Council and Session, and intimated to his co-trustees and to the company, is entitled to have his name removed from the register; no deed of transfer is necessary.[72] When one of several trustees dies, shares registered in the names of the trustees vest in the surviving trustees, and the executors of the deceased trustee are not liable as members even though no intimation of the death has been given to the company.[73] The last surviving trustee, however, is in a different

[67] *Pugh and Sharman's Case* (1872) L.R 13 Eq. 566; *Richardson's Case* (1875) L.R. 19 Eq. 588.

[68] As to the purpose of such entry, see, *per* Cairns L.C. in *Muir* v. *City of Glasgow Bank* (1879) 6 R. (H.L.) 21 at p. 26.

[69] *Muir* v. *City of Glasgow Bank* (1879) 6 R. (H.L.) 21; (1878) 6 R. 392, following *Lumsden* v. *Buchanan* (1865) 3 M.(H.L.) 89.

[70] *Per* Lord Selborne in *Buchan* v. *City of Glasgow Bank* (1879) 6 R. (H.L.) 44 at p. 50.

[71] Trusts (Scotland) Act 1921, s.21; *Bell* v. *City of Glasgow Bank* (1879) 6 R. (H.L.) 55; (1879) 6 R. 548.

[72] 1921 Act, s.19(1); *Dalgleish* v. *Land Feuing Co. Ltd.* (1885) 13 R. 223.

[73] *Oswald's Trustees* v. *City of Glasgow Bank* (1879) 6 R. 461.

position from the other trustees in that his death does not automatically terminate his liability as a member.[74]

The liability of trustees to the company is *in solidum*, not *pro rata*, *i.e.* the company may hold any one of the several trustees liable for the full amount due on shares.[75]

Trustees who have been made liable for calls in respect of shares forming part of the trust estate are entitled to full relief from the trust estate without reference to their own payments or ability to pay; the trust estate may be made liable beyond what the trustees can personally pay, and the company may by diligence compel the trustees to make the right of relief available to the company.[76]

The persons for whom shares are held in trust are *not* members of the company, although their names may appear on the register.[77]

Disclosure of Substantial Shareholdings

Sections 198–220 contain provisions for securing the disclosure and registration of substantial individual interests in share capital carrying unrestricted voting rights. The aim is to ensure that directors,[78] shareholders and employees of a public company may ascertain the identity of, for instance, any person who may be in the process of buying shares in the company through nominees, who will only appear on the register, to gain control of it or of any person who is in a position to veto a special resolution of the company not only at the date of the request but also in respect of the previous three years.[79] In addition they allow companies to carry out their own investigations into such matters without necessitating intervention by the Secretary of State under sections 442–444.[80]

[74] *Low's Executors* v. *City of Glasgow Bank* (1879) 6 R. 830.
[75] *Cuninghame* v. *City of Glasgow Bank* (1879) 6 R. (H.L.) 98; (1879) 6 R. 679.
[76] *Cuningham* v. *Montgomerie* (1879) 6 R. 1333; contrast *Brownlie* v. *Brownlie's Trustees* (1879) 6 R. 1233.
[77] *Gillespie & Paterson* v. *City of Glasgow Bank* (1879) 6 R. (H.L.) 104; (1879) 6 R. 714.
[78] For the provisions relating to directors' shareholdings, see *post*, p. 363, and sections 324, 732 of and Schedule 13, Parts I, II and III to the 1985 Act.
[79] *Re Geers Gross* 1 W.L.R. 837.
[80] *Post*, p. 474.

Disclosure obligations—public companies

Section 198 requires any person who acquires or disposes of a substantial interest in shares, which is currently[81] defined as a three per cent. interest or more in "relevant share capital," to inform the company of that and of any significant change in the number of shares in which he is or was interested above the three per cent. level. "Relevant share capital" is defined as the voting shares of any public company. In adding up any individual's interest to ascertain whether he has passed the disclosure threshold, sections 204–208 provide for the attribution to individuals of interests in shares. These attributed interests are added to those already clearly held by the person to ascertain whether or not he is obliged to make disclosure of his interest in shares under this part of the Act.

Under section 202 any person obliged to disclose must within two days of the date upon which the obligation arose make the appropriate disclosure of his interest in writing to the company specifying the share capital to which it relates. He must also state either the number of shares in that public company in which he knows he was interested immediately after the time his obligation to notify arose together with the names of the registered holder(s) of those shares and the number of shares for each registered holder,[82] or state that he no longer has a notifiable interest if that is the case. Any known changes in those particulars must be subsequently notified by him to the company within two days of the day upon which he became aware of them and this obligation continues until he notifies the company that he has no longer any interest in those shares.

Section 198(4) states that the time an obligation arises is either the time the event or change of circumstances occurred or the time when the person becomes aware of those facts.

Sections 203 and 208 aim to make subject to the disclosure provisions interests in shares which arise indirectly. The notifiable interests in shares defined in section 208 include interests in shares on which a person has an option or a right to call for delivery or to acquire an interest in them. Section 203

[81] The figure may be changed by statutory instrument: s.210A.
[82] This is defined so as to include options held by nominees.

specifies various instances where a person is attributed with the interests which are ostensibly held by other persons and which are to be taken into account in ascertaining whether or not he is obliged to make notification under sections 198–202. Other persons' interests which come into this category as defined in section 203 include those of his spouse or any infant child or stepchild and 203(4) includes those interests, of any company which is accustomed to acting in accordance with his directors or in which he is entitled to control one third or more of the voting power at general meetings; and where that company which he "controls" itself has a one third shareholding in another company, the interest in shares of that other company is also attributable to him. The same is true where a person is entitled to exercise or control the exercise of one third or more of the voting power at general meeting and that company has the same right or control of the voting power at general meeting of another company.

Further important attributions of interests in shares are contained in sections 206 and 207 which deal with so-called "concert parties,"[83] *i.e.* those combinations of persons with agreements for the purpose of acquiring interests in shares. The aim is to prevent control in concert, in other words avoidance of the disclosure provisions by groups of persons secretly agreeing that while each acquires openly less than the disclosure threshold level they will secretly use the combined interests to gain control or to ensure a takeover or a special resolution at a meeting of the company. Sections 204 and 205 provide that each person involved in any such agreement is to be attributed with the interests of all the other parties to it even though some of those persons' interests may have been acquired before or outside of the so-called "concert party" agreement. The effect is that in ascertaining the obligation of each member of a concert party individually to notify his interests, the interests of all the other members are added to his interest or interests and if the total exceeds three per cent., he must make notification in accordance with section 204. In addition, under section 205 that person shall state that he is a party to such an agreement, the names and if known to him, the addresses of the other parties to the agreement, which, if any, of the shares to which the

[83] *Cf.* the City Code on Take-overs and Mergers, *post*, Chap. 31.

notification relates are shares in which he is interested by reason of attribution under section 204 and if that is the case, he must also notify the number of those shares.

In addition to the obligation to notify the company, section 206 obliges all the persons involved in a concert party to keep each other informed of facts relevant to their shareholding. This provision aims to give each and every member of a concert party the ability to know whether or not the interests attributed to him under section 204 (alone or together with any other interest he might have) are such as to necessitate his making a notification under sections 198–201. To do this he must know all the interests attributable to him and any changes in those interests.

Section 204, for example, may impose an obligation to disclose where two or more persons agree that one or more of them acquire interests in relevant shares of a particular "target" company. Once such interests have been acquired the obligation to disclose is not affected by any further acquisition under it or by a variation of or alteration in the membership of, the agreement. Section 205 states that each party to the agreement is deemed interested in all the shares in the target company held by any other party to the agreement irrespective of whether or not they were acquired pursuant to the agreement. Section 204(5) and (6) widely define an agreement to include any agreement, arrangement, undertaking, expectation or understanding whether express or implied, conditional or absolute which is legally binding except agreements to underwrite any offer of shares. An agreement which is not legally binding may give rise to the obligation to disclose if it involves mutuality in the undertakings, expectations or understandings of the parties to it.

Therefore all the concert party members must inform every other member of their existing interests, acquisitions and disposals of shares in that company and this obligation comes into being with the first acquisition of shares in that company in pursuance of the "concert party" agreement: section 206. Each party to the agreement has three days from the day on which the obligation arose within which to notify the other parties in writing of his interests in target company shares and of his current address. Failure to meet these obligations is made a criminal offence by section 210(3)(*c*).

Notifiable interests

Section 208 defines for the purpose of the duty to disclose the interests to be notified. Most significant is that a person is deemed to have an interest in shares if he enters into a contract for their purchase or where, even though he is not the registered holder, he is entitled to exercise or control the exercise of any right conferred by holding those shares or (trust aside) he has a right to call for delivery of the shares to himself or his order or he has a right to acquire an interest in shares or is under an obligation to take an interest in shares whether or not in any case that right or obligation is conditional or absolute. Joint interests are attributed equally to each person who has an interest and it is immaterial that the shares in which a person has an interest are unidentifiable. In this way contingent agreements which otherwise might be used to conceal an interest requiring disclosure are exposed.

Section 209 lists various interests in shares which do not give rise to the disclosure obligation under sections 198–202, for example an interest in shares as a security is an exempt security interest and disregarded if it is held by specified bodies which lend money in the course of business. Criminal liability for failure to meet the obligations imposed under this part of the Act is contained in section 210. Under section 210(3) failure to comply with sections 198–202 is made a criminal offence. This includes failure to fulfil an obligation to disclose; knowingly or recklessly making a false disclosure; failure (subject to the defence in section 210(4)) to give another person a notice required by section 206 and failure (without reasonable excuse) to secure that your agent notifies you immediately of acquisitions or disposals by him which may give rise to an obligation of disclosure under sections 198(3) or 206. The prosecutions must prove that the defendant knew enough to be aware that he had an interest or interests of the relevant amount and failed to report them but any interest which he has or had and does not know about will be irrelevant and will not make him liable for failure to make disclosure.

The Secretary of State may by regulations amend the notifiable percentage, the definition of relevant share capital, the time limits for notification and the definition of and exclusions from notifiable interests: section 210A.

Shares which are the subject of an offence may have imposed on them by the Secretary of State all the restrictions of Part XV of the Act.[84]

Register of substantial shareholders

By section 211 every public company must maintain a register of interests in shares notified to it in accordance with sections 198–202. It must record the relevant information against the name of the person obliged to provide such information together with the date of the entry and where the company is notified that a person has ceased to be party to an agreement to which section 204 applies it must record that fact against that person's name wherever his name appears in the register as a party to that agreement. These obligations must be fulfilled by the company within three days of notification. Section 211(5) and (6) prescribe the form that the register and the index to the register are to take and specifies that the company must make any necessary alterations in the index within 10 days of a name being entered on the register.

Any company that ceases to be a public company must keep the register and index to it for six years from the date it ceases to be a public company and in any case the register must, according to section 325 and Part IV of Schedule 13, para. 25, be kept together with the register of directors' interests[85] either at the company's registered office (if that is where its register of members is kept) or at the place where its register is kept in compliance with the terms set out in section 219. Section 211(10) states that the company and every officer[86] in default is made criminally liable to a fine for either failing to keep the register or failing to keep it in the manner prescribed and to a daily default fine for continued contravention.

Company's power to require information

Under section 212 a public company can require information from existing members about the capacity in which they hold their shares, and it is further empowered to make enquiries of

[84] *Post*, p. 254.
[85] *Post*, p. 363.
[86] *Post*, p. 347.

any person who it has been informed is or who its investigations reveal to be, interested in shares in the company. Members may be asked whether or not any voting rights on their shares are controlled by another person under some agreement and if that is the case, particulars of the parties and terms of the agreement may be required. Members and persons who also indicated that they were interested in shares during the three years prior to the date of notice under this section must disclose details of their present interests or any past interests in shares held within the previous three years or of any other past or present interest not referred to in a notice issued under this section. Such information, known to a member, must be disclosed to the company. Likewise the company may require similar information from any person named or revealed as a party to such an agreement as will enable it to cross check the information it receives concerning interests in shares. Section 212 is subject to change by regulations made by the Secretary of State under section 210A.

A public company is entitled to use section 212 to probe and discover the true beneficial owner, of its shares.[87] It is a failure to comply with the section if the person required fails to give a full and truthful answer so far as it lies within his knowledge, and this can include failure to disclose the precise nature of his interest in the shares.[88]

However, such a person must be given time not only to collect the information but to take legal advice to ensure that it is complete. In the case of UK residents the same day ought to suffice but two days would be needed for non-residents.[89]

The company, in turn, is obliged by section 213 to register the information received in response to an inquiry under section 212 including an indication of the fact and date of the requirement imposed by the company under section 212. Thus not only the company but the public has a right to know of the true owners of the shares.

Furthermore the company may be compelled to investigate and, under the power given in section 212, report on persons who hold the controlling interest in the company. This power of

[87] *Re Lonrho plc* (*No. 2*) (1988) 4 BCC 234.
[88] *Re TR Technology Trust plc* (1988) 4 BCC 244.
[89] *Lonrho plc* v. *Edelman* (1989) 5 BCC 68.

compulsion is provided by section 214 to a 10 per cent. minority of shareholders at the date of making the requisition provided they comply with the procedures laid down in the section, such as specifying the manner in which the company is to exercise its power and the giving of reasonable grounds for their request. There is, however, nothing to stop the members making the request, applying to the court if the company is slow in responding to a good request or to the Department of Trade and Industry in terms of sections 442–445; 454–457 and 732. Also if the company fails to comply with a valid requisition to exercise its powers of investigation then both it and every officer of it who is in default is liable to a fine specified in Schedule 24 to the Act. Likewise should any person validly[90] requested by the company fail to provide the requisite information in terms of section 212 he becomes subject to the penalties imposed by section 216. Under this provision the company can ask the court to impose restrictions set out in Part XV of the Act, including putting a stop on dividend payments to or the exercise of voting rights by that person.[91] Also persons who fail to comply or who knowingly or recklessly give false information are liable to imprisonment and/or a fine as shown in Schedule 24. But no offence justifying such an order or such other penalties would be committed if the person can prove that the notice seeking information is frivolous or vexatious.

The company is empowered by section 217 to remove out-of-date entries from the register of interests in shares which it is required to keep under section 211[92] if these entries are six years old and also if a person has ceased to be a member or it is that old and has been superseded by a later entry against the name of that person.

Section 217(2) imposes on the company the obligation to notify within 15 days any person whose name has been provided to it as a member and state what entries in consequence have been made against his name on the register of interests in shares and inform him of his right to apply to have the entry removed in accordance with the procedures in section 217. A person whose name appears in the registers of share interests as a party

[90] An invalid notice will have no effect: *Malaga Investments Ltd., Petitioners*, 1987 S.L.T. 603 (O.H.).
[91] See below.
[92] *Ante*, p. 251.

to an agreement to which section 204 applies and who ceases to be a party to that agreement may apply in writing to the company to record that fact (if satisfied) in every place where his name appears as a party to the agreement in the register. If a company refuses such a request the applicant may apply to the court for an order to remove the entry or to enter the fact that it is incorrect or that he has ceased to be a party to try such agreements. The company having removed any name from the register on request or under an order to do so must within 14 days make the necessary alterations to any associated index. Failure to comply with any of the obligations imposed by this section exposes the company and officers in default to a fine and a daily default fine for a continued contravention as set out in Schedule 24. According to section 218 the same applies where any deletion not authorised by section 217 occurs and in addition it requires the company to restore any improperly removed name to the register as soon as reasonably practicable.

Both the section 211 register of interests and the section 215 report on investigation must by virtue of section 210 be kept available for inspection without charge to members and non-members during business hours at either the company's registered office or the place where the register of members is kept. Again, failure to do so makes both company and any officer in default criminally liable and the court may by order compel an immediate inspection or order that a copy be sent to the person requiring it.

Restrictions for non-disclosure of interests in shares

If there is a breach of the compulsory notification provisions under sections 198 to 202[93] the Secretary of State may order that all or any of the restrictions set out in Part XV of the Act shall apply to those shares: section 209(5). Similarly if there is a failure to provide information as requested by a company under section 212[94] the company may go to court to ask for such restrictions to be imposed upon the shares: section 216.

Part XV of the Act contains sections 454 to 457. Under section 454 the restrictions are that:

[93] *Ante*, p. 246.
[94] *Ante*, p. 251.

(a) any purported transfer of the shares will be void;
(b) no voting rights exercised in respect of the shares;
(c) no further shares may be issued in respect of them (*e.g.* on a rights issue); and
(d) no dividends or other payments are to be made in respect of them.

Section 455 provides penalties for evasion or attempted evasion of the restrictions.

The restrictions may be lifted by the Secretary of State or the court as appropriate but only if either:

(i) the relevant facts about the shares have been disclosed and no unfair advantage has accrued to anyone as the result of non-disclosure[95]; or
(ii) the shares are transferred for valuable consideration, under a transfer approved or ordered by the court, in which case the court may pay the proceeds to those beneficially interested in the shares: sections 456, 457.

Under (ii) the transfer, *i.e.* a sale or exchange, must be approved by the court, it is not enough that the applicant is proposing to sell the shares at arms length. It is always a matter for the courts' discretion, but if the relevant facts have not been disclosed it is less likely to be exercised.[96]

Similarly in any case the question of costs is a matter for the court's discretion. In general the court will consider each party upon whom a notice has been served, or against whom an obligation has arisen, and ascertain whether that party has provided full information within its power and whether its default has caused or contributed to the costs incurred.[97]

Neither the court nor the Secretary of State has the power to make any qualified restrictions, they must either impose the full restrictions under section 454 or refuse to do so at all,[98] nor do they have the right to lift the restrictions otherwise than under section 456, even if innocent third parties become involved, *e.g.*

[95] See, *e.g. Re Ricardo Group plc* (1989) 5 BCC 388.
[96] *Re Geers Gross plc* [1987] 1 W.L.R. 837.
[97] *Re The Bestwood plc* (1989) 5 BCC 620; *Re Ricardo Group plc* (*No.2*) [1989] BCLC 766.
[98] *Lonrho plc* v. *Bond* (*No.* 2) (1989) 5 BCC 776.

if a take-over bid is being affected by it.[99] As a result of this the Secretary of State has taken the power to amend the share disclosure provisions and Part XV of the Act by regulations in order to allow for the protection of third parties, to allow the courts to make interim orders and to amend the rules as to the relaxation or removal of the various restrictions: section 135 Companies Act 1989.

Annual Return

Every company must make a return (called the annual return) to the registrar each year made up to a date not later than the company's "return date." That date is fixed initially at one year from the date of the company's incorporation, and subsequently it is one year from the date when the last return was made up. Because the only restriction is that an annual return must not be made up to a period of more than 12 months from the previous one, the return date may be brought forward so as to harmonise return dates within a group of companies. The return date concept, new under the 1989 Act, allows a "shuttle system" for annual returns. Under this system the registrar sends out a completed annual return based on last year's information to the company in advance of its return date. The company need only amend it, have it signed by a director or the secretary and return it to the registrar within 28 days of the return date. It is an offence for any director or officer of the company to fail to comply with these obligations: section 363.

The contents of the annual return for all companies are specified by section 364. The following information is required:

(a) address of the registered office;
(b) the type of company it is, according to a classification scheme laid down by the registrar;
(c) its principal business activities, according to a prescribed classification;
(d) the name and address of the company secretary (if that is a firm, the name and principal officer of the firm may be used, if it is a company it corporate name and registered office will suffice);

[99] It must be assumed that *Re Ricardo Group plc* (No. 2) [1989] BCLC 771 is wrongly decided.

(e) the name and address of all directors, including shadow directors[1];
(f) details of nationality, date of birth, business occupation, other directorships held and former names of all directors and shadow directors[1];
(g) details of corporate directors;
(h) location of the register of members[2] if it is not at the registered office;
(i) location of the register of debenture holders if it is not at the registered office; and
(j) notification of any election by a private company to dispense with the laying of accounts[3] or the holding of an annual general meeting.[4]

In addition, if the company has a share capital, section 364A requires the annual return to contain details of shares allotted or subscribed for, of each class of share, of current shareholders and those who have ceased to be shareholders since the previous return was made up, including details of as to which class of share is so held or has ceased to be held. Once a list of such shareholders has been given, subsequent returns need only specify any changes.

The required contents of an annual return can be amended by regulations made by the Secretary of State: section 365.

[1] *Post*, p. 347.
[2] *Ante*, p. 238.
[3] *Post*, Chap. 22.
[4] *Post*, p. 317.

Chapter 13

SHARES

A SHARE has been defined as "the interest of a shareholder in the company measured by a sum of money, for the purpose of liability in the first place, and of interest in the second, but also consisting of a series of mutual covenants entered into by all the shareholders *inter se* in accordance with [the Companies Act, s.14[1]]. The contract contained in the articles of association is one of the original incidents of the share."[2] The share is measured by a sum of money, namely, the nominal amount of the share, and also by the rights and obligations belonging to it as defined by the Companies Acts and by the memorandum and articles of the company. The undivided profits form an integral part of the shares to which they appertain.[3]

Each share in a company must be distinguished by its appropriate number, provided that it need not have a number if all the issued shares, or all the issued shares of a particular class, are fully paid up and rank *pari passu* for all purposes: section 182(2). Numbers are often dispensed with today under the proviso to section 182(2).

A share certificate, which specifies the shares held by the member and which is prima facie evidence of his title to the shares (section 186), is usually issued to a shareholder.

Shares in a company are personal[4] estate, transferable in the manner provided by the articles of the company: section 73.

A shareholder may borrow money on the security of his shares, *i.e.*, in England, he may give the lender a mortgage over

[1] *Ante*, p. 87.
[2] *Per* Farwell J. in *Borland's Trustee* v. *Steel Bros. & Co. Ltd.* [1901] 1 Ch. 279 at p. 288.
[3] *Carron Co.* v. *Hunter* (1868) 6 M. (H.L.) 106.
[4] The Scottish equivalent of "personal" is "moveable."

the shares to secure the payment of interest and repayment of the principal sum.[5]

Classes of Shares

A company is not bound to issue all its shares with the same rights but may confer different rights on different classes of shares. Such classes may be described as ordinary shares and preference shares but the name by which a class of shares is called gives only an indication of the rights attaching to it in any particular company, and to ascertain the rights reference must be made to the articles or the terms of issue of the shares.

Although the memorandum of association is required to set out the division of the nominal capital into shares of a fixed amount, it is not required to set out, and in practice it will not usually set out, the different classes of shares into which the capital is divided. However, the articles will normally give the company power to issue different classes of shares.

Table A, regulation 2, provides: "Subject to the provisions of the Act and without prejudice to any rights attached to any existing shares, any share may be issued with such rights or restrictions as the company may by ordinary resolution determine."

If there is no such provision in the articles, in the absence of a prohibition in the memorandum they may be altered by special resolution to give such a power.[6]

Where a company issues shares with rights which are not stated in its memorandum or articles or in any resolution or document to which section 380 applies, or varies the rights attached to shares otherwise than by amendment of its memorandum or articles or by resolution or document to which section 380 applies, section 128 requires the company to deliver particulars to the Registrar unless the shares are uniform with shares previously issued.

Preference shares

Preference shares are shares the issue of which was authorised by the memorandum or the articles and which are entitled to

[5] For assignation of shares in security in Scots law, see *post*, p. 298.

[6] *Andrews* v. *Gas Meter Co.* [1897] 1 Ch. 361 (C.A.), *ante*, p. 81; *cf. Liquidator of The Humboldt Redwood Co. Ltd.* v. *Coats*, 1908 S.C. 751, and *Crookston* v. *Lindsay, Crookston & Co. Ltd.*, 1922 S.L.T. 62 (O.H.).

some priority over the other shares in the company. They usually carry a right to preference in payment of dividend (if a dividend is declared) at a fixed rate, and a right to preference in the repayment of capital in a winding up. There may be several classes of preference shares, first, second and third, ranking one after the other.

The rights attached to preference shares are always a question of construction of the memorandum, the articles or the terms of issue of the shares. However, unless the articles, etc., otherwise provide, the rights which attach to preference shares are as described below. These prima facie rights differ according to whether the company is a going concern or in liquidation.

When the company is a going concern

1. When a right to a preferential dividend is given without more, it is a right to a *cumulative* dividend, *i.e.* if no preference dividend is declared in any year the arrears of dividend are carried forward and must be paid before a dividend is paid on the other shares.[7] If, however, the shares are declared to be non-cumulative preference shares, or the preferential dividend is to be paid out of the yearly profits,[8] or out of the net profits of each year,[9] the dividend will not be cumulative.

2. Preference shares are *non-participating*, *i.e.* they do not confer any right to a participaton in the surplus profits of the company, after payment of a specified rate of dividend on the ordinary shares, in the absence of anything to that effect in the articles, etc. Where a special resolution that the holders of preference shares were entitled to a cumulative preference dividend at the rate of 10 per cent. per annum and that such shares should rank, both as regards capital and dividend in priority to the other shares, the holders were only entitled to a 10 per cent. dividend in the distribution of profits—the provision defined the whole terms of the bargain between the shareholders and the company.[10] Sometimes, however, cumulative

[7] *Webb* v. *Earle* (1875) L.R. 20 Eq. 556; *Ferguson & Forrester Ltd.* v. *Buchanan*, 1920 S.C. 154. Interest is not payable on the arrears: *Partick etc. Gas Co. Ltd.* v. *Taylor* (1888) 15 R. 711.
[8] *Adair* v. *Old Bushmills Distillery* [1908] W.N. 24.
[9] *Staples* v. *Eastman Photographic Materials Co.* [1896] 2 Ch. 303 (C.A.); contrast *Miln* v. *Arizona Copper Co. Ltd.* (1899) 1 F. 935.
[10] *Will* v. *United Plantations Co. Ltd.* [1914] A.C. 11.

and participating preference shares are created, conferring a right to participate in surplus profits up to a fixed percentage, *e.g.* a right to a preferential dividend of seven per cent. may be given, together with a further right, after seven per cent. has been paid on the ordinary shares, to participate in the surplus profits equally with the ordinary shares until an additional seven per cent. has been paid, but no more.

3. Unless the articles, etc., otherwise provide, preference shares carry the *same voting rights* at general meetings as the other shares.[11] However if, as is common, the preference shareholders are expressly given a right to vote in certain specified circumstances, *e.g.* when there preference dividend is in arrears[12] or the rights attached to the preference shares are being varied, prima facie they have no right to vote in other circumstances.

The Jenkins Report recommended that holders of voteless preference shares should receive notices of general meetings and a copy of any chairman's statement which is circulated with the accounts. The majority of the Committee thought that the case for abolition of voteless shares had not been made out and rejected the suggestion that holders of voteless shares should be given a statutory right to attend and speak at the company meetings.

When the company is being wound up

1. In the absence of a provision in the articles, etc., arrears of cumulative preference dividend are not payable out of the assets in a liquidation, unless the dividend has been declared.[13] If, however, as is usual, the articles provide for the payment of arrears, such arrears are payable out of the surplus assets after payment of the company's debts, whether or not any undistributed profits are included in the assets.[14] If the articles

[11] See s.370(6), *post*, p. 332.

[12] Preference dividend is in arrears if it has not been paid even though that is because there are no available profits: *Re Bradford Investments plc* [1990] BCC 740.

[13] *Re Crichton's Oil Co.* [1902] 2 Ch. 86 (C.A.); *Re Catalinas Warehouses & Mole Co. Ltd.* [1947] 1 All E.R. 51; *Robertson-Durham* v. *Inches*, 1917, 1 S.L.T. 267 (O.H.).

[14] *Re Springbok Agricultural Estates Ltd.* [1920] 1 Ch. 563; *Re Wharfedale Brewery Co. Ltd.* [1952] Ch. 913. The rules as to the payment of dividends (*post*, Chap. 22) have no application to the surplus assets in a winding up.

provide only for payment of all arrears "due" at the date of winding up, no arrears will be payable unless dividends have been declared, because a dividend is not due until it has been declared.[15]

A provision that preference shares shall be entitled to "a fixed cumulative preferential dividend at the rate of x per cent. per annum . . . and . . . shall rank both as regards dividends and capital in priority to the ordinary shares, but shall not confer the right to any further participation in profits or assets," entitles the preference shareholders to receive arrears of dividends, although not declared, in priority to the repayment of capital to the ordinary shareholders—the early part of the provision applies to the state of affairs when the company is a going concern and the words "shall rank . . . as regards dividends . . . in priority to the ordinary shares" obviously apply in a winding up.[16] A similar provision omitting the word "preferential" and any reference to further participation in profits or assets confers no right to undeclared arrears of preference dividend in a winding up—it is not necessary to treat the words "shall rank . . . as regards dividends" as conferring priority in respect of arrears of cumulative preference dividend in a winding up, because there is no prior statement that the preference shareholders are to have a preference dividend.[17] A provision including the word "preferential" and merely omitting any reference to further participation in profits or assets also gives a right to arrears of preference dividend in a winding up in priority to the ordinary shares.[18]

2. Prima facie, preference shares have no priority in the repayment of capital in a winding up. However, such a right may be, and usually is, given by the articles, and its effect is that after the company's debts and liabilities, and any arrears of preference dividend which are payable, have been paid, the preference shareholders are entitled to repayment of their

[15] *Re Roberts and Cooper Ltd.* [1929] 2 Ch. 383.

[16] *Re Walter Symons Ltd.* [1934] Ch. 308; *Re F. de Jong & Co. Ltd.* [1946] Ch. 211 (C.A.).

[17] *Re Wood, Skinner & Co. Ltd.* [1944] Ch. 323; *Robertson-Durham* v. *Inches*, 1917, 1 S.L.T. 267 (O.H.). And see *Re William Bedford Ltd.* [1967] V.R. 490.

[18] *Re E. W. Savory Ltd.* [1951] 2 All E.R. 1036; *Re Wharfedale Brewery Co. Ltd.*, *ante*.

capital in full before the ordinary shareholders are repaid their capital.[19]

3. Where there are surplus assets available after the discharge of all the company's liabilities and the repayment of the capital to the shareholders, such surplus assets are divisible rateably among all classes of shareholders in the absence of any provision in the articles etc. to the contrary.[20] But, if, as is common, the articles set out the rights attached to a class of shares to participate in profits while the company is a going concern or to share in the property of the company in liquidation, prima facie those rights are exhaustive. Thus, articles giving preference shareholders priority in the repayment of capital in a liquidation but containing no reference to any further rights in the capital do not entitle the preference shareholders to participate in such surplus assets.[21]

The colliery assets of a coal mining company had been transferred to the National Coal Board under the Coal Industry Nationalisation Act 1946 and the company was to go into voluntary liquidation. Meanwhile the company proposed to reduce its capital by returning their capital to the holders of the preference stock. The articles provided that in the event of a winding up the preference stock ranked before the ordinary stock to the extent of repayment of the amounts, called up and paid thereon. *Held*, the proposed reduction was not unfair or inequitable. Even without it, the preference shareholders would not be entitled in a winding up to share in the surplus assets or to receive more than a return of their paid up capital. Accordingly, they could not object to being paid, by means of the reduction, the amount which they would receive in the proposed liquidation: *Wilsons and Clyde Coal Co. Ltd.* v. *Scottish Insurance Corpn. Ltd.*, 1949 S.C. (H.L.) 90; [1949] A.C. 462.

It follows from this decision that where the preference shareholders have priority as to repayment of capital on a winding up they should also be repaid first on a reduction of capital due to over-capitalisation,[22] and have no right to

[19] The preference shares were by the articles given priority in the return of capital in the cases cited in notes 16, 17, 18, *ante*.

[20] *Monkland Iron etc. Co. Ltd.* v. *Henderson* (1883) 10 R. 494; *Liquidators of Williamson-Buchanan Steamers Ltd., Petitioners*, 1936 S.L.T. 106 (O.H.); *Town and Gown Assocn. Ltd., Liquidator, Petitioner*, 1948 S.L.T. (Notes) 71 (O.H.).

[21] *Wilsons and Clyde Coal Co. Ltd.* v. *Scottish Insurance Corpn. Ltd.*, 1949 S.C. (H.L.) 90; 1948 S.C. 360; *Re The Isle of Thanet Electricity Supply Co. Ltd.* [1950] Ch. 161 (C.A.).

[22] *Ante*, p. 197.

complain about any variation of their class rights,[23] since it is in accord with their rights.[24]

If articles expressly give preference shareholders a right to share in surplus assets after the repayment of capital, they are entitled to share in accumulated profits in a liquidation even if the articles give the ordinary shareholders a right to exclusive enjoyment of accumulated profits not required for the preference dividend—the right of the ordinary shareholders depends on the appropriate resolutions being passed before a winding up.[25]

Preference shares contrasted with ordinary shares

Preference shares are more like debentures than like ordinary shares in that, if profits are available and if a dividend is declared on preference shares, it will be at a fixed rate just as debentures carry a fixed rate of interest (whether profits are available or not), whereas the rate of dividend on ordinary shares varies according to the amount of profits available.

Further, in the case of preference shares the right of the holders to vote at general meetings is usually restricted to when their special rights are being varied, or their dividend is in arrear,[26] and debentures normally confer no right to vote at general meetings, whereas ordinary shares usually confer a full right of voting.

The above may be said to be, at least in times of inflation when profits are high, the main disadvantages of preference shares. Another disadvantage is that in a prosperous business the preference shareholder is now regarded as a temporary member of the company, whose rights are limited to his preferential dividend and to priority in the return of capital on a winding up, and whose capital is liable to be returned to him whenever the company can raise the necessary money at a lower dividend rate.[27] The advantage of preference shares is that they are a safe investment. In particular, in a winding up, under

[23] *Post*, p. 265.
[24] *Re Saltdean Estate Co. Ltd.* [1968] 1 W.L.R. 1844; *House of Fraser plc* v. *A.C.G.E. Investments Ltd.* [1987] A.C. 387 (H.L.).
[25] *Dimbula Valley (Ceylon) Tea Co. Ltd.* v. *Laurie* [1961] Ch. 353.
[26] *Ante*, p. 261.
[27] *Ante*, p. 192.

normal articles the preference capital is repayable after payment of the company's debts and before the ordinary capital is returned.

Variation of class rights

1. Where a company's shares are divided into classes, "class rights" are special rights of a class of shares, *e.g.* a preferential right as to dividend attached to preference shares where a company's shares are divided into preference shares and ordinary shares.

It has been said that the term "class" must be confined to those persons whose rights are not so dissimilar as to make it impossible for them to consult together with a view to their common interest.[28]

Section 125 applies to alterations governing the rights attaching to any class of shares in a company whose share capital is divided into shares of different classes.[29] It has been held in one case that it is not necessary for those rights to be attached to particular types of shares as long as they are given to a class of members in their capacity as members or shareholders, *e.g.* a right of pre-emption over other shares. For the purposes of section 125 therefor the share capital of a company is to be regarded as being divided into different classes, if shareholders, *qua* shareholders enjoy different rights. It follows that the shares could come into or go out of a particular class on their acquisition or disposal by a particular individual.[30]

Class rights are usually given to preference shareholders and if the articles give the *ordinary* shareholders a right to the distributed profits after payment of a dividend on the preference shares, and a right to surplus assets on a liquidation, these are *not* class rights—they are no more than would be implied if the

[28] *Per* Bowen L.J. in *Sovereign Life Assurance Co.* v. *Dodd* [1892] 2 Q.B. 573 (C.A.) at p. 583. (This case concerned the forerunner of s.425, *post*, Chap. 30. An arrangement was made between a company in course of being wound up and its creditors. Insured persons whose policies had matured formed a distinct class of creditors from those whose policies had not.) See also *Re Hellenic and General Trust Ltd.* [1979] 1 W.L.R. 123.

[29] See *post.*

[30] *Cumbrian Newspaper Group Ltd.* v. *Cumberland & Westmorland Newspaper and Printing Co. Ltd.* [1987] Ch. 1.

articles did not refer to them.[31] However, it seems that the original ordinary shares in *Greenhalgh* v. *Arderne Cinemas*,[32] *post*, formed a class of shares within the meaning of an article providing for variation of the rights attached to a class of shares. Again, in *Lord St. David's* v. *Union-Castle Mail Steamship Co. Ltd.*,[33] where under the articles the large number of preference shares carried a right to vote when the preference dividend was in arrears and, such dividend being in arrears, the preference shareholders proposed to alter the articles so as to give themselves a right to vote on all resolutions, it was held that the proposed resolution would not affect the rights of the small number of ordinary shares unless the ordinary shareholders approved in accordance with an article providing for variation of class rights, *i.e.* class rights were attached to the ordinary shares.[34]

Class rights may be attached to a class of shares by the memorandum or the articles of the company, or by the terms of issue of the shares, or by a special resolution of the company in general meeting as in *Re Old Silkstone Collieries Ltd.*[35] They are usually concerend with voting, dividend, and the distribution of assets in the event of the company's being wound up but if the wider definition in the *Cumbrian Newspapers*[36] case is adopted they will be much wider than that.

2. If class rights are set out in the memorandum, or incorporated therein by reference to the articles,[37] they are only alterable if all the members of the company agree[38] unless the memorandum itself provides a method of alteration which must be complied with, or a method of alteration is provided by articles which were included at the time of the original incorporation of the company,[39] or the consent of the court is obtained to a scheme of arrangement under section 425.[40]

[31] *Hodge* v. *James Howell & Co.*, *The Times*, December 13, 1958 (C.A.).
[32] [1946] 1 All E.R. 512 (C.A.).
[33] *The Times*, November 24, 1934.
[34] See too, *Rights and Issues Investment Trust Ltd.* v. *Stylo Shoes Ltd.* [1965] Ch. 250, *ante*, p. 95.
[35] [1954] Ch. 169, *ante*, p. 198.
[36] *Ante*, p. 265.
[37] *Dimbula Valley (Ceylon) Tea Co. Ltd.* v. *Laurie* [1961] Ch. 353.
[38] s.125(5).
[39] s.125(4).
[40] *Post*, Chap. 30.

An alteration by a method provided by the memorandum will probably be subject to section 127, *post.* If the proposed variation relates to the authority to issue shares[41] or a reduction of capital,[42] the specified majority will be three quarters whatever the procedure provided by the memorandum or articles might say: section 125(3).

Any meeting held to vary the class rights must comply with the Act as to notice and conduct of meetings with a minimum quorum of the holders of at least one third of the nominal value of the class being at least two in number: section 125(6).

Under section 425 a company may make a binding compromise or arrangement with a class of members. Application must be made to the court to order a meeting of the class. Then the compromise or arrangement must be approved at the meeting by a simple majority in number representing three-fourths in value of those voting in person or by proxy. Finally, the court must approve it.

The power to alter the memorandum conferred by section 17[43] does not authorise any variation or abrogation of the special rights of any class of members.

3. The rights of different classes of shares are usually set out in the articles and the articles often provide for the variation of class rights. In any event the Act now implies such a variation procedure.

If the articles attach class rights to a class of shares and contain a "modification of rights clause" the class rights may in general be varied, with the consent of the specified proportion or resolution of the holders of shares of the class, by a valid alteration of the articles by a special resolution of the company in general meeting.[44] In two cases, *viz.* a variation relating to the directors' powers to issue shares[45] and one connected with a reduction of capital,[46] the required majority is three quarters whatever the articles may say: section 125(3).

Such modification of rights classes must be complied with: section 125(4). Any meeting held must comply with the Act as

[41] *Ante*, p. 164.
[42] *Ante*, p. 192.
[43] *Ante*, p. 83.
[44] *Ante*, p. 90.
[45] *Ante*, p. 164.
[46] *Ante*, p. 192.

to the notice and conduct of meetings with a minimum quorum of the holders of at least one third in nominal value of the class being at least two in number: section 125(6).

If the articles do not set out a modification of rights clause, the rights can nevertheless be varied either by the written consent of the holders of three quarters of the issued shares of that class or by an extraordinary resolution to that effect passed at a separate meeting of that class: section 125(2). Again the meetings provisions in the Act must be complied with: section 125(6). This implied procedure may eventually replace express clauses—Table A no longer contains one.[47]

There is no effective compliance with a modification of class rights unless those holding a sufficient majority of the shares of the class vote in favour of the modification in the bona fide belief that they are acting in the interests of the general body of members of the class, *i.e.* at the class meeting the majority shareholders must consider what is best for the shareholders as a class, not what is best in their own interests.

A reduction of capital was to be effected by cancelling the five per cent. £1 cumulative preference shares and allotting the holders an equivalent amount of six per cent. unsecured loan stock repayable 1985/90. The majority of the preference shareholders, who supported the reduction, were also holders of 52 per cent. of the company's ordinary stock and non-voting ordinary shares. Minority preference shareholders opposed the reduction. The court refused to confirm it. The majority preference shareholders had considered what was best in their own interests, based on their large equity shareholding, without considering what was best for preference shareholders as a class. Further, the reduction was unfair[48]—the advantages of the exchange into unsecured stock did not compensate for the disadvantages: *Re Holders Investment Trust Ltd.* [1971] 1 W.L.R. 582.

4. Where there is in the articles (or the memorandum) an express or implied power to vary class rights, the exercise of the power is subject to section 127. This section provides that if, in the case of a company with a share capital divided into different classes of shares, provision is made by the articles (or memorandum) for the variation or abrogation of the rights attached to any class of shares, subject to the consent of a

[47] This implemented para. 198 of the Jenkins Committee Report.
[48] *Ante*, p. 196.

specified proportion of the holders of the shares of the class or the sanction of a resolution passed at a separate meeting of the holders of such shares, and in pursuance of such provision the rights attached to any such class of shares are varied, an application can be made to the court to have the variation cancelled, whereupon it has no effect unless and until it is confirmed by the court. The section also applies to variations under the procedure implied by section 125(2); section 127(1)(*b*).

Those who can apply are the holders of not less than 15 per cent. of the issued shares of the class who did not consent to or vote for the variation. The application must be made within 21 days after the giving of the consent or the passing of the resolution. In England it is made by petition by one or more of the dissenting shareholders authorised in writing by the 15 per cent.: R.S.C., Ord. 102, r. 5. For Scotland, see R.C. 189.

The court may disallow the variation if, after hearing the various parties interested, it is satisfied that the variation would unfairly prejudice the shareholders of the class in question. If the court is not so satisfied it must confirm the variation.

The Company must, within 15 days, send a copy of the order made by the court to the Registrar of Companies: section 127(5).

The object of the section is to protect shareholders from being prejudiced by the voting of other shareholders who hold shares of another class in addition to those of the class affected by the variation.

For example, if a variation reduces the dividend on preference shares from seven per cent. to six per cent. per annum, and 80 per cent. of the preference shareholders are also ordinary shareholders, the requisite consent of the preference shareholders is likely to be obtained, since the variation will leave more profits for a dividend on the ordinary shares. This would be unfair to the 20 per cent. of the preference shareholders who are not ordinary shareholders and they could apply under section 127.

A variation of class rights, includes an abrogation of those rights: section 125(8).[49] However it has been held that class

[49] Preference shareholders rights are not abrogated by being repaid first on a reduction of capital: *House of Fraser plc* v. *A.C.G.E. Investments plc* [1987] A.C. 387, doubting *Frazer Brothers Ltd., Petitioners*, 1963 S.C. 139.

rights are *not* "varied" by the subdivision of other shares, under a power in the articles, which results in the holders of the shares with the class rights being outvoted by the holders of the other shares.

2s. ordinary shares, as regards voting, ranked *pari passu* with the 10s. ordinary shares. Each 10s. share was sub-divided into five 2s. ordinary shares. *held*, the voting rights of the original 2s. shares had not been varied. The only voting right attached to that class was one vote per share, and that right remained: *Greenhalgh* v. *Arderne Cinemas Ltd.* [1946] 1 All E.R. 512 (C.A.).[50]

Again, class rights are *not* "affected" by the creation or issue of new shares of the class ranking equally with the old.

Capital was being increased by the issue of 660,000 £1 preference shares ranking *pari passu* with the existing 600,000 £1 preference stock, and 2,640,000 ordinary shares of 10s. each ranking *pari passu* with the existing £3,300,00 ordinary stock. The new shares were to be issued to the ordinary stockholders and paid for out of the reserve fund. *Held*, the proposed issue of new capital did not "affect" the rights of the existing preference shareholders. Only the enjoyment of the rights was affected, the rights themselves were not: *White* v. *Bristol Aeroplane Co. Ltd.* [1953] Ch. 65 (C.A.).[51]

A modification of rights clause in the articles cannot be altered by special resolution without the appropriate consent of shareholders of the class under that procedure: section 125(7).

Deferred shares

Deferred shares, which are sometimes called founders or management shares, are usually of small nominal amount with a right to take the whole or a proportion of the profits after a fixed dividend has been paid on the ordinary shares. The rights of the holders of deferred shares depend on the articles or the terms of issue.

Deferred shares are rarely issued now and the modern tendency is to convert existing deferred shares into ordinary shares.

[50] And see the *Dimbula* case, *ante*, p. 266.

[51] And see *Re John Smith's Tadcaster Brewery Co. Ltd.* [1953] Ch. 308.

Non-voting ordinary shares

In recent years some companies have issued non-voting ordinary shares. The purpose of such issues is to enable the companies concerned to raise money and at the same time enable those with the majority of the existing voting shares to retain control. However, with the idea of ensuring that the public is not misled, the Stock Exchange requires non-voting shares to be designated as such.[52] This is usually done by describing the shares as A Ordinary shares, etc.

The Jenkins Report[53] recommended that holders of voteless equity[54] shares should receive notices of general meetings and a copy of any chairman's statement which is circulated with the accounts.

No par value shares

The memorandum of a limited company with a share capital must state the amount of share capital with which the company proposes to be registered and its division into shares of a fixed amount (s.2(5)(*a*)), and any provision in the memorandum or articles, or in any resolution, of a company limited by guarantee purporting to divide the undertaking into shares or interests is treated as a provision for a share capital, notwithstanding that the nominal amount or number of the shares or interests is not specified thereby (s.15(2)). The requirement that the nominal share capital must be divided into shares of a fixed amount means that *shares of no par value cannot be issued.*

Such shares would not give rise to the misleading impression which is often created by the nominal or par value of shares. After a company has been in existence for any length of time, the nominal value of the shares rarely bears any relation to the real value, and so gives no assistance to investors or creditors. For example, after some years, a share of a nominal amount of £1 issued at a price of £1 may be worth £2. Further, if dividends are expressed as a percentage of the nominal value of such share, where the real return is, say, six per cent. on the market

[52] Admission of Securities to Listing, page 9.04.
[53] Para. 140.
[54] *i.e.* ordinary and not preference shares.

value of the share, the dividend will be expressed as 12 per cent. of the nominal value, and this may give rise to the mistaken impression that the dividend is excessive.

The Report of the majority of the Gedge Committee[55] recommended that companies should be able to issue ordinary shares of no par value if they wished, and the Jenkins Report[56] recommended[57] the amendment of the Companies Act to allow the issue of preference and ordinary shares of no par value, but, as yet, effect has not been given to these recommendations. Shares of no par value can be issued in a number of countries, including the U.S.A.

Employees' shares

Some companies issue special shares to their employees. Modern tax legislation, however, in general only provides tax incentives for companies who provide their employees with ordinary shares, *i.e.* those not specifically available only to employees.

SHARE CERTIFICATES

Every company must complete the share certificates and have them ready for delivery within two months[58] after the allotment of any of its shares or after the date on which a transfer of its shares is lodged for registration, unless the conditions of issue otherwise provide, under a penalty of a default fine: section 185. The form of the certificate is governed by the articles. Table A, regulation 6, gives the right to a certificate without payment and provides that it shall be under the seal of the company,[59] and shall specify the shares to which it relates and the amount paid up thereon. If a quotation on the Stock Exchange is desired, the certificate must also have a footnote to the effect that no transfer will be registered without production of the share certificate.[60]

[55] (1954) Cmd. 9112.
[56] (1962) Cmnd. 1749.
[57] Para. 34.
[58] Fourteen days if the shares are quoted on the Stock Exchange: Admission of Securities to Listing, page 5.31.
[59] This can include the official seal for this purpose authorised under s.40.
[60] Admission of Securities to Listing, page 9.13.

If shares, debentures or debenture stock are allotted to a stock exchange nominee (SEPON Ltd.), or a transfer of shares, debentures or debenture stock to a stock exchange nominee is lodged with the company, the company is exempt from the obligation to prepare certificates under section 185: section 185(4). This is to facilitate the computerised system of transfers on the stock exchange.[61]

The certificate is a formal statement by the company under its common seal if it has one, or its official seal under section 40, or is otherwise signed in accordance with section 36A or 36B,[62] that the person named therein is the holder of the number of shares in the company specified in the certificate. It is prima facie evidence of the title of that person to the shares: section 186.[63] It is not, however, a document of title (as the register of members is).[64] The object of the certificate is to facilitate dealings with the shares, whether by way of sale or security, and so make them more valuable to their owner. On the other hand, a share certificate is not a negotiable instrument, so that its accidental loss or destruction is not a matter of great moment. The articles usually make provision for the granting of a new certificate in such a case.

Table A, regulation 7, provides: "If a share certificate is defaced, worn out, lost or destroyed, it may be renewed on such terms (if any) as to evidence and indemnity and payment of the expenses reasonably incurred by the company in investigating evidence as the directors may determine but otherwise free of charge, and (in the case of defacement or wearing out) on delivery up of the old certificate."

In England a share certificate is not a deed for the purposes of the Law of Property Act 1925, s.74,[65] which might otherwise validate it.[66]

[61] For future paperless transactions on the Stock Exchange, see s.207 C.A. 1989, *post*, p. 288.
[62] *Ante*, p. 111.
[63] See, *e.g.* *Woodhouse & Rawson Ltd.* v. *Hosack* (1894) 2 S.L.T. 279 (O.H.).
[64] *Ante*, p. 238.
[65] *Per* Clauson J. in *South London Greyhound Racecourses Ltd.* v. *Wake* [1931] 1 Ch. 496, at p. 503. *Quaere* whether it is a deed for the purposes of s.36A, *ante*, p. 111.
[66] If attested in the presence of a director and secretary.

Estoppel[67] as to statements in a certificate

The issue of a share certificate may give rise to an estoppel against the company. The company cannot deny the truth of the certificate against a person who has relied on the certificate and in consequence has changed his position.

T., the registered holder of shares, left the share certificate with her broker. T.'s signature was forged to a transfer in favour of S., T. did not reply to notice of the transfer sent to her by the company and a new certificate in the name of S. was issued by the company. A. bought from S. and paid for the shares on delivery of the share certificate and a new share certificate was issued to A. The fraud was subsequently discovered and T.'s name was restored to the register. *Held*, the company was liable to indemnify A. The giving of the certificate to S. amounted to a statement by the company, intended to be acted upon by purchasers of shares in the market, that S. was entitled to the shares, and A. having acted on the statement, the company was estopped from denying it. A. was entitled to recover from the company as damages the value of the shares at the time when the company first refused to recognise him as a shareholder, with interest: *Re Bahia and San Francisco Rlwy. Co* (1868) L.R. 3 Q.B. 584.

There is no estoppel in favour of a person, such as S. in the above case, who procures the granting of a certificate on a forged transfer[68] or forged power of attorney,[69] even if he has acted in good faith. In fact the company may be able to claim an indemnity from such a person.[70]

The company may be estopped from denying the title to shares of the person to whom it has issued a share certificate.[71]

D. bought 30 shares through a broker, L., who was also secretary of the company, and paid L. She received and returned to L. a transfer of shares executed to L.'s direction by his clerk, P., who was never a man of substance and who did not hold any shares. The transfer, which did not specify the numbers of the shares, was put before the board by L. and passed without production of P.'s certificate being required, and a new certificate prepared by L. was issued to the effect that D. held 30

[67] Personal bar is the Scottish equivalent of "estoppel." See Lord Kyllachy (Ordinary) in *Clavering, Son & Co.* v. *Goodwins, Jardine & Co. Ltd.* (1891) 18 R. 652 at p. 657.

[68] *Sheffield Corporation* v. *Barclay* [1905] A.C. 392, *post*, p. 293.

[69] *Starkey* v. *Bank of England* [1903] A.C. 114.

[70] *Post*, p. 294.

[71] *Balkis Consolidated Co. Ltd.* v. *Tomkinson* [1893] A.C. 396.

shares, numbers 115–144 inclusive. The chairman, who did not sign the certificate, did not notice that the shares were part of his holding (numbers 1–333). The board properly relied on the secretary to check transfers and certificates with the register. Two years later the board notified D. that P.'s transfer was invalid and declined to recognise her as a shareholder. L. was bankrupt by then and the company could not prove that he could not have reimbursed D. if, when the certificate was issued, the company had refused to issue it. *Held*, D. was entitled to damages: *Dixon* v. *Kennaway & Co.* [1900] 1 Ch. 833.

The company may be estopped from denying the amount stated to be paid up on shares.

B. lent money to a company on the security of fully paid shares in the company and was handed by the company share certificates for 10,000 shares of £1 each which the certificates stated to be fully paid up. No money had been paid on the shares, which had been issued direct by the company to B., but B. did not know this. On the company's going into liquidation, B. was placed on the list of contributories in respect of these shares. *Held*, the company was estopped by the certificate from denying that the shares were fully paid up and B. was entitled to have his name removed from the list of contributories: *Bloomenthal* v. *Ford* [1897] A.C. 156.[72]

The company may be made liable in damages to the person who has relied on the statement in the share certificate.[73]

If B., in the *Bloomenthal* case, had known that the shares were not fully paid up, there would have been no estoppel—there is no estoppel in favour of a person who knows the untruth of statements in a share certificate.[74] An original allottee, therefore, will seldom be in a position to benefit from the principle.[75]

The company is not estopped where a certificate is a forgery.[76]

[72] *Cf. Waterhouse* v. *Jamieson* (1870) 8 M. (H.L.) 88, in which it was held that statements in the memorandum and articles, which also appeared in share certificates, as to the amount paid up on shares could not be contradicted by the liquidator.

[73] *Clavering, Son & Co.* v. *Goodwins, Jardine & Co. Ltd.* (1891) 18 R. 652.

[74] See *Crickmer's Case* (1875) L.R. 10. Ch.App. 614. In England, if the shares had been transferred to a purchaser without notice that they were not fully paid up he could give a good title to a purchaser from him with or without notice: *Barrow's Case* (1880) 14 Ch.D. 432 (C.A.).

[75] *Liquidator of Scottish Heritages Co. Ltd.* (1898) 5 S.L.T. 336 (O.H.): contrast *Penang Foundry Co. Ltd.* v. *Gardiner*, 1913 S.C. 1203 (O.H.).

[76] See note 71, *ante*.

R. lent money to the secretary of a company for his own purposes on the security of a share certificate issued to R. by the secretary and certifying that R. was registered as transferee of the shares. The secretary issued the share certificate without authority, affixed the common seal and forged the signatures of two directors, so that the certificate apparently complied with the articles. R. sued the company for damages for refusal to register him. *Held*, in the absence of evidence that the company had held out the secretary as having authority to do more than the mere ministerial act of delivering share certificates, when duly made, to those entitled to them, the company was not estopped from disputing the claim or responsible for the secretary's act: *Ruben* v.*Great Fingall Consolidated* [1906] A.C. 439.

Transfer of Shares

There is a distinction between a transfer of shares and a transmission of shares. A transfer is by the act of the member, while a transmisson occurs by operation of law on the death or the bankruptcy of a member.[77] The procedure on transfer is set out below,[78] but there must be a valid agreement of transfer, either by gift or contract. In *Harvela Investments Ltd.* v. *Royal Trust Company of Canada* (*C.I.*) *Ltd.*[79] the House of Lords held that the holder of shares in a private company could not validly invite other parties to submit sealed bids for those shares and then accept a bid which is referential, *i.e.* one which is given as an amount above that submitted by the other bidder. If such bids were allowed one party could not lose and the other party could not win.

Restrictions on transfer

Every shareholder has a right to transfer his shares to whom he likes, unless the articles provide to the contrary.[80]

By the Companies Acts "it is provided that the shares in a company under these Acts shall be capable of being transferred in manner provided by the regulations of the company. The regulations of the

[77] *Post*, p. 294.
[78] *Post*, p. 285.
[79] [1986] A.C. 207 (H.L.).
[80] *Weston's Case* (1868) L.R. 4 Ch.App. 20: *O'Meara* v. *The El Palmar Rubber Estates Ltd.*, 1913, 1 S.L.T. 383 (O.H.). It is otherwise, *e.g.* where the company is being wound up and a transfer is prevented by I.A. 1986, s.127, *post*, Chap. 29.

company may impose fetters upon the right of transfer. In the absence of restrictions in the articles the shareholder has by virtue of the statute the right to transfer his shares without the consent of anybody to any transferee, even though he be a man of straw, provided it is a bona fide transaction in the sense that it is an out-and-out disposal of the property without retaining any interest in the shares—that the transferor bona fide divests himself of all benefit. . . . In the absence of restrictions it is competent to a transferor, notwithstanding that the company is *in extremis* to compel registration of a transfer to a transferee notwithstanding that the latter is a person not competent to meet the unpaid liability upon the shares. Even if the transfer be executed for the express purpose of relieving the transferor from liability, the directors cannot upon that ground refuse to register it unless there is in the articles some provision so enabling them": *per* Buckley L.J. in *Lindlar's Case* [1910] 1 Ch. 312 (C.A.) at p. 316.[81]

An article providing that on the bankruptcy of a member he shall sell his shares to particular persons at a particular price, which is fixed for all persons alike and is not shown to be an unfair price, is valid.[82] So, too, is an article providing that on the death of a member his shares must be offered to "the other members" at par, even though there is only one surviving member.[83]

In the case of a private company, the articles may, and usually do, restrict the right to transfer its shares.[84] In the case of a public company, shares must normally be free from restrictions on the right of transfer if a stock exchange quotation is to be obtained.[85]

Any restrictions on the transfer of shares are a derogation from the common law right of free transfer. It follows that: any rights conferred by the articles will not be extended to situations not covered by them[86]; the procedure laid down in the articles

[81] For Scottish authority to the same effect, see, *e.g.* Lord Kincairney (Ordinary) in *Stewart* v. *James Keiller & Sons Ltd.* (1902) 4 F. 657 at p. 667.

[82] *Borland's Trustee* v. *Steel Bros. & Co. Ltd.* [1901] 1 Ch. 279.

[83] *Jarvis Motors (Harrow) Ltd.* v. *Carabott* [1964] 1 W.L.R. 1101, where one of the two members of a company, who each held half of the shares, died, and the executors of the deceased had to offer his shares at par to the surviving member.

[84] Until the 1980 Act such restrictions were obligatory for private companies: *ante*, p. 45. The restriction on the transfer of shares in a private company is one reason why such shares are not dealt in on stock exchanges.

[85] Admission of Securities to Listing, page 9.01. The main advantage of a stock exchange quotation is that it makes the securities more marketable.

[86] *Furness & Co.* v. *Liquidators of "Cynthiana" Steamship Co. Ltd.* (1893) 21 R. 239.

for the exercise of the rights must be strictly followed[87]; and if the rights are not actively exercised the right of free transfer will revive.[88]

If there has been a registered transfer in breach of the articles the only remedy available to an aggrieved shareholder is rectification of the register. This is a discretionary remedy, however, and will not be granted to third parties for extraneous purposes.[89]

Such restrictions usually fall within one of two categories: pre-emption clauses and refusal clauses.

Pre-emption clauses

The articles of a private company usually contain a pre-emption clause, *e.g.* to the effect that no shares shall be transferred to any person not a member of the company so long as a member can be found to purchase them at a fair price to be determined in accordance with the articles.[90] Such a pre-emption clause does not entitle the company to refuse to register a transfer of shares from one member to another member of the company.[91] Where the value of shares for the purpose of such a clause falls to be fixed by the directors, the court will not review the directors' valuation provided that they have acted fairly and honestly.[92]

Sometimes the articles provide that a member desiring to sell any of his shares must inform the directors of the number of shares, the price and the name of the proposed transferee, and the directors must first offer the shares at that price to the other shareholders. In such a case, any member to whom the shares are offered cannot buy part only of the shares, and if none of the members is willing to buy all the shares the proposed transfer can be carried out.[93]

[87] *Neilson* v. *Ayr Race Meetings Syndicate Ltd.*, 1918, 1 S.L.T. 63 (O.H.).
[88] *Shepherd's Trustees* v. *Shepherd*, 1950 S.C. (H.L.) 60 (application for registration granted, the two directors having failed to agree to refuse registration).
[89] *Re Piccadilly Radio plc* [1988] BCLC 683. For rectification of the register, see p. 241, *ante*.
[90] *Post*, p. 314.
[91] *Delavenne* v. *Broadhurst* [1931] Ch. 234.
[92] *Stewart* v. *James Keiller & Sons Ltd.* (1902) 4 F. 657.
[93] *The Ocean Coal Co. Ltd.* v. *The Powell Duffryn Steam Coal Co. Ltd.* [1932] 1 Ch. 654.

A member whose shares have been offered to other members under a pre-emption clause has been held entitled to withdraw his offer at any time before its acceptance.[94]

Articles provided that no transfer of shares should take place so long as any other shareholder was willing to purchase at a price to be ascertained by agreement between the intending transferor and the directors, or, failing agreement, at a price to be fixed by the auditors, and that any shareholder who was "desirous of transferring" his shares should inform the secretary of the number of shares which he desired to transfer. *Held*, shareholders who, on a take-over bid accepted an outside offer to buy their shares, received the price, gave the purchaser general proxies, and agreed to execute transfers and deliver up the share certificates when called upon to do so, were "desirous of transferring" their shares and had to comply with the pre-emption clause, unless they gave notice that they had changed their minds before the other shareholders exercised their pre-emption rights: *Lyle & Scott Ltd.* v. *Scott's Trustees*, 1959 S.C. (H.L.) 64; [1959] A.C. 763. Such a dispute between the company and its members has been distinguished from a case involving a third party: *Williams* v. *MacPherson*, 1990 S.L.T. 279 (O.H.).

Many pre-emption clauses provide a machinery whereby the shares may be offered to the existing members, *e.g* by making the company secretary agent for their sale. In *Tett* v. *Phoenix Property and Investment Co.*[95] the articles simply provided that there should be no transfer if any member indicated that he was willing to purchase the shares. The Court of Appeal, reversing Vinelott J., implied a term into the articles requiring a transferor to take reasonable steps to give the other members a reasonable opportunity to offer to purchase the shares at a fair value. Strictly speaking such a clause is not a pre-emption clause since it simply forbids a transfer to outsiders where a member has indicated his willingness to buy.

Pre-emption clauses on the other hand do not prevent a shareholder declaring himself a trustee for a proposed transferee, or even on death allowing the executors to hold the shares on trust for a beneficiary. Unless the pre-emption clause expressly applies to such situations the other shareholders may not invoke it. There is no transfer upon which it can operate. It

[94] *J. M. Smith Ltd.* v. *Colquhoun's Trustee* (1901) 3 F. 981.
[95] [1986] BCLC 149 (C.A.).

may be different if the shareholder also gives the beneficiary an irrevocable proxy to vote with the shares.[96] In *Theakston* v. *London Trust plc* [1984] BCLC 390, one member agreed to sell his shares to another member but in fact the purchase price was paid by a non-member, in whose name the shares were charged and according to whose directions the "purchaser" was to vote. Harman J. held that this was a transfer from one member to another and so outside the pre-emption clause. The fact that the transferee had equitable obligations to an outsider did not affect that position.

If the provision in the articles relating to the offer of the shares to the existing shareholders before a transfer is made is disregarded, the directors cannot validly register the transfer since it is a transfer in breach of the articles.[97] In England the same is true in the case of a sale, in disregard of the articles, by a mortgagee under his power of sale.[98] However, a transfer by a shareholder, in breach of the pre-emptive rights given by the articles, to a person who has paid for the shares operates as a transfer of the *beneficial interest* in the shares, so that the transferee takes priority over a judgment creditor who subsequently obtains a charging order[99] on the shares.[1] There must be substantial compliance with the pre-emption procedure before a transfer outside its terms can be effective. If there is no such compliance the court can award an injunction to prevent such transfer.[2]

Articles may provide that the other members are bound to buy the shares of a member who wishes to transfer them.[3]

[96] *Safeguard Industrial Investments Ltd.* v. *National Westminster Bank Ltd.* [1982] 1 All E.R. 449 (C.A.).

[97] *Tett* v. *Phoenix Property and Investment Co. Ltd.* [1986] BCLC 149 (C.A.).

[98] *Hunter* v. *Hunter* [1936] A.C. 222.

[99] *Post*, p. 298.

[1] *Hawks* v. *McArthur* [1951] 1 All E.R. 22. In *Tett* v. *Phoenix Investment and Property Co. Ltd. supra*, Vinelott J. upheld *Hawks* v. *McArthur* and rejected any general argument to the contrary based on *Hunter* v. *Hunter, supra.* This part of his judgment was not challenged in the Court of Appeal.

Similarly, in Scotland, in a competition between a transferee and an arrester, the arrester was held not to be entitled to found on an alleged failure on the part of the company to observe the proper procedure relating to pre-emption and registration of transfers, with the result that the court declared that the shares had vested in the transferee: *National Bank of Scotland Glasgow Nominees Ltd.* v. *Adamson*, 1932 S.L.T. 492 (O.H.).

[2] *Curtis* v. *J. J. Curtis & Co. Ltd.* [1986] BCLC 86 (N.Z.).

[3] *Rayfield* v. *Hands* [1960] Ch. 1, *ante*, p. 89.

It has also been held that a company enforcing a power of sale under a lien on its own shares must itself comply with the pre-emption clause in its articles in effecting that sale: *Champagne Perrier-Jouet S.A.* v. *H. H. Finch Ltd.*[4]

Note what is said later as to the duty of care owed by an auditor who values shares in the knowledge that his valuation will determine the price to be paid under a contract.[5]

Directors' power to refuse transfers

In addition to containing a pre-emption clause, the articles of a private company usually contain an article that the directors may, in their absolute discretion and without assigning any reason therefor, refuse to register any transfer of any share. If the shares are transferred in breach of the pre-emption clause then the directors have no power to register the transfer—no question of discretion arises.[6] In other cases, if the directors refuse to register a transfer the court will not interfere unless it can be shown that the directors are exercising their discretion improperly.[7]

When directors have power to decline to register a transfer, whether their power is absolute or limited to certain specified grounds, they need not disclose their reasons for refusing registration and if, having considered the questions, they refuse registration without giving any reasons, their refusal cannot be questioned unless there is evidence (which will be hard to come by) that they have not acted in good faith.[8]

The directors' discretionary power is a fiduciary power and must be exercised in good faith, *i.e.* legitimately for the purpose for which it is conferred. In exercising it the directors must act in good faith in the interest of the company and with due regard to the shareholder's right to transfer his shares, and they must fairly consider the question at a board meeting.[9]

[4] [1982] 1 W.L.R. 1359.
[5] *Post*, p. 314.
[6] *Tett* v. *Phoenix Property and Investment Co. Ltd.* [1986] BCLC 149 (C.A.).
[7] See *Stewart* v. *James Keiller & Sons Ltd.* (1902) 4 F. 657.
[8] *Re Coalport China Co.* [1895] 2 Ch. 404; *Kennedy* v. *North British Wireless Schools Ltd.*, 1916, 1 S.L.T. 407; 1915, 1 S.L.T. 196 (O.H.).
[9] *Per* Chitty J. in *Re Bell Bros. Ltd.* (1891) 65 L.T. 245 at p. 245, and *per* Lawton L.J. in *Heron International Ltd.* v. *Lord Grade* [1983] BCLC 244 at p. 265; and see also Lord Trayner in *Stewart* v. *James Keiller & Sons Ltd.* (1902) 4 F. 657 at p. 678.

Articles gave the directors "an absolute and uncontrolled discretion" to refuse to register any transfer of shares. The two directors each held 4,001 of the 8,002 ordinary shares. F. died and his son, as the executor, applied for the shares to be registered in his name, S. refused, but offered to register 2,001 shares if 2,000 were sold to him at a fixed price. F.'s son applied for rectification of the register but failed. There was nothing to show that the director's power was not exercised in the company's interest: *Re Smith and Fawcett Ltd.* [1942] Ch. 304 (C.A.).

There is a presumption that the directors have acted *bona fide* and reasonably.[10]

If the articles empower the directors to decline to register transfers on certain grounds, *e.g.* on the ground that the transferor is indebted to the company, or that the transferee is a person of whom they do not approve, they can be interrogated as to the ground on which they have refused registration, although not as to the reasons for their refusal, unless the articles provide that they shall not be bound to specify the grounds for their refusal, in which case they cannot be interrogated at all.[11]

If the directors give reasons for their refusal, the court can decide whether they are sufficient to justify the refusal.

The articles empowered the directors to refuse to register a transfer if "in their opinion it is contrary to the interests of the company that the proposed transferee should be a member thereof." The directors declined to register transfers of single shares, stating that it was contrary to the interests of the company that shares should be transferred singly or in small amounts to outside persons with no interest in, or knowledge of, shipping. *Held*, this was a bad reason for refusing—refusal should have been on grounds personal to the transferee—and the transfers were directed to be registered: *Re Bede S.S. Co. Ltd.* [1917] 1 Ch. 123 (C.A.).

A formal active exercise of the right of refusal to register is required before the company is authorised to refuse to register shares in the names of the transferees. Where directors are equally divided and so come to no decision to decline to register, the transfer must be registered.[12]

[10] *Per* Lord Anderson (Ordinary) in *Kennedy* v. *North British Wireless Schools Ltd.*, 1916, 1 S.L.T. 407; 1915, 1 S.L.T. 196 (O.H.) at p. 198.

[11] *Berry and Stewart* v. *Tottenham Hotspur Football Co. Ltd.* [1935] Ch. 718.

[12] *Shepherd's Trustees* v. *Shepherd*, 1950 S.C. (H.L.) 60, *per* Lord Porter at p. 66; *Re Hackney Pavilion Ltd.* [1924] 1 Ch. 276.

Where the articles provided that no share should be transferred to a person not already a member of the company without the consent of the directors and, to prevent a particular transfer from being registered, a director purposely abstained from attending board meetings so that a quorum could not be obtained, it was held that the transferee was entitled to an order directing the company to register the transfer.[13]

In one case the board lost their right to veto a transfer because they were guilty of an unreasonable delay of four months in deciding whether or not to exercise the veto—the period of two months specified in section 183(5) for giving a transferee notice of the company's refusal to register a transfer was considered to be the outside limit after which there is unnecessary delay for this purpose, unless in an exceptional case it is impossible to constitute a board.[14] Where there are no properly appointed directors to constitute a quorum to decide whether to exercise the right of refusal, the transferee has, however, no right to registration until the end of the period within which a properly constituted board could have exercised the power, *i.e.*, two months. It follows that any purported registration during that period is invalid.[15]

In a rare case, the remedy of the transferee, or of the transferor, on a refusal to register a transfer is to apply to the court to rectify the register of members by substituting his name for that of the transferor under section 359. Unnecessary delay in registering a transfer does not in itself constitute a ground for rectification, and a transferor applying for rectification must be able to show that he has been prejudiced by the delay.[16] A winding-up petition is not the proper remedy for the transferor where registration of a transfer is refused.[17]

Form of transfer

Section 183(1), which was passed to make sure that there is an instrument which can be stamped with stamp duty, provides that it is unlawful for a company to register a transfer of shares

[13] *Re Copal Varnish Co. Ltd.* [1917] 2 Ch. 349.
[14] *Re Swaledale Cleaners Ltd.* 1 W.L.R. 1710 (C.A.).
[15] *Re Zinotty Properties Ltd.* [1984] 1 W.L.R. 1249.
[16] *Property Investment Co. of Scotland Ltd.* v. *Duncan* (1887) 14 R. 299.
[17] *Charles Forte Investments Ltd.* v. *Amanda* [1964] Ch. 240 (C.A.).

unless a "proper instrument of transfer" has been delivered to the company.[18] Consequently it is illegal to have an article that upon the death of a shareholder his shares shall be deemed to have passed to his widow, without any transfer.[19]

The form of the transfer may be that prescribed by the articles but a "proper instrument" for the purposes of section 183(1) does not necessarily mean an instrument complying with the formalities prescribed by the articles—it means an instrument such as will attract stamp duty.[20] The articles may require transfers to be made in writing under seal.

Table A, regulation 23, provides: "The instrument of transfer of a share may be in any usual form or in any other form which the directors may approve and shall be executed by or on behalf of the transferor and, unless the share is fully paid, by or on behalf of the transferee."

Formerly, the common form of transfer of shares had to be executed by the transferee as well as by the transferor and had to be attested.

Now, in the case of a company limited by shares, if shares are fully paid they may be transferred by a simplified form of transfer, namely a stock transfer under hand in the form set out in Schedule 1 to the Stock Transfer Act 1963.[21] Such a transfer need be executed only by the transferor and need not be attested: 1963 Act, s.1. Additional permitted forms were introduced for the computerised system of transfers on the stock exchange; *i.e.* where the transfer is to or from a stock exchange nominee.[22]

The 1963 Act applies to, *inter alia*, fully paid up registered securities issued by a company limited by shares, or by a statutory company or a chartered company (but not by a building society or an industrial and provident society), or, subject to exceptions, by the Government or by a local

[18] For the future paperless system of transfers on the Stock Exchange, see s.207 C.A. 1989, *post*, p. 288.

[19] *Re Greene* [1949] Ch. 333.

[20] *Re Paradise Motor Co. Ltd.* [1968] 1 W.L.R. 1125 (C.A.).

[21] As amended by the Stock Transfer (Amendment of Forms) Order 1974 (S.I. No. 1214).

[22] Introduced by the Stock Transfer (Addition of Forms) Order 1979 (S.I. No. 277).

authority, or which are units of a unit trust scheme: section 1. The expression "registered securities" means transferable securities the holders of which are entered in a register, and "securities" includes shares, stock, debentures, debenture stock, loan stock, bonds and units of a unit trust scheme: section 4.

Where a stock transfer has been executed for the purpose of a stock exchange transaction, particulars of the consideration and of the transferee may be either inserted in such transfer or, where there are several transferees, supplied by brokers' transfers, *i.e.* separate instruments in the form set out in Schedule 2 to the 1963 Act, identifying the stock transfer and specifying the securities to which each relates. The transferor need not sign a brokers' transfer: section 1.

Procedure on transfer

If a shareholder has sold all his shares comprised in one share certificate[23] to one person,[24] the transfer is effected as follows:

(1) the transferor sends the transferee a "proper instrument of transfer" required by sections 183(1) and complying with the articles or the Stock Transfer Act 1963, *ante*, and executed by the transferor, together with the share certificate relating to the shares comprised in the transfer;
(2) the transferee then executes the transfer if it is in accordance with the articles, and forwards it, with the share certificate and the registration fee, to the company for registration;
(3) within two months[25] after the transfer is lodged the company must either issue a new share certificate to the transferee or, where the directors are exercising a power to refuse registration, send *him* notice of its refusal to register the transfer: sections 183(5), 185(1). In the case of transfers on the stock exchange where a stock exchange nominee is the transferee, the company

[23] As to shares comprised in a share warrant, see *post*, p. 312.
[24] As to the procedure when, *e.g.* part only of the holding is being sold, see Certification of transfers, *post*.
[25] Fourteen days if the shares are quoted on a stock exchange: Admission of Securities to Listing, page 5.31.

is exempt from the obligation to prepare the new share certificate: section 185(4).

The Jenkins Report[26] recommended that the period be five weeks and that notice of a refusal be given to the transferor too.

The penalty for non-compliance is a default fine on the company and every officer who knowingly authorises or permits the default: sections 183(6), 185(5).

Table A contains the following provisions as to transfers of shares:

Regulation 24.—"The directors may refuse to register the transfer of a share which is not fully paid to a person of whom they do not approve and they may refuse to registrer the transfer of a share on which the company has a lien. They may also refuse to register a transfer unless—

(a) it is lodged at the office or at such other place as the directors may appoint and is accompanied by the certificate for the shares to which it relates and such other evidence as the directors may reasonably require to show the right of the transferor to make the transfer;
(b) it is in respect of only one class of shares; and
(c) it is in favour of not more than four transferees."

Regulation 26.—"The registration of transfers of shares or of transfers of any class of shares may be suspended at such times and for such periods (not exceeding 30 days in any year) as the directors may determine."

Regulation 27.—"No fee shall be charged for the registration of any instrument of transfer or other document relating to or affecting the title to any share."

A transfer may also be registered, at the request of the transferor, in the same manner and subject to the same conditions as if registration were applied for by the transferee: section 183(4).

Certification of transfer

If a holder of shares sells some only of his shares comprised in a share certificate, *e.g.* 250 shares out of 1,000, it will be unsafe for him to deliver his share certificate for 1,000 shares to

[26] Para. 483.

the purchaser. Similarly if he sells some of the shares to one person and the rest to another. The usual procedure in such cases is, therefore:

(1) the transferor executes the transfer and sends it, with the share certificate, to the company;
(2) the secretary indorses on the transfer the words "certificate lodged" or similar words, and returns the transfer so certificated to the transferor;
(3) the transferor hands over this certificated transfer to the transferee against payment of the price;
(4) the transferee executes the transfer if it is in the form prescribed by the articles, and forwards it to the company for registration;
(5) within two months[27] the company either issues new share certificates or, where a power to refuse registration is being exercised, informs the *transferee* of its refusal to register him: sections 183(5), 185(1), *ante*. This does not apply to transfers to a stock exchange nominee,[28] *ante*.

The certification of a transfer is a representation by the company to any person acting on the faith of the certification that there have been produced to the company such documents as show a prima facie title to the shares in the transferor, but it is not a representation that the transferor has any title: section 184(1). However, if a company *fraudulently or negligently* makes a false certification the company is liable in damages to a person who acts on the faith of it to his detriment: section 184(2).

Suppose that P transferred all his shares to X and his certificate was lodged by X with the company. Before registration was completed, P executed a transfer of some of the shares to Y, who sold them to B. Y's transfer to B was negligently certificated by the company and, on the strength of this, B paid Y. The company registered X and refused to register B. The company is liable in damages to B.

A certification is deemed to be made by the company if it is made by a person, such as the secretary, authorised to issue certificated transfers on the company's behalf and if it is signed

[27] See note 25, *ante*.
[28] And see the proposed new paperless system of transfers, p. 288, *post*.

by a person authorised to certificate transfers on the company's behalf: section 184(3).

When a transfer is certificated the company destroys the original certificate and issues new certificates. But if it *negligently* returns the original certificate with the certified transfer to the transferor and the transferor then fraudulently deals with the original certificate so as to inflict loss on a third party, *e.g.* the transferor purports to transfer *all* the shares comprised in the original certificate to the third party, the company is not liable to the third party. The reason is that the share certificate is neither a negotiable instrument nor a warranty of title on the part of the company issuing it, and the company owes no duty to the public as to the custody of the certificate. Further, the company is not estopped form denying the validity of the transferor's title to the shares *previously* transferred, because the proximate cause of the third party's loss is the fraud of the transferor and not the negligence of the company.[29]

Proposed paperless system for share transfers

Section 207 of the Companies Act 1989 allows the Secretary of State to issue regulations providing for a new paperless system of share ownership and share transfer. This is to enable the proposed TAURUS scheme of transfers on the Stock Exchange to proceed. It will radically change the existing law on share certificates and transfer procedures, but it is too early to say yet how it will operate in practice.

Rights as between vendor and purchaser

On a sale of shares the ordinary contract between the parties is that the vendor shall give to the purchaser a valid transfer and do all that is required to enable the purchaser to be registered as a member in respect of the shares, the purchaser's duty being

[29] *Longman* v. *Bath Electric Tramways Ltd.* [1905] 1 Ch. 646. The Scottish equivalent of "estoppel" is personal bar, but, in the absence of Scottish authority on certification, it seems doubtful whether a company would be entitled to deny the validity of a share certificate in the circumstances mentioned: *cf. Clavering, Son & Co.* v. *Goodwins, Jardine & Co. Ltd.* (1891) 18 R. 652.

to get himself registered.[30] The vendor's duty is not only to give a genuine transfer but also, where the vendor is not the transferor, one which is signed by a transferor willing that the transfer shall be registered.

Solicitors instructed stockbrokers to sell stock and enclosed the certificate and a blank transfer (*i.e.* a transfer in which the transferee's name had still to be inserted)[31] signed by the stockholder. The stockbrokers sold the stock but the stockholder repudiated the contract and the company, on her instructions, refused to register the transfer. The stockbrokers replaced the stock by a purchase on the Stock Exchange and sued the solicitors for an indemnity. *Held*, (1) the solicitors were principals of the stockbrokers as regards the sale, (2) it was the solicitor's duty to deliver a transfer executed by a transferor willing that it should be registered, and (3) the solicitors were liable. *Hichens, Harrison, Woolston & Co.* v. *Jackson & Sons* [1943] A.C. 266.

If the directors, in pursuance of a power in the articles, decline to register the transfer, the purchaser, unless he bought "with registration guaranteed," will be unable to sue the vendor for damages or rescind and recover the price from the vendor—there is no implied condition subsequent to such effect.[32] In such a case the vendor will be a trustee of the shares for the purchaser.[33] The vendor is, of course, under a duty to the purchaser not to prevent or delay the registration of the transfer.[34]

As from the time of the contract of sale the equitable or beneficial interest in the shares passes to the purchaser, and the vendor holds the legal title as quasi-trustee for the purchaser.[35] The purchaser does not obtain the legal or complete title until his name is entered on the register of members.[36]

[30] *Skinner* v. *City of London Marine Insce. Corpn.* (1885) 14 Q.B.D. 882 (C.A.).
[31] Such a transfer may be invalid in Scots law: *post*, p. 299.
[32] *London Founders Assocn. Ltd.* v. *Clarke* (1888) 20 Q.B.D. 576 (C.A.).
[33] *Stevenson* v. *Wilson*, 1907 S.C. 445; this quasi-trust would not, however, defeat a subsequent arrestment of the shares by a creditor of the transferor: *per* Lord Moncrieff (Ordinary) in *National Bank of Scotland Glasgow Nominees Ltd.* v. *Adamson*, 1932 S.L.T. 492 (O.H.) at p. 495.
[34] *Hooper* v. *Herts* [1906] 1 Ch. 549 (C.A.).
[35] See note 33, *ante*.
[36] See *per* Lord Gifford in *Morrison* v. *Harrison* (1876) 3 R. 406 at p. 411; see also *Tennant's Trustees* v. *Tennant*, 1946 S.C. 420.

Until the transfer is registered, the vendor will receive any dividends or other benefits declared on the shares and, in the case of partly paid shares, calls may be made on him. As between the vendor and the purchaser the rights and liabilities depend on the terms of the contract. The shares may be bought "cum" or "ex" dividends or rights, or with a specified sum paid. In the absence of any such agreement, the purchaser is entitled to dividends or other benefits declared after the *date of the contract.*[37]

In September, 1935, R. sold shares privately to W. In April, 1936, the company declared a dividend for the year ending December 31, 1935. *Held*, the sale being by private bargain and not governed by Stock Exchange rules, W. was entitled to the whole dividend and it was not apportionable between W. and R.: *Re Wimbush* [1940] Ch. 92.

Subject to contrary agreement, the purchaser must indemnify the vendor against calls made after the date of the contract.

X, owner of shares not fully paid up, sold to Y, giving him a blank transfer. Y, without being entered on the register, sold to Z, giving Z a blank transfer. Z was not entered on the register, and became bankrupt. The company made a call on X. *Held*, Y was bound to indemnify X, although Y had then no beneficial interest. The implied obligation arose out of the contract between them: *Spencer* v. *Ashworth, Partington & Co.* [1925] 1 K.B. 589 (C.A.).

Note: Z would have been liable to indemnify X only during the period of Z's beneficial ownership. The obligation would have arisen from the relationship of trustee and beneficiary between them.

Again, until the transfer is registered, the vendor is entitled to exercise any vote conferred by the shares but he must vote as directed by the purchaser.

An unpaid vendor of shares who remains on the register of members after the contract of sale retains *vis-à-vis* the purchaser the right to vote in respect of those shares unless the contract restricts such right.[38]

[37] *Black* v. *Homersham* (1878) 4 Ex.D. 24; *Re Kidner* [1929] 2 Ch. 121.

[38] *Musselwhite* v. *C. H. Musselwhite & Son Ltd.* [1962] Ch. 964, where a contract for the sale of shares provided that the transfer and share certificate should be held by a third party until the price was paid by instalments over a period of years.

Priorities

English law

The general rules are:

(1) The party who is on the register of members and therefore has the legal title has priority.
(2) If neither party is on the register, the party whose equitable title is first in time has priority.

For example, if X, the registered owner, is trustee of the shares for Y and, in breach of trust sells the shares to Z, who buys without notice of the trust and becomes registered as owner before the company knows of the trust, Z will have priority over Y. A company, however, is entitled to a reasonable time for the consideration of every transfer before it registers the transfer,[39] and therefore if Y, in the example just given, had given notice of his claim to the company before Z was actually registered as owner, he would have been entitled to priority over Z, as his equitable title would have been first in time.

C. assigned all his property to P. as trustee for C.'s creditors. The property included some shares. P. asked for the share certificates but was unable to obtain them from C.; he then gave notice of the assignment to the company. C., after the date of the assignment to P. sold the shares to X, who applied for registration. *Held*, P., having an equitable title which was prior in time, was entitled to registration: *Peat* v. *Clayton* [1906] 1 Ch. 659.

Entry on the register after notice of a prior equitable claim will not give priority.

In 1893 X transferred debentures of a private company to Y on trust for X for life with remainder to X's sons. The transfer was not registered. In 1894 one son sold his share of the debentures to Z. In 1911 X deposited the debentures with the bank as security for the company's overdraft. In 1914 the bank, on learning of the settlement and transfer to Y, took a transfer of the debentures from X, and were registered as owners. *Held*, Z was entitled to priority over the bank: *Coleman* v. *London County and Westminster Bank Ltd.* [1916] 2 Ch. 353.

[39] *Re Ottos Kopje Diamond Mines Ltd.* [1893] 1 Ch. 618 (C.A.).

It has been said[40] that even if a complete legal title has not been obtained, a person who has, as between himself and the company, a present, absolute, unconditional right to registration before the company learns of a better title, has the same priority as if he were actually registered. It is doubtful, however, whether anything short of registration will give priority, except perhaps in very special circumstances. Directors should refuse to register a transfer after receiving notice of an adverse equitable claim to the shares, unless the transfer has already been passed for registration.[41]

Delay in obtaining registration is dangerous to a transferee for two reasons: a later transferee may gain priority by obtaining registration first, or an earlier equity may come to light.

A husband mortgaged shares of which he was trustee for his wife. Before the mortgagee was registered the wife successfully claimed that her equitable title prevailed over that of the mortgagee: *Ireland* v. *Hart* [1902] 1 Ch. 522.

To protect himself such a transferee should issue a stop notice.[42]

Scots law

If there are competing claims for membership of a company, the person preferred is the one who first completes his title to the shares by having his name entered on the register; a mere assignation of shares, even though intimated to the company, does not make the assignee a member.[43] Where a competition arises between a transferee and an arrester, the transferee is preferred to the arrester as soon as the transfer has been registered.[44] In a question between a transferee whose transfer has been duly intimated to the company but not registered and a subsequent arrester, the intimation of the transfer has been held to cut out the arrestment.[45]

[40] *Per* Romer J. in *Moore* v. *North Western Bank* [1891] 2 Ch. 599 at pp. 602, 603.
[41] *Per* Joyce J. in *Ireland* v. *Hart* [1902] 1 Ch. 522 at p. 529.
[42] See p. 297, *post*.
[43] *Morrison* v. *Harrison* (1876) 3 R. 406.
[44] *National Bank of Scotland Glasgow Nominees Ltd.* v. *Adamson*, 1932 S.L.T. 492 (O.H.).
[45] *Jackson* v. *Elphick* (1902) 10 S.L.T. 146 (O.H.).

Directors may delay registration where they suspect that a transfer is affected by fraud or dishonesty[46] but, if they receive intimation of a competing interest in the shares from some party other than the transferee, they are entitled to register the transfer unless the intimation is followed up by a legal measure such as interdict.[47] The company must be made a party to any such interdict process, and interdict has been refused where it was alleged that share transfers, bearing that the beneficial interest remained in the transferors, had been executed by a body of trustees to certain of their own number and another person in order to give the transferees a qualification to act as directors; the possibility that the shares had been transferred in breach of trust was not, the court held, a matter which concerned the company or which made the registration of the transferees invalid.[48]

Forged transfers

A forged transfer of shares is a nullity and cannot affect the title of the shareholder whose signature is forged. If the company, therefore, has registered the forged transfer and removed the true owner of the shares from the register, it can be compelled to replace him.[49] It can then claim an indemnity from the person who sent the forged transfer for registration if it has sustained loss through acting thereon. No estoppel in favour of such a person arises from a share certificate issued to him even though he knows nothing of the forgery—he has not relied on the act of the company in issuing the certificate.

B. sent to the corporation for registration a transfer of stock which stood in the names of T. and H. The transfer was a forgery, T. having forged H.'s signature to the transfer, but B. was ignorant of this. The corporation registered the transfer. B. transferred the stock to third parties to whom certificates were issued. The corporation was estopped from denying that those registered were the stockholders entitled. H. subsequently discovered the forgery and compelled the corporation to buy him an equivalent amount of stock and to pay him the missing

[46] *Property Investment Co. of Scotland Ltd.* v. *Duncan* (1887) 14 R. 299.
[47] *Per* Lord M'Laren in *Shaw* v. *Caledonian Rlwy. Co.* (1890) 17 R. 466 at p. 482.
[48] *Elliot* v. *J. W. Mackie & Sons Ltd.*, 1935 S.C. 81.
[49] *Barton* v. *N. Staffordshire Rlwy. Co.* (1888) 38 Ch.D. 458.

dividends with interest. *Held*, B. was bound to indemnify the corporation upon an implied contract that the transfer was genuine: *Sheffield Corporation* v. *Barclay* [1905] A.C. 392.[50]

This right extends to an indemnity from a stockbroker who makes the application on behalf of the person with the forged transfer.[51] The company may not, however, be able to claim a complete indemnity if it is guilty of negligence in failing to spot the forgery. In such a situation it has been suggested that section 2(1) of the Civil Liability (Contribution) Act 1978 may prevent complete recovery.[51]

In an effort to prevent the registration of a forged transfer, companies usually, on a transfer being lodged for registration, write to the shareholder informing him of the transfer and of their intention to register it unless by return of post they hear that he objects. The neglect of the shareholder to reply to this communication does not estop him from proving that the transfer is a forgery.[52]

Transmission of Shares

Section 183(2) provides that section 183(1) *ante*,[53] does not prejudice any power of a company to register as shareholder any person to whom the right to any shares in the company has been transmitted by operation of law. Transmission of shares occurs on the death or the bankruptcy of a member, or, if the member is a company, on its going into liquidation.

On the death of a sole shareholder the shares vest in his personal representative[54] *i.e.* his executor or administrator.[55] The company is bound to accept production of the probate of the will or, in the case of an intestacy, letters of administration of the estate, or, in Scotland, the confirmation as executor, as sufficient evidence of the grant: section 187. Subject to any restrictions in the articles, the personal representative may be

[50] *Cf.* Lord Kyllachy (Ordinary) in *Clavering, Son & Co.* v. *Goodwins, Jardine & Co. Ltd.* (1891) 18 R. 652 at p. 657.

[51] *Yeung* v. *Hong Kong & Shanghai Bank Ltd.* [1980] 2 All E.R. 599 (P.C.).

[52] *Re Bahia and San Francisco Rlwy. Co.* (1868) L.R. 3 Q.B. 584, *ante*, p. 274. *Barton* v. *L. & N.W. Rlwy. Co.* (1890) 24 Q.B.D. 77 (C.A.).

[53] p. 283.

[54] *Re Greene* [1949] Ch. 333.

[55] Executor in Scots law: see p. 234, *ante*.

registered as a member or transfer the shares without himself becoming a member: section 183(3).[56]

Table A, regulation 30, provides: "Any person becoming entitled to a share in consequence of the death or bankruptcy of a member may, upon such evidence being produced as the directors may properly require, elect either to become the holder of the share or to have some person nominated by him registered as the transferee. If he elects to become the holder he shall give notice to the company to that effect. If he elects to have another person registered he shall execute an instrument of transfer of the share to that person. All the articles relating to the transfer of shares shall apply to the notice or instrument of transfer as if it were an instrument of transfer executed by the member and the death or bankruptcy of the member had not occurred."

When shares are jointly held, the surviving holder becomes the sole holder. Under Table A, regulation 29, the estate of the deceased joint holder is not released from any liability in respect of the shares.

MORTGAGE OF SHARES (ENGLISH LAW)

In England, a shareholder who borrows money on the security of his shares may give the lender either a legal mortgage or an equitable mortgage over the shares.

Legal mortgage

A legal mortgage of shares is effected by transfer of the shares to the lender (the mortgagee) followed by registration of the transfer by the company. There should also be a document setting out the terms of the loan and containing an agreement to retransfer the shares on repayment of the amount borrowed with interest. The document will empower the lender to sell the shares in the event of default by the borrower (the mortgagor). When exercising a power of sale the lender is under a duty to take reasonable care to obtain a proper price for the shares. He does not have to wait for a higher price but he must obtain the true market value at the shares. Any clause in the deed which

[56] *Ante*, p. 23.

purports to exclude this liability for negligence must be expressly worded to that effect.[57]

This form of mortgage gives the lender complete security up to the value of the shares. He will be entitled to dividends and to exercise any voting rights in respect of the shares, unless it is agreed that the dividends shall be paid to the borrower and that he shall exercise the voting rights as the borrower directs.[58]

However, restrictions on the transfer of shares contained in the articles[59] may prevent this kind of mortgage being made. Further, it might not be advisable where the shares are not fully paid because the lender on the register would be personally liable for calls.

Equitable mortgage

1. An equitable mortgage of shares may be made by depositing the share certificate with the lender as security for such a loan. In such a case the lender can enforce his security by applying to the court for a sale of the shares or for an order for transfer and foreclosure.[60]

2. A method more commonly adopted is for the borrower to deposit with the lender the share certificate together with a blank transfer, *i.e.* a transfer signed by the borrower with the transferee's name left blank. In such a case the lender has an *implied* power to sell the shares if default is made by the borrower in making repayment at the agreed time or, if no time for repayment is agreed, within a reasonable time after notice.[61] The implied power of sale includes power to insert the name of the buyer in the blank transfer if, as is usual, the articles provide for transfers to be in writing. The borrower is under an implied obligation not to delay registration of the transfer so filled up.[62]

3. If the articles require transfers to be by deed, the lender cannot fill up a blank transfer unless he is authorised by deed. In such a case an equitable mortgage may be made by deposit

[57] *Bishop* v. *Bonham* [1988] BCLC 656 (C.A.).
[58] *Siemens Brothers & Co. Ltd.* v. *Burns* [1918] 2 Ch. 324.
[59] *Ante*, p. 276.
[60] *Harrold* v. *Plenty* [1901] 2 Ch. 314.
[61] *Hooper* v. *Herts* [1906] 1 Ch. 549.
[62] *Powell* v. *London and Provincial Bank* [1893] 2 Ch. 555 (C.A.).

of the share certificate plus a transfer by deed to the lender. If the borrower defaults, the lender can lodge the transfer for registration.

No equitable mortgage is in itself absolutely secure because the borrower remains on the register and may sell the shares and procure the registration of the purchaser with priority over the lender, who would have no remedy against the company.

C. deposited his share certificate and a blank transfer with R. as a security for a loan. Upon the certificate was printed: "Without the production of this certificate no transfer of the shares mentioned therein can be registered." C. sold the shares to Y. and induced the company to register Y. as owner of the shares without the production of the share certificate. R. sued the company for wrongfully registering the shares in Y's name. *Held*, the company was not liable as it owed no duty of care to R., and the statement on the certificate was only a warning to the owner of the shares to take care of the certificate and not a statement of fact giving rise to an estoppel: *Rainford* v. *James Keith & Blackman Co. Ltd.* [1905] 1 Ch. 296.[63]

However, the mortgagor must exercise any voting rights as directed by the mortgagee.[64]

Stopnotice

To obtain complete protection, an equitable mortgagee of shares should serve a stop notice. This is done by filing an affidavit setting out the facts, and a notice in the prescribed form, in the Central Office of the Supreme Court or in a District Registry and serving an office copy of the affidavit and a duplicate notice on the company. The effect of the notice is that, whilst it continues in force, if the company receives any request to register a transfer of the shares in question it must give notice in writing to the person who has served the notice. Within eight days, such person must apply for an injunction restraining the transfer or the company will be at liberty to register the transfer.[65]

[63] Reversed on the facts [1905] 2 Ch. 147 (C.A.). On the facts the company was affected with notice of R's charge and he was able to recover the price of the shares which had been paid to the company in repayment of a loan made by the company to C.

[64] *Wise* v. *Landsell* [1921] 1 Ch. 420.

[65] R.S.C., Ord. 50, rr. 11–15. See also the Charging Orders Act 1979.

Charging order

A judgment creditor of the registered owner of shares may obtain an order charging the shares with payment of the judgment debt,[66] after which, until the order is discharged, the company cannot permit a transfer except with the authority of the court. A charging order will not have priority over a mortgage created by deposit of the share certificate and a blank transfer before the date of the charging order, as the judgment creditor can be in no better position than the judgment debtor at the time when the order was made.

Assignation of Shares in Security (Scots Law)

The only effective way of assigning shares in security is by the execution and registration of a transfer in favour of the lender. See the section headed "Legal mortgage," *ante.*[67]

No form of the equitable mortgage recognised by English law gives the lender any real security in competition with the general creditors of the borrower.[68] Accordingly, where a borrower delivers the share certificate to the lender and undertakes to transfer the shares to the lender when requested to do so, a transfer executed within six months before the borrower's sequestration or his granting of a protected trust deed is reducible as an unfair preference under section 36 of the Bankruptcy (Scotland) Act 1985.[69] For the purposes of that section the day on which a preference was created is the day on which the preference became "completely effectual,"[70] and that would only be so when the transfer had been registered. It may be, however, that where a completed transfer has been delivered to the lender along with the share certificate so that the lender is in a position to have himself registered as a

[66] R.S.C., Ord. 50, rr. 2–7.

[67] p. 295.

[68] *Gourlay* v. *Mackie* (1887) 14 R. 403; *per* Lord Gifford in *Morrison* v. *Harrison* (1876) 3 R. 406 at p. 411; *cf. Guild* v. *Young* (1884) 22 S.L.R. 520 (O.H.).

[69] This provision is the successor to the repealed Bankruptcy Act 1696 (Scots Act 1696, c. 5) which made fraudulent preferences reducible on the ground of notour bankruptcy.

[70] Bankruptcy (Scotland) Act 1985, s.36(3).

member without further interposition of the borrower, registration of the transfer on the eve of the borrower's sequestration is not open to challenge as an unfair preference provided the delivery of the documents to the lender was made more than six months before the borrower's sequestration.[71] A blank transfer may be invalid under the Blank Bonds and Trusts Act 1696 (Scots Act 1696 c. 25) which declares null "bonds, assignations, dispositions or other deeds" subscribed blank in the name of the person or persons in whose favour they are conceived.

Stop notices and charging orders are not part of Scots law. When a company called on to register a transfer receives intimation from some person other than the transferee that that other person has an interest in the shares, the company is entitled to proceed to register the transfer unless the intimation is followed up by an application for interdict or other legal measure.[72]

Shares are subject to arrestment at the instance of the creditors of the shareholder, whether the arrestment is in execution,[73] or merely to found jurisdiction.[74] Where competition arises between a transferee and an arrester the tranferee has the preferable right to the shares as soon as his transfer has been lodged, even although it is not registered before the lodging of the arrestment.

In January S. transferred 200 shares to M. and 1,000 shares to F., and the transfers were received by the secretary of the company on January 19, and February 2, respectively. Because of an arrestment lodged the previous November against S. at the instance of a bank, the transfers were not registered. On March 30, arrestments were executed at the instance of D. against S. *Held*, the transfers to M. and F. were preferable to D.'s arrestments: *Harvey's Yoker Distillery Ltd.* v. *Singleton* (1901) 8 S.L.T. 369 (O.H.).

[71] *Guild* v. *Young* (1884) 22 S.L.R. 520 (O.H.), decided under the 1696 Act, can give at best slender support to the proposition. Whereas the 1696 Act affected only *voluntary* preferences conferred by the bankrupt on favoured creditors, section 36 of the 1985 Act applies to any *transaction entered into* by the debtor. Although section 36 is not restricted to the challenge of voluntary preferences, it is submitted that the registration by a creditor of an already executed transfer in circumstances such as arose in *Guild* v. *Young* would not be classed as a *transaction entered into* by the debtor.

[72] *Per* Lord M'Laren in *Shaw* v. *Caledonian Rlwy. Co.* (1890) 17 R. 466 at p. 482.

[73] *Sinclair* v. *Staples* (1860) 22 D. 600.

[74] *American Mortgage Co. of Scotland Ltd.* v. *Sidway*, 1908 S.C. 500.

"An arrestment can only attach property belonging truly and in substance to the common debtor. Now these shares did not belong in substance to Singleton at the time of the arrestment, because he had by that time done all in his power to dispose of them by executing the transfers": *per* Lord Stormonth Darling (Ordinary) at p. 370.

An arrester is not entitled to found on any irregularity in the registration procedure to the effect of defeating the transferee's title.[75] Intimation to the company of a transfer, even without registration, has the effect, in a question between the transferee and a subsequent arrester of cutting out of the arrestment.[76]

CALLS ON SHARES

A call on shares is a demand by the directors that a member pay to the company money which is unpaid on his shares, whether on account of the nominal value of the shares or by way of premium.[77] If, when shares are issued, the full amount of each share is not payable at once as in the privatisation issues, the terms of issue will provide that part is payable on application, part on allotment and the remainder by instalments at fixed dates, in which case the instalments are not calls,[78] as the obligation of the shareholder to pay is not dependent on a call from the company. However, in a rare case, the company may not require all the nominal amount of a share, or the full amount of a premium on a share, to be paid at or soon after allotment but may leave part to be called up in accordance with the provisions of the articles as and when required by the company or, in the event of a winding up, by the liquidator. If so, a shareholder is bound to pay the whole or part of the balance unpaid on his shares "as and when called on," in accordance with the provisions of the articles. Calls must be made in the manner laid down in the articles.

[75] *National Bank of Scotland Glasgow Nominees Ltd.* v. *Adamson*, 1932 S.L.T. 492 (O.H.); for an arrestment made effective by the granting by the court of a warrant to sell the shares, see *Valentine* v. *Grangemouth Coal Co. Ltd.* (1897) 35 S.L.R. 12 (O.H.).

[76] *Jackson* v. *Elphick* (1902) 10 S.L.T. 146 (O.H.).

[77] For Scots *dicta* on the nature of a call see Lord President M'Neill in *Wryght* v. *Lindsay* (1856) 19 D. 55 at p. 63; affd. (1860) 22 D. (H.L.) 5.

[78] But articles may provide that they shall be *deemed* to be calls: see Table A, reg. 16.

In England a call creates a specialty debt due from the shareholder to the company (s.14(2)), and so the period within which an action can be brought for payment of it is 12 years.[79] In Scotland a call remains enforceable until the expiry of 20 years.[80] Table A, regulation 15, provides for payment of interest from the date fixed for payment until actual payment.

If authorised by the articles, a company may make arrangements on the issue of shares for a difference between the shareholders in the amounts and times of payment of calls: section 119(*a*). Table A, regulation 17, authorises such an arrangement. Such a power does not entitle directors to make calls on all the shareholders except themselves,[81] at any rate without the knowledge and sanction of the other shareholders—the directors' power to make calls must be exercised bona fide for the benefit of the company as a whole, and not so as to give themselves an advantage over other shareholders.[82]

Any arrangement made under section 119(*a*) must be made at the time of the issue of shares. If no such arrangement is made, the rule is that "prima facie it is entirely improper for the directors to make a call on some members of a class of shareholders who stand in the same relation to the company as the other members of the class without making a similar call on all the other members of that class."[83]

Table A, regulations 18 to 22, provides for forfeiture for non-payment of a call or an instalment.[84]

In an action to enforce payment of a call it is no defence for the shareholder to say that he has repudiated the contract because of misrepresentations in the prospectus or listing particulars. To succeed he must show that he has taken steps to have his name removed from the register of members.[85]

[79] Limitation Act 1980, s.8(1).
[80] Prescription and Limitation (Scotland) Act 1973, s.7.
[81] *Alexander* v. *Automatic Telephone Co.* [1900] 2 Ch. 56 (C.A.).
[82] *Post*, p. 399.
[83] *Per* Sargant J. in *Galloway* v. *Hallé Concerts Society* [1915] 2 Ch. 233 at p. 239.
[84] *Post*, p. 307.
[85] *First National Reinsurance Co.* v. *Greenfield* [1921] 2 K.B. 260; *Scottish Amalgamated Silks Ltd.* v. *Macalister*, 1930 S.L.T. 593 (O.H.); see, however, *Liquidators of Mount Morgan (West) Gold Mine Ltd.* v. *M'Mahon* (1891) 18 R. 772.

Calls made by a liquidator in the course of a winding up are in some respects different from calls made by directors during the active existence of the company.[86]

Payment in advance of calls

If authorised by the articles, a company may accept payment from a member of the whole or a part of the amount remaining unpaid on his shares, although no part of this amount has been called up: section 119(*b*).

When a payment in advance of calls has been made the consequences are:

(1) the shareholder's liability to the company is extinguished or reduced, as the case may be;
(2) he becomes a creditor to the extent of the payment in advance, so that interest on it can be paid out of capital,[87] *i.e.* whether profits are made by the company or not;
(3) the company cannot be compelled to repay the payment,[88] except in a winding up, *post*;
(4) the company cannot repay without the consent of the shareholder[89];
(5) in a winding up he will rank after the other creditors but will be entitled to repayment of the advance with interest in priority to the other shareholders who have not paid in advance.[90]

The power of receiving payment in advance of calls is a fiduciary power and must be exercised by the directors bona fide for the benefit of the company as a whole, and not for the private ends of the directors. Accordingly, where directors, knowing the company to be insolvent, paid the amount remaining unpaid on their shares and on the same day appropriated the money in payment of their fees, it was held

[86] *Mitchell, Petitioner* (1863) 1 M. 1116; *Liquidators of Benhar Coal Co. Ltd., Petitioners* (1882) 9 R. 763.
[87] *Lock* v. *Queensland Investment and Land Mortgage Co.* [1896] A.C. 461; *Myles, Petitioner* (1893) 1 S.L.T. 90 (O.H.).
[88] *Per* Lindley and Kay L.JJ. in *Lock* v. *Queensland Investment etc. Co.* [1896] 1 Ch. 397 (C.A.) at pp. 405, 407.
[89] *London and Northern Steamship Co.* v. *Farmer* (1914) 111 L.T. 204.
[90] *Re Exchange Drapery Co.* (1888) 38 Ch.D. 171.

that they still remained liable on the shares.[91] However, although directors are trustees of their powers for the shareholders,[92] they are not yet established as trustees for the company's creditors,[93] and where, the company being insolvent, they paid in advance the amount of their calls and applied the money in discharging the company's bank overdraft, which they had guaranteed, it was held that their shares were fully paid up.[94]

Lien on Shares (English Law)

The articles of a private company may give the company a lien on the shares held by a member for his unpaid call or instalment, or for some other debt due from him to the company. Public companies however may only have a lien on such shares for an unpaid call or instalment on those shares: section 150. By way of exception a money-lending or credit company have have a lien on any of its shares for non-payment of a debt owed by the shareholder in the ordinary course of the company's business.

Such a lien is an equitable charge upon the shares, and gives rise to the same rights as if the shares had been expressly charged by the member in favour of the company.[95]

Table A, regulation 8, provides: "The company shall have a first and paramount lien on every share (not being a fully paid share) for all moneys (whether presently payable or not) payable at a fixed time or called in respect of that share. The directors may at any time declare any share to be wholly or in part exempt from the provisions of this regulation. The company's lien, on a share shall extend to any amount payable in respect of it."

The articles of a private company may extend regulation 8 to include any debt owed by a member to the company. Where a director had incurred a debt by virtue of the company paying bills on his behalf, the company was held to have a lien on his shares even though it was also, by virtue of another article, prohibited from making a loan to that director on security of its shares. The company had not made a loan to the director, he had simply become indebted to the company:

[91] *Sykes' Case* (1872) L.R. 13 Eq. 255.
[92] *Post*, p. 395.
[93] *Post*, p. 397.
[94] *Poole's Case* (1878) 9 Ch.D. 322 (C.A.).
[95] *Everitt* v. *Automatic Weighing Machine Co.* [1892] 3 Ch. 506.

Champagne Perrier-Jouet S.A. v. *H. H. Finch Ltd.* [1982] 1 W.L.R. 1359.

The articles may grant a lien on shares which are fully paid but in such a case an official quotation on the Stock Exchange cannot be obtained.[96] If the lien given by the articles extends only to shares not fully paid, the company can alter its articles so as to give a lien on all shares, even if only one member will be affected by the alteration.[97]

Table A, regulation 24, empowers the directors to decline to register the transfer of a share on which the company has a lien.

A shareholder against whom a lien is to be enforced can compel the company to assign its lien to his nominee who is willing to pay off the amount of the lien.[98]

How a lien is enforced

A lien is enforced, like any other equitable charge, by a sale. If the articles do not give the company power to sell the shares, an application for an order for sale may be necessary. It is probable that the company has the implied power of sale given by the Law of Property Act 1925, s.101, to a mortgagee whose mortgage is made by deed. However, since it is uncertain that the articles, which create the lien, are a deed for the purposes of section 101,[99] to avoid the necessity of an application to the court the articles usually give an express power of sale.

Table A provides: "9. The company may sell in such manner as the directors determine, any shares on which the company has a lien, if a sum in respect of which the lien exists is presently payable, and is not paid within 14 clear days after notice, has been given to the holder of the share, or the person entitled to it in consequence of the death or bankruptcy of the holder, demanding payment and stating that if the notice is not complied with the shares may be sold."

Further, articles usually give the company power to nominate someone to execute the transfer.

[96] Admission of Securities to Listing, page 9.01.
[97] *Allen* v. *Gold Reefs of West Africa Ltd.* [1900] 1 Ch. 656 (C.A.), *ante*, p. 92.
[98] See note 95, *ante*.
[99] See s.14, *ante*, p. 87.

Table A provides: "10. To give effect to sale the directors may authorise some person to execute an instrument of transfer of the shares sold to or in accordance with the direction of the purchaser. The title of the transferee of the shares shall not be affected by any irregularity in or invalidity of the proceedings in reference to the sale."

The first part of article 10 is necessitated by section 183(1), which requires a proper instrument of transfer to be produced before a transfer is registered.

Table A continues: "11. The net proceeds of the sale, after payment of the costs, shall be applied, in payment of so much of the sum for which the lien exists as is presently payable, and any residue shall (upon surrender to the company for cancellation of the certificate for the shares sold and subject to a like lien for any moneys not presently payable as existed upon the shares before the sale) be paid to the person entitled to the shares at the date of the sale."

However the sale of the shares is subject to any restrictions on the transferability of those shares contained in the articles of a private company, *e.g.* a pre-emption clause requiring them to be offered to existing shareholders.[1]

A lien cannot be enforced by forfeiture even if power to forfeit is contained in the articles.

The articles of a company provided that the company should have a lien on shares for the debts of the shareholder, and also provided that the lien could be enforced by forfeiture. *Held*, (1) forfeiture for debts generally, as distinct from debts due from the shareholder as a contributory, amounted to an illegal reduction of capital; (2) power to forfeit on failure to redeem after notice amounted to a clog on the shareholder's equity of redemption, and was invalid and *ultra vires*: *Hopkinson* v. *Mortimer, Harley & Co. Ltd.* [1917] 1 Ch. 646.

Priority of lien

When a third party advances money on the security of shares, a question may arise as to whether the third party has priority over the company's lien. In such a case, if the third party gives notice of his security to the company before the company's lien arises, the third party will have priority, but otherwise not.

The articles of a company gave "a first and paramount lien and charge" on shares for debts due from the shareholder. A shareholder created an equitable mortgage of his shares by depositing the share

[1] *Champagne Perrier-Jouet S.A.* v. *H. H. Finch Ltd.* [1982] 1 W.L.R. 1359.

certificate with a bank as security for an overdraft and the bank gave notice of the deposit to the company. The shareholder subsequently became indebted to the company whereupon a lien arose in favour of the company. *Held*, the bank had priority as the company's lien arose after notice of their equitable mortgage. The notice was not notice of a trust contrary to what is now section 360 but notice affecting the company, in its character of trader, with knowledge of the bank's interest: *Bradford Banking Co.* v. *Briggs & Co.* (1886) 12 App.Cas. 29.

It seems that the position may be different even if the articles contain a clause like Table A, regulation 5,[2] relieving the company of the obligation to take notice of equities in relation to shares.[3]

Similarly, where the shareholder is a trustee, the company's lien will prevail over the claims of the beneficial owners unless the company is given notice, before the lien arises, that the shareholder is a trustee.

Trustees held shares in a company, the articles of which gave the company a lien on shares standing either in a single name or in joint names for any debt due from any of the holders, either separately or jointly with any other person. There was also an article like Table A, regulation 5. Long after the registration of the shares in the trustee's names, one of the trustees incurred a liability to the company. It was *not* alleged that the company had notice of the trust before the lien arose. *Held*, the company's lien prevailed over the title of the *cestuis que trust*: *New London and Brazilian Bank* v. *Brocklebank* (1882) 21 Ch.D. 302 (C.A.).

The title of the beneficial owners, however, will have priority if the company has notice, before the lien arises, that the shareholder is a trustee of the shares.[4]

The company has no lien on the shares registered in the name of a trustee for debts due to it from the beneficial owner.[5]

If a lien in favour of the company has arisen and the shareholder sells part only of his shares, the purchaser can require the company to discharge the lien primarily out of the shares not sold.[6]

[2] *Ante*, p. 244.
[3] *Champagne Perrier-Jouet S.A.* v. *H. H. Finch Ltd.* [1982] 3 All E.R. 713, 720–721.
[4] *Mackereth* v. *Wigan Coal Co. Ltd.* [1916] 2 Ch. 293.
[5] *Re Perkins* (1890) 24 Q.B.D. 613 (C.A.).
[6] *Gray* v. *Stone* (1893) 69 L.T. 282.

A lien does not cease on the shareholder's death, but may be enforced against his executors.[7]

Lien on Shares (Scots Law)

A company has at common law and independently of any provision in its articles a lien on shares held by a member for debts due by the member to the company.[8] Articles, however, usually make express provision to the same effect. The lien enables the company to refuse to register any transfer of the shares until the transferor's debt to the company has been satisfied.

A company whose articles expressly limit the lien to partly paid shares may alter the articles so as to extend the lien to all shares, but if such an alteration is not made until after a transfer of fully paid shares has been presented for registration the transferee's right to be registered is not affected by that alteration.[9]

A lien can be enforced by a sale only if the power of sale has been conferred by the articles, or a warrant is obtained from the court. A lien in respect of debts other than calls or instalments could not be enforced by forfeiture, since that would be an illegal reduction of capital.

Where X, a shareholder, has assigned his shares in security to Y who has completed his title to the shares by being registered as the holder of them, the company is no longer entitled to a lien on the shares in respect of debts due to it by X, since X is not the registered holder.[10]

For the provisions of section 150 and of Table A on lien, see "Lien (English Law)," above.

Forfeiture of Shares

Although a forfeiture of a member's shares by the company is recognised by the Act, the directors may forfeit shares only if

[7] *Allen* v. *Gold Reefs of West Africa Ltd.* [1900] 1 Ch. 656 (C.A.), *ante*, p. 92.
[8] *Hotchkis* v. *Royal Bank* (1797) 3 Paton 618; (1797) M. 2673; *Burns* v. *Lawrie's Trustees* (1840) 2 D. 1348; *Bell's Trustee* v. *Coatbridge Tinplate Co. Ltd.* (1886) 14 R. 246.
[9] *Liquidator of W. & A. M'Arthur Ltd.* v. *Gulf Line Ltd.*, 1909 S.C. 732.
[10] *Paul's Trustee* v. *Thomas Justice & Sons Ltd.*, 1912 S.C. 1303.

expressly authorised to do so by the articles and only for non-payment of a call or an instalment: section 143(3)(*d*).

Table A provides:

Regulation 18 "If a call remains unpaid after it has become due and payable the directors may give to the person from whom it is due not less than 14 clear days' notice requiring payment of the amount unpaid together with any interest which may have accrued. The notice shall name the place where payment is to be made and shall state that if the notice is not complied with the shares in respect of which the call was made will be liable to be forfeited."

Regulation 19 "If the notice is not complied with any share in respect of which it was given may, before the payment required by the notice has been made, be forfeited by a resolution of the directors and the forfeiture shall include dividends or other monies payable in respect of the forfeited shares and not paid before the forfeiture."

Forfeiture, being in the nature of a penal proceeding, is valid only if the provisions of the articles, *e.g.* as to notice, are strictly followed. Any irregularity will avoid the forfeiture.[11] To protect purchasers of the forfeited shares against possible irregularities in the forfeiture, the articles usually provide, as does Table A, regulation 22, that the title of the purchaser shall not be affected by any invalidity in the proceedings in reference to the forfeiture.

The power of the directors to forfeit shares must be exercised in good faith and not for the purpose of relieving shareholders with whom the directors are friendly from their liability.[12]

Forfeiture for non-payment of other debts due to the company is invalid.[13] Similarly, an article which authorises the forfeiture of shares held by a member who sues the company or the directors is invalid.[14]

An invalid forfeiture can be restrained by injunction.[15]

Forfeited shares may be sold or reissued by a private company according to the provisions of the articles.

A public company however must cancel the forfeited shares unless they are disposed of within three years. In the interim

[11] *Johnson* v. *Lyttle's Iron Agency* (1877) 5 Ch.D. 687 (C.A.).

[12] *Re Esparto Trading Co.* (1879) 12 Ch.D. 191; *Gower's Case* (1868) L.R. 6 Eq. 77.

[13] *Hopkinson* v. *Mortimer, Harley & Co.* [1917] 1 Ch. 646, *ante*, p. 305.

[14] *Hope* v. *International Financial Socy.* (1876) 4 Ch.D. 237 (C.A.).

[15] See note 11, *ante*. The procedure in Scots law would be an interdict.

period the company may not vote with the shares. If this cancellation takes the public company below the authorised minimum capital it must re-register as a private company: section 146.

A forfeiture cannot be cancelled without the consent of the person whose shares have been forfeited.[16]

Forfeited shares can be reissued at less than the amount which has been paid on them.

A company had forfeited a number of shares of £5 5s. each, £2 5s. paid, and proposed to reissue them at the price of 30s. a share. *Held*, the company could do so, as it was not bound to treat the forfeited shares as if nothing had been paid upon them: *Morrison* v. *Trustees, etc., Corpn. Ltd.* (1898) 68 L.J.Ch. 11 (C.A.).

The purchaser of the reissued shares is liable for the payment of all future calls duly made, including one for the amount of the call which occasioned the forfeiture.[17] Consequently, there is no issue of shares at a discount, as the company has already received the amount paid up. The purchaser should be credited with any subsequent payments made by the ex-owner.[18]

The effect of the forfeiture on the former owner of the shares is to discharge him from his liability on the shares.[19] "The company on forfeiture gets its shares back, and the shareholder who has had his shares forfeited is wholly discharged from his liability."[20] To prevent this position from arising, the articles usually preserve the liability of the former owner.

Table A provides:

Regulation 21 "A person any of whose shares have been forfeited shall cease to be a member in respect of them and shall surrender to the company for cancellation the certificate for the shares forfeited but shall remain liable to the company for all monies which at the date of

[16] *Larkworthy's case* [1903] 1 Ch. 711.

[17] *New Balkis Eersteling Ltd.* v. *Randt Gold Mining Co.* [1904] A.C. 165, where the purchaser was to hold the shares "discharged from all calls due prior to such purchase."

[18] *Re Randt Gold Mining Co.* [1904] 2 Ch. 468, *Re Bolton*, below, shows that the converse is true.

[19] *Stocken's Case* (1868) L.R. 3 Ch.App. 412; in *Goldsmith* v. *Colonial Finance etc. Corpn. Ltd.* [1909] 8 C.L.R. 241, Griffith C.J., at p. 249, and Barton J., at p. 253, thought that what Lord Cairns L.J. said in *Stocken* was founded on the particular article there in question.

[20] *Per* Luxmore J. in *Re Bolton* [1930] 2 Ch. 48, *post*, at p. 59.

forfeiture were presently payable to him to the company in respect of those shares with interest at the rate at which interest was payable on those monies before the forfeiture or, of no interest was so payable, at the appropriate rate (as defined in the Act) from the date of forfeiture until payment but the directors may waive payment wholly or in part or enforce payment without any allowance for the value of the shares at the time of forfeiture or for any consideration received on their disposal."

Such an article makes the person whose shares have been forfeited for non-payment of calls liable as a debtor to the company, and not as a contributory,[21] so that where, more than a year after the forfeiture, the company went into liquidation, it was held that the former owner of the shares was still liable.[22]

The company cannot recover more than the difference between the calls due and the amount received on reissue.

B. underwrote two blocks of shares in a company. The issue to the public was a failure and B. was consequently allotted (*inter alia*) 8,200 £1 shares in the company. He was unable to pay the calls on these shares, which were forfeited. They were then reissued so that the company received the balance of the calls in full, but to obtain the new allottees the company had to pay £1,018 by way of commission. B. became bankrupt. The articles provided that the holder of forfeited shares should remain liable for calls notwithstanding the forfeiture and the company attempted to prove for the balance of calls due from B. *Held*, the company could not receive payment of the calls twice over and could only prove for the actual loss sustained *viz.* the £1,018 commission: *Re Bolton* [1930] 2 Ch. 48.

A surety for calls is released on forfeiture of the shares without his consent.[23]

Surrender of Shares

The Act does not give a company any express power to accept a surrender of his shares by a member. A company's articles, however, frequently give power to the directors to accept a surrender of shares where they are in a position to forfeit such

[21] *Post*, Chap. 29.

[22] *Ladies' Dress Assocn. Ltd.* v. *Pulbrook* [1900] 2 Q.B. 376 (C.A.); *cf. Ferguson* v. *Central Halls Co. Ltd.* (1881) 8 R. 997, and *Liquidators of Mount Morgan (West) Gold Mine Ltd.* v. *M'Mahon* (1891) 18 R. 772.

[23] *Re Darwen and Pearce* [1927] 1 Ch. 176.

shares, *i.e.* for non-payment of calls or instalments on those shares: section 143(3)(*d*).

A surrender of shares is lawful where it is accepted to save the company from going through the formalities of forfeiture.[24]

"These [surrenders of shares] have been admitted by the Courts upon the principle, as I understand it, that they have practically the same effect as forfeiture, the main difference being that the one is a proceeding *in invitum*, and the other a proceeding taken with the assent of the shareholder, who is unable to retain and pay future calls on his shares."[25]

Surrender in these circumstances has been described as an "apparent exception" only to the principle of maintenance of capital,[26] since "the extinction of the obligation of a bankrupt shareholder can injure nobody."[27]

Following section 143 a company may only acquire its own shares in a few cases in addition to a surrender in lieu of forfeiture. These have been considered above.[28] It appears that in all those cases, *e.g* a purchase by the company, a surrender of shares may be used as the method of acquisition. No other forms of surrender appear to be valid.

In particular, a surrender of partly paid shares, not liable to forfeiture, is unlawful, as it (*a*) releases the shareholder from further liability in respect of the shares, (*b*) amounts to a purchase by the company of its own shares, and (*c*) is a reduction of capital without the sanction of the court.

A company sustained a loss of £4,000 and the directors agreed to share the loss between themselves. They therefore surrendered shares to the amount of £4,000. The shares were £11 each, £10 paid, and the intention was that the directors should be released from the remaining £1 a share unpaid. The company subsequently became more prosperous and the directors took proceedings to have the surrender declared invalid. *Held*, the surrender was invalid as amounting to a purchase by the company of its own shares: *Bellerby* v. *Rowland & Marwood, Steamship Co. Ltd.* [1902] 2 Ch. 14 (C.A.).

[24] *e.g. General Property Investment Co. Ltd. and Liquidator* v. *Craig* (1890) 18 R. 389.

[25] *Per* Lord Watson in *Trevor* v. *Whitworth* (1887) 12 App.Cas. 409 at p. 429.

[26] *Ante*, p. 191.

[27] *Per* Lord M'Laren in *Gill* v. *Arizona Copper Co. Ltd.* (1900) 2 F. 843 at p. 860.

[28] *Ante*, Chap. 10.

Shares which have been validly surrendered can be reissued in the same way as forfeited shares, if the articles authorise their reissue.

SHARE WARRANT

A share warrant is a document issued by a company either under its common seal or otherwise in compliance with section 36A or 36B as appropriate,[29] stating that the bearer of the warrant is entitled to the shares specified therein: section 188.

Before share warrants can be issued the following conditions must be satisfied:

(1) the company must be a company and limited by shares;
(2) there must be authority in the articles. (Table A does not authorise the issue of share warrants);
(3) the shares must be fully paid up: section 188.

When the issue of share warrants is authorised, the articles usually provide for such matters as the deposit of the share warrant with the company a certain number of days before any right is exercised, and for the giving of notices of meetings by advertisement.

On issuing a share warrant, the company must strike out of its register of members the name of the holder of the shares as if he had ceased to be a member and make the following entries in the register:

(1) the fact of the issue of the warrant;
(2) a statement of shares included in the warrant, distinguishing each share by its number, so long as the share has a number;
(3) the date of issue of the warrant: section 355(1).

The bearer of a share warrant may, however, if the articles so provide, be deemed to be a member of the company either to the full extent or for any purposes defined in the articles: section 355(1).

[29] *Ante*, p. 111.

A share warrant can, subject to the articles, be surrendered for cancellation, whereupon the holder is entitled to be entered in the register of members: section 355(2).

Stock warrants to bearer can be issued on the same terms as share warrants.[30]

A share warrant differs from a share certificate[31] in the following respects:

(1) the bearer of a warrant is not entered in a register: section 355;
(2) he is entitled to the shares specified in the warrant: section 188(1);
(3) the shares are transferable by delivery of the warrant: section 188(2);
(4) a warrant is a negotiable instrument and if it is stolen and afterwards gets into the hands of a bona fide purchaser for value without notice of the fraud, he can enforce against the company payment of coupons for dividends due in respect of such share warrant[32];
(5) coupons for dividends may be attached to a warrant: section 188(3).

Dividends are advertised, and then collected upon the handing over of the appropriate coupon. This procedure is necessary because the company does not know to whom to send the dividend;

(6) holding a share warrant is not enough where the articles require a director to hold a specified share qualification: section 291(2).[33]

Share warrants are not very common. This is because until 1979, they could only be issued with Treasury consent and had to be deposited with an authorised depositary, because of the serious consequences of loss or theft, and also because of the heavy stamp duty. Another reason is that the company has to advertise in newspapers to get in touch with the shareholders. With the abolition of exchange controls in 1979 there are fewer restrictions on their use.

[30] *Pilkington* v. *United Railways of Havana* [1930] 2 Ch. 108.
[31] *Ante*, p. 272.
[32] *Webb Hale & Co.* v. *Alexandria Water Co. Ltd.* (1905) 93 L.T. 339.
[33] *Post*, p. 361.

Section 189 makes special provision for certain offences in connection with share warrants in Scotland.

Valuation of Shares

Articles of private companies often provide that a member who wants to sell his shares must first offer them to the existing members at a price to be fixed by the auditors. Similar provisions are often applicable in the case of a member's death.[34] In valuing the shares for this purpose, the auditor is not obliged to explain the basis of his valuation or to give his reasons for it, and in such circumstances there can be no action to have the valuation set aside by a party who is dissatisfied with it, if it is of the right property by the right man who is acting in good faith.[35] These are known as "non-speaking" certificates. If, however, he does give an explanation, *i.e.* by a "speaking" certificate, the court can inquire into it and, if satisfied that the valuation has been made on the wrong basis, can declare that it is not binding, *i.e.* the valuation can be impeached for[36] fraud, mistake or miscarriage, but on matters of opinion the court will not interfere.[37] In this respect it is irrelevant either that the transaction has been completed or that the auditors might be liable in negligence.[38]

In valuing a minority shareholding a valuer should allow for a discount to reflect that fact.[39] If there is an actual offer by a third party subsequent to the date of valuation the valuer may use that as evidence of value at that date. It would be different if there was a subsequent change in the market conditions.[40] For

[34] *Ante*, pp. 278 *et seq.*

[35] *Baber* v. *Kenwood Manufacturing Co. Ltd.* [1978] 1 Lloyd's Rep. 175.

[36] The Scottish equivalent of "impeached for" is "challenged on the ground of."

[37] *Dean* v. *Prince* [1954] Ch. 409 (C.A.). In this case the articles of a private company provided that a deceased director's shares should be purchased by the surviving directors at a price to be certified by an auditor as a fair value. The director who held a controlling interest died. The auditor stated that he had not regarded the company as a going concern but had valued on a "break-up" basis because in his opinion the shares had no value on any other basis because of losses made by the company. *Held*, the auditor was right. See further *Jones* (*M.*) v. *Jones* (*R.R.*) 1 W.L.R. 840, where the valuation was not made by the stipulated expert.

[38] *Burgess* v. *Purchase and Sons* (*Farms*) *Ltd.* [1983] Ch. 216.

[39] *Howie* v. *Crawford* [1990] BCC 330, *cf. Re Bird Precision Bellows Ltd.* [1986] Ch. 658.

[40] *Re ESC Publishing Ltd.* [1990] BCC 335.

the purpose of valuing the shares of a private company with high returns but little or no assets, the value of the company is the capitalised sum of the future profits.[41]

An auditor may be liable in negligence to either party, however, even though the valuation may not be liable to be set aside. To be liable in this way an auditor must be acting as a valuer and not as an arbitrator, *i.e.* settling a dispute between at least two parties which was sent to him to resolve in such a way that he had to exercise a judicial discretion.[42] An auditor of a private company who, on request, values its shares in the knowledge that this valuation will determine the price to be paid under a contract owes a duty of care to both the vendor and the purchaser. An agreement for valuation is not generally one for an arbitration. The function of a valuer is usually to settle a price so that no differences arise between the parties. His function is not to make an award after a difference has arisen. Only in the latter case will no duty of care arise.[43]

Even if a duty of care does arise, the standard of care expected of an ordinary auditor is not that of a specialist valuer. This "auditor standard" will only be displaced by express contrary intention.[44]

[41] *Buckingham* v. *Francis* [1986] BCLC 353.
[42] *Sutcliffe* v. *Thackrah* [1974] A.C. 727.
[43] See *Leigh* v. *English Property Corporation* [1976] 2 Lloyd's Rep. 298.
[44] *Whiteoak* v. *Walker* (1988) 4 BCC 122.

Chapter 14

GENERAL MEETINGS

THIS chapter is concerned with general meetings, *i.e.* meetings of the members or shareholders of a company and certain other persons (the auditors, the personal representatives of a deceased member and the trustee in bankruptcy of a bankrupt member). The various kinds of general meeting are dealt with first and it will be seen that the Act requires that subject to an election by a private company to the contrary, certain meetings, *e.g.* an annual general meeting, are held and allows other meetings, called extraordinary general meetings, to be held, usually when the directors think fit. Then the notice that the members must be given of general meetings is explained. Thirdly, proceedings at general meetings are dealt with—how many members must be present to constitute a meeting and enable it to transact business, who takes the chair, how a vote is taken and so on. Fourthly, the various kinds of resolution that may be passed at a meeting, including elective resolutions, are explained. Finally, the effects of written resolutions which do not require a meeting at all are discussed.

If a company has more than one class of shares, class meetings, *i.e.* meetings of the holders of the shares of a certain class, may be held. Some of the sections referred to below, *e.g.* section 369 with regard to the length of notice for calling meetings, also apply to meetings of any class of members of a company as they apply to general meetings of the company. Section 125(6) provides that the provisions of the Act and the articles relating to general meetings apply to class meetings, except that a quorum shall be two persons at least holding or representing by proxy one-third of the issued shares of the class and that any holder of shares of the class present in person or by proxy may demand a poll.

KINDS OF GENERAL MEETING

Annual general meeting

By section 366 the general rule is that, subject to an election by a private company to the contrary, under section 366A[1] every company must hold an annual general meeting, specified as such in the notice calling it, every year, with an interval of not more than 15 months between one annual general meeting of the company and the next. The word "year" means calendar year, *i.e.* the period January 1 to December 31.[2] A limited exception is that as long as a company holds its first annual general meeting within 18 months of incorporation it need not hold it in the year of incorporation or, sometimes in the following year, *e.g.* a company incorporated on October 1, 1991, might hold its first annual general meeting in March 1992.

The directors must call the annual general meeting. The object of section 366 is to ensure that those members who wish to do so can meet together and confront the directors at least once a year. The usual business at an annual general meeting is: the declaration of a dividend, the consideration of the accounts, balance sheets and the reports of the directors and auditors, the election of directors in place of those retiring, and the appointment of, and the fixing of the remuneration of, the auditors.

If default is made in holding an annual general meeting, the Secretary of State (for Trade and Industry) may, on the application of any member of the company, call or direct the calling of a meeting and give such ancillary directions as he thinks expedient, including a direction that one member present in person or by proxy shall be deemed to constitute the meeting: section 367.

Under section 366A a private company may, by an elective resolution,[3] dispense with the holding of an annual general meeting. It may also by such a resolution elect not to lay its annual accounts at the meeting,[4] and not to appoint its auditors

[1] *Infra.*
[2] *Gibson* v. *Barton* (1875) L.R. 10 Q.B. 329.
[3] *Post*, p. 340.
[4] *Post*, Chap. 22.

annually,[5] which dispenses with a large part of its annual business. Any member may, despite a section 366A election being in force, require an AGM to be held by giving notice to that effect to the company at least three months before the end of the year in question, and section 366 will then apply. If the election is revoked no meeting need be held in that year if there are less than three months of the year remaining.

Extraordinary general meetings

Any general meeting of a company, other than an annual general meeting, is an extraordinary general meeting. Table A, regulation 36, so provides and regulation 37 provides that the directors *may*, whenever they think fit, convene an extraordinary general meeting.

Further, by section 368, despite anything in the articles, the directors are *bound* to convene an extraordinary general meeting on the requisition of the holders of not less than one-tenth of the paid-up capital of the company carrying the right of voting at general meetings or, if the company has no shares capital, of members representing not less than one-tenth of the total voting rights. The requisition must state the objects of the meeting and be signed by the requisitionists. If the directors do not, within 21 days of the deposit of the requisition at the registered office of the company, proceed to convene the meeting, the requisitionists, or the holders of more than half their voting rights, may convene it themselves so long as it is held within three months after such deposit.[6] The reasonable expenses of the requisitionists in convening the meeting must be repaid by the company, which must retain them out of any remuneration of the directors in default.

Under a long awaited amendment to section 368 by the 1989 Act,[7] the directors, if requested to hold a meeting under that section, must fix the actual date of the meeting within 28 days of its being summoned, thus allowing a maximum 49 day period in

[5] *Post*, Chap. 23.

[6] This right may be abrogated if the requisionists are themselves directors who have, by failing to attend board meetings, been the cause of the directors' default: *Thyne* v. *Lauder*, 1925 S.N. 123 (O.H.).

[7] Sched. 19 para. 9.

total. Prior to this amendment directors could call a meeting within 21 days for a date at any time in the future.[8]

Section 142 requires the directors of a public company to call a general meeting in the event of a serious loss of capital. In such a case the meeting must be convened within 28 days for a date not later than 28 days after the notice convening the meeting.[9]

By section 371, if for any reason it is impracticable to call a meeting in any manner in which meetings may be called, or to conduct a meeting in the manner prescribed by the articles or the Act, the conduct may, either of its own motion or on application by any director or any member entitled to vote at the meeting, order a meeting to be called, held and conducted in such manner as the court thinks fit, and may give such ancillary directions as it thinks expedient, including a direction that one member present in person or by proxy shall be deemed to constitute the meeting.

E. Ltd. had three members, A, B and C. A and B were directors and held five per cent. of the shares each. C, who was not a director, held 90 per cent. of the shares. No general meetings were held. The articles provided that a quorum at a meeting should be two members. A and B frustrated C's efforts to call a meeting under section 368 by refusing to attend. C gave special notice to his intention to move ordinary resolutions to remove the directors at the next extraordinary general meeting, and asked the court to call a meeting under section 371 and to direct that one member should be a quorum. C's application was opposed by the directors. *Held*, the application should be granted because(1) otherwise C would be deprived of his right to remove the directors under section 303, (2) the directors were in breach of their statutory duty by not holding an annual general meeting: *Re El Sombrero Ltd.* [1958] Ch. 900.[10]

O Ltd. had two members, A and B who were the sole directors. A owned 51 per cent. of the votes and B the remainder. They fell out and A called a meeting to dismiss B as a director. B refused to attend so that the quorum provisions for meetings (two) could not be complied with. On A's application under section 371, the court ordered a meeting with a quorum of one, otherwise there would be a deadlock situation. The quorum provisions did not give B a veto. A's conduct in

[8] *Re Windward Islands (Enterprises) U.K. Ltd.* [1983] BCLC 293; *McGuinness & Anor., Petitioners* (1988) 4 BCC 161.

[9] *Ante*, p. 204.

[10] For a Scottish instance, see *Edinburgh Workmen's Houses Improvement Co. Ltd., Petitioners*, 1935 S.C. 56.

dismissing B was a matter for other proceedings: *Re Opera Photographic Ltd.* (1989) 5 BCC 601.

The Jenkins Report[11] recommended that section 371 should be amended so that personal representatives of deceased members should be treated, for the purpose of the section, as members of the company, *i.e.* able to apply under the section, and as having the same voting rights as the dead members would have had. This would enable the company to appoint directors when all directors and shareholders have died.

A private company may dispense with meetings for the majority of items by using the written resolution procedure, *post*.

NOTICE OF GENERAL MEETINGS

Length of notice for calling meetings

The effect of section 369 is that notwithstanding a provision in the articles providing for shorter notice:

(1) an annual general meeting must be called by not less than 21 days' written notice:

(2) any other general meeting of a limited company must be called by not less than 14 days' written notice, unless a special resolution is to be proposed, in which case, by section 378, not less than 21 days' such notice is required.

Table A, regulation 38, provides that the notice shall be clear notice, *i.e.* exclusive of the day on which it is served or deemed to be served and of the day for which it is given.[12]

A meeting may be called by shorter notice than that specified above or in the articles if that is agreed to by—(1) all the members entitled to attend and vote in the case of an annual general meeting; or (2) a majority in number of the members holding not less than 95 per cent. of the shares giving the right to attend and vote or, in the case of a company without a share

[11] Para. 31.

[12] In Scotland articles may be so worded as not to require *clear* notice, *e.g.* a provision that "days shall be reckoned, excluding the first and including the last of such days," allows the day of the meeting to be counted: *The Aberdeen Comb Works Co. Ltd., Petitioners* (1902) 10 S.L.T. 210.

capital, representing not less than 95 per cent. of the total voting rights, in the case of any other meeting. A private company may by an elective resolution[13] reduce the percentage of members required to sanction short notice to 90 per cent: sections 369(3), (4); 378(3).

If a resolution is to be passed on short notice, it must be appreciated that the resolution is being so passed.[14]

Sections 369(3), (4) and 378(3) are derived from cases like *Re Express Engineering Works Ltd.*[15] and *Re Oxted Motor Co. Ltd.*[16] which established that it is competent to all the shareholders to waive formalities as regards notice of meetings, etc.

In the *Express Engineering* case five persons formed a private company in which they were the sole shareholders. They sold to the company for £15,000 a property which they had just brought for £7,000. The price was to be paid by the issue of debentures for £15,000 by the company. The transaction was carried out at a "board" meeting of the five individuals who appointed themselves the directors. The articles forbade a director to vote in respect of a contract in which he was interested. It was held that there was no fraud and the company was bound in the matter by the unanimous agreement of the members. Consequently the debentures were valid.

In the *Oxted Motor* case both members of a company waived the normal length of notice of a meeting at which an extraordinary resolution for voluntary winding up was validly passed.

The *Express Engineering* case was applied in *Re Bailey, Hay & Co. Ltd.*[17] where short notice was given of a meeting to pass an extraordinary resolution for voluntary winding up but all five corporators attended and the resolution was passed by the votes of two shareholders, the other shareholders abstaining from voting. The resolution was deemed to have been passed with the unanimous agreement of all the corporators and those who abstained were treated as having acquiesced in the winding-up.

Service of notice of meetings

Section 370 provides that, unless the articles provide to the contrary, notice of the meeting of a company is to be served on

[13] *Post*, p. 340.
[14] *Re Pearce Duff & Co. Ltd.* [1960] 1 W.L.R. 1014.
[15] [1920] 1 Ch. 466 (C.A.), followed in the Victorian case of *E. H. Dey Pty Ltd.* v. *Dey* [1966] V.R. 464.
[16] [1921] 3 K.B. 32.
[17] [1971] 1 W.L.R. 1357.

every member of the company as required by Table A. Section 387(1) requires that notice of every general meeting be given to the auditors.

If notice of a meeting is not given to every person entitled to notice, any resolution passed at the meeting will be of no effect.

A committee of a club met and passed a resolution expelling Y from the club. X, a member of the committee, was not summoned to the meeting, as she had previously informed the chairman that she would be unable to attend meetings. *Held*, the omission to summon X invalidates the proceedings of the committee: *Young* v. *Ladies' Imperial Club Ltd.* [1920] 2 K.B. 523 (C.A.).

To obviate this result it is usually provided in the articles, as in Table A, regulation 39, that the accidental omission to give notice to, or the non-receipt of notice by any person entitled to receive notice shall not invalidate the proceedings at that meeting.

In *Re West Canadian Collieries Ltd.* [1962] Ch. 370, the omission to give notice of a meeting to a few members, because the plates for these members were inadvertently kept out of the machine when the envelopes for the notices were being addressographed, was an accidental omission within an article like Table A, article 39.

However, in *Musselwhite* v. *C. H. Musselwhite & Sons Ltd.* [1962] Ch. 964,[18] the omission to give notice of a general meeting to the unpaid vendors of shares who remained on the register of members, because the directors erroneously believed the vendors were no longer members, was due to an error of law and was not accidental omission within such an article.

Nature of notice of meetings

The articles of a company will contain provisions dealing with the nature of the notice to be given of meetings. Table A, regulation 38, provides that the notice of a meeting shall state the time and place, of the meeting and, the general nature of the business to be transacted.

Notice of an annual general meeting was in common form and included in the business was "to elect directors." C., the retiring director, offered himself for re-election, but was not elected. A motion

[18] *Ante*, p. 290.

was proposed for the election of three new directors to fill up the places of the retiring director and two vacancies, but the chairman refused to accept it. *Held*, the refusal was wrong, as the notice sufficiently specified the general nature of the business to bring it within the competence of the meeting to elect directors up to the number permitted by the articles: *Choppington Collieries Ltd.* v. *Johnson* [1944] 1 All E.R. 762 (C.A.).

Notice of the business to be transacted must "state the resolution to be passed in such way as fairly to state the purpose for which the meeting is convened, so that every shareholder may make up his mind whether he will or will not attend with knowledge of the result of his act."[19]

Directors of a holding company had from 1907 to 1914 been receiving remuneration as directors of a subsidiary company without the knowledge of the shareholders of the holding company. Special resolutions, authorising the directors to retain the remuneration and altering the altering the articles to allow the directors to receive remuneration as directors of subsidiary companies, were proposed and an extraordinary general meeting summoned to pass them. The notice did not specify the amount of the remuneration, which was £44,876. The resolution was passed. A shareholder brought an action on behalf of himself and all other shareholders of the company against the company and its directors claiming, *inter alia*, a declaration that the resolution was not binding upon the company. *Held*, the resolution was not binding as the notice was insufficient: *Baillie* v. *Oriental Telephone etc. Co. Ltd.* [1915] 1 Ch. 503 (C.A.).

A notice convening a meeting stated that it was being held for receiving the directors' report, and the election of directors and auditors. The directors' report sent therewith stated that the meeting would be asked to confirm the appointment of R. as director. *Held*, the notice and the report together were sufficient notice of this special business: *Boschoek Proprietary Co Ltd.* v. *Fuke* [1906] Ch. 148.

The notice of a general meeting at which a special resolution or an extraordinary resolution is to be proposed must specify the intention to propose the resolution as a special resolution or an extraordinary resolution[20] as the case may be: section 378. There must be complete identity between the substance of the

[19] Stiebel's *Company Law* (3rd. ed.), p. 335.

[20] Strictly interpreted in *Rennie* v. *Crichton's* (*Strichen*) *Ltd.*, 1927 S.L.T. 459 (O.H.), in which a notice of a resolution for voluntary winding up was held invalid because it did not specify the intention to propose the resolution *as an extraordinary resolution*; for *obiter dicta* to the contrary see *North of Scotland etc. Steam Navigation Co. Ltd.*, *Petitioners*, 1920 S.C. 94.

resolution as passed and the substance of the resolution set out in the notice. Thus in a resolution for a reduction of capital a change in the amount proposed to be reduced of £321 out of a total of £1,356,900 as shown in the notice was held to invalidate the notice. Changes because of grammatical or clerical errors or the use of more formal language might however be allowed.[21]

Where a meeting has been requisitioned under section 368, *ante*,[22] it may competently deal with business additional to that specified in the requisition, provided adequate notice of the additional business has been duly given.[23]

Every notice calling a meeting of a company with a share capital must contain a statement, given reasonable prominence, that a member entitled to attend and vote may appoint a proxy to attend and vote instead of him, and that the proxy need not be a member of the company: section 372.

Notice of members' resolutions and statements

If some of the members of a company themselves wish to move a resolution at an *annual general meeting*, or to circulate to members a statement relating to any proposed resolution or the business to be dealt with at *any general meeting*, they can do so under section 376. The section provides that on the written requisition of members holding not less than one-twentieth of the voting rights of the members entitled to vote at the relevant meeting, or of one hundred members on whose shares there has been paid up an average sum of not less than £100 a member, the company must:

(1) give notice to every member entitled to receive notice of the annual general meeting of any resolution which may properly be moved and is intended to be moved at that meeting;
(2) circulate to every member entitled to receive notice of any general meeting any statement, of not more than 1,000 words, relating to any proposed resolution or the business to be dealt with at the meeting.

[21] *Re Moorgate Mercantile Holdings Ltd.* [1980] 1 All E.R. 40.
[22] p. 318.
[23] *Per* Lord Hill Watson (Ordinary), in *Ball* v. *Metal Industries Ltd.*, 1957 S.C. 315 (O.H.) at p. 316.

The notice of the resolution must be given, and any statement must be circulated, with the notice of the meetings or, if that is impracticable, as soon as possible afterwards. The company is not bound to circulate a statement if, on the application of the company or any aggrieved person, the court is satisfied that the rights given by the section are being abused to secure needless publicity for defamatory matter: section 377(3).

The requisition must be signed by the requisitionists and deposited at the registered office: (1) at least six weeks before the meeting when notice of a resolution is required; and (2) at least one week before the meeting in any other case. A sum to cover the company's expenses shall be borne by the company, in which case the deposit will be returned): section 377(1).

If the directors call an annual general meeting for a date six weeks or less after deposit of the requisition, the requisition is deemed to have been properly deposited.

Special notice

Section 379 provides that where under the Act special notice is required of a resolution, notice of the intention to move it must be given *to the company* not less than 28 days before the meeting at which it is to be moved, and the company must give notice of the resolution *to the members* when it gives them notice of the meeting (or, if that is not practicable, either by advertisement in a newspaper having an appropriate circulation or in any other mode allowed by the articles, not less than 21 days before the meeting). To close a loophole which would otherwise allow directors to avoid the provision by claiming that the notice had not been given in time, the section also provides that if the directors call a meeting for a date 28 days or less after the notice has been given to the company, the notice is deemed to have been properly given. The notice to the company may be left at or sent by post to the registered office: section 725.[24]

Special notice is only required by sections 293, 303 and 388 (appointment of a director who has attained the age of 70, removal of directors and the appointment and removal of auditors respectively).

[24] *Ante*, p. 65.

Section 379 does not confer any rights on a shareholder to have a resolution to which it applies circulated if he cannot fulfil the requirements of section 376, above. It simply confers a right to receive notice in a special way if the resolution is being proposed in due form.[25]

Proceedings at General Meetings

Quorum

Under Table A, regulation 40, no business is to be transacted at a general meeting unless a quorum of members is present. Formerly this article only required a quorum when the meeting proceeded to business and so in England was satisfied if a quorum was present at the beginning of the meeting.[26] This was not the law in Scotland, however[27] and the new wording agrees with that law.

The quorum must be an effective quorum, *i.e.* it must consist of members qualified to take part in and decide upon questions before the meeting,[28] and where articles require a quorum of members to be "present" (without any such addition as "personally or by proxy") that word means "present in person."[29]

By section 370, unless the articles otherwise provide, a quorum is two members present in person for any company. Table A, regulation 40, also fixes two members present in person or by proxy as a quorum in the case of any company. As to a quorum at a class meeting, see section 125(6), *ante*.[30]

Strictly, since the word "meeting" prima facie means a coming together of more than one person, one person cannot constitute a meeting,[31] even where he attends in more than one

[25] *Pedley* v. *Inland Waterways Association Ltd.*, [1977] 1 All E.R. 209.

[26] *Re Hartley Baird Ltd.* [1955] Ch. 143, distinguished in *Re London Flats Ltd.* [1969] 1 W.L.R. 711.

[27] *Henderson* v. *Louttit & Co. Ltd.* (1894) 21 R. 674.

[28] *Henderson's case*, above, *per* Lord President Robertson at p. 676.

[29] *M. Harris Ltd. Petitioners*, 1956 S.C. 207, in which a member represented by an attorney was held not to be "present."

[30] p. 267.

[31] *Sharp* v. *Dawes* (1876) 2 Q.B.D. 26 (C.A.), applied in *Re London Flats*, above; *cf. Souter, Petitioner*, 1981 S.L.T. (Sh. Ct.) 89, in which a single creditor was held not to constitute a committee of inspection.

capacity or holds proxies for the other persons.[32] However, in *East* v. *Bennett Bros. Ltd.*[33] It was held that one member, who held all the shares of a class, constituted a class meeting. Further, under sections 366[34] and 371,[35] the Secretary of State and the court, respectively, may direct that one member shall be deemed to constitute a meeting.

If a quorum is not present within half an hour of the time appointed for the meeting, Table A, regulation 41, provides that the meeting shall stand ajourned to the same day in the next week at the same time and place, or to such time and place as the directors may determine, and if at the ajourned meeting a quorum is not present within half an hour, the members present shall form a quorum. It is thought that a single member can constitute a quorum at an adjourned meeting.[36]

Chairman

Section 370 provides that, unless the articles otherwise provide, the members present at a meeting may elect any member as a chairman. However, the articles usually provided who is to be chairman. Table A, regulation 42, states that the chairman of the board of directors shall preside a every general meeting of the company, or if there is no such chairman, or if he is not present within 15 minutes after the time appointed for the meeting or is unwilling to act, the directors present shall elect one of themselves to be chairman. Regulation 43 provides that if no director is willing to act as chairman or if no director is present within 15 minutes, the members present may elect one of their number to be chairman of the meeting.[36a]

[32] *James Prain & Sons Ltd., Petitioners*, 1947 S.C. 325. This case was distinguished in *Neil M'Leod & Sons Ltd., Petitioners*, 1967 S.C. 16, in which the requisite quorum of three *members* personally present was held to be constituted by two individuals, one of whom attended in two capacities (*i.e.* as a member holding shares in his own right and as a member entitled to vote in respect of a trust holding).

[33] [1911] 1 Ch. 163.

[34] *Ante*, p. 317.

[35] *Ante*, p. 319.

[36] See *Jarvis Motors (Harrow) Ltd.* v. *Carabott* [1964] 1 W.L.R. 1101.

[36a] In *Re Bradford Investments plc* [1990] BCC 740, it was held that where no directors are present and there is a dispute as to who may vote then any member may appoint a chairman. This could later be challenged only if the voting rights were themselves subject to challenge.

It is the duty of the chairman:

(1) to preserve order;
(2) to see that the proceedings are regularly conducted,[37]
(3) to take care that the sense of the meeting is properly ascertained with regard to any question properly before it,[38]
(4) to decide incidental questions arising for decision during the meeting, *e.g.* whether proxies are valid.[39]

He must allow the minority of the shareholders to have a reasonable time to put forward their arguments, but at the expiration of that time he is entitled, if he thinks fit, to put a motion to the meeting that the discussion be terminated.[40]

The chairman has no casting vote unless expressly given one by the articles.[41] Table A regulation 50, gives him a casting vote.

Adjournment

A chairman can only adjourn a meeting at his own will in cases of disorder, or where due to inadequacy of space it is impossible for all those entitled to take part in the debate or vote. In such a case he need not put a motion for an adjournment. If the chairman exercises this common law power of adjournment he must act not only in good faith but alsoreasonably in deciding when to reconvene the meeting, so that adjourning to another location for the afternoon of a morning meeting was held not to be reasonable since it did not give all members a reasonable opportunity for attending.[42] If, in any other case, he purports to so adjourn the meeting it may elect another chairman and proceed with the business.[43]

The chairman is not bound to adjourn a meeting, even if the majority desire him to do so,[44] unless the articles otherwise provide.

37 *Byng* v. *London Life Association Ltd.* [1990] Ch. 170 (C.A.).
38 *National Dwellings Society* v. *Sykes* [1894] 3 Ch. 159.
39 *Post*, p. 330.
40 *Wall* v. *London and Northern Assets Corporation* [1898] 2 Ch. 469 (C.A.).
41 *Nell* v. *Longbottom* [1894] 1 Q.B. 767.
42 *Byng* v. *London Life Association Ltd.* [1990] Ch. 170 (C.A.).
43 See note 38.
44 *Salisbury Gold Mining Co. Ltd.* v. *Hathorn* [1897] A.C. 268.

Table A, regulation 45, provides: "The chairman may, with the consent of a meeting at which a quorum is present (and shall if so directed by the meeting), adjourn the meeting from time to time and from place to place, but no business shall be transacted at any adjourned meeting other than the business which might properly have been transacted had the adjournment not taken place. When a meeting is ajourned for the fourteen days or more, at least seven clear days' notice shall be given specifying the time and place of the adjourned meeting and the general nature of the business to be transacted. Otherwise it shall not be necessary to give any such notice,"

Conduct of a meeting

In *Byng* v. *London Life Association Ltd.*,[45] it was held that a meeting could be properly held in more than one room provided that all the rooms are properly provided with audio-visual links so that those in all the rooms can see and hear what is going on in the other rooms and that all due steps are taken to direct to the overflow rooms those unable to get into the main meeting.

Where there are insufficient audio-visual links, as in that case, the main meeting may still constitute a meeting although it will be incapable of proceeding to business. The chairman may therefore validly adjourn this "meeting." There is no rule of law that a meeting at which members are validly excluded is a nullity for that purpose.[46]

Subject to provisions of the Companies Act and the articles, the way in which the business at a meeting is to be conducted is decided by the meeting itself.

"There are many matters relating to the conduct of a meeting which lie entirely in the hands of those persons who are present and constitute the meeting. Thus it rests with the meeting to decide whether notices, resolutions, minutes, accounts, and such like shall be read to the meeting or be taken as read; whether representatives of the Press, or any other persons not qualified to be summoned to the meeting, shall be permitted to be present, or if present shall be permitted to remain; whether and when discussion shall be terminated and a vote taken; whether the meeting shall be ajourned. In all these matters, and they are only instances, the meeting decides, and if necessary a vote must be taken to ascertain the wishes of the majority. If no objection is taken by any constituent of the meeting, the meeting must be taken to

[45] [1990] Ch. 170 (C.A.).
[46] Mustill L.J. dissented on this point.

be assenting to the course adopted": *per* Lord Russell of Killowen in *Carruth* v. *I.C.I. Ltd.* [1937] A.C. 707,[47] at p. 761.

Voting

1. *A show of hands*

The common law rule is that, unless the articles otherwise provide, a resolution put to a meeting is normally decided in the first instance by a show of hands.[48] Further, on a show of hands each member entitled to vote and present in person has one vote only, *i.e.* proxies[49] are not counted. In practice articles do not provide otherwise, *e.g.* Table A, regulation 46, below, provides that a vote shall be by a show of hands unless a poll is demanded and article 54 provides that subject to any rights or restrictions attached to any class of shares,[50] every member present in person shall have one vote on a show of hands, *i.e.* proxies cannot vote.

Table A provides:

Regulation 55 "In the case of joint holders the vote of the senior who tenders a vote, whether in person or by proxy, shall be accepted to the exclusion of the votes of the other joint holders; and seniority shall be determined by the order in which the names of the holders stand in register of members."

Regulation 56 "A member in respect of whom an order has been made by any court having jurisdiction (whether in the United Kingdom or elsewhere in matters concerning mental disorder may vote, whether on a show of hands or on a poll, by his receiver, curator bonis or other person authorised in that behalf appointed by that court, and such receiver, curator bonis or other person may, on a poll, vote by proxy. Evidence to the satisfaction of the directors of the authority of the person claiming to exercise the right to vote shall be deposited at the office, or at such other place as is specified in accordance with the articles for the deposit of instruments of proxy, not less than 48 hours before the time appointed for holding the meeting or adjourned meeting at which the right to vote is to be exercised and in default the right to vote shall not be exercisable."

[47] *Ante*, p. 198.
[48] *Re Horbury Bridge Coal Co.* (1879) 11 Ch.D. 109 (C.A.).
[49] *Post*, p. 331.
[50] *Ante*, p. 259.

Regulation 57 "No member shall vote at any general meeting or at any separate meeting of the holders of any class of shares in the company, either in person or by proxy, in respect of any share held by him unless all monies presently payable by him in respect of that share have been paid."

Regulation 58 "No objection shall be raised to the qualification of any voter except at the meeting or adjourned meeting at which at which the vote objected to is tendered, and every vote not disallowed at the meeting shall be valid. Any objection made in due time shall be referred to the chairman whose decision shall be final and conclusive."

In *Marx* v. *Estates & General Investments Ltd.*,[51] Brightman J. said that there is much to be said for an article like regulation 58. In that case a proxy form, which was liable to stamp duty because it authorised a proxy to vote at more than one meeting but which was unstamped, was not void but a valid authority capable of being stamped, and since the company had accepted it without objection at the meeting the votes cast by the proxy were valid. Further, by virtue of regulation 58 the objection taken several days after the meeting was made too late.

A bankrupt shareholder may vote if he is still on the register.[52] A shareholder, even if he is a director, can vote although he has an interest in the question to be voted on, provided that the majority of the members do not unfairly oppress the minority.[53]

"The shareholder's vote is a right of property, and prima facie may be exercised by a shareholder as he thinks fit in his own interest": *per* Lord Maugham in *Carruth* v. *I.C.I. Ltd.* [1937] A.C. 707, at p. 765.

Table A, regulation 47, provides that, unless a poll is demanded, a declaration by the chairman that a resolution has on a show of hands been carried, or carried by a particular majority, or lost, and an entry to that effect in the minutes, is conclusive evidence of the fact without proof of the number or proportion of the votes recorded for or against.[54] See also section 378(4), *post.*[55]

[51] [1976] 1 W.L.R. 380.

[52] *Morgan* v. *Gray* [1953] Ch. 83, *ante*, p. 236.

[53] *Post*, Chap. 18.

[54] Where a show of hands has been taken and the minutes record the passing of the resolution but omit any mention of the show of hands, further evidence may be required to establish the validity of the procedure: *Fraserburgh Commercial Co. Ltd., Petitioners*, 1946 S.C. 444.

[55] p. 339.

2. *A poll*

Although a show of hands can be taken quickly, it is not an accurate method of ascertaining the wishes of the members of a company because the votes of those voting by proxy are not counted. Again, it does not pay due regard to the wishes of a member holding a large number of shares since he has only one vote on a show of hands. Consequently, although the right to demand a poll exists at common law,[56] section 378(4) gives a statutory right to demand a poll in the case of a special or an extraordinary resolution and articles always make provision for taking a poll. The effect of Table A, regulation 46, is that a poll may be demanded before, or on the declaration of the result of, a show of hands, *i.e.* it is not necessary to have a show of hands before a poll is taken.[57] A proper demand for a poll does away with the need for, or the result of, a show of hands.

The number of votes which a member has on a poll depends upon the articles. Section 370(6) states that unless the articles otherwise provide a member shall have one vote in respect of each share or each £10 of stock held by him, and regulation 54 and 59 of Table A provide that, subject to any rights or restrictions attached to any class of shares, on a poll every member present in person or proxy shall have one vote for each share of which he is the holder, *i.e.* proxies can be counted.

A poll is complete when the result is ascertained, not on an earlier day when the votes are cast.[58]

Section 373 provides that, on any question other than the election of the chairman or the adjournment of the meeting, any article is void in so far as it excludes the right to demand a poll or requires more persons to demand a poll than (*a*) five members entitled to vote at the meeting, or (*b*) members representing one-tenth of the voting rights, or (*c*) members holding one-tenth of the paid-up capital conferring a right to vote. Further, a proxy has the same right to demand a poll as the member he represents. If articles could require a considerable number of members to demand a poll the right would

[56] *R.* v. *Wimbledon Local Board* (1882) 8 Q.B.D. 459 (C.A.).
[57] *Per* Jenkins L.J. in *Holmes* v. *Keyes* [1959] Ch. 199 (C.A.) at p. 212, although see *per* Lord Blanesburgh in *Carruth's* case, *ante*, at p. 755.
[58] *Holmes* v. *Keyes*, *post*, p. 361.

be worthless. It is essential that a proxy be able to demand a poll—he has no vote on a show of hands.

Table A, regulation 46, provides that in addition to the members in (*b*) or (*c*), *ante*, a poll may be demanded by the chairman or by two members having the right to vote at the meeting, and, by article 48, that the demand for a poll may be withdrawn, but only with the consent of the chairman.

The poll is taken as laid down in the articles. Table A, regulation 51, provides that a poll demanded on the election of a chairman or on a question of adjournment shall be taken forthwith. If demanded on any other question, it shall be taken at such time as the chairman directs. Where, under articles similar to Table A, a poll was demanded on a question of adjournment and taken, but the scrutineers informed the chairman that the result could not be announced within the time during which the meeting hall was available, it was held that the meeting subsequently convened to hear the result was a continuation of the original meeting, with the result that no proxies deposited between the date of the original meeting and the date of the continuation meeting were valid, as the articles required proxies to be deposited 48 hours before the meeting.[59]

On a poll, a member entitled to more than one vote need not cast all his votes or cast them all in the same way: section 374. This provision was introduced to meet the difficulties of a large trust corporation which might hold shares in a company on behalf of two or more different trusts, whose respective intrests might well require different exercises of its votes.[60]

Proxies

Although there is no common law right to vote by proxy,[61] section 372 gives such a right.

The section contains the following provisions: Any member entitled to attend and vote at a company meeting may appoint

[59] *Jackson* v. *Hamlyn* [1953] Ch. 577, applying *Shaw* v. *Tati Concessions Ltd.* [1913] 1 Ch. 292.

[60] *Per* Walton J. in *Northern Counties Securities Ltd.* v. *Jackson & Steeple Ltd.* [1974] 1 W.L.R. 1133, at p. 1147.

[61] *Per* Lord Hanworth M.R. in *Cousins* v. *International Brick Co. Ltd.* [1931] 2 Ch. 90 (C.A.) at p. 100.

another person, whether a member of the company or not, to attend and vote as his proxy, and if the company is a private company, to speak as his proxy. The Jenkins Report[62] recommended that a proxy be allowed to speak at a meeting of any company. Every notice calling a meeting must state this right of a member to appoint a proxy. Unless the articles otherwise provide, a proxy can only vote on a poll, a member of a private company cannot appoint more than one proxy to attend on the same occasion, and a member of a company without a share capital cannot appoint a proxy. Articles cannot require the instrument appointing a proxy to be deposited with the company more than 48 hours before a meeting or an adjourned meeting. If articles could require the instrument to be deposited a considerable time before a meeting the right to appoint a proxy would be worthless.

A proxy is appointed by an instrument in writing in accordance with the articles. There are two forms of proxy in use—a general proxy appointing a person to vote as he thinks fit, having regard to what is said at the meeting, and a special proxy appointing a person to vote for or against a particular resolution. A special proxy is often called "a two-way proxy." The Stock Exchange requires two-way proxy forms to be sent to shareholders.[63]

The articles usually provide for the form and proof of proxies.

Table A contains the following provisions:

Regulation 59.—"On a poll votes may be given either personally or by proxy. A member may appoint more than one proxy to attend on the same occasion."

Regulation 60.—The instrument appointing a proxy must be in writing signed by the appointer; it also prescribes the form of a general proxy.

Regulation 61.—Prescribes the form of a special proxy.

Regulation 62.—The instrument must be deposited at the registered office at least 48 hours before the holding of the meeting or adjourned meeting—24 hours in the case of a poll—otherwise it is invalid.

Regulation 63.—A vote by proxy is valid notwithstanding the revocation of the proxy, as long as no intimation in writing of such

[62] Para. 468.

[63] Admission of Securities to Listing, page 5.35.

revocation has been received by the company as the registered office before the commencement of the meeting or adjourned meeting.

It has been held that directors acting bona fide in the interests of the company are entitled to send out to the shareholders proxy papers in favour of named directors at the expense of the company.[64] However, section 372(6) provides that if invitations to appoint a proxy by a person or one of a number of persons specified in the invitations are issued at the company's expense to some only of the members entitled to vote at a meeting, every officer of the company who knowingly and wilfully authorised or permits their issue is liable to a fine, although an officer is not liable by reason only of the issue to a member, at his written request, of a form of appointment naming the proxy or of a list of persons willing to act as proxy, if the form or list is available to every member entitled to vote. If this were not so the directors might send the proxy papers to friendly shareholders only. The Jenkins Report[65] recommended that proxy forms issued by a board of directors should permit the member the instruct his proxy to vote for or against (or to exercise his discretion in respect of) each resolution dealing with special business.

It is the duty of the chairman to decide on the validity of proxies. If the articles provide, as does Table A, regulation 58, that votes tendered at a meeting and not disallowed shall be deemed to be valid, the court will not review the chairman's decision, even if it is wrong, in the absence of fraud or bad faith on his part.[66] Where articles do not incorporate Table A a mere misprint or some quite palpable mistake on the face of a proxy form does not entitle the company to refuse to accept the proxy.[67]

Where proxy forms were sent out to all the stockholders in a company and the chairman was named as their proxy, it was

[64] *Peel* v. *L. & N.W. Rlwy. Co.* [1907] 1 Ch. 5 (C.A.).

[65] Para. 468.

[66] *Wall* v. *Exchange Investment Corporation* [1926] Ch. 143 (C.A.). And see *Marx* v. *Estates and General Investments Ltd.* [1976] 1 W.L.R. 380, *ante*, p. 331.

[67] *Oliver* v. *Dalgleish* [1963] 1 W.L.R. 1274, where the proxies referred to the "annual general meeting" instead of the "extraordinary general meeting" and there was no other meeting which could be confused with that the date of which was stated in the proxies.

held that he was bound to demand a poll in order to ascertain the sense of the meeting, and bound to exercise all the proxies in accordance with the instructions which they contained.[68]

A shareholder who has given a proxy is free to attend the meeting and vote in person, in which case the vote tendered by the proxy may properly be rejected.[69] He does not thereby revoke the proxy and the proxy may, *e.g.*, vote on a second resolution on which the shareholder does not vote.[70]

A corporation, whether a company within the meaning of the Act or not, may, if it is a member of another corporation which is such a company, by resolution of its directors or other governing body authorise such person as it thinks fit to act as its representative at any meeting of the company of any class of members of the company. The representative is entitled to exercise on behalf of the corporation the powers which the corporation could exercise if it were an individual shareholder of the company: section 375. Such a representative is *not* a proxy and may vote on a show of hands as well as on a poll, and may address the meeting even if the company is not a private company.

In one case,[71] where no committee of inspection had been appointed and no directions had been received from the body of creditors or the court, the liquidator in a creditors' voluntary winding up was held to be within the phrase "or other govering body" in section 375, *ante*, and entitled to appoint himself as representative of the company at general meetings of subsidiary companies.

Minutes

Every company must keep minutes of all proceedings of general meetings. Such minutes, signed by the chairman of the meeting at which the proceedings were held or of the next succeeding meeting, are evidence of the proceedings: section

[68] *Second Consolidated Trust Ltd.* v. *Ceylon, etc. Rubber Estates Ltd.* [1943] 2 All E.R. 567.

[69] *Cousins* v. *International Brick Co. Ltd.*, *ante*, where the proxy had not been revoked under Table A, art. 63, *ante*.

[70] *Ansett* v. *Butler Air Transport Ltd.* (*No.* 2.) (1958) 75 W.N. (N.S.W.) 306.

[71] *Hillman* v. *Crystal Bowl Amusements Ltd.* [1973] 1 W.L.R. 162 (C.A.).

382(1), (2). Unless the articles so provide, they are not conclusive evidence, and so, if a resolution has been passed, but is not entered in the minutes, other evidence to prove it will be admitted.[72] However, when the articles provide that the minutes, signed by the chairman, shall be "conclusive evidence without any further proof of the facts therein stated," as between those bound by the articles, namely the company and the members *qua* members,[73] evidence cannot be called to contradict the minutes unless they have been fraudulently written up.[74]

When minutes have been duly made, there is a presumption that all the proceedings were in order, and all appointments of directors, managers or liquidators are deemed to be valid: section 382(4).

The books containing minutes of general meetings are to be kept at the registered office and open to the inspection of any member without charge. A member is entitled to be furnished, within seven days, with a copy on payment of the prescribed fee. If inspection is refused or copies are not sent, the court can compel immediate inspection of the books[75] or direct that copies be sent to those requiring them: section 383. The minute books may be bound, or loose-leaf provided that adequate precautions are taken for guarding against falsification: section 722. Section 723, *ante*, enables the company to use a computer to keep the minutes.

RESOLUTIONS

Kinds of resolution

In the absence of a contrary provision in the Act or in the memorandum or the articles the company in general meeting acts by ordinary resolution. Sometimes, however, the Act or the memorandum or articles require a special resolution, an

[72] *Re Fireproof Doors* [1916] 2 Ch. 142; *cf. Fraserburgh Commercial Co. Ltd., Petitioners*, 1946 S.C. 444.
[73] *Ante*, p. 88.
[74] *Kerr* v. *Mottram* [1940] Ch. 657.
[75] By the member himself or by a named expert on his behalf: *M'Cusker* v. *M'Rae*, 1966 S.C. 253.

extraordinary resolution or an elective resolution. Any of these types of resolution may be effected by the written resolution procedure, *post*.

An *ordinary resolution*, which is not defined in the Act, is a resolution passed by a simple majority of the votes of the members entitled to vote[76] and voting in person or, where allowed, by proxy, at a meeting of which notice has been duly given. The length of the notice depends upon a number of factors including the kind of meeting at which the resolution is passed.[77]

Section 378 defines an *extraordinary resolution* as a resolution passed by at least a three-fourths' majority of [the votes of] the members entitled to vote[78] and voting, in person or, where allowed, by proxy, at a general meeting of which notice specifying the intention to propose the resolution as an extraordinary resolution has been duly given. Again the length of the notice depends upon a number of factors including the kind of meeting at which the resolution is passed.

A *special resolution* is defined as a resolution passed by a majority of at least three-fourths of [the votes of] the members entitled to vote[79] and voting, in person or, where allowed, by proxy, at a general meeting of which at least 21 days' notice specifying the intention to propose the resolution as a special resolution has been given: section 378(2).

The words in brackets must read into section 378 because voting may be on a show of hands, in which case each member will usually have one vote, or on a poll, in which case each member will usually have one vote for each of his shares.

In England a provision in the articles that the day of service is to be included in the number of days' notice to be given does not apply to notice of a special resolution, *i.e.* the period of not less than 21 days prescribed by section 378 is a period of not less than 21 clear days, exclusive of the day of service of the notice and of the day on which the meeting is to be held. Articles cannot curtail the length of time which Parliament has said must elapse between the date on which the notice is served

[76] *Ante*, p. 264, and see *Re Bradford Investments plc* [1990] BCC 740.
[77] *Ante*, p. 317.
[78] See note 76.
[79] See note 76.

and the date on which the meeting is held.[80] In Scotland the requisite notice under section 378(2) means a notice of not less than 21 days computed by excluding the day on which the notice is received by the shareholder but including the day on which the meeting is to be held.[81] We have seen[82] that less than 21 days' notice of a special resolution may be given if it is so agreed by a majority in number of the members holding not less than 95 per cent. of the shares giving the right to attend and vote at the meeting: section 378(3).

At a meeting at which a special resolution or an extraordinary resolution is submitted to be passed, a declaration of the chairman that the resolution is carried is, unless a poll is demanded, conclusive evidence of the fact without proof of the number of proportion of the votes recorded in favour of or against the resolution: section 378(4). This provision prevents a resolution from being challenged on the ground, *e.g.*, that certain shareholders were not qualified to vote.[83] If, however, the declaration of the chairman is fraudulent, or shows on the face of it that the proper majority has not been obtained, it is not conclusive.

A special resolution was put to the meeting. The chairman then said: "Those in favour 6; those against 23; but there are 200 voting by proxy,[84] and I declare the resolution carried." *Held*, the declaration was not conclusive, and the resolution was not passed: *Re Caratal (New) Mines Ltd.* [1902] 2 Ch. 498.[85]

Further, the chairman's declaration is not conclusive where the resolution has not been effectively submitted to the meeting, *e.g.* if a show of hands has not been taken as required by the articles.[86]

[80] *Re Hector Whaling Ltd.* [1936] Ch. 208, applied in *Thompson* v. *Stimpson* [1961] 1 Q.B. 195.

[81] *Neil M'Leod & Sons Ltd., Petitioners*, 1967 S.C. 16, *per* Lord President Clyde at p. 20.

[82] *Ante*, p. 320.

[83] *Grahams' Morocco Co. Ltd., Petitioners*, 1932 S.C. 269.

[84] Those "voting" by proxy could not vote on a show of hands.

[85] A corresponding Scottish case is *Cowan* v. *Scottish Publishing Co. Ltd.* (1892) 19 R. 437.

[86] *Citizens Theatre Ltd., Petitioners*, 1946 S.C. 14; *cf. Fraserburgh Commercial Co. Ltd., Petitioners*, 1946 S.C. 444.

The chairman can put a resolution to the meeting without its being seconded, unless the articles prohibit it.

Elective resolution

The Companies Act 1989 introduced the concept of an elective resolution which a private company may use to elect out of any of five internal requirements of the Acts. The Secretary of State has the power to add additional areas of election by regulations: 1989 Act, sections 115–117.

An elective resolution may be made by a private company for any one of the following purposes:

(i) to apply section 80A in relation to the authority of directors to allot shares[87];
(ii) to dispense with the laying of accounts and reports before a general meeting[88];
(iii) to apply section 366A to dispense with the holding of an annual general meeting[89];
(iv) to reduce the percentage required for sanctioning short notice of meetings or special resolutions[90];
(v) to dispense with the annual appointment of auditors.[91]

An elective resolution requires at least 21 days' notice in writing both of the terms of the resolution and of the meeting. It must then have the unanimous consent of all those entitled to attend and vote at the meeting—one shareholder can therefore prevent it being pursued. The election can be revoked at any time by an ordinary resolution and is automatically revoked if the company is re-registered as a public company. No company may contract out of this elective regime by its articles: section 379A.

An elective resolution and one revoking an elective resolution must be registered in the same way as a special resolution:

[87] *Ante*, p. 165.
[88] *Post*, Chap. 20.
[89] *Ante*, p. 318.
[90] *Ante*, p. 321.
[91] *Post*, Chap. 21.

section 380. Both may be effected by the written resolution procedure, *post*.

Amendments

A positive amendment, pertinent to the subject-matter of the resolution, is proposed, it must be voted upon first. If the chairman refuses to put a proper amendment to the meeting, the resolution, if passed, is not binding.[92]

An amendment cannot be moved if it goes beyond the notice convening the meeting. Because notice of special business must state the resolution to be passed in such a way as fairly to state the purpose for which the meeting is convened,[93] there is little scope for amendment where a resolution is special business. Where a notice of a meeting stated that it was to pass, with such amendments as should be determined, a resolution that three named persons be appointed directors, an amendment to elect two other directors as well was held valid.[94] Again, there is little scope for amendment of special and extraordinary resolutions since, as we have seen, the notice of a special resolution or an extraordinary resolution must set out in substance the exact wording of the resolution.[95] However, where a notice of a meeting stated that it was to pass special resolutions to wind up voluntarily and to appoint X as liquidator, and the second resolution was dropped and a new one to appoint Y as liquidator was passed, it was held that Y's appointment was valid because as soon as the resolution to wind up was passed a liquidator could be appointed, without notice, under the Act.[96]

Registration and copies of certain resolutions

A printed copy of certain resolutions and agreements, or a copy in some other form approved by him, must be forwarded to the Registrar within 15 days after they are passed or made

[92] *Henderson* v. *Bank of Australasia* (1890) 45 Ch.D. 330 (C.A.).
[93] *Ante*, p. 323.
[94] *Betts & Co. Ltd.* v. *Macnaghten* [1910] 1 Ch. 430.
[95] *Re Swindon Town Football Co. Ltd.* [1990] BCLC 467, 468, *per* Harman J.
[96] *Re Trench Tubeless Tyre Co.* [1900] 1 Ch. 408 (C.A.).

and, where articles have been registered, a copy must be annexed to every copy of the articles issued subsequently: section 380(1), (2).

Section 380 applies to, *inter alia*, special and extraordinary resolutions, elective resolutions, written resolutions and other resolutions agreed to by all the members which would otherwise not have been effective unless passed as special resolutions or extraordinary resolutions, and resolutions agreed by all the members of a class of shareholders. This section also applies to certain ordinary resolutions, *e.g.* one to vary or revoke the authority of the directors to issue shares under section 80, or to revoke an elective resolution section 380(4).

A resolution passed at an adjourned meeting is treated as having been passed on the date on which it was in fact passed, and is not deemed to have been passed on the date of the original meeting: section 381.

It will be remembered that a printed copy of a resolution effecting an increase of capital, or a copy in some other form approved by the Registrar, must also be filed within 15 days: section 123.

When various resolutions required

The company in general meeting acts by ordinary resolution unless another kind of resolution is required by the Act or by the memorandum of the articles. Thus an ordinary resolution is enough under section 384 (appointment of auditors).[97] In practice an increase of capital is effected by an ordinary resolution.[98] An ordinary resolution is *expressly* provided for by sections 303 (removal of a director) and 386 (removal of an auditor).

An extraordinary resolution is required is a few cases, for example by section 84 of the Insolvency Act 1986[99] (initiation of a creditors' voluntary winding up, when the company is insolvent), and by section 165 of that Act[1] (to sanction the exercise of certain of the powers of the liquidator in a members' voluntary winding up).

[97] *Post*, Chap 21.
[98] *Ante*, p. 186.
[99] *Post*, Chap. 28.
[1] *Ibid*.

A special resolution is required for the more important matters, for example by section 4 (alteration of objects), section 9 (alteration of articles), section 135 (reduction of capital), section 84 of the Insolvency Act 1986[2] (initiation of a members' voluntary winding up), and section 110 of that Act (authority for the liquidator in a members' voluntary winding up to sell the company's business to another company for cash or shares on the other company).

An elective resolution is required for one of the five purposes set out above.

The Written Resolution Procedure

The courts have evolved the doctrine that if all the members assent to a transaction *intra vires* the company, the company is bound and it is not necessary that they should hold a meeting in one room or one place to express that assent simultaneously.

In *Parker & Cooper* v. *Reading*[3] there was no actual meeting but the members individually and at different times informally ratified a debenture granted by the directors, which although *intra vires* the company, was beyond the powers of the directors because two directors had been invalidly appointed.

Parker & Cooper was applied in *Re Duomatic Ltd.*[4] in which it was held that where it can be shown that all shareholders who have a right to attend and vote at a general meeting of the company assent to some matter which a general meeting of the company could carry into effect, that assent is as binding as a resolution in general meeting. This principle was subsequently applied to such an assent to vary the articles of a company even though no formal special resolution to that effect had been passed. It was held to be a basic principle that all the shareholders acting together could do anything which was *intra vires* the company: *Cane* v. *Jones*.[5]

Further, Table A, regulation 53, provides that a written resolution signed by all the members entitled to attend and vote at general meetings shall be as effectual as if passed at a general meeting of the company duly convened and held. The Jenkins

[2] See note 98.
[3] [1926] Ch. 975.
[4] [1969] 2 Ch. 365.
[5] [1981] 1 All E.R. 533.

Report[6] recommended that the Act should expressly provide that in the case of any company such a resolution shall be equivalent to an ordinary or special resolution duly passed at a general meeting and that has been largely achieved in part by the courts and regulation 53.

However, Nourse J. in *Re Barry Artist Ltd.*,[7] whilst approving the use of a written resolution, *i.e.* one signed by all the members, as a special resolution for a reduction of capital, stated that he would not do so again since the reduction of capital procedure requires confirmation by the court.[8] This decision cast doubt on the exact parameters of regulation 53. Could it apply where the resolution is part of a wider process, *e.g.* authorising a private company to give financial assistance for the acquisition of its own shares?

As a result, the 1989 Companies Act added four new sections, 381A, 381B, 381C and 382A and a new Schedule 15A into the 1985 Act to provide for a statutory framework to allow any private company to pass a resolution without holding any meeting, provided all those who could have attended the meeting and voted sign the resolution instead. This basic right is given by section 381A. No notice requirements apply and, provided all the relevant members sign a document which accurately states the resolution, it need not be the same document or even identical wording. Moreover, a signature can be delegated to another. Thus several letters can be sent for signature.

Under section 381A(3) the date of the resolution is the date when the last relevant member signs it; until then the resolution has no validity at all and so is subject to a veto by any member. The date of the resolution is also the date of the passing of the resolution for the relevant provisions of the Act unless, because of the procedure under section 381B, the date when it comes into effect is later (see below). A written resolution under this procedure can be used to effect all types of resolution and is to be deemed to be duly passed for all purposes. Under Schedule 15A, however, the procedure cannot be used to dismiss a director under section 303 or an auditor under section 391. It is

[6] Para. 468.
[7] [1985] BCLC 283.
[8] *Ante*, p. 192.

also subject to modifications in the case of certain procedural resolutions.

Section 381B requires that a copy of every proposed written resolution must be sent to the auditors who may do one of four things, with the following consequences:

(i) do nothing for seven days from receipt. In that case the resolution will be effective either from that time or the date of the resolution (*i.e.* when the last person signs), whichever is later;

(ii) within seven days notify the company that it does not concern them as auditors. In that case the resolution will be effective either from the time of notification or the date of the resolution, whichever is later;

(iii) within seven days notify the company that it does concern them as auditors but that no meeting need be held. In that case the consequences are as in (ii) above;

(iv) within seven days notify the company that it does concern them as auditors and that it should be considered by a meeting. In that case the resolution has no effect even if it has already been signed by all the members. At any meeting called the auditor then has a right to attend and speak: section 390(2).

It is apparent from section 381B that it will be politic to send a copy of any written resolution to reach the auditors at least seven days before is is intended to initiate the written resolution procedure.

Under section 382A, written resolutions must be recorded in the same way as ordinary resolutions. If the procedure is being used to effect a special, extraordinary or elective resolution it must be registered as such.

It is clear from section 381C(2) that nothing in the new written resolution procedure will affect the doctrine laid down in *Re Duomatic*[9] etc., as to informal resolutions being allowed if all the relevant members assent. But its relationship with the articles, and regulation 53 of Table A (*ante*) in particular is unclear. Regulation 53 allows a company to pass a written

[9] [1969] 2 Ch. 365.

resolution without the need to consult the auditors, etc. Is it still possible to use that regulation and so avoid any reference to the auditors under section 381B above, at least where no regulatory process is involved?

Section 381C(1) is ambiguous. It states that:

> "Section 381A and 381B have effect notwithstanding any provision of the company's memorandum or articles."

This was intended to prevent companies restricting the new procedure by their articles but it is arguable that it could equally prevent the articles providing a simpler procedure and so could render regulation 53 subject to the new procedure.

The new written resolution procedure is available even on those occasions where a resolution is required as part of a complex authorisation procedure, by adapting that procedure to the written resolution process: Schedule 15A. The six areas affected are: a disapplication of pre-emption rights[10]; exemption by a private company from the financial assistance provisions[11]; approval of off-market purchases contracts and contingent purchase contracts by a company in relation to its own shares[12]; approval by a company for the redemption or purchase of its own shares out of capital[13]; approval of directors' service contracts,[14] and funding of directors' expenditure.[15] These variations are dealt with in relation to their subject area but in general any voting prohibition is lifted in such a way that it becomes irrelevant whether the restricted person signs the resolution or not, and any necessary documents are required to be sent to each relevant member in advance of his signing rather than in advance of the meeting.

[10] *Ante*, p. 165.
[11] *Ante*, p. 228.
[12] *Ante*, p. 210.
[13] *Ante*, p. 214.
[14] *Post*, p. 369.
[15] *Post*, p. 388.

Chapter 15

DIRECTORS

THE management of a company is usually entrusted to a body of persons called "directors." It will be seen later that the Act requires a public company to have at least two directors and a private company to have at least one. The exact name by which a person occupying the position of director is called is immaterial as, under section 741(1), in the Act the expression "director" includes any person occupying the position of director by whatever name called. Section 744 also provides that in the Act the expression "officer" in relation to a corporation includes a director or manager. Some of the statutory rules applicable to directors also apply to "shadow directors." Section 741(2) provides that these are persons in accordance with whose instructions the directors are accustomed to act other than on purely professional advice.

It has recently been held that the right to appoint two out of five directors does not make the appointor a shadow director. It was also decided in that case that the appointor is not as such vicariously liable for the acts of his appointee director: *Kuwait Asia Bank EC* v. *National Mutual Life Nominees Ltd.* [1990] BCC 567.

Among other things, this chapter deals with the appointment, remuneration and vacation of office of directors. It also shows that the directors of a company act as a board, that normal articles (*e.g.* Table A, regulation 70) give the directors extensive powers to manage the company's business (and that so long as the directors act within their powers, the company in general meeting cannot overrule them), and that articles usually empower the directors to appoint a managing director and delegate any of their powers to him.

The most important topics dealt with in the chapter are the fiduciary duties and duties of care which a director owes to his company in exercising these powers. Recent statutory developments have further restricted the powers of the directors and provide for disclosure by them of many transactions involving themselves and the company.

It should be noted that in a private company the directors are usually substantial shareholders. In a public company, the directors normally have few shares, their fees and other emoluments, rather than their dividends, being their main sources of profit from the company, with the result that management and ownership of the company are divorced.

Number and Appointment of Directors

Every public company registered on or after November 1, 1929, must have at least two directors. Companies registered before that date, and every private company, must have at least one director: section 282. The Jenkins Committee recommended that every company should have at least two directors.[1] Apart from section 282, the number of directors is regulated by the articles.

As to the *first directors*, section 13(5) provides that the persons named in the statement of first directors and secretary, which must be delivered for registration with the memorandum, shall, on the incorporation of the company, be deemed to have been appointed as the first directors and secretary, and any appointment by any articles delivered with the memorandum shall be void unless the person concerned is named as a director or secretary in the statement.

Subsequent directors are appointed in the way laid down in the articles, *e.g.* by the company in annual general meeting.

Table A provides:

"Regulation 73. At the first annual general meeting all the directors shall retire from office, and at every subsequent annual general meeting one-third of the directors who are subject to retirement by rotation or, if their number is not three or a multiple of three, the number nearest to one-third shall retire from office; but, if there is only one director who is subject to retirement by rotation, he shall retire."

"Regulation 74. Subject to the provisions of the Act, the directors to retire by rotation shall be those who have been longest in office since

[1] *Ante*, p. 47.

their last appointment or re-appointment, but as between persons who became or were last re-appointed directors on the same day those to retire shall (unless they otherwise agree among themselves) be determined by lot."

The articles also usually contain a clause, as does Table A in regulation 78, providing that casual vacancies, *i.e.* vacancies occurring between two annual general meetings, may be filled by the directors. Regulation 79 also provides that the directors may appoint additional directors to hold office until the next annual general meeting but so that the total number of directors fixed in accordance with the articles is not exceeded. Where there are articles similar to regulations 78 and 79 the power of appointing additional directors has not been delegated to the directors so as to exclude the inherent power of the company in general meeting to appoint directors.[2]

The appointment of directors at a general meeting, except in the case of a private company, must be voted on individually unless a resolution to the contrary has first been agreed to by the meeting without any vote being given against it. A motion for the appointment of two or more persons as directors of a public company by a single resolution is void (although the operation of section 285,[3] by which the acts of the "directors" are valid, is not excluded and no provision in the articles for the automatic reappointment of retiring directors in default of another appointment applies): section 292.

Table A, regulation 75, provides that if the company at the meeting at which a director retires by rotation does not fill the vacancy, the retiring director, if offering himself for re-election, is deemed to have been re-elected unless (*a*) another person is elected, (*b*) a resolution not to fill the vacancy is passed, or (*c*) a resolution for his re-election is lost. In the absence of a provision like (*c*), a retiring director will be deemed to be re-elected even though a resolution that he be re-elected is lost.[4] It is also provided, by regulation 76, that no person, other than the retiring director or a person recommended by the directors, is eligible for election as a director unless notice of intention to propose him, signed by a member entitled to vote, is left at the

[2] *Worcester Corsetry Ltd.* v. *Witting* [1936] Ch. 640.
[3] *Ante*, p. 127.
[4] *Grundt* v. *Great Boulder Proprietary Mines Ltd.* [1948] Ch. 145 (C.A.).

registered office not less than 14 nor more than 35 days before the meeting, together with a signed notice of his willingness to act.

The articles may appoint a named person a permanent director of the company, so that no re-election is necessary in his case. This was common in the case of the former exempt private companies.[5] The appointment of such a director, when the only contract he has is that contained in the articles, can be terminated by an alteration of the articles, or by his removal under section 303,[6] or by the company's going into liquidation.

The articles appointed F. governing director of the company for his life, or until he should resign or be removed by a special resolution of the company, at a salary of £300 a year. F. acted for 16 years, when the company went into voluntary liquidation. *Held*, F.'s employment was conditional on the continued existence of the company and ceased automatically when it was wound up, so that F. could not claim damages for breach of contract: *Re T. N. Farrer Ltd.* [1937] Ch. 352.

Power may be given to a particular person or company to nominate one or more directors; this is often done in the case of subsidiary companies.

Assignment of office by directors

If the articles or any agreement contains power for a director to assign his office to another person, an assignment is of no effect unless and until it is approved by a special resolution of the company: section 308.

Alternate directors

Although the Act does not say so, section 308, above, does not prevent the appointment by a director, if authorised by the articles and subject thereto, of an alternate or substitute director to act for him in certain circumstances. Because of the wide definition of the word "director" in section 741 it seems that an

[5] *Ante*, p. 9.
[6] *Post*, p. 373.

alternate is a director for the purposes of the Act, so that particulars with respect to him must be shown in registers such as the register of directors, *post.*[7]

PERSONS WHO CANNOT BE DIRECTORS

Certain persons cannot be appointed or act as directors:

Age

A person who has reached the age of 70 cannot be *appointed* director *unless* the company is private and not the subsidiary of a public company, *or* the articles otherwise provide, *or* he is appointed or approved by a resolution of which special notice, stating his age, has been given: section 293. The exceptions are such as to make this section ineffective.

A person who is *first* appointed a director of a company, other than a private company which is not the subsidiary of a public company, after he has reached the age at which the directors retire under the Act[8] or the articles, must give notice of his age to the company: section 294.

Bankruptcy

An undischarged bankrupt must not act as director of, or be concerned in the promotion, formation or management of, a company without the leave of the court by which he was adjudged bankrupt,[9] under penalty of imprisonment or a fine or both: Company Directors Disqualification Act 1986, section 11. Such a person may be personally liable if he acts whilst disqualified—see below.

In England, on an application for leave to act as director, notice must be given to the Official Receiver, who can oppose the application if he is of opinion that it is contrary to the public interest.

[7] p. 362. And see the Jenkins Report, para. 83.

[8] See s.293, *supra*.

[9] For Scotland, substitute "sequestration of his estates was awarded" for "he was adjudged bankrupt."

Disqualification orders other than on insolvency

The law relating to disqualification orders was consolidated from the Companies Act 1985 and the Insolvency Act 1985 into the Company Directors Disqualification Act 1986.

Conviction of indictable offence

A person cannot, without leave of the court, be a director of or be concerned in any way, whether directly or indirectly, in the management of a company if he has been convicted of an indictable offence in connection with the promotion, formation, management or liquidation of a company, or with the receivership or management of a company, or if in a winding up it has appeared that he has been guilty of fraudulent trading[10] or that he has been guilty, while an officer, of fraud or breach of duty in relation to the company, or that he has been persistently in default in relation to the Act,[11] and the court has made a disqualification order that he shall not be a director or be concerned in management for up to 15 years[12]: sections 1 to 5 of the Company Directors Disqualification Act 1986. Such an order would also prevent such a person being a liquidator, administrator receiver or manager of a company or being concerned in the promotion of a company. In *R.* v. *Georgiou*[13] it was held that for an offence to be connected with the management of a company it need not be linked to any misconduct in relation to the company's affairs. It could include carrying on an unlawful business through the medium of a company.

The period of disqualification must date from conviction, not, *e.g.*, from the convicted person's release from prison.[14] The restriction on taking part in the management of the company is very wide. In particular the words "be concerned in" the management do not mean "take part in," and so include acting as a management consultant.[15]

[10] *Post*, Chap. 29. This applies whether or not he is actually convicted of the offence.
[11] *Infra*.
[12] Disqualification orders may run concurrently.
[13] (1988) 4 BCC 322 (C.A.). See also *R.* v. *Austen* (1985) 1 BCC 99 528.
[14] *R.* v. *Bradley* [1961] 1 W.L.R. 398 (C.C.A.).
[15] *R.* v. *Campbell* [1984] BCLC 83 (C.A.).

An application for such a disqualification order may be made by the Secretary of State, the official receiver, the liquidator or any past or present member or creditor of the company concerned. Ten days' notice must be given and the person concerned may appear and give evidence or call witnesses.

When making an application the Secretary of State, official receiver or liquidator may give evidence and call the attention of the court to any matters which seem to him to be relevant. In *Re Gilgate Properties Ltd.* (1981) 131 N.L.J. 579, this was held to include inspectors' reports and a report of the City Panel on Takeovers and Mergers (*post*). The ordinary rules of evidence did not apply.

In *R.* v. *Young* [1990] BCC 549, the director had had a three and a half year record of successful business after committing the offence before the matter came to court. On the offence he was given a conditional discharge but disqualified for two years. This was quashed by the Court of Appeal (Criminal Division) on the basis of the intolerable delay and his recent record. Disqualification was a punishment which should be linked to the conditional discharge.

Persistent default

A person may alternatively be disqualified from being a director of or being concerned in the management of a company if he has been persistently in default in relation to any provision of the Companies Acts which requires any document to be delivered, or notice of any matter to be given, to the Registrar.[16]

The fact that a person has been persistently in default in relation to any provision of the Companies Acts may be conclusively proved by showing that in the five years ending with the date of the application he has been adjudged guilty (whether or not on the same occasion) of three or more defaults. A person is to be treated as being adjudged guilty of a default if:

[16] This includes acting as a liquidator, administrator, promoter, receiver, etc. The conditions for application for, and breach of, an order are as set out above.

(*a*) he is convicted of any offence by virtue of any contravention of or failure to comply with any provision of the Companies Acts (whether on his own part or on the part of the company); or

(*b*) a default order is made against him under sections 244 or 713 or sections 41, 170 of the Insolvency Act 1986, *post.*

However, it is not necessary to show three such convictions. In *Re Arctic Engineering Ltd.*[17] failure to send 35 required returns to the Registrar was held to be sufficient evidence for the making of an order.

An order made on this basis may only last for five and not 15 years.

Successive convictions or default orders

Alternatively a disqualification order may be made if a person is convicted of any offence by virtue of or failure to comply with any provision of the Act and in the five year period up to that conviction he has been convicted of other such offences or received default orders (see above), totalling three in number. In this case the court making the conviction can impose the disqualification order which may last for 15 years.

In *Re Civica Investments Ltd.*,[18] the judge said that deciding the length of the disqualification was similar to the passing of a sentence in a criminal case. Elaborate reasoning was therefore unnecessary for, as more of the cases arose, it would be undesirable for the judge to be taken through the facts of previous cases. The five year period was a maximum and should be reserved for serious cases. In the case before him, since most of the defaults had been remedied the judge imposed a one year disqualification only.

Register of disqualification orders

Section 18 of the Company Directors Disqualification Act provides that the prescribed officer of any court which makes an order that a person shall not, without the leave of the court, be a director of or be concerned in the management of a company

[17] [1986] 1 W.L.R. 686.
[18] [1983] BCLC 458.

for a specified period or grants leave in relation to such an order, must furnish the Secretary of State with particulars of the order or the grant of leave where the order is made under that Act.

The Secretary of State must maintain a register of such orders and grants of leave, which register is open to inspection on payment of such fee as may be specified by the Secretary of State in regulations made by statutory instrument.[19]

Disqualification orders relating to insolvency or a DTI investigation

If the court is satisfied that a person is or has been a director[20] of a company which has become insolvent[21] within the past two years,[22] and that his conduct as such makes him unfit to be concerned in the management of a company,[23] it must make a disqualification order against him for at least two years: Company Directors Disqualification Act, section 6. The conduct may relate to one or more companies as specified.[24] The application for such an order must be made by the Secretary of State (or the official receiver if the company is in compulsory liquidation), if it appears to him to be in the public interest, as the result of information received from a liquidator,[25] administrator,[26] administrative receiver[27] or the official receiver.[28] Those officials are under a duty to report information about a director's conduct in such matters to the Secretary of State: Company Directors Disqualification Act 1986, section 7. Although the proceedings are civil and not criminal they do

[19] See the Companies (Disqualification Orders) Regulations 1985 S.I. 1985 No. 829.
[20] Including a shadow director.
[21] See *infra.*
[22] This time limit runs from the date of the earliest of the insolvent acts (see below): *Re Tasbian* [1990] BCC 318; *Official Receiver* v. *Nixon, The Times*, February 6, 1990. The court may give leave outside that period, see *Re Probe Data Systems Ltd.* (*No.* 2) [1990] BCC 21 and *Re Crestjoy Products Ltd.* [1990] BCC 23. Time runs from the lodging of the application: *Secretary of State for Trade and Industry* v. *Josolyne*, 1990 S.L.T. (Sh.Ct.) 48.
[23] See, *infra.*
[24] *Re Bath Glass Ltd.* (1988) 4 BCC 130.
[25] See Chaps. 27 and 28, *post.*
[26] See Chap. 26, *post.*
[27] See Chap. 25, *post.*
[28] See Chap. 27, *post.*

involve penal consequences for the director and natural justice requires that he should know the substance of the charges he has to meet. Only if there will be no injustice will a modified charge be allowed during the proceedings.[29] A company becomes insolvent for this purpose: (a) when it goes into liquidation at a time when its assets are insufficient to pay its debts etc.; (b) when an administration order is made in respect of the company; (c) when an administrative receiver is appointed: Company Directors Disqualification Act, section 6(2).

The director must be given ten days clear notice before the institution of proceedings. Failure to do so will make the proceedings invalid under section 16(1) of the Company Directors Disqualification Act. The court may, however, grant leave for the proceedings to be commenced later even if the two year period has expired as a result of the defective initial proceedings.[30]

In deciding whether a person's conduct makes him unfit to be concerned in the management of a company, section 9 of the Company Directors Disqualification Act 1986 requires the court to have regard to the matters specified in Schedule 1 to that Act. These are: (a) any misfeasance, breach of duty or misapplication of assets[31]; (b) failure to comply with the requirements under the Companies Act relating to books and records, returns and accounts[32]; and, where the company has become insolvent; (c) responsibility for the cause of insolvency or for losses of customers who furnished advance payments, involvement in any transaction (or preference) which can be set aside[33]; and (d) failure to comply with the statutory requirements relating to insolvency. The court may only, however, have regard to matters of which the director has had notice and not to those which it regards as having emerged from the evidence: *Re Sevenoaks Stationers (Retail) Ltd.* [1990] BCC 785.

[29] *Re Churchill Hotel (Plymouth) Ltd.* (1988) 4 BCC 112; *Re Lo-Line Electric Motors Ltd.* [1988] Ch. 477.

[30] *Re Cedac Ltd.* [1990] BCC 555; *Re Jaymor Management Ltd.* [1990] BCC 303.

[31] *Re Keypack Homecare Ltd.* (*No.* 2) [1990] BCC 117; *Re T. & D. Services Ltd.* [1990] BCC 592.

[32] See, *e.g. Re Rolus Properties Ltd.* (1988) 4 BCC 446; *Re. T. & D. Services Ltd., ante.*

[33] See Chap. 29, *post.*

The courts have laid down various general tests to decide whether a director's conduct is deserving of disqualification. In *Re Dawson Print Group Ltd.*[34] Hoffman J. said:

> "There must, I think, be something about the case, some conduct which if not dishonest is at any rate in breach of standards of commercial morality, or some really gross incompetence which persuades the court that it would be a danger to the public if he were allowed to continue to be involved in the management of companies, before a disqualification order is made."

In *Re Churchill Hotel (Plymouth) Ltd.*[35] Peter Gibson J. construed this to mean that gross incompetence without a breach of commercial morality would suffice for a disqualification, whilst the statement was approved by Browne-Wilkinson V.C. in *Re McNulty's Interchange Ltd.*[36] together with his own test in *Re Lo-Line Electric Motors Ltd.*[37] that:

> "Ordinary commercial misjudgment is in itself not sufficient to justify disqualification. In the normal case, the conduct complained of must display a lack of commercial probity although I have no doubt that in an extreme case of gross negligence or total incompetence disqualification could be appropriate."

The Court of Appeal in *Re Sevenoaks Stationers Retail Ltd.* [1990] BCC 765, stated that incompetence to a marked degree would suffice; it need not be total.

The general theme of these criteria is the protection of the public. The same idea is sometimes phrased by reference to the test being whether the director has forfeited the right to enjoy the privileges of limited liability by failing to perform the attendant duties.[38]

Disqualification orders have been refused where the director's conduct was only imprudent and improper[39] and where there

[34] (1987) 3 BCC 322, 324.

[35] (1988) 4 BCC 112, 117.

[36] (1988) 4 BCC 533, 536.

[37] [1988] Ch. 477, 479. See also *Re Chartmore Ltd.* [1990] BCLC 673.

[38] This test was used by Vinelott J. in *Re Stanford Services Ltd.* (1987) 3 BCC 326, Peter Gibson J. in *Re Bath Glass Ltd., ante*, Mervyn Davies J. in *Re Majestic Recording Studios Ltd.* (1988) 4 BCC 519, and Hoffman J. in *Re Ipcon Fashions Ltd.* (1989) 5 BCC 773.

[39] *Re Bath Glass Ltd.*, *ibid.*

was a reasonable reliance on advice which indicated that the director had none of the badges of a man who had exploited limited liability in a cynical way, with disregard for proper responsibility, or by incompetence.[40] On the other hand, an order was made against a director who had assumed a position which could not be shirked by leaving everything to others, since that indicated that he was a danger to the public.[41]

The major area of dispute has been the relevance of a director allowing his company to run up arrears of money which it ought to have paid over to the tax authorities. The significant point is that these debts are not trading debts in the ordinary sense since they arise out of the use for other purposes of money which the company actually receives on behalf of the Crown, *e.g.* VAT collected from suppliers, income tax deducted at source from employees' wages under the Pay As You Earn system and national insurance contributions similarly deducted and not handed over to the correct authorities. In *Re Dawson Print Group Ltd.*[42] Hoffman J. rejected the idea that in some way these sums amounted to quasi-trust moneys so that misappropriation was a serious matter. Failure to pay such debts was not a sufficient breach of commercial morality as to justify a disqualification. In *Re Stanford Services Ltd.*,[43] Vinelott J., whilst deciding that failure to set aside sums to cover those debts was not in itself a breach of commercial morality, stated that the Crown was nevertheless an involuntary creditor and if a company went into liquidation with such sums owing and irrecoverable the directors would be regarded as either being improperly informed as to the company's financial position or as acting improperly in using the money to finance the company's current trade.

Vinelott J.'s approach has been subsequently endorsed by Peter Gibson J. in *Re Churchill Hotel* (*Plymouth*) *Ltd.*[44] and Browne-Wilkinson V.C. in *Re Lo-Line Motors Ltd.*,[45] but in *Re C.U. Fittings Ltd.*[46] Hoffman J. refused to make an order where

[40] *Re Douglas Construction Services Ltd.* (1988) 4 BCC 553.
[41] *Ibid.*
[42] *Ante.*
[43] *Ante.*
[44] *Ante.*
[45] *Ante.*
[46] (1989) 5 BCC 210.

the company had not used the Crown's money as working capital for its trade but had been winding down its business, and in *Re Keypack Homecare Ltd.* (*No. 2*),[47] Harman J. refused to regard a single quarter of VAT arrears and PAYE arrears being paid off by agreement with the Inland Revenue, as indicating a serious lack of commercial probity.

In *Re Sevenoaks Stationers (Retail) Ltd.* [1990] BCC 765 (C.A.), the Court of Appeal regarded non-payment of Crown debts as important, not because of the fact that they were such debts, but because their non-payment indicated that the director was only paying those creditors who were pressing for their debts at the time to the detriment of other creditors, including the Crown. Viewed in that light such non-payment was a factor to be taken into account when deciding whether a director was unfit to be concerned in the management of a company.

If the judge decides to make a disqualification order under section 6 of the Company Directors Disqualification Act, he has a discretion as to how long that order should apply for provided it is for at least two years and no more than 15. In *Re Lo-Line Electric Motors Ltd.*,[48] a director was disqualified for only three years on the basis that it was no longer suggested that he was consciously dishonest, and lack of dishonesty and better management since were taken into account in imposing a similar disqualification in *Re D. J. Matthews* (*Joinery Design*) *Ltd.*[49] Absence of personal dishonesty and the employment of a chartered secretary reduced the disqualification to two years in *Re Rolus Properties Ltd.*,[50] whilst in *Re Cladrose Ltd.*[51] the fact that one director was a chartered accountant was, where the other was not, held to be a relevant factor. Again, in *Re Majestic Recording Studios Ltd.*,[52] a director was disqualified from acting as a director for five years but was given leave to continue as a director of his family company provided he had an independent chartered accountant to act with him. In *Re T & D Services Ltd.* [1990] BCC 592, Vinelott J. disqualified a director

[47] [1990] BCC 117.
[48] *Ante.*
[49] (1988) 4 BCC 513.
[50] (1988) 4 BCC 446.
[51] [1990] BCC 11.
[52] *Ante.* See also *Re Chartmore Ltd.* [1990] BCLC 673.

for ten years where the director had misappropriated property from the company, failed to keep accounts or make returns and accumulated several months of unpaid Crown debts.

In *Re Sevenoaks Stationers (Retail) Ltd.* [1990] BCC 765 (C.A.), the Court of Appeal suggested that the period of disqualification should be used in three bands. The band over ten years should be used only for very serious cases such as a second disqualification; that between 5 and ten years for serious first cases and that from two to five years for minor cases. The Court of Appeal noted that the High Court was imposing lower periods than the County Court.

The Secretary of State may also apply for a disqualification order against a person if it appears to him to be expedient in the public interest following a report by inspectors,[53] or from the production of books and papers[54] or the entry and search of premises.[55] The court will make an order if it is satisfied that the person's conduct makes him unfit to be concerned in the management of the company; Company Directors Disqualification Act, section 8.

Personal liability of persons acting whilst disqualified through bankruptcy or by a disqualification order

Any person disqualified by reason of his personal bankruptcy under section 11 of the Company Directors Disqualification Act 1986 or by a disqualification order and who becomes involved in the management of the company[56] is personally liable for all debts incurred whilst he was so involved. This liability extends to those who although not disqualified themselves act or are willing to act on the orders of someone who is so disqualified and whom he knows is so disqualified. Anyone who has so acted is presumed to be willing to act in the future. The liability extends to debts incurred whilst they were so acting or willing to act: Company Directors Disqualification Act 1986, section 15.

[53] Under s.437, see p. 472.
[54] Under s.447, see p. 478.
[55] Under s.448 see p. 479.
[56] This includes acting as a director or directly or indirectly taking part in the management of the company: C.D.D.A. 1986 s.15(4). See *R.* v. *Campbell, supra.*

SHARE QUALIFICATION OF DIRECTORS

A share qualification is a specified number of shares which a person must hold in the company to qualify him for appointment as a director of it. There is no share qualification unless the articles otherwise provide, as they sometimes do. The Admission of Securities to Listing do not require a qualification, nor does Table A provide for one.

It should be remembered that in the case of a private company a director will in any event usually be a substantial shareholder.

When a qualification is imposed, a director not already qualified must obtain his qualification within two months of his appointment or the shorter time fixed by the articles: section 291(1). Where he is appointed by a resolution decided on a poll (on which each member usually has one vote for each of his shares) the two months' period, within which his name must be entered in the register of members, runs from midnight on the day on which the votes are counted and the result of the poll ascertained, not from midnight on an earlier date on which the votes are cast.[57]

If a director fails to obtain his qualification within the appropriate period, or if he thereafter ceases to hold it, his office is vacated and he is liable to a fine until he ceases to act as director: section 291(3).

A provision in the articles that "no person shall be eligible to, or shall continue in, the office of director" unless he holds a specified number of shares does not apply to persons who are expressly and unconditionally named as directors in the articles.[58]

Qualification shares need not be obtained from the company; the director may obtain them by transfer from a member,[59] but he should not obtain them by way of gift from a promoter.[60]

Where articles provide that a first director is to "be deemed to have agreed to take" his qualifying shares from the company,

[57] *Holmes* v. *Keyes* [1959] Ch. 199 (C.A.).

[58] *Liquidator of the Consolidated Copper Co. etc. Ltd.* v. *Peddie* (1877) 5 R. 393.

[59] *Brown's Case* (1874) L.R. 9 Ch. 102.

[60] *Eden* v. *Ridsdales Railway Lamp Co. Ltd.* (1899) 23 Q.B.D. 368, *post*, p. 405.

a person who has accepted office as one of the first directors and has acted as such is bound to accept an allotment of shares made in accordance with that provision.[61]

Shares held jointly with another person are a sufficient qualification, unless the articles otherwise provide.[62]

The holding of a share warrant does not constitute the holding of qualification shares, as the shares can be transferred at any time by delivery of the warrant: section 291(2).

REGISTER OF DIRECTORS AND SECRETARIES

Section 288(1) provides that a company must keep at its registered office a register of its directors and secretaries. In the case of an individual director, section 289 provides that the register must contain his name[63] and any former name,[64] address, nationality and business occupation, together with particulars of any other present or past directorships held by him (except directorships of companies of which the company is the wholly owned subsidiary, or which are wholly owned subsidiaries either of the company or of another company of which the company is the wholly owned subsidiary) and the date of his birth. The obligation relating to past directorships only relates to the previous five years and does not apply to dormant companies, *post.* The register is open to inspection by members without fee and by others on payment of the prescribed fee.

Within 14 days of any change in the directors or secretary or in the particulars contained in the register, the company must notify the Registrar of the change and the date when it occurred. A notification of a person having become a director or secretary must contain his signed consent to act as such: section 288(2).

Section 711 requires the Registrar to publish in the *Gazette* notice of the receipt by him of any notification of a change

[61] *The Kingsburgh Motor Construction Co. Ltd.* v. *Scott* (1902) 10 S.L.T. 424 (O.H.).

[62] *Grundy* v. *Briggs* [1910] 1 Ch. 444.

[63] A corporate director will use its corporate name. A Scottish partnership can use its firm name.

[64] This does not include the maiden name of a married woman, the previous name of a peer or a name changed before the director was 18 or more than 20 years ago.

among the directors of a company. Further, section 42 provides that a company cannot rely against other persons on any change among its directors if it had not been officially notified at the material time and is not shown by the company to have been known at that time to the person concerned, or if the material time is less than 16 days after official notification and it is shown that the person concerned was unavoidably prevented from knowing of the event at that time. Such official notification does not constitute notice to anyone—section 42 has a purely negative effect.[65]

PARTICULARS OF DIRECTORS ON BUSINESS LETTERS

No company may state, in any form, the name of any of its directors[66] in a business letter, either in the text or as a signatory, unless it states in legible characters the name of every director of the company: section 305. Initials or recognised abbreviations of forenames may be used.

DISCLOSURE OF DIRECTORS' SHAREHOLDINGS, ETC.

Obligation of director to notify company of his interests in shares in, or debentures of, it or associated companies

Subject to any exceptions made by the Secretary of State,[67] a person who becomes a director when he is interested in shares in or debentures of the company or its subsidiary, holding company or co-subsidiary, must, within five days[68] (or, if he does not know of the interest, within five days after it comes to his knowledge), give the company written notice of his interests and of the number of shares of each class in, and the amount of debentures of each class of, the company and each of the associated companies: section 324(1).

A person in accordance with whose directions the directors are accustomed to act is deemed to be a director of the company.

[65] *Official Custodian of Charities* v. *Parway Estates Ltd.* [1985] Ch. 151.
[66] This includes shadow directors.
[67] See the Companies (Disclosure of Directors' Interests) (Exceptions) Regulations 1985. (S.I. 1985 No. 802).
[68] Excluding Saturdays, Sundays and bank holidays.

A director must (within five days, if he knows of the event and that its occurrence gives rise to the obligation; otherwise within five days after he becomes aware that the occurrence of the event gives rise to the obligation) give the company written notice if, while he is a director:

(i) an event occurs in consequence of which he becomes or ceases to be interested in shares in or debentures of the company or an associated company; or
(ii) he contracts to sell any such shares or debentures; or
(iii) he assigns a right given to him by the company to subscribe for shares in or debentures of the company; or
(iv) he is granted by an associated company a right to subscribe for shares in or debentures of that other company, or he exercises or assigns such a right;

stating the number or amount, and class, of shares or debentures involved: section 324(2). Certain other matters such as the price or other form of consideration must be stated too.

Contravention of section 324, or making to the company a statement known to be false or recklessly making a false statement, gives rise to liability to two years' imprisonment or a fine or both. Proceedings can, in England or Wales, be instituted only by or with the consent of the Secretary of State or the Director of Public Prosecutions.

If it appears that section 324 has been contravened the Secretary of State may order an investigation: section 446.[69]

Rules for giving effect to obligation to disclose

Schedule 13 contains the following rules for giving effect to section 324, *ante*:

(1) An interest in shares or debentures includes any form of interest in such shares or debentures even if the exercise of a right conferred by ownership is or may be made subject to restraint or restriction.

(2) An interest under a trust whereof the property comprises shares or debentures is deemed an interest in the shares or debentures if it would otherwise not be so.

[69] *Post*, p. 478.

(3) A person is deemed interested in shares or debentures if a company is interested in them and—

(*a*) it or its directors are accustomed to act in accordance with his directions; or

(*b*) he is entitled to exercise or control the exercise of one-third or more of its voting power at any general meeting; or he is so entitled to exercise the votes of one company which in turn can exercise any voting power at the general meeting of another company, he is deemed interested in the relevant shares of that second company.

(4) A person is deemed interested in shares or debentures if—

(*a*) he enters into a contract for the purchase of them whether for cash or other consideration; or

(*b*) he has a right, otherwise than by virtue of having an interest under a trust, to call for delivery of them or to acquire an interest in them or is under an obligation to take an interest in them; or

(*c*) not being a registered holder, he is entitled (otherwise than by virtue of having been appointed a proxy or as representative of a corporation) to exercise any right conferred by the holding thereof.

(5) Each person with a joint interest is deemed to have an interest.

(6) It is immaterial that the shares or debentures are unidentifiable.

(7) Interests in reversion or remainder, or (as regards Scotland) in fee, are disregarded so long as a person is entitled to receive, during the lifetime of himself or another, income from trust property comprising shares or debentures.

(8) An interest in England and Wales as bare trustee or as custodian trustee, or in Scotland as simple trustee, is disregarded.

(9) An interest subsisting by virtue of, *inter alia*, an authorised unit trust scheme[70] is disregarded.

(10) An interest of the Church of Scotland General Trustees or of the Church of Scotland Trust is disregarded.

[70] *Post*, Chap. 19.

(11) Delivery to a person's order of shares or debentures in fulfilment of a contract to purchase by him or in satisfaction of his right to call for delivery thereof, or failure to deliver to him in accordance with such a contract or right, or the lapse of his right to call for delivery, is deemed an event in consequence of which he ceases to be interested in them.

Extension of obligation to disclose to interests of spouses and children

For the purposes of section 324, *ante*, an interest of the spouse of, or of a child under the age of majority of, a director (not being himself or herself a director) in shares or debentures is treated as the director's interest, and a contract, assignment or right of subscription entered into, exercised or made by, or a grant made to, such a spouse or child is treated as that of the director: section 328(1)(2).

Within five days after the event in question comes to his knowledge, a director must notify the company in writing if, while he or she is a director—

(*a*) the company grants the director's spouse or child a right to subscribe for shares in or debentures of the company; or
(*b*) such spouse or child exercises such a right: section 328(3).

In each case the like information as is required by section 324, *ante*, must be stated: section 328(4). If section 328(4) appears to have been contravened the Secretary of State may order an investigation: section 446.[71]

In section 328, "son" includes step-son and adopted son, and "daughter" includes step-daughter and adopted daughter.

Register of directors' shareholdings, etc.

Section 325 contains provisions for securing that information furnished under section 324,[72] and certain other information about directors' interests, is recorded and made available.

[71] *Post*, p. 478.
[72] *Ante*, p. 363.

Every company must keep a register for the purposes of section 324 and whenever it receives information from a director in consequence of that section, within three days[73] thereafter it must inscribe in the register, against his name, the information and the date of inscription.

When a company grants a director a right to subscribe for shares or debentures it must, within a similar time, inscribe against his name the date of the grant, the period during or time at which it is exercisable, the consideration for the grant, the description of the shares or debentures and the number or amount thereof, and the price to be paid. When such a right is exercised there must be inscribed that fact (identifying the right), the number or amount of shares or debentures involved, the fact that they were registered in his name or the names of the persons in whose names they were registered, together with the number or amount registered in the name of each person.

The entries against the names in the register must appear in chronological order. If a director requires it, the nature and extent of his interest in shares or debentures must also be recorded.

The company is not, by virtue of anything done for the purposes of section 325, affected with notice of, or put upon inquiry as to, the rights of any person in relation to shares or debentures.

Inspection of register

The register must be kept at the registered office or where the register of members is kept[74] and must be open to the inspection of members without charge and other persons on payment of the prescribed fee per inspection. Except where it has always been kept at the registered office the company must notify the Registrar of the place where the register is kept. Any person may require a copy of the register or part thereof on payment of the prescribed fee. Any copy must be sent by the company within 10 days after the requirement is received. The

[73] Excluding Saturdays, Sundays and bank holidays.
[74] *Ante*, p. 238.

register must also be produced at the commencement of the annual general meeting and remain open and accessible during the meeting to any person attending.[75]

Index of names

Unless the register is in the form of an index the company must also keep an index of the names inscribed therein. The index must give a sufficient indication to enable the information against each name to be readily found and must be altered within 14 days after the date on which a name is entered in the register.

Contravention of section 325

There are default fines[76] and other fines for contravention of section 325, and the court is empowered to order inspection of the register and delivery of a copy: section 326.

Duty of company to notify recognised investment exchange of acquisition of its securities by director

Section 329 provides that when a company, whose shares or debentures are listed on a recognised investment exchange, is notified of any matter by a director under section 324 or section 328 *ante*, and that matter relates to shares or debentures listed on an investment exchange, the company must notify that exchange of the matter before the end of the following day (Saturdays, Sundays and Bank Holidays in any part of Great Britain being disregarded).

If there is default in complying with the section the company and every officer in default is guilty of an offence and liable on summary conviction to a fine and further to a default fine, although proceedings in England and Wales cannot be instituted except by, or with the consent of, the Secretary of State or the Director of Public Prosecutions.

[75] *Ante*, p. 316.
[76] Sched. 24.

DIRECTORS' SERVICE CONTRACTS

Section 318 provides that, subject as below, every company must keep a copy of each director's contract of service[77] or of any variation thereof, or a memorandum thereof setting out its terms if it is not in writing, at one place. This obligation extends to the directors of its subsidiary companies, if any. The place may be:

(1) the company's registered office; or
(2) the other place where the register of members is kept; or
(3) its principal place of business in England, if the company is registered in England, or in Scotland if the company is registered in Scotland.

The documents must be kept open to the inspection of members without charge.

Notice of such place and of any changes in it must be given to the Registrar except where the documents have always been kept at the registered office.

Contracts requiring a director to work wholly or mainly outside the United Kingdom are excluded although a memorandum of the duration of the contract, and, if appropriate, the name and place of the subsidiary company, must be kept. Also excluded are those where the unexpired term of the contract is less than 12 months or the contract can be terminated by the company without payment of compensation within 12 months.

There are default fines[78] for contravention of section 318 and the court is empowered to order an inspection.

To prevent possible abuse by directors granting themselves long-term service contracts in order to obtain large compensation payments in the event of a dismissal, section 319 limits the length of such contracts without the approval of a general meeting at which a copy of the proposed contract is available, and where such a copy has been available for inspection at the registered office for the previous 15 days.[79] Any term in such a

[77] This applies also to "shadow directors."
[78] See note 75, *supra*.
[79] Such a resolution may be passed using the written resolution procedure provided the agreement etc. is supplied to each relevant member prior to his signature: Sched. 15A para. 7; *ante*, p. 343.

contract which entitles a director[80] to employment with the company for longer than five years must be approved by the company in general meeting.

Any term in breach of this section is void and replaced by one which enables the company to terminate the contract at any time, subject to reasonable notice. This requirement cannot be avoided by negotiating several consecutive five year agreements, since no second contract may succeed the first if that contract has more than six months left to run.

In addition to the disclosure rules noted above such contracts are to be set out in the company's accounts (*post*).

Dealing by Directors in Certain Options

The Jenkins Report[81] stated that a director should not deal in options, in securities of his company or of the group to which the company belongs—a director who speculates in such a way with special inside information is clearly acting improperly. However, it was said that the prohibition should not extend to options to subscribe for securities given to directors by the company or another member of the group—the terms of such options are a matter for the company.

Accordingly, section 323, as extended by section 327, penalises the dealing by directors,[82] their spouses or children, in options to buy or sell quoted shares in, or quoted debentures of, the company or associated companies.

A director who buys a right to call for delivery, or a right to make delivery, or, at his election, a right either to call for or to make delivery, at a specified price and within a specified time of a specified number of relevant shares or a specified amount of relevant debentures, is liable to two years' imprisonment or a fine or both: section 323.

"Relevant shares" and "relevant debentures" mean, respectively, shares in, or debentures of, the company or its subsidiary, holding company or co-subsidiary, as respects which a stock exchange listing has been granted in Great Britain or elsewhere.

[80] This includes a shadow director.
[81] Para. 90.
[82] Including shadow directors.

Buying a right to subscribe for shares or debentures is not penalised, nor is buying debentures which carry a right to subscribe for or convert into shares.

Section 327 extends section 323 to the spouse of, or child under the age of majority of, a director, not being herself or himself a director of the company, except that it is a defence for such a spouse or child, charged with an offence under section 323, to prove that he had no reason to believe that his spouse or parent was a director of the company in question. "Child" includes step-child and adopted child.

If it appears that section 323 has been contravened the Secretary of State may order an investigation: section 446.[83]

VACATION OF OFFICE BY DIRECTORS

A director may cease to be such for various reasons, *e.g.* death, dissolution of the company, retirement by rotation under articles like Table A, regulations 73 and 74, *ante*,[84] or retirement under an age limit, disqualification, under the terms of the articles, removal under section 303, or because they are subject to a disqualification order by a court.[85]

Retirement of directors under age limit

A director must retire at the end of the first annual general meeting after he reaches 70 *unless*:

(1) the company is a private company which is not the subsidiary of a public company; or
(2) the articles otherwise provide; or
(3) he was appointed or approved by the company in general meeting by a resolution, *i.e.* an ordinary resolution, of which special notice, stating his age, was given: section 293.

If a director should have to retire under this section he may be reappointed by an ordinary resolution of which special

[83] *Post*, p. 478.
[84] p. 348.
[85] *Ante*, p. 352.

notice,[86] stating his age, has been given. The result is that the section is a weak one and unimportant in practice. In particular, the articles may alter the age limit or provide that directors shall not be obliged to retire on reaching any age. The Jenkins Report[87] recommended that the section be strengthened, simplified and made to apply to all companies.

Disqualification of directors under the articles

The articles usually provide for the vacation of office by directors on the happening of certain events, *e.g.* bankruptcy or resignation.[88]

Table A provides:
Regulation 81: "The office of a director shall be vacated if—

- (a) he ceases to be a director by virtue of any provision of the Act or he becomes prohibited by law from being a director; or
- (b) he becomes bankrupt or makes any arrangement or composition with his creditors generally; or
- (c) he is, or may be, suffering from mental disorder and either—
  - (i) he is admitted to hospital in pursuance of an application for admission for treatment under the Mental Health Act 1983, or in Scotland, an application for admission under the Mental Health (Scotland) Act 1984, or
  - (ii) an order is made by a court having jurisdiction (whether in the United Kingdom or elsewhere) in matters concerning mental disorder for his detention or for the appointment of a receiver, curator bonis or other person to exercise powers with respect to his property or affairs; or
- (d) he resigns his office by notice to the company; or
- (e) he shall for more than six consecutive months have been absent without permission of the directors from meetings of directors held during that period and the directors resolve that his office be vacated."

When the articles provide that a director shall vacate his office if he absents himself from board meetings for a certain

[86] *Ante*, p. 325.
[87] Para. 85.
[88] These matters are distinct from those who cease to be directors because they are subject to a disqualification order made by the court; *ante*, p. 351.

time, the office will not be vacated if the absence is involuntary, as where the director is ill and unable to travel.[89] On the other hand, if the director is absent because his doctor has advised that his health will be benefited by going abroad, the office will be vacated.[90]

On the happening of any of the events mentioned in the articles, the vacation of office is automatic and the board of directors has no power to waive the offence or condone the act.[91] Similarly, on the resignation of a director the office is automatically vacated, so that the resignation cannot be withdrawn without the consent of the company.[92]

In *Lee* v. *Chou Wen Hsien*[93] the articles provided that a director should vacate his office if he was "requested in writing by all his co-directors to resign." The Privy Council held that a notice in the correct form validly removed the recipient from his directorship even if it was made with an ulterior motive. Any challenge had to be made on the basis that the other directors had acted in breach of their fiduciary duty which was in any event owed to the company and not to an individual director.[94] The clause was so drafted that the dismissal was automatic on the giving of the correct notice.

Removal of directors

By section 303 a company may by ordinary resolution[95] remove a director before the expiration of his period of office, *notwithstanding* anything in the articles or in any agreement between him and the company. Special notice[96] must be given of any resolution to remove a director or to appoint another person in place of a removed director at the meeting at which he is removed. On receipt of notice of an intended resolution to

[89] *Mack's Claim* [1900] W.N. 114.
[90] *McConnell's Claim* [1901] 1 Ch. 728.
[91] *Re The Bodega Co. Ltd.* [1904] 1 Ch. 276.
[92] *Glossop* v. *Glossop* [1907] 2 Ch. 370.
[93] [1985] BCLC 45 (P.C.).
[94] *Post*, p. 394.
[95] This is a rare case where the Act *expressly* provides for an ordinary resolution. The written resolution procedure is not available for such a purpose: Sched. 15A para. 1; *ante*, p. 343.
[96] See note 86, *ante*.

remove a director the company must send a copy to the director concerned, who is entitled to have his representations in writing of a reasonable length sent to the members of the company or read out at the meeting and also to be heard on the resolution at the meeting. The director may be deprived of the former right if the court is satisfied that it is being abused to secure needless publicity for defamatory matter.

It has been held that nothing in the Act prevents the articles giving a director's shares special voting rights, *e.g.* three votes per share on a poll, on a resolution to remove him.[97]

Subsection (5) provides that nothing in section 303 deprives a removed director of any compensation[98] or damages payable to him in respect of the termination of his appointment as director or of any appointment, *e.g.* as managing director, terminating with that as director; and nothing in the section derogates from any power of removal which may exist apart from the section, *e.g.* a power of removal given by the articles of the company. For example, as will be explained later,[99] he will be entitled to damages if he has a contract of service, outside the articles, appointing him managing director for a specified period which has not yet expired, and his removal is inconsistent with such contract. Section 318, *ante*,[1] enables members to inspect the service contract and thus ascertain how much it will cost to remove a director.

A director validly removed from office may, if he is a member, in appropriate circumstances, be entitled to an order under section 459 where the affairs of the company have been conducted in an unfairly prejudicial manner,[2] or an order that the company be wound up by the court on the ground that winding up is just and equitable.[3]

Proceedings of Directors

Table A, regulation 88, provides that subject to the articles, the directors may regulate their proceedings as they think fit.

[97] *Bushell* v. *Faith* [1970] A.C. 1099.
[98] *e.g.* for unfair dismissal. See *Parsons* v. *Parsons Ltd.* [1978] I.C.R. 456.
[99] p. 385.
[1] p. 369.
[2] *Post*, p. 457.
[3] *Re Westbourne Galleries Ltd.* [1973] A.C. 360, *post*, p. 453.

Regulation 88 further provides that a director may, and the secretary on the requisition of a director must, at any time summon a board meeting.

Every director is entitled to have reasonable notice of a meeting except that regulation 88, *ante*, provides that notice need not be given to a director who is absent from the United Kingdom. What is reasonable notice depends on the practice of the company, but if a director wishes to complain of the shortness of the notice he should act promptly, otherwise the court will not interfere.[4]

If notice is not properly given, the proceedings at the meeting are void.

Application was invited for 106,000 shares, and the directors resolved not to allot until 14,000 shares were applied for. A subsequent meeting was held at which two directors, a quorum, were present, when a resolution was passed to allot the shares applied for, about 3,000. The meeting was held at a few hours' notice at 2 o'clock. This was much shorter notice than had ever been given before. One director did not receive notice until next day, and another gave notice that he could not attend until 3 o'clock. *Held*, the allotment was void: *Re Homer District Gold Mines* (1888) 39 Ch.D. 546.

A quorum is that number of directors which must be present to make the proceedings of the board valid. The articles usually fix a quorum. Table A, regulation 89, provides: "The quorum for the transaction of the business of directors may be fixed by the directors and unless so fixed at any other number shall be two."

If the number of directors sinks below the quorum, the directors cannot act unless the articles provide, as they usually do, that the continuing directors can act.

Table A, regulation 90, provides that if the number of directors is less than the number fixed as the quorum, the continuing directors or director may act only for the purpose of filling vacancies or of calling a general meeting.

In ascertaining whether a quorum is present, those directors who are incompetent to vote on the matter under discussion

[4] See *Browne* v. *La Trinidad* (1887) 37 Ch.D. 1 (C.A.).

must not be counted.[5] Directors, however, can attend the meeting even if they are unable to vote.[6] One transaction cannot be split up into two resolutions so as to qualify directors to vote.

Y. and D., two directors of a company, had made advances to the company in consideration of receiving debentures. The company had four directors, three of whom were a quorum. A resolution was passed granting a debenture to Y. Y. did not vote on this resolution. Another resolution was then passed granting a debenture to D., on which D. did not vote. The two debentures ranked equally among themselves. *Held*, the issue of the two debentures formed one transaction in which Y. and D. were equally interested and that the two resolutions were invalid for want of a quorum: *Re North Eastern Insurance Co. Ltd.* [1919] 1 Ch. 198.

If an act is invalid owing to some informality in the constitution of the board it will in most cases be binding on the company, either because of section 35A or section 285, *ante*,[7] or because of subsequent ratification by a properly constituted board.[8]

The articles deal with the election of a chairman. By Table A, regulation 91, the directors may elect a chairman of their meetings and determine the period for which he is to hold office. The chairman has no casting vote at common law,[9] nor does he have one by virtue of Table A.

Table A, regulation 93, provides that a resolution in writing, signed by all the directors entitled to receive notice of a meeting of the directors, shall be as valid as if it had been passed at a board meeting duly convened and held. (The position is the same at common law.[10])

Section 382 provides that minutes of proceedings at directors' meetings must be entered in books kept for the purpose, and such minutes signed by the chairman of the meeting at which

[5] *Re Greymouth Point Elizabeth Ry., etc. Co. Ltd.* [1904] 1 Ch. 32. See also Table A, reg. 89 as to alternate directors, and reg. 95.
[6] *Grimwade* v. *B.P.S. Syndicate Ltd.* (1915) 31 T.L.R. 531.
[7] Chap. 6. But if the third party is a director the transaction will be voidable under s.322A.
[8] *Re Portuguese Consolidated Copper Mines Ltd.* (1890) 45 Ch.D. 16 (C.A.).
[9] *Wall* v. *London and Northern Assets Corpn.* [1898] 2 Ch. 469 (C.A.).
[10] *Re Bonelli's Telegraph Co.* (1871) L.R. 12 Eq. 246.

the proceedings were had, or by the chairman of the next succeeding meeting, are evidence of the proceedings. Where minutes have been duly made there is a presumption that the meeting was duly held and convened, that all proceedings were duly had and that all appointments of directors and managers were valid.

By section 722 the minutes may be kept in a bound book, or in a loose-leaf book provided that adequate precautions are taken for guarding against falsification. Minutes may also be kept on a computer under section 723.

If the minutes are incomplete, a resolution duly passed can be proved by other evidence.[11]

Although section 722 contains no provision for the inspection of the minutes, the Court of Session may, on the petition of a director presented to the *nobile officium*, ordain a company to make them available for inspection by the director and by a named accountant on his behalf.[12]

Powers of Directors

The powers of the directors depend on the articles since, apart from requiring that certain things, *e.g.* alterations to the articles (s.9) or the capital (ss.121, 135) or the delegating of authority to issue shares (s.80), shall be done by the members in general meeting, the Act leaves the distribution of powers between the general meeting and the board to the articles, which always give the directors extensive powers.

Table A provides:

Regulation 70: "Subject to the provisions of the Acts, the memorandum and the articles and to any directions given by special resolution, the business of the company shall be managed by the directors who may exercise all the powers of the company. No alteration of the memorandum or articles and no such direction shall invalidate any prior act of the directors which would have been valid if that alteration had not been made or that direction had not been given. The powers given by this regulation shall not be limited by any special power given

[11] *Re Fireproof Doors Ltd.* [1916] 2 Ch. 142.
[12] *M'Cusker* v. *M'Rae*, 1966 S.C. 253.

to the directors by the articles and a meeting of directors at which a quorum is present may exercise all powers exercisable by the directors.

If they act within the powers given to them by such an article, directors are not bound to obey resolutions passed by the shareholders at a general meeting; such resolutions cannot override a decision of the directors or control the exercise of their powers in the future.[13] The directors' powers can be altered for the future by an alteration of the articles in the proper way,[14] but the articles cannot be altered with retrospective effect. And it may be that the directors can be removed from office in the proper way.[15]

"A company cannot by ordinary resolution dictate to or overrule the directors in respect of matters entrusted to them by the articles. To do that it is necessary to have a special resolution": *per* Plowman J. in *Bamford* v. *Bamford* [1970] Ch. 212 at p. 220.

The articles of a company contained an article like the predecessor at Table A, regulation 70, except that it was stated to be "subject to such regulations as might be made by the company by extraordinary resolution." The majority of the shareholders arranged a sale of the company's undertaking and requisitioned a meeting at which an ordinary resolution requiring the directors to seal the contract was passed. *Held*, the directors were not bound to obey the resolution: *Automatic Self-Cleansing Filter Syndicate Co. Ltd.* v. *Cuninghame* [1906] 2 Ch. 34 (C.A.).

The articles contained an article like the predecessor of Table A, regulation 70, and also provided that no resolution of the directors to acquire or dispose of premises was to be valid unless neither A nor B dissented. (A and B were the managing directors.) The directors resolved to acquire premises. B dissented. An ordinary resolution to the same effect as the board resolution was passed at an extraordinary general meeting of the company. *Held*, the ordinary resolution was inconsistent with the articles and the company was restrained from acting on it: *Salmon* v. *Quin & Axtens Ltd.* [1909] 1 Ch. 311 (C.A.); [1909] A.C. 442.

"This Court decided not long since, in [the *Automatic Self-Cleansing* case], that even a resolution of a numerical majority at a general meeting of the company cannot impose its will upon the directors when

[13] *Automatic Self-Cleansing Filter Syndicate Co. Ltd.* v. *Cuninghame* [1906] 2 Ch. 34 (C.A.); *Salmon* v. *Quin and Axtens Ltd.* [1909] 1 Ch. 311 (C.A.); [1909] A.C. 442; *Breckland Group Holdings Ltd.* v. *London and Suffolk Properties Ltd.* [1989] BCLC 100; *cf. Marshall's Valve Gear Co. Ltd.* v. *Manning Wardle & Co. Ltd.* [1909] 1 Ch. 267.

[14] *Ante*, p. 90.

[15] *Ante*, p. 373.

the articles have confided to them the control of the company's affairs": *per* Farwell L.J. in [1909] 1 Ch. 311 at p. 319, quoting Buckley L.J. in *Gramophone & Typewriter Ltd.* v. *Stanley* [1908] 2 K.B. 89 (C.A.).

"Thus, as it seems to me, there is little doubt that the law is that, where matters are confided by articles such as article 80 to the conduct of the business by the directors, it is not a matter where the general meeting can intervene": *per* Harman J. in *Breckland Group Holdings Ltd.* v. *London & Suffolk Properties Ltd.* [1989] BCLC 100 at p. 106.

In accordance with the principle set out above, a resolution passed by a company in general meeting that the directors should make an advance of money to the shareholders pending the declaration of a dividend was held to be inoperative.[16]

The powers of the board may also be regulated by a shareholders' agreement. In *Breckland Group Holdings Ltd.* v. *London and Suffolk Properties Ltd.*,[17] the company had adopted regulation 70 of Table A and also had a shareholders' agreement that no litigation could be brought without the approval of a director appointed by each of the two shareholders. Harman J. decided that a combination of regulation 70 and the agreement precluded any interference by the general meeting in a decision whether to bring proceedings on behalf of the company.

If directors are unable to exercise one of their powers because of deadlock on the board or because their number has fallen below the number required for a quorum, the company in general meeting may exercise the power.[18]

The position is similar if a company has no directors.[19] Where a company has no directors and two individuals, acting without the authority of the company, commence an action in the company's name, the company in general meeting or, if the company is being wound up, the liquidator can ratify the proceedings.[20]

[16] *Scott* v. *Scott* [1943] 1 All E.R. 582.

[17] *Supra.*

[18] *Barron* v. *Potter* [1914] 1 Ch. 895, where the articles gave the board of directors power to appoint an additional director and, owing to differences between the directors, no board meeting could be held for the purpose. *Held*, the company retained power to appoint additional directors in general meeting.

[19] *Per* Lord Hailsham of St. Marylebone in *Alexander Ward & Co. Ltd.* v. *Samyang Navigation Co. Ltd.*, 1975 S.C. (H.L.) 26 at p. 47.

[20] *Alexander Ward* case, *ante*.

If directors exceed or improperly exercise their powers, their action can be ratified by an ordinary resolution of the company in general meeting.[21] If they act contrary to the company's articles or memorandum it can be ratified by a special resolution.[22]

By way of defence to a take-over bid directors allotted 500,000 shares at par for cash to a third company which was the principal distributor of the products of the company to be taken over. The articles provided that the unissued shares were to be at the directors' disposal. Two shareholders brought an action against the three directors, the third company, and the company, claiming a declaration that the allotment was invalid in that the directors had not acted bona fide in the interests of the company. *Held*, assuming that the allotment was *intra vires* the company and the directors but not bona fide in the interests of the company and therefore voidable, it could after full disclosure be ratified by an ordinary resolution at a general meeting: *Bamford* v. *Bamford* [1970] Ch. 212 (C.A.), approving *Hogg* v. *Cramphorn Ltd.*, *post.*[23]

If directors improperly refuse to exercise a power to initiate an action in the company's name, a minority shareholders' action may be brought by way of exception to the rule in *Foss* v. *Harbottle.*[24]

In one case where the directors directed the company to plead guilty to a charge of conspiracy to defraud, the court granted an injunction to prevent the company so pleading because the company's interests would thereby suffer, *e.g.* the loss of a potential civil action against an individual defrauder: *Re A Company*: *F.F.I.* (*U.K. Finance*) *Ltd.* v. *Lady Kagan* (1982) 132 N.L.J. 830.

Power to manage the business of the company does not give directors power to fix their own remuneration.[25] The articles, however, may empower them, as does Table A, regulation 87, to pay a gratuity or pension or allowance on retirement to a director who has held a salaried office with the company, or to his widow or dependants.

[21] *Grant* v. *United Kingdom Switchback Rlwys. Co.* (1888) 40 Ch.D. 135 (C.A.).
[22] s.35; see Chaps. 3 and 6.
[23] p. 400.
[24] *Cook* v. *Deeks* [1916] A.C. 554, *post* p. 440.
[25] *Foster* v. *Foster* [1916] 1 Ch. 532.

The directors cannot delegate their powers unless empowered to do so by the articles. It will be seen later[26] that the articles usually provide for delegation to a managing director. They may also provide for delegation to a committee of directors.[27] However, such a delegation must be validly authorised by the articles or such a committee will have no authority to enter into the transaction. In *Guinness plc* v. *Saunders*,[28] a committee of the directors set up to conduct a take-over bid had no authority under the articles to authorise special payments to the directors involved. Such payments could only be authorised by the full board. It followed that the payments were unauthorised, and therefore reclaimable from the directors concerned.

Remuneration of Directors

Directors as such are not servants of the company,[29] but managers or controllers of the company's affairs. Accordingly they have no claim to payment for their services unless, as is usual, there is a provision for payment in the articles.[30]

If there is no authorisation, either in the articles or elsewhere, for payment a director cannot make a claim for payment by way of quantum meruit or in equity for special work performed. Thus in *Guinness plc* v. *Saunders*, *ante*, the House of Lords refused such a claim by a director who had successfully negotiated a take-over bid for the company but whose remuneration was not properly authorised either by the directors or the company.

Table A provides:

Regulation 82: "The directors shall be entitled to such remuneration as the company may by ordinary resolution determine and, unless the resolution provides otherwise, the remuneration shall be deemed to accrue from day to day."

Regulation 83: "The directors may be paid all travelling, hotel and other expenses properly incurred by them in connection with their

[26] p. 390.
[27] See Table A, reg. 72.
[28] [1990] 1 All E.R. 652 (H.L.).
[29] *Post*, p. 393.
[30] *Per* McCardie J. in *Moriarty* v. *Regent's Garage Co. Ltd.* [1921] 1 K.B. 423, at p. 446; *cf.* Lord President Inglis in *M'Naughtan* v. *Brunton* (1882) 10 R. 111 at p. 113.

attendance at meetings of directors or committees of directors or general meetings or separate meetings of the holders of any class of shares or of debentures of the company or otherwise in connection with the discharge of their duties."

It should be remembered that a director may hold some other position with the company, *e.g.* he may also be the managing director, in which case he will be a servant of the company as regards that other position and will receive a salary fixed by his contract of service or employment with the company.[31]

Where the company pays remuneration to its directors under an express power, such as regulation 82, the court will not inquire into the reasonableness of the remuneration even if it is paid out of capital, unless at the suit of a dissenting shareholder.

If remuneration is voted to the directors, it constitutes a debt due from the company and is consequently payable not only out of profits but also out of capital.[32] As was shown earlier,[33] a clause in the articles that directors shall receive a certain sum as remuneration, although it cannot be directly enforced against the company, is binding if the directors have accepted office on the footing of the articles.[34]

A director who is entitled to remuneration for his services is not entitled to his travelling and other expenses in attending board and other meetings unless the articles expressly so provide.

The articles, which were not like Table A, regulation 83, provided that each director should be paid £200 a year by way of remuneration for his services, and that the company should pay all costs and expenses which any officer of the company should incur in the discharge of his duties. Y. was appointed a director, and shortly afterwards the directors passed a resolution that all reasonable travelling expenses should be reimbursed to the directors. *Held*, the resolution was *ultra vires* the directors, and Y. must repay the travelling expenses received.

[31] *Anderson* v. *James Sutherland* (*Peterhead*) *Ltd.*, 1941 S.C. 203, in which a managing director was held to be a person "employed by the company in any capacity" within an article which enabled the directors to remove such a person from membership when he was dismissed as managing director for misconduct (assaulting a co-director by the firing of a revolver at a directors' meeting). Such contracts are subject to the general law: see *Horcal* v. *Gartland* [1984] BCLC 549.

[32] *Re Lundy Granite Co.* (1872) 26 L.T. 673.

[33] p. 90.

[34] *Re New British Iron Co.* [1898] 1 Ch. 324.

His expenses of attending directors' meetings were covered by his remuneration: *Young* v. *Naval and Military Society* [1905] 1 K.B. 687.[35]

Unless authorised by the articles, directors cannot vote remuneration to one of themselves or appoint one of their number to a salaried position with the company. It has been said that "Directors have no right to be paid for their services, and cannot pay themselves or each other, or make presents to themselves out of the company's assets, unless authorised so to do by the instrument which regulates the company or by the shareholders at a properly convened meeting."[36]

The article governing directors' remuneration was the same as the predecessor of regulation 82.[37] The *directors* passed a resolution appointing K., one of the directors, "overseas director" at a salary of £1,800 a year. In pursuance of this appointment K. was obliged to go, and did go, to Australia. He sued for arrears of salary. *Held*, the appointment was *ultra vires* the board, so that K. could not recover the arrears of salary and was liable to refund salary already received: *Kerr* v. *Marine Products Ltd.* (1928) 44 T.L.R. 292.

A resolution of the directors to forgo fees to which they are entitled is binding on them and on the company if the company is a party to the agreement.[38] Otherwise the directors may rescind the resolution and claim for fees.[39]

On a liquidation, directors are not entitled to preferential payment of fees owing to them, since as directors they are not servants of the company.[40] It is otherwise with regard to salary owing to them where they hold some other position with the company.[41]

When a director ceases to be a director during a year of office, a question arises as to whether he is entitled to have his remuneration apportioned. If, *e.g.*, the articles say that he is to

[35] See also *Marmor Ltd.* v. *Alexander*, 1908 S.C. 78 and *Tomlinson* v. *Liquidators of Scottish Amalgamated Silks Ltd.*, 1935 S.C. (H.L.) 1; 1934 S.C. 85.

[36] *Per* Lindley L.J. in *Re George Newman & Co.* [1895] 1 Ch. 674 (C.A.) at p. 686.

[37] *Ante*, p. 381.

[38] *West Yorkshire Darracq Agency Ltd.* v. *Coleridge* [1911] 2 K.B. 326.

[39] *Re Consolidated Nickel Mines Ltd.* [1914] 1 Ch. 883.

[40] *Re Newspaper Proprietary Syndicate Ltd.* [1900] 2 Ch. 349.

[41] *Post*, Chap. 29.

be paid "at the rate of" so much a year, he is entitled to be paid for the period during which he was a director.[42] On the other hand, if he is to be paid £1,000 a year, or in any way other than at the rate of so much a year, it has been held that he is entitled to be paid only for each complete year he serves, and not for any broken period.[43]

Disclosure of directors' emoluments

Any provision in the articles as to the directors' remuneration must usually be disclosed in a prospectus or listing particulars issued by the company.[44]

By section 232 and Schedule 6, Part I, a note to the accounts which must be laid before the company in general meeting must show certain particulars of directors' salaries, pensions, etc.

The particulars are:

(1) The aggregate amount of the directors' emoluments.

These include fees, including those paid for accepting the position of director, and percentages, sums paid as expenses allowances which are charged to income tax,[45] contributions paid in respect of the directors under any pension scheme, and the estimated money value of any other benefits received otherwise than in cash. The accounts must distinguish between emoluments in respect of services as directors and other emoluments such as sums received by the directors as salaried employees of the company.

(2) The aggregate amount of directors' or past directors' pensions.

This does not include pensions paid under a pension scheme where the contributions are substantially adequate for the maintenance of the scheme, but does include a pension paid to a director's widow or other dependant.

(3) The aggregate amount of any compensation paid to directors or past directors for loss of office.

This includes sums paid on a director's retirement from office.

[42] *Swabey* v. *Port Darwin Gold Mining Co.* (1889) 1 Meg. 385, although despite the report, the articles did not contain the words "at the rate of," as pointed out in *Inman's* case, *post.*

[43] *Salton* v. *New Beeston Cycle Co.* [1899] 1 Ch. 775; *Inman* v. *Ackroyd & Best Ltd.* [1901] 1 Q.B. 613 (C.A.), followed in *Liquidator of the Fife Linoleum etc. Co. Ltd.* v. *Lornie* (1905) 13 S.L.T. 670 (O.H.).

[44] *Ante*, Chap. 7.

[45] See Income and Corporation Taxes Act 1988, ss.153–168.

These amounts must include all relevant sums received from the company, the company's subsidiaries and any other person. The amount shown under (3), above, must distinguish between sums received from the company, the company's subsidiaries and other persons.

(4) With respect to each person who has been chairman of the directors' meetings during the year, his emoluments so far as attributable to his period of office (unless his duties were mainly discharged outside the United Kingdom).

(5) With respect to all the directors (other than any whose duties were mainly discharged abroad), the number whose several emoluments did not exceed £5,000, exceeded £5,000 but not £10,000,[46] and so on in bands of £5,000.

(6) If the emoluments of one or more directors exceed the chairman's emoluments, his emoluments or the greater or, as the case may be, the greatest emoluments.

Emoluments include all such amounts (other than contributions paid in respect of a person under a pension scheme) as are caught by (1) above.

(7) The number of directors who have waived rights to receive emoluments and the aggregate amount of such emoluments.

Heads (4)–(7) do not apply if the company is a subsidiary company or the aggregate amount of the directors' emoluments for that year does not exceed £60,000.

Each director is under a duty to give notice to the company of such matters relating to himself as may be necessary to enable the above information to be shown in the accounts, under penalty of a fine: section 232.

Compensation to Directors for Loss of Office

It is unlawful for a company to make to a director any payment by way of compensation for loss of office, or as consideration for or in connection with retirement, unless particulars of the proposed payment, including the amount, are disclosed to the members and the proposal is approved by the company: section 312. It was held in *Re Duomatic Ltd.*[47] that disclosure must be made to *all* members, even those with no right to attend and vote at general meetings, whilst the payment is still a proposed payment, although in *Wallersteiner* v. *Moir*[48] Lord Denning

[46] Sched. 6, para 4.
[47] [1969] 2 Ch. 365.
[48] [1974] 1 W.L.R. 991 (C.A.) at p. 1016.

M.R. said that he imagined that payment could be later approved by the company in general meeting.

The section does not apply to a payment to a *managing director as such.*[49] Nor does it apply to a payment to a director who does not retire.

It is unlawful for anyone to make to a director a payment by way of compensation for loss of office, etc., in connection with the transfer of the whole or part of the company's undertaking or property unless particulars are disclosed and approved. If such a payment is not disclosed the director holds it upon trust for the company: section 313.

When, in connection with a transfer of all or any of the shares in the company resulting from (*a*) an offer made to the general body of shareholders, (*b*) an offer made with a view to the company becoming the subsidiary of another, (*c*) an offer made with a view to an individual obtaining control of not less than one-third of the voting power at a general meeting, or (*d*) any other offer conditional on acceptance to a given extent, a payment is to be made to a director as compensation for loss of or retirement from office, he must take reasonable steps to see that particulars of the proposed payment, including the amount, are sent with any notice of the offer for their shares given to the shareholders. If this is not done, or the payment is not, before the transfer of the shares, approved by a meeting of the shareholders summoned for the purpose, the director holds the payment on trust for the persons who have sold their shares as a result of the offer: sections 314 and 315.

Sections 313, 314 and 315 cannot be avoided, *e.g.* by paying more than the market value for a director's shares, because section 316 provides that, in connection with sections 313 and 315, the price paid to a director for any of his shares in the company in excess of the price which could have been obtained by other shareholders, or the money value of any valuable consideration given to him, is deemed to have been a payment to him of compensation for loss of office. References in sections 313 to 315 to payments of compensation for loss of office exclude bona fide payments of damages for breach of contract or of pensions in respect of past services. But these provisions have been held not to protect an *ex gratia* payment in lieu of

[49] *Lincoln Mills* v. *Gough* [1964] V.R. 193.

pension made on the eve of liquidation in the case of a company whose directors had no power to make such payments.[50]

The provisions of sections 312 to 315 do not apply, however, to payments which the company is already bound to make, *e.g.* under a director's service contract.[51] Such payments are not voidable because the director intends to breach his fiduciary duty to the company.[52]

SUBSTANTIAL PROPERTY TRANSACTIONS INVOLVING DIRECTORS

Section 320 is intended to prevent directors abusing their position by stripping the company of its assets. The section provides that no contract may be made without the approval of the general meeting, between a director and his company involving the transfer, either way,[53] of a non-cash asset, if its value exceeds £100,000 or 10 per cent. of the company's net assets, provided it is not less than £2,000.

This section applies equally to "shadow directors"[54] and persons "connected with a director."[55]

Any arrangement entered into in breach of this section is voidable by the company (unless restitution of the status quo is impossible). Further, the director concerned and any director who authorised the transaction are liable to account to and indemnify the company for any loss.

The section does not apply if the director concerned received the assets solely by virtue of being a member (*e.g.* on a general reduction of capital), or the transaction was entered into during the course of the winding up of an insolvent company. Most transactions within a group of companies are also excluded as are transactions on a recognised investment exchange made

[50] *Gibson's Executor* v. *Gibson*, 1978 S.C. 197 (O.H.).

[51] *Taupo Totara Timber Co. Ltd.* v. *Darey Kevin Rowe* [1977] 3 W.L.R. 466 (P.C.).

[52] *Horcal Ltd.* v. *Gartland* [1984] BCLC 549.

[53] Thus applying both to sales to the company by a director, *e.g. Pavlides* v. *Jensen* [1956] Ch. 565; and sales to a director by his company, *e.g. Daniels* v. *Daniels* [1978] 2 W.L.R. 73. The amounts were raised by the Companies (Fair Dealing by Directors) (Increase in Financial Limits) Order 1990.

[54] s.320(3). *Ante*, p. 347.

[55] s.346. This includes his minor children, spouse, partners, or any company in which he and his other associates control one-fifth of the equity share capital or votes.

through an independent broker by a director of a group which includes the market maker concerned: section 321.

Disclosure of such arrangements in the accounts is required by section 232.

Directors are also under a general duty to disclose their interests in contracts to the board of directors: section 317, *post*. This includes disclosure of the arrangements detailed in section 320.

LOANS TO DIRECTORS

Following certain major scandals in the 1970s the rules relating to loans to directors were strengthened and now appear in sections 330 to 342.

Section 330 prohibits various categories of loans and other credit transactions between a company and its directors, "shadow directors"[56] and "persons connected with its directors."[57] A subsidiary is equally restrained as regards its holding company.[58]

All companies are prohibited from making loans to, giving guarantees for and security for loans to, their directors or "shadow directors." The strength of this provision appears, however, to be somewhat weakened by the decision of Walton J. in *Champagne Perrier-Jouet S.A.* v. *H. H. Finch Ltd.*,[59] that where a company paid a great many bills for one of its directors it had not made a loan to that director. "Money paid to B at the request of A is quite definitely not a loan."[60] This would seem to be an obvious loophole in the general embargo on loans.

In addition, however, public companies, and companies forming part of a group which includes a public company, may not make loans, give guarantees or securities to persons connected with such directors. Further, public companies may not make "quasi-loans" to their directors, etc., nor may they provide credit facilities for such persons. A "quasi-loan" is defined (s.331(3)) to include the provision of credit card

[56] See note 54, *supra*.
[57] See note 55, *supra*.
[58] This includes a wholly-owned subsidiary, unlike s.320 above.
[59] [1982] 1 W.L.R. 1359.
[60] *Ibid*. p. 1364.

facilities, *e.g.* where the company is the cardholder and the card is used by the director. A credit transaction is one where goods or services are provided on the undertaking that payment will be made later.

These prohibitions cannot be avoided by directors assigning their liabilities to their company or by "back to back" deals, *i.e.* where two companies each make what appear to be separate provisions for each other's directors.

Sections 332 to 338 provide certain exceptions to the prohibitions of section 330. The effect is to allow all loans up to a total of £5,000 outstanding for each director; to allow all credit transactions, if they are on normal commercial terms; to provide an exemption for loans to cover expenses incurred by a director for company purposes, provided the transaction has the prior approval of the general meeting[61] or is ratified within six months, subject to a maximum of £20,000 for directors of public companies; to allow quasi-loans up to £1,000 outstanding at any one time if the terms require repayment within two months; and to allow credit transactions up to £10,000 outstanding at any one time per director.

In addition moneylending companies[62] may make loans and quasi-loans to directors on normal commercial terms subject to a maximum of £100,000 outstanding at any one time apart from "authorised banks."[63] Directors of such companies may also be allowed to participate in subsidised house purchase schemes up to a limit of £100,000.

The various sums used in sections 334 to 338, *i.e.* £10,000, £20,000 and £100,000, are sums outstanding at any time and are calculated in accordance with section 339.

Section 341 provides that the civil consequences of a breach of section 330 are the same as those for a breach of section 320 (substantial property transactions), *ante*.[64] In addition section 342 provides for a series of criminal offences for public companies and their directors who know or have reasonable causes to believe that section 330 has been breached.

[61] The various amounts and purposes must be disclosed at the relevant meeting: s.337. If the written resolution procedure, *ante*, p. 343, is used such disclosures must be made to each relevant member before he signs the resolution: Sched. 15A.

[62] s.338(2).

[63] s.338(4).

[64] p. 387.

Sections 232 to 237 require particulars of all loans etc., whether prohibited or not, to be disclosed in the accounts unless they are less than £2,000 in total. This includes disclosure of the principal terms of the transaction and the true beneficiary. Authorised banks[65] are subject to special rules. Auditors must disclose any breach of the disclosure requirements in their report.

MANAGING DIRECTOR

Unless the directors are empowered to appoint a managing director[66] by the memorandum[67] or the articles, the directors cannot appoint a managing director.[68] When the articles empower the directors to appoint a managing director, the company in general meeting cannot itself make such an appointment without first altering the articles.[69]

Table A, regulation 84, provides that the directors may appoint *one or more of their number* to the office of managing director for such period and on such terms as they think fit, and, *subject to the terms of any contract of service*, may revoke such appointment; that a director so appointed shall not, whilst holding that office, retire by rotation,[70] but that the appointment shall be automatically determined if he ceases to be a director.

A managing director has two functions and two capacities, those of director and managing director. As managing director he is usually a party to a contract of employment or service with the company.[71] In a family company, however, if there is no

[65] See note 63, *supra*.
[66] For a discussion of the general nature of the post of managing director, see *Anderson* v. *James Sutherland* (*Peterhead*) *Ltd*., 1941 S.C. 203 *ante*, p. 382; also *Hindle* v. *John Cotton Ltd*. (1919) 56 S.L.R. 625 (H.L.) (managing director held to be an "employee" within the meaning of the articles) and opinions in *Kerr* v. *Walker*, 1933 S.C. 458.
[67] *Re Scottish Loan & Finance Co. Ltd*. (1944) 44 S.R. (N.S.W.) 461.
[68] *Per* Swinfen Eady J. in *Boschoek Proprietary Co. Ltd*. v. *Fuke* [1906] 1 Ch. 148 at p. 159.
[69] *Thomas Logan Ltd*. v. *Davis* (1911) 104 L.T. 914; 105 L.T. 419.
[70] *Ante*, p. 348.
[71] *Per* Lord Normand in *Anderson* v. *James Sutherland* (*Peterhead*) *Ltd*., 1941 S.C. 203 at p. 218; *per* Jenkins L.J. in *Goodwin* v. *Brewster* (1951) 32 T.C. 80 at p. 96.

express contract of service the managing director may not be regarded as an employee.[72]

Subject to the articles, the powers and duties of a managing director depend upon his contract of service with the company.

C. was appointed a managing director of H. Co. His service agreement provided that he should perform the duties and exercise the powers in relation to the business of H. Co. and the businesses of its existing subsidiary companies which might from time to time be assigned to or vested in him by the directors. Later the directors resolved that C. should confine his attention to a particular subsidiary company. C. sued for damages for breach of contract. C.'s action was dismissed: *Caddies* v. *Harold Holdsworth & Co.* (*Wakefield*) *Ltd.*, 1955 S.C. (H.L.) 27; [1955] 1 All E.R. 725 (H.L.).

As has been seen in Chapter 6, a managing director may have implied power to enter into certain agreements on behalf of the company even though there has been no express delegation of the power to him by the board.[73] On the other hand the implied authority of a managing director is not limitless. He has no such implied power to act contrary to the articles and resolutions of the company and/or the board[74] or to use the company's money to bribe someone for the benefit of the company.[75]

Where a managing director is appointed under an article like Table A, regulation 84, above, his appointment may be prematurely determined by his removal from his directorship,[76] *e.g.* under section 303,[77] but the company will be liable in

[72] *Parsons* v. *Albert J. Parsons & Sons Ltd.* [1979] I.C.R. 271 (C.A.).

[73] *Allison* v. *Scotia Motor etc. Co. Ltd.* (1906) 14 S.L.T. 9 (O.H.) (implied power to engage a works manager for a period of five years).

[74] *Guinness plc* v. *Saunders* [1990] 1 All E.R. 652.

[75] *E. Hannibal & Co. Ltd.* v. *Frost* (1988) 4 BCC 3.

[76] *Southern Foundries* (*1926*) *Ltd.* v. *Shirlaw* [1940] A.C. 701, *ante*, p. 96; *Nelson* v. *James Nelson & Sons Ltd.* [1914] 2 K.B. 770 (C.A.); *Carrier Australasia Ltd.* v. *Hunt* (1939) 61 C.L.R. 534. In the *Nelson* case the articles empowered the board to appoint a managing director and to revoke the appointment. The board appointed the plaintiff managing director, the agreement providing that he was to hold the office so long as, *inter alia*, he efficiently performed the duties. The board revoked his appointment whilst he was still fulfilling the conditions of the agreement and he was held entitled to damages for breach of contract. In the *Carrier Australasia* case the articles empowered the company to remove a director, subject to the provisions of any agreement. The articles were altered so as to delete the words "subject to . . . any agreement" and then the managing director was removed from his directorship. He was held to be entitled to damages.

[77] *Ante*, p. 373.

damages if this is in breach of his contract of service, as it usually will be. In fact the company will often have to pay a large sum by way of liquidated damages.

S. was appointed managing director of N. Ltd., a subsidiary of L. Co., for 10 years. The articles of N. Ltd. included regulation 68 of Table A in the 1929 Act (which provided that a managing director's appointment should be automatically determined if he ceased to be a director or if the company in general meeting resolved to terminate his appointment). M. Co. bought the shares in L. Co., and at a general meeting of N. Ltd. resolutions were passed removing S. from office as a director and terminating his service agreement. S. sued for damages for wrongful dismissal. *Held*, S. succeeded. It was an implied term of the service agreement that N. Ltd. would do nothing of its own motion to put an end to the state of circumstances which enabled S. to continue as managing director: *Shindler* v. *Northern Raincoat Co. Ltd.* [1960] 1 W.L.R, 1038, applying *Stirling* v. *Maitland* (1865) 34 L.J. Q.B. 1 and *Southern Foundries* (*1926*) *Ltd.* v. *Shirlaw* [1940] A.C. 701.[78]

R. was appointed managing director at £7 a week, the duration of his appointment not being specified. Article 68 of Table A in the 1929 Act was one of the articles. Later, the directors dismissed R. on a month's notice and their action was confirmed by the company in general meeting. R. sued for damages for wrongful dismissal on the ground that he was not given reasonable notice. *Held*, the claim failed, because R.'s contract incorporated article 68 which empowered the company to dismiss him without notice by a resolution in general meeting. In the absence of any contract independent of article 68 and the directors' resolution appointing him, there was no ground for implying a term as to reasonable notice: *Read* v. *Astoria Garage* (*Streatham*) *Ltd.* [1952] Ch. 637 (C.A.).

Where directors have a discretionary power to dismiss a managing director, this power must be exercised in good faith in the interests of the company and not for some ulterior purpose such as appropriation of the managing director's shares.[79]

In practice a managing director's remuneration will be specified in his contract of service which the directors will negotiate on behalf of the company.

If, where the appointment of a managing director is in fact void, he performs services which are accepted by the company, it has been held that he is entitled to reasonable remuneration.

[78] *Ante*, p. 96.
[79] *Hindle* v. *John Cotton Ltd.* (1919) 56 S.L.R. 625 (H.L.).

The articles authorised the directors to appoint one of their number managing director. By contract under the company's seal, C. was appointed managing director at a salary. The seal was affixed to the contract by a resolution of the board of directors but none of the directors had acquired his qualification shares. C. himself acted as managing director, but also failed to acquire his qualification shares. *Held*, C.'s contract was void and C. was not properly appointed managing director. His claim for remuneration in contract failed but the alternative claim in quasi-contract succeeded, *i.e.* he was entitled to payment on a *quantum meruit* basis arising from the performance of his services and their acceptance by the company: *Craven-Ellis* v. *Canons Ltd.* [1936] 2 K.B. 403 (C.A.).[80]

A managing director has been held not to be a "servant" of the company so as to be entitled to preferential payment of his salary on a winding up.[81]

Position of Directors

As a company has no physical but only a legal existence, the management of its affairs is entrusted to human instruments called "directors" whose exact position in relation to the company is rather hard to define.[82] Directors as such are not servants of the company, but are rather managers who in some respects may be said to be (1) quasi-trustees or fiduciaries, and (2) agents for the company. The result is that they owe fiduciary duties and certain duties of care to the company, *i.e.* the members as a body, as will be explained later.

"The Directors are a body to whom is delegated the duty of managing the general affairs of the Company. A corporate body can only act by agents, and it is of course the duty of those agents so to act as best to promote the interests of the corporation whose affairs they are conducting. Such agents have duties to discharge of a fiduciary nature towards their principal. And it is a rule of universal application that no one, having such duties to discharge, shall be allowed to enter into engagements in which he has, or can have, a personal interest conflicting, or which possibly may conflict, with the interests of those whom he is bound to protect": *per* Lord Cranworth L.C. in *Aberdeen Rlwy. Co.* v. *Blaikie Bros.* (1854) 1 Macq. 461 at p. 471.

[80] In *Guinness plc* v. *Saunders* [1990] 1 All E.R. 652 the House of Lords refused a *quantum meruit* claim by a director, but in rather different circumstances, where there was no doubt as to the validity of the appointment.

[81] *Re Newspaper Proprietary Syndicate Ltd.* [1900] 2 Ch. 349, *post*, Chap. 29.

[82] *Quaere* whether there is any contract between a company and its directors arising out of the appointment alone: *Newtherapeutics Ltd.* v. *Katz* [1990] BCLC 700.

"The directors are the mere trustees or agents of the company—trustees of the company's money and property—agents in the transactions which they enter into on behalf of the company": *per* Lord Selborne L.C. in *Great Eastern Rlwy. Co.* v. *Turner* (1872) L.R. 8 Ch. 149 at p. 152.

"The director's functions are in one view those of an agent, and in another those of trustee. But the former predominate over the latter": *per* Lord Johnston in *McLintock* v. *Campbell*, 1916 S.C. 966 at p. 980.

Since a director's fiduciary duties only apply to his acts *qua* director, his acts *qua* shareholder are not so affected. Thus, a director has the same right as any other shareholder to transfer his shares to a man of straw in order to avoid payment of a call,[83] and he may exercise his voting power at general meetings, even though the effect is to increase his own remuneration[84] or to prevent the calling up of a loan made by the company to himself.[85]

On the other hand, the fiduciary nature of a director's position will not allow a director of a listed company who is negotiating the sale of his strategic shareholding in the company to insist on a service contract with the company from the purchasers, nor may he promise the purchasers the right to appoint directors. Such matters are for the company, and attempts at such a bargain are "commercially disreputable": *Wilton Group plc* v. *Abrams* [1990] BCC 310.

Directors as fiduciaries

Directors have been described as trustees (1) of the company's money and property,[86] and (2) of the powers entrusted to them. More properly they may be regarded as being in a fiduciary position to the company because the company's money and property are not vested in them but in the company. They are liable as if they were trustees.

Thus they must act as regards the company's property as if they were trustees for the company although of course the company is the legal owner. Such property must be applied for

[83] *M'Lintock* v. *Campbell*, 1916 S.C. 966.
[84] *Harris* v. *A. Harris Ltd.*, 1936 S.C. 183.
[85] *Baird* v. *J. Baird & Co.* (*Falkirk*) *Ltd.*, 1949 S.L.T. 368 (O.H.).
[86] *Per* Lord Selborne L.C. in *Great Eastern Rlwy. Co.* v. *Turner* (1872) L.R. 8 Ch. 149 at p. 152.

the specified purposes of the company and a misapplication of it is a breach of fiduciary duty.[87] Where a person has improperly profited from his fiduciary position the court has equitable jurisdiction to award interest on the judgment for damages for misfeasance or breach of duty as a director.[88]

In an action to recover moneys of the company misapplied by them, directors can in England rely on the Limitation Act 1980, s.21, as if they were trustees,[89] *i.e.* the action must be brought within six years except where they have been guilty of fraud, or where the property is still in their possession or has been previously converted to their own use.

Directors are fiduciaries of their powers in the sense that, as will be explained later,[90] they must exercise them for the purposes for which they were conferred and bona fide for the benefit of the company as a whole. They must not put themselves in a position where their duty and interest conflict.

Directors had power to issue the unissued shares of the company. The company was in no need of further capital, but the directors made a fresh issue to themselves and their supporters with the object of maintaining control of the company and resisting the election of three additional directors which would have made the two existing directors a minority on the board: *Held*, the allotment of the shares was invalid and void. Directors are not entitled to use their power of issuing shares merely for the purpose of maintaining their control or the control of themselves and their friends over the affairs of the company, or merely for the purpose of defeating the wishes of the existing majority of shareholders. The power to issue shares is primarily given to directors for the purpose of enabling them to raise capital when required for the company: *Piercy* v. *S. Mills & Co. Ltd.* [1920] 1 Ch. 77.[91]

The importance of directors owing fiduciary duties is that liability may arise even if there is no loss or common law fraud involved. Those affected, *i.e.* the company, can recover under the remedy of account which requires simply that the fiduciary,

[87] *Selangor United Rubber Eastates Ltd.* v. *Craddock* (*No.* 3) [1968] 1 W.L.R. 1555, *post*, p. 416.
[88] *Wallersteiner* v. *Moir* (*No.* 2) [1975] Q.B. 373 (C.A.), where the interest awarded was compound interest at one per cent. per annum above the official bank rate or minimum lending rate in operation at the time.
[89] *Re Lands Allotment Co.* [1894] 1 Ch. 616 (C.A.), *cf. John S. Boyle Ltd.* v. *Boyle's Trustees*, 1949 S.L.T. (Notes) 45 (O.H.).
[90] p. 399.
[91] *Cook* v. *Barry Henry, & Cook Ltd.*, 1923 S.L.T. 692 (O.H.). See now s.80.

the director, has abused his powers or made a profit out of his position. Unlike the common law remedy of damages no loss need be shown.

Since directors owe fiduciary duties to the company it follows that if there is a fraudulent or dishonest breach of such a duty and company property is misapplied, anyone who receives such property with knowledge of the breach of duty will be liable to the company as a constructive trustee. Knowledge for this purpose has traditionally meant actual or constructive notice,[92] but in *Re Montague's S.T.*,[93] it was doubted whether anything less than actual notice or deliberate ignorance would suffice. In addition anyone who assists in the breach will also be liable to account to the company if he has knowledge of the breach. For this purpose knowledge is either actual knowledge or wilfully shutting one's eye to the obvious or, possibly, wilfully and recklessly failing to make the enquiries which an honest and reasonable man would have made. Failure to make such enquiries, however, will not suffice unless he would have obtained the information from the presumed answers. There is no assumption that he would have been told the truth.[94]

In a few, exceptional, cases the directors have been held to be in a position of trust *vis-à-vis* the shareholders, *i.e.* so that their fiduciary duties extend to their actions in such cases. In one case the directors of a family company were so treated because of the nature of the company, the dominant position of the directors, their inside knowledge and the methods used.[95]

Directors as agents

Directors are agents through whom a company acts,[96] and it is largely because they are agents that they owe fiduciary duties and certain duties of care to the company.

[92] *Selangor United Rubber Estates Ltd.* v. *Cradock* (*No. 3*) [1968] 2 All E.R. 1073, *Belmont Finance Ltd.* v. *Williams Furniture Ltd.* (*No.* 2) [1980] 1 All E.R. 393, *International Sales and Agencies Ltd.* v. *Marcus* [1982] 3 All E.R. 551.

[93] [1987] Ch. 264.

[94] *Belmont Finance Ltd.* v. *Williams Furniture Ltd.*, *supra*, *Baden*, *Delvaux and Lecuit* v. *Société General etc.* [1983] BCLC 325.

[95] *Coleman* v. *Myers* [1977] 2 N.Z.L.R. 225.

[96] See, *e.g. per* Lord Selborne L.C. in *Great Eastern Rlwy. Co.* v. *Turner* (1872) L.R. 8 Ch. 149 at p. 152. See Chap. 6.

"Directors of a company are fiduciary agents, and a power conferred upon them cannot be exercised in order to obtain some private advantage or for any purpose foreign to the power": *per* Dixon J. in *Mills* v. *Mills* (1938) 60 C.L.R. 150 at p. 186.

Like other agents, directors incur no personal liability on contracts made by them on behalf of the company, within the scope of their authority.[97]

E. contracted to supply goods to a company of which H. was chairman of directors, payment to be made by the issue of £600 of the company's debentures. The contract was made at a board meeting at which H. was chairman. E. constantly pressed for the debentures, but none was issued, and eventually the company was wound up. *Held*, H. was not liable to an action at the suit of E.: *Elkington & Co.* v. *Hürter* [1892] 2 Ch. 452.

If, however, directors exceed the powers given to them by the memorandum and articles they will be liable for breach of warranty of authority.[98] Their actions may be ratified by the company in general meeting even if they have acted contrary to the company's constitution.[99]

Directors may be *specifically appointed* agents for the shareholders to negotiate a sale of the company's shares. If so, the shareholders are liable for their fraud.

R., managing director of N. Ltd., by frauds of which the other directors were ignorant, made N. Ltd. profitable, and negotiated with E. Ltd. for the sale of the shares in N. Ltd. without disclosing that the profits were based on dishonest trading. The negotiations were reported to the shareholders who, in ignorance of R.'s fraud, authorised R. to complete the sale on the basis of his negotiations. The fraud was subsequently discovered and the shareholders were sued for damages. *Held*, they were liable as R. was their agent to negotiate the sale of their shares, and they were liable for his fraud even though it preceded his appointment as agent: *Briess* v. *Woolley* [1954] A.C. 333.

Further, directors may *hold themselves out* to the shareholders as agents for the shareholders, in which case the directors must disclose any profit made by them to the shareholders.

[97] Directors may be personally liable under s.349(4), *ante*, p. 61.
[98] *Firbank's Exors.* v. *Humphreys* (1886) 18 Q.B.D. 54 (C.A.).
[99] See Chap. 6.

Directors entered into negotiations for the amalgamation of the company with other companies. Before the negotiations were completed they induced a number of shareholders to give them options on their shares at par, representing that this was necessary to effect the amalgamation. The directors then exercised the option and thereby made a handsome profit. *Held*, they had to account for this profit to the shareholders: *Allen* v. *Hyatt* (1914) 30 T.L.R. 444, distinguishing *Percival* v. *Wright*, below.

Duties of Directors

Under the general law directors (and other agents of the company) owe fiduciary duties[1] and certain duties of care[2] only to the company, *i.e.* the members as a body, and, except in cases like *Allen* v. *Hyatt*, *Coleman* v. *Myers* and *Re A Company ante*, not to the individual shareholders.[3]

The directors of a company bought shares from X. They did not disclose to him that negotiations were being conducted for the sale of all the company's shares at a higher price than that asked by X. The negotiations proved abortive. X sued to have his sale set aside on the ground that the directors ought to have disclosed the negotiations. *Held*, the sale was binding, as the directors were under no obligation to disclose the negotiations to X: *Percival* v. *Wright* [1902] 2 Ch. 421.

In *Dawson International plc* v. *Coats Patons plc*[4] it was stated that if the directors chose to give shareholders advice about a take-over bid they must act in good faith and not fraudulently but this was a fiduciary duty that was owed to the company, *i.e.* the members present and future and not the current members as vendors of their shares. On the other hand the directors' duties to their company may override any undertakings they have given to a third party, *e.g.* as to recommending acceptance of an offer for part of the company's business, where the two are in

[1] *Per* Lord Cranworth L.C. in *Aberdeen Rlwy. Co.* v. *Blaikie Bros.* (1854) 1 Macq. 461 at p. 471, *ante*, p. 393.

[2] *Per* Romer J. in *Re City Equitable Fire Insurance Co. Ltd.* [1925] Ch. 407 at p. 428.

[3] Nor to applicants for shares: *Brown* v. *Stewart* (1898) 1 F. 316; *Wilson* v. *Dunlop, Bremner & Co. Ltd.*, 1921, 1 S.L.T. 35 (O.H.) and 354.

[4] (1988) 4 BCC 305 affm'd other grounds (1989) 5 BCC 405 (Scotland).

conflict: *John Crowther Group plc* v. *Carpets International plc* [1990] BCLC 460.

Section 309, first introduced in 1980, provides that directors must also have regard to the interests of the employees as a whole. However, the employees have no collective right to enforce this. In fact since the duties of directors are owed to the company and not the individual shareholders or employees, the enforcement of the duties may be a problem where the directors in breach of duty control the company, as will be explained later.[5]

In *Nicholson* v. *Permakraft (N.Z.) Ltd.* [1985] N.Z.L.R. 242, Cooke J. also suggested that a director's fiduciary duty could, in certain circumstances, be owed to the company's creditors as well as the members. A payment made to the prejudice of current or continuing creditors, when a likelihood of loss to them ought to have been known, could, he said, amount to misfeasance against the company. On the other hand in *Re Welfab Engineers Ltd.* [1990] BCC 600, directors were held not to be in breach of their duty to the company in selling the business of the company as a going concern for a lower price than could have been obtained for the premises alone. The directors were held not to be required to act as liquidators.

Fiduciary duties

The fiduciary duties of directors are:

(1) to exercise their powers for the purposes for which they were conferred and bona fide for the benefit of the company as a whole,[6] as defined above;

(2) not to put themselves in a position in which their duties to the company and their personal interests may conflict.[7]

As to duty (1), directors' discretionary power to refuse to register a transfer of shares is a fiduciary power.[8] The directors'

[5] Chap. 17.
[6] And not, *e.g.* for his fellow directors: *Lee* v. *Chou When Hsien* [1985] BCLC 45 (P.C.); *ante*, p. 373.
[7] *Guinness plc* v. *Saunders* [1990] 1 All E.R. 652 (H.L.).
[8] See *Re Smith and Fawcett Ltd.* [1942] Ch. 304 (C.A.), *ante*, p. 282.

power to issue shares is also a fiduciary power even though it is now subject to the controls of section 80, *ante*, and the exercise of such a power is invalid if it is not exercised for the purpose for which it was granted, which is primarily to raise capital when required by the company. Thus an issue of shares has traditionally been held to be invalid if the directors are motivated by self-interest, *e.g.* a desire to preserve their control of the company.[9]

Directors, in an endeavour to secure control in order to forestall a takeover bid, issued unissued shares in the company to trustees to be held for the benefit of employees, the shares being paid for by the trustees out of an interest-free loan from the company. *Held*, the issue exceeded the directors' fiduciary power, it being immaterial that it was made in the bona fide belief that it was in the interests of the company. Since the directors did not hold the majority of the shares before the new issue, the issue could be ratified by the company in general meeting, the votes carried by the shares issued to the trustees not being exercised: *Hogg* v. *Cramphorn Ltd.* [1967] Ch. 254.

The reasoning in *Hogg* v. *Cramphorn* was criticised and distinguished in Canada in the case of *Teck Corporation Ltd.* v. *Millar*[10] on the basis that it was an exception to the general rule that directors must act bona fide in what they consider to be the best interests of the company. It was not correct to say that issuing shares otherwise than to raise capital was always a breach of duty. Directors were entitled to consider the reputation, experience and policies of anyone seeking to take-over the company. If they decided on reasonable grounds that the take-over would cause substantial damage to the company's interests they were entitled to use their powers to protect the company. This decision has since been applied in many Canadian cases, *e.g. Olson* v. *Phoenix Industrial Supply Ltd.*,[11]

[9] *Piercy* v. *S. Mills & Co. Ltd.* [1920] 1 Ch. 77, *Hogg* v. *Cramphorn Ltd.* [1967] Ch. 254; *Bamford* v. *Bamford* [1970] Ch. 212 (C.A.); *Ngurli* v. *McCann* (1954) 90 C.L.R. 425, where there was no take-over bid, shares were issued to a shareholder to give him control of the company, the interests of the company as a whole were not considered, and an attempted ratification was a fraud on the minority and so ineffective; *cf. Teck Corporation Ltd.* v. *Millar* (1972) 33 D.L.R. (3d) 288.

[10] (1972) 33 D.L.R. (3d) 288. See also *Heilowe's Nominees Pty. Ltd.* v. *Woodside* (*Laker Entrance*) *Oil Co. N.L.* (1971) 45 A.J.L.R. 162.

[11] (1984) 9 D.L.R. (4th) 451.

where the test was stated as being whether the directors honestly believed that they were acting in the best interests of the company, and whether there were reasonable grounds for their belief.

This divergence of view was considered by the Privy Council in the case of *Howard Smith Ltd.* v. *Ampol Petroleum Ltd.*[12] where on similar facts to *Hogg* v. *Cramphorn*, the judge had established (i) that the primary purpose of the allotment was not to raise money but to destroy the existing majority block of shares and (ii) that the directors were not motivated by self-interest. The Privy Council rejected both extreme arguments—*i.e.* that once no self-interest is discovered there can be no breach of duty, and that an allotment of shares can only be made to raise capital—any other purpose being wrong. Instead they considered that no limitation can be placed in advance on the exercise of the directors' powers. The court must examine the substantial purpose for which the power was exercised and whether that purpose was proper or not. The court must respect the directors' opinion on questions of management but in other cases it is a question for decision in each case. Although *Teck's* case was concerned with an area of management this was not—it was a question of altering an existing majority shareholding into a minority one. In *Mutual Life Insurance* v. *The Rank Organisation,*[13] Goulding J. applied this distinction between areas of management and others in upholding a rights issue which was not available to certain U.S. shareholders. Unlike the *Howard Smith* case it did not upset the *status quo* but maintained the investment policy of the company. The test applied was that applied in *Olson's* case above.

In *Rolled Steel Products (Holdings) Ltd.* v. *British Steel Corporation*,[14] the Court of Appeal suggested that the question of whether a power had been exercised bona fide for the benefit of the company could be answered by applying the tests laid down by Eve J. in *Re Lee Behrens & Co. Ltd.*[15] and formerly applied to determine whether an act was *ultra vires* the company

[12] [1974] A.C. 821 (P.C.). See also *Ashburton Oil N.L.* v. *Alpha Mineral N.C.* (1971) 45 A.J.L.R. 162.

[13] [1985] BCLC 11.

[14] [1984] BCLC 466 (C.A.). See also *Woods* v. *Cann* (1963) 80 W.N. (N.S.W.) 1583, and *Mills* v. *Mills* (1938) 60 C.L.R. 150 *per* Lathom C.J.

[15] [1932] 2 Ch. 46.

or not.[16] These tests are: (1) is the transaction reasonably incidental to the carrying on of the company's business; (2) is it a bona fide transaction; (3) is it done for the benefit and prosperity of the company.

If directors exercise a power for a proper purpose and in good faith, their judgment is not open to review by the courts.[17] However, although it would be wrong for the courts to question the correctness of the management's decision on a question of management, if bona fide arrived at, when the question is whether directors exercised a power for one purpose or another, the courts are entitled to look at the situation objectively in order to ascertain how substantial an alleged requirement may have been.[18]

Where a director is also a shareholder in the company he may promote his own interests so long as his dominant motive is to benefit the company.[19]

A nominee director, *e.g.* a director appointed by a shareholder, owes the same duties to the company as any other director.[20]

Because a director owes a fiduciary duty, where in England a company owes a statute-barred debt, a balance sheet signed by a director (whose signature was necessary to its validity) who is himself interested in the debt, cannot constitute an acknowledgment for the purposes of what is now the Limitation Act 1980, ss.29 and 30, and the time within which an action may be brought does not run afresh,[21] unless it is sanctioned by every

[16] Chap. 3, *ante*.

[17] See the *Howard Smith* case, *ante*, at p. 835 and *per* Barwick C.J., McTiernan J. and Kitto J. at p. 493 in *Harlowe's* case, quoted in the *Howard Smith* case at p. 836.

[18] *Howard Smith* case, *ante*.

[19] *Mills* v. *Mills* (1938) 60 C.L.R. 150 where the directors believed that the bonus issue was in the best interests of the company and it was immaterial that one director derived some benefit from the passing of the board resolution.

[20] *Per* Lord Denning in *Meyer* v. *Scottish C.W.S. Ltd.*, 1958 S.C. (H.L.) 40 at pp. 67, 68; [1959] A.C. 324 at pp. 366, 367; *per* Ungoed-Thomas J. in *Selangor United Rubber Estates Ltd.* v. *Cradock* (*No.* 3) [1968] 1 W.L.R. 1555, at pp. 1613, 1614; *cf.*, *e.g. per* Jacobs J. in *Re Broadcasting Station 2 GB Pty. Ltd.* [1964–65] N.S.W.R. 1648; at p. 1663, where he said that so long as the nominee directors believed that the interests of the shareholder who nominated them were identical with those of the company, they could follow the wishes of the shareholder without a close personal analysis of the issues.

[21] *Re Transplanters (Holding Company) Ltd.* [1958] 1 W.L.R. 822.

member of the company, in which event it cannot be said that the directors are in breach of their fiduciary duty.[22]

The Jenkins Report merely recommended[23] (1) that the Companies Act should provide that a director must observe the utmost good faith towards the company in any transaction with it or on its behalf and must act honestly in the exercise of his powers and the discharge of his office, (2) that a director who commits a breach of such statutory duty should be liable to the company for any profit made by him and for any damage suffered by the company as a result of the breach, and (3) that such statutory duty should be in addition to and not in derogation of the general law duties of a director.

Secret benefits of directors

Because a director is in a fiduciary position,[24] he must not make a secret profit by reason of that position. If he does, he must account for it to the company. It is immaterial that the company itself could not have obtained the profit. The company in general meeting may consent to such a profit being made or kept.

A. was a director of B. Co. and, on the company's behalf, contracted for the building of fishing smacks. Unknown to the company, he was paid a commission on the contract by the shipbuilders. A. was also a shareholder in an ice company which, in addition to dividends, paid bonuses to shareholders who were owners of fishing smacks and who employed the ice company in supplying ice to the fishing smacks. A. employed the ice company in respect of B. Co.'s fishing smacks and received the bonus. *Held*, A. must account to B. Co. for both the commission and the bonus, although the bonus could never have been received by B. Co. as it was not a shareholder in the ice company: *Boston Deep Sea Fishing Co.* v. *Ansell* (1888) 39 Ch.D. 339 (C.A.).

R. Ltd. owned one cinema and wanted to buy two others with a view to selling the three together, R. Ltd. formed a subsidiary company to buy the two cinemas, but was unable to provide all the capital required, so all the directors of R. Ltd. except one subscribed for some of the shares in the subsidiary themselves. The cinemas were acquired

[22] *Re Gee & Co. (Woolwich) Ltd.* [1975] Ch. 52, applying *Re Duomatic Ltd.* [1969] 2 Ch. 365.

[23] Para. 99(a)(i), (iii) and (iv).

[24] p. 398.

and the shares in R. Ltd. and the subsidiary sold at a profit. *Held*, the former directors who subscribed for shares in the subsidiary themselves must account to R. Ltd. for the profit they made, because it was only through the knowledge and opportunity they gained as directors of R. Ltd. that they were able to obtain the shares. The one former director who did not himself subscribe but merely found someone else to do so was under no liability nor was a solicitor who was invited to subscribe by the directors: *Regal* (*Hastings*) *Ltd.* v. *Gulliver*[25]

A director must not divert to his own use a "maturing business opportunity" which his company is pursuing even after his resignation, at least if his resignation is prompted by that desire.[26] Nor may he use confidential information obtained in his capacity as a director for his own use, but this does not apply to general information, *e.g.* as to a particular marker.[27]

In the *Regal* case the directors could have protected themselves by a resolution (either antecedent or subsequent) of the Regal shareholders in general meeting,[28] and the case was distinguished in *Lindgren* v. *L. & P. Estates Ltd.*[29] where the directors were released from liability by the company retaining them on the board, after it had knowledge of the facts (the alleged breach of duty was that the directors had merely "rubber-stamped" the decisions of other persons).

"The rule of equity which insists on those, who by use of a fiduciary position make a profit, being liable to account for that profit, in no way depends on fraud, or absence of bona fides; or upon such questions or considerations as whether the profit would or should otherwise have gone to the plaintiff [*i.e.* the company], or whether the profiteer was under a duty to obtain the source of the profit for the plaintiff, or whether he took a risk or acted as he did for the benefit of the plaintiff, or whether the plaintiff has in fact been damaged or benefited by his action. The liability arises from the mere fact of a profit having, in the stated circumstances, been made. The profiteer, however honest and well-intentioned, cannot escape the risk of being called upon to account": *per* Lord Russell of Killowen in the *Regal* case at p. 144.

[25] [1967] 2 A.C. 134 (Note), applied in *Phipps* v. *Boardman* [1967] 2 A.C. 46.

[26] *Industrial Development Consultants Ltd.* v. *Cooley* [1972] 1 W.L.R. 443; *Island Export Finance Ltd.* v. *Umunna* [1986] BCLC 460.

[27] *Island Export Finance Ltd.* v. *Umunna* (*ante*).

[28] *Per* Lord Russell of Killowen at p. 150.

[29] [1968] Ch. 572 (C.A.), in which it was also held that the prospective directors of a company owe no duty to it and that directors of a parent company owe no duty to, and are not debarred from contracting with, a subsidiary with an independent board.

In a case before the Privy Council the managing director of a company obtained licences for the company to develop a mine but it was unable to proceed due to financial problems. He resigned and with the knowledge of the directors, he developed the mine himself. The Privy Council held that he was not liable to account for his profits since the rejection by the company and the knowledge of the board excused him: *Queensland Mines Ltd.* v. *Hudson* (1978) 18 A.L.R. 1 (P.C.). This decision also has some Canadian support,[30] but seems to be out of line with the established UK position as established by the *Regal* case.[31]

Another example of the principle that a director must not make a secret profit out of his position is that a director must not, without the consent of the company, accept from a promoter any gift, *e.g.* of shares or money, either while any negotiations between the promoter and the company are still going on or after they have been completed.[32]

The Jenkins Committee recommended[33] (1) that the Companies Act should provide that a director of a company must not make use of any money or other property of the company, or of any information acquired by virtue of his position as a director or officer of the company, to gain directly or indirectly an improper advantage for himself at the expense of the company, (2) that a director who commits a breach of such statutory duty be liable to the company for any profit made by him and for any damage suffered by the company as a result of the breach and (3) that such statutory duty be in addition to the general law duties of a director.

Contracts of directors with their company

A consequence of the general duty of a director towards the company not to allow conflict between duty and interest,[34] is

[30] *Peso Silver Mines Ltd.* v. *Cropper* (1966) 58 D.L.R. (2d) 1.

[31] For Scotland see Lord Young in *Great North of Scotland Railway Co.* v. *Urquhart* (1884) 21 S.L.R. 377, 382, and *Laughland* v. *Millar, Laughland & Co.* (1904) 6 F. 413 (contract for indirect secret benefit of director held unenforceable).

[32] *Eden* v. *Ridsdales Railways Lamp Co. Ltd.* (1899) 23 Q.B.D. 368 (C.A.); *Archer's Case* [1892] 1 Ch. 322 (C.A.); *Henderson* v. *The Huntington Copper etc. Co. Ltd.* (1877) 5 R. (H.L.) 1; *Scottish Pacific Coast Mining Co. Ltd.* v. *Falkner, Bell & Co.* (1888) 15 R. 290.

[33] Para. 99(a)(ii), (iii) and (iv).

[34] *Ante*, p. 399.

that even if he makes no profit, a director must not be interested in a contract or proposed contract with the company unless the articles permit it, as they usually do, *e.g.* Table A, regulation 85. If this rule is broken the contract is prima facie voidable by the company.

This is so even if his interest is only that of a shareholder in another company which contracts with the company of which he is a director.

T. Co. bought some shares in L. Co. from N.B. Co. H. was a shareholder in both T. Co. and N.B. Co. and also a director of T. Co. As such director he voted for the purchase and N.B. Co. had notice of it. H. did not disclose the nature of his interest (his shareholding in N.B. Co.) as required by the articles of T. Co., which also provided that a director was not to vote in respect of any contract in which he was concerned. *Held*, the contract was voidable at the option of T. Co.: *Transvaal Lands Co.* v. *New Belgium* (*Transvaal*) *Land*, *etc. Co.* [1914] 2 Ch. 488 (C.A.).

"Where a director of a company has an interest as shareholder in another company or is in a fiduciary position towards and owes a duty to another company which is proposing to enter into engagements with the company of which he is a director, he is in our opinion within this rule. He has a personal interest within this rule or owes a duty which conflicts with his duty to the company of which he is a director. It is immaterial whether this conflicting interest belongs to him beneficially or as trustee for others": *per* Swinfen Eady L.J., reading the judgment of the court, at p. 503.

His interest may be that of a partner in a firm which contracts with his company.[35]

It is usual to provide in the articles that a director who is interested in a contract with the company must declare his interest as required by section 317 *post*, that he shall not vote on any such contract, and that if he does vote his vote shall not be counted. The effect of this is to allow the director to contract with the company, on disclosing his interest, and to keep any profit he may make.[36]

Table A, regulation 85, provides: "Subject to the provisions of the Act and provided that he has disclosed to the directors the nature and

[35] *Aberdeen Rlwy. Co.* v. *Blaikie Bros.* (1854) 1 Macq. 461.
[36] *Costa Rica Ry.* v. *Forwood* [1901] 1 Ch. 746 (C.A.).

extent of any material interest of his, a director notwithstanding his office—

(a) may be a party to, or otherwise interested in, any transaction or arrangement with the company or in which the company is otherwise interested;

(b) may be a director or other officer of, or employed by, or a party to any transaction or arrangement with, or otherwise interested in, any body corporate promoted by the company or in which the company is otherwise interested; and

(c) shall not, by reason of his office, be accountable to the company for any benefit which he derives from any such office or employment or from any such transaction or arrangement or from any interest in any such body corporate and no such transaction or arrangement shall be liable to be avoided on the ground of any such interest or benefit."

Regulation 86: "For the purposes of regulation 85—

(a) a general notice given to the directors that a director is to be regarded as having an interest of the nature and extent specified in the notice in any transaction or arrangement in which a specified person or class of persons is interested shall be deemed to be a disclosure that the director has an interest in any such transaction of the nature and extent so specified; and

(b) an interest of which a director has no knowledge and of which it is unreasonable to expect him to have knowledge shall not be treated as an interest of his."

Section 317 provides that a director who is any way interested in a contracted or proposed contract with the company must declare the nature of his interest at a board meeting. This includes any arrangement or transaction whether or not it is a contract, and a director is deemed to have such an interest in any loan etc. controlled by section 330.[37] Where a director is interested in a proposed contract, the declaration must be made at the meeting of the directors at which the question of entering into the contract is first considered. Otherwise, the declaration must be made at the first meeting after the director becomes interested in the contract or proposed contract. However, a general notice by a director that he, or a person connected with him, is a member of a specified company or firm and is to be regarded as interested in all contracts made with that company

[37] *Ante*, p. 388.

or firm is a sufficient declaration of interest if it is given at a meeting of the directors or the director takes reasonable steps to secure that it is brought up and read at the next meeting of the directors after it is given. Compliance with statutory duty is enforced by a fine.

It should be noted that only the nature of the interest need be declared, that the declaration of interest need not be to the company in general meeting and that a general declaration of interest is sufficient.

The section also provides that it does not prejudice the operation of any rule of law restricting directors from having an interest in contracts with the company. This means that the section does not imply in the articles a provision allowing a director to contract with the company.

If the articles do not contain such a provision and a director is interested in a contract with the company, the contract may be affirmed by the company in general meeting and, if the director is a member of the company, he can cast the votes conferred by his shares in favour of the resolution, so long as it is not a fraud on the minority of the shareholders.[38]

If a director does not disclose his interest in a contract with his company in accordance with section 317, the director is guilty of a breach of statutory duty and liable to a fine. But failure to make such disclosure also brings the general equitable rules as to conflict of interest and duty into play thus making the contract voidable at the company's option,[39] and the director must account to it for any secret profit which he has made out of the contract.[40]

Section 310 *post*[41] is qualified by section 317, which is a statutory extension of the general law in that, *e.g.* it imposes a penalty for a breach of the section.

The Jenkins Report[42] recommended that section 317 be amended so as to require a director to disclose only material

[38] *N.-W. Transporation Co.* v. *Beatty* (1887) 12 App.Cas. 589 (P.C.).

[39] *Hely-Hutchinson* v. *Brayhead Ltd.* [1968] 1 Q.B. 549 (C.A.), where it was too late to avoid because *restitutio* was impossible; approved by H.L. in *Guinness plc* v. *Saunders* [1990] 1 All E.R. 652.

[40] *Per* Lord Cairns L.C. in *Parker* v. *McKenna* (1874) L.R. 10 Ch.App. 96, at p. 118.

[41] p. 414.

[42] Para. 99.

interests in contracts, including contracts which do not come before the board.

One specific aspect of directors' duties relates to insider dealing. This is dealt with in Chapter 19, *post*.

Directors competing with company

Under the general law, apart from the case where a director has a service agreement with the company which requires him to serve only the company, there is authority to the effect that he may become a director of a rival company, *i.e.* that in this way he may compete with the first company, provided that he does not disclose to the second company any confidential information obtained by him as a director of the first company, and that what he may do a rival company he may do for himself[43] or a rival firm. However, it has been said that he must not subordinate the interests of the first company to those of the second and that if he does so it is at the risk of an application under section 459.[44] (Remedy in case of unfairly prejudicial conduct).[45]

Duties of care

Directors' duties of care towards the company cannot be said to be unduly burdensome, as will be seen from the three propositions laid down by Romer J. in *Re City Equitable Fire Insurance Co. Ltd.*[46] These were:

(1) A director need not exhibit in the performance of his duties (*i.e.* his functions) a greater degree of skill than may

[43] *London & Mashonaland Exploration Co.* v. *New Mashonaland Exploration Co.* [1891] W.N. 165; *per* Lord Blanesburgh in *Bell* v. *Lever Bros. Ltd.* [1932] A.C. 161 at p. 195.

[44] *Per* Lord Denning in *Meyer* v. *Scottish C.W.S. Ltd.*, 1958 S.C. (H.L.) 40 at p. 68; [1959] A.C. 324 at p. 368.

[45] *Post*, Chap. 18.

[46] [1925] Ch. 407, at p. 428. The *City Equitable* case was applied in *Huckerby* v. *Elliott* [1970] 1 All E.R. 189. For a similar description of a director's duties, see Lord Justice-Clerk Moncreiff in *Western Bank* v. *Baird's Trustees* (1872) 11 M. 96 at p. 112, and on the extent to which directors are entitled to rely on other officials, see *Western Bank* v. *Addie* (1867) 5 M. (H.L.) 80; (1865) 3 M. 899, and *Lees* v. *Tod* (1882) 9 R. 807.

reasonably be expected from a person of his knowledge and experience (*i.e.* the particular director's own knowledge and experience). A director of a life insurance company, for instance, does not guarantee that he has the skill of an actuary or of a physician. He must take such care, however, in the performance of his duties as an ordinary man might be expected to take on his own behalf.

(2) A director is not bound to give continuous attention to the affairs of his company. His duties are of an intermittent nature to be performed at periodical board meetings. He is not, however, bound to attend all such meetings, though he ought to attend whenever, in the circumstances, he is reasonably able to do so.[47]

(3) In respect of all duties that, having regard to the exigencies of business, and the articles of association, may properly be left to some other official, a director is, in the absence of grounds for suspicion, justified in trusting that official to perform such duties honestly.

As to (1) *ante*, a greater degree of skill than that indicated by Romer J. must be shown by an executive director, such as a finance or legal director—it is an implied term of his contract of service that he will use reasonable skill in the performance of the duties of his office, *i.e.* the degree of skill which may reasonably be expected of a person in such a position.[48]

Further, the duties of directors have been said to vary according to the nature of the company and of its business, *e.g.* the responsibilities of directors of small private companies consisting of only two members differ from the responsibilities of directors of a large public company.[49]

The directors of an insurance company left the management of the company's affairs almost entirely to B., the managing director. Owing to B.'s fraud a large amount of the company's assets disappeared. Items appeared in the balance sheet under the headings of "loans at call or at short notice" and "cash at bank or in hand," but the directors never inquired how these items were made up. Had they done so, they would have discovered that the loans were chiefly to B. and to the company's general manager, and that the "cash at bank or in hand" included £73,000 in the hands of a firm of stockbrokers in which B. was

[47] But see *Dorchester Finance Co. Ltd.* v. *Stebbing* [1989] BCLC 498 (*infra*).
[48] *Lister* v. *Romford Ice and Cold Storage Co. Ltd.* [1957] A.C. 555.
[49] *Per* Lord Johnson in *Brenes & Co.* v. *Downie*, 1914 S.C. 97 at p. 104.

a partner. *Held*, the directors were negligent: *Re City Equitable Fire Insurance. Co.* [1925] Ch. 407.

In *Dorchester Finance Co. Ltd.* v. *Stebbing*,[50] however, Foster J. held that in applying the standard of care to directors no distinction could be made between executive and non-executive directors. In that case two non-executive directors were held to be liable in negligence for signing blank cheques to be signed by the managing director at a later date. Both were, however, professional men.

What is said below as to the relief of directors from liability for breach of duty in connection with their fiduciary duties applies also to their duties of care. As to relief by a resolution of the company in general meeting, it was held in *Pavlides* v. *Jensen*[51] that if the directors by their negligence had sold the company's mine at an undervalue, it was open to the company by a vote of the majority to decide that proceedings should not be taken against them.

Part II of the Supply of Goods and Services Act 1982 implies certain terms into a contract for the supply of services in England, including those of directors. However, the main term, as to the exercise of reasonable care and skill, has been excluded, by statutory instrument, from directors' contracts. Another term, as to supply of services within a reasonable time, is, however, implied by the Act into directors' contracts.

Other liabilities

In certain cases a director may be personally liable for some wrong or debt connected with his company. In *C. Evans and Sons Ltd.* v. *Spritebrand Ltd.*,[52] the Court of Appeal discussed a director's liability for torts committed by his company. They decided that a director is not automatically liable for such torts even if it is a small company over which he exercised total control. It is necessary to examine the role he played in regarded to the commision of the tort. On the other hand it would not always be necessary to prove that the director had acted recklessly or knowing that the company's acts were

[50] [1989] BCLC 498.
[51] [1956] Ch. 565, *post*, p. 437.
[52] [1985] 1 W.L.R. 317.

tortious. If the tort itself required negligence or recklessness then the director's state of mind might well be relevant, but for torts of strict liability different considerations could apply.

On the other hand, a director will be personally liable in tort to a third party if he makes a personal statement in connection with the company's business which is either negligent or deceitful and which he knows is being relied upon by the person receiving it. This is a separate personal liability.[53]

Liability for acts of co-directors

A director is not liable for the acts of his co-directors of which he has no knowledge and in which he has taken no part,[54] as his fellow directors are not his servants or agents to impose liability on him.[55] Moreover, if an improper investment is made at a directors' meeting, a director who was not present at the meeting is not liable for the investment merely because he was present at a meeting at which the minutes of the meeting authorising the investment were confirmed.[56]

If a director is fraudulent, his co-directors are not liable for not discovering his fraud in the absence of circumstances to arouse their suspicions.

A bank sustained heavy losses by advances to customers made improperly. The irregular nature of the advances was concealed by means of fraudulent balance sheets, the work of the general manager and the chairman. *Held*, a co-director was not liable for not having discovered the frauds, as he was not, in the absence of circumstances of suspicion, bound to examine entries in the company's books to see that the balance sheets were correct: *Dovey* v. *Cory* [1901] A.C. 477.

Non-attendance at board meetings has been held not to impose liability on a director for the acts of the board.[57]

Where more than one director is alleged to have neglected his duties of care, both or all are jointly and severally liable, with the result that if an action is brought by the company against

[53] *Thomas Saunders Partnership* v. *Harvey*, *The Independent*, May 5, 1989.
[54] *Perry's Case* (1876) 34 L.T. 716.
[55] *Cullerne* v. *London and Suburban Bldg. Socy.* (1890) 25 Q.B.D. 485 (C.A.).
[56] *Re Lands Allotment Co.* [1894] 1 Ch. 616 (C.A.).
[57] *Re Denham & Co.* (1884) 25 Ch.D. 752; *cf. Dorchester Finance Co. Ltd.* v. *Stebbing* [1989] 8 BCLC 498.

only one of them he is not entitled to plead that all parties interested have not been called.[58] However, the director sued is entitled to contribution from the other directors.

Contribution between directors

When directors have misapplied the company's funds, as by paying dividends out of capital or advancing money for an unauthorised purpose, a director who has been sued for the misapplication is entitled to contribution from the other directors who were parties to it.[59] If, however, the money misappropriated has been applied for the sole benefit of one of the directors, that director is not entitled to obtain contribution.[60]

Relief of directors from liability for breach of duty

By a resolution in general meeting

Since directors' fiduciary duties are owed to the members as a body, the majority of the members in general meeting may, after full disclosure of all material circumstances, waive a breach of fiduciary duty by a director.[61] If the breach involves acting contrary to the company's memorandum or articles such ratification must be by a special resolution.[62] In any case, however, if he is a member, the director may vote in favour of waiver, provided that there is no fraud on the minority of the members.

The directors of a company contracted to buy a ship from a vendor who was a director. (This was a breach of duty by him since the articles contained no clause authorising a director to contract with the

[58] *Liquidators of Western Bank* v. *Douglas* (1860) 20 D. 447, the reason being that the action is based on delict and not on contract: *per* Lord Justice-Clerk Inglis at p. 476.

[59] *Ramskill* v. *Edwards* (1886) 31 Ch.D. 100; see also (for England) Civil Liability (Contribution) Act 1978, and (for Scotland) Law Reform (Miscellaneous Provisions) (Scotland) Act 1940, s.3.

[60] *Walsh* v.*Bardsley* (1931) 47 T.L.R. 564.

[61] *Bamford* v. *Bamford* [1970] Ch. 212 (C.A.), *ante*, p. 380.

[62] s.35(3). See Chap. 6, *ante*.

company. Further, there was at the time no section like the present section 199, *post*). At a general meeting a resolution affirming the contract was carried, against the wishes of the minority shareholders, by reason of the fact that the vendor held the majority of the shares in the company. *Held*, the resolution was valid. As a shareholder, the vendor was merely using his voting power to his own advantage, and there was no question of a fraud on the minority—there was no unfairness or impropriety: *N.-W. Transportation Co.* v. *Beatty* (1887) 12 App.Cas. 589 (P.C.).

Two directors of a construction company negotiated for a construction contract in the usual way in which the company's business was carried on, and then took the contract in their own names. A meeting of the company was called, and by their votes as holders of three-quarters of the shares a resolution was passed declaring that the company had no interest in the contract. *Held*, the benefit of the contract belonged to the company and the directors must account to the company for it, and the purported ratification was a fraud on the minority and ineffective: *Cook* v. *Deeks* [1916] 1 A.C. 554 (P.C.).

The general meeting may give advance authority for an exercise of power by the directors which would otherwise involve a breach of their fiduciary duty.[63]

However, if the fiduciary duty is owed to employees or creditors, *ante*, it is not clear how far the members can waive the breach. Further in *Multinational Gas and Petrochemical Co.* v. *Multinational Gas and Petrochemical Services Ltd.*[64] whilst two members of the Court of Appeal adopted the traditional approach to waiver, May L.J. thought that such a waiver would only apply whilst those who approved the act remained in control, so that their ratification would not bind a liquidator or purchaser of the company.

Not by a provision in the articles

Under the general law a director can be exempted from liability for breach of duty by a provision in the articles of the company. However, section 310, first introduced in 1929, states that, subject as below, any provision, whether in the articles or

[63] *Winthrop Investments Ltd.* v. *Winns Ltd.* [1975] 2 N.S.W.L.R. 666 (C.A.). But not, according to Samuels J.A., if to do so would be to usurp the directors' powers. The notice convening the meeting must set out clearly the nature of the contemplated breach of the directors' duty, and state that the directors seek to be absolved from such breach and that the meeting will be asked to authorise the breach and waive its consequences.

[64] [1983] Ch. 258.

in any contract with the company or otherwise, for exempting a director or other officer or the auditor from liability for negligence, default, breach of duty or breach of trust in relation to the company, or indemnifying him against such liability, is void.

One problem with the section is that it appears to be inconsistent with regulation 85 of Table A (and similar articles) which allow a director to have an interest in a transaction etc. subject to disclosure to the board. Insofar as this attempt to relieve the director from the conflict of interest rule (*supra*) is it not exempting him from a breach of duty or trust and so void under section 310? In *Movitex Ltd.* v. *Bulfield*[65] Vinelott J. resolved the difficulty by deciding that the conflict of interest rule was a disability imposed by equity and not a duty owed by the director. Thus by modifying the rule the articles are removing a disability and not exempting a breach of duty under section 310.

The section goes on to provide that the company may, in pursuance of a provision in the articles, etc., indemnify such a person against any liability, *i.e.* against any costs, incurred by him in defending any proceedings, civil or criminal, in which judgment is given in his favour or in which he is acquitted,[66] or in connection with any application under section 727 in which relief is granted to him by the court.

There is a further exemption provided by the section in relation to indemnity insurance policies taken out by companies in favour of their directors as cover for any such liability for breach of duty. Any such policy must be disclosed in the Directors' Report however.[67]

By the court

Section 727 provides that if, in proceedings for negligence, default, breach of duty or breach of trust against a director or other officer or auditor of a company, it appears that he has acted honestly and reasonably, and that, having regard to all the circumstances, including those connected with his appointment,

[65] [1988] BCLC 104.
[66] *Cf. Tomlinson* v. *Liquidators of Scottish Amalgamated Silks Ltd.*, 1935 S.C. (H.L.) 1.
[67] See Chap. 20, *post*.

he ought fairly to be excused, the court may relieve him, wholly or partly, from liability on such terms as it thinks fit.

A director does not act reasonably unless he does everything which a normal man would do in the conduct of his own affairs.

B. and G., two of the directors of a company were present at a finance committee in June at which it was resolved to sell £60,000 War Bonds and to reinvest the proceeds at B.'s discretion. In September, G. inquired about the reinvestment of the proceeds and was told that they had been temporarily invested on the Stock Exchange. B. misappropriated the proceeds of sale. *Held*, (1) G. was negligent in allowing the money to remain in B.'s hands longer than was reasonable and in not making inquiries as to its permanent investment, and (2) though G. had acted honestly, he had not acted reasonably and ought not to be granted relief: *Re City of London Insurance Co.* (1925) 41 T.L.R. 521.

In *Selangor United Rubber Estates Ltd.* v. *Cradock* (*No. 3*)[68] directors of a public company who disposed of virtually all its assets without regard for minority shareholders, and without consideration, but blindly at the behest of the majority shareholder who nominated them to the board, did not act reasonably and could not be relieved. In *Re Duomatic Ltd.*[69] a director dealing with payment to another director of compensation for loss of office, who did not seek legal advice but dealt with the matter himself without a proper exploration of what should be done on the company's behalf, did not act reasonably.

Similarly in *Gibson's Executor* v. *Gibson*, 1978 S.C. 197 (O.H.), Lord Dunpark held that directors of a moribund company who had made an *ex gratia* payment of £5,000 to one of their number in lieu of pension could not "fairly" be excused for their breach of duty.

Section 727 only applies to proceedings against a director for breach of duty by, on behalf of or for the benefit of the company as a whole[70] or penal proceedings against a director for breach of the Companies Acts. It does not apply to claims against a director by a third party to enforce a debt, *e.g.* arrears of general betting duty.[71] It has no relevance either to a claim by a company for recovery of money paid to a director under an unauthorised and void contract, since that is not founded on a breach of duty,[72] or to a claim for wrongful trading.[73]

[68] [1968] 1 W.L.R. 1555.
[69] [1969] 2 Ch. 365.
[70] As defined above. See, *e.g. Re Welfab Engineers Ltd.* [1990] BCC 600.
[71] *Customs and Excise Commissioners* v. *Hedon Alpha* [1981] 2 All E.R. 697 (C.A.).
[72] *Guinness plc* v. *Saunders* [1990] 1 All E.R. 652 (H.L.).
[73] *Re Produce Marketing Consortium Ltd.* [1989] BCLC 513; *post*, p. 418.

DIRECTORS AND INSOLVENCY

We have already seen that in certain circumstances a director may be disqualified from office following an insolvent liquidation of his company and that personal liability may follow if he acts in breach of such an order.[74] In addition, however, the Insolvency Act 1986 provides three more controls on directors of insolvent companies. The general principles involved are to make directors seek a liquidation early rather than late if the company is insolvent and to prevent directors "hopping" from one insolvent company to another by using so-called Phoenix companies. These provisions are in addition to others which apply more generally on a liquidation, see Chapter 29, *post*.

Liability for wrongful trading

As mentioned above one of the principle aims of the Insolvency Act 1986 is to encourage directors to put their company into liquidation when all reasonable expectation of saving it has gone. Before 1986 the only remedy available to a liquidator against a director who had allowed his company to incur debts after all reasonable hope had gone was to institute proceedings for fraudulent trading. This remedy still exists and can give rise to both civil and criminal consequences.[75] But it requires proof of intent to defraud creditors and in practice that is often difficult to establish. Under section 214 of the Insolvency Act 1986 there is now an additional liability on directors and shadow directors[76] for those guilty of wrongful trading in such circumstances.[77]

To establish wrongful trading the liquidator of a company must show that the company has gone into an insolvent liquidation,[78] that the director, prior to the liquidation, knew or ought to have concluded that there was no reasonable prospect that the company could avoid going into insolvent liquidation,

[74] *Ante*, p. 360.
[75] *Post*, Chap. 27.
[76] *Ante*.
[77] No defence under s.727 is available against a claim for wrongful trading: *Re Produce Marketing Consortium Ltd.* [1989] BCLC 513; *ante*, p. 416.
[78] This is defined as where its assets are insufficient for the payment of its debts and other liabilities and the expenses of winding up.

and that he took insufficient steps in the circumstances to minimise the potential loss to the company's creditors: Insolvency Act 1986, section 214(2)(3). Note that no dishonesty need be involved, simply unreasonable behaviour or negligence. To decide whether a director ought to have concluded that an insolvent liquidation was unavoidable the court must ask whether that would have been the conclusion of a reasonably diligent person having both the general knowledge, skill and experience that might reasonably be expected of a person carrying out that particular director's duties, with the company (including those entrusted to him even if he doesn't actually carry them out) and the general knowledge, skill and experience actually known or ascertained by that director: Insolvency Act 1986, section 214(4)(5).

In construing these provisions Knox J. in *Re Produce Marketing Consortium Ltd.* (*No. 2*),[79] held that each director had to be judged by what might reasonably be expected of a person fulfilling his functions in a reasonably diligent way, always bearing in mind certain minimum standards such as the preparation of annual accounts, etc. Further such a director must be judged not only on the facts as known to him but those which he would have known had the company complied with its obligations under the Act, *e.g.* as to the publication of accounts.

If wrongful trading is established the court may require the director to make a contribution to the company's assets: Insolvency Act 1986, section 214(1). Such an order is to be compensatory, *i.e.* to provide an amount equal to that by which the company's assets were depleted by the directors' conduct, and not penal. The absence of fraudulent intent can be taken into account but is not in itself a reason for fixing a low or nominal figure. Any amount is payable with interest from the date of winding up.[80] Following such an order the court may also make a disqualification order against the director: Company Directors Disqualification Act 1986, section 10.

Restriction on use of insolvent company's name

Another abuse prior to 1986 was the so-called "Phoenix" company operation. The liquidator would dispose of the

[79] [1989] BCLC 520.
[80] *Re Produce Marketing Consortium Ltd. (No. 2)* [1989] BCLC 520.

company, its name and assets to the existing directors, who would purchase it with other funds and then continue to trade in exactly the same way as before the insolvent liquidation leaving the creditors of the old company stranded. With the new controls on liquidators and extended rights of creditors in the Insolvency Act 1986 it may have been thought that such practices might come to an end. However, section 216 of the Insolvency Act 1986 is intended to make sure. Where a company goes into insolvent liquidation,[81] anyone who was a director (or shadow director[82]) of that company at any time in the previous year cannot be a director of a company using the name[83] or trading name of the insolvent company for five years unless he has leave of the court. This prohibition extends to being concerned in the promotion, formation, management or taking part in the business of a company using the insolvent company's name. Breach of this section is a criminal offence.

Personal liability of delinquent directors etc.

Section 212 of the Insolvency Act 1986 provides that if in a winding up it appears that any person who is or has been an officer[84] of the company, or a promoter, or manager, liquidator, administrator[85] or administrative receiver[86] of a company, has misapplied or retained or became accountable for any money or other property of the company, or has been guilty of any misfeasance or breach of trust or other[87] duty to the company the court may on the application of the official receiver.[88] the liquidator or any creditor or contributory,[89] examine his conduct and order him to repay or restore the assets or to contribute to the assets of the company as the court thinks just. A

[81] See note 78, *supra*.
[82] *Ante*.
[83] Or any name which is so similar as to suggest an association with the previous company.
[84] This includes a director, manager or secretary.
[85] *Post*, Chap. 26.
[86] *Post*, Chap. 25.
[87] See the Jenkins Committee Report, para. 503.
[88] Not applicable in Scotland.
[89] *Post*, Chap. 29.

contributory can only bring such an action with the leave of the court.

This section replaced section 631 of the Companies Act 1985 which had established a similar summary procedure whereby directors and others could be called to account swiftly for any breach of duty or misfeasance prior to the liquidation. In many ways it is identical with section 631 and many of the cases on that section will still apply. The main differences are that section 212 applies to administrative receivers and includes breaches of duty other than breaches of trust, *i.e.* negligence.[90] Although "misfeasance" is not a Scots law term, the section does apply to Scotland.

Section 631 was held to be procedural only. It gave a summary remedy, not a new cause of action.[91] It has been said that it "did not create any new liability, any new right but only provide a summary mode of enforcing rights which must otherwise have been enforced by the ordinary procedure of the Courts." Also, that the applicant "must show something which would have been the ground of an action by the company if it had not been would up." Further, that the word "misfeasance" in the section meant "misfeasance in the nature of a breach of trust, that is to say, it refers to something which the officer . . . has done wrongly by misapplying or retaining in his own hands any monies of the company, or by which the company's property has been wasted, or the company's creditor improperly pledged. It must be some act resulting in some actual loss to the company."[92] There seems no reason why all this should not apply equally to section 212 of the Insolvency Act 1986.

A summons[93] was taken out by the liquidator against the secretary of a company for sums overdrawn by him on account of his salary on the instructions of the managing director. *Held*, as this was a claim for repayment of an ordinary debt due from the secretary without any

[90] Thus overriding the earlier case law on s.631—see *Re B. Johnson & Co. (Builders) Ltd.* [1955] Ch. 634.

[91] *Coventry and Dixon's Case* (1880) 14 Ch.D. 660 (C.A.). See Lord President Inglis in *Liquidators of City of Glasgow Bank* v. *Mackinnon* (1881) 9 R. 535 at p. 564 and Lord Guest (Ordinary) in *Lord Advocate* v. *Liquidators of Purvis Industries Ltd.*, 1958 S.C. 338 (O.H.) at p. 342.

[92] *Per* James L.J. in *Coventry and Dixon's Case* at p. 670.

[93] In Scotland the application to the court would take the form of a note in the petition process (compulsory winding up): R.C. 218M, or a petition (voluntary winding up): R.C. 189.

wrongful conduct on his part, no order on the summons ought to be made: *Re Etic Ltd.* [1928] Ch. 861.

Section 631 was "limited to cases where there has been something in the nature of a breach of duty by an officer of the company as such which has caused pecuniary loss to the company. Breach of duty of course would include a misfeasance or a breach of trust in the stricter sense, and the section will apply to a true case of misapplication of money or property of the company, or a case where there has been retention of money or property which the officer was bound to have paid or returned to the company": *per* Maugham J. at p. 875.

Instances of misfeasance under section 631 were the improper receipt by a director of his qualification shares from a promoter,[94] the overpayment of a director when he knew the company was insolvent,[95] or of an *ex gratia* payment in lieu of pension on the eve of liquidation,[96] the certifying by an auditor of erroneous accounts whereby dividends were paid out of capital,[97] the receipt by the secretary of a secret profit from a person who sold a mine to the company,[98] the acts of a director in procuring the company to buy shares in another company from himself at an over-value, and making an unsecured loan to enable him and his co-directors to pay calls[99] and failure by a liquidator to make proper provision for the equal ranking and payment of all preferential claims.[1] No set-off was allowed to a claim for misfeasance under that section.[2]

The court has a discretion as to the amount to be ordered to be paid on an application under section 212 of the Insolvency Act 1986.

A liquidator negligently admitted a proof, which he should have disallowed, and as a result the company paid £30,000 to a creditor. An

[94] Which occurred in *Eden* v. *Ridsdales Railway Lamp Co. Ltd.* (1889) 23 Q.B.D. 368 (C.A.).
[95] *Blin* v. *Johnstone*, 1988 S.L.T. 335.
[96] *Gibson's Executor* v.*Gibson*, 1978 S.C. 197 (O.H.).
[97] See *Re Kingston Cotton Mill Co.* (*No.* 2) [1896] 2 Ch. 279 (C.A.) *post*, p. 618.
[98] *McKay's Case* (1875) 2 Ch.D. 1 (C.A.).
[99] *Re V.G.M. Holdings Ltd.* [1942] Ch. 235 (C.A.).
[1] *Lord Advocate* v. *Liquidators of Purvis Industries Ltd.*, 1958 S.C. 338 (O.H.) *post*, Chap. 29.
[2] *Ex p. Pelly* (1882) 21 Ch.D. 492 (C.A.).

attempt to recover this failed, as there was no mistake of fact on the liquidator's part. *Held* the liquidator was liable for misfeasance under section 631, but the court, in the exercise of its discretion, ordered him to pay only such a sum as would enable the creditors to be paid in full with interest at five per cent.: *Re Home and Colonial Insce. Co. Ltd.* [1930] 1 Ch. 102.

Further, the court's power under section 631 was not merely to specify a sum by way of compensation but to apportion it between co-defendants in such a way and with such priority of liability as the court thought fit.[3] Again there is no reason to suppose that section 212 of the Insolvency Act 1986 has altered this.

Directors' Powers and Shareholders' Control

We have seen that in modern public companies the directors have usually only a small shareholding, their salaries and other emoluments, rather than their dividends, being their main sources of profit from the company, with the result that management and ownership of the company have become divorced.[4]

We have also seen that the articles commonly delegate extensive powers to the directors, although there can be no delegation of powers which are required by the Act to be exercised by the company in general meeting, *e.g.* those of altering the articles (s.9), or the capital (ss.121, 135).[5] The Jenkins Committee[6] thought that wide delegation is necessary if the directors are to manage the company efficiently and that members are persistently reluctant to concern themselves with management.

The Committee[7] also thought that as a general rule directors exercise their powers in what they conceive to be the best interests of the company. Again, the Act provides shareholders with theoretically powerful weapons if they choose to use them, *e.g.* the powers of requisitioning meetings and of requiring the giving of notice of members' resolutions to be proposed at

[3] *Re Morecambe Bowling Ltd.* [1969] 1 W.L.R. 133.
[4] *Ante*, p. 347.
[5] *Ante*, p. 377.
[6] Paras. 104 and 109 of the Report.
[7] Para. 110 of the Report.

meetings (ss.368 and 376[8]), and there are various sources of information available to members, *e.g.* the balance sheet and profit and loss account (s.240[9]), and, even if practical considerations (the large number of shareholders in the company, the lack of interest normally shown by the general body of shareholders, the difficulty of rallying support) make such weapons difficult for the small investor to wield, the institutional investors (such as insurance companies) are not always willing to submit to any major abuse of power by the directors. In fact in many cases they have established unofficial, but powerful, Investor Protection Committees, to safeguard their interests. Further, where quoted companies are concerned, the Stock Exchange requirements and the sanction for them in the shape of a suspension of quotation provide some protection.[10]

However, there are cases where directors abuse their power[11] and the Committee made certain recommendations[12] designed to protect the vital interests of shareholders without hampering directors in their conduct of the day-to-day business of the company. There are remedies available for such a breach and these are set out in Chapter 18, *post.*

[8] *Ante*, pp. 318, 324.
[9] *Post*, Chap. 20.
[10] Jenkins Report, para. 106.
[11] *Ibid.* para. 111.
[12] *Ibid.* para. 122.

Chapter 16

THE SECRETARY

EVERY company must have secretary and a sole director cannot also be secretary: section 283(1), (2). The secretary may be an individual or a Scottish firm or a corporation, but a corporation cannot be the secretary if its sole director is also the sole director of the company: section 283(4). A company may have all the partners of a firm as joint secretaries: see section 290. That section also requires disclosure of the identity of the secretary in the register of directors and secretaries to be kept by the company under section 288.

Section 286, first introduced in 1980, requires the directors of a public company to secure that the secretary is a person who appears to them to have the requisite knowledge and experience to be a secretary. In addition a public company secretary must have either been a public company secretary for three out of the five years before his present appointment, or be a barrister, advocate or solicitor, or a member of one of the professional accountancy bodies or of the Institute of Chartered Secretaries and Administrators, or be someone who because of his position or qualifications appears to the directors to be capable of discharging the duties of a public company secretary. A private company secretary need have no such qualifications.

The secretary is usually appointed by the directors, but sometimes he is named in the articles.[1]

Table A, regulation 99, provides: "Subject to the provisions of the Act, the secretary shall be appointed by the directors for such

[1] As to which see *Eley* v. *Positive Life Assurance Co. Ltd.* (1876) 1 Ex.D. 88 (C.A.), *ante*, p. 89.

term, at such renumeration and upon such conditions as they may think fit; and any secretaries so appointed may be removed by them."

The position of a company's secretary has changed a great deal in the last 100 years. In 1887 it was said that: "a secretary is a mere servant; his position is that he is to do what he is told, and no person can assume that he has any authority to represent anything at all; nor can anyone assume that statements made by him are necessarily to be accepted as trustworthy without further Inquiry."[2] Even in 1902 his duties were described as "of a limited and of a somewhat humble character."[3] Accordingly, it has in the past been held that a company is not liable for the acts of its secretary in fraudulently making representations to induce persons to take shares in the company,[4] or in issuing a forged share certificate.[5] The secretary is, however, the proper official to issue share certificates, and so the company is estopped or barred from denying the truth of genuine share certificates issued by him without the authority of the company.[6] He may also, with a director, validly execute a deed on behalf of the company whether or not that company has a common seal.[7]

It has also been held that the secretary has no independent authority to bind the company by contract.[8]

L., a director of N. Co., without any authority from the company, made a contract with H. The contract was confirmed by a letter written by the secretary on behalf of the company. *Held*, the secretary, as such, had no power to bind the company, and N. Co. was not liable on the contract: *Houghton & Co.* v. *Nothard, Lowe & Wills Ltd.* [1928] A.C. 1, *ante*.[9]

[2] *Per* Lord Esher M.R. in *Barnett, Hoares & Co.* v. *South London Tramways Co.* (1887) 18 Q.B.D. 815 (C.A.), at p. 817.
[3] *Per* Lord Macnaghten in *George Whitechurch Ltd.* v. *Cavanagh* [1902] A.C. 117, at p. 124.
[4] *Barnett, Hoares & Co.* v. *South London Tramway Co.*, *ante*.
[5] *Ruben* v. *Great Fingall Consolidated* [1906] A.C. 439, *ante*, p. 276.
[6] *Clavering, Son & Co.* v. *Goodwins, Jardine & Co. Ltd.* (1891) 18 R. 652.
[7] S.36A. *Ante*, p. 111.
[8] *Williams* v. *The Chester and Holyhead Ry. Co.* (1851) 15 Jur. 828. He may of course have actual authority to do anything: see *UBAF Ltd.* v. *European Banking Corp.* [1984] Q.B. 713.
[9] Chap. 6.

Similarly, it has been held that he cannot borrow money on behalf of the company.

At the request of the secretary, a director, C., lent £17,353 to the company to discharge debts guaranteed by the company. The loans were confirmed by a meeting of the directors at which C. and one other director were present. The articles provided that two directors were a quorum, but that a director could not vote in respect of a contract in which he was interested. The company went into liquidation. *Held*, C. was not entitled to recover the money advanced. The secretary had no power to borrow on behalf of the company and his request was not made or confirmed at a properly constituted meeting of the directors: *Re Cleadon Trust Ltd.* [1939] Ch.286 (C.A.).

Also, without the authority of the company, he cannot issue a writ in the company's name[10] or lodge defences in the company's name,[11] and it is not his duty as secretary to instruct the company to its legal rights.[12]

The secretary of a company is not "an official who *virtute officii* can manage all its affairs with or without the help of servants, in the absence of a regular directorate": *per* Lord Parker in *Daimler Co. Ltd.* v. *Continental Tyre Co. Ltd.* [1916] 2 A.C. 307 at p. 337.

Again, the secretary cannot according to the older cases register a transfer until he is authorised to do so by the directors[13]; nor, without such authority, strike a name off the register of shareholders[14], and he cannot summon a general meeting on his own authority[15].

However, the changed position of the company secretary was taken into account in *Panorama Developments* (*Guildford*) *Ltd.* v. *Fidelis Furnishing Fabrics Ltd.*[16] where it was said[17] that a company secretary is a much more important person now than he was in 1887. He is the chief administrative officer of the company with extensive duties and responsibilities. This appears

[10] *Daimler Co. Ltd.* v. *Continental Tyre, etc., Co. Ltd.* [1916] 2 A.C. 307.
[11] *Edington* v. *Dumbar Steam Laundry Co.* (1903) 11 S.L.T. 117 (O.H.).
[12] *Niven* v. *Collins Patent Lever Gear Co. Ltd.* (1900) 7 S.L.T. 476 (O.H.).
[13] *Chida Mines Ltd.* v. *Anderson* (1905) 22 T.L.R. 27.
[14] *Re Indo-China Steam Navigation Co.* [1917] 2 Ch. 100.
[15] *Re State of Wyoming Syndicate* [1901] 2 Ch. 431.
[16] [1971] 2 Q.B. 711 (C.A).
[17] *Per* Lord Denning M.R. and Salmon L.J., at pp. 716, 717.

not only in the modern Companies Acts but in the role which he plays in the day-to-day business of the company. He is no longer a mere clerk. He regularly makes representations on behalf of the company and enters into contracts on its behalf which come within the day-to-day running of its business. So much so that he may be regarded as held out as having authority to do such things on behalf of the company. He is certainly entitled to sign contracts connected with the administrative side of a company's affairs, such as employing staff and ordering cars. All such matters come within the ostensible or apparent authority of a company's secretary.

The secretary, purportedly on behalf of the company, fraudulently hired cars, ostensibly for the purpose of meeting customers, and used the cars for his own private purposes. *Held*, the secretary had ostensible authority to enter into contracts for the hire of cars on behalf of the company and the company was liable to pay the hire charges: *Panorama Developments (Guildford) Ltd.* v. *Fidelis Furnishing Fabrics Ltd.* [1971] 2 Q.B. 711 (C.A.).

On the other hand it appears that he still has no ostensible or apparent authority to make representations about the company in relation to a commercial transaction, *e.g.* a syndicated loan.[18]

This new status of the company secretary was recognised by the introduction in the 1980 Act of a qualification standard for public company secretaries: section 286 *ante*.

The duties of the secretary depend on the size and nature of the company, and on the arrangement made with him. In any case he will be present at all meetings of the company, and of the directors, and will make proper minutes of the proceedings. He will issue, under the direction of the board, all notices to members and others. In practice he will usually countersign every instrument to which the seal of the company is affixed. Alternatively, he is one of those whose signature will validate a document as a document under seal by virtue of sections 36A and 36B (Chap. 6, *ante*). He or his department will conduct all correspondence with shareholders in regard to transfers and otherwise, will certify transfers, and will keep the books of the company, or such of them as relate to the internal business of the company, *e.g.* the register of members, the share ledger, the

[18] *UBAF Ltd.* v. *Euopean American Banking Corp.* [1984] Q.B. 713.

transfer book, the register of charges, etc. He will also make all necessary returns to the Registrar, *e.g.* the annual return, return of allotments, notice of increase of capital, etc.

If a provision requires or authorises a thing to be done by or to a director and the secretary it is not satisfied by the thing being done by or to the same person acting both as director and as secretary: section 284.

If a person is secretary of two companies, a fact which comes to his knowledge as secretary of one company is not notice to him as secretary of another company, unless it was his duty to the first company to communicate his knowledge to the second company.

H. was secretary to two companies, A. Co. and B. Co. B. Co. drew a bill on a third company, C. Co., and indorsed it in favour of A. Co. The bill was dishonoured by C. Co. and no notice of dishonour was given to B. Co. It was claimed that as H., in his capacity of secretary, knew of the dishonour, no notice was necessary. *Held*, notice to H., as secretary of A. Co., was not notice to B. Co.: *Re Fenwick, Stobart & Co.* [1902] 1 Ch.507.

In England a full-time secretary has been held to be a "clerk or servant" so as to be entitled to preferential payment of his salary on a winding up but a part-time secretary is not.[19] Since that decision the relevant wording has been amended to "employee."

The secretary is an officer of the company: section 744. In some instances therefore he is in the same position as a director so that a provision in the articles or in any contract for relieving him from liability is void: section 310.[20] Again, the court can relieve him from liability in certain cases: section 727.[21] The disclosure in the accounts of loans etc. to the secretary is less stringent than that for directors.[22] Under Schedule 6 only the aggregate amounts outstanding need to be disclosed together with the number of officers involved.

[19] *Cairney* v. *Back* [1906] 2 K.B. 746 *post*, p. 823. Scottish cases in which a secretary was held not be a "clerk or servant" for this purpose are *Scottish Poultry Journal Co.* (1896) 4 S.L.T. 167 (O.H.), *Clyde Football etc. Co. Ltd.* (1900) 8 S.L.T. 328 (O.H.) and *Laing* v. *Gowans* (1902) 10 S.L.T. 461 (O.H.).
[20] *Ante*, p. 414.
[21] *Ante*, p. 415.
[22] *Ante*, p. 390.

A secretary has been held to have no lien over the books of the company coming into his possession in the course of his duties.[23]

[23] *Gladstone* v. *M'Callum* (1896) 23 R.783 (minute book); *Barnton Hotel Co. Ltd.* v. *Cook* (1899) 1 F.1190 (register of members and other books and documents at secretary's own premises).

Chapter 17

CONTROLLING MEMBERS' DUTIES

In this chapter the term "controlling members" means those members of a company who between them possess sufficient voting power to pass the appropriate resolution in general meeting, usually an ordinary resolution.

We have seen that the company in general meeting may waive a breach of fiduciary duty by a director who contracts with the company as in the *N. W. Transportation* case,[1] or by one who makes a secret profit out of his position as in *Regal* (*Hastings*) *Ltd.* v. *Gulliver*,[2] or may waive a breach of a directors's duty of care, as in *Pavlides* v. *Jensen*.[3] In general therefore the majority of the company may exercise their votes to control the company provided that they comply with the Companies Acts. It has often been stated that although the directors of a company owe a fiduciary duty [4] to the company, as such, shareholders do not: "When voting, a shareholder may consult his own interests."[5]

Until recently it has thus been accepted that a share is a piece of property which is to be enjoyed and exercised for the owner's personal advantage.[6] Thus a shareholder may bind himself by contract to vote in a particular way, where a director may not.

> "When a director votes as a director for or against any particular resolution in a directors' meeting he is voting as a person under a fiduciary duty to the company for the proposition that the company should take a certain course of action. When a shareholder is voting for or against a particular resolution he is voting as a person owing no

[1] (1887) 12 App. Cas. 589 (P.C.).
[2] [1942] 1 All E.R. 378 (H.L.).
[3] [1956] Ch. 565.
[4] *Ante*, p. 393.
[5] *Per* Megarry V.-C. in *Estmanco* (*Kilner House*) *Ltd.* v. *G.L.C.* [1982] 1 All E.R. 437, 444.
[6] See, *e.g. N.W. Transportation* v. *Beatty*, *supra*.

fiduciary duty to the company and who is exercising his own right of property, to vote as he thinks fit. The fact that the result of the voting at the meetint (or at a subsequent poll) will bind the company cannot affect the position that, in voting, he is voting simply in exercise of his own property rights . . . a director is an agent, who casts his vote to decide in what manner his principal shall act through the collective agency of the board of directors; a shareholder who casts his vote in general meeting is not casting it as an agent of the company in any shape or form. His act therefore, in voting as he pleases, cannot in any way be regarded as an act of the company": *per* Walton J. in *Northern Counties Securities Ltd.* v. *Jackson and Steeple Ltd.* [1974] 1 W.L.R. 1133, at p. 1144.

In *Greenwell* v. *Potter*,[7] where executors and trustees of a will who held shares agreed to sell some to G., who stipulated that he should nominate X as a director and that the executors should, when X retired by rotation, vote for his re-election, it was held that the executors were bound by the agreement. It may be mentioned that there was a voting agreement in *Greenhalgh* v. *Mallard*[8] but it was held that the shareholders who agreed to vote in a certain way were under no obligation to retain their shares and there was no continuing obligation running with the shares.

This right to vote has however always been subject to the doctrine of the fraud on the minority so that the majority cannot waive a breach of a director's fiduciary duty by approving a misappropriation by him of the company's property which would be a fraud on the minority. That is what the majority tried to do in *Cook* v. *Deeks.*[9]

The same is true where there is an attempted confirmation of a share issue made by a director in order to give him control of the company and benefit the majority to the detriment of the minority, *i.e.* the general meeting cannot then waive the director's breach of duty.[10]

Members cannot, by resolution in general meeting, expropriate the company's property.

The shareholders in E. Co., which was formed with the object of constructing a submarine telegraph, were H. Co. with 3,000 shares, M. with 2,000 and thirteen other persons with 325 between them. H. Co. was to make and lay cables for E. Co. The directors of E. Co., who were nominees of H. Co., and H. Co. decided not to pursue an action

[7] [1902] 1 Ch. 530. See also *Puddephatt* v. *Leith* [1916] 1 Ch. 200.
[8] [1943] 2 All E.R. 234 (C.A.).
[9] [1916] 1 A.C. 554, *post*, p. 440
[10] *Ngurli* v. *McCann* (1954) 90 C.L.R. 425.

in which E.Co was claiming a concession to construct the telegraph, procured the passing of a resolution in general meeting to put E. Co. into voluntary winding up and concealed the fact that they had agreed to end the agreement between E. Co. and H. Co. so that H. Co. could sell the cable to a third company. M. brought an action on behalf of himself and the other shareholders, except those who were defendants, in which he joined E. Co. as a defendant. He claimed, *inter alia*, a declaration that H. Co. was a trustee of the resulting profit for M. and the other shareholders in E. Co. *Held*, M. succeeded. The majority shareholder had obtained certain advantages by dealing with something which was the property of the whole company: *Menier* v. *Hooper's Telegraph Works* (1874) L.R. 9 Ch.App. 350.

As regards the property of other members of the company, we saw in Chapter 4 that, on the authority of *Sidebottom* v. *Kershaw, Leese & Co.*,[11] an alteration of the articles by special resolution in general meeting in order to enable some members to acquire the shares of other members must be bona fide for the benefit of the company as a whole.

Further, we saw that cases such as *Greenhalgh* v. *Arderne Cinemas Ltd.*,[12] and *Shuttleworth* v. *Cox Bros. Ltd.*,[13] established the rule that in making any alteration to the articles the general meeting must act bona fide for the benefit of the company as a whole. Similarly, a class meeting of preference shareholders sanctioning a modification of the special rights of the preference shares must act bona fide for the benefit of the class as a whole.[14]

It was said in a Scottish case[15] that: "Prima facie, the shareholders are the best judges of their own affairs, and it is only where it appears that some sinister motive has operated, or that interests other than the interest of the company have plainly prevailed, that the Court will entertain a complaint. The test always is—is the thing complained of a thing done in the interest of the company?—or, to put it perhaps more accurately, is the action of the majority irreconcilable with their having proceeded upon any reasonable view of the company's interest?" In the case in question a resolution of a general meeting to issue unissued shares to the managing director at a lower premium than would have been obtained on the market was valid. In another Scottish case it was

[11] [1920] 1 Ch. 154 (C.A.), *ante*, p. 94.
[12] [1951] Ch. 286 (C.A.), *ante*, p. 94.
[13] [1927] 2 K.B. 9 (C.A.).
[14] *Re Holders Investment Trust Ltd.* [1971] 1 W.L.R. 583, *ante*, p. 268.
[15] *Per* Lord Kyllachy (Ordinary) in *Cameron* v. *Glenmorangie Distillery Co. Ltd.* (1896) 23 R. 1092 at p. 1095.

said[16] that "The question ... is whether the resolution complained of ... can be held to be so oppressive and extravagant that no reasonable man could consider it to be for the benefit of the Company."

Thus controlling members do owe a duty to the company, *i.e.* the corporators as a body, to act bona fide for the benefit of the company as a whole and not to commit a fraud on the minority.

It has been said in one case, however, that the controlling members may in fact be subject to more stringent controls than the accepted doctrine of a fraud on the minority, although not being subject to the full fiduciary duties of a director.

In *Clemens* v. *Clemens Bros. Ltd.*[17] the defendant owned 55 per cent. of the issued shares of a family company. She was one of five directors and proposed to give the other directors shares and to set up a trust for long-service employees. The plaintiff, who was the defendant's niece, held 40 per cent. of the shares and was not a director. The defendant proposed resolutions to increase the capital so that the plaintiff's shares would fall below 25 per cent. of the total and her right to veto special resolutions would be lost. It was also clear that she would never now obtain control of the company. The judge held that the defendant was not entitled to exercise her majority votes as an ordinary shareholder in any way she pleased. That right was subject to equitable considerations which could make it unjust to exercise them in a particular way. In this case such considerations applied and the resolutions would be set aside.

One interpretation of this case is that it shows that the majority do not have unrestricted voting rights if it is "unjust" in the particular circumstances.

In *Estmanco* (*Kilner House*) *Ltd.* v. *Greater London Council*[18] Megarry V.-C., however, accepted the general proposition that the shareholders do not owe any fiduciary duties but affirmed that in altering the articles they are subject to the doctrine of fraud on the minority, *i.e* they must act in what they believe to be in the best interests of the company as a whole. In that case the majority shareholder wished to deprive the company of a right of action under a contract and proposed, and carried, a

16 *Per* Lord Wark (Ordinary) in *Harris* v. *A. Harris Ltd.* 1936 S.C. 183 at p. 192.
17 [1976] 2 All E.R. 268.
18 [1982] 1 All E.R. 437.

resolution to that effect. A minority shareholder sought to bring an action on behalf of the company[19] to prevent this. Megarry V.-C. considered the situation thus[20]:

> "Plainly there must be some limit to the power of the majority to pass resolutions which they believe to be in the best interests of the company and yet remain immune from interference by the courts. It may be in the best interests of the company to deprive the minority of some of their rights or some of their property, yet I do not think that this gives the majority an unrestricted right to do this, however unjust it may be, and however much it may harm shareholders whose rights as a class differ from those of the majority."

More recently, in *Re Swindon Town Football Club Ltd.* [1990] BCLC 467, Harman J. accepted that the general rule that shareholders are entitled to vote in their own interest remains the law and is the correct proposition, even though it has not been followed on every modern occasion. The judge also accepted the proposition that: "The company is entitled to consider lawful resolutions, however silly, and, if thought fit, to pass them, and it is not for the court to tell the company that it should not be silly." (p. 469).

[19] *Post*, p. 441.
[20] [1982] 1 All E.R. 437, 444.

Chapter 18

MAJORITY RULE AND MINORITY PROTECTION

THIS chapter attempts to present in a coherent form a number of matters, some of which have been explained already and others of which have been referred to.

One of the matters which has been referred to on more than one occasion is the rule in *Foss* v. *Harbottle* to the effect that the company is usually the proper plaintiff in an action to enforce the duties of directors and controlling members.

Majority rule and its counter balance, minority protection, are dealt with—under the general law, the wishes of the majority of the members normally prevail over those of the minority but the majority must not perpetrate a fraud on the minority.

Statutory protection of the minority against the majority is explained: for example, under sections 122 and 124 of the Insolvency Act 1986 even a single member can have the company wound up by the court if that is just and equitable and under sections 459 to 461 of the Companies Act, a single member can obtain other relief from the court under the so-called alternative remedy where the company's affairs are being conducted in an unfairly prejudicial manner to some or all of the members.

Finally the protection afforded by Department of Trade and Industry investigations is set out, although these necessarily involve an element of public control as well. The rules relating to insider dealing—a particular abuse of directors' and others' duties—are explained in Chapter 19.

THE RULE IN FOSS *v.* HARBOTTLE[1]

The rule is that, as one would expect, the proper plaintiff[2] in an action to redress an alleged wrong to a company on the part of

[1] "It is common ground between the parties, and those familiar with the complications of the rule in *Foss* v. *Harbottle* will not find this a matter of surpise, that difficult questions do arise," *per* Knox J. in *Smith* v. *Croft* (*No.* 2) [1987] BCLC 206, 208.

[2] The Scots term is "pursuer."

anyone, whether director, member or outsider, or to recover money or damages alleged to be due to it, is prima facie the company and, where the alleged wrong is any irregularity which might be made binding on the company by a simple majority of members, no individual member can bring an action in respect of it.[3]

In other words, the company is normally the proper plaintiff in an action to enforce a duty owed to the company by directors or controlling members, and where the breach of duty can be condoned by an ordinary resolution of the members in general meeting, no individual member or minority of members may sue. A general meeting may be held so that the members may by ordinary resolution decide whether to sue or not. If such a meeting has been held and the breach of duty condoned not only does this prevent a single shareholder from bringing an action it also prevents the liquidator from subsequently doing so.[4] It also follows that where the wrong may be ratified by a special resolution and such a resolution is passed no action will lie.[5] It is for this reason also that the employees of a company, to whom the directors now owe a duty following section 309,[6] first introduced in 1980, may find it impossible to enforce such a right. Only the members have the right to enforce it.

It has been said[7] that there are two branches of rule and these have been described[8] as—

(1) the proper plaintiff principle,
(2) the internal management principle.

Two members took proceedings on behalf of themselves and all other members except those who were defendants against the directors of a company to compel them to make good losses sustained by the company owing to the directors buying their own land for the

[3] See *per* Lord Davey delivering the judgment of the court in *Burland* v. *Earle* [1902] A.C. 82 (P.C.) at pp. 93, 94.

[4] *Multinational Gas and Petrochemical Co.* v. *Multinational Gas and Petrochemical Services Ltd.* [1983] Ch. 258 (C.A.). But see also the dissenting judgment of May L.J. to the contrary.

[5] See s.35(3); Chap. 6., *ante*.

[6] *Ante*, p. 399.

[7] *Per* Jordan C.J. in *Australian Coal etc. Employees' Fedn.* v. *Smith* (1937) 38 S.R. (N.S.W.) 48.

[8] *Per* Street J. in *Hawkesbury Development Co. Ltd.* v. *Landmark Finance Pty. Ltd.* (1970) 92 W.N. (N.S.W.). 199.

company's use and paying themselves a price greater than its value. *Held*, as there was nothing to prevent the company from taking the proceedings, if it thought fit to do so, the action failed: *Foss* v. *Harbottle* (1843) 2 Ha. 461; 67 E.R. 189.[9]

A minority shareholder sought to bring an action on behalf of himself and to all other shareholders, save three who were directors, against those directors and the company for damages, alleging that the directors had been negligent in selling an asset of the company for less than its market value. Most of the shares in the company were held by another company the directors of which were also directors of the first company. *Held*, since the sale of the mine was *intra vires* the company, and there was no allegation of fraud by the directors or appropriation of assets of the company by the majority shareholders in fraud of the minority, the action was not maintainable. It was open to the company, on the resolution of a majority of the shareholders, to sell the mine at a price decided by the company in that manner, and it was open to the company by a vote of the majority to decide that, if the directors by their negligence had sold the mine at an undervalue, proceedings should not be taken by the company against the directors. *Semble*, it is sometimes admissible to go behind the apparent ownership of shares to discover whether a company is in fact controlled by wrongdoers, *e.g.* where the shares are held by nominees: *Pavlides* v. *Jensen* [1956] Ch. 565.[10]

The rule avoids multiplicity of suits. The reason for the last part of the rule is that litigation at the suit of a minority of the members is futile if the majority do not wish it.

"If the thing complained of is a thing which in substance the majority of the company are entitled to do, or if something has been done irregularly which the majority of the company are entitled to do regularly, or if something has been done illegally which the majority of the company are entitled to do legally, there can be no use in having

[9] Applied in the *Hawkesbury* case, *ante*. In a corresponding Scottish case, *Orr* v. *Glasgow etc. Rlwy. Co.* (1860) 3 Macqueen 799, "the ground of action . . . was that the directors were also directors of a rival company, and that they had acted in the interests of this latter company to the prejudice of the shareholders of the first. The action was dismissed on the ground that although the transaction complained of was beyond the powers of the directors, it was competent for the shareholders to sanction it, and therefore that a single shareholder, or a minority, had no title to sue," *per* Lord Kinnear (Ordinary) in *Rixon* v. *Edinburgh Northern Tramways Co.* (1889) 16 R. 653 at p. 656.

[10] Scottish illustrations are *Lee* v. *Crawford* (1890) 17 R. 1094 (action against director for payment to the company of funds alleged to have been illegally lent to officials of the company), *Cameron* v. *Glenmorangie Distillery Co. Ltd.* (1896) 23 R. 1092 (directors carrying out shareholders' resolution to allot to managing director unissued shares at a premium considered by a shareholder to be inadequate) and *Brown* v. *Stewart* (1898) 1 F. 316 (claim for damages against directors on ground that they had acted recklessly in commencing business when so few shares had been applied for).

litigation about it, the ultimate end of which is only that a meeting has to be called, and then ultimately the majority gets its wishes": *per* Mellish L.J. in *MacDougall* v. *Gardiner* (1875) 1 Ch.D. 13 (C.A.) at p. 25.[11]

Another modern rationale for the rule is that it prevents the company being subjected to a long and expensive litigation to no ultimate purpose if an independent majority of the company do not wish to pursue the claim. As a result the rule is dealt with as a preliminary issue before any full trial is held.[12]

Under this rule, the court will not, for example, interfere with irregularities at meetings at the instance of a shareholder.

The articles empowered the chairman, with the consent of the meeting, to adjourn a meeting, and also provided for taking a poll if demanded by five shareholders. The adjournment was moved, and declared by the chairman to be carried; a poll was then demanded and refused by the chairman. A shareholder suing on behalf of himself and all other shareholders except those who were directors brought an action against the directors and the company for a declaration that the chairman's conduct was illegal and an injunction to restrain the directors from carrying out certain arrangements without the shareholders' approval. *Held*, the action could not be brought by a shareholder; if the chairman was wrong, the company alone could sue: *MacDougall* v. *Gardiner* (1875) 1 Ch.D. 13 (C.A.).

Nor will the court grant a declaration that the accounts are not in the correct form at the instance of a shareholder: *Devlin* v. *Slough Estates Ltd.* [1983] BCLC 497.

Derivative actions—exceptions to the rule in Foss v. Harbottle

The rule is subject to a number of exceptions, in which cases a minority of shareholders, or even an individual shareholder, may bring a minority shareholders' action, usually under R.S.C., O. 15, r. 12,[13] *i.e.* the minority shareholders sue on behalf of themselves and all other shareholders except those

[11] *Cf.* Lord Hunter in *Harris* v. *A. Harris Ltd.*, 1936 S.C. 183 at p. 198.

[12] *Prudential Assurance Co. Ltd.* v. *Newman Industries* (*No.* 2) *Ltd.* [1982] Ch. 204 (C.A.); *Smith* v. *Croft* (*No. 3*) [1987] BCLC 355; *post*, p. 442.

[13] Not applicable to Scotland. There is no special form for a "derivative action" in Scots law: the minority shareholder would require to proceed in his own name. For procedural problems in Scotland see Allan L. Mackenzie, *The Problem of Enforcement of Directors' Duties in Scotland*, 1981 S.L.T. (News) 257, and A. A. Paterson, *The Derivative Action in Scotland*, 1982 S.L.T. (News) 205.

who are defendants, and may join the company as a defendant. The directors are usually defendants. This action is brought instead of an action in the name of the company.

"The form of the action is always 'A.B. (a minority shareholder) on behalf of himself and all other shareholders of the company' against the wrongdoing directors and the company": *per* Lord Denning M.R. in *Wallersteiner* v. *Moir* (*No.* 2) [1975] Q.B. 373 (C.A.) at p. 390.

This type of action is a *derivative action*, *i.e.* the right to sue derives from that of the company. The shareholders as such have no such right. If their own personal rights are being infringed they may bring a *representative* action, *post*.

The nature of the derivative action is that is a "procedural device for enabling the court to do justice to a company controlled by miscreant directors or shareholders."[14] It follows that the court is entitled to examine the conduct of whoever intends to start such proceedings—he must be doing so for the benefit of the company and not for some other purpose; *i.e.* he must be a proper person to bring a derivative action. A particular person might not be a proper person because his conduct is tainted in some way which under the rules of equity may bar relief; *e.g.* he might not come with "clean hands" (*e.g.* having participated in the wrong) or he may have been guilty of delay.[15]

A husband was the majority shareholder and his wife the minority shareholder of a company. The husband had appropriated money belonging to the company for his own use, but the wife had previously brought matrimonial proceedings and had been awarded a sum in respect of that money by the court. The Court of Appeal decided that she was not a proper person to bring a derivative action on behalf of the company since she had, with knowledge of the facts, elected to pursue the matrimonial claim, and it would be inequitable to allow a double claim. A defendant to a derivative action can raise any defence which he could have raised had the action been brought by the shareholder personally: *Nurcombe* v. *Nurcombe* [1985] 1 W.L.R. 370 (C.A.).

[14] *Nurcombe* v. *Nurcombe* [1985] 1 W.L.R. 370, *per* Lawton L.J. at p. 376. See also *Wallersteiner* v. *Moir* (*No.* 2) [1975] Q.B. 373, *per* Lord Denning M.R. at p. 390.

[15] *Towers* v. *African Tug Co.* [1904] 1 Ch. 588.

It also follows from the nature of a derivative action that if the company has no right to bring an action then no derivative action can be allowed.[16] A minority shareholder cannot have a larger right to relief than the company itself would have if it were the plaintiff. If therefore there is a valid reason why the company should not sue, it will equally prevent a minority shareholder suing on its behalf.[17]

A derivative action may be brought in the following cases:—

(1) Where the wrong complained of is a fraud by the majority of the members on the minority and the wrongdoers are in control of the company in general meeting, *i.e.* they control the majority of the shares in the company, and they will not permit an action to be brought in the name of the company. If the aggrieved minority could not bring a minority shareholders' action in this case ther grievance would never reach the courts. Where an action is brought under this exception the wrongdoers are usually both directors and controlling shareholders.

In *Cook* v. *Deeks*[18] a shareholder brought a minority shareholders' action to compel the directors to account to the company for the profits made out of the construction contract which they took in their own names.[19]

In Scotland it has been held that the minority must have first made a definite attempt to obtain the company's co-operation: it is not sufficient for them to plead that the majority had the power to outvote them; *per* Lord Kyllachy (Ordinary) in *Lee* v. *Crawford* (1890) 17 R. 1094 at p. 1096; *Brown* v. *Stewart* (1898) 1 F. 316.

Recent cases have widened this exception to the rule in two ways and, possibly, narrowed it in another. First as to the meaning of "fraud" in this context:

In *Daniels* v. *Daniels*[20] the minority shareholders of a company were allowed to bring an action where the directors

[16] See *Watts* v. *Midland Bank plc* [1986] BCLC 15, 20, *per* Peter Gibson J.

[17] *Smith* v. *Croft* (*No.* 3) [1987] BCLC 355.

[18] [1916] 1 A.C. 554.

[19] See also *Menier* v. *Hooper's Telegraph Works* (1874) L.R. 9 Ch.App. 350. For Scotland see also *Rixon* v. *Edinburgh Northern Tramways* (1889) 16 R. 653 and *Hannay* v. *Muir* (1898) 1 F. 306.

[20] [1978] 2 All E.R. 89.

had authorised the sale of company land to one of them at a price alleged to be well below its market value. The directors objected that since fraud had not been alleged the action should not be allowed.

Templeman J. laid down a wider definition of "fraud" for this purpose: "If minority shareholders can sue if there is fraud, I see no reason why they cannot sue where the action of the majority and the directors, though without fraud, confers some benefit on those directors and majority shareholders themselves.[21] The judge distinguished *Pavlides* v. *Jensen*, above, on the grounds that in that case the directors had not benefited by their "negligence." The essence of this decision is that since fraud is often impossible to prove it may be presumed from such obvious facts.

In *Estmanco* (*Kilner House*) Ltd. v. *Greater London Council*[22] the majority shareholder proposed to alter a contract it had with the company in order to deprive the minority shareholders of certain rights. The majority shareholder then proposed a resolution whereby the company should not sue for breach of contract. When a minority shareholder sought to sue on the company's behalf the majority shareholder argued that since it had acted bona fide for the benefit of the company there was no fraud on the minority to allow such an action.

Megarry V.-C. refused to accept that test of fraud on the minority as applicable for the purposes of bringing an action. It only related to the alteration of the company's articles.[23] In this case the action of the majority shareholder injured one category of shareholder to the benefit of another. Fraud in this sense is abuse of a power.

Further in *Re A Company*: *FFI* (*U.K. Finance*) *Ltd.* v. *Lady Kagan* (1982) 132 N.L.J. 830, the judge granted an injunction, at the request of a shareholder, to prevent the company pleading guilty to a charge of conspiracy to defraud at the instigation of the directors, on the basis that this would damage the company's potential civil claims against others. Improper influence appeared to have been used.

The second development concerns the requisite element of "control" by the majority. It has always been accepted, as stated above, that this means actual voting control. But in *Prudential Assurance Co. Ltd.* v. *Newman Industries Ltd.* (*No.* 2)[24]

[21] *Ibid.* p. 96.
[22] [1982] 1 All E.R. 437.
[23] *Ante*, p. 90.
[24] [1982] 1 All E.R. 354 (C.A.); [1980] 2 All E.R. 841.

Vinelott J. was prepared to extend the exception when the alleged fraud was committed by directors who did not exercise actual voting control but who exercised control *in practice*. Large public companies, such as *Newman*, are in fact controlled by less than 50 per cent. of the votes. The Court of Appeal in that case did not express any opinion on this point.

It may be, however, that following Knox J.'s decision in *Smith* v. *Croft* (*No. 3*),[25] *infra*, if a majority of the independent shareholders do not wish to sue, then no action may be brought, even when the defendants are in control.

(2) Where the act is one which is illegal, or, prior to the 1989 Act, contrary to the company's constitution.[26]

The members cannot ratify an illegal act. However, if the act is merely contrary to the company's constitution it may be condoned, and any action against the directors waived, by separate special resolutions under section 35(3).[27] An individual shareholder still has the right to seek an injunction to prevent such an act, which is not subject to the rule in *Foss* v. *Harbottle*, and this is preserved by sections 35(2) and 35A(4)[28] unless the company is already bound. It follows that an act contrary to the company's constitution is better regarded as falling within (3) below following the changes made by the 1989 Act, rather than under this head.

Even if the act is illegal, *e.g.* under the Companies Act, however, the majority may validly resolve to take no action to remedy the wrong done and if that resolution is made in good faith and in what the majority consider to be for the benefit of the company, it will bind the minority.[29]

In *Smith* v. *Croft* (*No. 3*),[30] the action involved alleged payments by the directors in breach of section 151, *i.e.* the financial assistance rules,[31] which if proved would have been

[25] [1987] BCLC 355.
[26] *Flitcroft's Case* (1882) 21 Ch.D. 519 (C.A.). And see the *Hawkesbury* case, referred to in note 8.
[27] *Ante*, Chap. 6.
[28] *Ante*, Chap. 6.
[29] *Taylor* v. *National Union of Mineworkers* (*Derbyshire Area*) [1985] BCLC 237.
[30] [1987] BCLC 355.
[31] *Ante*, p. 219.

illegal. The judge held that an individual shareholder did not have an absolute right to bring a derivative action on that basis to recover the money so spent, as distinct from preventing it beforehand. Such a right of recovery would only be available if the company had such a right. In that case a majority of the independent shareholders[32] did not wish the action for recovery to be brought and the judge regarded that as a sufficient reason to disallow the action.

"Ultimately the question which has to be answered ... is: 'Is the plaintiff being prevented improperly from bringing these proceedings on behalf of the company?' If it is an expression of the corporate will of the company by an appropriate independent organ that is preventing the plaintiff from prosecuting the action he is not improperly but properly prevented and so the answer to the question is No. The appropriate independent organ will vary according to the constitution of the company concerned and the identity of the defendants, who will in most cases be disqualified from participating by voting in expressing the corporate will"; *per* Knox J. [1987] BCLC 355, 403.

(3) Where the matter is one which can be validly done or sanctioned, not by a simple majority, but only by some special majority, *e.g.* a special resolution, which has not been obtained. If an action could not be brought in this case the company could, in breach of the memorandum or articles, do *de facto* by ordinary resolution that which according to its regulations can only be done by a special resolution.

Thus in *Baillie* v. *Oriental Telephone Co. Ltd.*,[33] a shareholder was able to bring a minority shareholders' action to restrain the company from acting on a special resolution of which insufficient notice had been given.[34]

Acts contrary to the company's constitution may be ratified by a special resolution, so that the above rule applies in that case. However, it may be that in all such cases, where an action is for recovery of loss to the company, a majority of the independent

[32] That is a question of fact in each case.
[33] [1915] 1 Ch. 503 (C.A.), *ante*, p. 323.
[34] And see *Dunn* v. *Banknock Coal Co. Ltd.* (1901) 9 S.L.T. 51 (O.H.).

shareholders may be able to prevent such an action being brought, following the decision in *Smith* v. *Croft* (*No. 3*), *supra*.

(4) It was assumed, although not decided, in *Heyting* v. *Dupont*[35] that there may be a further exception to the rule in *Foss* v. *Harbottle*—namely where justice demands that an action be brought, *e.g.* where all that is alleged is damage to the company arising from a director's misfeasance in withholding an asset of the company without fraud or *ultra vires*.

The company was to exploit an invention of the defendant's consisting of a machine for making plastic pipes and the defendant withheld the company's patent application. However, the company could not have exploited the invention because it was in a state of paralysis owing to discord, so there was no damage to the company and therefore justice did not require that exception be made. Again, there is some authority to the effect that justice may demand that exception be made where the directors are in breach of duty which the company in general meeting could but will not condone and although the directors are not controlling shareholders they prevent the company suing because an article like Table A, regulation 70, gives them most of the powers of the company.[36]

In the *Prudential* case[37] Vinelott J. based his decision on the derivative action against the directors on the doctrine that a minority action could be allowed if "the interests of justice require that a minority action should be permitted."[38] The Court of Appeal did not need to discuss the rule in *Foss* v. Harbottle because the company had actually adopted the case, but expressed the opinion that any exception based on the justice of the case was not a practical one.

Procedure

The real difficulty is that the question of whether a minority shareholder should be allowed to bring a derivative action ought

[35] [1964] 1 W.L.R. 843 (C.A.), *per* Russell and Harman L.JJ. at pp. 851, 854.
[36] See *per* Hudson J. in *Kraus* v. *J.G. Lloyd Pty. Ltd.* [1965] V.R. 232 at pp. 236, 237.
[37] *Ante*, p. 441.
[38] [1980] 2 All E.R. 841 at p. 877.

to be a preliminary issue tried before the merits of the case, *e.g.* alleged fraud, are debated. If the justice exception is used it will in effect need a full trial of the issues to decide how justice will be best served. The Court of Appeal in the *Prudential* case thought that in such a preliminary action the minority shareholder should be required to establish at least a prima facie case that (a) the company is entitled to the relief claimed, and (b) the action falls within the proper boundaries of the rule restricting members' actions on behalf of the company.

This procedure was approved by Knox J. in *Smith* v. *Croft* (*No. 2*)[39] as a half way house between assuming for procedural purposes either that all allegations are true or requiring the plaintiff to prove everything as a preliminary issue, as happened in the *Prudential* case.

On the other hand, the court may now authorise civil proceedings to be brought on behalf of the company by such persons and on such terms as it shall direct, as the result of a petition under section 459, *post*.

The minority shareholders' action is called a derivative action[40] to indicate that the right being enforced is that of the company. If the company is in liquidation such an action should be taken over by the liquidator if he is willing to do so.[41] The Legal Aid Act 1988 makes no provision for legal aid in a minority shareholders' action but it is open to the court in such an action to order the company to indemnify the plaintiff against the costs of the action. The minority shareholder should apply for the sanction of the court soon after issuing his writ. If granted he will be given such indemnity. It would be unlawful as being contrary to public policy for a solicitor to accept a retainer for the plaintiff(s) to conduct the action on a contingency fee basis (*i.e.* he is paid the fee if he wins but not if he loses).[42]

It has been held that applications for indemnity should be made *inter partes* and that the court will apply the same criteria as when deciding whether there is a triable case. Further it was

[39] [1987] BCLC 206.

[40] *Per* Lord Denning M.R. at p. 390 and Scarman L.J. at p. 406 in *Wallersteiner* v. *Moir* (*No.* 2) [1975] Q.b. 373 (C.A.). Scarman L.J. said that the American description of a minority shareholders' action, brought to obtain redress for the company, as a stockholders' derivative action, is apt.

[41] *Fargro Ltd.* v. *Godfroy* [1986] BCLC 370.

[42] *Wallersteiner* case, *ante*.

said in that case that costs should not be awarded unless financially necessary.[43] This contradicts an earlier case,[44] where an indemnity order was granted on the basis of whether an honest, independent and impartial board would have authorised the action and the fact that the minority shareholder was not impecunious was held not to be a ground for refusing the indemnity order.

Representative actions

In *Hogg* v. *Cramphorn*[45] the plaintiff was held to be justified in suing in a representative capacity in respect of the alleged wrongful disposition of the company's money by the directors which could be condoned by a resolution in general meeting, so that the action should have been dismissed unless it was not a *derivative* representative action but an individual rights *representative* action.

A member of a company may enjoy a right alone or in common with other members of the company and the rule in *Foss* v. *Harbottle* has no application where individual members sue, not in right of the company, but in their own right to protect their *individual* rights as members[46]—in such a case a member can bring an action in his own name and may sue on behalf of himself and other members, and the breach of duty owed to an individual shareholder cannot be ratified by a majority of shareholders. Thus in *Pender* v. *Lushington*[47] a shareholder was able to enforce the article giving him a right to vote at meetings and compel the directors to record his vote.[48] Similarly, actions for damages by shareholders in their own right do not come within the rule. Thus where the defendant owes a duty to the shareholder personally, no restrictions apply.[49]

[43] *Smith* v. *Croft* [1986] 1 W.L.R. 580.
[44] *Jaybird Group Ltd.* v. *Greenwood* [1986] BCLC 319.
[45] [1967] Ch. 254, *ante*, p. 400.
[46] *Per* Sir Geo. Jessel M.R. in *Pender* v. *Lushington* (1877) 6 Ch.D. 70 at pp. 80, 81.
[47] (1877) 6 Ch.D. 70.
[48] See also *Ngurli* v. *McCann* (1954) 90 C.L.R. 425, as explained in *Provident International Corpn.* v. *International Leasing Corpn. Ltd.* (1969) 89 W.N. (Pt. 1) (N.S.W.) 370.
[49] *R.P. Howard Ltd.* v. *Woodman, Matthews & Co.* [1983] Com.L.R. 100.

Circumstances in which an individual member can sue in his own name include actions to prevent:

(1) the company from acting illegally or contrary to the memorandum[50];
(2) proposed acts where a special majority is required and has not been obtained[51];
(3) the company from acting contrary to its articles.

It used to be thought that where the wrong complained of damaged the rights of individual members, in the sense of lowering the value of their shares, as well as being a breach of duty to the company, the individual members could sue for the damage to themselves as proper plaintiffs and so avoid the rule in *Foss* v. *Harbottle*. One member could thus sue on behalf of the others in a *representative action*. In the *Prudential* case[52] the minority shareholder used this form of action in addition to the derivative action. The claim was based on the loss suffered by the shareholders as result of the directors' alleged fraud on the company. Because the company had lost money, the shareholders' profit expectations had been diminished. This argument failed, however, in the Court of Appeal. The alleged loss to the shareholders was neither separate nor distinct from that suffered by the company. Only one loss had occurred and only one action could be allowed. Such actions would "subvert" the rule in *Foss* v. *Harbottle*. However, if the payment of damages to the company would not compensate the shareholders for the loss they have suffered *e.g.* because as a result of the directors' breach of duty the shareholders' former company has been acquired by another at a lower value than would otherwise have occurred, a representative action may still be brought.[53]

The rule does not apply where a shareholder relies on a statutory right, *e.g.* a right to have the register of members rectified under section 359.

[50] *Per* Lord Campbell L.C. in *Simpson* v. *Westminster Palace Hotel* (1860) 8 H.L.C. 712, 11 E.R. 608 at p. 610; *Russell* v. *Wakefield Waterworks Co.* (1875) L.R. 20 Eq. 474, at p. 481. See also ss.35(3) and 35A(4), *ante*, Chap. 6.
[51] *Edwards* v. *Halliwell* [1950] 2 All E.R. 1064 (C.A.).
[52] *Ante*, p. 441.
[53] *Heron International Ltd.* v. *Lord Grade* [1983] BCLC 244, 262 *per* Lawton L.J.

MAJORITY RULE AND MINORITY PROTECTION

Majority rule

The members of a company can express their wishes at general meetings by voting for or against the resolutions proposed. However, the will of the majority of the members usually prevails and if the appropriate majority is obtained a resolution binds all the members, including those who voted against it. Sometimes the majority is a simple majority and sometimes it is a three-quarters majority—for example, an ordinary resolution is a resolution passed by a simple majority of the votes of the members entitled to vote and voting; a special resolution is a resolution passed by a three-quarters majority of the votes of such members.[54] This can be said to be the first example of what is called "majority rule."

Further, it should be remembered that, subject to a few restrictions, the articles of a company, which constitute a contract binding the company and the members, can be altered by special resolution.[55]

Another example of majority rule, as we have seen, is the rule in *Foss* v. *Harbottle*, by which, subject to certain exceptions, if a wrong to a company is alleged, or if there is an alleged irregularity in its internal management which is capable of confirmation by a simple majority of the members, the court will not interfere at the suit of a minority of the members.[56]

Minority protection

Both under the general law and under the Companies and other Acts there is some protection of the minority of the members against the acts of the majority.

Examples of minority protection are:—

(1) Under the general law, the doctrine that the majority of the members must not commit a fraud on the minority but must act bona fide for the benefit of the company as a whole.[57]

[54] *Ante*, p. 338.
[55] *Ante*, p. 90.
[56] *Ante*, p. 435.
[57] *Ante*, p. 432.

(2) The other exceptions to the rule in *Foss* v. *Harbottle*,[58] in which cases an individual member may bring a minority shareholders' action.

(3) The various sections intended to protect a minority of members. Some apply on a general basis, thus under sections 122 and 124 of the Insolvency Act 1986[59] a member can petition the court to wind up the company on the ground that it is just and equitable that the company be wound up. And under section 459[60] of the Companies Act a member can petition the court for other relief where the company's affairs are being conducted in an unfairly prejudicial manner to some or all of the members, including himself. Other minority sections enable a number of shareholders to challenge the majority on specific issues. For example, under section 5, dissentient holders of 15 per cent. of the issued shares can apply to the court for cancellation of an alteration of objects.[61] Again, under section 127, where class rights are varied in pursuance of a clause in the articles, dissentient holders of 15 per cent. of the issued shares of the class can apply for cancellation of the variation.[62] Finally, under sections 442 and 443,[63] 200 members or the holders of one-tenth of the issued shares can apply to the Department of Trade and Industry for an investigation of the company's affairs or of the ownership of the company.

Some of these minority sections will now be examined in detail.

Winding up by the Court on the "Just and Equitable" Ground

Under sections 122 and 124 of the Insolvency Act 1986 a contributory may petition that a company be wound up by the court and where the court is of opinion that it is just and equitable that the company should be wound up, the court may order winding up.

[58] *Ante*, p. 438.
[59] *Infra*.
[60] *Post*, p. 457.
[61] *Ante*, p. 72.
[62] *Ante*, p. 268.
[63] *Post*, p. 474.

A member of a company is a contributory, and it has been held that a holder of fully paid-up shares is a contributory.[64] Thus in appropriate circumstances even a single member can petition for a winding up. We shall see[65] that section 124 of the 1986 Act generally prevents a contributory from petitioning unless he has held his shares for at least six months.

In petitioning for a winding up on the just and equitable ground a member is not confined to such circumstances as affect him as a shareholder, *i.e.* he is not confined to cases where his position as a shareholder has been worsened by the action of which he complains; he is entitled to rely on any circumstances of justice or equity which affect him in his relations with the company or with the other shareholders,[66] although it may be otherwise on a petition under section 459. The relationship between petitions for winding up and those under section 459 is dealt with *post*.[67]

The court will not, as a rule, order a winding up on a contributory's petition unless he alleges in the petition, and proves at the hearing, at least to the extent of a prima facie case, that there will be assets for distribution among the shareholders or that some disadvantage would accrue to him by virtue of his membership which could be avoided or minimised,[68] a purely private advantage will not suffice.[69] The reason is that unless there are such assets the contributory has no interest in a winding up. The courts will not normally strike out a petition before the hearing on that basis, however, unless it has no doubts about the matter. Thus even where the company's only asset was a non-assignable lease with no clear market value the judge let the petition go to trial since it might have been of some value to the company.[70] Further, a

[64] *Re National Savings Bank Assocn.* (1866) L.R. 1 Ch.App. 547; *Walker and Others, Petitioners* (1894) 2 S.L.T. 230 and 397 (O.H.).

[65] *Post*, Chap. 27.

[66] *Ebrahimi* v. *Westbourne Galleries Ltd.* [1973] A.C. 360.

[67] p. 467.

[68] *Re Rica Gold Washing Co.* (1879) 11 Ch.D. 36 (C.A.); *Re Martin Coulter Enterprises Ltd.* [1988] BCLC 12; *Re Instrumentation Electrical Services Ltd.* (1988) 4 BCC 301.

[69] *Re Chesterfield Catering Co. Ltd.* [1976] 3 All E.R. 294. If the petitioner is also a creditor and the company is insolvent the petition may be amended to one seeking a winding up on the grounds of insolvency: *Re Commercial and Industrial Insulations Ltd.* [1986] BCLC 191.

[70] *Re Martin Coulter Enterprises Ltd.* [1988] BCLC 12.

contributory's petition which is opposed by the majority of the contributories will usually not be granted except where the conduct of the majority is something of which the minority have a right to complain,[71] or the main object of the company has failed.[72] The petitioner need not establish that the other members have not acted bona fide in the interests of the company.[73] If directors who are not contributories wish to bring a petition they must be acting unanimously.[74]

An order for winding up on the just and equitable ground will be made in the following circumstances, some of which do not involve oppression of the minority:

(1) Where the main object of the company has failed or the company is engaging in acts which are entirely outside what can fairly be regarded as having been within the general intention or common understanding of the members when they became members.[75]

A company was formed to acquire the English portion of the aircraft business of M. Blériot, a well-known airman. M. Blériot refused to carry out the contract. *Held*, the company should be wound up because its substratum had gone: *Re Blériot Aircraft Co.* (1916) 32 T.L.R. 253.

A company formed to purchase, charter and work ships and to carry on the business of shipowners lost its only vessel. Its remaining asset was a balance of £363 in the bank. A majority in number and value of shareholders petitioned for compulsory winding up, but a minority of shareholdings petitioned for compulsory winding up, but a minority of shareholders desired to carry on the business as charterers. *Held*, it was just and equitable that the company should be wound up: *Pirie* v. *Stewart* (1904) 6 F. 847.

(2) If the company is a "bubble," *i.e.* there is no bona fide intent on the part of the directors to carry on business in a proper manner.[76]

[71] *Re Middlesborough Assembly Rooms Co.* (1880) 14 Ch.D. 104 (C.A.); *Re Tivoli Freeholds Ltd.* [1972] V.R. 445.

[72] *Re German Date Coffee Co.* (1882) 20 Ch.D. 169; *Pirie* v. *Stewart* (1904) 6 F. 847; *Re Perfectair Holdings Ltd.* (1989) 5 BCC 837; contrast *Cox* v. "*Gosford*" *Ship Co. Ltd.* (1894) 21 R. 334 and *Galbraith* v. *Merito Shipping Co. Ltd.*, 1947 S.C. 446.

[73] See note 66.

[74] *Re Instrumentation Electrical Services Ltd.* (1988) 4 BCC 301.

[75] See note 72.

[76] *Re London and County Coal Co.* (1866) L.R. 3 Eq. 355.

The court will not order a solvent company to be wound up merely because it is making a loss or is deeply indebted if the majority of the shareholders are against a winding up,[77] or if no meeting of shareholders has been held to consider winding up.[78]

(3) Where the company was formed to carry out a fraud, or to carry on an illegal business.

T.E.B. and his sons were relatives of, and had been employed by, persons who carried on the business of piano manufacturers under the name of J. B. & Sons. They left J. B. & Sons and formed a company called T. E. B. & Sons Ltd. for carrying on a similar business. A prospectus was issued which stated that the price paid for the business was £76,650, when it was really only £1,000 in cash together with £5,000 in shares in the company. Money was subscribed by the public and most of this money found its way into the hands of the persons who were the real, though not the ostensible, promoters. J. B. & Sons obtained an injunction restraining the company from using the name B., and it was found that the company was formed to filch as much trade as possible from J. B. & Sons. Numerous actions were brought against the company for fraud in the prospectus. *Held*, the company should be wound up: *Re Thomas Edward Brinsmead & Sons* [1897] 1 Ch. 45; 406 (C.A.).

Fraudulent misrepresentation in the listing particulars or prospectus[79] or fraud in the course of business with the outside world[80] are not, by themselves, grounds for winding up the company, as the majority of the shareholders may waive the fraud, or there may be a change of management; but fraud in the real, though not the ostensible, object of the company will be such a ground.

(4) Where the mutual rights of the members are not exhaustively defined in the articles, *e.g.* where they entered into membership on the basis of a personal

[77] *Re Suburban Hotel Co.* (1867) L.R. 2 Ch.App. 737 (company making a loss), *Black* v. *United Collieries Ltd.* (1904) 7 F. 18 (company deeply indebted). See also *Galbraith* v. *Merito Shipping Co. Ltd.*, 1947 S.C. 446, *per* Lord Mackay, at p. 458.

[78] *Cox* v. "*Gosford*" *Ship Co. Ltd.* (1894) 21 R. 334; *Scobie* v. *Atlas Steel Works Ltd.* (1906) 8 F. 1052.

[79] *Re Haven Gold Mining Co.* (1882) 20 Ch.D. 151 (C.A.).

[80] *Re Medical Battery Co.* [1894] 1 Ch. 444.

> relationship involving mutual confidence or an understanding as to the extent to which each is to participate in the management of the company's business, and that confidence is not maintained or the petitioner is excluded from the management.

From about 1945 E. and N. were partners in a carpet dealing business with an equal share in the management and profits. In 1958 they formed a private company to take the business over. E. and N. were the first directors and each held 500 £1 shares. The articles provided that shares could not be transferred without the directors' consent. Later, N.'s son, G., was appointed a director and E. and N. each transferred 100 shares to him. The company made good profits which were all distributed by way of directors' remuneration, *i.e.* no dividends were paid. After a disagreement between E. and N., with whom G. sided, N. and G. at a general meeting removed E. as director by ordinary resolution under section 184, and thereafter excluded him from the conduct of the company's business. E. petitioned for an order under section [122(*g*) of the Insolvency Act 1986] that the company be wound up on the ground that it was just and equitable. *Held*, (by the House of Lords) that it was just and equitable that the company be wound up. After a long association in partnership, during which he had had an equal share in the management and profits. E. had joined in the formation of the company; the inference was indisputable that he and N. had done so on the basis that the character of the association would, as a matter of personal faith, remain the same; and E. had established that N. and G. were not entitled, in justice and equity, to make use of their legal powers of expulsion. Furthermore E. was unable to dispose of his interest in the company without the consent of N. and G.: *Ebrahimi* v. *Westbourne Galleries Ltd.* [1973] A.C. 360.

Per Lord Wilberforce at pp. 374, 375: " . . . there has been a tendency to create categories or headings under which cases must be brought if the [just and equitable] clause is to apply. This is wrong. Illustrations may arise but general words should remain general and not be reduced to the sum of particular instance."

And at p. 379: "The words [just and equitable] are a recognition of the fact that a limited company is more than a mere legal entity, with a personality in law of its own: that there is room in company law for recognition of the fact that behind it, or amongst it, there are individuals, with rights, expectations and obligations inter se which are not necessarily submerged in the company structure. That structure is defined by the Companies Act and by the articles of association by which shareholders agree to be bound. In most companies and in most contexts, this definition is sufficient and exhaustive, equally so whether the company is large or small. The 'just and equitable' provision does not . . . entitle one party to disregard the obligation he assumes by entering a company, nor the court to dispense him from it. It does, as equity always does, enable the court to subject the exercise of legal rights to equitable considerations; considerations, that is, of a personal character arising between one individual and another, which may make it unjust, or inequitable, to insist on legal rights, or to exercise them in a particular way.

It would be impossible, and wholly undesirable, to define the circumstances in which these considerations may arise. Certainly the fact that the company is a small one, or a private company, is not enough. There are very many of these where the association is a purely commercial one, of which it can safely be said that the basis of association is adequately and exhaustively laid down in the articles. The superimposition of equitable considerations requires something more [than the fact that the company is a small one, or a private company], which typically may include one, or probably more, of the following elements: (i) an association formed or continued on the basis of a personal relationship, involving mutual confidence—this element will often be found where a pre-existing partnership has been converted into a limited company; (ii) an agreement, or understanding, that all, or some (for there may be 'sleeping members'), of the shareholders shall participate in the conduct of the business; (ii) restriction on the transfer of the members' interest in the company—so that if confidence is lost, or one member removed from management, he cannot take out his stake and go elsewhere."

Ebrahimi v. *Westbourne Galleries* was applied in *Re A. & B.C. Chewing Gum Ltd.*,[81] where the petitioners held one-third of the company's shares on the basis that they should have equal control with the two individual respondents, who were brothers and directors of the company and owned the other two-thirds of the shares. To achieve equality of control, the articles were altered so as to provide, *inter alia*, that the petitioners could appoint and remove a director representing them, and that decisions at board meetings should be unanimous. The petitioners, the respondents and the company also signed and sealed a shareholders' agreement setting out the way in which the day to day business was to be conducted. The respondents refused to recognise the petitioner's removal of their director and the appointment of another in his place. This was not a case of one side making use of its legal rights to the prejudice of another

[81] [1975] 1 W.L.R. 579.

—the petitioners were excluded from their legal and contractual rights. Their right to management participation was repudiated.

Weinberg and Rothman were the sole shareholders in and directors of a company, with equal rights of management and voting power. After a time the became bitterly hostile to one another and disagreed about the appointment of important servants of the company. All communications between them were made through the secretary. The company made large profits in spite of the disagreement. *Held*, mutual confidence had been lost between W. and R. and the company should be wound up: *Re Yenidje Tobacco Co. Ltd.* [1916] 2 Ch. 426 (C.A.).

Whether it is just and equitable to wind up a company depends on facts which exist at the time of the hearing and a petitioner is confined to heads of complaint set out in his petition.[82]

It is a matter therefore for the petitioner to establish mutual confidence and/or entitlement to management participation. If he can establish neither, then the matter will be left to be dealt with under the company's articles.[83] Such confidence or entitlement may be shown either by the very nature of the company and the relationship between the member/directors, as in a quasi-partnership company similar to that in the *Ebrahimi* case, *supra*, or by representations being made to the petitioner to a similar effect.[84] The remedy is even available to someone who is part contingent creditor and part contingent shareholder, *i.e.* a co-venturer with capital at stake who has a right to take shares, and who has been wrongfully excluded from the management he was intended to have, although it will not be available if he is pursuing a separate action for damages based on the same facts.[85]

If the petitioner can establish that the affairs of the company are not being managed in a proper manner then if the petition is not due to be heard for some time, the court

[82] *Re Fildes Bros. Ltd.* [1970] 1 All .R. 923.
[83] *Re A Company* (1988) 4 BCC 80.
[84] *Tay Bok Choon* v. *Tachansan Sdn. Bhd.* (1987) 3 BCC 132 (P.C.).
[85] *Re A Company* (1987) 3 BCC 575.

will appoint a receiver[86] to manage the company's affairs to preserve the status quo and avoid any prejudice to either side. The jurisdiction is exercised by analogy with partnership law.[87]

A shareholder is not entitled to a winding-up order on the "just and equitable" ground if his object is not a company purpose but the securing for himself of an advantage in a question between himself and other shareholders.[88] But he will not be barred even if he is himself guilty of misconduct if that is not the cause of the breakdown in confidence.[89]

If, in the case of a contributories' petition, the court is of opinion that it is just and equitable that the company should be wound up and some other remedy, *e.g.* accepting an offer to purchase his shares, or seeking an order under sections 459–461, *post*, is available to the petitioners, the court *must* nevertheless making a winding-up order unless it is of the opinion that the petitioners are acting unreasonably in not pursuing the other remedy: Insolvency Act 1986 section 125(2).

In *Re A Company*,[90] Warner J. decided that where the petitioner had a potential claim under section 459, that did not making it unreasonable for him to maintain a claim for a winding up order since it was not plain and obvious that the relief that he would get at the hearing would be relief under section 459. The question would be resolved by the judge at the hearing. Even if the winding up petition was damaging to the company it did not follow that a petitioner claiming his rights as a quasi-partner was being unreasonable in preventing a petition. The position is even clearer where the court has already refused an application under section 459.[91]

With regard to a bona fide offer being made by the other members under the articles for the petitioner's shares, *i.e.* at a valuation by an independent valuer, the Court of Appeal in

[86] Under s.37 of the Supreme Court Act 1981.
[87] *Re A Company* [1987] BCLC 133.
[88] *Anglo-American Brush etc. Corpn. Ltd.* v. *Scottish Brush etc. Co. Ltd.* (1882) 9 R. 972.
[89] *Vujnovich* v. *Vunovich* (1989) 5 BCC 740 (P.C.).
[90] (1989) 5 BCC 18.
[91] *Vujnovich* v. *Vujnovich* (1989) 5 BCC 740.

Re Abbey Leisure Ltd.,[92] overruling the judge below and other earlier decisions, decided that this was not an automatic reason for striking out the winding up petition. There was nothing unreasonable in the petitioner refusing to accept the risk that a valuer's decision might apply a discount for his minority shareholding, since the machinery in a winding up to determine claims against the company was preferable to their worth being estimated by an accountant. If the essence of the decision to allow petitions based on equitable considerations in *Ebrahimi* v. *Westbourne Galleries Ltd.*[93] was that the company's constitution, *e.g.* as to dismissal of a director might be overriden, then it could be likewise equitable to ignore the shares valuation provisions in the articles.

Alternative Remedy for Unfairly Prejudicial Conduct

Section 210 of the 1948 Act, now repealed, provided that any member who complained that the affairs of the company were being conducted in a manner oppressive to some part of the members, including himself, could petition for an order under that section.

That section however suffered from several drawbacks. It required proof of oppression sufficient to justify putting the company into liquidation. This oppression had to be continuous.[94] The conduct had to be "a visible departure from the standards of fair dealing,"[95] or "burdensome, harsh and wrongful."[96] Future oppression could not be anticipated.[97] In addition only one of three remedies could be sought and this had to be specified in advance in the petition. Economic oppression[98] and oppressive conduct of affairs[99] were, however, held to justify a petition. But allegations of negligence did not suffice.[1]

[92] [1990] BCC 60.
[93] [1973] A.C. 360, *ante*.
[94] *Re Jermyn Street Turkish Baths Ltd.* [1971] 1 W.L.R. 1042 (C.A.).
[95] *Elder* v. *Elder and Watson*, 1952 S.C. 49, 55.
[96] *Meyer* v. *Scottish C.W.S. Ltd.*, 1958 S.C.(H.L.) 40, 47; [1959] A.C. 324, 342.
[97] *Re Five Minute Car Wash Service Ltd.* [1966] 1 W.L.R. 745.
[98] *Meyer* v. *Scottish C.W.S. Ltd.* [1959] A.C. 324.
[99] *Re H.R. Harmer Ltd.* [1959] 1 W.L.R. 62 (C.A.).
[1] *Re Five Minute Car Wash, etc., ante.*

Above all the section was too closely allied to the rules regulating liquidation. In 1980 it was repealed and replaced by what are now sections 459 to 461 of the 1985 Act.[2]

Under section 459 any member[3] of the company can petition the court for an order on the ground that the affairs of a company are being or have been conducted in a manner which is unfairly prejudicial to the interests of its members generally or of some part of the members (including at least himself) or that any actual or proposed act or omission of the company (including an act or omission on its behalf) is or would be so prejudicial.[4]

The reference to all of the members being affected, as distinct from some part of the members, was added by a 1989 Act amendment, to avoid confusion caused by conflicting decisions on whether if all the members were affected a petition would lie.[5]

If the company is a small private company all the members should be joined as respondents since they may well be affected by the petition. This might not be the case in a larger company, however.[6] Unlike a derivative action the petitioner cannot ask for an indemnity against costs[7] but the court may in appropriate circumstances appoint a receiver pending a full hearing of the petition.[8]

Meaning of unfairly prejudicial conduct

The alleged conduct may be past, present or future.[9] It may be by an act or omission and be by an agent (*e.g.* the directors). There is no definition of what is "unfairly prejudicial" conduct.

[2] For details of s.210, see the twelfth edition of this work.

[3] A creditor cannot petition under s.459. The Secretary of State may, however, do so following an investigation, *post*, s.460. Executors of members may also bring a petition: s.459(2). A person who has assented to registration as a shareholder is a member for the purpose of presenting a petition: *Re Nuneaton Borough Association Football Club Ltd.* (1989) 5 BCC 377.

[4] s.459(1). This remedy is not available to an employee but only to members: *Re A Company* [1986] BCLC 391.

[5] *Re A Company* [1988] 1 W.L.R. 1068, *cf. Re Sam Weller Ltd.* (1989) 5 BCC 810.

[6] *Re A Company* (1987) 3 BCC 375.

[7] *Ante*, p. 445 *Re A Company* [1987] BCLC 82.

[8] *Re A Company* [1987] BCLC 133.

[9] See, *e.g. Re Kenyon Swansea Ltd.* (1987) 3 BCC 259.

It is clearly wider than oppression and is no longer allied to the rules for winding-up so that there is no compelling reason for the courts to insist that such conduct must be continuous.

Clearly the conduct must be both unfair and prejudicial. The early decisions suggested that a restricted interpretation would be given to this phrase. Thus in *Re A Company*,[10] the judge rejected a petition by the executors of a will for infant shareholders who wished to sell their shares to release funds for the beneficiaries. Although the directors had refused to consent to the sale (it was a private company) the petition failed because the conduct did not affect the petitioners *qua* shareholders but as executors. The judge also thought that no petition could be brought unless the act complained of had affected the value of the petitioners' shareholding.

In that case, the judge justified the restriction *qua* shareholder, by giving the example of a shareholder who lives next door to company property which is developed in a way detrimental to his property. However, suppose the conduct affects a shareholder as an employee or director? In the classic case we have been dealing with in the previous section, of the exclusion of a director from management in a company formed on the basis of management participation, can such an exclusion amount to unfairly prejudicial conduct for the purposes of a section 459 petition? In *Re Westbourne Galleries Ltd.*[11] the petitioner failed under section 210 of the 1948 Act (even though he succeeded in winding up the company). Would he have succeeded under section 459?

In *Re A Company*,[12] Vinelott J. said that he thought it unlikely that such persons were intended to be excluded from section 459, even though it would not strictly affect his rights as a shareholder. In *Re R.A. Noble & Sons (Clothing) Ltd.*[13] Nourse J. adopted the following observations of Slade J. in *Re Bovey Hotel Ventures Ltd.*,[14] as to the scope of "unfairly prejudicial" conduct: (1) all cases successful under section 210 of the 1948 Act would fall within section 459, and section 459

[10] [1983] BCLC 126. See also *Re Carrington Viyella plc*, *The Financial Times*, February 16, 1983.
[11] [1973] A.C. 360, *ante*, p. 453.
[12] [1983] BCLC 151, 158.
[13] [1983] BCLC 273.
[14] Unreported, July 31, 1981.

could include cases which would not have succeeded under section 210; (2) it would be sufficient for a member to show that the value of his shareholding had been seriously diminished or at least seriously jeopardised by a course of conduct by those who had *de facto* control of the company; (3) the test of unfairness is objective—there is no need to show any conscious knowledge on the part of the controller that it was unfair, or any other evidence of bad faith. It would be a question of whether a reasonable bystander would regard it as unfairly prejudicial.

Nourse J. then accepted that exclusion from management participation could amount to unfairly prejudicial conduct in cases such as *Re Westbourne Galleries*, even though the value of the petitioner's shareholding would not have been seriously diminished. Financial hardship of that type was not necessary. However, in *Coulson, Sanderson and Ward Ltd.* v. *Ward*,[15] Slade L.J. considered that mere exclusion from management participation would not necessarily found a petition under section 459 since what was being complained of was the acts of the directors *inter se* and not the conduct of the affairs of the company.

In *Re A Company*,[16] Hoffman, J. considered that exclusion from a "legitimate expectation" of taking part in a company's long term management would be unfairly prejudicial, and in *Re A Company*[17] he said that in each such case the question was whether the terms on which the relationship came to an end were unfairly prejudicial to any of the participants. More recently, in *Re Ringtower Holdings plc*,[18] Peter Gibson J. accepted that if management participation was a legitimate expectation then its demise could found an unfairly prejudicial petition.

Whatever the position may be in relation to management exclusion cases there is no doubt that in other areas the restrictions of the early cases have not been continued. In *Re A Company*[19] Hoffman J. allowed a petition to proceed where the directors of a private company had made an inaccurate

[15] *The Financial Times*, October 18, 1985.
[16] [1986] BCLC 376.
[17] [1986] BCLC 362.
[18] (1989) 5 BCC 82.
[19] [1986] BCLC 382.

statement to their shareholders in recommending acceptance of a bid from another company owned by them. It was unfair conduct because it affected the shareholders' right to sell their shares to a higher bidder and it affected them *qua* member because one of the interests of a shareholder was in being able to sell his shares at the best price. The judge rejected the argument that it only affected them in their capacity as vendors of the shares.

In some cases the judges have adopted the "legitimate expectation" approach, adopted by Hoffman J., *supra*. Thus in *Re Blue Arrow plc*,[20] Vinelott J., although taking into consideration the wider equitable rights of the petitioner, rejected a petition by the president of a company when the articles were altered to allow her to be removed by a majority of the directors since she had no legitimate expectation that this would not happen on the company becoming a public company.

In most cases it is, however, a question of whether particular actions can be regarded as both unfair and prejudicial. In *Re D.R. Chemicals Ltd.*,[21] whilst the action of a majority shareholder/director in allotting shares to himself to increase his shareholding from 60 per cent. to 96 per cent. was not only a breach of the pre-emption rules of the Companies Act[22] but was also a "blatant case" of unfairly prejudicial conduct, the fact that after that date the minority director/shareholder was paid no remuneration was not since he took no further part in the running of the company. Similarly, in *Re Ringtower Holdings plc*[23] late presentation of accounts was regarded as non-prejudicial and where pre-emption provisions in the articles were deleted and the company re-registered as a private company as part of a management buy-out by the majority, this was not unfair to the minority since the offer was available to them even though it might be prejudicial since they would be locked into the company if they refused the offer.

The conduct complained of must be unfair to the petitioner[24] and it must relate to the way in which the affairs were

[20] [1987] BCLC 586. See also *Re Posgate and Denby Agencies Ltd.* (1986) BCC 99, 352.
[21] (1989) 5 BCC 39.
[22] *Ante*, p. 165.
[23] (1989) 5 BCC 82. See also *Re A Company* (1989) 5 BCC 792.
[24] *Re Piccadilly Radio plc* (1989) 5 BCC 692.

conducted or be attributable to an act or omission on the part of the company and not from the acts of a shareholder carried out in a personal capacity outside the course of the company's business, *e.g.* as a creditor.[25]

If the conduct of the controller is prima facie "above board" it may still, because of surrounding circumstances, be "unfairly prejudicial" for the purposes of section 459.

L owned one third of the shares of a company and was a director. He was removed from his directorship by the other two shareholders and presented a petition under section 459. An emergency general meeting of the company was then called to increase the company's capital and to give the directors power to allot the new shares. The majority shareholders only intended to issue the shares *pro rata* by way of a rights issue. L sued for an injunction to prevent this rights issue. Harman J. granted the injunction. Although the proposed rights issue was prima facie fair since it would not alter the balance, it might in certain circumstances amount to unfairly prejudicial conduct *e.g.* (i) if it was known that the dissenting shareholder could not afford to take up the offer and this was the reason for making it, or (ii) if the dissenting shareholder was engaged in litigation and the offer was designed to deplete his available funds. The judge also said that when a section 459 petition had been presented the status quo between the parties should be preserved until the hearing except where a change was absolutely essential: *Re A Company*.[26]

In deciding whether to grant a petition under section 459 the conduct of the petitioner is relevant only to the extent either that it might make the conduct of the controllers although prejudicial not unfair, or that it might affect the remedy which the court may make. There is no general rule, as with the old section 210, that the petitioner must come "with clean hands."[27]

X owned 250 an Y Ltd. 750 shares in a company which ran degree courses. Y Ltd. appropriated the students to its own courses and X was dismissed as a director and teacher. He set up another college and took several intending students with him. Nourse J. held that such an act was not a bar to his petition—on the facts there was no justification for Y Ltd.'s action: *Re London School of Electronics*.[28]

[25] *Re A Company* [1987] BCLC 141.
[26] [1985] BCLC 80.
[27] *Cf.* derivative actions, *ante*, p. 439.
[28] [1986] Ch. 211.

It has also been held that a petition can be brought against a former controller of a company for unfairly prejudicial conduct whilst he was a member.[29] Nor is it a bar that some of the shares are then subject of disputed ownership.[30] On the other hand a single petition covering a group of companies has been rejected on the basis that a separate petition must be brought for each company.[31]

Court orders

If the court is satisfied it may make such order as it thinks fit.[32] No specific request need be made in advance.[33] However, the section provides five possible orders[34] which the court may make.[35]

(1) an order regulating the affairs of the company in the future,[36]
(2) an order to restrain the doing or continuing of an act or to rectify an omission,[37]
(3) an order authorising civil proceedings to be brought in the name and on behalf of the company by such persons and on such terms as the court may direct[38];

The respondent to a petition argued that the petitioner was too emotionally involved and vindictive to be given control of any

[29] *Re A Company* [1986] 1 W.L.R. 281.
[30] *Re Garage Door Associates Ltd.* [1984] 1 W.L.R. 35.
[31] *Re A Company* [1984] BCLC 307.
[32] s.461(1).
[33] *Cf. ante*, p. 457.
[34] For interim orders see p. 465, *post*.
[35] s.461(2).
[36] This order could be made under s.210 and was in *Re H.R. Harmer Ltd. ante*. In practice such orders usually now merge with those under (5) below to provide a solution: see, *e.g. Re A Company* (1989) 5 BCC 792; but see also *McGuinness* v. *Bremner plc*, 1988 S.L.T. 891 (O.H.) where such an order was made under this head alone.
[37] This was new in 1980. An instance occurred in *Whyte, Petitioner*, 1984 S.L.T. 330, in which the court pronounced orders restraining a company from holding a meeting, and from passing a resolution removing a director and replacing him with another, and restraining two shareholders from moving or voting in favour of such resolutions.
[38] This was new and intended to alleviate the rule in *Foss* v. *Harbottle*, *ante*.

litigation. The Court of Appeal still authorised proceedings to be brought but subject to certain conditions: (i) protection of creditors; (ii) the control of the litigation to be solely the affair of the petitioner's solicitor to the entire exclusion of the petitioner; (iii) no other legal proceedings to be commenced without legal opinion in support; and (iv) no direct communication between the petitioner and respondent: *Re Cyplon Developments Ltd.*[39]

(4) an order altering the company's memorandum or articles. This will have automatic effect without any resolution of the company usually required for such alterations.[40] Such alterations may not be re-altered without the court's consent.[41]

(5) an order providing for the majority to buy out the minority or a purchase of the minority's shares by the company itself.[42] In the latter case it will arrange for the reduction of capital accordingly;

In making an order as to the purchase of shares the court has very wide powers. In one case it even made an order that the petitioner buy out the controller's shares[43] but that was unusual. Usually the issue is one of the purchase of a minority shareholder's shares. That raises two questions. By what method are those shares to be valued and at what date? As to the former it appears that when the shareholding is in a management participation company (*i.e.* an incorporated partnership such as that in *Re Westbourne Galleries Ltd.*[44]) so that the shares were taken up initially and are still held by the shareholder as part of the management agreement, then the sale is in effect one from an unwilling vendor. The shares should therefore be valued pro rata according to the value of the shares as a whole. On the other hand where the shareholding has simply been acquired as a minority shareholding it should be valued at a discounted value as a minority shareholding.[45] Similarly where the petitioner has chosen to accept the ending of the management participation agreement and to remain as a

[39] Unreported, March 3, 1982.
[40] s.461(4).
[41] s.461(3).
[42] This is an exception to s.143, *ante*, Chap. 10.
[43] *Re Bovey Hotel Ventures Ltd.*, Unrep. June 10, 1982 (C.A.).
[44] *Ante*, p. 453.
[45] *Re Bird Precision Bellows Ltd.* [1985] 3 All E.R. 523 (C.A.); *Re London School of Electronics* [1986] Ch. 211.

minority shareholder his shares will be valued at the discounted price.[46] The court will adopt special valuation rules where the company is in a special position, *e.g.* a football club where the valuation depends upon prestige rather than profits.[47]

Although the date of valuation is prima facie the date of the purchase order[48] this is not a general rule and if the value of the shareholding has been affected by the unfairly prejudicial conduct and the valuation date can be the date when the contract began[49] or the date of the bringing of the petition.[50] The court has no power to make an interim order for payment pending an order for the purchases of the shares except where the only dispute is as to the valuation and the interim order is on the lowest possible contended valuation.[51]

A copy of any order requiring a company to alter its memorandum or articles must be filed with the registrar within 14 days.[52]

Effect of offer to buy out the petitioner

If there is a breakdown in relations between director/shareholders so that one of them brings a petition under section 459 on the basis of unfairly prejudicial conduct, the most likely order that the court will make is that one side, usually the majority shareholders, buy out the other. As we have seen such an order will provide for the method and date of the valuation of the shares. In several cases, however, the majority will have already made an offer to purchase the petitioner's shares under the terms of the company's articles and the court is then faced with the problem as to whether such an offer, providing usually for valuation by an independent valuer such as the company's auditors, in effect settles the matter and accordingly no court order is necessary.

In *Re A Company*[53] the articles actually required the dismissed director to offer his shares to the other shareholders.

[46] *Re D.R. Chemicals Ltd.* (1989) 5 BCC 39.
[47] *Re A Company* (1989) 5 BCC 792.
[48] *Re D.R. Chemicals Ltd.*, *supra*.
[49] *Re OC (Transport) Services Ltd.* [1984] BCLC 251.
[50] *Re London School of Electronics*, *ante*; *Re Cumana Ltd.* [1986] BCLC 430 (C.A.).
[51] *Re A Company* (1987) 3 BCC 41; *Ferguson* v. *Maclennon Solmon Co.* [1990] BCC 702.
[52] s.461(5).
[53] [1987] 1 W.L.R. 102.

The majority intended to invoke this provision and on that basis Hoffman J. refused to allow a section 459 petition based on that dismissal to continue. The articles had made provision in advance for what was to happen if there was a breakdown in relations. As in all such cases it was clear that one party had to leave and on the facts that had to be the petitioner on the terms of the articles. The judge did not, however, confine this principle to cases where the petitioner was obliged to sell his shares, but to all cases where there is a dispute leading to a section 459 petition except where the majority have been guilty of bad faith or plain impropriety or the articles provide an arbitrary or artificial method or valuation.

> "It is almost always clear from the outset that one party will have to buy the other's shares and it is usually equally clear who that party will be. The only real issue is the price of the shares . . . . Not many such petitions go to full hearing. They are usually settled by purchase of the petitioner's shares at a negotiated price. But the presentation of such a petition is a powerful negotiating tactic . . . . In these circumstances it seems to me that if the articles provide a method for determining the fair value of a party's shares, a member seeking to sell his shares upon a breakdown of relations with other shareholders should not ordinarily be entitled to complain of unfair conduct if he has made no attempt to use the machinery provided by the articles . . . . I therefore do not consider that in the normal case of breakdown of a corporate quasi-partnership there should ordinarily be any 'legitimate expectation' that a member wishing to have his shares purchased should be entitled to have them valued by the court rather than the auditors pursuant to the articles.[54]

This approach has since been followed in several cases. In *Re A Company*,[55] such an offer was held to render the section 459 petition inappropriate, and the exact words of Hoffman J. quoted above were applied by Peter Gibson J. in *Re A Company*,[56] by Hoffman J. again in *Re A Company*[57] and Judge Paul Baker QC in *Re Castleburn Ltd.*[58] In the latter case it was also said that if the valuers make a mistake the petitioner

[54] [1987] 1 W.L.R. 102, 110.
[55] (1987) 3 BCC 624.
[56] (1988) 4 BCC 80.
[57] (1989) 5 BCC 218.
[58] (1989) 5 BCC 652.

has a remedy to attack the valuation without resorting to a section 459 petition.

On the other hand the court will still order a valuation under section 461 if the valuer under the articles cannot be seen to be wholly independent of the directors and to have no connection with the unfairly prejudicial conduct.[59] Nor will an offer to purchase some shares prevent a petition where the petitioner claims to be entitled to other shares in the company.[60] Finally, the Court of Appeal in *Re Abbey Leisure Ltd.*,[61] in rejecting the idea that an offer under the articles would automatically bar a winding up petition on the just and equitable ground[62] and reversing Hoffman J. on that point, refused either to confirm or reject the idea that it would automatically bar an unfairly prejudicial petition. The position cannot therefore be regarded as finally settled.

Joint petitions for a just and equitable winding up and the alternative remedy

In practice many petitions based on management exclusion cases seek either a just and equitable winding up under section 122 of the Insolvency Act 1986 (*ante*) or relief under section 459 to 461 as alternatives. Prior to 1980 it was generally easier to obtain a winding-up order (*e.g. Re Westbourne Galleries Ltd.*, *ante*). This may still be the position in some cases today. In *Re R.A. Noble and Sons*,[63] Nourse J. refused to grant a petition under section 459 on the grounds that objectively the management exclusion had not been unfair since it was partly due to the petitioner's disinterest. The judge did, however, make a winding up order since the exclusion had been the substantial cause of the breakdown in mutual confidence. Thus for a winding up the question is whether the management exclusion was a substantial cause of the subjective breakdown of the underlying equitable obligation of mutual trust whereas for

59 *Re Boswell & Co. (Steels) Ltd.* (1989) 5 BCC 145.

60 *Re A Company* (1989) 5 BCC 18.

61 [1990] BCC 60.

62 *Ante*, p. 457.

63 [1983] BCLC 273. See also *Coulson Sanderson & Ward Ltd.* v. *Ward*, *The Financial Times*, October 18, 1985; *Teague, Petitioner*, 1985 S.L.T. 469 (O.H.) (provisional liquidator appointed) and *Re A Company* (1989) 5 BCC 18.

an alternative remedy petition the exclusion must amount to unfairly prejudicial conduct affecting the petitioner *qua* member.[64]

Further, it may be easier to bring a winding up petition rather than a section 459 petition if the majority have made an offer for the petitioner's shares.[65]

INVESTIGATIONS AND POWERS TO OBTAIN INFORMATION

Statutory provision is made for a number of forms of inspection.[66] These comprise investigation of a company's affairs, investigation of the ownership of a company, investigation of share dealings, and inspection of companies' books and papers.

Investigations of a company's affairs

Appointment of inspectors

1. In the case of a company with a share capital, *on the application of not less than 200 members or of members holding not less than one-tenth of the shares issued, or on the application of the company*, the Secretary of State *may* appoint one or more inspectors to investigate the affairs of the company and to report on them. The application must be supported by evidence showing that the applicant or applicants have good reason for requiring investigation. Security, not exceeding £5,000, for the costs of the inquiry, may be required by the Secretary of State (for Trade and Industry): section 431.

An inspector is usually a Queen's Counsel, a Chartered Accountant or an official of the Department of Trade and Industry. In serious cases two inspectors will be appointed.

2. The Secretary of State *shall* appoint an inspector or inspectors *if the court by order*,[67] *declares that an investigation ought to be made*: section 432(1).

[64] Re A Company [1990] BCC 221.

[65] *Re Abbey Leisure Ltd.* [1990] BCC 60.

[66] *e.g.* the investigation into the affairs of House of Fraser Holdings plc, after the disputed take-over of that company.

[67] The procedure in England is to apply to the Companies Court by originating motion under R.S.C., O. 102, r. 4. For Scotland, see R.C. 189.

3. The Secretary of State *may on his own initiative*, appoint inspectors if it appears—

(i) that a company's affairs are being or have been conducted with intent to defraud its creditors or the creditors of any other person or otherwise for a fraudulent or unlawful purpose or in a manner which is unfairly prejudicial to part of its members, or that any actual or proposed act or omission of the company is or would be so prejudicial or that it was formed for a fraudulent or unlawful purpose; or

(ii) that the promoters or the persons managing its affairs have been guilty of fraud, misfeasance or other misconduct towards the company or its members; or

(iii) that the members have not been given all the information as to the company's affairs which they might reasonably expect: section 432(2).

Inspectors appointed under this head may be appointed on the basis that any report they may make is not to be for publication. In such a case the usual rules as to availability and publication (*post*) will not apply: section 432(2A).[68]

If the Secretary of State appoints inspectors under these headings the company has no right to state its case before the inspectors are appointed. The only requirement is that the decision to appoint is made in good faith.[69]

Powers of inspectors

1. An inspector may, if he thinks it necessary, investigate any other body corporate which is or has been either the company's subsidiary[70] or holding company[70] or a subsidiary of its holding company or a holding company of its subsidiary: section 433(1).

2. He may call for the production of documents[71] by past or present officers and agents (including bankers, solicitors and

[68] This is intended to speed up investigations to decide whether any offences have been committed. It is also a result of the House of Fraser Holdings plc investigation, and the unsuccessful attempt by Lohnro plc to have the report published before the Secretary of State was willing to do so: see (1989) 5 BCC 633 (H.L.).

[69] *Norwest Holst Ltd.* v. *Department of Trade* [1978] 3 All E.R. 280.

[70] *Ante*, p. 51.

[71] Documents include information held in an electronic form, *e.g.* on a computer, and the inspectors may require such information in a legible form: section 434(6).

auditors) of the company or related company, whose duty it is to produce to the inspector all documents of or relating to the company or related companies which are in their custody or power, to attend before the inspector when required and to give the inspector all reasonable assistance. These powers extend to persons other than officers or agents if the inspectors consider that they are or may be in possession of any information which they believe to be relevant to the investigation[72]: section 434(1)(2).

3. The inspector may examine any person on oath for the purposes of an investigation: section 434(3).

If an officer or agent refuses to perform his duties under section 434 the inspectors may certify that refusal to the court which may punish him as if he were in contempt of court: section 436.

A solicitor or barrister need not disclose a privileged communication made to him, except as regards the name and address of his client, and a banker need not disclose any information which is confidential by virtue of banking business relating to his customers other than the company unless either the customer consents or the Secretary of State authorises the disclosure: section 452.

An answer given by a person to a question put under powers given by section 434 (or section 446) may be used in evidence against him: section 434(5).

In general all evidence given to an inspector is admissible against him in both subsequent criminal and civil proceedings. This includes unsworn evidence. Section 434(5) is not limited to public interest proceedings brought by a public authority. Thus the section permits the evidence to be used in subsequent proceedings by the company or its liquidator to redress wrongs done to the company, *e.g.* against the company's auditors.[73]

4. An inspector may at any time, and, if directed to do so, must inform the Secretary of State of any matters coming to his knowledge as a result of their investigation: section 437(1A). If matters have come to light which have led to the affair being placed in the hands of the appropriate prosecuting authority the

[72] This could include partners and members of unincorporated associations not covered by s.433, *supra*.

[73] *London and County Securities Ltd.* v. *Nicholson* [1980] 3 All E.R. 861.

Secretary of State may direct the inspector either to take no further steps or to proceed only as directed by him. In such a case no final report will be made unless either the inspectors were appointed by a court order or the Secretary of State so directs: section 437(1B).

It has been held that the inspectors' function is investigatory and not judicial but they must, in view of the consequences which may follow from their report, act fairly and, before they condemn or criticise a person, give him a fair opportunity to answer what is alleged against him.[74] It is sufficient for the inspectors to put to witnesses what has been said against them by other persons or in documents to enable them to deal with those criticisms in the course of the inquiry; it is not necessary for the inspectors to put their tentative conclusions to the witnesses in order to give them an opportunity to refute them.[75]

It has been said[76] that the considerations which are to be borne in mind in respect of an inquiry under the Companies Act are:

(*a*) it is a very special kind of inquiry. It is not a trial. There is no accused, no prospecutor, no charge. It is simply an investigation;

(*b*) there is no one to present a case to the inspector. There is no "counsel for the Commission." The inspector has to do it all himself;

(*c*) the investigation is in private. This is necessary because witnesses may say something defamatory of someone else, and it would be quite wrong for it to be published without the party affected being able to challenge it;

(*d*) the inspectors have to make their report. They should state their findings on the evidence and their opinions on the matters referred to them. They should make it

[74] *Re Pergamon Press Ltd.* [1971] Ch. 388 (C.A.), where the persons who were required to give evidence were not entitled to see the traanscripts of evidence of witnesses. In *Testro Bros. Pty. Ltd.* v. *Tait* (1963) 109 C.L.R. 353, the majority of the High Court of Australia held that the inspector need not, before making a report on the compnay's affairs, give the company an opportunity of answering or explaining matters which, if unanswered or unexplained, might give rise to adverse findings or comment in the report.

[75] *Maxwell* v. *Department of Trade and Industry* [1974] 1 Q.B. 523 (C.A.).

[76] *Per* Lord Denning M.R. in *Maxwell's* case, *ante*, at p. 533.

with courage and frankness, keeping nothing back. Before they condemn or criticise a person they must act fairly by them.

Inspectors' report

The inspectors may make interim reports, and on the conclusion of the investigation they must make a final report to the Secretary of State.

The Secretary of State may send a copy of a report to the company's registered office, and if he thinks fit, may furnish a copy on request and on payment of the prescribed fee to any member of the company or other company dealt with in the report, or to any person whose conduct is referred to in the report, or to the auditors of the company, or to the applicants for the investigation, or to any other person whose financial interests appear to be affected by it, *e.g.* creditors. He may also order the report to be printed and published. Where the appointment was under section 432 in pursuance of a court order, a copy *must* be furnished to the court: section 437. Section 437 has no application where the inspectors were appointed under section 432 on the basis that their report would not be published.[77]

In exercising his decision as to publications the Secretary of State must act reasonably and according to relevant considerations. He is entitled to withhold publication in the public interest if publication would inhibit a criminal investigation and/or prejudice the fair trail of anyone subject to such investigation.[78]

Proceedings on inspectors' report

Section 124A of the Insolvency Act 1986 provides that if it appears to the Secretary of State from the inspectors' report, or from any information obtained under an investigation,[79] that it is expedient in the public interest that the company be wound

[77] *Ante*, p. 469.
[78] *R.* v. *Secretary of State for Trade and Industry, ex p. Lonrho plc* [1989] 1 W.L.R. 525 (H.L.).
[79] *Post*, p. 479.

up, he may present a petition that it be wound up by the court if the court thinks it just and equitable that the company be wound up.[80] No evidence of fraud or misfeasance is necessary.

In addition a minority shareholder may use an inspector's report to support his own petition to wind up the company on the just and equitable ground under section 122(*g*) of the 1986 Act.[81]

If from the report, etc., it appears that civil proceedings ought in the public interest to be brought by any company, section 438 empowers the Secretary of State to bring such proceedings in the name and on behalf of the company. The Secretary of State must indemnify the company against costs or expenses incurred by it in connection with any such proceedings. If civil proceedings are properly brought under this section and there is no evidence to show that the company will be able to pay the defendant's costs if the defence is successful, the defendant is fully protected by the indemnity provision in the section and security cannot be ordered under section 726.[82]

Under section 460 the Secretary of State may bring a petition for an alternative remedy consequent on a report.[83]

Expenses of investigation

The expenses of an investigation of a company's affairs are defrayed in the first instance by the Secretary of State but the following persons are liable to repay him:

(1) any person convicted on a prosecution instituted as a result of the investigation, or ordered to pay the costs of proceedings brought by virtue of section 438, *ante*, may in the same proceedings be ordered to repay;
(2) any company in whose name proceedings are brought is liable to repay in the extent of money or property recovered by it as a result of the proceedings;
(3) a company dealt with by an inspectors' report, where the inspectors were appointed otherwise than of the Secretary of State's own motion and except where it

[80] *Ante*, p. 449.
[81] *Re St. Piran Ltd.* [1981] 3 All E.R. 270.
[82] *Selangor United Rubber Estates Ltd.* v. *Cradock* [1967] 1 W.L.R. 1168.
[83] *Ante*, p. 458.

was the applicant, is liable except so far as the Secretary of State otherwise directs;

(4) the applicants for the investigation, where the inspector was appointed under section 431, *ante*, or section 442(3), *post*, are liable to such extent as the Secretary of State may direct: section 439.

Extension of Secretary of State's powers of investigation

The investigation powers apply to all companies incorporated outside Great Britain which are carrying on business in Great Britain or have at any time carried on business therein, subject to any adaptations the Secretary of State may specify by statutory instrument: section 453. Sections 431, 438, 442 to 445 and 446 do not apply to such companies, however.

Inspection: Investigation of the ownership of a company[84]

Appointment of inspectors

1. Where he considers that there is good reason to do so, the Secretary of State (for Trade and Industry) *may* appoint one or more inspectors to investigate and report on the membership of a company, for the purpose of determining the true persons who are, or have been, financially interested in the success or failure of the company, or able to control or materially influence its policy: section 442(1). The scope of the investigation may be defined either as to time or the matters to be investigated: section 442(2).

2. Unless the application is vexatious, the Secretary of State *must* appoint an inspector, on the application, with regard to particular shares or debentures, of those members who can apply under section 431[85] for an investigation of the company's affairs provided the applicants give security as to costs not greater than £5,000. The appointment shall not exclude from the scope of the investigation any matter stated by the applicants unless the Secretary of State is satisfied that it would be unreasonable to investigate it. The Secretary of State may,

[84] *e.g.* the investigation, by Mr. J. B. Lindon Q.C. of the membership of the Savoy Hotel Limited, *post*, p. 477.

[85] *Ante*, p. 468.

however, refuse to appoint inspectors if the powers to require information as to persons interested in shares (*post*) will be sufficient: section 442(3).

Powers of inspectors. Inspectors' report

An inspector appointed under section 442, above, has the same power as an inspector appointed to investigate the affairs of a company has under sections 431 and 432. Section 437 applies to the report of inspectors appointed under section 442.[86]

In addition, the sections apply in relation to all persons whom the inspector reasonably believes to be or to have been financially interested in the success or failure of the company or related company, or able to control or materially influence its policy. However, the Secretary of State may furnish the company or any person with an abbreviated copy of the report if he is of the opinion that there is good reason for not divulging part of it: section 443(3).

Expenses of investigation

The expenses of an investigation under section 442 are defrayed initially by the Secretary of State but may be recovered in the same way as in an investigation into a company's affairs: section 439, *ante*.

Power to require information as to persons interested in shares, etc.

Where it appears that there is good reason to investigate the ownership of any shares or debentures of a company, and that it is unnecessary to appoint an inspector for the purpose, the Secretary of State (for Trade and Industry) may require any person whom he reasonably believes to have or to be able to obtain any information as to the present and past interests in the shares or debentures and the names and addresses of the persons interested therein and of any persons who act or have

[86] *Ante*, pp. 472 *et seq*.

acted for them in relation to the shares or debentures to give them such information.

A person is deemed to have an interest in a share or debenture if he has a right to acquire or dispose of it or any interest therein, or to vote in respect thereof, or if his consent is necessary for the exercise of any right of other persons interested therein, or if such other persons can be required or are accustomed to exercise their rights in accordance with his instructions.

Failure to give information required under this section, or making a statement known to be false in a material particular, or recklessly making a statement false in a material particular, is punishable by imprisonment or a fine or both: section 444.

Power to impose restrictions on shares, etc.

If the Secretary of State has difficulty in finding out the relevant facts about any shares or debentures, they may direct that the shares or debentures shall be subject to restrictions: section 445. The restrictions prevent transfers and agreements to transfer, the exercise of voting rights, the issue of further shares or debentures in right of the shares or debentures or to the holder thereof, including an agreement to transfer such rights, and, except in a liquidation, payment or agreement to transfer payment of any sums due from the company on the shares or debentures, whether in respect of capital or otherwise, *e.g.* payment of a dividend: section 454.[87]

If an order is made any person aggrieved may appeal to the court for the order to be lifted. The court may only lift an order if it is satisfied either that all the relevant facts about the shares have been disclosed and that no unfair advantage has accrued to anyone by the earlier failure to disclose or the shares are to be transferred for a valuable consideration[88] and the court approves the transfer: section 456(3).

Where an order has been made either the Secretary of State or the company may apply to the court for a further order that the shares be compulsorily transferred free from some or all of

[87] This includes payment on a take-over bid: *Re Ashbourne Investments Ltd.* [1978] 2 All E.R. 418.

[88] This will include, *e.g.* accepting a take-over offer of shares in the offeror company. It is no longer restricted to sales for cash.

the restrictions. The proceeds of a compulsory transfer are to be paid into a separate fund against which the owners can claim, subject to the payment of costs.

Contravention of such restrictions renders the person or company concerned liable to penalties, although a prosecution in England can be instituted only by or with the consent of the Secretary of State: sections 455 and 732.

The Savoy Hotel Investigations

In 1953 there was heavy buying of Savoy Hotel stock on the Stock Exchange. The real buyers were unknown since the buying was through nominees. The object of the buyers was to obtain control of the Savoy Hotel Limited and develop its assets. 224 members of the company applied to the Board of Trade under sections 442 and 444 and Mr. J. B. Lindon Q.C. was appointed to investigate the ownership of the company. From the inspector's interim report,[89] it appeared that Land Securities Investment Trust Limited, of which Mr. Harold Samuel was chairman and principal shareholder, had bought Savoy stock carrying 20 per cent. of the votes of a poll at a general meeting of Savoy Hotel Limited, and Princes Investments Limited, controlled by Mr. Charles Clore, had bought stock carrying nine per cent. of the votes.

The Berkeley Hotel Company Limited was a subsidiary of the Savoy Company, with substantially the same directors, and it would have been possible to make a large immediate profit by turning the Berkeley Hotel into offices. To put the Berkeley Hotel out of the reach of anyone who might obtain control of the Savoy Company, the Savoy directors formed Worcester Buildings Company Limited and sold the Berkley Hotel to the Worcester Company at a price satisfied by the issue to the Berkeley Company of fully paid preferences shares in the Worcester Company. The Worcester Company gave the Berkeley Company a lease of the hotel for 50 years at a rent. The hotel could not be used otherwise than as a hotel without the consent of the Worcester Company. However, the Worcester Company was controlled by a number of ordinary shares of small nominal amount which were issued for cash to the trustees of the Savoy Company's benevolent fund. The cash was provided from the fund, which had been transferred to the trustees. The Board of Trade, under section 432, appointed Mr. E. Milner Holland Q.C. to investigate the affairs of the Savoy Company. His report[90] stated that, on the analogy of *Piercy* v. *Mills & Co.*,[91] the transaction was an invalid use of the powers of management of the Savoy directors, even though they thought they were acting for the benefit of the companies and their shareholders,

[89] Dated November 28, 1953, and published by H.M.S.O.
[90] Dated June 14, 1954, and published by H.M.S.O.
[91] [1920] 1 Ch. 77.

and even though they had legal advice that they could act as they did. The purpose of the transaction was to deny to the majority holding voting control of the Savoy Company the power, by exercise of that control, to cause the Berkeley Hotel to be used otherwise than as a hotel.

Inspection: Investigation of share dealings

Section 446, provides that if it appears to the Secretary of State (for Trade and Industry) that sections 323[92] or 324[93] or 328(3)–(5)[94] (these sections being concerned with penalisation of dealing in options by, and notification of interests of, directors or their spouses or children) may have been contravened, he may appoint one or more competent inspectors to investigate and report to him.

Sections 434 to 437,[95] which impose on officers and agents the duty to assist inspectors, apply with one or two modifications. Thus section 446 applies, *e.g.* to any individual who is, or an officer of a company which is, an authorised person under the Financial Services Act 1986 (see Chap. 19, *post*).

Section 452[96] (savings for lawyers and bankers) applies.

The expenses of such an investigation are dealt with in the same way as with other investigations: section 439, *ante*.

Inspection: Inspection of a company's books and papers

This is dealt with in sections 447 to 451 as follows—

Power of Secretary of State to require production of documents

Section 447 provides that the Secretary of State (for Trade and Industry) may, if he thinks there is good reason to do so, require a company to produce such documents[97] as may be specified.

Without prejudice to any lien he may have, production of documents may be required from any person who appears to be

[92] *Ante*, p. 370.
[93] *Ante*, p. 363.
[94] *Ante*, p. 366.
[95] *Ante*, p. 470.
[96] *Ante*, p. 470.
[97] Documents include information stored on computers and any copies required must be given in a legible form.

in possession of them to any officer or other competent person.[98] Copies or extracts may be taken, and explanations may be required from such person or from present or past officers or employees of the company. If the documents are not produced, the person required to produce may be required to state, to the best of his knowledge and belief, where they are: section 447.

Nothing in that section compels a lawyer to produce a document containing a privileged communication made by or to him: section 452.

Non-compliance with a requirement to produce documents or provide an explanation or make a statement renders the company or person concerned liable to imprisonment or a fine or both. Where a person is charged with failing to produce documents it is a defence for him to prove that they were not in his possession or under his control and that it was not reasonably practicable for him to produce them: section 447.

If a person provides or makes an explanation or statement which he knows to be false, or recklessly provides or makes a false explanation or statement, he is liable to imprisonment or a fine or both: section 451.

Entry and search of premises

If a justice of the peace, or in Scotland the sheriff or a magistrate, is satisfied, on information on oath laid by or on behalf of the Secretary of State or anyone authorised, that there are reasonable grounds for suspecting that there are on any premises any documents, in any form, of which production has been required under any investigation provision, and which have not been produced, he may issue a warrant authorising any constable and any other named person and other constables to enter and search the premises and take possession of any documents either appearing to be such or relevant to the investigation or to take steps to preserve them, or to take copies of them or to require any person named in the warrant to provide an explanation of them or state where they may be found.

[98] Thus such low-key investigations may be undertaken by private firms.

A similar warrant may also be issued if the magistrate etc., is satisfied on information under oath that there are reasonable grounds for believing that an offence has been committed (punishable with at least two years imprisonment), that there are premises on which documents relevant to that offence are kept, that the Secretary of State could require such documents and that such documents might not be produced but might be tampered with.

Any documents of which possession is taken may be retained for three months or, if within that period there are commenced criminal proceedings (being proceedings to which the documents are relevant), until the conclusion of the proceedings.

Penalties are imposed for obstructing the exercise of a right of entry or search, or of a right to take possession of documents: section 448.

Provision for security of information

No information or document obtained under section 447, *ante*, may, without the previous written consent of the company, be published or disclosed, except to a competent authority (including the Secretary of State (for Trade and Industry), his officer, an inspector appointed under the Act, the Lord Advocate, the Director of Public Prosecutions, any constable and any procurator fiscal, any designated authority under the Financial Services Act 1986,[99] the City Panel on Takeovers and Mergers,[1] the Treasury or an officer thereof), unless the publication or disclosure is required, *inter alia*:

(1) with a view to the institution of, or for the purposes of, any criminal proceedings or an application for the disqualification of a director[2];
(2) for the purpose of the examination of any person by an inspector appointed under the Act in the course of his investigation;
(3) for the purpose of enabling the Secretary of State to exercise his functions under the Companies Act, the Company Securities (Insider Dealing) Act 1985, the

[99] Chap. 19, *post*.
[1] Chap. 31, *post*.
[2] *Ante*, p. 360.

Insurance Companies Act 1982, the Insolvency Act 1986 and the Financial Services Act 1986;

(4) for the purposes of any disciplinary proceedings against public servants for misconduct, etc.

Publication or disclosure of any information or document in contravention of the section is punishable by imprisonment or a fine or both: section 449.

The Secretary of State may disclose any information obtained under any of the investigation sections to certain other bodies concerned in financial regulation, *e.g.* the Bank of England and overseas regulatory authorities; and in any other case where it is not restricted by the section concerned: section 451A.

Penalisation of destruction, etc., of company documents

Section 450 provides that an officer of a company or an insurance company, who destroys, mutilates or falsifies, or is privy to the destruction, etc., of a document affecting or relating to the property or affairs of the company is guilty of an offence unless he proves that he did not intend to conceal the state of affairs of the company or to defeat the law. Similarly if he fraudulently parts with, alters or makes an omission in, any such document. The penalty is imprisonment or a fine or both.

Investigation to assist overseas regulatory authorities

The Companies Act 1989 introduced new powers to allow the Secretary of State to compel the divulging of information and documents "for the purpose of assisting an overseas regulatory authority which has requested his assistance in connection with inquiries being carried out by it or in its behalf": section 82 C.A. 1989. These powers are designed to enable the UK to comply with its obligations under various conventions on the mutual co-operation between countries relating to financial markets. As such they apply equally to the investigations into insider dealing set out in Chapter 19.

An overseas regulatory authority is one which is concerned with functions similar to the Secretary of State with regard to companies, financial services, insurance companies, to the Bank of England or any other UK regulatory authority (see Chapter

19, *post*), or to the control of insider dealing, companies or financial services: section 82.

The Secretary of State, or his agent or other competent person, cannot exercise these powers unless he is satisfied that the assistance requested is for the purposes of its regulatory functions, and may take into account when making his decision whether he would be given reciprocal help of this nature, the seriousness of the matter, the public interest and above all whether the alleged breach relates to a law which has no close parallel in the UK or to an asserted jurisdiction which is not recognised by the UK Finally, the Secretary of State may require the overseas authority to contribute towards the costs incurred.

The powers exercisable by the Secretary of State are similar to those given to inspectors appointed under section 432 (company investigation) and 442 (company ownership). Thus they include powers to require the production of documents, the giving of evidence on oath and to require such assistance as the person concerned is reasonably able to give: section 83 C.A. 1989. The standard exemptions for professional privilege are included by section 84, and section 85 imposes criminal sanctions for failure to comply or the giving of false or misleading information.

The restrictions on the disclosure of information so obtained are broadly similar to those relating to domestic investigations under section 449: sections 86 and 87 C.A. 1985.

Chapter 19

INVESTOR PROTECTION

COMPANIES operate their finances largely through the medium of shares and debentures, and public companies, in particular, rely on the marketability of those securities. Company law is, however, for the most part concerned with the legal aspects of shares and debentures from the company's angle—its rights and obligations *vis-à-vis* the issuing and redemption, etc. of company securities, and with the rights of the holders of those investments *vis-à-vis* the company, *e.g.* voting rights. However, there is another area of law which applies to company securities simply because they are investments—the law relating to investor protection. This area of the law is concerned to regulate the conduct of those engaged in the investment industry, either as advisers, market makers or in the marketing process, to regulate the conduct of the markets in various types of investment, including insurance, and to prevent abuses of the system by those with restricted or "inside" knowledge.

Four aspects of the law on investor protection are relevant to company law. Since shares and debentures are investments, regulation of the terms on which they are advertised and, if appropriate, quoted on the Stock Exchange, falls within this area. The legal framework for such issues was the subject of Chapter 7. Secondly, the classical UK take-over by one company of another involves the offeror company making an offer for some or all of the issued shares of the target company. This is an area where orderly conduct of the market and equal treatment of shareholders are regarded as being of paramount concern. The rules relating to such take-overs are the subject of Chapter 31.

This chapter is concerned with the other two areas. First it outlines the general system of regulation of the investment industry, since some of those concerned will be involved in the marketing and market making etc. of company securities. It should be stressed that this is merely an outline of what is a complex area and a subject in its own right distinct from company law. The second part deals with the law relating to insider dealing—*i.e.* the process of dealing in shares or other securities with special "inside" knowledge of their potential value. This is particularly relevant to company law and is contained in a separate Act, the Company Securities (Insider Dealing) Act 1985, part of the 1985 consolidation. The more general rules on investment can be found in the Financial Services Act 1986 which created a new framework for investor protection.

Control of the Investment Industry

The Financial Services Act 1986

To a large extent the control of the investment industry has, until recently, been largely ignored by the law. Certain areas, such as banking and insurance have always been regulated to some degree but the law relating to the marketing and dealing in investments was patchy and inadequate. The Prevention of Fraud (Investments) Act 1958 and its satellite rules, the Licensed Dealers (Conduct of Business) Rules 1983 (formerly of 1960), applied in practice to very few dealers and were often found to be wanting. Other financial centres, such as New York or Paris, created statutory regulatory authorities to deal with the area of investor protection.

In the United Kingdom Professor Gower was commissioned to write a report, the Review of Investor Protection.[1] In due course a white paper "Financial Services in the United Kingdom"[2] was published and the resulting legislation is contained in the Financial Services Act 1986. The 1958 Act and its machinery (most of its criteria were dispensed with by 10 General Permissions to issue circulars etc.) were repealed. The solution for the United Kingdom has been to impose a statutory form of self-regulation upon the investment industry which is almost but not quite a contradiction in terms.

[1] 1984 Cmnd. 9125.
[2] 1985 Cmnd. 9432.

All references to sections in this part of this chapter are to the Financial Services Act 1986, unless otherwise stated.

Initial control on investment personnel

Section 3 provides the central plank in the new system of regulation. No person shall carry on, or purport to carry on, investment business in the United Kingdom unless he is either an authorised person or an exempted person. Schedule 1 elaborately defines the concepts of investment and investment business for this purpose. There are 11 classes of investments, including shares and debentures. Investment business includes dealing, arranging deals, managing or advising on investments—although certain activities, *e.g.* employee share schemes, are excluded. Breach of section 3 is a criminal offence,[3] and there are civil penalties on deals made in breach—*e.g.* the contract is voidable and money paid is recoverable.[4–5]

Authorised persons

Authorised persons only may carry on an investment business. There are in fact five ways a person may be so authorised.

(1) By being a member of a recognised self-regulating organisation (SRO). SROs are organisations recognised as such for the purpose of the Act which have their own rules and codes of conduct which can be enforced on their members. SROs must apply for recognition and their rules and procedure(s) must be of a sufficiently high standard as to ensure an adequate level of protection for investors, bearing in mind the nature of the investment business, the kinds of investors and the costs of compliance.[6] If necessary their rules can be altered by the court. There are five SRO's currently recognised. The one most closely connected with corporate securities is the Securities Association (T.S.A.).

[3] s.4. See also s.200 which provides offences relating to false claims and the supply of false information in relation to authorisation, etc.
[4–5] ss.5, 6.
[6] ss.7–14, and Sched. 2.

Traditionally, dealings on the Stock Exchange have centred round jobbers, *i.e.* market makers, and brokers who act as intermediaries between the investor and the jobber. Since 1986, however, that distinction has broken down, and multi-media financial institutions have arisen which can be advisers, dealers and market makers at the same time. Special rules have had to be devised to prevent the obvious conflicts of interest.

(2) By being a member of a recognised professional body.[7] In effect such recognised professional bodies, *e.g.* The Institute of Chartered Accountants, are equivalent to SROs for this purpose and subject to a similar process of recognition, etc.

(3) By being an authorised insurance company,[8] registered friendly society,[9] or the operator or trustee of a recognised collective investment scheme (unit trust).[10]

(4) By direct authorisation.[11] Any person or company can apply for direct authorisation. The grant, refusal or withdrawal of such authorisation is subject to an appeal to the Financial Services Tribunal established by the Act.[12]

(5) By being authorised in another member state of the European Community.[13]

Exempted persons

There are five categories of exempted persons or institutions which would otherwise be required to be authorised to conduct investment business. These categories can be extended or restricted by regulations.[14] The exempted persons are:

(1) the Bank of England[15];

(2) recognised investment exchanges.[16] These include the Stock Exchange and other financial exchanges. It should be remembered that members of these exchanges will need to be authorised persons, only the exchanges themselves are exempt;

[7] ss.15–21 and Sched. 3.
[8] s.22.
[9] s.23.
[10] s.24. See p. 488, *post*.
[11] ss.25–30.
[12] See p. 489, *post*.
[13] ss.31–34.
[14] s.46.
[15] s.35.
[16] ss.36–41 and Sched. 4.

(3) Lloyd's and their underwriters are exempt for the purpose of insurance business carried on there.[17] This aspect of the securities industry is governed by Lloyd's itself under a separate statute;

(4) listed money market institutions, approved by the Bank of England and the Treasury[18];

(5) appointed representatives, *i.e.* employees etc. of employers who take responsibility for them, (*e.g.* insurance salesmen)[19];

(6) various public officials exercising statutory functions, *e.g.* the official receiver.[20]

Subsequent control of investment business

Following changes made by the Companies Act 1989, the SIB (to whom overall control of the system has been delegated, *post*) promulgates general principles which may give rise to disciplinary proceedings only and requires SROs to adopt those for similar purposes. Beneath those, there are various rules laid down by the SIB governing, *e.g.* the conduct of business, which are designated as core rules to be adopted by all SROs. Below that second tier the SROs themselves have codes of practice, breach of which does not in itself constitute a breach of a rule but is evidence of such a breach. This three tier system provides the control of those authorised by the SROs.[21] These changes were made in an attempt to simplify the various rule books. There is some flexibility built into the system.

Section 47 of the Act creates criminal offences for deliberately or recklessly making a misleading statement or forecast and for deliberately engaging in misleading practices as to the market or value of an investment. This had been explained in Chapter 7 above. Rules can be made to allow cancellation of an investment agreement,[22] for the notification of certain events,[23]

[17] s.42.
[18] s.43. and Sched. 5.
[19] s.44.
[20] s.45.
[21] ss.47A, 47B, 63A, 63B, 63C.
[22] s.51.
[23] s.52.

for indemnity[24] and as to the handling of client's money.[25] Unsolicited investment calls are also controlled and can amount to a criminal offence.[26] There is also provision for the establishment of a compensation fund to protect investors in the event of an investment business being unable to meet any claims under the Act.[27]

Investment advertisements are also strictly controlled and limited to authorised and exempt persons.[28] In general those which may be made by way of exemption from that general rule are listing agreements, prospectus-linked advertisements and other cases where no prospectus would need to be issued if an offer of unlisted shares was being made.[29] Prohibited persons may not be employed in connection with an investment business.[30] There are various sanctions for breach of the principles, rules or prohibition including the making of public statements as to misconduct, injunctions, restitution orders and actions for damages.[31] No action for damages lies in the case of a breach of a principle, however, and in all cases such an action will only be available to private investors.[32]

In addition there are various powers of intervention against those directly authorised. These include a restriction of business, dealing with assets, vesting assets in a trustee (that can apply to SROs if they request it) and the requirement to maintain assets in the jurisdiction.[33]

Unit trusts

Unit trusts (*i.e.* trusts which make investments and which themselves sell their beneficial units as investments) and overseas open-ended investment companies are referred to in the Act as collective investment schemes. Such schemes may not be promoted in the UK unless they are authorised unit trusts or

[24] s.53.
[25] s.55.
[26] s.56.
[27] s.54.
[28] ss.57, 58.
[29] See *ante*, p. 140.
[30] s.59.
[31] ss.60–62.
[32] s.62A.
[33] ss.64–71.

recognised overseas schemes, or the promotion is to an authorised person or a professional investor.[34] Open-ended investment companies are not allowed under UK company law since no company may purchase all its own shares.[35]

Financial Services Tribunal, information, audit and fees

The Financial Services Tribunal was created to hear appeals relating to direct authorisation and the disqualification of prohibited persons. It only relates to appeals from individuals and not dissatisfied SROs. It is seen as a judicial rather than a regulatory body. The Act provides for its constitution, jurisdiction and procedure.[36] It will consist of both legally qualified and other experienced personnel and will sit in panels of three.

There is a register of all directly authorised persons, SROs, recognised professional bodies and exchanges, authorised unit trusts and recognised schemes and prohibited persons. The register is open to inspection. In addition there are powers to obtain information and for investigation and to carry out audits on those engaged in an investment business.[37] There are also powers to charge fees both initial and periodical to assist in the costs of administration.[38]

Administration of authorisation and control

Although the Financial Services Act refers to the powers of recognition and control being in the hands of the Secretary of State, in fact the unique feature of the structure set up by the Act is that the Secretary of State is able to delegate most of his powers in this respect to a private sector company. The Act specifically provides for such delegation, with appropriate safeguards and caveats, to the Securities and Investments Board Ltd. (SIB). SIB has in fact most of the general principle and rule-making powers and is concerned with direct authorisation, recognition and control of bodies such as SROs.[39]

[34] ss.75–95.
[35] *Ante*, Chap. 10.
[36] ss.96–101.
[37] ss.102–111.
[38] ss.112, 113.
[39] ss.113–118.

Certain powers are, however, retained by the Secretary of State, largely there relating to extending exemption from the Act, overseas aspects, the Tribunal and powers of investigation. He also retains control of whether to bring a prosecution under the Act (jointly with the Director of Public Prosecutions).[40]

INSIDER DEALING

Introduction

The Company Securities (Insider Dealing) Act 1985 deals with certain forms of insider trading and makes them criminal offences.[41] Provisions to regulate dealings in a company's shares came about because of widespread concern prior to 1980 about the misuse of confidential information by officers of the company in particular but also by their associates, their families and friends to whom information about the company had been relayed by them, or the misuse by others outside the company such as accountants, auditors and bankers who might equally have access to restricted information about the company which would affect the value of its shares on the market.

Insider dealing occurs where an individual or organisation buys or sells securities while knowingly in possession of some piece of confidential information which is not generally available and which is likely, if made available to the general public, to materially affect the price of these securities. So, for example, there is insider trading where a company director knows that the company is in a bad financial state and sells his shares in it knowing that in a few days time this news will be made public together with an announcement of a cut in dividend payment. Likewise, the director would be insider dealing if, on being informed, before it was generally known by the public, that the company has discovered oil or gold on its own land, he bought more shares in the company in the not unrealistic expectation of an increase in their market value as a result of the subsequent public announcement.

[40] s.201.

[41] This Act as amended by the Financial Services Act 1986 and the Companies Act 1989 consolidates the provisions first introduced in sections 68–73 of the Companies Act 1980.

Ethical and legalobjections

The moral or ethical reasons[42] for prohibiting such activities is that the use of inside information is clearly unfair to those who deal with the insider. One of the difficulties, however, is that in many cases it is seen as a victimless crime in that it is difficult to identify those who have lost by the insider dealing where, as the law currently requires, it takes place on a Stock Exchange dealing.

From the point of view of company law, perhaps a more significant reason for attempting to regulate insider trading by law is that the insider with access to confidential information is thereby in a potential conflict-of-interest situation. For example he may be in such a position within the company as to be able to dictate or at least influence when the public disclosure of price-sensitive information is to be made. In that situation his decision and his own desire to trade advantageously in the company's shares may conflict; in other words the best interests of the company may wrongly take second place to his own self interest. Directors are duty bound, subject to the exceptions contained in section 309 of the Companies Act 1985 and section 187 of the Insolvency Act 1986,[43] only to act bona fide in the best interests of the company as a whole.[44]

Furthermore, such unethical conduct is likely to bring not only the reputation of the company concerned but also of the securities market in this country into disrepute with the possible risk of a consequent adverse investment effect. For this reason in particular the Financial Services Act 1986 extended the scope of the provision aimed at preventing the abuse of information obtained by persons in their official capacity in connection with

[42] There are some economic arguments in favour of the practice.

[43] The first of these enjoins directors in the performance of their functions to have regard to the interests of the company's employees as well as those of its members (but without providing employees with any legal sanction for failure to do so). The latter section now permits a company to make provision for the benefit of its employees or ex-employees on the cessation or transfer of the whole or part of its business even if it is not in the best interests of the company and permits a liquidator to make over assets to employees in satisfaction of the amount decided to be provided to them in such circumstances.

[44] *Hutton* v. *W. Cork Rly*. (1883) 23 Ch.D. 654 C.A.; *Re Lee Behrens & Co.* [1932] Ch. 46; *Evans* v. *Brunner Mond & Co.* [1921] 1 Ch. 359; *Parke* v. *Daily News* [1962] Ch. 927; and *Re Roith* [1967] 1 W.L.R. 479.

the new regulation of the securities and investment industry and provided the innovation of investigations into suspected insider dealing. In turn the Companies Act 1989 has allowed for investigations at the request of overseas regulators since insider dealing may well take place on an international scale.

Methods of control

Given that it is recognised as wrong for a director or another to deal in a company's shares knowing of some development which will affect the price of the shares and to which other members or the public generally are not privy, then the question arises how to put an end to such unethical activity. The universal condemnation of this malpractice has produced differing solutions for its eradication.

In the United States of America, which has been in the forefront of the attack on insider trading, the solution adopted is to make the insider disgorge his ill-gotten gains to the company itself or to the individual with whom he dealt.

In the United Kingdom on the other hand, the solution now contained in the Company Securities (Insider Dealing) Act 1985 is to prohibit, under pain of criminal penalty, an individual connected with a company from trading or dealing on a recognised stock exchange, or through an off-market dealer, in securities of that company. He is prohibited from such activity if he is in possession of unpublished price-sensitive information concerning the company. Likewise, he is subject to a penalty if he attempts to have someone else dealing on his behalf and he must not communicate the information he possesses to any other person if he has reasonable cause to believe that that person might deal in the shares, taking unfair advantage of such confidential information.

The European Community has adopted a directive co-ordinating the regulation of insider dealing in all Member States.[45] As such the directive, which is to be implemented by June 1992, will not require many changes to the 1985 Act but the Government is considering using the opportunity to simplify and update some of its provisions. These are outlined at the end of this chapter.

[45] Dir. 89/592/EEC, O.J. L 334/30.

Previous controls—civil liability

Prior to the implementation of the 1980 Companies Act, the only statutory restrictions on insider trading by company officers were the prohibitions on option dealings by directors and the requirement that a register of their share dealings and the dealings of their spouses and children be maintained and available for inspection by an interested person.[46] These 1967 statutory provisions were ineffective because although they purported to create a legal duty or obligation to disclose share dealings, yet they provided no remedy for failure to comply with the Act's requirements.

Also by that time there were sanctions conceived and imposed by the Stock Exchange Authorities and the City Panel under the City Code on Take-overs and Mergers.[47] These, however, are only an extra-statutory form of self regulation and open to criticism because they have no legal backing.[48] Despite that, these bodies have devised strict rules, for example, relating to the disclosure of director's personal interests in shares in relation to certain profitable transactions such as take-over bids; for absolute secrecy before any significant announcement is made, and for regulating dealings by insiders in the shares while negotiations continue.[49] In theory any breach of the rules, at the Panel's direction will be investigated by it or the Stock Exchange Authority, and improprieties chastised or corrected by appropriate action.

At common law officers of a company had always been freely permitted to hold and deal in the shares of their company. The only sanction which the common law imposed was to make actionable the use of certain confidential information belonging to the company. Such information included industrial or trade secrets and details concerning customers.[50] The misuse of such

[46] See Chap. 15, *ante*.
[47] See Chap. 31, *post*.
[48] They rely on private reprimand, public censure or the withdrawal of access to the facilities of the securities market.
[49] The City Code on Take-overs and Mergers.
[50] See *British Industrial Plastics* v. *Ferguson* [1938] 4 All E.R. 504; *Cranleigh Precision Engineering Ltd.* v. *Bryant* [1965] 1 W.L.R. 1293; *Measure Bros* v. *Measures* [1910] 1 Ch. 336, [1910] 2 Ch. 248; *Printers & Finishers Ltd.* v. *Holloway* [1965] 1 W.L.R. 1.

information by directors, whether it occurred during the course of, or after the termination of, corporate office, was actionable.

The reason why the common law imposed no clear prohibition on the use of insider information in share dealings stems largely from the decision in *Percival* v. *Wright*.[51] In this case where directors had purchased a member's shares in the knowledge that there was a ready buyer for all the shares of the company at a higher price than they paid him, it was held that the transaction could not be set aside for the directors' failure to disclose the negotiations which were already taking place at a higher price. There was said to be no duty to disclose because there was no fiduciary relationship between the directors and individual shareholders. The director's duty was owed by the company alone. Subsequently in the case of *Allen* v. *Hyatt*[52] the courts did recognise special but very limited circumstances in which a duty might be owed by directors to individual shareholders. In that particular case the directors had profited through share purchases from members and were held accountable to them because they had purported to act as agents for the members by inducing the latter to give them purchase options over each member's shares supposedly to facilitate a proposed amalgamation. Unless some special relationship of this type could be shown so as to establish a legal duty to disclose all relevant information, the officer retained his profit without adverse legal consequences.

Initiation of reform

The Cohen and the Jenkins Committee Reports and the more recent 1973 White Paper on company law declared their opposition to insider dealing.[53] All recommended more mandatory disclosure and statutory restrictions to prevent the abuse of inside information. The Jenkins Committee also recommended the provision of remedies similar to those in America to compensate parties injured by the insider's activities.[54] This

[51] [1902] 2 Ch. 421.
[52] (1914) 30 T.L.R. 444.
[53] The Cohen Committee Report 1945 (Cmnd. 6659, para. 8b). The Jenkins Committee Report 1962 (Cmnd. 1749, paras. 93–100). The Company Law Reform White Paper (July 1973, Cmnd. 5391).
[54] 1962 Cmnd. 1749 at para. 98.

latter recommendation was not implemented specifically by the 1980 Companies Act or any other enactment,[55] despite the impression to the contrary given by an early decision in Scotland.[56] The concern and aim of the 1980 legislation was not the compensating of any injured parties or the forcible disgorging of wrongfully acquired gains. The only intendment of the relevant part of that legislation, and likewise of the current Company Securities (Insider Dealing) Act 1985 which was purely a consolidation measure, was to make insider trading or dealing a criminal offence. The hope was and is that all who possess material corporate information will feel compelled (*in terrorem*) to refrain from dealing until that information has been properly made available to the general public.

THE 1985 "INSIDER DEALING" ACT

The Company Securities (Insider Dealing) Act 1985 as amended by the Financial Services Act 1986 prohibits only some forms of insider dealing. In detail, section 1 prohibits dealings on a recognised stock exchange[57] in shares by insiders and those who obtain information from them ("tippees"). Also it prohibits the procuring of such deals, the provision of information to make such deals possible, and dealing by persons who have made or withdrawn a take-over offer or dealing by persons who have access to any such information. Section 2 originally prohibited dealings by Crown servants or by "tippees" who are knowingly in receipt of information from Crown servants who have or have had access to prescribed information. This prohibition has been extended now to cover a broader class of persons called "public servants" which includes Crown servants and the members, officers and servants of the designated agencies and self regulating organisations involved in the regulation of the investment industry and any persons performing a public function in that connection whom the Secretary of State deems

[55] See, however, Powers of Criminal Courts Act 1973, ss.35–38 and Criminal Justice (Scotland) Act 1980, ss.58–67, which enable compensation to be awarded.

[56] *P.F.* v. *Bryce*, August 21, 1981, Edinburgh Sheriff Court (unreported).

[57] That is on the Stock Exchange and any other recognised investment exchange. By the Insider Dealing (Recognised Stock Exchange) Order 1989, S.I. 1989/2165 NASDAQ is so recognised.

to be "public servants."[58] Section 4 prohibits dealing in advertised securities using an off-market dealer who is making a market in those securities.

Prescribed information

The information, the use of which is the concern of these provisions, is only what is termed "unpublished price-sensitive" information. This as defined in section 10 consists of information which relates to specific matters concerning the company in question, either directly or indirect, and which is not generally known to those persons who are accustomed or likely to deal in those securities but which would, if generally known to them, be likely materially to affect the market price of those securities.

The definition in the EC Directive on Insider Dealing is[59]: "information which has not been made public of a precise nature relating to one or several issuers of transferable securities, which, if it were made public, would be likely to have a significant effect on the price of the transferable security or securities in question."

Criminal law implications

Contravention of the prohibitions is made a criminal offence by section 8. Sections 1, 2, 4 and 5 make very clear that the prosecution, to secure a conviction, must prove both of the traditional pre-requisites of the criminal law. First the *actus reus*, the doing of something which is prohibited,[60]—in this instance the act of dealing or trading in securities as an insider, or counselling, procuring or imparting of prescribed information to enable such dealings to take place. Secondly, the prosecution must prove *mens rea* or the requisite criminal intent or guilty state of mind. Depending on the nature of the offence and the

[58] See Financial Services Act 1986, s.173. Under the Insider Dealing (Public Servants) Order 1989, S.I. 1989/2164 these now include officers and employees of the Bank of England, Lloyd's and the Monopolies and Mergers Commission.

[59] Dir. 89/592/EEC Art. 1., *post* p. 503.

[60] In limited circumstances an *actus reus* may result from an omission to act, *e.g.* *R.* v. *Dytham* [1979] 3 W.L.R. 467.

precise wording of any statutory provision defining the offence, the *mens rea* element may be satisfied by proof of either intention, recklessness or negligence.

In relation to the principal offence of dealing in securities, section 1 specifies a number of factual and mental elements which are to be proved. The accused must be proved:

(a) to be "knowingly connected" with the company;
(b) to have information by virtue of that connection;
(c) to have been reasonably expected not to disclose the information by reason of that connection;
(d) to have known that the information is unpublished, price-sensitive information in relation to the securities of the company[61]; and
(e) to have dealt in those securities on the Stock Exchange or, if they are advertised securities, through an off-market dealer.

In relation to the other offences of counselling or procuring dealing or communicating information, the prosecution must prove, in addition on the other alleged facts, that the accused "knew or had reasonable cause to believe" that dealing would occur on a Stock Exchange or outside Great Britain. An accused with knowledge that the dealing would be either on a recognised Exchange or an unrecognised or off-market Exchange but does not know or care which, will be caught by the section.

Technically the words "knowingly" or "to know" indicate the traditional requirement of *mens rea* as to all the elements of *actus reus* or offence.[62] This means that the prosecution will only satisfy the necessary *mens rea* element if it can prove intention as opposed to either recklessness or negligence. This may be achieved by showing that the defendant voluntarily did the *actus reus* intending the forbidden consequence to occur or the forbidden circumstance to be produced.[63] Intention may also be inferred by a jury if the prosecution can show that the

[61] The directive requires only that a person knows that he has inside information.

[62] But it has not invariably been held to do so—see Smith and Hogan, *Criminal Law* (4th ed.), at p. 102.

[63] See *Hyam* v. *D.P.P.* [1975] A.C. 55; *Mohan* [1976] Q.B. 1; *Belfon* [1976] 1 W.L.R. 741, and *Cunningham* (1981) Cr.App.R. 253.

defendant foresaw that particular consequence of his act as virtually certain to occur.[64] Generally words like "knowingly" will include the state of mind of a person who suspects the truth but deliberately avoids finding out, "shutting his eyes to an obvious means of knowledge" or "deliberately refraining from making enquiries the results of which he might not care to have. 'Connivance,' as this attitude of mind is sometimes called, is closely akin to recklessness."[65] Recklessness consists of either being aware of a risk and unjustifiably taking it or failing to consider that there is a risk in circumstances in which the risk should have been evident.[66] Clearly there is a degree of overlap between conscious disregard, which is the first limb of recklessness, and knowing conduct, which is intentional. At very least, evidence of conscious disregard may raise the implication that the defendant did act "knowingly."[67] Proof of "connivance" even more certainly would satisfy the requirement that the accused "knew" or was "knowingly connected."

Corporate connection—primary insiders

For the purpose of the principal offences specified in section 1, a person according to section 9 is connected with a company, and therefore an insider, if he is a director of that company or a related company such as a subsidiary or he is an officer or employee of either or he is in a position involving a professional or business relationship between himself and that company or any related company. In addition such a position must be reasonably expected to give him access to unpublished price-sensitive information about the securities of either company.

The ambit of this provision is such as to include a company's independent auditors, brokers and other financial or legal advisers. Any individual who is, or who at any time in the preceding six months has been, so knowingly connected may not deal in securities of that company if he had information which as stated above he gained by virtue of his position which is

[64] *R.* v. *Moloney* [1985] A.C. 905; *R.* v. *Hancock & Shankland* [1986] A.C. 455; *Nedrick* [1986] 1 All E.R. 1.

[65] Smith and Hogan, *Criminal Law* (4th ed.), at p. 103.

[66] *Cf. R.* v. *Stephenson* [1979] Q.B. 695; *R.* v. *Caldwell* [1981] 1 All E.R. 961; *R.* v. *Lawrence* [1981] 1 All E.R. 975 and *R.* v. *Seymour* [1983] 2 A.C. 493.

[67] See *Derry* v. *Peek* (1889) 14 App.Cas. 337.

confidential and which he knows to be unpublished price-sensitive information.

Also, such a person may not deal in the securities of any other company if the confidential, connected information which he possesses is known similarly by him to be unpublished price-sensitive information relating to the securities of that other company and relates to any transaction, actual or contemplated, involving both the company with which he is connected and the other company, or involving one of them and the securities of the other, or relates to the fact that any such transaction is no longer contemplated.

Outsiders prohibited—secondary insiders or tippees

Section 1(3) and (4) necessarily close an otherwise convenient loophole by prohibiting persons who receive unpublished price-sensitive information from dealing in securities of the company to which it relates. Any persons, sometimes referred to as "tippees," who obtain information, directly or indirectly, from another who is or was connected with the company within the period of six months prior to the receipt of the information is now caught by the dealing prohibition. The recipient or "tippee" must be shown either to know or to have reasonable cause to believe that the imparter of the information held it by virtue of being connected with the company and that because of the latter's position it would be reasonable to expect him not to disclose it.

In *Attorney-Generals Reference No. 1 of 1988*[68] the House of Lords held that a tippee could obtain information within the meaning of section 1(3) even if he did not actually actively seek the information but merely received it.

Section 2 as amended,[69] deems any public servant or ex-public servant connected with any company about which he received prescribed information in his capacity either as a Crown servant or as a member, officer or servant of the regulatory agencies or organisations charged with the supervision of the investment industry or as a person in that connection who appears to perform a public function and is deemed by the Secretary of

[68] [1989] A.C. 971.
[69] Financial Services Act 1986, s.173.

State to be a public servant. Such persons may not deal in the securities to which that information relates until that confidential information has become general knowledge or ceases to be price-sensitive.

Statutory exceptions

Section 3 as amended,[70] provides for certain exceptions or defences. A person with information may deal if he does so otherwise than with a view to profit or avoidance of a loss for himself or another which the defendant must prove to avoid conviction if the offence is otherwise made out.[71] This would seem to cover the situation where circumstances compel the realisation of securities despite the knowledge of unpublished price-sensitive information. Other exemptions in that section apply to liquidators, receivers and trustees in bankruptcy acting in good faith in performance of their duties and to any jobber (*i.e.* any individual, partnership or company dealing in securities on a recognised stock exchange and recognised as such by the Council of the Stock Exchange) acting in good faith in the course of business.

Also exempt[72] from the prohibition on the use of inside information are those who obtain such knowledge in the course of a business as a market maker and that knowledge is of the usual kind for him to acquire in the ordinary course of his business. A market maker is defined as any person recognised by a recognised stock exchange who holds himself out as willing to buy and sell securities at prices specified by him in compliance with the rules of that exchange.[73]

Section 6[74] relaxes the prohibitions on insider dealing in so far as transactions to stabilise the price of securities are concerned provided they are made in conformity with the rules made under section 48 of the Financial Services Act 1986 and concern

[70] Financial Services Act 1986, s.174.

[71] An argument that s.3 required the prosecution to prove a profit motive was rejected by the Court of Appeal in *R.* v. *Cross* [1990] BCC 237. *Quaere* whether this is correct in the light of the general principles of statutory interpretation laid down in *Hunt* [1987] A.C. 352.

[72] Financial Services Act 1986, s.174(1).

[73] Financial Services Act 1986, s.174(2).

[74] Substituted by Financial Services Act 1986, s.175.

one of the following types of securities namely: company stocks or shares; debentures; government or public securities such as loan stock or bonds; instruments entitling to shares, or securities such as warrants and certificates representing securities. Furthermore this exemption only applies if the stabilisation transaction occurs during the period before or after the issue of those securities as is specified in the rules made under that Act. Section 7 protects trustees and personal representatives who know they have inside information and who act on the advice of a person who does not appear to be prohibited by the Act from dealing.

Investigations into insider dealing

When the offence of insider dealing was first made law by the Companies Act 1980 no provision was made or mechanism included whereby alleged or suspected abuse of inside information might be investigated by a regulatory body other than the police. Despite the fact that this was a serious drawback to any effectiveness that the legislation might have had, no amendment was made to rectify that weakness prior to the consolidation of the Companies Act in 1985. The existing provisions were simply reproduced in the separate enactment entitled the Companies Securities (Insider Dealing) Act 1985. Since the consolidation, however, the government decided by way of the Financial Services Act 1986 to empower the Secretary of State to appoint investigators into what appears to him to be a contravention of the Companies Securities (Insider Dealing) Act. In investigating alleged insider dealing the investigators have been provided with wide powers[75] similar to those vested in an inspector appointed under the Companies Act 1985.[76] The investigators are empowered to require any person who may be able to give information concerning the sale or purchase of securities to disclose it; to produce documents; to attend before the investigators and be questioned on oath by them subject only to legal professional privilege and a more limited exception in the case of bankers.[77] The evidence provided may be used in

[75] Financial Services Act 1986, s.177.
[76] Companies Act 1985, Part XIV, ss.431–453, *ante*, p. 468.
[77] A journalist has no such exemption: see *Re an Inquiry under the Company Securities (Insider Dealing) Act 1985* [1988] A.C. 660.

evidence against that person or any other person where is discloses prohibited insider dealings.

The Secretary of State may vary the terms of the investigation and direct the inspectors to take no further steps. Any person convicted of an offence as a result of an inquiry may be required to contribute towards the costs of the inquiry.

Statutory penalties

The penalties specified in section 8 for contravention of sections 1, 2, 4 or 5 are: (a) on conviction on indictment, a term of imprisonment not exceeding seven years or a fine, or both and (b) on summary conviction, a term of imprisonment not exceeding six months or a fine not exceeding the statutory maximum, or both.[78] This section also provides that proceedings in England and Wales may only be instituted by, or with the consent of the Secretary of State or the Director of Public Prosecutions. The aim of this provision is to prevent malicious private prosecutions and it also reflects the fact that most prosecutions will be the product either of an investigation by the Department of Trade and Industry under the Companies Act 1985[79] or, more likely today, as a result of an investigation under section 177 of the Financial Services Act 1986.

If a person fails to co-operate with an investigation conducted under 177 of the Financial Services Act 1986 then he may become liable for the special penalties provided by section 178 of that Act. Section 178 authorises the investigators to certify that failure to the court which may inquire into the facts and if it decides that there is no reasonable excuse for the non-co-operation it may punish that person as if he had committed a contempt of court.[80] Alternatively the court may direct that the Secretary of State may use the powers given to him under section 178(3). These powers entitled the Secretary of State to

[78] The maximum term was increased to seven years by the Criminal Justice Act 1988.

[79] See ss.431–432 of the Companies Act 1985; see p. 469, *ante*.

[80] The penalty for this common law offence is entirely at the discretion of the court and may result in imprisonment and/or a fine. A journalist has no defence to such an action on the grounds of public interest: *Re An Inquiry etc.*, *ante*.

cancel that person's authorisation to carry on investment business; to disqualify him from becoming authorised or to impose on him any number of restrictions or prohibitions in relation to the carrying on of investment business. Although the Secretary of State is also empowered to revoke the previous penalty notice such a revocation does not necessarily revive any authorisation held by that person prior to the original penalty notice.

Finally, section 8(3) of the Company Securities (Insider Dealing) Act 1985 states that although insider dealing is illegal the transactions which do occur remain valid. This is a recognition of the difficulties that would be involved in any attempt by statute to put the parties fairly back into their original positions or the position they would have been in but for the mischief of the insider with whom they dealt. Once bona fide purchasers or third parties have intervened that task becomes virtually impossible if injustice is to be avoided. Further, although this legislation makes no provision for compensating or indemnifying either any injured party with whom the insider dealt or the shareholders or company generally, for the profits wrongfully gained through the misuse of insider information, this does not preclude legal action in equity against such a director, in particular to recover the profits made by his insider trading in breach of his fiduciary duty[81] and the criminal courts themselves do have the power to award compensation in any criminal proceedings to individuals who have actually suffered a loss as a result of the convicted person's criminal activity. In fact the courts must state why they are not awarding compensation in cases where they decline to do so.[82]

Changes proposed following the EC directive

The Government has suggested that it will make the following changes to the Insider Dealing Act, partly to comply with the provisions of the Insider Dealing directive of December 1989[83]:

[81] *Phipps* v. *Boardman* [1967] A.C. 46. See, however, the difficulty that arises in this connection because of the rule in *Foss* v. *Harbottle* (1843) 2 Ha. 461.

[82] See Powers of Criminal Courts Act 1973, ss.35 and 38, and Criminal Justice (Scotland) Act 1980, ss.58–67, as amended.

[83] Dir. 89/592/EEC Art. 1.

(i) changes to the definition of inside information
– omission of the need to show that it would be reasonable to expect the insider not to disclose the information except in the performance of his functions;
– changes in the wording to indicate how specific that information must be, adopting the directive's wording[84];

(ii) all transactions involving a professional intermediary will be covered, but no liability for face to face transactions;

(iii) changes as to the definition of an insider
– no time limit for connection with a company
– inclusion of shareholders
– professional and businessmen caught if they have access to the information by virtue of the exercise of their business, etc.;

(iv) new defence for actions done in good faith by those with a conflict of interest and duty; this replaces specific defences, *e.g.* for market makers.

[84] *Ante*, p. 496.

Chapter 20

ACCOUNTS

INTRODUCTION

WHEN the original legislation was passed in the 1850s enabling limited liability companies to be set up merely by registration, the intention was primarily to provide a minimum framework which would facilitate economic development in a manner consistent with *laissez-faire* capitalism.[1] The view which implicitly seems to have been taken was that companies would find it in their own interests to disclosure a certain amount of reliable information, so reducing uncertainty in the minds of creditors, shareholders and other interested parties, and to the extent that they might be reluctant to do this it would be up to both the individuals dealing with a company, its officers and agents, and to its members to protect their interests by making appropriate contracts with the parties concerned. The justification for intervention in this process could only exist if it were perceived that the benefits to society that might be expected to result would more than offset the costs of complying with any regulations imposed.

Against this background it is hardly surprising that in the latter half of the nineteenth century disclosure requirements were minimal, the view in particular being taken that record-keeping and the preparation of financial statements for a company were really a domestic matter, of concern only to the

[1] See T. Hadden, *Company Law and Capitalism* (2nd ed., 1977), Weidenfeld and Nicolson, London, Chap. 1 and *passim*. The idea has been given a new lease of life recently with the development of the economic theory of agency: see, for instance, W. H. Beaver, *Financial Reporting: An Accounting Revolution* (2nd ed., 1989), Prentice Hall, Englewood Cliffs, N.J., Chap. 2 and *passim*.

directors and shareholders, unless the rights of third parties were directly affected.[2] As a result the only guidance in accounting matters in the early legislation was to be found in the model articles given in Table A.[3] At the same time the non-interventionist philosophy was reflected in a number of decisions concernig the payment of dividends by companies, the overall view apparently being that the courts should not in general interfere in the business decision-making process unless there were good grounds for believing that the rights of certain interested parties were being prejudiced—a laudable policy given the fact that from an economic viewpoint there is no necessary connection between profit, however calculated, and the distribution decision.[4]

Towards the end of the nineteenth century views about mandatory disclosure gradually began to change. The formal accounts were beginning to be used for purposes (such as a basis for assessing income tax liabilities) which were different from those apparently originally intended. Moreover, specific examples of inequality of information and manipulation of data arose, and at a time when a third of new companies failed within a short space of time[5] the view that unsecured creditors had insufficient information on which to base their decisions gained a certain currency. The result was that the statutory audit was introduced in 1900, and in 1908 the 10,000 businesses in the newly created "public" class of company were required to file their balance sheets. However, the 30,000 or so "private" concerns were still exempted from this provision.

[2] See *In re Spanish Prospecting Co. Ltd.* [1911] 1 Ch. 92; *Edwards* v. *Saunton Hotel Co. Ltd.* [1943] 1 All E.R. 176; *Young* v. *Brownlee and Co. Ltd.*, [1911] S.C. 677.

[3] See H. C. Edey and Prot Panitpakdi, *British Company Accounting and the Law 1844–1900*, in *Studies in the History of Accounting*, ed. A. C. Littleton and B. S. Yamey, 1956, Sweet and Maxwell, London (pp. 356–379). (In fact, under the original 1856 Act what became Schedule A from 1862 onwards was designated as Schedule B).

[4] See *post*, Chap. 22; E. A. French, *The Evolution of the Dividend Law of England*, in *Studies in Accounting* (3rd ed., 1977), ed. W. T. Baxter and S. Davidson, Institute of Chartered Accountants in England and Wales, London (pp. 306–331); and R. C. Morris, *Distribution Policy*: *An Economic Rationale*, *Accountancy*, October 1982 (pp. 80–82).

[5] See H. A. Shannon, *The Listed Companies of 1866–1883*, in *Essays in Economic History*, Vol. 1, ed. E. M. Carus-Wilson, 1954, Edward Arnold, London.

By 1925 the numbers of companies registered had risen to around 95,000 (of which some 85,000 were private), but the 1929 Companies Act nevertheless did not extend the duty to file accounts to private companies, nor did it substantially expand the disclosure requirements for company financial statements. However, the climate of opinion began to change in the 1930s, it being increasingly recognised that the affairs of the modern corporation are often of interest to a much wider constituency than just the existing body of shareholders.[6] The gradual shift in opinion was given added impetus by the Royal Mail debacle[7] and the creation of the Securities and Exchange Commission in the United States, events which forced lawyers and accountants in Great Britain to question the accepted wisdom in relation to the disclosure of a company's financial affairs. The result was that the Cohen Committee[8] on company law reform of 1945 was charged with considering the needs of the public as well as shareholders and creditors. It recommended that so-called reserve accounting should be outlawed; that the preparation of group accounts (where appropriate) should be mandatory; and that for the first time companies should be required to prepare an income statement worthy of the name. By that time there were some 200,000 registered companies, of which over 90 per cent. enjoyed private status, but the 1948 Companies Act only required public and a small proportion of (non-exempt) private companies to file their annual accounts.

The Jenkins Committee[9] on company law reform, reporting in 1962, favoured further compulsory disclosure, and it proposed that exempt private companies (which comprised some 75 per cent. of the 400,000 or so companies then registered) should be required to file their financial statements, the purpose being to benefit unsecured creditors. A requirement to this effect was included in the 1967 Companies Act, and this led to a rapid increase in the number of company searches, which rose from 600,000 in 1960 and 1.3 million in 1969 to 2.6 million in 1980.[10] The Act also greatly extended the disclosures which had to be

[6] See Hadden, *op. cit.*, *passim*.
[7] *R.* v. *Kylsant* [1932], 1 K.B. 442.
[8] (1945) Cmnd. 6659.
[9] (1962) Cmnd. 1749.
[10] By 1985 the number of searches had risen to 3.1 million and by 1989 to over 4 million.

made in the income statement and in notes to the accounts and the directors' reports (*e.g.* turnover, hire charges, movements in fixed assets and segmental analysis of activities).

The late 1960s and the 1970s witnessed an upsurge in activity aimed at regulating the ways in which companies report their financial affairs, most of it of a quasi-legal nature. Thus ever since the First World War the authorities had set government contract prices by using a formula relying in part on published accounting figures, and with the growing economic significance of such business the rules were gradually tightened up. Elsewhere, successive governments between 1965 and 1979 attempted to monitor and control price increases, first through the National Board for Prices and Incomes (1965–1971) and later through the Price Commission (1973–1979), and these bodies (like the Monopolies Commission and the Restrictive Trade Practices Court before them) relied heavily on accounting information, which for the Price Commission had to be prepared following certain specified rules. Meanwhile companies had had for many years to keep detailed records to ensure PAYE, national insurance contributions and excise duties were properly accounted for, and the introduction of the value added tax in 1973 made this even more necessary. In addition, powers were taken in the Industry Act 1975 which meant that certain companies might be required to disclose supplementary information to ministers and to trade unions.

Even in the nineteenth century companies had to consider the direct "economic consequences" of what they reported in their financial statements in terms of what they might involve in cash payments (*e.g.* with regard to corporate taxation and profit sharing contracts). However, by the 1960s and 1970s interest in the accounting and business community had for many years been much more closely focused on the "signalling properties," primarily for the 3,000 or so British listed companies, for which it was important to try to indicate to investment analysts the trend in permanently sustainable earnings, but also with respect to the much larger number of unlisted public and private companies trying to influence the opinions of third parties, such as credit suppliers and bank lenders. The economic consequences of such signals for companies are indirect in the sense that they only affect their costs of capital, as reflected in their relative share prices and borrowing costs, but the necessary information can be conveyed to interested parties by alternative means (*e.g.* the chairman's report, presentations to stockbrokers and institutional investors, or press releases).[11]

One of the effects of the advent of new regulations in the late 1960s and the 1970s was to exacerbate conflicts of interest between different parties with respect to the information reported in company financial statements. This development in turn was largely responsible for the leading accountancy bodies setting up the Accounting Standards Committee (ASC) in 1969, and over the next 20 years it issued a number of mandatory statements, concerning the preparation and publication of companies' annual accounts, two of the most important relating to the preparation of supplementary flow of funds and current cost accounting statements, the latter following the publication of a lengthy government report on the matter.[12] The ASC's efforts were backed up by the statements of the International Accounting Standards Committee (IASC), set up in 1973, and the International Stock Exchange's Listing Agreement, published in 1972, the latter applying to British quoted companies. Elsewhere, the OECD and the United Nations have both published disclosure guidelines concerning the activities of international concerns.

Another major factor, of more direct relevance to changes introduced in the Companies Acts 1980 and 1981, was the EC's attempts to harmonise accounting regulations within the Common Market countries, the avowed aim being to encourage the efficient allocation of capital within the European Community. These two Acts incorporated most of the accounting and disclosure proposals contained in the EC's Second, and Fourth Council Directives, dealing respectively with capital

[11] For a discussion of the economic consequences phenomenon and its role in moulding financial reporting practice, see R. L. Watts and J. L. Zimmerman, "Positive Accounting Theory," 1986, Prentice Hall, Englewood Cliffs, N.J.

[12] (1975) Cmnd. 6225. With an abatement of the general rate of inflation and a lack of interest in such supplementary data on the part of analysts (who presumably estimate the likely impact of relative price changes on future sustainable permanent cash flow earnings by referring to other sources of information), the over-complicated standard (SSAP 16) requesting listed and other large companies to publish supplementary current cost accounting statements was withdrawn in September 1986.

maintenance and distributions; and individual company accounts. Similarly, the Companies Act 1989 implemented the requirements of the Seventh and Eighth Council Directives, the former relating to group accounts and the latter to eligibility for appointment as a company auditor. The opportunity was also taken when framing the legislation to reform the institutional framework for setting accounting standards along lines suggested in a report by a committee chaired by Sir Ron Dearing, which was published in September 1988.[13] As a result, a broadly based Financial Reporting Council is to be set up to guide the work of a standard setting body, the Accounting Standards Board.[14]

What is perhaps surprising about recent developments has been the lack of debate in a succession of discussion documents[15] about the economic rationale for requiring greater disclosure by companies, particularly as further regulation seems to imply an increasing degree of market failure. Yet it should be remembered that the data contained in a set of published accounts are only part of a much wider information set available to decision makers, be they shareholders, potential investors, creditors or employees, and there is an impressive amount of empirical evidence suggesting that financial and other markets are efficient in obtaining and processing information perceived to be relevant.[16] Now that the law of negligence has gradually been extended through *Hedley Byrne* v. *Heller*[17] and subsequent cases to offer some protection to third parties, there is even more reason to question the validity of extending disclosure requirements, particularly since the costs of complying with the regulations are far from negligible, but this is a matter which rather surprisingly does not seem up till now to have greatly concerned lawyers and accountants, though businessmen and the government are at last beginning to question the wisdom of the

[13] "The Making of Accounting Standards," September 1988.

[14] See *post*, p. 550, for a discussion of the status of accounting standards under s.256 of the Companies Act 1985.

[15] *e.g.* (1973) Cmnd. 5391; (1979) Cmnd. 7654.

[16] See for instance, Beaver, *op. cit.*, especially Chaps. 5–6.

[17] [1964] A.C. 465. However, the House of Lords has more recently decided that in a takeover situation auditors owe no duty to members of the public at large who rely on a company's accounts when deciding to buy its shares: *Caparo Industries plc* v. *Dickman* [1990] 2 W.L.R. 358 (see *post*, p. 623).

policies being pursued.[18] It is therefore against this background that the current legislative rules should be viewed.

In what follows, this chapter deals, first, with the accounting records which must be kept by a company; secondly, with the reference period for which accounts must be prepared; thirdly, with the regulations for laying them before the company in general meeting and filing copies with the Registrar of Companies; fourthly, with the form and content of the annual accounts and the accounting principles which must be applied in their preparation; fifthly, with the regulations concerning group accounts; sixthly, with the directors' report; seventhly, with the auditor's report; eighthly, with a note on special requirements for banking and insurance companies; ninthly, with the powers of the Secretary of State to alter the accounting requirements of the Act; tenthly, with some brief details of other accounting and disclosure regulations; and finally with the question of whether the inclusion of a debt in a signed balance sheet amounts to an acknowledgment of its existence by the company.

Accounting Records

Section 221 of the Companies Act 1985 requires every company to ensure that adequate accounting records are kept, sufficient to show and explain its transactions. Moreover, they must be such as to disclose with reasonable accuracy at any time the financial position of the company, and also enable a balance sheet and profit and loss account to be prepared so as to give a true and fair view of the company's financial position and profit or loss. Parent companies are equally required in relation to subsidiaries to which the provisions of section 221 do not apply to take reasonable steps to ensure such undertakings keep sufficient accounting records so that the group accounts give a true and fair view.

In particular, the accounting records must contain (a) entries from day to day of all monies received and expended, with details of transactions, and (b) a record of assets and liabilities. In addition, a company dealing in goods must keep statements of stock held at the end of each financial year and of stocktakings from which the year end statements are made up,

[18] (1985) Cmnd. 9571, para. 5.13; (1986) Cmnd. 9794, paras. 8.3–8.6.

as well as records of all goods sold and purchased (other than in ordinary retail trade transactions), showing goods, buyers and sellers so as to allow identification. However, there is no requirement to keep statements of work in progress.[19]

Section 222 requires that the accounting records must be open for inspection by the officers of the company at all times, but there is no express statutory provision authorising the court to compel inspection. However, it was held in *M'Cusker* v. *M'Rae*[20] that the Court of Session may, on the petition of a director presented to the *nobile officium*, ordain a company to make the accounting records available for inspection by the director and by a named accountant on his behalf.

If the accounting records are kept outside Great Britain, such accounts and returns must be kept in Britain as will disclose the position of the business at intervals not exceeding six months and will enable the directors to ensure that any balance sheet or profit and loss account prepared by them gives a true and fair view of the company's financial position and profit or loss.

The accounting records must normally be kept for a minimum period of three years for a private company, or six years for a public company.

Failure to keep accounting records as required is an offence for which officers of the company are liable, the penalty being imprisonment and/or a fine.

A shareholder has no right to inspect the books of account of the company unless one is given to him by the articles. In this regard Table A, article 109 (S.I. No. 805, 1985) provides that "No member shall (as such) have any right of inspecting any accounting records or other book or document of the company except as conferred by statute or authorised by the directors or by ordinary resolution of the company."

For the purposes of the Companies Act, accounting records need not be kept in bound books, so long as adequate safeguards are taken to prevent their falsification and the records are capable of being reproduced in a legible form (sections 722–723; S.I. 1985 No. 724).

[19] The scope of the requirements of s.221 is reviewed in counsel's opinion for the Auditing Practices Committee, "Legal Requirements for Accounting Records," 1979.

[20] 1966 S.C. 253. See also *Conway* v. *Petronius Clothing Co. Ltd.* [1978] 1 W.L.R. 72.

ACCOUNTING REFERENCE PERIODS

Section 223(1)–(2) of the Companies Act 1985 provides that the directors of a company must prepare accounts based on an *accounting reference period* for its *financial year.*[21] This commences on the day after the date to which the last accounts were prepared and ends on the last day of the company's normal financial year. However, in order to accommodate natural week ends, the directors may at their discretion move such reference date to up to seven days before or after the last day of the company's normal financial year.

The *accounting reference date*, which under section 224(1) determines the accounting reference period, is either chosen by the company itself, giving notice of such date in prescribed form to the Registrar of Companies (section 224(2); or, failing that, it will be March 31, for companies incorporated prior to the implementation of the Companies Act 1989, and for those incorporated thereafter the end of the month in which the anniversary of its incorporation falls (section 224(3)).[22] Where the company opts to choose the date, prescribed notice must be given within nine months of incorporation, and the reference period must be not less than six nor more than 18 months (section 224(2)(4)), while the period covered by the profit and loss account must begin with the first day of that accounting reference period and end not more than seven days before or more than seven days after the reference period, as the directors may determine (section 223(2)).[23]

Section 225 of the 1985 Act makes provision for alteration of the accounting reference period. Under its terms notice may be given to the Registrar in prescribed form at any time during an

[21] Corresponding requirements for oversea companies are contained in s.701.

[22] According to a survey of a sample of year ends of listed companies, about 40 per cent. have year ends at December 31, 20 per cent. at March 31, 10 per cent. at September 30 and 6 per cent. at June 30. (M. Barron, "Year-end Heterogeneity in Calculations of Industry and Economy Averages of Accounting Numbers," *Accounting and Business Research*, Autumn 1986). Statistics recently published by the Department of Trade and Industry for the entire population of 1,073,200 companies which had been allocated Accounting Reference Dates at March 31, 1989, show 39 per cent. had March year ends, 18.6 per cent. December year ends, 7 per cent. September year ends, 6.6 per cent. June year ends, and 6.2 per cent. April year ends.

[23] Barron, *op. cit.*, found 15 per cent. of the companies in his sample availed themselves of the concession to vary the year end date by up to 7 days.

accounting reference period specifying a new accounting reference date, the effect of which will be to alter the current and subsequent accounting reference periods of the company. This may be done after the end of a reference period so as to change the date by which the accounts would normally be laid and filed only if the company is a holding or subsidiary company and the change is made in order that the accounting reference dates of the companies may coincide or if an administrative order under Part II of the Insolvency Act 1986 is in force. However, the change cannot be made in any case if the period allowed for laying and delivering accounts in relation to the previous accounting reference period has expired.

Notice under section 225 must state whether the new period is to be shorter or longer than the current reference period, and in any case extension is not possible if a current period plus the extension is more than 18 months in duration, except where an administrative order under Part II of the Insolvency Act 1986 is in force. Moreover, not more than one extension will generally be allowed within a period of five years except to bring the reference periods of holding and subsidiary companies into line.

Laying the Accounts Before the Company in General Meeting and Filing Them With the Registrar

A company's directors must lay before the company in general meeting in respect of each financial year copies of its accounts and the directors' and auditors' reports. Failure to do so within the periods specified in section 244 renders the directors' liable to fines (section 241 of the Companies Act 1985).

A company's directors are also required to deliver copies of the accounts and directors' and auditors' reports to the Registrar of Companies within the time intervals specified in section 244. Where documents are in a foreign language they must be accompanied by a certified English translation. Failure to comply with these provisions renders the directors liable to a fine and, for continued contravention, to a daily default fine. Moreover, if they still fail to file the accounts and reports within 14 days of receiving a notice requiring them to do so, the Court may make a direction ordering them to make good the default within a specified time, in which case it can also order them to bear the costs. However, it will be a defence to show that all reasonable steps were taken to ensure compliance (section 242 of the Companies Act 1985).[24]

In addition to the liability incurred by directors when accounts are not filed, a civil penalty can be imposed on the company. The size of this depends on whether the company is public or private, and it escalates according to the length of the delay (section 242A of the Companies Act 1985).

Where a parent company has an unconsolidated subsidiary which is either registered and operates outside Great Britain, or is an unincorporated business, the subsidiary will not be liable to file its individual accounts with the Registrar. In such circumstances, copies of the subsidiary's latest accounts (*i.e.* for a period ending not less than 12 months before the parent company's year end) have to be filed, together with the auditors' report. Where appropriate these will be its group accounts. Moreover, where necessary a certified English translation must be included. Exemptions from these requirements are available where such a business does not prepare or publish its accounts elsewhere, or where its activities are so different from those of the rest of the group that consolidation would be inappropriate (section 243 of the Companies Act 1985).

The periods allowed for laying and delivering a company's accounts and the directors' and auditors' reports are normally 10 months after the reference period for a private company and seven months for a public company, although if either has interests outside the U.K. the directors can give notice to the Registrar and claim a further three months' extension. Certain modifications are allowed where companies are in their first accounting reference period or where they shorten their accounting reference periods; moreover, the Secretary of State has powers to extend the period for laying and delivering accounts by giving notice in writing.

[24] A number of research studies in the late 1980s suggest that as many as a third of active companies were failing to file their accounts. This is a much lower proportion than the 58 per cent. recorded in May 1984 at the time of an adverse report by the Public Accounts Committee, but it is double the figure given for June 1986 by the Department of Trade and Industry. The Department, which prosecutes directors from about 1,500 companies each year for late delivery of accounts, has since initiated an advertising campaign to improve compliance rates and claims that these are continuing to improve.

The modified rules for a company in its first reference period are that, where such a reference period is greater than 12 months in length, the accounts must nevertheless be laid and delivered within 22 months of its date of incorporation if it is a private company, or 19 months if it is a public company, but both subject to a three months' extension if it has overseas interests. However, this is subject to the proviso that there should always be a minimum allowed period of three months between the end of the reference period and the last date for laying and delivering accounts. Where a company's reference period is shortened under section 225,[25] the period allowed for laying and delivering the accounts is that which expires later of (a) the period normally allowed, and (b) three months from the date of the notice of the change in the accounting reference period given under section 225 (section 244 of the Companies Act 1985).

It should be noted, however, that quoted companies are required by The International Stock Exchange's Listing Agreement to issue their annual reports and accounts within six months of the end of the financial period to which they relate.

Abbreviated accounts

Section 246 of the Companies Act 1985 offers concessions to small and medium sized private companies or groups, as defined in sections 247–249 of the Act, permitting them to file abbreviated (formerly "modified") financial statements with the Registrar of Companies (see *post*, pages 520; 526–528; 549–550; 580; 582–583), though it should be noted that these concessions do not affect the information that must be provided to members of the company. It is estimated that some 90 per cent. of all registered companies qualify as small companies (Cmnd. 9794, para. 8.5). However, many of the 1.1 million companies registered at March 31, 1989 can be regarded as "inactive," only some 450,000 being registered for VAT. Nevertheless, in the year ending on that date 717,000 had filed financial statements, of which 56.8 per cent. submitted full accounts, 31.8 per cent. modified small sized company accounts, 0.5 per cent. modified medium sized company accounts, and 2.8

[25] *Ante*, p. 514.

per cent. group accounts. A further 8 per cent. were classified as dormant. This bears out research which suggests that fewer than half of the companies and groups eligible file modified accounts. Moreover, most of these appear to be larger "small" entities, which are apparently able to afford the luxury of preparing two different sets of accounts and can perhaps ignore the potential information requirements of their creditors that might be satisfied by a close scrutiny of their detailed financial statements.

Approval by directors

A company's annual accounts have to be approved by its board of directors, and the balance sheet and the copy delivered to the Registrar must be signed on their behalf by one of their number. Moreover, every copy of the balance sheet which is laid before the company in general meeting or which is otherwise circulated and published must state the name of the signatory. Failure to observe these requirements renders the company and its defaulting officers liable to a fine. Equally, directors who approve the accounts without taking reasonable steps to ensure they comply with the requirements of the Companies Acts or to prevent their being approved are liable to a fine (section 233 of the Companies Act 1985).

In the case of an abbreviated set of accounts delivered to the Registrar for a small or medium sized private company or group under the provisions of sections 246–249 and Schedule 8, a statement must be included immediately above the signature indicating that the directors have relied on the exemptions and that the company is entitled to benefit from them (Schedule 8, para. 7).

Section 711 of the 1985 Act provides that the Registrar must cause to be published in the *Gazette* notice of the receipt by him of any document delivered by a company in pursuance of section 242, *i.e.* its annual accounts, including the directors' and auditors' reports, and (where relevant) the group accounts.

Directors of an unlimited company are not required to deliver accounts and annexed reports to the Registrar. However, this privilege is lost if any connected company has limited liability or the company itself is a promoter of a trading stamp scheme (section 254 of the Companies Act 1985).

Dispensing with the obligation to lay accounts

A private company may by elective resolution in accordance with section 379A dispense with the laying of its annual accounts and the directors' and auditors' reports before the company in general meeting. Such a resolution relates to the financial statements for the year in which it is made, and the election carries over to subsequent financial years. However, the financial statements still have to be circulated to members, and references in the Act to the laying of accounts are therefore to be interpreted in such circumstances as referring to the documents so circulated (section 252 of the Companies Act 1985).

Where an election is in force dispensing with the requirement to lay annual accounts and the directors' and auditors' reports before a company in general meeting, copies of these statements must be sent to members at least 28 days before the period allowed for laying and delivering accounts, together with a notice of their rights to require the laying of accounts and annexed reports before a general meeting. Failure to do so renders the company and its officers liable to fines. An objecting member or auditor must then inform the company within 28 days of the accounts being circulated, and the directors must then convene a general meeting within 21 days, failing which the objecting party may do so himself. Such a meeting must be held within three months. Where an objecting party has to convene a meeting, he may recover reasonable expenses from the company (section 253 of the Companies Act 1985).

Revision of defective accounts and reports

Where a company's annual accounts and/or directors' report do not comply with the provisions of the Companies Acts, the directors may voluntarily revise them. Where the financial statements have been laid before the company in general meeting or delivered to the Registrar, the revisions need only deal with the corrections and consequential effects. However, the Secretary of State will be able to make regulations by statutory instrument concerning such revisions in respect of the extent of replacing or supplementing the original documents, the function of the auditors in relation to the amendments, remedial steps with regard to publication of the revised information, and the general application of the provisions of the Companies Acts (section 245 of the Companies Act 1985).

The Secretary of State is also empowered to give notice to a company's directors indicating respects in which he believes the financial statements laid before the company or delivered to the Registrar may not comply with the Acts' requirements. The notice must specify a period up to one month, in which time the directors must either explain satisfactorily the accounts or prepare revised financial statements, failing which the Secretary of State may apply to the Court. Moreover, the same actions can be applied against revised accounts (section 245A of the Companies Act 1985).

Further, the Secretary of State (or a person he nominates by statutory instrument) can apply to the Court for a declaration that the accounts are in breach of the Acts and for an order requiring directors to prepare revised financial statements. The order may give directions with respect to the audit, the revision of the directors' report or summary financial statement, steps to be taken by directors to bring the making of the order to the notice of those likely to rely on the defective accounts, and any other pertinent matters. The Court may also order that some or all of the directors approving defective accounts should be liable to pay all or part of the costs of the action. Such proceedings can also be applied against revised accounts (sections 245B and 245C of the Companies Act 1985).

The right to receive accounts

The general rule under section 238 of the 1985 Act is that a copy of a company's annual accounts, together with copies of the auditors' and directors' reports, must be sent to every member, debenture holder, and other person entitled to receive notice of general meetings at least 21 days before the date of the meeting at which they will be laid.[26] If all the members entitled to attend and vote so agree, a shorter time will suffice. Failure to comply renders the company and every officer in default liable to a fine.

[26] However, it is only necessary to send a copy to one joint holder.

Under section 239 any member or debenture holder is entitled to a copy on demand without charge. Failure to comply within seven days with such a demand renders the company and every officer in default liable to a fine and, for continued contravention, a daily default fine.

Publication of financial statements

Section 240 sets out the requirements concerning the publication of a company's accounts. It distinguishes between a company's "statutory" and "non-statutory" accounts, the former being defined as the full individual or group accounts properly delivered to the Registrar. However, statutory accounts also include abbreviated individual or group accounts where properly filed under sections 246–249.[27] Such statutory accounts must be accompanied by the relevant auditors' report.

Where non-statutory[28] accounts are published, a statement must accompany them indicating (a) that they are not the statutory accounts; (b) whether statutory accounts for the year in question have been delivered to the Registrar; and (c) whether the auditors have made a report on the statutory accounts, and if so whether or not it was qualified. The non-statutory accounts must not be published with the auditors' report relating to the statutory accounts (section 240(3) of the Companies Act 1985).

A company which is obliged to prepare group accounts must not publish its individual accounts without also publishing its group accounts (section 240(2) of the Companies Act 1985).

A company which contravenes these requirements and any defaulting officers are liable to be fined.

Non-statutory accounts include preliminary announcements made by quoted companies subject to The International Stock Exchange's Listing Agreement. Other summarised financial statements qualifying as non-statutory accounts would appear to be the simplified statements often circulated by large companies to their employees, but not the summary financial statements circulated to their shareholders by listed companies (see *post*).

[27] Prior to the Companies Act 1989 those were known as "modified" accounts. For the requirements with respect to filing accounts, see p. 514.

[28] Prior to the Companies Act 1989 these were known as "abridged" accounts.

Summary financial statements

Under regulations made by statutory instrument by the Secretary of State, a listed company need not send its members copies of its annual accounts and the directors' and auditors' reports, as required by section 238, *ante*. Instead, under section 251 it can send them a summary financial statement, although those wishing to receive the full accounts must be sent them.

The Act provides that the summary financial statement must be derived from the company's annual accounts and the directors' report in such a form and containing such information as is specified in the regulations.[29] Moreover, it must include statements (a) indicating that it only contains summarised financial information; (b) by the auditors as to whether the information given is consistent with the full accounts and the directors' report; (c) whether the full auditors' report is qualified, and if so include that full report; and (d) whether the full auditors' report contains a statement concerning the accounting records and/or the adequacy of the information and explanations received, and if so include such statements in full.

Failure to observe these conditions renders the company and every defaulting officer liable to a fine.

THE ANNUAL ACCOUNTS

Neither the law nor the accountancy profession has satisfactorily defined the role and purpose of the annual accounts of a company, though the traditional view is that they primarily represent "a stewardship record." Thus the Jenkins Committee expressed the opinion that "a profit and loss account is an historical record. It shows as the profit or loss the difference between the revenue for that period covered by the account and the expenditure chargeable in that period."[30]

Unfortunately the only objective historical record of a company's affairs is afforded by its cash account—any attempt to measure profit inevitably involves valuation, either of the business itself as a going concern, or (more usually) of the individual net assets it owns. Yet experience seems to suggest

[29] The current regulations appear in S.I. 1990 No. 515.
[30] (1962) Cmnd. 1749, para. 333.

that what potential users want above all *is* a measure of profit, even though this must inevitably involve an element of subjectivity in its calculation. The traditional accounting approach, substantially influenced no doubt by the needs of the auditing side of the accountancy profession, has been to value the net assets according to a reasonably flexible set of conservatively biased rules, the overall effect of which is to delay the recognition of profit through time. However, when there is a significant systematic rise in prices over a given period the expenses (representing assets used up) that are matched against current revenues can give rise to a misleadingly inflated profit figure, thus defeating the accountants' aim to exercise prudence in determining the income figure. Another result is that the asset values in a balance sheet are even less likely to approximate to current market values (if indeed that is what is deemed desirable) than might be the case in a period when increases in the general price level are relatively small.

In practice most classes of user of financial statements are well aware of the shortcomings of conventional accounts, and certainly for listed companies they seem primarily to look upon published profit figures as one amongst several signals they receive concerning a company's relative performance and its likely future prospects. In such circumstances the main purpose of the profit calculation would therefore appear to be to enable users of the accounts to compare reported outcomes against what was expected, and this is even true for unquoted companies where alternative sources of information (except at the wider industry level) are rather more limited. Where the reported income and other accounting figures are used not as one of a number of signals of likely future performance, but rather as the basis of a particular calculation (such as a share of profits, the liability to corporation tax, or a restriction under a debt covenant), the interested parties must specify more carefully the exact accounting conventions that are to be adopted in preparing the company's relevant annual financial statements.

It is against this background, then, that the statutory disclosure requirements contained in the Companies Acts (and most specifically in the Companies Act 1985, Sched. 4) should be seen. They establish a basic minimum of information which must be disclosed and be subjected to audit, thus increasing its credibility in the eyes of the reader and so hopefully reducing his uncertainty about future likely outcomes. Many companies will disclose more, either in the statutory accounts themselves and in supplementary statements demanded by the ASC (such as the flow of funds statement and, formerly, current cost accounts) and by International Stock Exchange requirements (which *inter alia* provide that listed companies should publish half-yearly interim accounts); or, alternatively, by other means (*e.g.* for quoted companies through the chairman's report, press releases, or news leaked onto the market via stockbroker's reports; and for unquoted companies by disclosing relevant information directly to bank managers, other major creditors and employee representatives).

Basic principles

Section 226 of the Companies Act 1985 requires the directors of a company to prepare for each financial year its "individual accounts" (*i.e.* its end year balance sheet and a profit and loss account). Likewise, section 227 requires the directors of a company which is a parent company (see *post*) to prepare group accounts (see pp. 564 *et seq*). These sections establish two basic principles with regard to a company's or group's financial statements: first, that insofar as they are prepared under these sections of the Act they must comply as to their form and content with the provisions of Schedules 4 and 4A to the Act; and, secondly, that the balance sheets and profit and loss account and notes thereto must give a true and fair view of the company's or group's financial position and its profit or loss for a given period.

Where a company does not trade for profit, the financial statements will include an income and expenditure account instead of the profit and loss account, together with the balance sheet and notes to the accounts (section 262(2)).

For the purpose of determining whether group accounts should be prepared, a parent undertaking is essentially defined in relation to a subsidiary if (a) it holds a majority of the voting rights; (b) it is a member of the subsidiary and has power to appoint or remove a majority of its directors; or (c) it can exert a dominant influence over the subsidiary (*e.g.* by virtue of a contract) or the companies are managed on a unified basis (section 258 of the Company Act 1985). Further guidance on the interpretation of these terms is given in Schedule 10A, which deals with such matters as voting rights, powers to appoint and remove a majority of directors, and rights to exercise a dominant influence.

Where a group relationship exists, the parent company must prepare group as well as individual company accounts, and they will generally be in the form of consolidated accounts comprising (a) a consolidated balance sheet dealing with the state of affairs of the parent company and its subsidiary undertakings, and (b) a consolidated profit and loss account dealing with the profit or loss of the parent company and its undertakings (section 227(1)–(2) of the Companies Act 1985). However, where a parent undertaking prepares a consolidated profit and loss account, it need not publish a separate individual profit and loss account as long as it discloses how much of the consolidated profit or loss has been dealt with in the company's individual accounts and that it is taking advantage of this exemption (section 230 of the Companies Act 1985).

The requirement for the individual and group financial statements to give a true and fair view is an overriding one, so where information additional to the minimum specified in the Acts is necessary for the financial statements to give a true and fair view, such extra information must be included in those statements. Likewise, where the circumstances are such that strict compliance with a requirement of the Act would not result in a true and fair view, the company must depart from that requirement, full particulars of the reasons for the departure and its effect being disclosed in the notes to the accounts (sections 226(4)–(5) and 227(5)–(6) of the Companies Act 1985; Sched. 4, para. 15).

Despite the fact that it is an overriding requirement that the financial statements should give "a true and fair view" of a company's financial affairs, the exact meaning of the phrase is unfortunately unclear, a matter which was highlighted in the early 1980s by the presence of an alternative current cost set of accounts in the annual reports of most listed companies. However, it seems that adherence to normal accounting practice would be prima facie evidence of giving a true and fair view. Thus the claim that accounts were misleading because they included property at original cost rather than at current market value was rejected by the Courts because normal practice had been followed.[31]

More recently, the status of accounting standards[32] in helping to clarify the meaning of the phrase has been examined in the case of *Lloyd Cheyham and Co. Ltd.* v. *Littlejohn and Co.*[33] There Woolf J. considered the evidential role of such standards and held that "while they are not conclusive ... and they are not ... rigid rules, they are very strong evidence as to what is the proper standard which should be adopted ... " Nevertheless, it is clear that the "true and fair view override" cannot be used with impunity, as was demonstrated in the *Argyll Foods* case.[34] There the company wished to record "economic substance" at the expense of "legal form" and chose—with the agreement of its auditors—to consolidate into its group financial statements for the year ending December 1974 the accounts of a company, even though it did not acquire full control until after the group's balance sheet date. In so doing it was in breach of the Companies Act and Statement of Standard Accounting Practice (SSAP) 14. The magistrates who heard the case decided that the accounts did not show a true and fair view, and subsequently the Department of Trade and Industry (which had brought the prosecution) issued a statement interpreting the decision as confirming its view that the "true and fair view override" is confined to the disclosure requirements of the Companies Acts and that it does not enable companies to depart from the other provisions (*e.g.* definitions) in the Acts. In such circumstances it would seem appropriate where necessary to indicate the underlying economic substance in notes to the accounts or in supplementary pro-forma statements.

The figures included in the annual accounts have been given added significance as a result of sections 39–45 of the Companies Act 1980 (now sections 263–281 of the 1985 Act), which prescribe that distributable profit is generally the aggregate of accumulated realised net profts as reported in the

[31] *Re Press Caps Ltd.* [1949] Ch. 434.
[32] See *post*, pp. 550 *et seq.*
[33] [1986] PCC 389.
[34] Unfortunately the case is not reported, but the issues, evidence and decision have been examined at some length by R. K. Ashton in "The Argyll Foods Case: A Legal Analysis," *Accounting and Business Research*, Vol. 17, no. 65, Winter 1986, pp. 3–12.

latest audited (or, if relevant, interim) accounts. Moreover, public company can only a pay a dividend if the net assets (after payment of the dividend) at least equal its capital plus any reserves not available for distribution (see *post*, Chap. 22). Apart from introducing the problem of deciding which profits are actually realised and which are not—a somewhat arbitrary distinction and a matter anyway of some dispute amongst accountants[35]—such rules cannot ensure the protection of unsecured creditors, while at the same time they may possibly inhibit the efficient workings of the capital market.

Large, medium, and small sized companies

Although the directors of private companies have always had to prepare statutory accounts to lay before their shareholders in general meeting, prior to 1967 most were exempted from the need to file these financial statements with the Registrar of Companies. However, under the provisions of the Companies Act in that year, this dispensation ceased to operate, and, apart from exemptions for special classes of business (like banks and insurance and—at that time—shipping companies), the only concessions were for companies below a certain size which were permitted not to disclose details of turnover and directors' remuneration, the criteria (set in terms of the size of the amounts involved) being altered from time-to-time by statutory instrument. Exemptions were also granted in relation to a turnover criterion permitting companies not to disclose in their directors' reports the value of exports, the average number of employees and their aggregate remuneration, and turnover and pre-tax profit or loss by each class of business. It was the view of the Bolton Committee of enquiry on small firms that these concessions did not seriously prejudice the work of credit agencies and the interests of unsecured creditors.[36]

Using a size criterion to determine the extent of disclosure in the accounts filed with the Registrar of Companies was a

[35] Section 262(3) of the 1985 merely says that "realised" profits and losses are "such profits or losses of the company as fall to be treated as realised in accordance with principles generally accepted . . . with respect to the determination for accounting purposes of realised profits or losses." See *post*, p. 629.

[36] (1972) Cmnd. 4811, Chap. 17.

principle established by section 5(1) of the Companies Act 1981, and now confirmed in section 246 of the 1985 Act. Briefly, while all limited companies (other than investment companies and companies engaged in banking and insurance—see *post*, pages 584–586 must prepare and lay detailed accounts before their members in general meeting in accordance with one or other of a set of prescribed forms of financial statement given in Schedule 4 to the Act (section 241), medium and small sized non-public companies can avail themselves of concessions whereby they need only *file* "abbreviated" accounts (see *ante*, page 516).

In order to qualify for this exemption, small or medium sized companies or groups must neither be nor include public companies, banks, insurance companies or authorised persons under the Financial Services Act 1986 (section 246(3)–(4) of the Companies Act 1985).

A company qualifies as small or medium sized where it meets the criteria described below:

(1) in its first financial year; or
(2) subsequently in the current and previous years; or
(3) it was so qualified in the previous financial year.

The qualifying criteria are that it should meet at least two of three conditions concerning annualised turnover, balance sheet totals and the average weekly number of employees as follows:

		Small sized	Medium sized
(1)	annualised turnover	≤£2m	≤£8m
(2)	balance sheet total	≤£975,000	≤£3.9m
(3)	average weekly number of employees	≤50	≤250

(section 247 of the Companies Act 1985).

The concessions available to qualifying small and medium sized private companies are summarised below on pages 549–550. However, a parent company will not qualify unless it meets the conditions necessary to exempt it from the need to prepare group accounts under section 249, described below.

In order to file abbreviated accounts, a qualifying small or medium sized company must obtain a report from its auditors stating whether in their opinion the company is entitled to the exemptions (Sched. 8, para. 8(1)). The directors must also append to the filed accounts a statement indicating that advantage is being taken of the exemptions and the grounds for doing so (Sched. 8, para. 7). The abbreviated accounts must also be accompanied by a signed special auditors' report stating that in their opinion the company is entitled to the exemptions and that the accounts have been properly prepared in accordance with the provisions of Schedule 8. Included in this report will be the audit report required under section 235, which refers to the full accounts (Sched. 8, para. 8(2)–(4)).

A parent company of a group which qualifies as a small or medium sized group need not prepare group accounts, either for delivery to the Registrar or for presentation to the shareholders at a general meeting. However, to take advantage of this exemption, the company's auditors must provide the directors with a report stating that in their opinion the company is entitled to do so, and this must be attached to the company's individual accounts. However, a group is not eligible for the exemption if any of its members are public companies, banks, insurance companies or authorised persons under the Financial Services Act 1986 (s.248, Companies Act 1985).

To qualify as a small or medium sized group and thus be eligible not to prepare group accounts, it must meet the criteria:

(1) in its first financial year; or
(2) subsequently in the current and previous years; or
(3) it was so qualified in the previous financial year.

The qualifying criteria are that it should meet at least two of the conditions concerning annualised turnover, balance sheet totals and the average weekly number of employees as follows:

		Small sized		Medium sized	
		Net	Gross	Net	Gross
(1)	annualised turnover	≤£2m	≤£2.4m	≤£8m	≤£9.6m
(2)	balance sheet total	≤£1m	≤£2.1m	≤£3.0m	≤£4.7m
(3)	average weekly number of employees	≤50		≤250	

(Net means after set-offs required by Sched. 4A when consolidated accounts are being prepared, and gross means before those set-offs) (section 249 of the Companies Act 1985).

Form and content of accounts[37]

1. *General rules*

The approach adopted in the EC's Fourth Council Directive (on which the first Schedule to the 1981 Act and now the fourth Schedule of the 1985 Act are substantially based) was essentially prescriptive in nature, reflecting the influence of continental Europe. Thus Section A of Part I of the fourth Schedule to the 1985 Act establishes the general rules in relation to the form and content of the accounts, indicating that one of the prescribed formats (four for the profit and loss account and two for the balance sheet) must be used (para. 1) and be adhered to year by year unless there are special reasons justifying a change (para. 2). However, some flexibility is allowed—where necessary, directors may give greater detail than prescribed (para. 3(1)) or adapt the formats to reflect the special nature of a company's business (para. 3(3)), and certain items (indicated in the model statements by Arabic numerals) can be combined if the combination facilitates an assessment of the company's performance or position (para. 3(4)). Comparative figures for the previous accounting period are also to be shown (para. 4), but individual items may not be set off against each other (para. 5).

2. *Balance sheet*

Section B of Part I of the fourth Schedule to the Companies Act 1985 sets out two alternative formats of balance sheet, the contents of which are in fact identical. The first (reproduced below) equates net assets to the aggregate of the share capital and reserves, and is thus not dissimilar to the vertical layout commonly used in the United Kingdom before the Act came into effect. Not surprisingly it is therefore the most widely used layout, particularly for larger companies. The second format equates assets against claims, a method of presentation more commonly used in continental European countries.

[37] In the remainder of this chapter, paragraph references are to the fourth Schedule to the 1985 Act, unless otherwise indicated.

Balance sheet—Format I

A *Called up share capital not paid*

B *Fixed assets*

I Intangible assets

1 Development costs
2 Concessions, patents, licences, trade marks and similar rights and assets
3 Goodwill
4 Payments on account

II Tangible assets

1 Land and buildings
2 Plant and machinery
3 Fixtures, fittings, tools and equipment
4 Payments on account and assets in course of construction

III Investments

1 Shares in group undertakings
2 Loans to group undertakings
3 Participating interests
4 Loans to undertakings in which the company has a participating interest
5 Other investments other than loans
6 Other loans
7 Own shares

C *Current assets*

I Stocks

1 Raw materials and consumables
2 Work in progress
3 Finished goods and goods for resale
4 Payments on account

II Debtors

1 Trade debtors
2 Amounts owed by group undertakings
3 Amounts owed by undertakings in which the company has a participating interest
4 Other debtors
5 Called up share capital not paid
6 Prepayments and accrued income

III Investments

1 Shares in group undertakings
2 Own shares

3 Other investments

IV Cash at bank and in hand

D Prepayments and accrued income

E Creditors: amounts falling due within one year

1 Debenture loans
2 Bank loans and overdrafts
3 Payments received on account
4 Trade creditors
5 Bills of exchange payable
6 Amounts owed to group undertakings
7 Amounts owed to undertakings in which the company has a participating interest
8 Other creditors including taxation and social security
9 Accruals and deferred income

F Net current assets (liabilities)

G Total assets less current liabilities

H Creditors: amounts falling due after more than one year

1 Debenture loans
2 Bank loans and overdrafts
3 Payments received on account
4 Trade creditors
5 Bills of exchange payable
6 Amounts owed to group undertakings
7 Amounts owed to undertakings in which the company has a participating interest
8 Other creditors including taxation and social security
9 Accruals and deferred income

I Provisions for liabilities and charges

1 Pensions and similar obligations
2 Taxation, including deferred taxation
3 Other provisions

J Accruals and deferred income

K Capital and reserves

I Called up share capital

II Share premium account
III Revaluation reserve
IV Other reserves
1 Capital redemption reserve
2 Reserve for own shares
3 Reserves provided for by the articles of association
4 Other reserves
V Profit and loss account

Preliminary expenses, issuing expenses and commissions, and research expenditure are not permitted to be treated as assets in a company's balance sheet (Sched. 4, para. 3(2)). Intangible assets, such as patents and trade marks, can however be included if they were either acquired for valuable consideration or were created by the company itself. Similarly, only goodwill acquired for valuable consideration can be shown as an asset in a balance sheet, but its cost must be written off systematically over a period which must not exceed its estimated useful economic life (para. 21). The amount of each item to be shown under the head "Debtors" must be split between those amounts receivable within one year of the balance sheet date and those receivable later than that; and in determining the amount to be shown under "Net current assets," amounts shown as "Prepayments and accrued income" have to be taken into account.

As regards claims, where there are debenture loans these have to be split between convertible and non-convertible loans; and the amounts of allotted and paid-up share capital have also to be shown separately. Payments received on account for orders must be shown under creditors unless disclosed as a deduction from stocks of finished goods.

A "participating interest" is an interest held by an undertaking in the shares of another undertaking which it holds on a long-term basis. Moreover, such a holding must be for the purpose of securing a contribution to its activities by the exercise of control or influence arising from or related to that interest. Normally a holding of 20 per cent. of a company's shares, including convertibles and options, will give rise to the presumption of there being a "participating interest" unless the contrary is shown (section 260 of the Companies Act 1985).

A provision is "any amount retained as reasonably necessary for the purpose of providing for any liability or loss which is either likely to be incurred, or certain to be incurred but uncertain as to amount or as to the date on which it will arise" (Sched. 4, para. 89).

A company will normally only hold its own shares where it has acquired them by forfeiture or surrender. Where it purchases or redeems its own shares they must be cancelled (sections 146 and 160(4)).

For the rules relating to share premium and capital redemption reserve accounts, see Chapters 9–10.

Medium and large sized companies, as defined previously, have to file a full balance sheet, but small companies need only submit an abbreviated statement, duly signed by a director, that discloses only those items that are preceded by a letter or a Roman numeral. However, the aggregate amounts of debtors and creditors have to be divided between amounts receivable or payable within one year and those receivable or payable beyond that period. Details can be disclosed either in the balance sheet itself or in the notes to the accounts (Sched. 8, para. 1(2)).

3. *Profit and loss account*

Of the four profit and loss account formats given in the fourth Schedule to the 1985 Act, the first two (reproduced below) are presented in a vertical form (and are therefore probably the most likely to be used in the United Kingdom), while the third and fourth show expenses on the left and income on the right. Formats 1 and 3 classify expenses by function, whereas formats 2 and 4 classify them by type. Format 1 is the layout most commonly used by large companies.

Profit and loss accounts—Format 1

1 Turnover
2 Cost of sales
3 Gross profit or loss
4 Distribution costs
5 Administrative expenses
6 Other operating income
7 Income from shares in group undertakings
8 Income from participating interests
9 Income from other fixed asset investments
10 Other interest receivable and similar income
11 Amounts written off investments

12 Interest payable and similar charges
13 Tax on profit or loss on ordinary activities
14 Profit or loss on ordinary activities after taxation
15 Extraordinary income
16 Extraordinary charges
17 Extraordinary profit or loss
18 Tax on extraordinary profit or loss
19 Other taxes not shown under the above items
20 Profit or loss for the financial year

Profit and loss accounts—Format 2

1 Turnover
2 Change in stocks of finished goods and in work in progress
3 Own work capitalised
4 Other operating income
5 (*a*) Raw materials and consumables
(*b*) Other external charges
6 Staff Costs:
(*a*) wages and salaries
(*b*) social security costs
(*c*) other pension costs
7 (*a*) Depreciation and other amounts written off tangible and intangible fixed assets
(*b*) Exceptional amounts written off current assets
8 Other operating charges
9 Income from shares in group undertakings
10 Income from participating interests
11 Income from other fixed asset investments
12 Other interest payable and similar income
13 Amounts written off investments
14 Interest payable and similar charges
15 Tax on profit or loss on ordinary activities
16 Profit or loss on ordinary activities after taxation
17 Extraordinary income
18 Extraordinary charges
19 Extraordinary profit or loss
20 Tax on ordinary profit or loss
21 Other taxes not shown under the above items
22 Profit or loss for the financial year

Where the format classifies expenses by function (*i.e.* formats 1 and 3) the amounts to be shown under cost of sales, distribution costs and administrative expenses are to be net of depreciation charges and provisions for diminution in the value of assets. However, the amounts of any such charges or provisions for both tangible and intangible fixed assets must be disclosed separately in the notes to the financial statements. In addition, any interest or similar charges payable to group companies must be shown separately.

Apart from the above, whichever format is adopted the following items must be disclosed separately in the profit and loss account:

(i) profit or loss on ordinary activities before taxation;
(ii) the aggregate amount of any dividends paid or proposed; and
(iii) movements to or from reserves (Sched. 4, paras. 3(6), (7)).

Large sized companies have to choose one of the four profit and loss account formats and file the full version. However, medium sized companies are permitted to file an abbreviated statement. Effectively, the following items can be combined and be shown as one item, "gross profit or loss":

(*a*) where expenses are classified by function—turnover, cost of sales, gross profit or loss and other operating income; and
(*b*) where expenses are classified by type—turnover, change in stocks of finished goods and work in progress, own work capitalised, other operating income, raw materials and consumables, and other external charges (Sched. 8, para 7).

The directors of a small company are exempted from having to file a profit and loss account (Sched. 8, para. 2).

Various Statements of Standard Accounting Practice (SSAPs) issued by the ASC affect the calculation and presentation of items in the profit and loss account, and they can be accommodated either in the notes or in the body of the statement as supplementary disclosures. The most important in this regard are probably the standards on earnings per share (SSAP 3), which requires listed companies to show this figure on the face of the statement itself; on associated companies (SSAP 1), which requires partial consolidation of associated companies' profits; on group accounts (SSAP 14), which deals with the methods of consolidation; on extraordinary items (SSAP 6), which indicates how and where such items should be disclosed; on taxation (SSAPs 8 and 15), which indicate how current and deferred tax charges should be disclosed; on foreign currency translation (SSAP 20); on accounting for leases and hire purchase contracts (SSAP 21); on accounting for goodwill (SSAP 22); on accounting for acquisitions and mergers (SSAP 23) and on segmental reporting (SSAP 25). In addition, SSAP 10 requires all except the smallest of companies to publish a supplementary statement of source and application of funds (see *post*, page 562).

Notes to the financial statements

Much of the information which was required to be disclosed either in the accounts or in the directors' report between 1967 and 1981, but which cannot be accommodated in the model formats given in the fourth Schedule to the 1985 Act, has to be revealed in notes to the financial statements, which themselves form an integral part of the accounts. These notes may be contained in the accounts themselves or in a separate document annexed to the accounts (section 261 of the Companies Act 1985). Most of the details of items which are to be disclosed in note form are given in the fourth Schedule, paras. 35–38, and in the fifith and sixth Schedule. However, items in the model statements required by the fourth Schedule which are preceded by Arabic numerals can also be relegated to a note if necessary (Sched. 4, para. 3(4)). Conversely, items required to be shown in notes may, where feasible, be shown on the face of the accounts (Sched. 4, paras 3(1) and 35).

1. *General notes*

The accounting policies used by a company must be disclosed, in particular indicating the depreciation and foreign currency translation methods employed, a requirement which substantially meets the conditions of SSAP 2 (paras. 36 and 58(1)). There must also be a statement indicating whether the accounts have been prepared in accordance with applicable accounting standards[38] and giving particulars of any material departure from such standards and the reasons for it (para. 36A).

Other SSAPs relevant in this context are group accounts (SSAP 14), associated companies (SSAP 1), the treatment of

[38] See *post*, pp. 550–552.

government grants (SSAP 4), accounting for value added tax (SSAP 5), depreciation (SSAP 12), research and development (SSAP 13), stocks and work in progress (SSAP 9), taxation (SSAPs 8 and 15), foreign currency translation (SSAP 20), accounting for leases (SSAP 21), accounting for goodwill (SSAP 22), accounting for acquisitions and mergers (SSAP 23), and accounting for pension costs (SSAP 24). Exposure drafts (EDs) of proposed accounting standards which are relevant in this context have also been published, *e.g.* on related party transactions (ED 46); and reflecting the substance of transactions in assets and liabilities (ED 49).

Corresponding amounts for the previous financial year (adjusted if necessary to make them comparable), have to be given for all items disclosed in the notes, except for movements on reserves, provisions, fixed asset and depreciation accounts; loans and other transactions with directors and officers of the company under the sixth Schedule to the Act; and information on subsidiaries and significant shareholdings that has to be disclosed under Parts I and II of the fifth Schedule to the Act; *i.e.* Balance Sheet items (B), (C) (D)(ii)–(iv), and (I) as referred to below on pages 537–544 (Sched. 4, para. 58).

2. *Balance Sheet*

The following details must be disclosed by way of notes:

(A) *Share capital and loan stock*

- (i) Authorised share capital and number and nominal value of each class of shares allotted (para. 38).
- (ii) Where redeemable shares (either preference or equity) have been alloted the notes must disclose the earliest and latest dates of redemption, whether the company is obliged to redeem them or merely has the option to do so, and whether any premium is payable on redemption, and if so the amount (para. 38).
- (iii) Where shares or debentures have been allotted during the year, the reasons for making the issue, the classes of securities involved and the amount/number issued or allotted, and the aggregate nominal value and the consideration received for each class. Moreover, in respect of debentures particulars must be disclosed of

any redeemable debentures the company has power to re-issue, and the nominal amount and book value of any debentures held by a nominee or trustee of the company (paras. 39, 41).

(iv) Where options or similar rights exist in relation to shares, the number, description and amount of the shares involved, the period during which the right is exercisable, and the price payable have to be disclosed (para. 40).

(B) *Reserves and provisions*[39]

The aggregate amounts of each reserve and provision (including any material amount included in the category "other provisions") at the beginning and end of the financial year must be disclosed, together with details of movements to and from such reserves and provisions during the year (para. 46). In addition, the amount of any provision for deferred taxation other than the amount of any provision for other taxation must be disclosed separately (para. 47); while under the terms of SSAP 15 the balance on the deferred tax account has to be shown separately. Other requirements in relation to the presentation of tax liabilities in the balance sheet and profit and loss account and accompanying notes are to be found in SSAP 8.

(C) *Fixed assets*[40]

For each item under this heading, both tangible and intangible assets, and also for long-term investments, the notes must disclose in respect of cost or valuation the aggregate amounts at the beginning and end of the year, the amounts of any acquisitions, disposals and transfers, and the effect of applying the alternative accounting valuation rules (see below). In addition, details must be given of the cumulative amounts of provisions for depreciation or for the diminution in the value of assets at both the beginning and end of the financial year, and the amounts of any additions, reductions through asset

[39] "Provisions" are defined in Sched. 4, paras. 88–89.
[40] "Fixed assets" are defined in s.262(1), Companies Act 1985.

disposals, and any other adjustments to such provisions made during the year (para. 42).

Where a fixed asset (other than listed investments) has been revalued, the notes must disclose the year in which the assets were severally valued and the several values; and in the years of each valuation the names or qualifications of the valuers and the bases of valuation (para. 43). Land and buildings must be divided among freeholds, long leaseholds (*i.e.* with more than 50 years of lease unexpired at the year end) and short leaseholds (paras. 44, 83).

(D) *Investments*

Certain details of investments must be disclosed, regardless of whether they are shown as fixed or current assets.

(i) *Listed investments*

The following information must be shown with respect to listed investments: their amount, split between investments listed on a recognised stock exchange, together with their quoted value (and estimated market value where this is higher) if it (or they) differ from the value(s) shown in the balance sheet; and unlisted investments. The latter category includes securities traded on the Unlisted Securities Market (USM) and the over-the-counter (OTC) market, but there is no requirement (as there was under para. 5A of the second schedule to the 1967 Act) to disclose either the directors' valuation of the unlisted securities or other information relating to them (paras. 45 and 84).

(ii) *Holdings in subsidiary undertakings*

For companies required to prepare group accounts, the following information must be disclosed in respect of all subsidiary undertakings of the parent company at its year end: their names; the countries in which they are incorporated (and, if in Great Britain, the country of registration) or, if they are unincorporated, their principal places of business; whether they are included in consolidated group accounts and, if not, the reasons why not; how they qualify as subsidiaries under section

258 of the Act, except where this is a result of majority holdings of voting shares; and the proportions of each class of a subsidiary's shares held by the parent company and by the group as a whole.

With respect to each subsidiary not included in consolidated accounts, the aggregate of its year end capital and reserves and the profit or loss as shown in its last accounts must be disclosed, except where (a) the investment is dealt with by the equity consolidation method; (b) the investee company is not required by the Act to deliver a copy of its accounts and does not publish them elsewhere; (c) the holding is less than half the nominal value of the subsidiary's shares; or (d) it is immaterial (Sched. 5, para. 17).

With respect to all subsidiaries, the parent company's directors must give reasons when their financial year ends differ from that of the parent company. They must also disclose the dates of the subsidiaries' most recent year ends, either for each subsidiary or the earliest and latest of such dates if there are several whose financial years do not coincide with that of the parent. Qualifications in auditors' reports on subsidiary undertakings' accounts, or material disclosures in such accounts which have avoided such qualifications, must also be revealed by the parent company if not disclosed in the group accounts (Sched. 5, paras. 19, 18).

Details must also be disclosed of shares and debentures in the parent company held by subsidiary undertakings (Sched. 5, para. 20).

Similar disclosures must be made by a company which has subsidiary undertakings but is not required to prepare group accounts (Sched. 5, paras. 1–6). However, in such circumstances the company has to disclose the reason why it is not preparing group accounts and, if the reason is that all the subsidiaries fall within the exemptions specified in section 229, a statement for each subsidiary indicating which exclusion applies (Sched. 5, para. 1(4)–(5)).

(iii) *Joint ventures*

A company which is required to prepare group accounts, and which accounts for an undertaking as a joint venture using the method of pro rata proportional consolidation, must disclose the undertaking's name; its principal place of business; the basis of its joint management; the proportion of its capital held by undertakings included in the consolidation; and, where its financial year does not coincide with that of the company, its most recent year end (Sched. 5, para. 21).

(iv) *Associated undertakings*

A company which is required to prepare group accounts, and which has an undertaking included in the consolidation that has an interest in an associated undertaking, must disclose the following in respect of such an associated undertaking: its name; the country in which it is incorporated (and, if in Great Britain, the country of registration) or, if it is unincorporated, its principal place of business; and the proportions of each class of the associate's shares held by the parent company and by the group as a whole (Sched. 5, para. 22).

(v) *Other significant holdings*

Companies, whether required to prepare group accounts or not, must disclose the following information (if not otherwise given) with respect to companies in which they hold either more than 10 per cent. of the nominal value of any class of share, or the amount invested as shown in the investor company's individual accounts exceeds 10 per cent. of its assets: their names; the countries in which they are incorporated (and, if in Great Britain, the country of registration) or, if they are unincorporated, their principal places of business; and the proportions of each class of the investee company's shares held (Sched. 5, paras. 7–9; 23–24).

For holdings in excess of 20 per cent. of the shares in an undertaking, the aggregate amount of the investee company's year end capital and reserves and of its annual profit or loss must also be disclosed, except where (a) the investment is dealt with by the equity consolidation method; (b) the investee company is not obliged to deliver a copy of its accounts and does not publish them elsewhere; (c) the holding is less than half the nominal value of the subsidiary's shares; (d) it is immaterial; or (e) the investor company is exempt from preparing group accounts as its accounts are included in the financial statements of a larger group (Sched. 5, paras. 9 and

25). Similar criteria are to be applied in respect of a group (rather than just the parent company) where this is relevant (Sched. 5, paras. 26–28).

In addition to the above, The International Stock Exchange's Listing Agreement requires, for all investments in which there is a participation of 20 per cent. or more, details of the countries in which the investee operates to be disclosed.

(E) *Creditors*

For each item under heading H in format 1 of the balance sheet (page 531, *ante*) and its equivalent in format 2, the following must be disclosed:

- (i) Amounts payable (other than by instalments) more than five years hence.
- (ii) The aggregate amount of any instalments payable five or more years hence.
- (iii) The terms of payment and any applicable rate of interest.
- (iv) The aggregate figure for secured creditors and the nature of securities given.
- (v) The amount and period of any arrears of fixed cumulative dividends (paras. 48, 49, 85).

(F) *Guarantees and financial commitments*

Under para. 50 of the fourth Schedule the following items must be disclosed:

- (i) The amount of third party liabilities secured by charges on the company's assets.
- (ii) The amount, nature and security provided (if any) in relation to any contingent liability. (SSAP 18 requires additional disclosures for such items).
- (iii) The aggregate of capital expenditure (a) contracted for, and (b) authorised by the directors but not contracted for.
- (iv) Pension commitments (a) provided for, and (b) not provided for. (Further guidance on how this should be done is given in SSAP 24 and Technical Release (TR) 756).

(v) Any other commitments relevant to a proper understanding of the company's affairs.

Commitments undertaken on behalf of (a) subsidiaries of the company; (b) parent or fellow subsidiary undertakings must be stated separately both from each other and from the company's other commitments (para. 59A).

(G) *Dividends*

The aggregate amount of proposed dividends has to be disclosed (paras. 3 and 51).

(H) *Loans made for the purchase of a company's shares*

Details of any outstanding loan made for the purpose of acquiring the company's shares under sections 153(4) or 155 of the Act (see *ante*, Chapter 11) must be disclosed in aggregate for each item in which they are included (para. 51).

(I) *Credit transactions with directors and officers of the company*

Under Parts II and III of the sixth Schedule to the Act, particulars must be disclosed in notes to the accounts of any material credit transaction or arrangement with a director, shadow director, connected person or officer other than a director which are permitted under sections 330–338 (see pages 388–389). Under paras. 22 and 29 of the sixth Schedule, the information to be disclosed is generally:

(i) The fact that the transaction, loan, arrangement or agreement was made or existed during the financial year; and
(ii) The name of the director or connected person; and/or the number of officers concerned.

With regard to directors and connected persons, the value of credit transactions has to be disclosed, as well as the nature of any material interest; while for loans and similar arrangements the following details must be given:

(i) Principal and interest at the beginning and end of the financial year, the maximum amount of the liability during the year, interest due but not paid, and related bad debt provisions; and

(ii) The liability of the company or its subsidiaries under guarantees or security and other similar arrangements at the beginning and end of the year, the maximum potential liability, and expenses or liabilities incurred in discharging the guarantee or security arrangement (Sched. 6, para. 22(2)).

With regard to officers other than directors, disclosure must be made of loans and other equivalent arrangements in terms of the aggregate amounts outstanding at the end of the year, together with the number of persons concerned, under the following headings:

(i) Loans or security therefor and similar arrangements;

(ii) Quasi-loans or security therefor and similar arrangements; and

(iii) Credit transactions or security therefor and similar arrangements (Sched. 6, para. 29).

Such disclosures also apply when the company is a recognised bank or, for groups of companies, where the holding company or a subsidiary is a recognised bank (Sched. 9, Part IV).

Exemptions from the disclosure requirements for directors, connected persons and officers of the company are permitted on a number of grounds, most notably in relation to service contracts and where the values of the items or interest are small (generally if they do not exceed £5,000 in aggregate at any time during the year for each director; or, for officers other than directors, £2,500) (Sched. 6, paras. 17–21, 23–26, 29(2)).

3. *Profit and loss account*

(A) *Segmental analysis*

(i) Where, in the opinion of the directors, a company has carried on two or more classes of business which differ substantially the notes must for each class show the turnover and the pre-tax profit or loss. Turnover in this context means revenues from ordinary activities net of trade discounts, VAT and other duties. (This treatment of VAT is consistent with the terms of SSAP 5.) In determining the source of turnover or of profit or loss the directors are to have regard to the way in which the company's activities are organised (paras. 55 and section 262(1) of the 1985 Act).

(ii) Where, in the opinion of the directors, a company has supplied goods and services to two or more geographical *markets* the turnover must be disaggregated as between such markets (para. 55). By contrast The International Stock Exchange requires a geographical analysis of turnover and contribution to trading results of trading (*i.e.* manufacturing, etc.) *operations* abroad.

(iii) Segmental information need not be disclosed if the directors are of the opinion that its publication would be detrimental to the company's best interests, but if this is the case the fact that such an analysis is being withheld must be stated (para. 55(5)).

SSAP 25 and International Accounting Standard 14 indicate that in addition the segment assets employed should be disclosed.

(B) *Other sources of income*

Income from listed investments and, where it comprises a substantial part of the company's revenue, net rents from land must be disclosed (para. 53). (Before the Companies Act 1981 there was also a requirement to disclose income from unquoted investments.)

(C) *Extraordinary items*

Particulars must be disclosed of prior year transactions included in the profit and loss account; extraordinary items (gross and net of associated tax); and exceptional items (*i.e.* those which arise as a result of the ordinary activities of the business but are abnormal by virtue of their size or incidence) (para. 57). (These requirements are substantially the same as the terms of SSAP 6 as revised, July 1986).

(D) *Taxation*

The notes must disclose the amounts of the charges to both United Kingdom corporation and United Kingdom income taxes, together with a note of the gross amount of the former before any double taxation relief, and details of any overseas taxation borne. Moreover, the tax associated with any extraordinary item must also be shown separately. In addition, the basis of the United Kingdom corporation tax charge must be disclosed, together with details of any special circumstances that affect any liability to taxation (para. 54).

Further requirements concerning the calculation and disclosure of taxation are given in SSAPs 8 and 15.

(E) *Specific expenses*

Under para. 53 of the fourth Schedule details of the following must be disclosed:

(i) Interest on loans outside the group, analysed between (a) bank loans, overdrafts and other loans repayable either in a lump sum within five years or by instalments with the last instalment payable within that period; and (b) any other loans.
(ii) Hire charges for plant and machinery (SSAP 21 covers the treatment of leased assets).
(iii) Amounts set aside for the redemption of (a) share capital; and (b) loans.

In addition, under section 390A(3)–(4) of the 1985 Act auditors' remuneration (including expenses) must be disclosed in a note to the accounts.

(F) *Employees and their remuneration*

Details must be disclosed of the following:

(i) The average number of employees in the financial year, found by summing the number of employees (both full- and part-time) week-by-week and dividing by the number of weeks in the period. This figure is then broken down into such categories of employee as the directors select, having regard to the company's organisation (para. 56). (The data are to relate to all employees, not just to those working in the United Kingdom, as was the requirement under section 18 of the 1967 Act.)

(ii) Insofar as they are not disclosed in the profit and loss account, the aggregate amount of each of the following: (a) wages and salaries payable; (b) social security costs, including contributions to state run pension schemes; and (c) other pension costs incurred, comprising contributions to a private pension scheme by the company, any other sums set aside for that purpose, and any pension payments (paras. 56 and 94).

(iii) Under section 232 of the Act and paragraphs 1, 7–9 of the sixth Schedule (a) directors' emoluments; (b) directors' pensions; (c) compensation payments to directors for loss of office; and (d) sums paid to third parties in respect of directors' services.

(iv) Under section 232 of the Act and paragraphs 2–5 of the sixth Schedule, where the total emoluments of all the directors exceed £60,000 in the year in question, the emoluments of the chairman, the highest paid director (if other than the chairman), the number of directors who did not receive emoluments, and the number of directors who received emoluments in the following bands; £0 up to £5,000; over £5,000 and up to £10,000; over £10,000 and up to £15,000; and so on, the bands rising by increments of £5,000. It is only necessary to show those bands for which there are entries, and for these purposes emoluments include amounts waived as well as paid.

(v) Under section 232 of the Act and paragraph 6 of the sixth Schedule the number of directors who have waived rights to receive emoluments and the aggregate amount of those emoluments.

For the purposes of (iii)–(v), above, "emoluments" where relevant refers to remuneration from a group of companies and includes fees and percentages, expenses allowances so far as charged to United Kingdom income tax, and the estimated money value of any other benefits received otherwise than in cash (Sched. 6, para. 1). In addition, for (iii) it includes contributions paid in respect of a director under a pension scheme (Sched. 6, paras. 1, 2). The amounts to be brought into account for a financial year are the sums receivable in respect of that year, whenever paid, or, in the case of sums not receivable in respect of a period, the sums paid during that year. With regard to remuneration, the details given in the parent company's accounts must relate to the emoluments, etc., of its directors or employees from all sources, including subsidiaries. (Sched. 6, paras. 10–11).

For the purposes of (iv)–(v), above, such disclosure is not required of a company which is neither a subsidiary nor a parent company if the aggregate amount of the emoluments disclosed as a result of (iii), above, does not exceed £60,000 (Sched. 6, para. 2).

4. *Other notes*

Certain other information has to be disclosed in notes to the financial statements (or sometimes on the face of the accounts themselves) in order to comply with the provisions of the Companies Act 1985 on accounting principles and rules (discussed below), and provisions of various accounting standards and (for quoted companies) The International Stock Exchange's Listing Agreement. Moreover, as indicated above (page 524), where there is a departure from strict compliance with a requirement of the Act to ensure the financial statements reflect a true and fair view, the reasons for the departure and its effect have to be disclosed in a note to the accounts (para. 15). In this context, the professional accountancy bodies in the British Isles suggest a material difference between reported and distributable profits should be disclosed in a note (see *post*, Chapter 22).

Under paragraphs 11 and 31 of the fifth Schedule, a company which is a subsidiary must state the name and country of incorporation of its ultimate parent company. In addition, under paragraphs 10 and 30, it must give similar details relating to the parent company of both the largest group for which group accounts are drawn up and of which it is a member and also the smallest such group. In so doing, if the parent is incorporated in

Great Britain, it must also disclose its country of registration; and if the parent undertaking is unincorporated, its principal place of business.

Companies are also required to disclose certain particulars where they have made arrangements during a year which attract merger relief (Sched. 5, paras. 10 and 29: see *post*, page 573).

5. *Abbreviated financial statements*

Under section 246 and paragraph 5 of the eighth Schedule to the Act, the directors of a *medium sized*[41] private company may omit from the statements that they file with the Registrar of Companies the statement indicating that their accounts have been prepared in accordance with applicable accounting standards,[42] as well as detailed information concerning their trading operations (see *ante*, page 535) and turnover and pre-tax profit by line of business and geographical market (*i.e.* profit and loss account note (A) on page 544, *ante*).

The concessions offered to *small sized*[42] private companies under paragraphs 1–4 of the eighth Schedule are more far reaching—of the items which may be disclosed in notes listed above, only the following have to be disclosed:

1. General notes:	Accounting policies, including in particular the bases of foreign currency translations.
2. Balance sheet[43]:	(A) Share capital and loan stock: items (i) and (ii), and in so far as it relates to shares (but not to loan stock) (iii).
	(C) Fixed assets, but only in respect of categories preceded by letters and roman numerals.
	(E) Creditors, items (i), (ii) and (iv).
	(I) Transactions with directors and officers of the company.

[41] See *ante*, pp. 526–528 for the requirements for a private company to qualify as medium or small sized; and p. 528 for the requirement that a statement should be included above the directors' signatures indicating the company is entitled to benefit from the disclosure exemptions. See *post*, p. 580 for the concession concerning the directors' report; and p. 528 on the requirement to attach a "special" auditor's report to the accounts.

[42] See *post*, pp. 550 *et seq*.

[43] The letters and Roman numbers correspond to the items referred to above on pp. 537–544.

3. Profit and loss account:	None
4. Other notes:	None of those required by Sched. 4 to the 1985 Act (*e.g.* relating to accounting principles and rules, except in so far as they can be interpreted as accounting policies), nor those required under Sched. 6 Part I, disclosing the remuneration of directors, or under Sched. 5 concerning subsidaries in respect of alignment of their year ends, qualifications in their audit reports, the holdings of shares in the parent company, and arrangements attracting merger relief.

Comparative amounts for previous years must still be given where appropriate for such items as are disclosed in notes.

Accounting principles and rules

Prior to 1981 successive Companies Acts gave little guidance as to what accounting principles and rules should be followed in preparing the annual accounts of companies. However, the view taken by the Cohen and Jenkins Committees on company law reform, reporting respectively in 1945 and 1962, was that in general the traditional historical cost convention used by accountants was appropriate, and it was largely left to the professional accountancy bodies themselves to formulate such rules as they deemed necessary.[44] The supposed inadequacy of such rules was highlighted in the late 1960s in a number of instances referred to the City Panel on Take-Overs and Mergers (see Chapter 31), and this led to the creation of the Accounting Standards Committee (ASC) in 1969, whose avowed aim was to codify the different practices and narrow the choice between them. In the 20 years since then the ASC has succeeded in deflecting much of the criticism formerly directed at the accountancy profession, and while it has provided a useful framework for codifying conventions and agreeing standard

[44] (1945) Cmnd. 6659, and (1962) Cmnd. 1749, respectively; the relevant paragraphs are 98 for Cohen and 333 for Jenkins.

forms of presentation, it has not greatly changed the substance of accounting practice. Only in relation to current cost accounting, on which its hand was forced by the report of the government-appointed Sandilands Committee[45] did it take a new initiative, and even then in this respect the requirement under SSAP 16 that listed companies should publish supplementary current cost financial statements was quietly dropped in 1986.

In the circumstances, it is perhaps not surprising that in the late 1980s there was considerable debate about the ways in which accounting standards should be promulgated and be monitored. As a result, a report ("The Making of Accounting Standards") was published in September 1988 by a committee chaired by Sir Ron Dearing. Briefly, it proposed that a broadly based Financial Reporting Council should be created to guide the work of the standard setting body, the Accounting Standards Board, which would determine its pronouncements on the basis of a two thirds majority. The standards themselves would not be incorporated into law, but directors would be required to state in notes to the accounts whether a company's financial statements were drawn up in accordance with applicable standards; and a new statutory power should exist enabling the Secretary of State to apply to the Courts for an order requesting revision of a company's accounts that do not give a true and fair view. The Accounting Standards Board would also publish guidance on so-called "emerging issues," and a Review Panel would examine contentious departures from accounting standards by large companies.

In order to facilitate the creation of the new order, the Companies Act 1989 introduced a requirement into the fourth Schedule of the 1985 Act requiring companies to state whether their accounts are drawn up in accordance with applicable standards; and by section 19 inserted a new section 256 into the 1985 Act indicating that "accounting standards" are standards issued by bodies prescribed by statutory regulations and which are relevant in the circumstances to a company's accounts. Moreover, the Secretary of State is specifically empowered to delegate authority concerning the issuing of standards, the overseeing of the promulgation of such standards, the investigation of departures from such standards, and taking steps to

[45] (1975) Cmnd. 6225.

ensure such compliance. This is in addition to the Secretary of State's powers under section 257 of the 1985 Act to alter by statutory instrument the regulations concerning the contents of annual accounts laid before a company in general meeting or filed with the Registrar.

In the meantime, while the ASC was developing standards in the 1970s, the EC was itself addressing the question of identifying so-called accounting principles which could be consistently applied within the European Communities, and its ideas were included in its Fourth Council Directive of 1978. For the most part these related to the historical cost convention, widely applied in a particularly conservative manner in most continental countries, largely to delay profit recognition for tax purposes. However, it was necessary to accommodate current (replacement) cost accounting, used for over 40 years by some major companies in the Netherlands, and also the practice whereby many major listed companies in the United Kingdom have in recent years taken to revaluing all or part of their fixed assets, partly it seems as a way of signalling to the public changes in managerial expectations. Moreover, it was also perceived to provide a framework within which any new form of current price level or current cost system of accounting could be accommodated—a matter of some importance since there were moves afoot in the late 1970s to introduce such systems in various continental countries as well as in the United Kingdom.

The result was that Part II of the first Schedule to the 1981 Act was divided into three sections: 1, accounting principles; 2, historical cost accounting rules; and 3, alternative accounting rules; and this now constitutes Part II of the fourth Schedule to the 1985 Act.

1. *Accounting principles and conventions*

Paragraphs 10–15 of the fourth Schedule to the 1985 Act reiterate the four so-called principles or concepts contained in SSAP 2 which, so long as they are consistent with the statements presenting a true and fair view, are supposed to underlie the preparation of annual accounts: going concern concept, consistency concept, accruals concept, and prudence doctrine. The going concern concept implies that the net realisable values of fixed assets will not normally be the relevant values to use in the accounts—indeed, they will only be appropriate where liquidation is envisaged. Consistent application of accounting policies both within a set of accounts and over time is necessary to try and ensure comparability from year to year and reduce opportunities to manipulate results. As a result the user should have a better chance of being able to identify the permanent (as opposed to transitory) element in profit, which should improve his forecasting ability. The accruals concept requires that revenues and expenses reported should relate to the financial year in question, regardless of when cash is actually received or spent. In practice, however, accountants rarely take the accruals principle to its logical conclusion, preferring to apply the prudence doctrine, which SSAP 2 (but not the 1985 Act) indicates should prevail where there is conflict between the two. Paragraph 12 of the Schedule specifies two rules in relation to the prudence doctrine: (a) that only realised profits should be included in the income statement (though section 262(3) of the 1985 Act defines such profits only in terms of best accounting practice at the time), and (b) that all liabilities and losses that have arisen and are likely to arise should be taken into account. Moreover, they must be included even when they only become apparent after the end of the accounting year, which is consistent with the terms of SSAP 17 on accounting for post balance sheet events.

Paragraph 14 of the Schedule indicates that each asset and liability must be valued separately. Since an asset is undefined this might technically cause problems—for instance, where a machine is owned, is it the machine itself or its component parts that constitute(s) the asset(s)? However, the main purpose of the requirement seems to be to try to ensure that assets which may reasonably be regarded as separate (such as different lines of stock) are valued on an individual rather than a group basis. In fact, the standard on stock valuation, SSAP 9, requires use of the individual item valuation basis, though for tax purposes the group basis remains acceptable.[46]

Paragraph 15 of the Schedule permits directors to depart from any of the principles referred to above if their application is

[46] *IRC* v. *Cock, Russell and Co.* [1949] 29 T.C. 387.

inconsistent with the overriding requirement of sections 226 and 227 to present a true and fair view. However, particulars of such a departure, the reasons and the effect must be disclosed.

2. *Historical cost accounting rules*

(A) *Fixed assets*

Section 262(1) of the 1985 Act defines fixed assets as those assets intended for use on a continuing basis, and the basic rule is that they should be shown at either the purchase price of production cost (the meaning of which terms is discussed below), net of any depreciation or diminution in value (para. 17). The latter apply where a fixed asset is wasting in nature and has a limited useful economic life, cost (net of estimated scrap value) being written off "systematically" over such life (para. 18). Additional depreciation *may* be provided for fixed asset investments in respect of a decline in value (para. 19(1)), and *must* be for any fixed asset (including a fixed asset investment) where such decline in value is expected to be permanent (which is consistent with the terms of SSAP 12) (para. 19(2)). The basis of such valuation is not defined, but under the going concern concept it will presumably normally be current value in use. Charges for additional depreciation, and amounts written back if such provisions are deemed no longer necessary, must be separately disclosed in the profit and loss account itself or in the notes thereto. Moreover, as regards the former, a distinction must be drawn between charges made under para. 19(1) and those under para. 19(2).

(B) *Intangible fixed assets*

(i) The original amount at which acquired goodwill is shown in the accounts must be written off "systematically" over a period chosen by the directors which must not exceed its useful economic life. The period of, and the reasons for choosing such period, must be disclosed in a note (Sched. 4, para. 21).

The current accounting standard on goodwill, SSAP 22, requires purchased goodwill, including that arising on consolidation, either to be written off immediately against reserves, or to be amortised through the profit and loss account over its estimated useful economic life. However, in an exposure draft issued in 1990 (ED 47), the ASC proposed that purchased goodwill should properly be regarded as a wasting fixed asset and should therefore be shown in a consolidated balance sheet. It should then be amortised over a period not exceeding 20 years.

The amount attributed to purchased goodwill is the difference between the fair value of the consideration given and the fair value of the separable net assets acquired. ED 53 indicates that such fair values will generally be the replacement costs of the relevant assets at the date which the parent company effectively acquired control over them.

Under the 1981 and 1985 Acts, the amount written off goodwill year by year has to be disclosed in the profit and loss account, but where it is written off immediately against reserves on acquisition (which is currently the preferred method) such disclosure would not appear to be necessary. However, SSAP 22 requires that the amount of goodwill recognised as a result of any acquisitions during the year should be shown separately for each acquisition where material, even where it is written off immediately to reserves. Moreover, movements in goodwill must be shown in a note to a group's consolidated accounts (Sched. 4A, para. 14: see *post*, page 568).[47]

(ii) Paragraph 20 permits development costs to be "capitalised" (a term defined in section 262(1) of the 1985 Act) and be shown in the balance sheet, and then only in "special circumstances." Where this is done notes must disclose the reasons for capitalising such development costs and the period over which they are being written off. Development expenditure is defined in SSAP 13 (though not in the Act)—it is essentially identifiable expenditure related to a specific project which can reasonably be expected to be recovered in

[47] SSAP 22 is currently being reviewed. The revised draft, ED 47, requires that goodwill should be amortised over an economic life of 20 years, or (in exceptional cases) 40 years.

> the future, and upon capitalisation is to be amortised on a systematic basis. Where such expenditure is capitalised a further note to the accounts will generally be required by section 269 and paragraph 20 to indicate that such unamortised expenditure is not being treated as a realised loss in calculating distributable profits and the justification for such treatment (which under section 262(3) of the 1985 Act is likely to be that it is consistent with accepted accounting principles and practice).

The Act does not specifically refer to research expenditure, which however is distinguished from development expenditure in SSAP 13 as expenditure which cannot be related to a specific project and cannot reasonably be expected to be recovered in the future. The accounting standard requires that such expenditure should be written off immediately against revenues in the profit and loss account, and this would appear to be consistent with the intention of the Act, given its specific use of the word "development."

The reason for such interest in the treatment of intangible assets appears to be that debt covenants frequently contain clauses which specifically refer to a maximum ratio of debt to assets so as to provide the lender with a margin of security. This seems to encourage companies to engage on the one hand in off balance sheet financing (a topic which is the subject of a standard on leasing, SSAP 21, and a more general draft one, ED 49) so as to reduce the face value of debt; and on the other to capitalise spending by creating or maintaining intangible assets, such as goodwill. A recent manifestation of the latter has been the practice of some large companies of putting brands into their balance sheets, a move which has been the subject of critical comment by the professional accountancy bodies. This culminated in the publication in 1990 of a draft accounting standard (ED 52) which proposes that intangibles should only be recognised separately if they are acquired for valuable consideration and can properly be regarded as separable assets.

In passing, it should perhaps be noted that attempts to engage in off balance sheet financing and/or to put intangible assets into a balance sheet are not costless to companies. When lenders see what is happening they will presumably respond by raising the cost of borrowing in the future, which will in part reflect their distrust of the company's management.

(C) *Current assets*

(i) Such assets are defined in section 262(1) of the 1985 Act as any assets not intended for use on a continuing basis in the company's activities. In general they are to be valued at the lower of, on the one hand, purchase price or production cost (the meaning of which is discussed below); and, on the other, net realisable value (paras. 22–23). This is slightly more restrictive than previous accounting practice, where the rule was the lower of original cost and market value at the balance sheet date, the latter in some circumstances being capable of interpretation for stocks, both for tax and financial reporting purposes, as replacement cost rather than net realisable value.[48]

Accounting practice in showing debtors net of a bad debts provision is consistent with this rule. Small companies may well determine such provisions in relation to specific debts, as is required for calculating the company's liability to corporation tax.[49] However, larger companies may well prefer to use general bad debt provisions for financial reporting purposes.

Where the going concern assumption is reasonable, accounting practice is generally to value work-in-progress at cost since net realisable value (which would usually be far lower) is irrelevant in such circumstances. Moreover, it is also common practice, in line with the terms of SSAP 9, for profits to be recognised gradually over the period of long-term contracts, although so as to ensure these are "realised" they have now under the revised standard to be included in the turnover and debtors figures.

Paragraph 23 of the fourth Schedule indicates that where an asset has been written down to net realisable

[48] *B.S.C. Footwear Ltd.* v. *Ridgway* [1971] T.R. 121; SSAP 9.
[49] Income and Corporation Taxes Act 1970, s.130(1).

value, but such value has subsequently risen, even if not fully up to cost again, the amount of the provision so made and no longer required must be written back.

(ii) Under paragraph 27 of the fourth Schedule, the purchase price or production cost of each class of stocks and similar fungible items (that is, assets where individual units—such as shares held—are indistinguishable from each other), may be determined using the most appropriate of any one of four methods: first in first out (FIFO), last in first out (LIFO), weighted average cost, and any similar method. In addition, para. 25 (referred to below) effectively permits use of the base stock method for stocks of raw materials and consumables. LIFO and base stock methods are not acceptable for tax purposes in the United Kingdom[50] and in such circumstances, because of the need to keep a second set of stock records, it is generally impractical to use the former for financial reporting purposes. Moreover, SSAP 9 suggests that neither LIFO nor base stock methods provide reasonable approximations to the cost of stocks. Nevertheless, some companies (notably in the sugar and base metal industries) continue to use the base stock method, and overseas subsidiaries of many British companies often use LIFO to obtain certain tax advantages, thus securing nominal qualification in the auditors' report for the group accounts as they do not technically comply with the terms of SSAP 9.

(iii) As discussed under D(ii) below, where stocks and work-in-progress are valued at production cost, the latter *may* include a reasonable proportion of manufacturing overheads. Presumably these can comprise either just variable or both variable and fixed overhead costs. Tax law is fairly flexible on this matter,[51] but SSAP 9 in fact *requires* that for financial reporting purposes a reasonable proportion of manufacturing

[50] The relevant cases are, respectively: *Minister of National Revenue* v. *Anaconda American Brass Ltd.* [1956] A.C. 85; and *Patrick* v. *Broadstone Mills* [1953] 33 T.C. 44.

[51] *Ostime* v. *Duple Motor Bodies* [1961] 39 T.C. 537.

overheads (including a proportion of fixed costs) should be included in the valuation of stocks and work-in-progress.

(iv) Whatever method of stock valuation is used, any *material difference* between the purchase price or production cost and the "relevant alternative amount" must be shown in a note to the accounts. Such "relative alternative amount" will normally be replacement cost at the balance sheet date, but an acceptable approximation very often will be a value based on the most recent purchase price or production cost (paras. 27(3), (4), (5)).

(D) *Purchase price and production cost*

(i) Purchase price is defined in paragraph 26(1) of the fourth Schedule and section 262(1) of the 1985 Act as the actual price paid for an asset, including expenses incidental to its acquisition.

(ii) Production cost is the sum of (a) the purchase price of raw materials and consumables used; and (b) direct production costs incurred (but, in the case of current assets, excluding distribution costs); plus (c) other costs that *may* be included, being a reasonable proportion of indirect costs in so far as they relate to the period of production. These latter may include interest on borrowed capital, where appropriate, but if this is the case, the fact and the amount involved must be disclosed in a note (para. 26).

(iii) Where there is no record for an asset of its original purchase price or production cost, or of related expenditure, the earliest value ascribed to it may be used instead, but this fact must be disclosed in the accounts or the notes thereto (paras. 28 and 51(1)).

(iv) Paragraph 25 permits tangible fixed assets and stocks of raw materials and consumables to be shown at a fixed quantity and fixed value where they are constantly being replaced and (a) their overall value is not material to the assessment of the company's state of affairs; and (b) their quantity, value and composition is not subject to material variation.

(v) Under paragraph 24, where an amount owed to a creditor is greater that the value of the asset received, the difference may be treated as an asset rather than an expense, analogous to acquired goodwill. However, it must be written off by "reasonable amounts" each year and must be completely written off before repayment of the debt. Any such asset in the balance sheet must be disclosed either in the statement or in the notes thereto. There is no reference to systematic amortisation in these provisions, as there is in relation to acquire goodwill, nor apparently is it necessary to indicate the period over which the asset is being written off.

3. *Alternative accounting rules*

If they so determine, companies may adopt any of the alternative accounting rules outlined in Section C of Part II of the fourth Schedule to the 1985 Act. Such rules apply only to the main financial statements, which as a result can be prepared not only in terms of the historical cost convention, but can instead be modified to take into account selective revaluations or be completely re-stated in current cost terms.

The Accounting Standards Committee introduced a standard on current cost accounting in 1980 (SSAP 16) which permitted those companies to which it applied (generally listed companies and companies meeting two of three criteria: turnover over £5m per annum; total assets in the historical cost accounts in excess of £2.5m; and average number of employees over 250) to present current cost accounts either as supplementary statements (which became usual practice) or as the main financial statements. Only in the latter case did the alternative accounting rules apply to the current cost accounts prepared so as to comply with SSAP 16. Following considerable opposition to the experiment in certain quarters, the ASC declared the standard to be non mandatory in 1985, and it was withdrawn in April 1988. Nevertheless, as Technical Release (TR) 707 acknowledges, it and the ASC's handbook, "Accounting for the effects of changing prices", provide guidance to any companies still wishing to prepare current cost accounts.

The alternative rules outlined in the fourth Schedule (paras. 31–34) are as follows:

(i) Intangible assets, other than goodwill, may be shown at current cost.
(ii) Goodwill (for which current cost has no clear meaning) should be shown at its cost of acquisition, less amortisation, unless it is written off immediately.
(iii) Tangible fixed assets may be stated either at their market values on the dates they were last valued or at current cost. (The latter could either be the second-hand value or the current cost new less notional depreciation.)
(iv) Fixed asset investments may be stated either at their market values on the dates they were last valued or at a value determined on an appropriate basis given the company's circumstances, in which case the method and reasons for using it must be disclosed. (Such a basis might be the equity "net assets" basis appropriate for accounting for associated companies under SSAP 1.)
(v) Current asset investments and stocks may be stated at their current costs.
(vi) As regards wasting fixed assets, depreciation should be based on the revalued amounts, not the purchase price or production cost. The charge to the profit and loss account can either be that based on the current value or just be the historical cost charge. However, in the latter case the difference between the two must be disclosed either in the accounts or in the notes thereto. This would appear to allow such differences to be debited or credited direct to the revaluation reserve.
(vii) Accumulated unrealised holding gains arising from revaluations which result from application of the alternative accounting rules must be credited to a revaluation reserve, and this must be shown separately in the balance sheet. Amounts can only be transferred from the revaluation reserve to the profit and loss account where the amount in question was (a) previously charged to the profit and loss account; (b) it represents a realised profit; or (c) it is applied wholly

or partly in paying up bonus shares allotted to members of the company. Otherwise the balance of the reserve has to be reduced where there is no longer any justification for its existence (*e.g.* where there has been a subsequent decline in the value of an asset previously revalued upwards). An explanation of the tax effects of increases or reductions in the revaluation reserve (such as the tax that would be payable if the asset were sold at its revalued amount) must be disclosed in a note to the accounts.

(viii) Where alternative rules are applied the notes must state the items affected, the basis of valuation of each balance sheet item, and (with the exception of stocks) for each of the latter items, including provisions separately, either the corresponding amount under the historical cost convention or the differences between the two sets of figures. Alternatively the basis of valuation, and the corresponding amount or differences, can be disclosed on the face of the balance sheet rather than in notes.

A draft accounting standard issued in 1990 (ED 51) suggests that the directors of a company should adopt a clear policy when deciding to revalue fixed assets on a selective basis. Consequently they should identify different classes of asset which they might wish to revalue and then reappraise those values on an agreed basis. Moreover, another draft standard (ED 55) suggests that current asset investments for which there are readily observable market values should be "marked to market".

Non-statutory requirements

The most important additional disclosure required of companies by the Accounting Standards Committee is a flow of funds statement. Under the provisions of SSAP 10 all companies with an annual turnover or gross income of more than £25,000 must publish such a statement, which should give a true and fair view of changes in the financial position of a company (or, where appropriate, group). This should be capable of reconciliation with the profit and loss account and balance sheet, but may nevertheless include supplementary disclosures. For the most part SSAP 10 concentrates on identifying working capital (*i.e.* net current asset) movements, but the ASC issued a draft accounting standard (ED 54) in 1990 which would instead summarise only cash transactions.

As was indicated on pages 551 and 560, between 1981 and 1985, companies meeting certain conditions were also required to publish (consolidated) current cost accounts. The conditions were that they should either be listed companies or meet two of three size criteria. However, subsidiaries, insurance and property companies, and investment trusts were exempted. Basically, for the profit and loss account, the current cost statements showed adjustments required to bring depreciation and cost of sales charges to their current cost equivalents and a working capital adjustment to offset the impact of inflation on the company's net investment in debtors. These adjustments were deducted from historical cost profit before charging interest and taxation to show current cost operating profit. An amount called the gearing adjustment was then added back, net of interest charged, to produce the pre-tax current cost profit figure.

Other accounting standards which require companies to make additional disclosures include SSAP 3 on earnings per share for listed companies; SSAP 15 on deferred taxation; SSAP 17 on post balance sheet events; SSAP 18 on contingent liabilities; SSAP 19 on investment properties; SSAP 21 on leases and hire purchase contracts; and SSAP 24 on pension commitments. In addition, ED 46 and International Accounting Standard 24 on related party disclosures; and International Accounting Standard 23 on capitalisation of borrowing costs give further guidance on matters which should be disclosed in a company's financial statements.

Amongst the requirements imposed on quoted companies by The International Stock Exchange's Listing Agreement are provisions for the publication of half-year and preliminary profit statements. The former (which is incidentally the subject of an EC Council Directive) may be important in terms of the requirement of section 272 that for a public company the declaration of an interim dividend should be related to accumulated realised profits, determined if necessary in interim accounts. These should be prepared on a basis consistent with the requirements of the Act with regard to a company's statutory annual accounts (see *post*, Chapter 22). Other matters referred to in the Listing Agreement include under its para. 10 disclosure in the annual report of reasons for any significant departure from standard accounting practice; an explanation of a substantial difference between trading results and any profit forecast made by the company; details of loans repayable in less than a year, in periods between one and two years and between two and five years, and beyond five years; and a statement as to whether or not for tax purposes the company is a close company (*i.e.* is under the control of a limited number of people).

Group Accounts

Some users of accounting statements may only be interested in the financial affairs of the particular *legal entity* with which they are dealing, most obviously unsecured creditors. However, others (such as existing and potential shareholders) may instead be rather more interested in the affairs of an *economic entity*, since those are likely to be more relevant for their decision-making needs. Such an entity can extend as far as a colluding group of companies between which there are no formal legal links; or it may exist where companies are tied together economically in a joint venture arrangement or even sometimes by the existence of a long term contract. This latter notion of a group, where undertakings are managed on a central and unified basis, is essentially the view taken in Germany and adopted in the EC's Seventh Council Directive on company law harmonisation.[52] The traditional British view is somewhat narrower, section 736 of the Companies Act determining the existence of a group where the holding company either controls the composition of the board of directors of a subsidiary, or controls more than half its voting rights. However, the Companies Act 1989 has inserted a new section 258 into the 1985 Act which introduces new criteria for determining whether a company should prepare group accounts. Essentially this adopts the broader view taken in the EC's Seventh Directive, the critical

[52] Seventh Council Directive on Company Law Harmonization, O.J. 1983, L. 193 (83/349/EEC).

element being whether "a parent company" exercises a dominant influence (see *ante*, pages 523–524).

The advantage to a user of financial statements of having access to a set of group accounts, however the term "group" is defined, is that the statements can be prepared so as to eliminate the often sizeable internal, intra-group transactions and show a more complete picture of the group financial structure. However, the preparation of full consolidated accounts may of necessity mean some particularly interesting piece of information will be lost—for instance, the fact that one subsidiary has been operating at a loss may no longer be apparent. Nevertheless, the potential significance of group accounts has long been recognised, and many large public companies in the United Kingdom began publishing them on a voluntary basis in the 1920s, long before section 150 of the 1948 Companies Act made their preparation compulsory.[53] Moreover, it is interesting that several large economic entities, most notably Unilever and Royal Dutch-Shell, publish joint venture accounts as well as the strictly legal accounts for their British participant companies, and it is these supplementary statements which are accorded most prominence in the group annual reports and which are critically scrutinised by professional financial analysts.

General requirements

(i) *The accounts of the parent company*

As indicated above (page 524), a parent company must prepare its individual accounts for its shareholders. One reason for this is that the dividend declared by a parent company must be based on these accounts and not on the group accounts (see *post*, page 628). The fourth Schedule balance sheet formats include various headings which are appropriate for individual parent and subsidiary companies—*viz.* those on pages 530–532, *ante*, marked as B III 1, 2; C II 2; C III 1; E 6; and H 6. In addition, under para. 59 a parent company and a subsidiary

[53] See J. Kitchen, "The Accounts of British Holding Company Groups: Developments and Attitudes to Disclosure in the Early Years," *Accounting and Business Research*, Spring 1972, pp. 114–136.

undertaking must disclose separately under the above headings the amounts owed to and from, and any interests in, a parent company or any fellow subsidiary, or any subsidiary. Set-offs cannot normally be used in making such disclosures, and amounts owing also have to be analysed between those due within one year and those not.

(ii) *Group accounts*

By section 227 of the 1985 Act, where at the end of its financial year a company is a parent company, its directors must prepare a consolidated profit and loss account and balance sheet. Such accounts must give a true and fair view of the group's position and profit or loss, so far as concerns the members of the company, and comply with the provisions of Schedule 4A concerning the form and content of group accounts. However, if there is a conflict, either sufficient additional information must be disclosed to ensure a true and fair view is given, or there must be departure from the requirements of Schedule 4A, explaining the reasons for such action and its effect.

Under section 228, sub-groups need not prepare group accounts if the immediate parent undertaking of the sub-group prepares audited group accounts under the law of an EC member state and the subsidiary undertaking is wholly owned by the sub-group parent, or it holds more than 50 per cent. of the shares and there is no request by a minority holding either half the remaining shares or five per cent. of the total shares for such sub-group accounts to be prepared. However, exemption from the obligation to prepare group accounts is conditional also on the company indicating that it is taking advantage of the concession; stating the name of the parent and its country of incorporation (or, if it is unincorporated, its principal place of business); delivering copies of the group accounts and auditors' report (if necessary with an English translation) to the Registrar; and not having securities listed on a stock exchange within the EC.

Under section 229, subsidiary undertakings may be excluded from consolidation where (1) their inclusion individually or collectively would not be material in giving a true and fair view; (2) long term restrictions hinder the parent's right to manage;

(3) the information required for the preparation of group accounts cannot be obtained without disproportionate expense or undue delay; and (4) the interest of the parent is only temporary. In addition, they must be excluded from consolidation where their activities are so fundamentally different that such accounts would not give a true and fair view. In this respect, SSAP 14 and its draft successor, ED 50, require in the latter case that the financial statements of the subsidiary should be disclosed together with the parent company's accounts, although ED 50 would also require that equity consolidation should be applied. SSAP 14 in addition regards grounds (2) and (4) as being sufficient to require exclusion from consolidation. In the case of the former it requires equity consolidation (see *post*, page 574) as does Schedule 4A, para. 18; and in the case of the latter that the investment in the subsidiary should be shown as a current asset.

Under Schedule 4A, group accounts must be prepared so far as possible to comply with the provisions of Schedule 4 as if the undertakings included in the consolidation were a single group (Sched. 4A, para. 1(1)). For such purposes, as already mentioned (*ante*, pages 565–566), dealings with or interests in, on the one hand, a parent undertaking or fellow subsidiaries; and, on the other, subsidiaries, must be shown separately in aggregate (Sched. 4, para. 59). For this, unconsolidated subsidiaries are to be regarded as part of the group (Sched. 4A, para. 1(2)). Moreover, the formats for accounts under Schedule 4 are to be modified to include an item for "minority interests" (Sched. 4A, para. 17).

Where a parent company is treated as an investment company,[54] the group is to be similarly treated (Sched. 4A, para. 1(3)).

For the purpose of consolidation, the accounts must incorporate in full the information contained in the individual accounts of the undertakings included in the consolidation. However, if the financial year of a subsidiary does not coincide with that of the parent,[55] the group must deal with the subsidiary's state of affairs at the end of its financial year ending last before that of the parent company's, providing it is within

[54] See p. 584.
[55] See p. 514.

three months of the latter. Otherwise, interim accounts must be used (Sched. 4A, para. 2). Moreover, the parent company should try to apply standard accounting rules when undertaking a consolidaton. If it does not, it should disclose this in a note (Sched. 4A, para. 3). Likewise, any differences between the accounting rules used in preparing a parent company's individual accounts and its group accounts should be disclosed in a note (Sched. 4A, para. 4).

Where an acquisition takes place in a financial year, the name of the undertaking acquired must be disclosed in a note, stating whether the combination has been accounted for using the acquisition or merger methods of accounting. In addition, details of the fair value of the consideration given must be disclosed, giving details in the case of an acquisition of the book values and fair values of the assets and claims and of the goodwill. Similarly, details of any adjustments made, in particular to the consolidated reserves, must be given where the merger method is used. Further, the profit or loss of the undertaking acquired must be stated for the period from the beginning of its financial year up until the combination and for its previous financial year (Sched. 4A, para. 13). The parent company must also show movements in the goodwill figure shown in the group accounts (Sched. 4A, para. 14).

Where there has been a disposal of an undertaking in the year that significantly affects the figures shown in the group accounts, the name of the undertaking and the amount of profit or loss attributable to it must also be disclosed in a note (Sched. 4A, para. 15).

Additional guidance on how those provisions should be implemented is given in two draft accounting standards issued by the ASC in 1990: ED 50 on "Consolidated accounts"; and ED 53 on "Fair value in the context of acquisition accounting."

Methods of consolidation

There are several different ways of preparing consolidated accounts, and it may be helpful to examine them briefly with the help of some examples.

Let it therefore be assumed there are two companies, X and Y, whose summarised balance sheets at December 31, 1985, are as shown in Figure 1.

	X	*Y*
Net assets	£5,000,000	£2,000,000
Ordinary £1 shares	1,500,000	500,000
Distributable reserves	3,500,000	1,500,000
	£5,000,000	£2,000,000

Figure 1

(i) *The acquisition method*

First, let it be supposed that X acquires for cash the entire share capital of Y at December 31, 1985, the cash being part of its net assets of £5m. The going concern value of Y is agreed as £3m. The consolidated balance sheet would generally be shown as in Figure 2(a), though in practice the net assets would be added together line-by-line for each different asset and liability category identified. It can be seen that goodwill is created as an asset: it represents the difference between the going concern value of Y at the date of acquisition and the book value of the net assets acquired by the X group. It can also be seen that the pre-acquisition profits of Y, the subsidiary, are no longer free for distribution. Only the post-acquisition profits of the subsidiary will be added in to the group's free reserves.

Now let it be supposed that the consideration given to acquire Y was not cash, but instead was new shares issued by X. It is now necessary to value the consideration given and received. If

		X Group		*X Group*
Goodwill	(£3m−£2m)	1,000,000	(£3m−£2m)	1,000,000
Other net assets	(£5m−£3m;+£2m)	4,000,000	(£5m+£2m)	7,000,000
		£5,000,000		£8,000,000
Ordinary share capital (X only)		1,500,000	(£1.5m+£.75m)	2,250,000
Share premium		—	(£3m−£.75m)	2,250,000
Distributable reserves (X only at date of acquisition)		3,500,000		3,500,000
		£5,000,000		£8,000,000

Figure 2 *(a)* *(b)*

the shares of X and Y are both quoted this may be relatively easy to assess, though depending on the dates chosen there may be slight differences in the total values of the shares issued and acquired. However, where the companies are unquoted it will be necessary either to assess the value by appraisal or to use the nominal value of the shares given as consideration. The latter gives rise to a problem which will be discussed below. For the moment, let it be assumed here that 750,000 new shares are issued in X to acquire the entire share capital of Y, the one third stake in the new combined enterprise and its future earning power being regarded by both parties as acceptable consideration. Given a market share price in X of £4 per £1 nominal share unit, the consolidated balance sheet appears as in Figure 2(b).

The method of consolidation shown in Figure 2 is known as the *acquisition* (or, in the United States, the *purchase*) method, reflecting the "parent company approach" to group consolidation, and it is that which has been most commonly used in the United Kingdom. Moreover, it can easily be adapted to allow for a situation where less than the entire equity in a subsidiary is acquired. Thus in the case of 2(b), above, let it now be assumed that only three quarters of the share capital in Y is acquired for an issue of 562,500 shares in X, the value of the transaction being assessed at £2.25m. The consolidated balance sheet is then as shown in Figure 3, the goodwill only relating to the majority stake acquired. The minority interest comprises the outside shareholders' stake in a subsidiary's share capital and both its pre- and post-acquisition reserves.

	X Group
Goodwill (£2.25m−¾×£2m)	750,000
Net assets	7,000,000
	£7,750,000
Ordinary share capital (X only) (£1.5m+£.5625m)	2,062,500
Share premium (£2.25m−£.5625m)	1,687,500
Distributable reserves (X only at acquisition)	3,500,000
Minority interest (¼×£2m)	500,000
	£7,750,000

Figure 3

It would technically be possible, without altering the basic technique, to allow the accounts to reflect a wider entity concept than the parent company approach by showing a notional goodwill figure for the *whole* group (here presumably £750,000 × $^4/_3$ = £1m) and crediting the appropriate share (here £250,000) to the minority interest, but this is never done in practice.

The above examples should have made it clear that the goodwill figure has little economic significance. It merely measures the *historic* difference between the going concern value of *part* of the group (typically the majority share in a subsidiary) and the corresponding book value at the date of purchase. Going concern values, even for parts of businesses, change from day-to-day as expectations of future likely outcomes alter; moreover, goodwill as such has no separate existence from the business as a whole, as do most other assets which appear in balance sheets.

Schedule 4A, paras. 7–9, indicate that it is the acquisition method of consolidation as there described which must be applied under the 1985 Act, except where specific conditions described below exist. The main requirement is that at the date of acquisition, the net assets of the company acquired must be included in the consolidated balance sheet at their fair value.

(ii) *The merger method*

A very different approach to consolidation, known as the *merger* (or, in the United States, the *pooling*) method avoids some of the problems identified above and it is probably more appropriate if it is deemed necessary to try to reflect a wider entity concept than the narrow parent company approach. Quite apart from avoiding the creation of goodwill on acquisition, it also has the advantage of bringing all or some of the pre-acquisition profits of the technical subsidiaries into the group balance sheet as distributable reserves.[56] It is therefore

[56] This is largely for presentational purposes, since only the parent company can distribute profits as dividends to its shareholders, not the group. However, where merger relief as described below is given, pooled group accounts show the effective position from an overall perspective.

particularly attractive where two companies of more or less equal size merge their activities.

To illustrate the technique, return to the facts used to derive the consolidated balance sheet in Figure 2(b). If it is argued that the value of the shares issued is their par value of £750,000, only £250,000 (the difference between the par values of shares issued and acquired by X) of the pre-acquisition profits of Y has to be regarded as non-distributable. The consolidated balance sheet would then appear as in Figure 4.

	X Group
Net assets (£5m+£2m)	£7,000,000
Ordinary share capital (X only) (£1.5m+£.75m)	2,250,000
Distributable reserves (3.5m+(£1.5m−£.25m))	4,750,000
	£7,000,000

Figure 4

The merger method is apparently the normal method of consolidation for share exchanges in Germany, probably reflecting the fact that it offers a reasonable reflection of the economic entity group concept (though strangely the EC's Seventh Council Directive favours the parent company approach).[57] It is also popular in the United States, though it has been abused there, some companies using it to inflate reported group profits in the year of acquisition. However, empirical evidence suggests the investing public sees through such manoeuvres.[58]

In Great Britain the method was used by a growing number of leading quoted companies in the late 1960s to account for mergers between large groups. A draft accounting standard was published on the subject in 1971, but doubts were expressed about the validity of the merger treatment in view of the decision in *Head (Henry) & Co., Ltd.* v. *Ropner Holdings Ltd.*,[59] concerning the need to establish a share premium account (see *ante*, Chapter 9). The decision in that case was

[57] *Op. cit.*, article 19.
[58] Hong, H., R. S. Kaplan and G. Mandelker, "Pooling *v.* Purchase: The Effects of Accounting for Mergers on Stock Prices", *The Accounting Review*, January 1978, pp. 31–47.
[59] [1952] Ch. 124.

confirmed in *Shearer* v. *Bercain Ltd.*,[60] which was widely regarded by the accountancy profession as closing the door on the merger method of consolidation. However, the 1981 legislation, in what has become sections 131–134 of the 1985 Act, provided relief to *individual companies* from what is now section 130, making it legitimate to use the approach as long as the necessary conditions are met—the main one is that the acquiring company should secure at least 90 per cent. in nominal value of each class of the share capital of the company being taken over (see *ante*, Chapter 9).

An accounting standard was issued in April 1985 by the ASC, SSAP 23, relating to *groups*, which indicates the circumstances where merger and acquisition accounting methods may be appropriate. Briefly, if a business combination meets all four of the conditions outlined in SSAP 23, the group *may* use either the merger or acquisition method of accounting for consolidation purposes; if it does not, it *must* use the acquisition approach. The four conditions are: (i) the offer must be to holders of all voting shares; (ii) the offeror secures 90 per cent. of each class of equity shares and 90 per cent. of the voting rights; (iii) immediately prior to the offer, the offeror does not hold 20 per cent. or more of the voting rights; and (iv) not less than 90 per cent. of the fair value of consideration given for equity shares is in the form of equity share capital, with similar conditions in respect of non-equity voting shares. By contrast, paragraph 10 of Schedule 4A merely prescribes that the parent company must hold at least 90 per cent. of the relevant shares as a result of offering its or its subsidiary's equity shares; and that the fair value of consideration other than equity shares given did not exceed 10 per cent. of the value of the shares issued.

Where a company takes advantage of the merger relief provisions of the Act under section 130, it must under paras. 10 and 29 of Schedule 5 disclose as a note to its accounts the name of the company, details of the shares allotted and of those received or cancelled in exchange, the accounting treatment adopted, and the effect on any group profit and loss account for the year of including pre-acquisition profits or losses of the merged subsidiary. Moreover, where the group disposes directly

[60] [1980] 3 All E.R. 295.

or indirectly of shares and/or assets in the merged company within 2–3 years of the merger, and in so doing makes a profit included in the income statements, such a profit has to be disclosed.

In February 1990 the ASC issued proposals for revising SSAP 23 (ED 48), which would make it mandatory (rather than optional) for companies meeting certain specified conditions to use the merger method. The conditions proposed aim to identify the substance of a merger rather than just apply a series of rules, and the draft standard offers a broader series of tests that need to be applied to reach the appropriate conclusions.

(iii) *The proprietary methods*

A third approach to consolidation is the proprietary approach, which eliminates recognition of the outside interest in both the balance sheet and the profit and loss account and is usually applied where the ownership stake is 50 per cent. or less. The concept can be implemented in one of two ways: either (a) by proportional consolidation, where income, assets and liabilities are separately added in to the holding company's accounts on a *pro rata* basis item by item; or (b) by the equity method of consolidation, where an investment is shown in the group balance sheet *pro rata* to its current net asset value, the net changes each year usually being dealt with in the profit and loss account. Both methods are accommodated within the EC's Seventh Council Directive,[61] though proportional consolidation, not uncommon on the Continent, is rarely practised by British companies, although its use is not unknown. The equity method has long been used in the United States to account for joint ventures and for subsidiaries not fully consolidated, and since the early 1970s it has been employed in Britain to account for associated companies, an accounting standard on the subject (SSAP 1) being issued in 1971. However, it should be noted that there is more than one way of showing the equity value of an investment in a consolidated balance sheet—the Seventh Directive implies that the goodwill (or premium) on acquisition should be shown separately, although this only became standard British practice in 1982.[62]

[61] *Op. cit.*, articles 32–33.
[62] *Op. cit.*, article 33; *cf.* SSAP 1, as revised, April 1982, paras. 8 and 26.

Paragraph 19 of Schedule 4A indicates that where an undertaking is jointly managed with one or more independent third parties, it may be accounted for by the method of proportional consolidation. Paragraph 20 indicates that an associated company is one in which an undertaking has a participating interest and exercises a significant influence. This is normally presumed if it holds over 20 per cent. of the voting rights. In such circumstances, the equity method of accounting is to be used, with the standard format of accounts modified accordingly and with goodwill being treated as under the acquisition method (Sched. 4A, paras. 21–22).

Further guidance on the application of these procedures is given in ED 50.

Unrealised intra-group profits

One further point relating to consolidated accounts, which is of some relevance in relation to distributable profits as defined in sections 263–281 of the 1985 Act, concerns the treatment of unrealised inter-company profits. Briefly, if one member of a group sells goods to another, such goods as are in stock at the balance sheet date will potentially include an element of unrealised profit. This can logically be eliminated in one of two ways—either by adopting a "single entity" approach and treating the transactions as though they had never taken place: this means writing back the unrealised profit against the company which sold the goods, with the minority interest in the selling company bearing its appropriate share; or, alternatively, by adopting a "separate entity" approach, in which case any unrealised profit must be written back against the company which holds the goods, with the minority interest in that company (if any) again bearing its appropriate share. In practice, however, British companies in the past have tended either to write back the whole of the unrealised profit regardless against the majority's profits; or, eliminate the majority's profit only against the company which sold the stock.[63]

[63] See D. A. Egginton, "Unrealised Profit and Consolidated Accounts", *Accountancy*, May 1965, pp. 410–415; and article 26(1)(c), (2) and (3) of the EC's Seventh Council Directive.

Paragraph 6 of Schedule 4A merely states that intra-group debts and claims and intra-group transactions should be eliminated when group accounts are prepared; and that unrealised profits may be eliminated "in proportion to the group's interest in the shares of the undertakings." However, ED 50 gives further guidance on how this requirement may be implemented.

Directors' Report

Section 234 of the Act requires that for each financial year the directors should prepare a report which contains a fair review of the development of the company and its subsidiaries during the year and the position at the end of it. It should also indicate the amount recommended as dividend and the amount proposed to be carried to reserves.

Before the 1981 Companies Act, legislation permitted any item otherwise required to be disclosed in the accounts or notes thereto to be shown instead in the directors' report, though corresponding figures for the previous year had to be given and the item was still subject to audit. Moreover, certain additional matters were required to be dealt with in the report. Several are now dealt with directly in notes to the accounts (contracts with the company (except service contracts) in which a director has an interest, new issues of shares and debentures and the reasons therefor, directors' options to subscribe for the company's securities, turnover and profit or loss before tax of different classes of activity, and the average weekly number of United Kingdom employees and their total remuneration for the year). However, since 1981 it has not been necessary to disclose particulars of exports where annual turnover exceeds £50,000—this item had to be shown in the directors' report between 1967 and 1981.

This shift in emphasis reflects the approach of the EC's Fourth Council Directive towards the directors' report, where the intention was that it should merely supplement the financial details given in the accounts with certain narrative information about the company's activities and its future prospects. Now the Companies Act not merely requires that directors should give a fair review of the development of the business, but also that their report should include particulars of any important events affecting the company or its subsidiaries that have occurred since the end of the financial year; and an indication of likely future developments in the business. In addition, the directors are required to report on the activities of the business in the field of research and development (Sched. 7, para. 6). However, the Act gives no guidance indicating the form of the review or the level of detail it should contain.

As well as requiring the above disclosures in the directors' report, section 234 of the Act indicates that it should state the names of the persons who were directors of the company during the year; the principal activities of the group and any changes therein; and various matters specifically referred to in Schedule 7 to the Act. Failure to comply with the requirements makes the offending directors liable to a fine, although it is a defence to prove that all reasonable steps were taken to secure compliance.

Briefly, the items requiring disclosure in the directors' report may be summarised as follows:

(i) A fair review of the development of the business of the company and its subsidiaries during the financial year ending with the balance sheet date and of their position at the end of it (section 234(1)(*a*)).

(ii) Amount recommended to be paid by way of dividend (section 234(1)(*b*)).

(iii) Amount proposed to be carried to reserves (section 234(1)(*b*)).

(iv) Names of directors at any time during the year under review (section 234(2)).

(v) Principal activities of the company and its subsidiaries and significant changes in those activities (section 234(2)).

(vi) Significant changes in the company's or its subsidiaries' fixed assets (Sched. 7, para. 1(1)).

(vii) An indication of the difference between the book amount and the market values of land and buildings if, in the opinion of the directors, the difference is of such significance that it should be drawn to the attention of the members or debenture holders (Sched. 7, para. 1(2)).

(viii) Interests of directors and their immediate families at the beginning and end of each year in shares or debentures of the company or its group undertakings, if such information is not shown in a note to the accounts. Details of options granted or exercised are also to be disclosed (Sched. 7, paras. 2, 2A, 2B). The International Stock Exchange's Listing Agreement also requires disclosure of any changes in such holdings between the financial year end and a date within one month of the notice of the annual general meeting being issued.

(ix) Details for a company or group of its UK charitable and political contributions where in aggregate they exceed £200, as follows:

	£
U.K. charitable organisations	xxx
Political donations of over £200 each:	
U.K. political organisations (by party, etc.)	xxx
Individuals (by name)	xxx
Others under £200 each (Total)	xxx
	xxx

"Giving money for political purposes" is defined as giving, directly or indirectly, a donation or subscription to—

(1) a political party in the United Kingdom; or

(2) a person who, to the company's knowledge, is carrying on, or proposing to carry on, activities which can at the time reasonably be regarded as likely to affect public support for such a political party.

Money given for charitable purposes to a person ordinarily resident outside the United Kingdom is ignored. "Charitable purposes" mean exclusively charitable purposes (Sched. 7, paras. 3–5).

(x) Particulars of any important events affecting the company which have occurred since the end of the year (Sched. 7, para. 6(a)). SSAP 17 additionally requires disclosure in the accounts and in the notes thereto of events which require adjustment to the accounting figures and those which do not.

(xi) An indication of future likely developments in the business of the company and of its subsidiaries (Sched. 7, para. 6(b)).

(xii) An indication of the activities (if any) of the company and its subsidiaries in the field of research and development (Sched. 7, para. 6(c)). SSAP 13 requires disclosure in the accounts or notes thereto of deferred development expenditure at the beginning and end of the year, movements during the year, and the accounting policy adopted.

(xiii) In respect of purchases of its own shares during the year by the company, the number and nominal value of the shares; the percentage of called-up capital so purchased; aggregate consideration paid; and the reasons for such purchase. In respect of other acquisitions of its own shares, either directly by the company, or by persons with financial assistance from the company where the company has a beneficial interest in the shares, or where such shares are made subject to a charge; the maximum number and nominal value held at any time during the year, and percentage of called-up capital; the amount of any charge; the number and nominal value disposed of or cancelled during the year, and the percentage of called-up capital; and the consideration received in respect of disposals (Sched. 7, paras. 7–8).

(xiv) For companies where the weekly average number of employees in the United Kingdom during the financial year exceeded 250, a statement of the company's policy in respect of applications for employment from disabled persons; employees who have become disabled; training, career development and promotion of disabled persons (Sched. 7, para. 9).

(xv) For companies of such classes as may be prescribed by regulations made by the Secretary of State, a statement as may be so prescribed about the arrangements in force for securing the health, safety and welfare at work of the company and its subsidiaries, and for protecting other persons against risks to health and safety arising out of, or in connection with, the activities at work of those employees (Sched. 7, para. 10).

(xvi) Where during the year a company has had on average more than 250 employees in the United Kingdom, a statement describing action taken to introduce, maintain or develop arrangements aimed at providing relevant information to those employees, consulting them or their representatives on a regular basis, encouraging their involvement in the business, and making them more aware of the financial and economic factors affecting its performance (Sched. 7, para. 11).

Under section 234A, the directors' report must be approved by the board, and both it and the copy delivered to the Registrar must be signed on the board's behalf by a director or the secretary. Moreover, the name of such a person must appear on each copy laid before the company in general meeting or otherwise circulated or published. Failure either to sign the report or to show the name of the signatory on circulated copies renders the company and its defaulting officers liable to a fine.

Under section 235(3) the auditor has a statutory duty to consider whether or not the information contained in the directors' report is consistent with the financial statements. Moreover, he is required to draw attention in his report to any inconsistency between the two for the year in question.

The directors of a small company need not file a directors' report with the annual accounts delivered to the Registrar (Sched. 8, para. 4).

Under International Stock Exchange regulations the following information not directly relating to items disclosed elsewhere in the financial statements has to be detailed by a listed company's directors: reasons for departing from standard accounting practice; explanations of significant differences between outcomes and any forecasts made; substantial holdings in the company's shares etc.; whether or not the company is a close company for tax purposes; particulars of any agreement to waive dividends; directors' interests in contracts with the company; and contracts with the company; and contracts with substantial shareholders. Several of these matters are also covered by ED 46 and by International Accounting Standard 24 on related party disclosures.

Auditors' Report

Section 235(1) of the Act requires a company's auditors to make a report to its members on all accounts laid before the company in general meeting during the auditors' tenure of office (see *post*, page 608). The report should state whether, in the opinion of the auditors, the financial statements comply with the Companies Act and give a true and fair view of the state of the company's (and, where appropriate, the group's) affairs at the balance sheet date and of its (or, where appropriate, the group's) profit and loss account for the year ended on that date (section 235(2)). Under sections 235 and 237, the auditors must state the fact if in their opinion any of the following is the case:

- (i) Proper accounting records have not been kept (s.237(2)).
- (ii) Proper returns have not been obtained from branches not visited by them (s.237(2)).
- (iii) The financial statements are not in agreement with the accounting records and returns (s.237(2)).
- (iv) Full information and explanations regarded as necessary for the audit have not been obtained (s.237(3)).
- (v) The information relating to the year given in the directors' report is not consistent with the financial statements (s.235(3)).

In addition, if the requirements of Schedule 6 are not complied with in the accounts (*i.e.* concerning disclosure of chairman's and directors' emoluments, waived emoluments, pensions, and compensation for loss of office; and details of loans and other credit transactions favouring directors and officers), it is the auditors' duty to include in their report, so far as they are reasonably able to do so, a statement giving the required information (s.237(4)).

Under section 236, the auditors' report and the copy delivered to the Registrar must state the names of the auditors and be signed by them. Moreover, their names must appear on each copy of the report laid before the company in general meeting or otherwise circulated or published. Failure to ensure that the original report or the copy delivered to the Registrar are signed, or that copies circulated carry the names of the auditors, renders the company and its defaulting officers liable to a fine.

Where the audit report is qualified and the company proposes to pay a dividend, the auditors must indicate whether the qualification is material in determining whether the distribution can lawfully be made (section 271(3)–(5)). Auditors belonging to the main professional accountancy bodies in the United Kingdom (which is the vast majority—see below, pages 596 *et seq.*) are also required by those bodies to refer in their reports to any breaches of accounting standards. This has meant that in recent years audit qualifications for listed companies have become more common, though empirical research seems to suggest that the investing public is able to distinguish between material and merely technical qualifications.[64] Moreover, although professionally qualified accountants tend to follow a pattern of recognised procedures in carrying out company audits, the professional accountancy bodies have attempted to codify auditing practices through a series of Auditing Standards and Guidelines published by the Auditing Practices Committee and the International Auditing Practices Committee, which largely reflect the methods employed by the leading practising firms of accountants that audit the accounts of most large and medium sized limited companies.

In addition to the general requirements stated above, where a company's directors propose to rely on exemptions in relation to its size (*e.g.* where a parent company is exempted under sections 248–249 from the obligation to prepare group accounts; or where as a company under sections 246–247 wishes to file abbreviated accounts with the Registrar), the auditors must provide them with a report that states whether, in their opinion, the necessary conditions for such a privilege have been met (s.248(3)–(4) and Sched. 8, para. 8(1)). Moreover, where advantage is taken of such exemptions, "special" auditors'

[64] M. Firth, "Qualified Audit Reports: Their Impact on Investment Decisions," *The Accounting Review*, July 1978, pp. 642–650. See also pp. 611–612, *post*, for the nature of audit qualifications.

reports must be attached to the company's financial statements. (In the case of the abbreviated accounts, these would be those filed with the Registrar rather than the full accounts laid before the company and circulated to its members). The auditors must state in such "special" reports whether, in their opinion, the requirements for exemption have been met. Additionally, the "special" report attached to filed abbreviated accounts must be properly signed by the auditors and reproduce the text of their report relating to the accounts laid before the shareholders in general meeting (Sched. 8, para. 8(2), (4)). However, under section 240, the auditors' report must not be published with non-statutory accounts, although the latter must be accompanied by a statement indicating that such a report has been made on the statutory accounts and whether or not it is qualified. Similarly, under section 251 a summary financial statement circulated by a listed company to its members must include a report by its auditors indicating (i) whether in their opinion such a statement (a) is consistent with its full accounts and the directors' report; and (b) complies with the requirements of section 251 and the regulations relating to summary financial statements; and (ii) whether the auditors' report on the full accounts was qualified, and if so setting out that report together with further material necessary to understand the qualification.

Special Classes of Company

Dormant companies

Under section 250 of the 1985 Act a dormant company, which is one in which no significant accounting transaction occurred during the period in question, need not have appointed auditors and hence need not file an auditors' report with the accounts. Instead, the directors must include a statement immediately above their signatures on the balance sheet to the effect that the company was dormant throughout the relevant period. To qualify for such exemption the company must meet the following three conditions: (i) it was not required to prepare group accounts during the previous financial year; (ii) it was classed as a small company during the previous financial year; and (iii) it has been dormant since the end of the previous financial year.

Investment companies

Companies qualify for special treatment if they are investment companies within the meaning of section 266 of the 1985 Act (which effectively applies to investment trust companies) and was not during the year prohibited from making a distribution under section 265 (Sched. 4, para. 73: see *post*, pages 634–636). The provisions of the 1985 Act are adapted in three ways for such companies: (i) revaluations of investments need not be credited or debited to the revaluation reserve; (ii) where the value of fixed asset investments is written down, such a debit need not be passed through the profit and loss account if it is either charged against a reserve to which investment revaluations have been credited, or is shown as a separate item under "other reserves"; (iii) disclosure must be made in a note of any distribution reducing the company's net assets to less than the aggregate of its called-up capital and undistributable reserves (which can arise if it chooses to apply the asset ratio test for distribution rather than the capital maintenance criterion: section 264) (Sched. 4, paras. 71–72).

Banking and insurance companies

Under the Companies Act 1948 the financial statements of banking and insurance companies did not have to be prepared and published in the full form required of other limited companies (Part III of the eighth Schedule of that Act, as amended).[65] Moreover, the EC's Fourth Council Directive was not intended to apply to banking and insurance companies, the reporting of whose financial affairs is the subject of other directives.[66] As a result, in framing the Companies Act 1981 the United Kingdom government took advantage of these concessions, and under section 255 of the 1985 Act qualifying companies (which include groups in which banking or insurance activities predominate) are permitted to prepare their financial statements under the old provisions, as modified. These are

[65] The concessions also used to apply to shipping companies, but the Jenkins Committee ((1962) Cmnd. 1749, para. 416) recommended that their exemption should be revoked. The EC's Fourth Council Directive also provided that such concessions should be phased out by 1987.

[66] That for banks is Council Directive 86/635 of December 8, 1986. The directive for insurance companies is still at the draft stage.

contained in sections 255 and 255A–D and Schedule 9 to the 1985 Act. Banking and insurance companies which take advantage of the concessions cannot submit modified accounts, and the financial statements must contain a statement that they have been prepared in accordance with the special provisions of the Act. The accounts must be accompanied by a modified directors' report, certain of the requirements of section 234 and Schedule 7 being excluded (section 255C and Sched. 10); and by an auditors' report which merely has to state whether in the auditors' opinion the accounts have been properly prepared in accordance with the Act (Sched. 9, para. 28A).

The broad effect of the concessions is to enable qualifying companies to conceal movements on reserve and fixed asset accounts, and for banks and insurance companies this is normally justified on the grounds that it is desirable not to undermine public confidence in such financial institutions. Yet the very fact that members of the public, as depositors or policy holders, have a direct interest in the financial affairs of such concerns has led successive governments to develop alternative means of monitoring their financial viability. In the case of banks and discount houses, the control machinery is informally operated and modified as the need arises by the Bank of England, although from 1979 the relationship between the Bank and the institutions it supervises has been formalised by the Banking Act of that year and has been further strengthened by the Banking Act 1987. Moreover, since 1970 the major clearing banks have developed their own liberal code concerning disclosure in their published accounts. Insurance companies are subject to the Insurance Companies Act 1982, and the Department of Trade also requires certain very detailed returns to be made.[67] For long term business (mainly life assurance) the conventional profit and loss account has relatively little significance, and more attention has to be paid to the actuarial report,[68] balance sheet, and other supplementary statements

[67] Most recently governed by S.I. 1983 No. 1811: The Insurance Companies (Accounts and Statements) Regulations 1983, as amended by S.I. 1988 No. 672.

[68] The significance of the actuarial valuation is in fact acknowledged in section 268 of the Companies Act 1985, which recognises actuarial surpluses or deficits as the appropriate measure of realised profits or losses available for distribution.

than to the income (*i.e.* fund) account. For short term business (*i.e.* for one year contracts concerning fire, theft, motor and similar insurance) the rules are slightly different and have been tightened up in recent years following the collapse of Fire, Auto and Marine in 1966[69] and Vehicle and General in 1971,[70] though again detailed returns have to be filed.[71]

Powers of the Secretary of State to Alter the Accounting Requirements of the Act

Under section 257 of the Act the Secretary of State can alter, add to or otherwise modify by statutory instrument the requirements relating to financial statements and annexed reports. Moreover, he also has powers to exempt oversea companies from certain requirements (section 700); while under sections 255(4) and 255A(6) he can, on application from, or with the consent of, a company's directors, modify the requirements of Schedule 9 with regard to a banking or insurance company.

Other Accounting and Disclosure Regulations

In recent years, beyond the conventional limits of company law, there has been lengthy debate, on the one hand about the extent of disclosure relating to such matters as the state of a company's industrial relations, the impact of its activities on society, and its dealings with national governments; and on the other how best to ensure proper disclosure to various groups of interested parties other than existing shareholders, most obviously employees and the government and its agencies. Many of these issues were examined in general terms in the ASC's 1975 discussion paper, *The Corporate Report*, and since its publication a number of large companies have responded by

[69] Part II of the Companies Act 1967, since substantially superseded by the Insurance Companies Acts 1974 and 1982.

[70] *Report of the Tribunal on the Vehicle and General Insurance Co. Ltd.*, February 18, 1972, H.C. 133.

[71] Insurance Companies Acts 1974 and 1982, and various Statutory Instruments, including S.I. 1983 No. 1811, as amended.

including in their annual reports some of the supplementary information it proposed in Value Added Statements, Employment Reports, Statements of Money Exchanges with Government and Transactions in Foreign Currency, and (less commonly) Statements of Corporate Objectives and Future Prospects. In the meantime various pieces of legislation (most notably the Industry Act 1975 and the Employment Protection Act 1975) have imposed new disclosure requirements on companies.[72]

As regards the extent of disclosure, the argument in relation to the state of industrial relations is fairly straightforward. Clearly investors and other interested parties may well be interested in learning something about such matters since this can potentially be at least as important in colouring their expectations about future likely outcomes as knowledge of a company's policy on research and development. Indeed, it is quite possible (and not unknown) for managers to seek short term advantage and higher immediate reported profits by neglecting training programmes and pressurising the work-force, but at the expense of long-term profitability. Various methods of human resource accounting have been proposed and experimented with to try to deal with these aspects of a company's affairs, but they are probably better dealt with in a narrative report. The same can generally be said of the impact of a company's activities on society, though some companies in the United States now publish narrative social balance sheets, listing the benefits they afford the community (*e.g.* through their general research and development programmes and their support of educational institutions, hospitals, etc.) as well as the costs (*e.g.* pollution).

As regards specific interest groups, the government most obviously requires accounting information from companies to assess their corporation tax liabilities. Briefly, a company's conventional annual accounts are used by the Inland Revenue as a starting point from which to calculate income subject to tax. The income itself has to be disaggregated by type into its schedular components, the most important source for most

[72] The disclosure requirements of the Industry Act 1975 were in fact repealed by the Industry Act 1980, but the disclosure provisions of the Employment Protection Act 1975 were only slightly amended by the Employment Act 1980.

companies being Schedule D Case I income, relating to trading profits. Adjustments have to be made to the reported figures for disallowable expenses (*e.g.* expenditure not wholly and exclusively incurred for the purpose of the trade, appropriations of profit, capital expenditure, depreciation, taxation, charges on income, etc.), and for capital allowances, before the liability to corporation tax can be assessed.

Another important piece of legislation concerning disclosure of financial and other information by companies to the government was the Industry Act 1975, which greatly extended the provisions of the Industry Act 1972. One of the aims of the legislation was to encourage companies to establish voluntary planning agreements with the authorities on an annual basis. The government would provide grants and loans, support export programmes, help find skilled workers, and make available its economic forecasts in return for information from the company concerning its long-term plans and specific aspects of its budgets concerning United Kingdom sales, exports, investment, productivity, employment and training. However, the Act further empowered ministers in certain circumstances to require companies to disclose past or budgeted information relating to specific matters for individual manufacturing establishments. The circumstances were defined in section 28 of the Act as being where such information was in the opinion of the relevant minister needed either to form or further national economic policies, or was needed for consultations between government, employers or workers on the outlook for a particular sector of manufacturing industry. Where the circumstances were met the minister could make out an order requiring the company to furnish him within a specified reasonable time with matters relating to the business in the United Kingdom of the undertaking concerning persons employed, capital expenditure, fixed capital assets, productive capacity and capacity utilisation, output and productivity, sales and exports of products, and certain details of research and development activity. After receiving the information specified in the order the minister was empowered to require the company to furnish the whole or part of the information to an authorised representative of each trade union recognised by the company within a reasonable period. The provisions, however, were repealed by the Industry Act 1980.

Employee representatives are still empowered to receive financial information under section 17 of the Employment Protection Act 1975 (which effectively embodies sections 56–57 of the Industrial Relations Act 1971, repealed in 1974).[73] If certain grounds for exemption do not apply, an employer is obliged by this section to disclose to trade union representatives material information relevant to collective bargaining procedures, and indeed any information relevant to collective bargaining which would be "in accordance with good industrial relations practice." The Advisory Conciliation and Arbitration Service (ACAS) has published a draft code to try to establish what constitutes such good practice, and it suggests relevant data should include work schedules, orders, market share, productivity figures, relevant cost structures, transfer prices, government financial assistance, intra-group loans and interest charged.

In several Continental countries legislation has established alternative means through which relevant information can be communicated to employee representatives, the most obvious being through works councils. Such committees have their informal counterparts in many British companies, but these latter do not enjoy the same legal status. However, it appears to be Common Market policy to encourage the creation of such councils throughout the Community. Another way of trying to ensure employee representatives are fully informed about a company's financial affairs is to give them board representation. This is the practice in West Germany where such representatives by law sit on supervisory boards which oversee the actions of executive directors. Yet although the EC's early drafts of the Fifth Council Directive on company law harmonisation[74] and the draft European company statute[75] contained provisions which would make this regular practice throughout the Community, little enthusiasm has been shown for the two-tier board structure in the United Kingdom, even though in practice many large British companies appoint non-executive directors to fulfil a

[73] This and the other disclosure provisions in ss.17–24 of the Act were only amended in minor respects by the Employment Act 1980.

[74] Draft Fifth Directive on Company Law Harmonization, J.O. 1972 C131/49. However, in 1982 the EC Commission agreed to drop the idea of making the two-tier board compulsory. See p. 17, *ante*.

[75] Draft European Company Statute, J.O. 1970 C124/1. See pp. 18–19, *ante*.

similar supervisory function. Moreover, proposals by the Bullock Committee[76] that employee representatives should be appointed as directors have found little support either amongst management or trade unions.

Elsewhere, a voluntary code of conduct has been established since December 1974 for companies operating in South Africa, and which since 1978 has been agreed under EC auspices (Cmnd. 7233 (1978) and Cmnd. 9860 (1986)). Under its terms, companies are expected to report annually on various aspects of their activities there, both to governments and to the public.

Acknowledgment of Debts

Finally, there is the question of whether or not the inclusion of a debt in the balance sheet amounts to an acknowledgment of that debt by the company.

In *Jones* v. *Bellgrove Properties Ltd.*[77] it was held that a statement in a balance sheet "To sundry creditors £7,638," the balance sheet being signed by the company's agents, a firm of chartered accountants, was an acknowledgment, within the meaning of section 24(2) of the Limitation Act 1939[78] (see now the Limitation Act 1980) of a debt of £1,807 owed to a shareholder and included in the £7,638. Consequently the right of action to recover the debt was by section 23(4) of the 1939 Act deemed to have accrued on the date of the acknowledgment and the action was not barred by the six-year limitation period fixed by section 2(1) of the 1939 Act. The *Jones* case was distinguished in *Re Transplanters* (*Holding Co.*) *Ltd.*[79] (where the directors had made the acknowledgment in favour of one of themselves) and considered in *Good* v. *Parry*,[80] but in *Consolidated Agencies Ltd.* v. *Bertram Ltd.*,[81] where a section of the Indian Limitation Act 1908, which was similar to but not

[76] (1977) Cmnd. 6706.
[77] [1949] 2 K.B. 700 (C.A.).
[78] Not applicable to Scotland; any similar question arising in Scotland would be governed by the Prescription and Limitation (Scotland) Act 1973.
[79] [1958] 1 W.L.R. 822.
[80] [1963] 2 Q.B. 418 (C.A.) (For there to be an acknowledgment the debt must be quantified in figures or it must be liquidated in the sense that it is capable of ascertainment by calculation or by extrinsic evidence without further agreeement of the parties).
[81] [1965] A.C. 470 (P.C.).

identical with section 23(4) of the 1939 Act, was construed, it was held that the word "acknowledgment" meant acknowledgment of a debt existing at the date of signature and, since the balance sheet was signed many months after the year to which it related, it was not an acknowledgment of such an existing debt but an acknowledgment of a past debt as at the date when the balance sheet was made up. It was said that the *Jones* case was rightly decided on its facts (no question arose there as to the date to which the acknowledgment related although it was taken to be the date of the annual general meeting) and that it is questionable whether a signature on a balance sheet, which must of necessity be made some time after the date to which the balance sheet has been made up, can amount to an acknowledgment of an existing debt. However, in *Re Gee & Co. (Woolwich) Ltd.*,[82] the *Consolidated Agencies* case was distinguished and it was held that a balance sheet, duly signed by the directors, is capable of being an effective acknowledgment of the state of the company's indebtedness as at the date of the balance sheet, so that the cause of action should, in an appropriate case, be deemed to have accrued at that date, being the date to which the signature of the directors relates. On the facts of the *Gee* case, the acknowledgment was effective even though it was made by the directors in favour of one of themselves, because it was sanctioned by every member of the company.

[82] [1975] Ch. 52.

Chapter 21

AUDITORS

INTRODUCTION

REFERENCE to the Auditors' Report and its content has already been made in Chapter 20 (see above, pages 581–583), and the position of the auditors has become a very important one. In particular, it has become increasingly recognised that where there is inequality (or "asymmetry") of information between parties, it is generally desirable, both as between the parties concerned and from a wider social perspective, that the accounts should be attested by an independent third party. This is necessary to avoid a breakdown in the market mechanism in two sets of circumstances. First, a prospective purchaser of a company's shares will require information before he commits himself to the transaction—just as a person buying a second-hand car will want to ensure he is not about to acquire a "pup" (or a "lemon," as Americans would call it). Economists have demonstrated that in the absence of reliable information, the market mechanism will become unstable and at the limit no trading will take place, a phenomenon they describe as being the result of "adverse selection." It is partly to avoid this that disclosure of validated information is required in a prospectus or listing particulars. The second situation arises where a "principal" (*e.g.* a shareholder) attempts to assess the performance of his "agent" (*e.g.* a manager) but has to rely in information given to him by the latter, who is clearly in a position to manipulate the data—a problem known to economists as one of "moral hazard." It is largely to counteract this that the device of a statutory audit has been developed.

As will be described below, the auditor is given wide powers by sections 389A, 391A, 392, 392A, and 394 of the Companies Act 1985, being able to enforce them by qualifying his report and, in an extreme case, by refusing to certify the accounts.

But just as it is important for readers of financial statements to have a guarantee that they have been properly prepared under an accepted set of conventions, it is also necessary for them to be able to rely on the word of those persons who certify them as having been so produced. This means, of course, that auditors should be recognised as fit and proper persons to carry out the duties of their office. Traditionally the market response to situations where the public wishes to purchase quality services (*e.g.* in medicine, architecture, law or accountancy) is for practitioners to organise themselves into professional bodies, which then set minimum standards for members. Self regulation along these lines can be very successful, but the position of professional bodies frequently enables them to restrict entry and exploit their monopoly power, making it necessary for central governments to intervene to try to redress the balance.

Prior to the Companies Act 1989 a person could only be appointed as an auditor of a company if he was a member of a professional body recognised by the Secretary of State (*i.e* The Institute of Chartered Accountants in England and Wales; The Institute of Chartered Accountants of Scotland; The Institute of Chartered Accountants in Ireland; and The Chartered Association of Certified Accountants) (section 389(1)(*a*) of the Companies Act 1985, now repealed). However, Part II of the 1989 Act, concerned with eligibility of company auditors, has introduced the provisions of the European Community's Eighth Council Directive[1] on company law harmonisation into British legislation. As a result two types of statutory supervisory body will now exist: Recognised Supervisory Bodies (RSBs), of which all company auditors must be members; and Recognised Qualifying Bodies (RQBs), which offer appropriate professional qualifications that are the prerequisite for membership of an RSB. In practice, the same organisation can simultaneously be both an RSB and an RQB, enabling the main professional bodies of public accountants to fulfil both functions.

The creation of the new institutional structure has required amendments to previous legislation concerning the appointment, resignation and removal of auditors, although this has also partly been the result of introducing the "elective regime" for private companies, whereby under section 252 of the 1985 Act

[1] Eighth Council Directive, 84/253 (O.J. 1984, L 126/20).

they can by unanimous resolution dispense with the holding of annual general meetings and the laying of accounts and reports before such meetings.[2] However, within the British context, the overall impact of Part II of the 1989 Act is unlikely to alter the position already achieved under self regulation with regard to the qualification of auditors, except to impose a more elaborate regulatory framework that will impose greater compliance costs on those involved—directly on auditors and indirectly on the customers for their services—while at the same time the authorities are continuing for the most part to rely on competition in the market place to ensure that professional bodies do not overexploit their monopoly power.

The most important matters dealt with in this chapter are the way in which auditors are appointed, their qualifications, and their powers and duties, including their duty to make a report to the members of the company.

Appointment of Auditors

Except where a company is dormant or where it is a private company electing to dispense with the laying of accounts, auditors will be appointed at a general meeting where the company's accounts are laid (section 384 of the Companies Act 1985). Moreover, except again where a private company elects to dispense with the laying of accounts, a company must appoint an auditor at each general meeting where accounts are laid until the next such meeting. However, the first auditors may be appointed by the directors before the first general meeting at which accounts are laid, or—failing action by them—by the company in general meeting (section 385 of the Companies Act 1985).

Where a private company has elected in accordance with section 252 to dispense with the laying of accounts,[3] auditors must be appointed by the company at a general meeting held within four weeks of accounts for the previous year being sent to members under section 238[4]; or, where such a meeting was held, the conclusion of a general meeting at which accounts for

[2] *Ante*, p. 518.
[3] *Ante*, p. 518.
[4] *Ante*, p. 519.

the previous year were laid. Such auditors hold office until the next date at which an appointment falls due. In the case of the first auditors of a private company taking advantage of an election under section 252, the directors (rather than the company in general meeting) can exercise the power of appointment, failing which the company in general meeting will appoint (section 385A of the Companies Act 1985).

Private companies may by elective resolution under section 379A opt to dispense with the obligation to appoint auditors annually, in which case the existing auditors will, so long as the election continues, be deemed to have been reappointed unless the company either is a dormant company or a resolution is passed ending the appointment (section 386 of the Companies Act 1985).

Where no auditors are appointed, a company shall within a week of the terms of such an appointment elapsing give notice to the Secretary of State so that he can fill the vacancy. Failure to give such notice renders the defaulting company and officers liable to be fined (section 387 of the Companies Act 1985).

A company's directors or the company in general meeting are empowered to fill a casual vacancy for the office of auditor. Where this is done by the company in general meeting, special notice is required, as it is when an auditor appointed to fill a casual vacancy by the directors is subject to reappointment by the company in general meeting. Copies of such notice have to be sent to the auditor concerned and to his predecessor if he resigned (section 388 of the Companies Act 1985).

A company which is dormant under the provisions of section 250 of the 1985 Act is exempt from the obligation to appoint auditors (section 388A(1) of the Companies Act 1985).

To qualify as dormant, the company must not have engaged in any significant accounting transaction other than the receipt of monies for its shares from subscribers to the memorandum of association during the period in question. It may then pass a special resolution exempting itself from the obligation under section 384 to appoint auditors. Such a special resolution may be passed either at an extraordinary general meeting held before the first general meeting where the accounts would normally be laid, so long as the company has been dormant since its formation; or at a general meeting where the accounts are to be laid but where the following conditions are met:

(*a*) the company is not required to prepare group accounts;

(*b*) the directors must be entitled to file small company accounts under section 246, or would be so entitled but for being a member of an ineligible group; and

(*c*) the company must have been dormant since the end of the previous year (section 250 of the Companies Act 1985).

In order to take advantage of the dormant company provisions, steps will also have to be taken to change its articles where they require it to appoint an auditor (as, indeed, would generally be the case for any company adopting Table A prior to the current form which took effect from July 1, 1985).

Where a company ceases to be dormant, the directors may appoint auditors to hold office until the next meeting at which accounts are to be laid. Alternatively, if the company elects under section 252 to dispense with laying accounts, they may either appoint auditors within 28 days of the annual accounts being sent to members under section 238 or, if a shareholder gives notice requiring the laying of accounts at a general meeting, at the beginning of that meeting. If the directors fail to exercise such powers, they may be exercised by the company in general meeting (section 388A(2)–(5)).

Professional Qualifications of Auditors

Supervisory bodies and professional qualifications

Recognised supervisory bodies

A Recognised Supervisory Body (RSB) is a body established in the U.K. which maintains and enforces rules as to

(a) the eligibility of persons seeking appointment or acting as company auditors; and

(b) the conduct of company audit work,

which are binding on persons seeking appointment or acting as company auditors either because they are members of that body or because they are otherwise subject to its control (section 30(1) of the Companies Act 1989).

Bodies wishing to become RSBs have to apply to the Secretary of State for recognition, and the conditions for granting or revoking recognition are specified in Schedule 11 to the 1989 Act. Prospective RSBs must submit their rules to the Secretary of State, but he may refuse to recognise a body if he is of the view that there are other bodies controlling the profession which have been, or are likely to be, recognised (Sched. 11, paras. 1–3). RSBs have to ensure that only individuals with appropriate qualifications and firms controlled by qualified persons are eligible for appointment as company auditors (paras. 4–5), and their rules must be such that only "fit and proper persons" can be so appointed (para. 6). Further, the RSB's rules should ensure that company audit work is conducted properly and with integrity and independence; that certain technical standards are applied; and that procedures exist for ensuring eligible persons maintain an appropriate level of competence (paras. 6–9). In addition, the RSB's rules must deal with monitoring and enforcement of compliance with its rules; admission and expulsion of members, the grant and withdrawal of eligibility for appointment as company auditor and disciplinary procedures; the investigation of complaints against its members and the body itself; and the provision by eligible persons of indemnity insurance and similar arrangements to meet claims arising from company audit work (paras. 10–13). In addition, RSBs must have rules requiring eligible persons to comply with sections 35 and 36 of the 1989 Act, respectively dealing with disclosure of auditors' names in a register and information about firms eligible for appointment as company auditors; have satisfactory arrangements for meeting the costs of complying with their rules; and be able and willing to promote higher standards of integrity in company audit work.

Under section 47 of the 1989 Act and Schedule 14, an RSB's rules and other guidance has to be submitted to the Director General of Fair Trading before recognition is granted so that he can assess whether they will restrict or prevent competition. However, RSBs and their officers, employees and members of their governing bodies are exempted from damages in respect of their discharging their statutory duties or failing to do so, unless it can be shown they have acted in bad faith. This effectively prevents them being joined in any action taken against auditors for negligence (section 48 of the Companies Act 1989).

Professional qualifications

Effectively the 1989 Act requires that auditors should hold an appropriate qualification. Usually this will be granted by a Recognised Qualifying Body (RQB), approved by the Secretary of State, but transitional arrangements provide that persons who were qualified as auditors immediately before January 1, 1990, continue to be eligible. Such provisions extend, first, to members of one of the four professional bodies recognised under section 389(1)(*a*) of the 1985 Act[5] and to students who have commenced their training before January 1, 1990, and who qualify before January 1, 1996, as long as their training is approved for this purpose by the Secretary of State (section 31(1), (4)–(5) of the Companies Act 1989). In addition, persons eligible for appointment as auditors immediately before January 1, 1990, have a 12 month period in which to notify the Secretary of State that they wish to continue to be treated as qualified. Such persons are essentially those authorised under section 13(1) of the Companies Act 1967 as being suitable to be appointed as auditors or who have received individual authorisation under the now repealed section 389(1)(*b*) on the basis of qualifications obtained outside the British Isles. However, in order to continue in practice, these auditors, like all others, will have to become members of an RSB (section 31(2)–(3)).

In order to offer recognised professional qualifications and become an RQB, a body must be approved by the Secretary of State (section 32 of the Companies Act 1989). The procedure for recognition is similar to that for an RSB, and the conditions for granting, refusing and revoking recognition are laid down in Schedule 12 to the Act, paras, 1–3. Basically, the qualification must only be open to persons who have attained university entrance level or have a sufficient period of professional experience (*i.e.* at least seven years in a professional capacity in finance, law and accountancy). Periods of theoretical instruction, up to a maximum of four years can count towards the necessary experience (Schedule 12, paras. (4)–(6)). Those who seek recognition must also pass an examination, which tests theoretical knowledge and the ability to apply it in practice, and they must have completed at least three years' practical training.

[5] *Ante*, p. 593.

However, certain exemptions are available for those who have passed equivalent examinations or who have obtained relevant practical experience. The subjects to be covered under the examination syllabus are to be defined by the Secretary of State by statutory instrument, and the practical training must be given by persons approved by an RQB. In fact, at least two thirds of it must be with a fully qualified auditor, a substantial part being on company audit work (Schedule 12, paras. (7)–(8)). In addition, the RQB must have rules and arrangements to ensure compliance with its regulations and procedures for ensuring the effective monitoring of continued compliance with such requirements (Schedule 12, para. 9).

With regard to those qualifying other than by membership of a professional body recognised under the now repealed section 389(1)(*a*) of the 1985 Act, anyone authorised under section 13(1) of the Companies Act 1967 will be treated as holding an appropriate qualification to audit an unquoted company, and this will be extended if the person indicates in writing to the Secretary of State that he wishes to retain that authorisation (sections 31(2) and 34 of the Companies Act 1989). Likewise, the Secretary of State may declare a professional qualification obtained outside the U.K. to be "an approved overseas qualification" under section 31(1) of the 1989 Act, which enables persons so qualified to audit the accounts of British companies. However, in considering whether or not to make such a declaration, the Secretary of State may take into account reciprocal arrangements for persons professionally qualified in the U.K. to audit overseas; and he may require additional qualifications to ensure an adequate knowledge of law and practice in the U.K. relevant to the audit of accounts. He may also withdraw recognition of an overseas qualification after a specified date if he is no longer satisfied that there is equivalent competence or there are inadequate reciprocal arrangements (section 33 of the Companies Act 1989).

Registers and fees

Under section 35 of the 1989 Act, the Secretary of State is empowered to make regulations through a statutory instrument requiring that a register be kept of all individuals and firms eligible for appointment as company auditors and of the qualified persons responsible for company audit work on their behalves. The register will give the names and addresses and indicate the relevant RSB. The regulations may require further information to be disclosed on the register, and the Secretary of State can impose further obligations on the RSBs, on persons eligible to be company auditors, and on anyone charged by one or more RSBs to keep the register. The regulations may also include provisions concerning the availability of the register for public inspection, for copies of entries being made available, and for appropriate fees to be charged for such services.

Similarly, under section 36 of the 1989 Act, the Secretary of State is empowered to make regulations through a statutory instrument requiring an RSB to make available to the public information about firms which are eligible under its rules to act as statutory auditors. The information to be disclosed will be the names and addresses of all directors and shareholders, if the firm is a company; or of all partners, if it is a partnership. The regulations may require further information to be disclosed, and the Secretary of State can impose further obligations on the RSBs, on persons eligible to be company auditors, and on anyone charged by one or more supervisory bodies to keep such information. The regulations may also include provisions concerning the availability of the information for public inspection, for copies of information being made available, and for appropriate fees to be charged for such services. However, the regulations may make different provisions for different types of information.

Section 45 of the 1989 Act provides for the payment of fees by applicants for recognition and of periodical fees payable by RSBs and RQBs. The regulations will be set by statutory instrument, and the fees will be paid into the consolidated fund.

Section 46 of the 1989 Act enables the Secretary of State, by order made by statutory instrument, to set up a body corporate to exercise his functions under Part II of the Act, concerning the eligibility for appointment as a company auditor. The order can delegate some or all of the Secretary of State's powers, except those preventing restrictive practices (section 47 and Schedule 14) and those determining his relations with such a delegated body. If such a delegation order is made, the Secretary of State will still be able concurrently to exercise his power to call for relevant information from an RSB or RQB under section 38 and to give directions so that such bodies should comply with European Community and other international obligations under section 40. Moreover, the delegated body will only be able to refuse or withdraw approval of an overseas qualification on the lack of reciprocity under section 33(3) with the consent of the Secretary of State. Provision is also made for the revocation in whole or in part of the delegation order or for its variation under a further order made by statutory instrument. The status, constitution and proceedings of a delegated body and the exercise by it of functions transferred by the Secretary of State are detailed in Schedule 13 to the Act.

The Secretary of State is empowered to require RSBs and RQBs both to notify him in writing of specified events and to disclose such information as he may reasonably require. He can also, as an alternative to revoking recognition, apply to the Court for an order directing an RSB or RQB to take the necessary steps to meet particular requirements and obligations, and he may also require such bodies to avoid actions that would be incompatible with international commitments (sections 37–40 of the Companies Act 1989).

Penalties for offences

A person or a partner or officer of a corporate body who supplies false or misleading information in relation to Part II of the 1989 Act, concerning eligibility for appointment as a company auditor, is liable to imprisonment and/or a fine. Similar penalties can be imposed where a person not on the register of auditors holds himself out as a registered auditor or where a body corporate which is not recognised as an RSB or RQB holds itself out as such. Proceedings, where necessary against an unincorporated body, must commence within 12 months of evidence coming to the notice of the prosecuting party, but action cannot be initiated more then three years after the offence took place (sections 41–44 of the Companies Act 1989).

Eligibility of partnerships

Prior to the 1989 Act, partnerships and corporate bodies could not be appointed as auditors, only individuals. However, to bring British law into line with that in a number of European Community countries and to limit the liability of individuals (though not of firms) in professional indemnity claims, section 25 specifically provides that a firm may be appointed as a company auditor. Where this is the case, when the membership of a partnership changes a succeeding practice will be eligible for appointment, so long as the members or the business are substantially the same as before. Provision is also made for the situation where part of a practice is taken over by another partnership or person eligible for appointment (section 26 of the Companies Act 1989). This clarifies the fact that in English law the appointment is of the partnership itself and not the individual partners and that the appointment will continue despite the routine cessations of partnerships when members join and leave. The position has always been different in Scotland where partnerships have a separate legal personality.

Where a corporate body is appointed as an auditor, it is necessary to ensure that the individuals responsible for the work hold appropriate qualifications and that the firm is controlled by qualified persons. Consequently, RSBs are required to have rules which deal with these matters and ensure that there are no potential conflicts of interest (paras. 4–5, 7, Schedule 11 to the Companies Act 1989).

Ineligibility because of lack of independence

The 1989 Act also defines the circumstances in which a person is ineligible for appointment as a statutory auditor on the grounds of lack of independence—*viz.* if he is an officer or employee of the company or a parent or subsidiary undertaking, or a partner or employee of such a person. A person may also be ineligible if there is a connection between him or any associate of his and the group of companies, the nature of such a connection being specified in regulations made by the Secretary of State (section 27 of the Companies Act 1989).

Appointment of an ineligible auditor

Acting as a statutory auditor when ineligible is an offence, and the guilty party is liable on conviction to a fine and on summary conviction to a fine not exceeding the statutory maximum. In the case of continued contravention, the person will be liable on a second or subsequent summary conviction to a fine of up to one tenth of the statutory maximum for each day on which the offence is continued. However, it is a defence to show that there was no knowledge and no reason to believe that the person concerned was ineligible. In this context, a person may either be ineligible or become ineligible. In the latter case, he should vacate office and give notice in writing to the company that he has resigned because of ineligibility (section 28 of the Companies Act 1989).

Where a company audit has been carried out by an ineligible person, the Secretary of State may direct that an eligible person be appointed, either to undertake a second audit or to review the first audit and report whether a second audit is needed. When such a direction is given, a copy will be sent to the Registrar of Companies, and the company must comply within 21 days. On receiving any report on the possible need for a second audit, the company must forward a copy to the Registrar within 21 days. Failure to comply with these provisions is an offence, liable on summary conviction to a fine not exceeding the statutory maximum; and in the case of continued contravention, on a second or subsequent summary conviction to a fine of one tenth of the statutory maximum for each day on which the offence takes place. Moreover the company is entitled to recover costs incurred complying with these provisions if the ineligible person knew he was ineligible (section 29 of the Companies Act 1989).

Vacation of Office by Auditors

Removal and resignation of auditors

A company may, by ordinary resolution, remove an auditor before his period of office has expired and notwithstanding any agreement with him. Where he is so removed, the company must give notice in prescribed form within two weeks, failing which both it and the defaulting officers are liable to a fine and, for continued contravention, a daily default fine. An auditor so removed retains his rights to compensation or damages in respect of the termination of his appointment; and he is also entitled under section 390 to receive all communications relating to general meetings when his term of office would normally expire or at which it is proposed to appoint his successor, and to attend and be heard at such meetings (section 391 of the Companies Act 1985).

Special notice is required for a resolution removing an auditor or appointing his successor, and such notice must be forwarded to the parties concerned. The auditor who is being removed or who is resigning may make representations of reasonable length to the company which, if requested, must circulate them with the resolution, failing which the auditor may require them to be read out at the meeting. However, application may be made to the Court by the company or other aggrieved party, and if such representations are deemed to be needlessly defamatory they need not be circulated or be read out at the meeting. In such circumstances, the Court may require the auditor to pay some or all of the costs involved (section 391 of the Companies Act 1985).

An auditor may resign by depositing notice in writing at a company's registered office, but under section 394 it must be accompanied by a statement indicating whether or not there are any special circumstances leading to such action. The auditor's period of office ends when such notice is lodged, unless it specifies another date. The company must deliver a copy of the notice to the Registrar within a fortnight of it being lodged at its registered office, failing which it and its defaulting officers are liable to a fine and, for continued contravention, a daily default fine (section 392 of the Companies Act 1985).

When an auditor's resignation letter is accompanied by a statement of circumstances leading to such action, as required by section 394, he may deposit a signed requisition calling on the directors to convene an extraordinary general meeting to receive such a statement and other explanations he may wish to give. He may also request the company to circulate a written explanation of reasonable length concerning the circumstances before such a meeting is convened, or before a meeting at which his term of office would normally have expired. The company must indicate in the notice of the meeting that such a statement has been made and circulate it to members of the company. The directors must convene a meeting within three weeks of the requisition being lodged, and it must be held within four weeks of the date of the notice of the meeting being given. Failure to do so renders every director who did not take reasonable steps to secure compliance liable to a fine. If the statement is not circulated, the auditor may require it to be read out at the meeting. However, application may be made to the Court by the company or other aggrieved party, and if such representations are deemed to be needlessly defamatory they need not be circulated or be read out at the meeting. In such circumstances, the Court may require the auditor to pay some or all of the costs involved (section 392A of the Companies Act 1985).

Where a private company by section 386 has elected to dispense with the annual appointment of an auditor, any member can deposit up to one notice in writing in each financial year at its registered office proposing that the appointment shall be terminated. The directors must then hold a general meeting within four weeks at which a resolution shall be put concerning the termination of the auditor's appointment. If the decision is to end the appointment, the auditor shall be deemed not to be reappointed when next he would be. Moreover, if notice was lodged within a fortnight of the accounts being circulated, any deemed reappointment that has taken place will be invalid. Where the directors fail to take steps to convene a general meeting within a fortnight of a member depositing notice, he may himself convene such a meeting, being reimbursed by the company for his expenses, which in turn may then recoup them from the defaulting directors. However, no compensation or damages are payable directly as a result of such termination of appointment, although an agreement between the company and the auditor may still provide for compensation for loss of office (section 393 of the Companies Act 1985).

Statement by a person ceasing to hold office as auditor

A person who for any reason has ceased to hold office as auditor is required to deposit at the company's registered office within specified periods a statement detailing any circumstances connected with his departure which he considers should be brought to members' or creditors' attention. Where the auditor considers there are no such circumstances, the statement should indicate that fact. However, where there are such circumstances, the company must either send copies of the statement to those persons entitled to receive copies of the accounts under section

238[6] or alternatively apply to the Court, in which case the auditor must be informed. For his part, the auditor must send a copy of his statement to the Registrar within four weeks of depositing it with the company, unless he receives notice within three weeks that the company has applied to the Court. If the Court is satisfied that the auditor is needlessly using his statement for defamatory purposes, it will direct that copies of it should not be circulated and may order the auditor to pay some or all of the costs involved. Moreover, the company will have to circulate another statement indicating the effect of the Court's order. If, however, the Court is not satisfied that the auditor's statement is vexatious, the company must circulate it within 14 days and notify the auditor, who will then send a copy to the Registrar within a week of being so informed (section 394 of the Companies Act 1985).

The specified periods within which a statement under section 394 should be deposited at a company's registered office are as follows:

- — resignation: to be deposited together with the notice of resignation forwarded to the company under section 392.
- — failure to seek reappointment: to be deposited not less than 14 days before the end of the time allowed for next appointing auditors.
- — in any other case: to be deposited within 14 days of the auditor ceasing to hold office (section 394(2) of the Companies Act 1985).

An individual auditor or a partnership acting as auditors are guilty of an offence if they breach the provisions of section 394, although it is a defence to show all reasonable steps were taken to comply. For its part, the company and every defaulting officer is liable to a fine; and, for continued contravention, a daily default fine.

Position of Auditors

The auditor is not a person included in the definition of "officer" in section 744. However, he is an officer of the

[6] *Ante*, p. 519.

company for the purpose of a misfeasance summons under section 212 of the Insolvency Act 1986[7] and for the purpose of offences under sections 206–211 and 218 of that same Act[8] (which sections also are concerned with offences by officers of companies in liquidation). An auditor is presumably an officer for the purpose of the Theft Act 1968,[9] s.19, *ante*[10] which is concerned with false statements by an officer of a body corporate, but an auditor appointed ad hoc for a limited purpose, *e.g.* appointed by the directors for a private audit, is not an officer.[11]

Under section 434(4) an auditor is specifically identified as an agent of the company for the purpose of an investigation into its affairs,[12] and he may be examined on oath by an inspector. Otherwise the auditor is not (in the absence of special contract) an agent of the company, and his normal certificate as to whether the accounts represent a true and fair view of the company's affairs under section 235 cannot constitute an acknowledgment by an agent for the purposes of the Limitation Act 1980.[13]

An auditor is treated in the same way as an officer by sections 310 (provisions relieving officers and auditors from liability) and 727 (relief of officers and auditors).[14]

There is no provision in the Companies Acts or in Table A to the effect that an auditor shall cease to hold office on becoming bankrupt or insane. His position in these respects should be compared with that of a director under section 302 and article 81 of Table A respectively.

REMUNERATION OF AUDITORS

The remuneration of the auditor of a company appointed by the directors or by the Secretary of State is fixed by the directors or

[7] *Re London and General Bank* [1895] 2 Ch. 16 (C.A.). S.212 of the Insolvency Act 1986 replaces s.631 of the 1985 Companies Act; it is dealt with *ante*, p. 419.

[8] ss.206–211 and 218 of the Insolvency Act 1986 replace ss.624–629 and 632 of the 1985 Companies Act.

[9] Not applicable to Scotland.

[10] *Ante*, pp. 157–158.

[11] *R.* v. *Shacter* [1960] 2 Q.B. 252 (C.C.A.).

[12] *Ante*, p. 468.

[13] *Re Transplanters* (*Holding Co.*) *Ltd.* [1958] 1 W.L.R. 822.

[14] *Ante*, pp. 414–416.

by the Secretary of State, as the case may be. In any other case it is fixed by the company in general meeting or as the company in general meeting may determine. "Remuneration" includes sums paid by the company in respect of his expenses (section 390A).

The auditor's remuneration (including expenses paid by the company) must be shown under a separate heading in the profit and loss account (section 390A(3)–(4) of the Companies Act 1985).[15]

The Secretary of State is empowered to introduce regulations by statutory instrument whereby a company will be required to disclose remuneration received by its auditors (including benefits in kind and expenses) for non-audit work. Such regulations can require disclosure of such remuneration not only in relation to the company's auditor but to his associates as well; and it can relate to associated undertakings of the company as well as the company itself. The regulations may also require the auditors to disclose the relevant information in their report or require it to be given in a note to the accounts, in which case the auditors will be obliged to supply the company's directors with the necessary data (section 390B of the Companies Act 1985).

Auditors' Report[16]

1. Report addressed to the members

The auditors must report *to the members*[17] on the annual accounts to be laid before the company in general meeting during their terms of office (section 235(1) of the Companies Act 1985).

[15] *Ante*, pp. 533 *et seq.*
[16] See also pp. 581–583, *ante*.
[17] The exact terms would normally be established in formal engagement letters (see the Auditing Practices Committee's (APC's) auditing guideline "Engagement Letters," May 1984; and International Auditing Guideline (IAG) 2. "Audit Engagement Letters," June 1980). However, the 1974 Labour Party Green Paper on Reform of Company Law made the point that while "In law, the auditors derive their position and authority from the shareholders to whom they report on [the] company's affairs; in practice, auditors work closely with the company's directors and senior executives and their relationship with shareholders particularly in non-director-controlled companies is frequently very tenuous indeed." (p. 31).

2. Content of the report

The report must state (except in the case of a banking or insurance company entitled to benefit under the provisions of Schedule 9[18])—

(*a*) whether in the auditors' opinion the annual accounts have been properly prepared in accordance with the Companies Act, 1985;

(*b*) whether in their opinion a true and fair view is given—

(i) in the case of an individual balance sheet, of the state of affairs of the company at the end of its financial year;

(ii) in the case of an individual profit and loss account, of the profit or loss of the company for the financial year; and

(iii) in the case of group accounts, of the state of affairs at the end of the financial year, and the profit and loss for the financial year, of the undertakings included in the consolidation as a whole, so far as concerns the members of the company (section 235(2) of the Companies Act 1985).

(*c*) whether, after due consideration, they are of the opinion that the information given in the directors' report for the financial year for which the annual accounts are prepared is not consistent with those accounts (section 235(3) of the Companies Act, 1985).

If the auditors think that proper accounting records or returns have not been kept or received, or that the balance sheet and (unless framed as a consolidated profit and loss account) the profit and loss account are not in agreement with the accounting records and returns, they must state that fact in the report (section 237(2)).

Further, if auditors fail to obtain all the information and explanations which, to the best of their knowledge and belief,

[18] *Ante*, pp. 584 *et seq.*.

are necessary for their audit, they must state that fact in the report (section 237(3)).

If the accounts do not contain particulars of the chairman's and directors' emoluments, waived emoluments, pensions and compensation for loss of office, the auditors' report must normally include the details (section 237(4)).

3. Signature on the auditors' report

The auditors' report and the copy delivered to the Registrar must state the names of the auditors and be signed by them. Similarly, all copies of the report laid before the company in general meeting or otherwise circulated must state the names of the auditors, and the penatly for default of these provisions is a fine (section 236 of the Companies Act 1985).

4. The duties of auditors in relation to the audit report

In preparing their report the auditors must carry out certain investigations, namely those which will enable them to form an opinion as to—

(*a*) whether proper accounting records have been kept by the company and proper returns adequate for their audit have been received from branches not visited by them;

(*b*) whether the company's individual accounts are in agreement with the records and returns (section 237(1)).

Guidance is given as to how such investigations should be undertaken in a series of Auditing Guidelines published by the Audit Practices Committee and the International Federation of Accountants concerning such general matters as planning, controlling and recording an audit; accounting systems; audit evidence; internal control, and review of financial statements. More detailed operational guidelines have been published concerning matters such as representations by management; attendance at stocktaking; events after the balance sheet date; auditing in a computer environment; quality control; audit sampling; reliance on internal audit; reliance on other specialists; reliance on the work of other auditors in respect of group accounts; analytical review; the auditor's responsibility for detecting and reporting fraud and other illegal acts; considerations in respect of going concern; and financial information issued with audited financial statements. Further advice is also available concerning the verification of debts; stocks and work-in-progress; the implications of goods sold subject to reservation of title; and ascertaining contingent liabilities.

The auditors perform their duty to the members by forwarding their report to the secretary. They are not responsible if the report is not put before the members.[19] However, an Australian case has held that they must pay due regard to the possibility of fraud and must warn the appropriate level of management promptly and without waiting for the general meeting to report to the shareholders.[20]

The articles cannot preclude the auditors from availing themselves of all the information to which they are entitled as material for their report.[21]

5. Qualified reports

The exact wording of reports by auditors is the subject of an Auditing Guideline issued by the APC ("Reports by auditors under company legislation in the United Kingdom," June 1989), and general guidance with respect to qualifications is given in an Auditing Standard ("The audit report," March 1989). Briefly, a distinction is drawn between "fundamental" and "material but not fundamental" qualifications, each of which may arise either as a result of uncertainty or through disagreement between the auditors and the company. A report must be qualified if an accounting standard is not complied with, although in some circumstances the auditors may concur with the treatment used so that the accounts overall give a true and fair view of the company's financial affairs, in which case the qualification can really be regarded as a technical one.

In recent years some two thirds of audit reports attached to the accounts of companies have referred to reliance by the auditor on management representations. These are necessary

[19] *Re Allen, Craig & Co (London) Ltd.* [1934] Ch. 483.
[20] *Pacific Acceptance Corpn. Ltd.* v. *Forsyth* (1970) 92 W.N. (N.S.W.) 29.
[21] *Newton* v. *Birmingham Small Arms Co. Ltd.* [1906] 2 Ch. 378.

where businesses are owner dominated or where the systems of internal control could be subject to management override. However, the revised Auditing Standard on "The audit report" issued in March 1989 makes the point that such a reference should be avoided wherever possible as it might be misconstrued as a form of qualification. It also makes the point that where an auditor wishes to draw attention to a particular circumstance without qualifying his opinion (an "emphasis of matter"), he should make this quite clear in his report.

6. Special audit reports

In the case of banking and insurance companies taking advantage of the special provisions of Schedule 9,[22] the report must state whether in the auditors' opinion the balance sheet and profit and loss account and, if applicable, group accounts, have been properly prepared in accordance with the provisions of the Act (para. 28A, Schedule 9 to the Companies Act 1985). However, the auditor of a bank has a wider responsibility than in an audit of an ordinary commercial company, and under section 47 of the Banking Act 1987 he has a duty not only to report to members but to the Bank of England as well. The procedures to be followed are detailed in an Auditing Guideline.

If the company qualifies as a small- or medium-sized company and wishes to take advantage of the filing concessions available to it, the auditors must prepare—

(*a*) a signed report for the directors stating whether, in their opinion, the necessary conditions for such a privilege have been met; and
(*b*) a signed special report appended to the accounts, which is the usual report together with a statement that the company fulfils the special filing requirements (para. 8, Schedule 8 to the Companies Act 1985).

Other special reports must be made where a parent company is exempted under sections 248–249 of the 1985 Act from the obligation to prepare group accounts; and when a summary

[22] *Ante*, pp. 584–586.

financial statement is circulated under the provisions of section 251. However, the full audit report must not be published with non-statutory accounts, although the latter must be accompanied by a statement indicating that such a report has been made and whether or not it is qualified (see *ante* p. 521).

Under section 270(2) of the 1985 Act, in order to determine whether a company has profits available for distribution,[23] and (if it is a public company) under section 264(1) to confirm that a distribution will not reduce the amount of the company's net assets below the aggregate of its called up share capital plus its undistributable reserves, reference must be made to certain items in the company's *relevant accounts*. Under section 270(3) such accounts will normally be the company's latest audited financial statements laid before the company in general meeting, but where necessary interim accounts or initial accounts must be prepared—the former is the case where a distribution would exceed the amount distributable according to the latest audited financial statements, and the latter where a company proposes to make a distribution during its first accounting reference period or before the date on which it lays its first audited financial statements before the shareholders (section 270(4)). Even private companies are required to prepare interim or initial accounts where appropriate to enable directors to make a reasonable judgment as to the profits available for distribution, but in addition public companies must ensure that certain requirements are met with respect to the relevant accounts (section 270(5)). With respect to the auditors, the annual accounts (where used as the relevant accounts) must be accompanied by the auditors' report required under section 235 (section 271(3)); while any initial accounts, where used, must be accompanied by a report of the auditors in which they state whether in their opinion they have been properly prepared (section 273(4)). Interim accounts, where used, need not be subjected to an audit. With regard to the annual or initial accounts, where the auditors' report is qualified, it must be stated in writing whether the qualification is material in determining the legality of the proposed distribution (sections 271(3), (4); 273(4), (5)). In the case where the annual accounts are used as the relevant accounts, the statement will be laid

[23] *Post*, Chap. 22.

before the shareholders in general meeting; whereas in the case where the initial accounts are used as the relevant accounts, the statement together with the accounts and audit report will merely have to be filed with the Registrar of Companies. It should be noted, incidentally, that a material qualification in this context can be either favourable or unfavourable in terms of the proposed distribution. Moreover, in relation to the realised profits of an insurance company with long term business—*e.g.* a life insurance company—covered by section 268 of the Act, and where the amount of distributable profits is effectively determined by an actuarial valuation, guidance has in the past been given by the leading bodies of professional accountants in the British Isles on the "Auditors' relationships with actuaries concerning actuarial valuations of long-term business funds of insurance companies."

As mentioned above, the audit report is addressed to members of the company (*i.e.* its shareholders), for whose benefit indeed the statutory accounts are basically prepared. It is therefore the case that, except in specific circumstances where they are with the auditors' knowledge referring to the accounts and the auditors' report for a specific purpose (see *post*, pages 622–623), third parties cannot rely on them in helping to reach a particular decision. As was made clear in an investigation into the affairs of an Australian company,[24] this is even true of creditors, including debenture stock holders. It may therefore be necessary for such parties, with the company's approval, to commission their own audit (if necessary by different accountants to those employed by the company to undertake the statutory audit), and guidance on how such a second audit should be undertaken and the form of a report in such circumstances was formerly given in an APC auditing guideline on "Auditors' reports to trustees under the terms of debenture and loan stock trust deeds." Similarly, a company's statutory auditors may undertake specific investigations which exceed their responsibilities in respect of a company's statutory accounts and their report on them to the shareholders under section 235—for example, with respect to the accounting records, systems and internal control that have been examined in the course of the statutory audit. In such circumstances, the

[24] See E. Stamp, "The Reid Murray Affair," *Accountancy*, August 1964.

letters of engagement should clearly specify the extent of such supplementary investigations, and an APC guideline on "Reports to management" to cover such audit work has been published. Auditors will also be commissioned to write reports in connection with the issue of listing particulars or a prospectus (see Chapter 7, *ante*), and the APC has issued guidance notes on the conduct of these audits.

Special reports are also required from auditors under company legislation in the following circumstances:

	Companies Act 1985
Re-registration of a private company as a public company	s.43(3)(*b*)
Allotment of shares by a public company otherwise than for cash	s.103(1)
Transfer of non-cash assets to a public company by a member of the company	s.104(4)(*b*)
Redemption or purchase by a private company of its own shares out of capital	s.173(5)
Financial assistance for acquisition of a private company's own shares	s.156(4)

The nature and form of these reports is fully discussed in the APC's Guideline, "Reports by auditors under company legislation in the United Kingdom," June 1989.

In addition, as explained in Chapter 13, articles of private companies often provide that a member who wants to sell his shares must first offer them to the existing members at a price to be fixed by the auditors. Similar provisions are often applicable in the case of a member's death. In such circumstances case law has established grounds under which the valuation can be set aside and/or the auditors may be liable in negligence.

Powers of Auditors

The auditors have a right of access at all times to the books and accounts and vouchers of the company, and are entitled to require from the officers of the company such information and explanations as they think necessary for the performance of their duties as auditors (section 389A(1)). (This power is in part necessary to enable them to obtain particulars of the directors' emoluments, including expenses charged to tax and benefits in kind,[25] which may not be ascertainable from an examination of the books.)

The auditors cannot require the information to be furnished in any particular form or that it should be certified in some way, as by the board of directors. There is no power to require the information to be supplied in writing, but auditors can reasonably say that they are not in a position to perform their duties without making further inquiries if they are asked to act on unrecorded oral statements. If proper information is not given, the auditors' remedy is to qualify their report.

If an officer of the company makes a statement to the auditors which purports to convey any information or explanation which they are entitled to require, and it is misleading, false or deceptive in a material particular, he is guilty of an offence and liable on conviction to imprisonment or a fine or both.

Auditors have the right to attend any general meeting of the company and to receive the same notices of general meetings as the members, and to be heard at any general meeting on any part of the business which concerns them as auditors. Where for a private company those entitled to attend and vote at a meeting agree under section 381A a resolution in writing without holding a meeting, the auditors are entitled to receive all relevant communications and shall give notice within seven days if, following section 381B, in their opinion the matter should be considered by the company in general meeting. They then have the right to attend such a meeting and be heard on matters which concern them as auditors (section 390 of the Companies Act 1985).

As mentioned previously, the APC has issued an auditing guideline concerning the reliance that can be placed on the work of other auditors in respect of group financial statements. The topic is also covered by IAG 5.[26] Incidentally, the consolidation of an overseas subsidiary's accounts may necessitate a formal qualification in the auditor's report. This can arise if in order to comply with the accounting requirements of the country in which it is registered, the subsidiary's financial statements have

[25] *Ante*, p. 384.

[26] For a recent survey of current practice in this area, see P. Moizer, S. Turley and D. Walker, "Reliance on Other Auditors: A UK Study," *Accounting and Business Research*, Autumn 1986.

been prepared using accounting principles and conventions which are unacceptable in Great Britain. This is sometimes the case with U.S. subsidiaries which for tax purposes use the LIFO system to determine the cost of stocks.

British subsidiaries and their auditors are required to give the parent company's auditors relevant information and explanations, in default of which they will be liable to a fine and possible criminal proceedings. Parent companies are equally required to obtain relevant information and explanations from overseas subsidiaries for the benefit of their auditors (section 389A of the Companies Act 1985).

Duties of Auditors

The duties of auditors depend on the terms of the articles as well as on the statutory provisions. However, Table A no longer gives any guidance on this point: prior to the 1985 Act an article provided that auditor's duties should be regulated in accordance with what are now substantially sections 235, 237 and 389A–394A (excluding 390B and 393); and Schedule 8, para. 8.

The auditors' duties may be summarised as follows—

(1) They must acquaint themselves with their duties under the articles and the Act.[27]

(2) They must carry out their duties with respect to the auditors' report as outlined above. In addition, they must ascertain and state the true financial position of the company by an examination of the books. This examination must be not merely to ascertain what the books show, but also to ascertain that the books show the true financial position.[28]

> "The duty of the auditor" is "not to confine himself merely to the task of verifying the arithmetical accuracy of the balance sheet, but to inquire into its substantial accuracy, and to ascertain that it . . . was properly drawn up, so as to contain a true and correct representation of the state of the company's affairs": *per* Stirling J. in *Leeds Estate Co.* v. *Shepherd* (1887) 36 Ch.D. 787 at p. 802.

[27] *Re Republic of Bolivia Exploration Syndicate Ltd.* [1914] 1 Ch. 139.

[28] *Per* Lindley L.J. in *Re London and General Bank* (*No.* 2) [1895] 2 Ch. 673 (C.A.) at pp. 682 *et seq.*

> An auditor "is not to be written off as a professional 'adder-upper and subtractor.' His vital task is to take care to see that errors are not made, be they errors of computation, or errors of omission or commission, or downright untruths. To perform this task properly he must come to it with an inquiring mind—not suspicious of dishonesty, I agree—but suspecting that someone may have made a mistake somewhere and that a check must be made to ensure that there has been none": *per* Lord Denning in *Fomento* (*Sterling Area*) *Ltd.* v. *Selsdon Fountain Pen Co. Ltd.* [1958] 1 W.L.R. 45 (H.L.) at p. 61.

The statutory duty of an auditor, *e.g.* to state whether in his opinion a true and fair view is given by the balance sheet and the profit and loss account, is a personal one, and if he adopts the opinion of the company's accountant, and he is sued by the company for wrongly stating that a true and fair view is given, it has been held in Australia that he has no cause of action against the accountant.[29]

(3) They must act honestly, and with reasonable care and skill.

> "An auditor is not bound to be a detective, or . . . to approach his work . . . with a foregone conclusion that there is something wrong. He is a watchdog, but not a bloodhound. He is justified in believing tried servants of the company in whom confidence is placed by the company. He is entitled to assume that they are honest, and to rely on their representations, provided he takes reasonable care. If there is anything calculated to excite suspicion he should probe it to the bottom; but in the absence of anything of that kind he is only bound to be reasonably cautious and careful": *per* Lopes L.J. in *Re Kingston Cotton Mill Co.* (*No.* 2) [1896] 2 Ch. 279 (C.A.) at p. 288.
>
> "It is the duty of an auditor to bring to bear on the work he has to perform that skill, care and caution which a reasonably competent, careful, and cautious auditor would use. What is reasonable skill, care and caution must depend on the particular circumstances of each case. An auditor . . . is not bound to do more than exercise reasonable care and skill in making inquiries. . . . He is not an insurer; he does

[29] *Dominion Freeholders Ltd.* v. *Aird* [1966] 2 N.S.W.R. 293 (C.A.) distinguishing *Hedley Byrne & Co. Ltd.* v. *Heller & Partners Ltd.*, [1964] A.C. 465.

not guarantee that the books do correctly show the true position of the company's affairs: ... he must be honest—*i.e.*, he must not certify what he does not believe to be true, and he must take reasonable care and skill before he believes that what he certifies is true ... Where there is nothing to excite suspicion very little inquiry will be reasonably sufficient. ... Where suspicion is aroused more care is obviously necessary; but, still, an auditor is not bound to exercise more than reasonable care and skill, even in a case of suspicion ... ": *per* Lindley L.J. in *Re London and General Bank* (*No. 2*) [1895] 2 Ch. 673 (C.A.) at p. 683.

It may be that entries in or omissions from the books ought to make the auditors suspicious. In such a case they must make full investigations into the suspicious circumstances, but they are not liable for "not tracking out ingenious and carefully laid schemes of fraud when there is nothing to arouse their suspicion."[30]

B. was the managing director of the company and the senior partner of E. & Co., stockbrokers. E. & Co. owed £250,000 to the company but on February 27, just before the close of the financial year, E. & Co. bought Treasury Bills for £200,000 and credited the company with them, thus reducing their debt to £50,000. The company's balance sheet accordingly showed an investment in Treasury Bills for £200,000, and a debt from E. & Co. for £50,000. On March 3, after the close of the financial year, E. & Co. sold the Treasury Bills and became debtors again for £250,000. This was done for three successive years. *Held*, although the transactions, when isolated, should have led the auditors to conclude that fraud had taken place, yet as they formed only one item in a large audit, there was no negligence on the part of the auditors: *Re City Equitable Fire Insurance Co. Ltd.* [1925] Ch. 407 (C.A.).

If payments are made or sums borrowed by the company, the auditors should see that they are authorised and made in accordance with the articles and the Act.[31]

"When it is [shown] that audited balance sheets do not [show] the true financial condition of the company and that damage had resulted, the onus is on the auditors to show that this is not the result of any breach of duty on their part."[32]

[30] *Per* Lopes L.J. in *Re Kingston Cotton Mill Co.* (*No. 2*) [1896] 2 Ch. 279 (C.A.) at p. 290.

[31] See *Thomas* v. *Devonport Corpn.* [1900] 1 Q.B. 16 (C.A.).

[32] *Per* Astbury J. in *Re Republic of Bolivia Exploration Syndicate Ltd.* [1914] 1 Ch. 139 at p. 171.

They must satisfy themselves that the securities of the company in fact exist and are in safe custody. This duty is discharged by their making a personal inspection of the securities in question. If, however, the securities are in the possession of a person who in the ordinary course of his business keeps securities for his customers, *e.g* a banker, and that person is regarded as trustworthy, the auditors may safely accept his certificate that the securities are in his custody.

The auditor accepted the certificate of the company's stockbrokers that they held securities on the company's behalf. In fact they did not hold the securities and the company suffered heavy loss. *Held*, by Romer J., the auditor was negligent, as he should have inspected the securities and either insisted on their being put in proper custody or reported the matter to the shareholders[33]: *Re City Equitable Fire Insurance Co. Ltd.* [1925] Ch. 407.

They must check the cash in hand and also the balance at the bank, by inspecting the pass book (or bank statement) or obtaining a certificate from the bank.[34]

Auditors are under no duty to take stock,[35] but this is part of the wider question of the auditors' duty as to the value of the assets.

The duty of the auditors as to the value to be placed on fixed assets is discussed in the previous chapter.[36] Apart from complying with the requirements of the fourth Schedule, if the auditors have formed an opinion that the assets are overvalued, they are bound to report it to the shareholders.

Auditors made a confidential report to the directors, calling their attention to the fact that the security for loans was insufficient, and that there was a difficulty in realisation. They also reported that in their opinion no dividend should be paid for the year. In their report to the shareholders, however, they merely said that the value of the assets was dependent upon realisation. A dividend of seven per cent. was declared out of capital. *Held*, the auditors were guilty of misfeasance and liable to make good the dividend paid: *Re London and General Bank* (*No.* 2) [1895] 2 Ch. 673 (C.A.).

[33] The Court of Appeal expressed no concluded opinion on this point. In any event, the articles protected the auditors from liability.
[34] *Fox & Son* v. *Morrish, Grant & Co.* (1918) 35 T.L.R. 126.
[35] *Re Kingston Cotton Mill Co.* (*No.* 2), *ante*.
[36] Chap. 20.

As to current assets, they are entitled to take the values of stocks and work in progress from the manager or other responsible official of the company, unless they have any reason to suppose them inaccurate.

The auditors accepted the certificate of J., the manager, a person of acknowledged competence and high reputation, as to the value of the stock-in-trade. This was grossly exaggerated, as a result of which dividends were paid out of capital. Had the auditors compared the amount of stock at the beginning of the year with the purchases and sales during the year, they would have been put on inquiry, but they did not do so. *Held*, the auditors were not liable, as they were entitled to rely on J.'s certificate in the absence of anything to excite suspicion: *Re Kingston Cotton Mill Co.* (*No.* 2) [1896] Ch. 279 (C.A.).

The facts were similar to those in the *Kingston Cotton Mill* case except that on discovery of the invoices with altered dates (by which the managing director had caused the price payable on purchases of stock made shortly before the end of each period of account to be included in the outgoings of the succeeding period) the auditor accepted the explanation of the managing director, whom he believed to be of the highest integrity when he should have examined the suppliers' statements and where necessary have communicated with the suppliers, and having ascertained the precise facts so far as possible he should have informed the board. By not taking these steps he failed in his duty and was liable for, *inter alia*, the amount of the dividends: *Re Thomas Gerrard & Son Ltd.* [1968] Ch. 455.

"The standards of reasonable care and skill are, upon the expert evidence, more exacting today than those which prevailed in 1896": *per* Pennycuick J. at p. 475.

If directors do not allow auditors time to conduct such investigations as are necessary in order to make the statements required to be contained in their report, the auditors must either refuse to make a report or make an appropriately qualified report: they are not justified in making a report containing a statement the truth of which they have not had an opportunity of ascertaining.[37]

Auditors are not concerned with the policy of the company or whether the company is well or ill managed.

"It is no part of an auditor's duty to give advice, either to directors or shareholders, as to what they ought to do. An auditor has nothing to do with the prudence or imprudence of making loans with or without

[37] *Per* Pennycuick J. in *Re Thomas Gerrard*, *ante*, at p. 477.

security. It is nothing to him whether the business of a company is being conducted prudently or imprudently, profitably or unprofitably. It is nothing to him whether dividends are properly or improperly declared, provided he discharges his own duty to the shareholders. His business is to ascertain and state the true financial position of the company at the time of the audit": *per* Lindley L.J. in *Re London and General Bank* (*No.* 2) [1895] 2 Ch. 673 (C.A.) at p. 682.

Auditors cannot be relieved from liability for any breach of duty by any provision in the articles or any contract (section 310), but in certain circumstances they may obtain relief from the court (section 727).[38]

In England the auditors can plead the Limitation Act after six years.[39]

Apart from the auditor's contractual duty of care to the company, he owes a duty of care to third persons with whom he is not in contractual or fiduciary relationship if, as a reasonable man, he knows that he is being trusted or that his skill and judgment are being relied on and he does not make it clear that he accepts no responsibility for information or advice which he gives.[40] For breach of this duty an action for negligence lies if damage results from the negligence.

The scope of this duty was defined originally as follows:

" . . . to whom do these professional people owe this duty? I will take accountants, but the same reasoning applies to . . . others. They owe the duty, of course, to their employer or client; and also I think to any third person to whom they themselves show the accounts, or to whom they know their employer is going to show the accounts, so as to induce him to invest money or take some other action on them": *per* Denning L.J. in *Candler* v. *Crane, Christmas & Co.* [1951] 2 K.B. 164 (C.A.) at p. 180.

This liability applies not only to persons to whom auditors show the accounts and those to whom they knew the company would show them but also to persons whom they ought reasonably to have foreseen at the time the accounts were prepared might rely on the accounts. Thus where the

[38] *Ante*, pp. 414–416.

[39] *Leeds Estate Co.* v. *Shepherd* (1887) 36 Ch.D. 787.

[40] *Hedley Byrne & Co. Ltd.* v. *Heller & Partners Ltd.* [1964] A.C. 465, disapproving *Candler* v. *Crane, Christmas & Co.* [1951] 2 K.B. 164 (C.A.). See also *Esso Petroleum Co. Ltd.* v. *Marden* [1976] 2 All E.R. 5 (C.A.) and *Yianni* v. *Edwin Evans & Sons* [1981] 3 All E.R. 592.

accountants knew at that time that outside finance was needed by the company, they ought to have foreseen that the accounts would be used by someone providing such finance, *e.g.* in the form of a take-over offer, and owed a duty accordingly. Nevertheless, they are only liable if reliance on the accounts caused the other person loss so that, *e.g.* where the take-over offer would have been made anyway, there is no liability: *JEB Fasteners Ltd.* v. *Marks, Bloom, & Co.* [1981] 3 All E.R. 289, affd. [1983] 1 All E.R. 583. However, such a view has recently been challenged in *Caparo Industries plc* v. *Dickman*,[41] where Lord Bridge argued that a wider duty of care to potential shareholders was not owed as they only stood to suffer pecuniary loss.

What constitutes professional skill and judgment where a reporting accountant or auditor is potentially liable is an interesting point. For instance, it is quite possible—even likely, perhaps—that over time as a result of inflation, the conventional historical cost accounts of many companies might show an upward trend in profits, whereas under current cost accounting principles the trend might instead be downwards.[42] However, it would seem likely that adherence to generally accepted principles, as codified by the accountancy profession, would provide a reasonable defence in such circumstances—though in view of the jury's attitude in the Royal Mail case in relation to a prospectus, where accounting principles acceptable at that time were properly followed, it is not clear that this would be adequate in a criminal prosecution.[43]

[41] [1990] 2 W.L.R. 358.
[42] For historical and current cost accounting rules, see pp. 550 *et seq.*, *ante*.
[43] *R.* v. *Kylsant* [1932] 1 K.B. 442 (C.C.A.). See p. 157.

Chapter 22

DIVIDENDS

INTRODUCTION

FROM an ideal economic perspective, a listed company's distribution policy should be determined as part of the overall investment decision taken by its directors, since it should only retain those funds on which it is expected to earn a risk-adjusted return greater than can be earned elsewhere by its shareholders. At one extreme, therefore, a company which has identified many profitable investment projects would make no distributions at all; however, shareholders wishing to secure a cash income for a particular year would either be able to sell off part of their holdings in order to realise some of the capital gain that will be reflected in the increasing value of their shares, or could use the enhanced value as security on which to raise a loan. At the other extreme, a company which has identified no profitable projects to justify reinvestment should logically distribute all its funds, including capital invested in the past. Moreover, it can be demonstrated that even the potential distortions introduced by the differential incidence of taxation can be substantially neutralised in the market, since certain types of investor prefer capital gains, while others will prefer dividend income. (Indeed, even the private investor may find the latter attractive if he is able to offset direct or indirect borrowing costs against such income.) A further complicating factor is that listed companies may well use the time series pattern of dividend as a signal of future likely prospects—*e.g.* a cut in dividend may reflect the directors' pessimism, and increase their optimism.[1]

[1] For a readable discussion of the economic rationale for dividend payout policies, see R. Brealey and S. Myers, "Principles of Corporate Finance" (3rd ed.), McGraw-Hill, London, 1988, ch. 16 and *passim*.

Elsewhere, the distribution policy for unlisted companies must take into account the fact that their shares are not readily marketable, and for private companies it may be preferable for tax purposes to distribute profits as directors' fees and salaries. However, for closely held companies (*i.e.* those whose shares are owned or controlled by a small group of persons), revenue law even deems that a certain amount of profits may be treated as distributed to shareholders, regardless of whether such dividend payments have been made or not.

But whatever the economic rationale may be, the law also has to take account of the existence of limited liability. Effectively this means the doctrine of (money) capital maintenance (see Chap. 9) must be applied so as to try to ensure a company's resources are not distributed in such a way as to prejudice the interests of unsecured creditors; or, indeed, of one class of security holders at the expense of another. In fact, it is not possible to provide fully effective protection to creditors and others in this way, but the general philosophy of money capital maintenance has nevertheless been behind the development of the law relating to the distribution of dividends as it has evolved over the past 130 years or so, although it is noticeable that in many of the cases around the turn of the century, judges went out of their way not to impose unreasonable restrictions which might potentially lead to a misallocation of resources within the economy.[2]

In view of the underlying rationale behind the law in this area, the realised profits test introduced by the Companies Act 1980, and confirmed in sections 263–281 of the 1985 Act (see below), can be viewed as a retrograde step. However, in practice it is unlikely to prove an effective constraint. In the rare cases in which companies might wish to distribute more than their accumulated realised profits, they could always convert unrealised gains into realised income by selling off assets (and, if necessary, buying or leasing them back); purchase their own shares under section 162 (see Chap. 10); or, as has happened on a number of occasions in recent years, apply to the court for a reduction of capital under section 135.

[2] See E. A. French, "The Evolution of the Dividend Law of England," in "Studies in Accounting" (3rd ed., 1977), ed. W. T. Baxter and S. Davidson, Institute of Chartered Accountants in England and Wales, London (pp. 306–331).

The Nature of a Dividend

Technically, a dividend is the share, received by a shareholder, of the company's profits legally available for dividend and divided among the members. Commercial companies are formed to earn profits for the shareholders out of which dividends can be paid,[3] and no express power to pay dividends is required in the memorandum or the articles. However, under section 281 provisions in the articles or memorandum may restrict either the amounts available for distribution or the circumstances in which a distribution may be made.

Sections 263(3) and 270(2) of the 1985 Act state that dividends must only be paid out of accumulated realised profits as reported in the statutory accounts.

Dividend must be distinguished from interest. Interest is a debt which, like all debts, is payable out of the company's assets generally. A dividend, however, is not a debt until it has been declared by the company, and dividends cannot be declared for payment out of the assets generally; they can be declared for payment only out of assets equivalent to the profits available for the purpose.

Profits Available for Dividend

As mentioned above and in the discussion in Chapter 9, it is a fundamental principle of company law that a company's subscribed money capital (*i.e.* issued share capital plus share premium) be maintained. Paid-up capital must not be paid to the shareholders except by leave of the court or under strictly defined circumstances. It must be spent only upon the objects defined in the memorandum. Any other expenditure is *ultra vires* and reduces the fund available for the company's creditors in satisfaction of their claims.[4]

W. guaranteed the preference dividends for three years and the company agreed to repay to W. on demand any sums paid by him

[3] Under s.30(3)(*b*)(ii) of the Act, a company may be prohibited from paying a dividend.

[4] See, *per* Jessel M.R. in *Flitcroft's Case* (1882) 21 Ch.D. 519 (C.A.) at p. 533.

under the guarantee. *Held*, the company's agreement was *ultra vires* and void, as it might involve capital being reduced otherwise than by expenditure on the company's objects: *Re Walters' Deed of Guarantee* [1933] Ch. 321.

The principle that a company's subscribed money capital must be maintained requires that a dividend, in money or kind,[5] declared by a company, should not be paid except out of accumulated realised profits. Prior to the 1980 Companies Act there were no statutory provisions governing the funds available for distribution to the shareholders as dividend. In the meantime, the courts for the most part took the view that they should not in general interfere in the business decision-making process unless there were good grounds for believing that the rights of certain interested parties were prejudiced. Unfortunately the decisions in a number of cases were nevertheless regarded by many accountants and lawyers as determining specific rules for distinguishing between on the one hand income, which could be applied for distributions, and on the other capital, which could not. Hardly surprisingly, given that they resulted from the peculiar circumstances of each case, these rules proved difficult to interpret.[6] In the circumstances, accountants tended to follow a conservative interpretation of the law and for the most part took the view that only accumulated realised profits should be regarded as available for distribution. The Jenkins Committee made several recommendations which would clarify the position by providing a statutory code to this effect.[7] These were eventually given effect, together with the requirements of the EEC's Second Council Directive on company law harmonisation, as sections 39–45 of the 1980 Companies Act, which have substantially become sections 263–281 of the 1985 Act. But apart from including provisions requiring that the fund from which distributions can be made

[5] *Post*, p. 642.

[6] *e.g.* the "rules" that before 1980 in England it was neither necessary to charge depreciation nor to make good past trading losses when determining distributable profits. In fact, the judgments in the main supporting cases (*Lee* v. *Neuchatel Asphalte Co.* (1889) 41 Ch.D. 1 (C.A.), and *Ammonia Soda Co.* v. *Chamberlain* (1918) 1 Ch. 266 (C.A.) respectively) seem to have been very much dependent on the particular circumstances of the cases. For a general discussion of this point, see French, *op. cit.*

[7] (1962) Cmnd., 1749, paras. 335–350.

should be the *accumulated realised profits* of a company, the 1980 Act also provided that these should be those shown in its statutory accounts, even though it might well be that to reflect properly the directors' performance to a company's shareholders the income figure reported in the financial statements should include unrealised gains.

Under section 263(2) of the 1985 Act, the rules apply to all *distributions* made by a company. A distribution is defined there as any payment of a company's assets to members of the company except: (a) an issue of bonus shares[8]; (b) the redemption or purchase by a company of its own shares[9]; (c) an authorised reduction of capital under section 135[10]; and (d) distributions on a winding up. Moreover, under section 263(1) such *distributions* may only be made out of the profits available for that purpose. In fact, there are two tests to ascertain such profits. The first, the realised profits test, applies to all companies; the second, the net assets test, only to public companies. It should be noted that with regard to a group, it is only the accumulated realised profits of the holding company that are available for distribution to shareholders of that company. Profits of a subsidiary can be transferred to the holding company by declaration of dividends by that subsidiary. However, any part of such revenues receivable by the holding company cannot be regarded by it as available for distribution to its shareholders if it represents a return of part of the purchase price shown in the accounts as being the consideration paid for the subsidiary. Under the acquisition method of consolidating the group accounts, this effectively means that only the subsidiary's post-acquisition profits may be transferred for distribution, but under the merger method (where it is available—see pages 185–186 and Chap. 20), all or some of the pre-acquisition profits may also be transferred for this purpose, depending respectively on whether the nominal value of shares issued by the holding company is less than or equal to the nominal value of the subsidiary company's shares acquired; or whether the nominal value of the shares issued is greater than the par value of shares acquired.

[8] *Post*, p. 644.
[9] *Ante*, Chap. 10.
[10] *Ante*, Chap. 9.

The Realised Profits Test

A company's profits available for distribution are its accumulated realised profits (so far as not already distributed or capitalised[11]) less its accumulated realised losses (so far as not already written off by a proper reduction of capital) (section 263(3)). There is no attempt to distinguish between income and capital profits or losses—the only criterion is whether they are *realised*. Unrealised profits, *e.g.* on a revaluation upwards of an asset in the accounts which produces a gain, cannot be used: the gain must be realised, *i.e.* the asset must effectively be sold at arm's length. Prior to 1980 a decision in a Scottish case[12] was in line with this principle, but one in a case in England was not.[13] Similarly under the provisions of the 1985 Act, realised losses (*e.g.* previous trading losses), must be deducted before a dividend can be declared—again in line with the decision in a Scottish case,[14] but not with that in an English one.[15] Unrealised profits cannot be used to pay up debentures or any amounts unpaid on issued shares (section 263(4)).

The notion of what is and is not a *realised* profit is specifically referred to in section 263(3) and defined in section 262(3) in the following terms:

"references to 'realised profits' and 'realised losses' . . . are to such profits or losses . . . as fall to be treated as realised profits, in accordance with principles generally accepted, at the time when the accounts are prepared, with respect to the determination for accounting purposes of realised profits or losses."

This is hardly illuminating, and the few cases in tax law dealing with the question of realisation are not necessarily relevant in this context. Given that the notion of what is and is not a realised profit is a subtle one, which has caused some controversy amongst accountants, the professional accountancy bodies in the British Isles issued two technical releases in September 1982 to offer guidance on the issue. The first[16] reached three conclusions:

[11] *Post*, p. 644.
[12] *Westburn Sugar Refineries Ltd.* v. *Inland Revenue*, 1960 S.L.T. 297.
[13] *Dimbula Valley (Ceylon) Tea Co. Ltd.* v. *Laurie* (1961) Ch. 353, 373.
[14] *Niddrie etc. Coal Co. Ltd.* v. *Hurll* (1891) 18 R. 805.
[15] *Ammonia Soda Co. Ltd.* v. *Chamberlain* (1918) 1 Ch. 266 (C.A.).
[16] TR 481: "The determination of realised profits and the disclosure of distributable profits in the context of the Companies Acts 1948 to 1981."

(i) Accounting standards[17] would constitute evidence of generally accepted accounting principles, and the profits calculated applying such standards should in general be regarded as "realised profits," even where the usual criteria for establishing "realisation" (such as receipt of cash, or the creation of a contractual obligation to pay a specific sum of money) are not met. This would mean, for instance, that the procedure of gradually recognising profits on long term contracts established in SSAP 9 (see *ante*, p. 557), and the inclusion in the profit and loss account of foreign currency translation gains and losses on net monetary items, where required by SSAP 20, would both give rise to "realised profits."

(ii) Where no accounting standard is applicable, a profit can be regarded as "realised" where the policy followed is consistent with the accruals concept and prudence doctrine outlined in SSAP 2 and Schedule 4 of the Act.

(iii) Where necessary a company must, in order for its accounts to show a true and fair view of its financial performance and position, depart from accepted accounting principles and include an unrealised profit in its income statement. However, where this is done, para. 15 of Schedule 4 requires that a note should be given with the accounts indicating the nature of the departure, the reasons for it, and the effect.

The second technical release[18] noted that accumulated profits and losses shown in the accounts may in fact differ from those available for distribution for a number of reasons (*e.g.* the

[17] The status of accounting standards has been examined in terms of clairfying the meaning of the phrase "a true and fair view" in the case of *Lloyd Cheyham and Co. Ltd.* v. *Littlejohn and Co.* [1986] PCC 389. In that case Woolf J. considered the evidential role of accounting standards and held that "while they are not conclusive . . . and they are not . . . rigid rules, they are very strong evidence as to what is the proper standard which should be adopted . . . " See also pp. 525 and 550 *et seq.*

[18] TR 482: "The determination of distributable profits in the context of the Companies Acts 1948 to 1981."

application of the net assets test to the accounts of public companies, discussed below). The statement concludes that, in order to show a true and fair view, a material difference between reported and distributable profits should be disclosed in notes to the accounts.

Apart from these general considerations, realised profits and losses are, under section 280(3), all profits and losses, whether capital or revenue (*i.e.* income), which are deemed to have been realised. It follows that when a company sells an undepreciated fixed asset (such as freehold land) which has been revalued in the accounts for consideration above its original cost, and the revaluation has been credited direct to reserves, the relevant part of the revaluation reserve has to be regarded as a realised profit, even though it has never been credited to the profit and loss account. Similar considerations relate to wasting fixed assets, although the provisions are more complex. Thus section 275 refers specifically to the question of depreciation provisions for such assets. Section 275(1) indicates that charges made to create or increase a depreciation provision in any one year are to be treated as realised losses, but under section 275(2) any additional depreciation charges made against an upward revaluation of the cost new of a similar asset do not have to be so treated, even though they will be reflected in the lower reported profit figure. In applying this latter provision, when there is no record of the original cost of an asset, or it cannot be obtained without unreasonable expense or delay, the calculations of any loss or gain in respect of that asset may be based on the earliest available record of its value since its acquisition by the company (section 275(3)). However, under section 275(1) a provision for a loss in value of one fixed asset cannot be offset against revaluation gains on other fixed assets unless *all* the company's fixed assets are revalued at the same time. For this purpose the revaluation of all the company's fixed assets may exclude goodwill. Moreover, under section 275(4), (5) the valuation does not have to be formal: it is sufficient that the directors are satisfied, after *considering* the value of a fixed asset against the value of all the company's fixed assets; and that the aggregate value is not less than the aggregate value at which such fixed assets are stated in the accounts. But where the directors take advantage of such a procedure, they must disclose in the notes to the accounts:

(i) that they have considered the value of some of the company's fixed assets, without actually revaluing those assets;

(ii) that they are satisfied that the aggregate value of the fixed assets whose value has been considered is not less than their value as stated in the accounts; and

(iii) that the asset that has diminished in value is recorded in the accounts after providing for that decline in value (section 275(6)).

With regard to development costs, section 269 specifically requires that where they are capitalised and shown as assets in a company's accounts, they should nevertheless be treated as a realised loss for the purpose of calculating distributable profits, unless there are special circumstances and the note required by para. 20 of Schedule 4 giving the reasons for treating such an item as an asset indicates the amount so involved.

Under section 263(5), where a company's directors are unable to determine whether a profit or loss made before December 22, 1980, is realised or unrealised, they may treat the profit as realised and the loss as unrealised.

Finally, when a company makes a distribution of a non-cash asset (*e.g.* part of its undertaking on a de-merger) any element of unrealised profits (*e.g.* on a revaluation) represented by those assets may be regarded as a realised profit (section 276). However, to make such a distribution the company has to be so empowered by its articles. Table A contains such a power in article 105 (see below, page 643). Moreover, the value attributed to the asset that is being distributed will have to be a fair value—*i.e.* generally its open market value in a transaction at arm's length.

The Net Assets Test

The realised profits test applies to all companies. A public company, however, is subject to a second, net assets, test. This means that even if it has profits available under the realised profits test, a public company may only make a distribution if, first, at the time the amount of its net assets is not less than the aggregate of its called-up share capital and its undistributable reserves; and, second, the amount of the proposed distribution will not lower the amount of those assets to less than that aggregate (section 264(1)).

The effect of the second test is that whereas a private company can make a distribution provided only that it has sufficient realised profits available, a public company can do so only if it has sufficient profits available after it has provided for any net unrealised losses.

Net assets

A public company's net assets for this purpose are the aggregate of its assets less the aggregate of its liabilities, including any provision for liabilities or charges in the accounts (section 264(2)). Uncalled share capital[19] may not, however, be used as an asset for this purpose (section 264(4)).

Called-up share capital and undistributable reserves

The net assets must be measured against the called-up share capital and undistributable reserves of the company. The called-up share capital is the aggregate amount of the calls made on its shares, whether or not they have been paid; any amount paid without being called; and any instalments due on the shares.[20] It is therefore more than the amount necessarily received by the company (section 737).

The undistributable reserves are those set out in section 264(3) of the 1985 Act:

(*a*) the share premium account[21];
(*b*) the capital redemption reserve[22];
(*c*) the excess of its accumulated unrealised profits over its accumulated unrealised losses, inasmuch as they have not previously been capitalised or written off, the only exception being a capitalisation resulting from a

[19] *Ante*, p. 174.
[20] *Ante*, p. 174.
[21] *Ante*, pp. 182 *et seq*.
[22] *Ante*, p. 213.

transfer of profits to capital redemption reserve on or after December 22, 1980; and

(*d*) any other reserve which cannot be distributed either by law (*e.g.* a revaluation reserve created under the alternative accounting rules (Sched. 4, para. 34)[23]) or by the company's memorandum and articles.

Investment and Insurance Companies

It would be inappropriate to apply the rules outlined above to certain types of company, and this is recognised in sections 265–268 of the 1985 Act, which relate to investment companies and insurance companies with long term (generally life assurance) business. Thus in the case of the former, it might well be that the value of the portfolio of an investment trust or property company may have fallen and be below the aggregate of its called up share capital and undistributable reserves, yet still be well in excess of its liabilities to third parties. In such circumstances, the Act provides alternative rules for determining distributable profits to the two generally available to public companies described above.

With regard to insurance companies, the natural time horizon of long term insurance business stretches over a period of anything up to 40 years rather than 12 months, and the appropriate valuation to determine profits and surplus is therefore determined by actuaries using compound interest to discount projected streams of premium and investment income to a present value, and deducting from that figure the corresponding discounted present value of projected payments to meet anticipated claims.

Investment companies

An investment company (see *ante*, page 584) is defined under section 266 as being a public company which has given notice in prescribed form to the Registrar of Companies of its intention to carry on a business as an investment company and

[23] *Ante*, Chap. 20.

(*a*) invests its funds in a portfolio of securities for the benefit of, and to spread risk for, its shareholders;
(*b*) fulfils the condition that none of its individual investments exceeds 15 per cent. in value of its total investments;
(*c*) whose memorandum and articles prohibits a distribution of its capital profits; and
(*d*) which retains no more than 15 per cent. of its income available for distribution in an accounting reference period.

In addition under section 351(1)(*c*) an investment company must indicate its status on its letter heads and on its order forms; while under paras. 71–73 of Schedule 4 and para. 1(3) of Schedule 4A the requirements with regard to the contents of its accounts are subject to modification from those generally applicable to other companies.

The conditions outlined above substantially coincide with those demanded of an approved investment trust if it is to secure tax and other privileges, although it would for these purposes also have to be resident in the UK, not be a "close" company and have its shares listed on a recognised stock exchange. The latter requirement would in fact subject it to various other conditions contained in The International Stock Exchange's Listing Agreement—*e.g.* no more than 20 per cent. of the group's assets could be invested in any one company; and it would have to disclose supplementary information with its accounts, including a summary of its 10 largest investments and an analysis of realised and unrealised surpluses, with a separate statement of profits and losses analysed between listed and unlisted investments.

A company which qualifies under section 266 as an investment company can take advantage of the alternative test for assessing profits available for distribution outlined in section 265(1) and described below, but it must also satisfy the following conditions

(*a*) its shares must be listed on a recognised stock exchange (section 265(4)(*a*)),
(*b*) during the previous accounting reference period the company must not have distributed any of its capital profits, nor must it have applied any unrealised profits or any capital profits in paying up debentures or

amounts unpaid on its issued shares (section 265(4)(*a*), (5)), and

(*c*) it must have given the necessary notice to the Registrar to qualify as an investment company under section 266 (section 265(6)).

Where these conditions are met, the alternative test of distributable profits prescribed under section 265(1) may be applied. This involves a realised profits test which, however, only applies to revenue and not to capital profits or losses; capital profits are thus excluded from the funds available for distribution. Moreover, for this purpose accumulated realised revenue profits are calculated as realised revenue profits less realised and unrealised revenue losses. The corresponding net assets test requires that the value of the assets must be a least 1½ time the aggregate of the company's liabilities (including provisions) both before and after the proposed distribution. However, where a distribution by an investment company reduces the amount of its net assets below the aggregate of its called up share capital and undistributable reserves, this fact must be dislcosed in the notes to its financial statements (Sched. 4, para. 72(1); Sched. 9, para. 13(4)).[24]

Under section 267 the Secretary of State may extend and modify by statutory instrument the provisions of sections 265–266 to companies whose principal business consists of investing in portfolios of securities, land and other assets with the objective of managing such portfolios and spreading risk for the benefit of the shareholders.

Insurance companies

For an insurance company which qualifies as such under the provisions of the Insurance Companies Act 1982, and which carries on long-term business, the profits and losses to be used in applying the general realised profits test described above on pages 629–632 are to be the result of amounts properly transferred to the profit and loss account of the company from surpluses or deficits on actuarial valuations. Moreover, any other profits or losses included in the company's profit and loss

[24] *Ante*, Chap. 20.

accounts are to be left out of account in applying the realised profits test (section 268).

RELEVANT ACCOUNTS

In deciding whether a company has distributable profits, reference must be made to its accounts. Moreover, in assessing whether a proposed dividend can properly be made, its effect on such accounts must be evaluated. For this purpose, where successive distributions are to be made by reference to one set of accounts, the amounts of the distributions, paid and proposed, must be accumulated (section 274). Under section 270(2) the items to be referred to in the relevant accounts are: (a) profits, losses and liabilities; (b) provisions (including those for depreciation); and (c) share capital and reserves (including undistributable reserves).

Section 270(3), (4) of the Act provides which are the relevant accounts for this purpose. The general rule is that the relevant accounts are the company's *last annual accounts* prepared in respect of the last preceding accounting reference period[25] (section 270(3)). However, in two cases other accounts may be used. First, such accounts as are necessary to enable a reasonable judgment to be made as to the amount of any relevant item—these are referred to as *interim accounts*. Second, if the distribution is proposed during the company's first year before any annual accounts are prepared, such accounts as are necessary for a reasonable judgment to be made. These are referred to as *initial accounts* (section 270(4)).

Last Annual Accounts

These must have been properly prepared for all companies (*i.e.* including banking and insurance companies) in accordance with the Companies Act in all material respects (section 271(2)). The auditors must have prepared either an unqualified report[26] on the accounts or, if it is qualified, they must state in writing whether their qualification is relevant to the question of distributable profits. Finally a copy of any such statement

[25] *Ante*, Chap. 20.
[26] *Ante*, Chap. 21.

must be laid before the company in general meeting (section 271(3)–(5)).

Interim accounts

A public company may only use interim accounts if they have been properly prepared in compliance with the format of accounts set out in section 228[27] and Schedule 4 to the Act in all material respects and be signed by the directors as required under section 233 (section 272(2), (3)). A copy must be sent to the Registrar with a certified English translation if appropriate (section 272(4), (5)). Section 272 does not apply to private companies, which may therefore use any interim accounts.

Initial accounts

A public company may only use initial accounts if they have been properly prepared in compliance with the format of accounts set out in section 226[27] and Schedule 4 to the Act in all material respects and be signed by the directors as required under section 233 (section 273(2), (3)). Further, there must be an auditors' report that the accounts have been so prepared and which is either unqualified, or, if qualified, accompanied by a statement that the qualification is irrelevant to the question of distributable profits (section 273(4), (5)). A copy of the accounts and the auditors' report must be sent to the Registrar with a certified English translation if appropriate (section 273(6), (7)). Section 273 does not apply to private companies, which may therefore use any initial accounts.

Banking and insurance companies.

The rules under sections 274–275 relating to distributions are modified for banking and insurance companies (in particular

[27] *Ante*, Chap. 20. The reference in ss.272(3) and 273(3) is only to s.226, relating to individual company accounts, and not to s.229, relating to group accounts, since only the holding company and not the group can declare dividends.

with respect to relevant accounts) by section 279 and Schedule 11.

The consequences of an unlawful distribution

Under section 270(5), a breach of the requirements of sections 270–273 relating to the relevant accounts for determining distributable profits constitutes a breach of the test of distributability. Moreover, shareholders cannot agree to waive these requirements.[28] Section 277(1) further provides that any shareholder who receives a distribution which he knows, or has reasonable grounds to believe, has been paid in breach of the 1985 Act rules, must repay that amount to the company. This is expressly made an addition to the shareholders' existing liabilities set out below, but it does not apply in relation either to financial assistance given by a company to a person to help him purchase its shares in contravention of section 151; or to any payment made by a company in respect of the redemption or purchase by the company of shares in itself (section 277(2)).

With regard to payments of dividends out of capital, it was established prior to the 1980 Act that directors who are knowingly parties to such payments (*e.g.* where debts known to be bad were entered as assets in reports and balance sheets, so that an apparent profit was shown, and the shareholders, relying on these documents, declared dividends) are jointly and severally liable to the company to replace the amounts of dividends so paid, with interest, and ratification is impossible so as to bind the company.[29] In such a case they are entitled to be indemnified by each shareholder who received dividends, *knowing them to be paid out of capital*, to the extent of the dividends received.[30] A shareholder who has knowingly received a dividend paid out of capital cannot individually, or on behalf of the company, maintain an action against the directors to replace the dividends so paid, at any rate until he has repaid the money he has received.[31]

[28] *Precision Dippings Ltd.* v. *Precision Dippings Marketing Ltd.* [1985] B.C.L.C. 385 (C.A.).

[29] *Flitcroft's Case* (1882) 21 Ch.D. 519 (C.A.); *Liquidators of City of Glasgow Bank* v. *Mackinnon* (1881) 9 R. 535.

[30] *Moxham* v. *Grant* [1900] 1 Q.B. 88 (C.A.).

[31] *Towers* v. *African Tug Co.* (1904) 1 Ch. 558 (C.A.); *Liquidators of City of Glasgow Bank* v. *Mackinnon* (1881) 9 R. 535.

PAYMENT OF DIVIDENDS

Dividends are paid in the manner laid down in the articles.

Table A, article 102, provides:

> "Subject to the provisions of the Acts, the company may by ordinary resolution declare dividends in accordance with the respective rights of the members, but no dividend shall exceed the amount recommended by the directors."

This relates to the final dividend, declared at the annual general meeting. As to an interim dividend, which is a dividend paid on some date between two annual general meetings of the company,[32] article 103 provides:

> "Subject to the provisions of the Acts, the directors may pay interim dividends if it appears to them that they are justified by the profits of the company available for distribution. If the share capital is divided into different classes, the directors may pay interim dividends on shares which confer deferred or non-preferred rights with regard to dividend as well as on shares which confer preferential rights with regard to dividend, but no interim dividend shall be paid on shares carrying deferred or non-preferred rights if, at the time of payment, any preferential dividend is in arrear. The directors may also pay at intervals settled by them any dividend payable at a fixed rate if it appears to them that the profits available for distribution justify the payment. Provided the directors act in good faith they shall not incur any liability to the holders of shares conferring preferred rights for any loss they may suffer by the lawful payment of an interim dividend on any shares having deferred or non-preferred rights."

Before recommending a dividend, directors should have a complete and detailed list of the company's assets and investments prepared for their information, and should not rely for their value merely on the opinion of the chairman or the auditors.[33]

In the absence of anything to the contrary in the articles,[34] a company cannot be compelled to declare a dividend and no action can be brought for its recovery until it has been

[32] *Per* P. O. Lawrence J. in *Re Jowitt* [1922] 2 Ch. 442, at p. 447.

[33] *Per* Romer J. in *Re City Equitable Fire Insce. Co. Ltd.* (1925) Ch. 407 at pp. 471, 474.

[34] For articles which were interpreted as requiring the whole profits to be divided, see *Paterson* v. *R. Paterson & Sons Ltd.*, 1917 S.C. (H.L.) 13; 1916 S.C. 452.

declared.[35] In England the declaration of a dividend creates a simple contract debt due from the company to the shareholder which will be barred in six years from the date of declaration.[36] In Scotland the period of prescription is five years.[37] However, Table A, article 108, provides that

> "Any dividend which has remained unclaimed for 12 years from the date when it became due for payment shall, if the directors so resolve, be forfeited and cease to remain owing by the company."

When preference shares entitle the holder to receive out of the profits of the company for each year a fixed dividend, the "profits of the company" are the profits available for dividend after setting aside such reserves as the directors think fit. If the whole of the profits are transferred to reserve the preference shareholders are not entitled to any dividend.[38]

More generally, the rights of holders of preference and other special shares must be observed, since infringement of such rights will give aggrieved members the right to apply for an injunction or other relief. Moreover, if dividends are paid infringing such rights, any class of members which suffers will be able to take legal action against the company, while the directors who wrongly paid the dividends will be liable to replace the sum involved.

When the articles, *e.g.* Table A, article 103 above, give the directors power to pay interim dividends, a resolution by the company in general meeting requiring the directors to declare an interim dividend is inoperative.[39]

In English law, unless the articles otherwise provide, dividends are payable to the shareholders in proportion to the nominal amounts of their shares, irrespective of the amounts paid up.[40] Section 119(c), however, permits a company, if so

[35] *Bond* v. *Barrow Haematite Steel Co.* [1902] 1 Ch. 353.

[36] *Re Compania de Electricidad de la Provincia de Buenos Aires Ltd.* [1978] 3 All E.R. 668.

[37] Prescription and Limitation (Scotland) Act 1973, s.6.

[38] *Re Buenos Ayres Great Southern Ry. Co. Ltd.* [1947] Ch. 384; *cf.* the Scottish case *Wemyss Collieries Trust Ltd.* v. *Melville* (1905) 8 F. 143, in which transfer of a sum to reserve was, on an interpretation of the articles, held to be valid, although preference shareholders were thereby deprived of an additional non-cumulative dividend.

[39] *Scott* v. *Scott* [1943] 1 All E.R. 582.

[40] *Birch* v. *Cropper* (1889) 14 App.Cas. 525.

authorised by its articles, to pay dividend in proportion to the amount paid up on each share where a larger amount is paid up on some shares than on others. Table A, article 104, accordingly provides that

"Except as otherwise provided by the rights attached to shares, all dividends shall be declared and paid according to the amounts paid up on shares on which the dividend is paid. All dividends shall be apportioned and paid proportionately to the amounts paid up on shares during any portion or portions of the period in respect of which the dividend is paid; but, if any share is issued on terms providing that it shall rank for dividend as from a particular date, that share shall rank for dividend accordingly."

In Scots law, if articles provide that "the directors may ... declare a dividend to be paid to the members in proportion to their shares" and define "shares" as shares in the nominal capital, dividends fall to be declared according to the nominal amounts of the shares, irrespective of the amounts paid up[41]; where, however, there is no provision in the articles as to how dividends are to be paid, the common law principle applicable is that they are payable in proportion to the amounts paid up on the shares.[42]

The articles usually provide, as does Table A, article 106, that dividends payable in cash may be paid by cheque sent through the post to the registered address of the shareholder, or to such persons and to such address as the shareholder may in writing direct. In the absence of such a provision in the articles, the company will have to issue a fresh dividend cheque to the shareholder should the cheque first sent be lost in the post.[43]

Unless power is given in the articles, dividends declared must be paid in cash, and a shareholder can restrain the company from paying them in any other way.

A company declared a dividend and passed a resolution to pay it by giving to the shareholders debenture bonds bearing interest and redeemable at par, by an annual drawing, over 30 years. The articles empowered the company to declare a dividend "to be paid" to the shareholders. *Held*, the words "to be paid" meant paid in cash, and a

[41] *Oakbank Oil Co. Ltd.* v. *Crum* (1882) 10 R. (H.L.) 11; (1881) 9 R. 198.
[42] *Hoggan* v. *Tharsis Sulphur etc. Co. Ltd.* (1882) 9 R. 1191.
[43] See *Thairlwall* v. *Great Northern Ry.* [1910] 2 K.B. 509.

shareholder suing on behalf of himself and the other shareholders could restrain the company from acting on the resolution on the ground that it contravened the articles: *Wood* v. *Odessa Waterworks Co.* (1889) 42 Ch.D. 636.

Accordingly, if it is desired to have the power to pay dividends otherwise than in cash, the articles should give such power, as they usually do. Table A, article 105, provides:

> "A general meeting declaring a dividend may, upon the recommendation of the directors, direct that it shall be satisfied wholly or partly by the distribution of assets and, where any difficulty arises in regard to the distribution, the directors may settle the same and in particular may issue fractional certificates and fix the value for distribution of any assets and may determine that cash shall be paid to any member upon the footing of the value so fixed in order to adjust the rights of members and may vest any assets in trustees."

CREATION OF A RESERVE

Section 234 of the Act requires that in their report the directors should state the amount, if any, which they recommend should be paid as dividend and the amount, if any, which they propose to carry to reserves. The articles therefore often contain provisions dealing with the creation of a reserve, and indeed there was an article to this effect in Table A to the 1948 Act (article 117). However, no corresponding article exists in the 1985 Table A (S.I. No. 805). Yet even where no power to create a reserve is included in its articles, a company may nevertheless create one as this is a business question for the decision of the company itself.[44] "The general practice of companies certainly is not to divide the total available profits, but to carry forward a part to make provision for meeting current liabilities."[45] Moreover, a reserve may at any time be distributed as dividend or be employed in any other way

[44] *Burland* v. *Earle* [1902] A.C. 83 (P.C.). Scottish cases decided on the interpretation of articles were *Cadell* v. *Scottish Investment Trust Co. Ltd.* (1901) 9 S.L.T. 299, affirming (1901) 8 S.L.T. 480 (O.H.) (power to carry forward profits to the next year instead of paying a larger dividend on deferred shares), and *Wemyss Collieries Trust Ltd.* v. *Melville* (1905) 8 F. 143 (transfer of profits to reserve fund instead of paying additional dividend on preference shares).

[45] *Per* Lord M'Laren in *Cadell* v. *Scottish Investment Trust Co. Ltd.* (1901) 9 S.L.T. 299 at p. 300.

authorised by the articles.[46] The fact that it has been used in the business does not show that it has been capitalised so as not to be available for dividend.[47]

Capitalisation of Reserves

Capitalisation of a company's profits is defined in section 280 as relating either to the creation of bonus shares; or to the transfer of profits to capital redemption reserve. However, to be able to issue so-called "bonus" shares credited as fully or partly paid, a company has to be so empowered by its articles.

Table A, article 110, accordingly provides:

"The directors may with the authority of an ordinary resolution of the company—

(*a*) subject as hereinafter provided, resolve to capitalise any undivided profits of the company not required for paying any preferential dividend (whether or not they are available for distribution) or any sum standing to the credit of the company's share premium account or capital redemption reserve;

(*b*) appropriate the sum resolved to be capitalised to the members who would have been entitled to it if it were distributed by way of dividend and in the same proportions and apply such sum on their behalf either in or towards paying up the amounts, if any, for the time being unpaid on any shares held by them respectively, or in paying up in full unissued shares or debentures of the company of a nominal amount equal to that sum, and allot the shares or debentures credited as fully paid to those members, or as they may direct, in those proportions, or partly in one way and partly in the other: but the share premium account, the capital redemption reserve, and any profits which are not available for distribution may, for the purposes of this regulation, only be applied in paying up unissued shares to be allotted to members credited as fully paid;

(*c*) make such provision by the issue of fractional certificates or by payment in cash or otherwise as they determine in the case of shares or debentures becoming distributable under this regulation in fractions; and

(*d*) authorise any person to enter on behalf of all the members concerned into an agreement with the company providing for the allotment to them respectively, credited as fully paid, of

[46] *e.g. Blyth's Trustees* v. *Milne* (1905) 7 F. 799.

[47] *Re Hoare & Co. Ltd.* [1904] 2 Ch. 208 (C.A.).

any shares or debentures to which they are entitled upon such capitalisation, any agreement made under such authority being binding on all such members."

Capitalising distributable reserves

When a company capitalises its distributable reserves, it reduces at a stroke its accumulated realised profits available for dividend and issues in their place to existing ordinary shareholders in proportion to their holdings shares or loan stock credited as fully paid up. From an accounting viewpoint, the distributable reserves figure in the balance sheet is reduced and the share or loan capital accounts increased by an equivalent offsetting amount. As a result, other things being equal, the net effect on the value of an individual's holding in the company remains unchanged. The term used to describe such issues as "bonus" issues is therefore misleading, and more appropriate descriptions are "capitalisation-," "scrip-" or "script-issues."

In practice, other things are not usually equal, and the effect will generally be to increase the value of a holding. Thus one reason for engaging in such an exercise is to provide more security for creditors (particularly to existing or prospective holders of loan stock), which alters the balance of risk bearing between them and the company's shareholders. Another is to achieve a subdivision of the equity capital, similar to that permitted under section 121 (see above, page 188): this can make the company's shares more marketable—*e.g.* if the market value per share has risen to £20 as a result of its retention of profits over time to finance growth, it may be preferable to reduce this to nearer £5 per unit. Moreover, in practice listed companies tend to use capitalisation issues as a means of signalling to the investing public that the company's future prospects are encouraging, often indicating specifically that it is not the directors' intention to reduce the dividend per share pro rata to the increase in the number of share units in issue, and there is empirical evidence which confirms that this news content is appreciated by the market.[48]

[48] *e.g.* E. F. Fama, L. Fisher, M. Jensen and R. Roll, "The Adjustment of Stock Prices to New Information," *International Economic Review*, Feb. 1969, 1–21; M. A. Firth. "An Empirical Investigation of the Impact of the Announcement of Capitalisation Issues on Share Prices," *Journal of Business Finance and Accounting*, Spring 1977, 47–60.

Capitalisation issues can also be used to credit partly-paid shares with a further amount paid up.

Capitalising undistributable reserves

A company which by its articles could, prior to the 1980 Act, use a reserve resulting from the revaluation of capital assets to pay for bonus shares, may continue to do so (1980 Act, s.45(1), now section 278 of the 1985 Act). Such a reserve could arise on a revaluation in the value of fixed assets made in good faith by competent valuers and not likely to fluctuate in the short term.[49] Moreover, by sections 130(2)[50] and 170(4)[51] of the Act respectively, a share premium account and a capital redemption reserve can be used to pay for unissued shares of the company to be allotted to members as fully paid bonus shares.

If bonus shares are to be issued:

(1) There must be authority in the company's articles.[52]
(2) Its nominal share capital must be sufficient.
(3) The members must resolve by ordinary resolution to capitalise profits or to apply the share premium account or the capital redemption reserve fund, and to issue bonus shares.[53]
(4) The shares must be allotted by the board in the proportions specified in the articles, usually the same proportions as those in which the members would have received a cash dividend.[54]
(5) A return of allotments and a contract between the members and the company (which may be signed on the members' behalf by the person authorised by the articles) must be delivered to the Registrar within one month after the allotment.[55] The Jenkins Report[56] recommended that it should be enough to file a copy

[49] *Dimbula Valley (Ceylon) Tea Co. Ltd.* v. *Laurie* [1961] Ch. 353.
[50] *Ante*, p. 184.
[51] *Ante*, p. 213.
[52] *Wood's case*, *ante*. See also Table A, article 110, *ante*.
[53] See Table A, article 110, *ante*.
[54] See Table A, article 110, *ante*.
[55] *Ante*, Chap. 8.
[56] (1962) Cmnd. 1749, para. 495.

of the resolution authorising the issue of the shares credited as fully paid up.

Chapter 23

DEBENTURES

THIS chapter is concerned with the borrowing of money by a company where the borrowing is on debentures or on debenture stock, and with fixed and floating charges which a company may create over its property in order to secure the principal sum borrowed and interest thereon until re-payment. Thus the chapter deals with the relationship between a company and its creditors, which is also central to the following chapters up to Chapter 29.

Perhaps the most important part of the chapter is that with regard to charges and the registration of charges, particularly registration with the Registrar of Companies under section 395. These provisions were substantially modified by the Companies Act 1989.

A COMPANY'S POWER TO BORROW MONEY

Prior to the substantial changes to corporate transactions contained in sections 35 and 35A and 322A of the 1985 Act as substituted by the 1989 Act[1] it was important to decide whether or not the company had the capacity, *i.e.* by virtue of an express or implied power, to borrow money, and it was possible for a loan to be *ultra vires* the company and so void.[2]

Following those changes, however, any borrowing is simply one type of transaction by a company and so its validity is now governed, as with all other corporate transactions, by the new provisions. It follows that unless the lender is either not acting in good faith[3] or is a director[4] no question of invalidity can arise

[1] Chap. 6, *ante*.

[2] For the position prior to the 1989 Act changes see the 13th (previous) edition of this work at pp. 607–11.

[3] So that s.35A cannot apply.

[4] Thus applying s.322A.

as a result of the company's constitution. Even if the lender is not acting in good faith or is a director, the transaction may still be ratified by the appropriate resolution. Ratification is also possible if the defect arises from a lack of authority on the part of those negotiating the loan on behalf of the company, if it arises under the general law of agency rather than from the company's constitution.[5]

DEBENTURES AND DEBENTURE STOCK

A debenture is a document which creates or acknowledges a debt due from a company. Such document need not be, although it usually is, under seal,[6] it need not give, although it usually does give, a charge on the assets of the company by way of security, and it may or may not be one of a series.[7] Thus debentures may be (1) secured, or (2) unsecured. A debenture is always for a specified sum, *e.g.* £100, which can only be transferred in its entirety. As will be seen, debentures may be collaterally secured by a trust deed.[8] Convertible debentures, *i.e.* debentures which the holder has the right to convert, at stated times, into shares in the company, have already been mentioned.[9]

It may be helpful to mention here that some of the differences between shares and debentures are:

(1) the holder of a debenture is a creditor, not a member, of the company; a shareholder is a member[10];
(2) debentures may be issued at a discount; shares, in general, may not be[11];
(3) a company may purchase its own debentures; it must not purchase its own shares except in accordance with specific procedures[12];

[5] *i.e.* because the agent has no authority to bind the company.
[6] N.B. the new provisions relating to the sealing of documents in s.36A, *ante*, p. 111.
[7] See *Lemon* v. *Austin Friars Investment Trust Ltd.* [1926] Ch. 1 (C.A.).
[8] *Post*, p. 652.
[9] See *Mosely* v. *Koffyfontein Mines* [1904] 2 Ch. 108, *ante*, p. 182.
[10] *Ante*, p. 231.
[11] *Ante*, p. 181.
[12] *Ante*, Chap. 10.

(4) interest at the specified rate on debentures may be paid out of capital; dividends on shares must be paid only out of distributable profits.[13]

Section 744, defines "debenture" as including debenture stock, bonds, and any other securities[14] of a company whether constituting a charge on the assets of the company or not. A mortgage of land by a company is a debenture.[15] Debentures, including debenture stock, loan stock, bonds and certificates of deposit are investments for the purposes of the Financial Services Act 1986,[16] see Chapter 19, *ante*.

Debenture stock is borrowed money consolidated into one mass for the sake of convenience. This is normally done by a trust deed,[17] which may give the trustees a charge on the company's property. Where there is no charge, debenture stock is commonly called unsecured loan stock. The main advantage of debenture stock is that it is transferable in fractional amounts, although the trust deed may specify the minimum fractional amount which can be transferred. Again, the debenture stockholders will be given simple debenture stock certificates instead of debentures.

Issue of Debentures

Debentures are issued in accordance with the provisions of the articles, usually by a resolution of the board of directors.

Debenture listing particulars, prospectuses and offers for sale were dealt with in Chapter 7.[18]

When debentures have been issued, the prospectus[19] cannot be looked at to ascertain the contract, but if the contract was intended to be contained in the prospectus and the debenture together, or if the prospectus contains a collateral contract the

[13] *Ante*, Chap. 22.
[14] "Securities," as used in s.744, does not include shares.
[15] *Knightsbridge Estates Trust Ltd.* v. *Byrne* [1940] A.C. 613, *post*, p. 662.
[16] Financial Services Act 1986, Sched. 1, para. 2.
[17] See note 8 above.
[18] *Ante*, p. 129; for an action of damages by a debenture holder against a promoter on the ground that by false and fraudulent representations of the promoter he had been induced to advance money to the company, see *Dunnett* v. *Mitchell* (1885) 12 R. 400.
[19] This presumably also applies to listing particulars.

consideration for which was the taking up of the debentures, the prospectus can be looked at.[20]

Debentures or debentures stock certificates must be completed and ready for delivery within two months after allotment or after the lodging of a transfer, unless the conditions of issue otherwise provide: section 185. As with shares this obligation does not apply to allotments, or transfers to SEPON on a stock exchange dealing.[21]

There is no objection to the issue of debentures at a discount[22] but when any commission, allowance or discount has been paid or made to any person in consideration of his subscribing or procuring subscriptions for debentures, particulars of the amount or rate of the commission or discount must be sent to the Registrar within 21 days. The omission to do this does not, however, affect the validity of the debentures. The deposit of debentures as security for a debt of the company does not, for this purpose, amount to the issue of debentures at a discount: sections 397(3) and 413(3).

A contract to take up debentures may be enforced by specific performance: section 195. This section provides an exception to the rule, laid down in *South African Territories Ltd.* v. *Wallington*,[23] that specific performance will not be granted of a contract to lend money since damages are an adequate remedy for breach of such contract.

Apart from the section, an agreement to issue debentures made in consideration of an actual advance of money has the effect in English law of putting the lender in equity in the same position as if the debentures had actually been issued.

A syndicate agreed to sell goods to a company on the terms that, as part payment, £3,000 debentures charged upon all the company's assets were issued. On this agreement the syndicate allowed the company to remove the goods, which were subsequently taken in execution by F. *Held*, although no debentures were actually issued, the syndicate was in the same position as if they had been and so F. was entitled subject to

[20] *Jacobs* v. *Batavia and General Plantations Trust Ltd.* [1924] 2 Ch. 329 (C.A.).
[21] Debenture stock traded on the Stock Exchange will also be subject to the prposed paperless transfer system proposed for late 1991.
[22] *Ante*, p. 182.
[23] [1898] A.C. 309.

the charge: *Simultaneous Colour Printing Syndicate* v. *Foweraker* [1901] 1 K.B. 771.

TRUST DEEDS

Debentures and debenture stock are usually secured by a trust deed.[24]

Contents of a trust deed

The main terms of a *debenture trust deed* are:

(1) a covenant by the company for payment to the debenture holders of the principal moneys and interest;
(2) clauses giving the trustees a legal mortgage by demise of the company's freeholds and leaseholds, which are specified,[25] and a floating charge over the rest of the undertaking and property;
(3) a clause specifying the events in which the security is to become enforceable, *e.g.* default in the payment of interest or principal moneys, order made or resolution passed for winding up, appointment of a receiver, cessation of business, breach of covenant by the company;
(4) a clause giving the trustees power to take possession of the property charged when the security becomes enforceable, to carry on the business and to sell the property charged and to apply the net sale moneys in payment of the principal and interest and to pay the balance to the company;
(5) power for the trustees to concur with the company in dealings with the property charged;
(6) covenants by the company to keep a register of debenture holders, to insure and to keep in repair the property charged;

[24] *Ante*, p. 649.
[25] In Scotland security over specifed heritable property would be created by the execution of a standard security which would be referred to in the trust deed.

(7) provision for meetings of debenture holders;
(8) power for the trustees to appoint a receiver when the security becomes enforeceable;
(9) provision for serving notices on the debenture holders by post.

A *debenture stock trust deed*, in addition to containing the foregoing terms, constitutes a stock by acknowledging that the company is indebted to the trustees in a specified sum and provides for the issue of debenture stock certificates.

A trust deed usually contains a clause providing that the rights of the debenture holders against the company or any property charged by the deed may be modified or compromised by extra-ordinary resolution of the debenture holders.

Advantages of a trust deed

The advantages of a trust deed are:

(1) the trustees will have a legal mortgage[26] over the company's land, so that persons who subsequently lend money to the company cannot gain priority over the debenture holders or debenture stockholders;
(2) events are specified on the happening of which the principal moneys and interest become payable, *e.g.* non-payment of interest or non-performance of the covenants in the deed; the appointment of trustees, who are usually paid, ensures that there are definite persons whose duty it is to take action on the happening of these events;
(3) the company is given a number of powers over the mortgaged property which it can exercise with the consent of the trustees, *e.g.* powers of sale, exchange or leasing. This enables the company to use the property advantageously for the purposes of its business without prejudicing the interests of the debenture holders or debenture stockholders;
(4) covenants are entered into by the company for insurance, repair and other matters, and can be enforced by the trustees;

[26] In Scotland a fixed security.

(5) power is given to the trustees to appoint a receiver or to enter into possession of the property and carry on the business of the company in case of urgency.

Liability of trustees

Trustees for debenture holders are in the same position towards their beneficiaries as any other trustees, and cannot purchase the debentures, the subject of the deed, without making full disclosure of all the information relating to them which is in their possession.[27] Any provision in a trust deed, or in a contract with the holders of debentures secured by a trust deed, for exempting the trustees from, or indemnifying them against, liability for breach of trust where they fail to show the degree of care and diligence required of them as trustees, is void, except that the trustees may be released from liability by a release given after the liability has arisen, and a provision in a trust deed for the giving of such a release by a majority of not less than three-fourths in value of the debenture holders present and voting in person or by proxy at a meeting summoned for the purpose is not void: section 192. (Contrast section 310 *ante*[28] as regards officers and auditors).

Section 727 (power of court to grant relief) *ante*[29] does not apply to the trustees although the Trustee Act 1925, s.61, and the Trusts (Scotland) Act 1921, s.32, do, and so in an appropriate case the court may relieve the trustees from liability.

Right to copy of trust deed

A debenture holder is entitled to require a copy of the trust deed on payment of the prescribed fee: sections 191, 356.

REGISTERED DEBENTURES

Debentures or debenture stock may be payable to either (1) the registered holder; or (2) the bearer.

[27] *Re Magadi Soda Co.* (1925) 41 T.L.R. 297.
[28] p. 414.
[29] p. 415.

Contents of a registered debenture

Where there is a trust deed the usual form of debenture payble to the registered holder is a document issued under the seal of the company and containing two clauses. The clauses are as follows:

(*a*) the company for valuable consideration received, covenants to pay the registered holder the principal sum on a specified day or on such earlier day as it becomes payable under the indorsed conditions, and in the meantime to pay interest by equal half-yearly payments on specified dates at a specified rate;

(*b*) the debenture is said to be issued subject to and with the benefit of the conditions indorsed thereon.

The indorsed conditions usually include the following:

(i) the debenture is said to be one of a series, each for securing a specified sum;

(ii) the registered holders of all the debentures of the issue are said to be entitled *pari passu* to the benefit and subject to the provisions of the trust deed, the date of execution of which and the parties to which are specified, and the charges conferred by the trust deed are recited.

This has the effect of putting all the debentures of the issue on an equal footing; in the absence of such a clause the debentures would rank according to the order in which they were executed[30]:

(iii) the company is empowered, at any time after a specified date, by giving not less than a specified number of months' notice, to pay off the principal moneys secured with interest to the date of payment;

(iv) provision is made for keeping a register of debenture holders at the registered office. We shall see that this will comply with section 190 and that a right of inspection is given by section 191;[31]

[30] *Gartside* v. *Silkstone and Dodworth Coal, etc., Co.* (1882) 21 Ch.D. 762.
[31] *Post*, p. 659.

(v) the company is not to be bound to recognise anyone as having any title to the debenture except the registered holder, or his personal representative, and is not to be bound to enter notice of any trust in the register.

Section 360, which provides that trusts are not to be entered on the register of members, does not apply to the register of debenture holders, and consequently such a clause is necessary. If the company does receive notice of a trust, the clause relieves it from the obligation of entering it on the register, but if it deals with the debentures as a trader, *e.g.* by advancing money on them, after notice of a trust, it will be bound by that trust[32]:

(vi) transfer of the debenture is provided for. Every transfer must be in writing, as will be explained later;

(vii) equities or, in Scots law, rights of compensation, between the company and any person other than the registered holder are excluded. This will be explained later;[33]

(viii) the principal moneys and interest are made payable at the company's registered office or at its bankers.

If this clause is not inserted it is the company's duty to follow the usual rule and seek out its creditor and pay him.

F. held 18 £100 debentures repayable in June, 1913, in the M. Corporation. Before the date of redemption F. died, and her executors neglected to present the debentures to the company for payment. In June, 1916, the company was sued for principal and interest. *Held*, as the debentures contained no clause to the effect set out above, it was the company's duty to seek out the debenture holder and pay her; as this had not been done, the company was liable to pay the principal with interest until the date of actual payment: *Fowler* v. *Midland Electric Corpn.* [1917] 1 Ch. 656 (C.A.).

(ix) the company is empowered to purchase any of the debentures of the issue at any time;

(x) interest is made payable by warrant on the company's bank payable to the order of the registered holder and sent by post to his registered address;

[32] *Bradford Banking Co.* v. *Briggs & Co.* (1886) 12 App.Cas. 29: *Mackereth* v. *Wigan Coal Co. Ltd.* [1916] 2 Ch. 293.

[33] *Post*, p. 668.

(xi) the principal monies are made immediately payable if the company defaults in the payment of interest for a specified number of months, or if a winding-up order is made or resolution passed, or if the security constituted by the trust deed becomes enforceable and the trustees enforce it.

The debenture holder is entitled to repayment of his principal on the company's going into liquidation, whether or not the date fixed for repayment has arrived.[34]

Transfer of registered debentures

Registered debentures are transferred in the manner laid down in the indorsed conditions (which usually require a transfer to be in writing under the hand of the registered holder or of his personal representatives) or by a stock transfer under the Stock Transfer Act 1963. As in the case of a transfer of shares[35] it is unlawful for a company to register a transfer of debentures unless a "proper instrument of transfer" has been delivered to the company: section 183(1).

The company must have the debenture or debenture stock certificate ready for delivery within two months of the lodging of the instrument of transfer unless the conditions of issue otherwise provide or the transfer is to SEPON, *i.e.* on a transfer under the stock exchange procedure: section 185. If registration of a transfer is refused, notice of refusal must be given to the transferee within two months: section 183(5).

Registered debentures are in England choses in action, and in Scotland incorporeal moveable property to the assignation of which the rule *assignatus utitur jure auctoris* ("the assignee acquires no higher right than his cedent had") applies. They are not negotiable instruments, and consequently a transferee takes them subject to all claims which the company may have against prior holders at the date of the transfer.

After a receiver had been appointed and a winding-up petition had been presented, P., a debenture stockholder, transferred £10,000

[34] *Hodson* v. *Tea Co.* (1880) 14 Ch.D. 859.
[35] *Ante*, pp. 283 *et seq.*

debenture stock to X, who was registered as the owner. P. was also a director of the company and a claim was made against him for money had and received by him while a director. *Held*, X was not entitled to payment until the amount due from P. to the company had been ascertained and deducted: *Re Rhodesia Goldfields Ltd.* [1910] 1 Ch. 239.

To avoid this result, the indorsed conditions usually provide that the principal and interest shall be paid to the registered holder without regard to any equities or rights of compensation existing between the company and any prior holder of the debenture. Such a clause amounts to a contract by the company that it will not rely on equities or rights of compensation, and its effect is to make the debentures more marketable.

A company was in liquidation. C., who had been a director of the company, transferred debentures to R. as security for a loan. The debentures contained a clause similar to that set out above. It was then discovered that C. had been guilty of misfeasance and he was ordered to pay a sum of money to the liquidator in respect thereof. The liquidator refused to register R.'s transfer. *Held*, the right to transfer and to have the transfer registered was not affected by the winding up, and R. was entitled to payment without regard to C.'s debt to the company: *Re Goy & Co. Ltd.* [1900] 2 Ch. 149.

A transferee cannot claim the benefit of such a clause unless either he is registered or the conditions specifically allow the holder to transfer the debenture free of equities.

B. held debentures containing a clause similar to that set out above. After a resolution for winding up had been passed he transferred them for value to C., who took without notice of any defect in B.'s title. Notice of transfer but no request for registration was given to the liquidator. C. claimed payment but the court found that B. had paid nothing for the debentures and had obtained them by misrepresentation. *Held*, notwithstanding the clause, C. took subject to the company's claim against B. *Re Goy & Co.*, *ante*, was distinguished on the ground that when the transfer in that case was sent for registration the company was not aware of and was not setting up any equities between itself and the transferor: *Re Palmer's Decoration and Furnishing Co.* [1904] 2 Ch. 743. Where the actual agreement specifically allowed the holder to transfer free of all equities it has been held that following such a transfer the issuing company is bound to register the transfer: *Hilger Analytical Ltd.* v. *Rank Precision Industries Ltd.* [1984] BCLC 301.

Section 184 (certification of transfers) *ante*[36] applies to transfers of debentures as well as to transfers of shares.

Register of debenture holders

A company is not required to keep a register of debenture holders but there are provisions regulating those companies which do. A company registered in England must not keep its register of debenture holders in Scotland, and vice versa. The register must be kept at the registered office or at any other office of the company where it is made up or, if it is made up by an agent, it may be kept at the agent's office: section 190. Debenture holders and shareholders in the company may, without fee, inspect the register of debenture holders within limits laid down by the Secretary of State. Other persons may inspect the register on payment of a prescribed fee. A copy may be demanded on payment of the prescribed fee: section 191. A computer may be used to keep the register of debenture holders: section 723.

The Jenkins Report[37] recommended that a company which issues a series of debentures ranking *pari passu* or debenture stock not transferable by delivery should be required to keep a register of the holders.

BEARER DEBENTURES

Debentures payable to bearer are in the same form as registered debentures except that they are expressed to be made payable to bearer and coupons for the interest are attached. The indorsed conditions are also in the same form with the necessary modifications for bearer, instead of registered, instruments.

Bearer debentures are negotiable instruments and consequently a transferee in good faith and for value takes them free from any defects in the title of a prior holder.

The B. Company owned some bearer debentures and kept them in a safe. The secretary fraudulently took them from the safe and deposited

[36] p. 286.
[37] Para. 306.

them with the bank, who took them in good faith and as security for advances to the secretary. *Held*, the debentures were negotiable instruments transferable by delivery and the bank was entitled to them as against the B. Company: *Bechuanaland Exploration Co.* v. *London Trading Bank* [1898] 2 Q.B. 658.

The courts take judicial notice of the fact that bearer debentures are negotiable instruments.[38]

Bearer debentures are transferable by delivery and no stamp duty is payable on transfer. Interest is payable by means of the coupons which are cut off and presented for payment to the company's bankers when the date of payment arrives.

Debentures to bearer issued in Scotland are expressly declared by section 197 to be valid and binding notwithstanding anything in the Blank Bonds and Trusts Act 1696 (Scots Act 1696 c. 25).[39]

Redeemable Debentures

Debentures may be (1) redeemable at the option of the company, or (2) irredeemable or perpetual.

Sometimes debentures are issued on the terms that the company is bound to redeem a certain number each year by "drawings" (in which case, in effect, the numbers of the debentures to be redeemable are drawn out of a hat),[40] or that it may purchase, *e.g.* on the Stock Exchange, or that it is bound to set aside a sinking fund for redemption purposes on a specified date. When debentures have been so redeemed, section 194 empowers the company to reissue them or issue other debentures in their place, unless—

(*a*) the company, in its articles or otherwise, has contracted not to reissue them; or

(*b*) the company has shown an intention to cancel the debentures by passing a resolution to that effect, or by some other act.

[38] *Edelstein* v. *Schuler* [1902] 2 K.B. 144.

[39] *Ante*, p. 298.

[40] For difficulties which may arise from the company's inability to trace the holders to whom repayment is due, see *United Collieries Ltd.* v. *Lord Advocate*, 1950 S.C. 458.

Under the general law, once a debenture was transferred to the company the debt was absolutely gone and the security ceased to exist.[41]

On a reissue of redeemed debentures, the person entitled to them has the same priorities as if the debentures had never been redeemed: section 194. The date of redemption of the reissued debentures cannot be later than that of the original debentures.[42]

Reissued debentures are treated as new debentures for the purpose of stamp duty: section 194.

PERPETUAL DEBENTURES

Debentures are not invalid merely because they are made irredeemable, or redeemable on the happening of a contingency, however remote, *e.g.* the winding up of the company, or on the expiration of a period, however long, *e.g.* 100 years after the issue of the debentures, *i.e.* the legal or contractual date for redemption may be postponed, despite any rule of equity to the contrary: section 193.

A company mortgaged 75 houses and other properties to secure £310,000 repayable by instalments over 40 years. There was no right of redemption before the 40 years expired. *Held*, the mortgage was a debenture and valid under what is now section 89: *Knightsbridge Estates Trust Ltd.* v. *Byrne* [1940] A.C. 613.

The issue of perpetual debentures amounts to the granting of a perpetual annuity.[43] If the debentures are secured by a floating charge, the money secured will become payable on the company's going into liquidation and the security will be enforceable on the class of assets charged as it exists at that time.[44]

In Scotland, the Conveyancing and Feudal Reform (Scotland) Act 1970, ss.11 and 18, conferred on the debtor in a standard security the right, which could not be varied by agreement, to redeem the security on giving two months' notice. The Redemption of Standard Securities (Scotland) Act 1971,

[41] *Re George Routledge & Sons Ltd.* [1904] 2 Ch. 474.
[42] *Re Antofagasta (Chile) and Bolivia Ry. Co.'s Trust Deed* [1939] Ch. 732.
[43] *Re The Southern Brazilian Rio Grande do Sul Ry. Co. Ltd.* [1905] 2 Ch. 78.
[44] *Hodson* v. *Tea Co.* (1880) 14 Ch.D. 859.

however, amended the 1970 Act on this point by providing that the condition relating to the debtor's right of redemption might be varied by agreement. The 1971 Act also, for the avoidance of doubt, declared that the provisions of the 1970 Act relating to the standard security do not affect the operation of section 193.

CHARGES SECURING DEBENTURES

A charge on the assets of a company given by a debenture or a trust deed in order to secure money borrowed by the company may be either (1) a specific or fixed charge, or (2) a floating charge. If the debentures are issued in a series and give a specific charge on the company's property, *e.g.* its land, they are always secured by means of a trust deed. The trust deed usually gives a floating charge, *e.g.* on the rest of the company's property, in addition to the fixed charge.

In practice many debentures are secured by both a fixed and a floating charge. Such charges are usually drafted to cover "all moneys" due by the company to the lender including contingent and future liabilities. In *Re Quest Cae. Ltd.*[45] it was held that such wording only covered debts arising as a result of transactions between the company and the lender so that where the lender subsequently acquired loan stock issued by the company to a third party it was not protected by the charge. The debt had not arisen by virtue of a transaction between the company and the lender.

Fixed charges (English law)

A fixed charge is a mortgage of ascertained and definite property, *e.g.* legal or an equitable mortgage of a specified factory, and prevents the company from realising that property, *i.e.* disposing of it free from the charge, without the consent of the holders of the charge. Where a charge is on fixed plant and machinery it will only apply to those items physically attached to the company's premises and not to all a company's fixed, *i.e.* capital, assets.[46]

[45] [1985] BCLC 266.

[46] *Re Hi-Fi Equipment (Cabinets) Ltd.* (1987) 3 BCC 478, not following *Tudor Heights Ltd.* v. *United Dominions Corporation Finance Ltd.* [1977] 1 N.Z.L.R. 532.

There is some doubt as to whether it is possible to create a fixed charge over present and future book debts. Slade J. in *Siebe Gorman & Co. Ltd.* v. *Barclays Bank Ltd.*[47] construed such a charge as being fixed and the Irish Court in *Re Keenan Bros. Ltd.*[48] considered that it was possible. Harman J. has admitted the possibility in two cases but in each decided that it did not include a credit balance at the company's bank, which was thus only included in the attached floating charge.[49]

Floating charges (English law)

In *Re Yorkshire Woolcombers Association Ltd.*[50] Romer L.J. said that if a charge has the three characteristics set out below it is a floating charge:

(1) it is a charge on a class of assets of a company, present and future;
(2) which class is, in the ordinary course of the company's business, changing from time to time;
(3) it is contemplated by the charge that, until the holders of the charge take steps to enforce it, the company may carry on business in the ordinary way as far as concerns the class of assets charged.

Thus a floating charge is an equitable charge on some or all of the present and future property of a company, *e.g.* the company's undertaking, *i.e.* all its property, present and future.[51] It is effective as to future property only when that property is acquired by the company. The company may, in the ordinary course of business, realise property which is subject to the charge. A floating charge will be valid even if the assets covered do not yet exist.[52]

However, when the security is enforceable, *e.g.* there is default with regard to payment of interest or repayment of the

[47] [1979] 2 Lloyds Rep. 142, relying on *Evans, Coleman & Evans Ltd.* v. *R. A. Nelson Construction Ltd.* (1959) 16 D.L.R. (2d) 123.
[48] [1986] BCLC 242; *cf. Re Armagh Shoes Ltd.* [1982] N.I. 59.
[49] *Re Brightlife Ltd.* [1987] Ch. 200; *Re Permanent Houses (Holdings) Ltd.* (1989) 5 BCC 151.
[50] [1903] 2 Ch. 284 (C.A.) at p. 295.
[51] *Re Panama, etc., Royal Mail Co.* (1870) L.R. 5 Ch.App. 318.
[52] *Re Croftbell Ltd.* [1990] BCC 781.

principal sum, and the debenture holders or the trustees enforce it, *e.g.* they appoint an administrative receiver of the property charged, the floating charge is said to crystallise, *i.e.* it becomes a fixed charge on the assets in the class charged at the time of crystallisation or, where the floating charge so provides, assets which come to the company after crystallisation.[53]

Crystallisation also occurs on the commencement of the winding up of the company, even if it is a voluntary winding up for the purpose of reconstruction,[54] or when the company ceases business.[55] The latter, which is a form of "implied automatic crystallisation" in that it needs no act or specific event to bring it about and so may be difficult for other creditors to judge, was disputed until recently. In coming to his decision on this point, Nourse J. pointed out that cessation of business prevents a company from dealing with its assets and so there is no reason why the charge should not crystallise. The judge, however, rejected another such ground, *i.e.* on the crystallisation of a second floating charge which is postponed to the relevant floating charge.[56]

It is possible that the charging deed may provide for crystallisation on a certain event, *e.g.* an attempt by the company to create another charge over the assets in the class charged, or simply by the giving of a notice to that effect. Such "express automatic crystallisation" is valid under English law following the decision of Hoffman J. in *Re Brightlife Ltd.*[57] The judge pointed out that floating charges were developed to enable companies to raise money without inhibiting their ability to trade, but this involved potential prejudice to other creditors who could suddenly find assets becoming subject to a charge on crystallisation without anyone else being aware. The appointment of an administrative receiver, administrator or liquidator were public acts, but the giving of a notice or the happening of an event would not be. The judge, however, considered that

[53] *N. W. Robbie & Co. Ltd.* v. *Whitney Warehouse Co. Ltd.* [1963] 1 W.LR. 1324 (C.A.); *Ferrier* v. *Bottomer* (1972) 126 C.L.R. 597.

[54] *Re Crompton & Co.* [1914] 1 Ch. 954.

[55] *Re Woodroffes (Musical Instruments) Ltd.* [1986] Ch. 366.

[56] It might be different if there is an express term to that effect—see *Stein* v. *Saywell* (1969) 121 C.L.R. 529.

[57] [1987] Ch. 200.

any restrictions on the contractual freedom of parties to a floating charge were matters for Parliament, and it would be "wholly inappropriate" for the courts to impose restrictions on the ground of public policy. The judge followed a decision of the New Zealand courts to a similar effect.[58]

Under section 410 the Secretary of State has the power to require registration not only of the floating charge but also of any provisions for automatic crystallisation. If those provisions are not registered they may render the automatic crystallisation void.[59]

The characteristics of a floating charge are therefore:

(1) it is an equitable charge on assets for the time being of the company[60];
(2) it attaches to the class of assets charged in the varying condition in which they happen to be from time to time,[60] *i.e.* it does not fasten on any definite property but is a charge on property which is constantly changing;
(3) it remains dormant, subject to any automatic crystallisation until the undertaking charged ceases to be a going concern, or until the person in whose favour it is created intervenes. His right to intervene may be suspended by agreement but if there is no agreement for suspension he may intervene whenever he pleases after default.[61] When this happens the charge is said to "crystallise" and becomes fixed[62];
(4) although it is an immediate and continuing charge, until it becomes fixed the company can, without consent, deal with the class of assets in the ordinary course of business, *e.g.* it has been held that a company can sell all or any of its business or property for shares or debentures of another company if the memorandum gives it power to do so, and the

[58] Re *Manurewa Transport Ltd.* [1971] N.Z.L.R. 909; *cf. R.* v. *Consolidated Churchill Copper Corpn. Ltd.* [1978] 5 W.W.R. 652. See also the Australian case of *Deputy Commissioner of Taxation* v. *Horsburgh* [1984] V.R. 773.

[59] *Post*, p. 687.

[60] *Per* Lord Macnaghten in *Governments Stock Investment Co. Ltd.* v. *Manila Ry. Co. Ltd.* [1897] A.C. 81, at p. 86.

[61] See note 54, above.

[62] *Evans* v. *Rival Granite Quarries Ltd.* [1910] 2 K.B. 979 (C.A.).

> debenture holders cannot prevent such a sale if the company remains a going concern[63]; similarly, a company with three businesses may sell one of the three.[64]

Where, before crystallisation of a floating charge over all the company's assets and undertaking, the company contracted to sell goods to a buyer to whom it owed money under a previous contract, and the goods were delivered after crystallisation, the company's right to sue for the debt due to it was embraced, when it arose, by the floating charge, but the debenture holder could not be in a better position to assert the rights under the previous contract than the company.[65]

Where there is a charge over the book debts of a company such a charge can be either a fixed or floating charge. The test is whether the company can deal with those debts and their proceeds freely in the normal course of business (a floating charge) or they are unusable in that context without the chargee's consent. Thus in *Re Keenan Bros. Ltd.*[66] where the charge required the company to pay all money it received in respect of book debts into specified bank accounts which could only be used with the consent of the bank, the Irish Supreme Court held that this created a fixed charge, overruling the judge below.[67]

The advantage of a floating charge from the *company's* point of view is that the company can give security for a loan to it by charging property which changes in the course of business and over which it is impracticable to create a fixed charge, *e.g.* the company's stock-in-trade. Further, until crystallisation the company can carry on business in the ordinary way.

[63] *Re Borax Co.* [1901] 1 Ch. 326.

[64] *Re H. H. Vivian & Co. Ltd.* [1900] 2 Ch. 654.

[65] *Rother Iron Works Ltd.* v. *Canterbury Precision Engines Ltd.* [1974] Q.B. 1 (C.A.) applied in *George Barker (Transport) Ltd.* v. *Eynon* [1974] 1 W.L.R. 462 (C.A.).

[66] [1986] BCLC 242 S.C. (Ir.) overruling [1985] BCLC 302.

[67] *cf. Re Armagh Shoes Ltd.* [1982] N.I. 59 where the charge applied to all "receivables . . . now or at any time belonging to the [company]" and was held to be a floating charge. See also *Re Brightlife Ltd.* [1987] Ch. 200 and *Re Permanent Houses (Holdings) Ltd.* (1989) 5 BCC 151, where Harman J. held that a credit balance at the bank was inappropriate to be covered by a fixed charge on book debts and was thus covered by the floating charge over all other assets.

A floating charge can be created only by a registered company not by a partnership or a sole trader. One reason is that such a charge created by a firm over chattels would be a bill of sale within the Bills of Sale Acts 1878 and 1882, and would have to be registered and, as a mortgage bill, would have to be in the statutory form and specify the chattels, which is impossible.

From the *chargee's* point of view, an important advantage is that, upon crystallisation of the floating charge, the chargee obtains priority in the payment of debts over unsecured creditors. However, there are a number of disadvantages attached to a floating charge from the chargee's point of view. For example:

(1) As will be seen, a floating charge is postponed to certain other interests.
(2) A floating charge may be invalidated under section 245 of the Insolvency Act 1986, *post*.[68]

Retention of title clauses

Sellers, particularly of raw materials, frequently protect themselves by inserting into the contract of sale a retention of title or "*Romalpa*" clause whereby they seek to retain title to the materials supplied until the buyer has paid for them. There have been many cases since the original decision in *Aluminium Industrie Vaassen BV* v. *Romalpa Aluminium Ltd.*[69] that such a clause could have the effect of retaining the legal title to the goods. Some clauses have failed, *e.g.* because the raw materials have ceased to exist,[70] or because they have created a floating charge which has thus been declared void for non-registration under the Companies Act[71] or because they have created a charge over the book debts of the company, which again is void for non-registration.[72] The distinction is always one of construction of the particular clause—is the buyer conferring a charge on

[68] *Post*, p. 675.
[69] [1978] 1 W.L.R. 676 (C.A.).
[70] *Borden (U.K.) Ltd.* v. *Scottish Timber Products Ltd.* [1981] Ch. 25.
[71] *Re Bond Worth Ltd.* [1980] Ch. 228. For registration see *post*, p. 678.
[72] *E. Pfeiffer Weinkellerei-Weineinkauf GmbH & Co.* v. *Arbuthnot Factors Ltd.* [1988] 1 W.L.R. 150.

his goods or the proceeds of sale of those goods[73] in favour of the seller,[74] or is the seller retaining title to *his* goods to provide himself with a security.[75] It may be indicative of the former if the seller attempts to retain title to the goods into which the raw materials have been incorporated.[76]

A seller supplied yarn to some fabric manufacturers. He included a clause whereby the ownership of the yarn was to remain with the seller and if it was incorporated into other goods the ownership of these other goods was to remain with the seller, in either case until payment. The Court of Appeal held that the first part of the clause was a valid retention of title clause whereas the second created a floating charge. Since only the unused yarn was claimed the seller was allowed to succeed: *Clough Mill Ltd.* v. *Geoffrey Martin* [1985] 1 W.L.R. 111 (C.A.).

Priority of charges (English law)

A company which has created a floating charge cannot later create another floating charge over some of the same assets ranking in priority to or *pari passu* with the original charge unless the provisions of the original charge allow this.[77]

On the other hand, since a company which has created a floating charge can, without the consent of the holders of the charge, deal with the class of assets in the ordinary course of business, it follows that the company can, in the ordinary course of business, create a later fixed charge, legal or equitable, over specific assets and with priority over the floating charge,[78] unless the floating charge provides that the company is not to create any mortgage or charge ranking *pari passu* with or in priority to the floating charge, in which case any fixed chargee taking *with notice of this provision* will be postponed to the floating charge. In spite of such a provision the holder of a specific charge will

[73] *Tatung (UK) Ltd.* v. *Galex Telesure Ltd.* (1989) 5 BCC 325.
[74] *Re Peachdart Ltd.* [1984] Ch. 131; *Specialist Plant Services Ltd.* v. *Braithwaite Ltd.* (1987) 3 BCC 119 (C.A.).
[75] *Hendy Lennox (Industrial Engines) Ltd.* v. *Grahame Puttick Ltd.* [1984] 1 W.L.R. 485, *Re Andrabell Ltd.* [1984] BCLC 522.
[76] *John Snow & Co. Ltd.* v. *D. B. G. Woodcroft & Co. Ltd.* [1985] BCLC 54.
[77] *Re Automatic Bottle Makers Ltd.* [1926] Ch. 412 (C.A.).
[78] *Wheatley* v. *Silkstone, etc., Coal Co.* (1885) 29 Ch.D. 715.

obtain priority over a floating charge on all the company's property if:

(1) taking a legal mortgage, he obtains his mortgage without notice of the provision, even though he has notice of the debentures[79]—the maxim "where the equities are equal the law prevails" will apply; or
(2) taking an equitable mortgage, he obtains the title deeds without notice of the debentures[80]—the maxim "where the equities are otherwise equal the earlier in time has priority" will not apply since the debenture holders left the title deeds with the company so as to enable it to deal with its property as if it was unincumbered so that the equities are not equal.

Further, registration of a floating charge under the Companies Act, *post*,[81] although constructive notice under certain circumstances of the charge, is not notice that the charge contains a provision prohibiting the creation of subsequent charges with priority over the floating charge.[82]

The following also have priority over a floating charge:

(1) an execution creditor if the goods are sold by the sheriff,[83] or the company pays out the sheriff to avoid a sale,[84] or the creditor obtains a garnishee order absolute[85] (not a garnishee order nisi),[86] *before* crystallisation of the floating charge;
(2) a landlord's distress for rent levied before crystallisation[87];

79 *English and Scottish Mercantile etc. Co. Ltd.* v. *Brunton* [1892] 2 Q.B. 700 (C.A.).
80 *Re Castell & Brown Ltd.* [1898] 1 Ch. 315.
81 pp. 678 *et seq.*
82 *Per* Eve J. in *Wilson* v. *Kelland* [1910] 2 Ch. 306 at p. 313; *Dempsey* v. *Traders' Finance Corpn.* [1933] N.Z.L.R. 1258 (C.A.).
83 *Re Standard Manufacturing Co.* [1891] 1 Ch. 627 (C.A.).
84 *Heaton and Dugard Ltd.* v. *Cutting Bros. Ltd.* [1925] 1 K.B. 655.
85 *Evans* v. *Rival Granite Quarries Ltd.* [1910] 2 K.B. 979 (C.A.).
86 *Norton* v. *Yates* [1906] 1 K.B. 112.
87 *Re Roundwood Colliery Co.* [1897] 1 Ch. 373 (C.A.). Where a floating charge crystallised before the company's landlord served a distress notice on the company's tenants which assigned their rents to the landlord, the chargee still took priority over the landlord, since the latter had notice of the crystallisation, which was on earlier assignment by the company to the chargee: *Rhodes* v. *Allied Dunbar Pension Services Ltd.* [1988] BCLC 186.

(3) the rights of persons such as one who has sold goods to the company under a hire-purchase agreement by which the goods are still the property of such person[88];

(4) the rights of preferential creditors: section 196, I.A. 1986 section 40.[89]

On the other hand a floating charge may not be postponed to the holder of a *Mareva* injunction over the assets. Such an injunction prohibits the company from removing its assets outside the United Kingdom. The holder of the floating charge may apply to have the injunction set aside and will succeed if the holders of the injunction are unsecured creditors.[90]

Fixed securities and floating charges (Scots law)

Before 1961 any attempt by a Scottish company to create a floating charge was of no effect, since such a charge violated the principle of the common law expressed in the maxim "*traditionibus, non nudis pactis, dominia rerum transferuntur*," *i.e.* "delivery, and not mere agreement, is required for the transfer of real rights."

"There is no principle more deeply rooted in the law than this, that in order to create a good security over subjects delivery must be given. If possession be retained no effectual security can be granted": *per* Lord Shand in *Clark* v. *West Calder Oil Co. Ltd.* (1882) 9 R. 1017 at p. 1033 (a case in which trustees for debenture holders to whom the company had assigned certain leasehold and moveable property in security were held to have no preference over the ordinary trade creditors of the company since no possession had followed on the assignation).

"The whole method of creating a floating charge ... is absolutely foreign to our law": *per* Lord President Dunedin in *The Ballachulish Slate Quarries Co. Ltd.* v. *Bruce* (1908) 16 S.L.T. 48 at p. 51 (an attempt to create a floating charge in English form on the uncalled capital and other assets of a company was held to give a debenture holder no valid security).

A company registered in Scotland and having a place of business and assets in England borrowed money under debentures which were in

[88] See *Re Morrison, Jones and Taylor Ltd.* [1914] 1 Ch. 50 (C.A.).

[89] pp. 713, 822.

[90] *Cretanor Maritime Co. Ltd.* v. *Irish Marine Management Ltd.* [1978] 1 W.L.R. 966 (C.A.).

English form and by which the company purported to create a floating charge over its whole undertaking, property and assets. *Held*, that no valid and effectual floating charge had been created even over the company's assets in England: *Carse* v. *Coppen*, 1951 S.C. 233.

"It is clear in principle and amply supported by authority that a floating charge is utterly repugnant to the principles of Scots law and is not recognised by us as creating a security at all. In Scotland the term 'equitable security' is meaningless. Putting aside the rare and exceptional cases of hypothec, we require for the constitution of a security which will confer upon the holder rights over and above those which he enjoys in common with the general body of unsecured creditors of a debtor, (*a*) the transfer to the creditor of a real right in specific subjects by the method appropriate for the constitution of such rights in the particular classes of property in question, or (*b*) the creation of a nexus over specific property by the due use of the appropriate form of diligence. A floating charge, even after appointment of a receiver, satisfies none of these requirements": *per* Lord President Cooper at p. 239.

Floating charges were introduced to Scots law by the Companies (Floating Charges) (Scotland) Act 1961, but there was no power under that Act to appoint receivers. Subsequently, on the recommendation of the Scottish Law Commission,[91] the Companies (Floating Charges and Receivers) (Scotland) Act 1972 was passed with the twofold purpose of:

(1) re-enacting with substantial modification the provisions of the Act of 1961; and
(2) making it competent under Scots law for receivers to be appointed.

The 1972 Act was consolidated by and appeared as sections 462 to 487 of the 1985 Act. Of these sections the first five (*i.e.* sections 462 to 466) relate to floating charges and are still applicable, but the remaining sections (*i.e.* sections 467 to 487) relating to receivers were amended by the Insolvency Act 1985 and in their amended form have now been consolidated by the Insolvency Act 1986, where they appear as sections 50 to 71.

Scottish floating charges and receivers have statutory definitions and statutory incidents which distinguish them in some respects from their English common law originals. The term "fixed security" is used in the statutory provisions to denote a security other than a floating charge.[92]

[91] *Report on the Companies (Floating Charges) (Scotland) Act 1961*, (1970) Cmnd. 4336.

[92] s.486.

Floating charges (Scots law)

The main characteristics of the Scottish floating charge are:

(1) It is a charge created by an incorporated company[93] over all or any part of the property (including uncalled capital) which may from time to time be comprised in its property and undertaking."

(2) It may be created for the purpose of securing any debt or other obligation (including a cautionary obligation) incurred or to be incurred by, or binding upon, the company or any other person. It is therefore possible, for instance, for a subsidiary company to create a floating charge over its own property to secure a debt due by its parent company (another person), or for a subsidiary company to guarantee a debt due by its parent company and create a floating charge over its own property to secure its liability under the guarantee.

(3) It can be created by a Scottish company only by the execution, under the seal of the company, of an instrument or bond or other written acknowledgment of debt or obligation which purports to create a floating charge. There is no longer any statutory form as there was under the 1961 Act. An alternative to execution by the company itself is execution by an attorney who has been authorised for that purpose by writing under the company's common seal. Where the floating charge relates to heritable property in Scotland, it takes effect on that property even although the instrument creating it has not been recorded in the Register of Sasines or registered under the Land Registration (Scotland) Act 1979: section 462.

(4) On the commencement of the winding up or on the appointment of a receiver it attaches (provided it is not invalid under section 399 of the 1985 Act[94] or

[93] Floating charges may also be created by industrial and provident societies registered in Scotland: Industrial and Provident Societies Act 1967, as amended by the Companies (Floating Charges and Receivers) (Scotland) Act 1972, s.10.

[94] Inserted by C.A. 1989, s. 95, *post*, p. 683.

section 245 of the Insolvency Act 1986[95]) to the property then comprised in the company's property and undertaking.

References in the Act to the crystallisation of a floating charge are, in relation to a Scottish floating charge, construed as references to the attachment of the charge.[96]

(5) Once attached it has the same effect as if it were a fixed security over the property for the principal of, and any interest due or to become due on, the debt or obligation to which it relates. The security extends to interest stipulated for from the date of attachment until payment.[97]

(6) It is postponed to the rights of certain creditors[98]: section 463.

The instrument creating a floating charge may contain:

(*a*) provisions prohibiting or restricting the creation of any fixed security or any other floating charge having priority over, or ranking equally with, the floating charge; or

(*b*) provisions regulating the order in which the floating charge is to rank with any other subsisting or future floating charges or fixed securities over the property or part of it: section 464.

A floating charge may be altered by an instrument of alteration: section 466.

The advantage of a floating charge from the *company's* point of view is that the company can give security for a loan to it by charging property such as stock-in-trade and other moveables which it would be impracticable to deliver to the lender. Until the floating charge has attached to the property the company can, in the ordinary course of business, realise any of its assets

[95] *Post*, p. 675.
[96] ss.419(4) and 420, inserted by C.A. 1989, s.104.
[97] *National Commercial Bank of Scotland Ltd.* v. *Liquidators of Telford Grier Mackay & Co. Ltd.*, 1969 S.C. 181, followed in *Royal Bank of Scotland Ltd.* v. *Williamson*, 1972 S.L.T.(Sh.Ct.) 45, and given statutory force by s.463(4).
[98] *Post*, p. 675.

without the consent of the creditor who is entitled to the benefit of the floating charge.

From the *creditor's* point of view, the two disadvantages exemplified on page 667, *ante*, in relation to English law, apply also in Scots law, but for the protection of the creditor it is provided that a Scots company may be wound up by the court "if there is subsisting a floating charge over property comprised in the company's property and undertaking and the court is satisfied that the security of the creditor entitled to the benefit of the floating charge is in jeopardy." The security of the creditor is deemed to be in jeopardy "if the court is satisfied that events have occurred or are about to occur which render it unreasonable in the creditor's interests that the company should retain power to dispose of the property which is subject to the floating charge": Insolvency Act 1986, section 122.

Priority of charges (Scots law)

Where all or any part of a company's property is subject both to a fixed security and to a floating charge, the fixed security has as a general rule priority over the floating charge. This is always so if the fixed security is one arising by operation of law (*e.g.* by a statutory provision). If the fixed security is not of that nature (*e.g.* is a standard security over heritable property under the Conveyancing and Feudal Reform (Scotland) Act 1970), the order of ranking may be regulated by provisions in the document which creates the floating charge or in any instrument of alteration. Where the right to a fixed security has become a real right before a floating charge has attached, the fixed security has priority of ranking over the floating charge.

Where there are two or more floating charges, the charges as a general rule rank with one another according to the time of their registration with the Registrar,[99] and if received by the Registrar by the same postal delivery they rank equally with one another. Here again the order of ranking may be regulated by provisions in the document creating a floating charge or in any instrument of alteration. There is, however, the following statutory restriction on the priority which may be obtained: where the holder of a floating charge which has been registered

[99] *Post*, p. 679.

receives a written intimation of the subsequent registration of another floating charge over the same property or part of it, the preference in ranking of the first floating charge is restricted to security for:

(*a*) the holder's present advances;
(*b*) future advances which he may be required to make;
(*c*) interest due or to become due on advances within (*a*) and (*b*), above; and
(*d*) expenses or outlays reasonably incurred by the holder: section 464.

The following have priority over a floating charge:

(1) the rights of any person who has effectually executed diligence on the property or any part of it, *e.g.* an inhibition registered after the granting of a floating charge but before the appointment of receivers: *Armour and Mycroft, Petitioners*, 1983 S.L.T. 453 (O.H.): section 463;
(2) the rights of persons such as one who has sold goods to the company under a hire-purchase agreement by which the goods are still the property of such person;
(3) certain *un*secured but preferential debts: Insolvency Act 1986, section 175.[1]

Avoidance of floating charges

To prevent those in control of insolvent companies from creating floating charges to secure past debts so as to gain priority over other unsecured creditors, section 245 of the Insolvency Act 1986 provides that floating charges created within 12 months prior to the commencement of a winding up or the presentation of a successful petition for an administration order[2] are invalid unless the company was solvent immediately after the charge was created, except insofar as money was paid or goods or services supplied to the company or a debt of the company was reduced or discharged, in consideration of and at the same time as or after the creation of the charge, with interest if appropriate.

[1] *Post*, Chap. 29.
[2] *Post*, Chap. 26.

The position is different if the floating charge is created in favour of a person who is connected with the company. In such cases the ambit of the section is widened to catch floating charges created within two years of the winding up or administration petition, as appropriate, and it is of no consequence that the company was solvent immediately after granting the charge.

The difficulty therefore is to establish whether money was paid, goods or services supplied or a debt reduced or discharged in consideration of the charge. The value of any goods or services so supplied are to be valued at the cost which could reasonably be expected to be paid for goods or services supplied at that time in the ordinary course of business and on the same terms (apart from the granting of a floating charge) as those on which they were supplied to the company. Section 245 replaced section 617 of the Companies Act 1985 which invalidated floating charges created within a year of a winding up except to the amount of any cash paid to the company in consideration and at the time of the charge (unless the company was solvent immediately after granting the charge). There are several decisions on whether "cash" was paid to a company for this purpose which will be relevant to the new wording of money etc. paid to the company.

Whether cash was paid at the time when the charge was created was a question of fact for section 617, and "a payment made on account of the consideration for the security, in anticipation of its creation and in reliance on a promise to execute it, although made some days before its execution, is made at the time of its creation within the meaning of the section.[3] Section 245 expressly requires it to be paid at the same time as or after the creation of the charge. *Quaere* whether this affects that statement.[4]

The words "in consideration for the charge" in section 617 meant "in consideration of the fact that the charge exists."

A company created a floating charge to secure its overdrawn current account with its bank. *Held*: (1) Every payment made by the bank to

[3] *Per* Neville J. in *Re Columbian Fireproofing Co. Ltd.* [1910] 1 Ch. 758, at p. 765.

[4] A decision on the old law which applies the quotation is *Re F. & E. Stanton Ltd.* [1929] 1 Ch. 180.

the company after the creation of the charge was "cash paid to the company" and was made in consideration of the charge. Consequently the charge was not invalid against the liquidator, and the bank was a secured creditor as to such payments. (2) The rule in *Clayton's Case*[5] applied. Each payment by the bank after the date of the charge was a provision of "new money" and there was nothing to displace the presumption that payments in by the company after the charge should be set in the first instance against the company's debt to the bank at the date of the charge: *Re Yeovil Glove Co. Ltd.* [1965] Ch. 148 (C.A.).

Section 245 of the Insolvency Act uses the phrase "so much of the consideration as consists of." *Quaere* whether *Re Yeovil Glove Co. Ltd.* is still valid?

In *Mace Builders (Glasgow) Ltd.* v. *Lunn*[6] it was held that the effect of section 617 was simply to render the charge invalid from the date of the winding up so that where the charge was repaid prior to the winding up the section had no effect. The wording of section 245 is not identical, however, and it may be that the position is now different.[7]

Cash was held to be paid to the company although it was only paid on condition that it be applied in paying a specified debt of the company.

Payments made direct to the company's creditors, though made on the company's behalf, have been held not to be within the phrase "cash paid to the company."[8]

D. was a director of the company and a partner in the firm of D. & Co. who supplied goods to the company. The company owed D. & Co. £1,954 and D. & Co. refused to supply any more goods until this debt was paid. In March D., who wished to save the company, agreed to lend the company £3,000 on the security of a floating charge if the company would, out of this sum, pay £1,954 to D. & Co. This was done. The company was insolvent at the time. In July the company went into liquidation. *Held*, the floating charge was valid, the whole £3,000 being cash paid to the company: *Re Matthew Ellis Ltd.* [1933] 1 Ch. 458.

The cash must, however, have been intended to benefit the company and not certain creditors.

[5] (1816) 1 Mer. 572.
[6] (1986) 130 S.J. 839 (C.A.).
[7] See also *Re Parkes Garage* [1929] 1 Ch. 139.
[8] *Libertas-Kommerz GmbH* v. *Johnston*, 1977 S.C. 191 (O.H.).

An insolvent company granted a floating charge to Z. to secure £900. The money was provided by D., for whom Z. was a nominee, and the same day as it was paid to the company the company paid £350 each to B. and S. for directors' fees and £200 to D., the amount guaranteed by D. in respect of the company's overdraft. Within 12 months the company went into liquidation. *Held*, the charge was invalid, as its object was to benefit B., S. and D. and not the company—in substance, no cash was paid to the company: *Re Destone Fabrics Ltd.* [1941] Ch. 319 (C.A.).

Cash was held not to be paid to the company where the substance of the transaction was the substitution of a better security for the company's debts.[9] It was also said that the section would apply irrespective of the motives of the chargee.[10] There seems no reason to suppose that the position will be any different under the new section.

Preferences and transactions at an undervalue

Any charge made by a company within *six* months[11] before the commencement of winding up, or presentation of a successful administration petition is void if it is a preference of any of the company's creditors, or, within a two year period, if it is part of a transaction at an undervalue, or within a three year period, if it is part of an extortionate credit transaction: Insolvency Act 1986, sections 238–244, Chap. 29, *post*.

Registration of Charges

Charges created by a company are required to be registered (1) in the company's own register of charges, and (2) with the registrar of companies.

Registration in company's own register of charges

Section 411 provides that every company must keep at its registered office a register of *all* charges over the company's property, whether or not they are also registrable with the registrar. A charge for this purpose means any form of fixed or

[9] *Re G. T. Whyte & Co. Ltd.* [1983] BCLC 311.
[10] *Ibid. per* Nourse J., p. 317.
[11] Two years for persons connected with the company.

floating security[12] (except one arising by law[13]) over the property or future property of the company, wherever it is situated: section 395. The register must give—

(*a*) a short description of the property charged;
(*b*) the amount of the charge;
(*c*) the names of the persons entitled thereto except in the case of bearer securities.

In addition the company must keep copies of all such instruments of charge, although a copy of one of a series of uniform debentures will suffice: section 411.

The omission to comply with section 411 merely results in a fine on every officer who is knowingly a party to the omission. The validity of the charge is *not* affected.[14]

The copies of the instruments of charge and also the company's register of charges, are open to the inspection of any creditor or member of the company without fee and to the general public on payment of a fee. That fee and opening hours are to be designated by the Secretary of State. In addition any person may request a copy of the instrument of charge or of the entry in the register, which must be sent to him within 10 days: section 412.

Registration with the registrar

Part XII of the 1985 Act in relation to the registration of company charges at Companies House was modified and rewritten in its entirety by Part IV of the 1989 Act.[15] The provisions for England and Scotland are now virtually identical, and are dealt with together. Unlike registration in the company's own register, the system of registration with the registrar can substantially affect the validity of a charge. In essence failure to register a charge or to register it accurately can make that charge void against a later registered charge, a subsequently appointed liquidator or administrator of the company or a subsequent purchaser of the property charged.

[12] *Quaere* whether this includes *all* retention of title clauses.
[13] *e.g.* an unpaid vendor's lien, solicitor's lien, etc.
[14] *Wright* v. *Horton* (1887) 12 App.Cas. 371.
[15] For an account of the provisions prior to the 1989 Act see the previous (13th) edition of this work, pp. 641 *et seq.*

Charges requiring registration

As we have seen, a charge is now defined in section 395 as any form of security interest over the property of a company other than an interest arising by operation of law,[16] wherever the property is situated. Property includes future property for this purpose. But not all such charges are registrable.

Section 396 provides for five classes of registrable charges.

(*a*) A charge on land or any interest in land.[17]
This category does not include rent charges, but any deposit of title deeds by a company to secure a debt is registrable since it creates an equitable charge on the land and not just a lien on the documents.[18]

(*b*) A charge on goods (or any interest in goods)
Goods in this context means any tangible moveable property.[19] The charge need not be in writing but the section excludes pledges and other possessory securities, *i.e.*, where the chargee is entitled to take possession of the goods or documents of title.

(c) A charge on:
- (i) goodwill
- (ii) intellectual property
- (iii) book debts
- (iv) uncalled share capital or unpaid calls on shares.

Intellectual property is defined as patents, trade marks, service marks, registered designs and copyright or design rights,

[16] These were excepted under the previous law, see, *e.g. London and Cheshire Insurance Co.* v. *Laplagrene Property Co.* [1971] Ch. 499 (unpaid vendor's lien). Whether a transaction amounts to a charge is a question of substance not of form: *Curtain Dream plc* v. *Churchill Merchanting Ltd.* [1990] BCC 341.

[17] Registration of such charges will also be necessary under the Land Registration Act 1925 or the Land Charges Act 1972, to protect the chargee against subsequent purchasers of the land. In Scotland the standard security requires to be recorded in the Register of Sasines or registered in the Land Register of Scotland.

[18] *Re Wallis & Simmonds* (*Builders*) *Ltd.* [1974] 1 W.L.R. 391.

[19] Thus it cannot include choses in action, *e.g.* shares in a racehorse, see *Re Sugar Properties* (*Derisley Wood*) *Ltd.* (1987) 3 BCC 88. It would, however, include computer software: *Welsh Development Agency* v. *Export Finance Co. Ltd.* [1990] BCC 393. In Scotland the definition is corporeal moveable property.

and any licence under or in respect of any such right. Book debts are still not defined as such but do include book debts of another company assigned to the company. What amounts to a book debt remains therefore a matter for the courts to decide.[20]

If a company which has entered into hire purchase agreements for the disposal of its products deposits the agreements on security for advances, there is a charge on the company's book debts.[21]

A charge on future book debts is registrable,[22] but where the subject matter of the charge at the date of its creation is the benefit of a contract, *e.g.* of insurance, it cannot be regarded as a charge which requires registration merely because it might ultimately result in a book debt.[23] The test is whether there is a charge on future book debts as and when they arise or simply an assignment of a contingent contractual right.[24]

(*d*) A charge securing an issue of debentures.[25]
(*e*) A floating charge on the whole or part of the company's property.

The section expressly excludes from registration, a ship-owner's lien on subfreights, which overrules a much criticised decision to the contrary.[26]

In deciding whether a charge requires registration, its nature at the date of creation, or at the date when the property subject to it is acquired by the company, is the relevant factor. If a charge is only partly within a registrable category then the registration provisions apply only to that part. The Secretary of State may change the categories of registrable charges by subsequent regulations. There are, for example, still surprising

[20] Thus the position of a credit balance at a bank remains in doubt following Harman J.'s express disclaimer in *Re Permanent Houses* (*Holdings*) *Ltd.* (1989) 5 BCC 151 that his decision in *Re Brightlife* [1987] Ch. 200 indicated that it could never be a book debt for registration purposes. In Scotland see *Tay Valley Joinery Ltd.* v. *C. F. Financial Services Ltd.*, 1987 S.L.T. 207.
[21] *Independent Automatic Sales Ltd.* v. *Knowles & Foster* [1962] 1 W.L.R. 974.
[22] *Ibid.*
[23] *Paul & Frank Ltd.* v. *Discount Bank* (*Overseas*) *Ltd.* [1967] Ch. 348.
[24] *Re Brush Aggregates Ltd.* [1986] BCLC 320.
[25] This means a group of debentures or an amount of debenture stock secured by the same charge: s.419(1).
[26] *Re Welsh Irish Ferries Ltd.* [1986] Ch. 471.

gaps in the system, *e.g.* a charge on shares held by a company in a subsidiary does not require registration.[27]

Duty to register prescribed particulars

It is the duty of a company creating a registrable charge or acquiring property subject to a registrable charge to deliver the prescribed particulars of the charge in the prescribed form to the registrar (in Cardiff or Edinburgh, as appropriate) within 21 days of such creation or acquisition. There are default fines which may be imposed on the company and its officials if this is not done, but the particulars may be delivered by any other person interested in the charge. There is no longer any duty on the company to send the instrument of charge itself to the registrar or for the registrar to check the furnished particulars against that instrument: section 398.

It is for the registrar to decide what particulars he requires, but he may under section 415 include details of any negative pledge, *i.e.* of any undertaking not to create other charges ranking in priority or *pari passu* with the charge.[28] Where the registrable charge is one securing an issue of debentures, the company must also deliver particulars within 21 days of each debenture or parcel of debenture stock being taken up, in addition to the particulars about the charge itself: section 408.[29] Failure to register the subsequent particulars does not affect the validity of the debentures, however.

Registration and the registrar's certificate

The registrar is obliged to keep a register of charges (in whatever form he decides) in which are filed the prescribed particulars and other notifiable matters; section 397(1)(2). The registrar is required to send the company, the chargee and any other person who delivered the particulars for registration a copy of both the particulars and his note of the date of delivery.

Under the previous system the registrar automatically sent out a certificate of registration which was conclusive evidence that all registration procedures had been complied with. This

[27] See the Jenkins Report (1962), para. 306.
[28] This is important when assessing the constructive notice effect of the register: see p. 686, *post*.
[29] For other notifications requirements, see p. 687, *post*.

protected the lender against all mistakes in the registration.[30] Now the lender must request a new style certificate which simply states the date on which the particulars were delivered to the registrar. This is conclusive evidence only that the particulars were not delivered on a later date and provides a rebuttable presumption that they were not delivered on an earlier date. It provides no guarantee therefore as to the accuracy of the particulars since the registrar no longer checks those against the charge itself: sections 397, 398(5). Thus although the certificate is useful in establishing whether delivery of the particulars took place within the required 21 days it is no guarantee that the charge has been correctly registered, *i.e.* either as to the amount of the loan or the extent of the security—accuracy can only be checked by a search of the register. Failure to register accurate particulars can have serious consequences.[31]

Effect of non-registration or late delivery

Failure to register the revised particulars within the 21 day period not only invokes the criminal law against those responsible,[32] but more importantly renders the charge void (subject to section 44, below) as against any administrator[33] or liquidator[34] of the company appointed under insolvency proceedings commencing after the creation of the charge and any other person who acquires, for value, an interest or right in the property charged after its creation, *e.g.* a subsequent chargee or purchaser[35]: section 399. The company itself cannot claim this invalidity[36] and an unregistered security which has been realised prior to the insolvency proceedings or acquisition of an interest is valid.[37]

Section 399 only applies to charges created by a company and not to property acquired by a company which is subject to a

[30] See, *e.g. R.* v. *Registrar of Companies ex p. Central Bank of India* [1986] Q.B. 1114.
[31] *Infra.*
[32] It is also a relevant factor under the Company Directors Disqualification Act 1986, *ante*, p. 353.
[33] *Post*, Chap. 26.
[34] *Post*, Chap. 27.
[35] The previous law did not apply to purchasers for value.
[36] *Re Monolithic Building Co. Ltd.* [1915] 1 Ch. 643.
[37] *Mercantile Bank of India* v. *Chartered Bank of India* [1937] 1 All E.R. 231.

charge, although the duty to register applies to both. If a charge does become void under this section the whole sum secured plus interest becomes repayable on demand: section 407. There are some limits on this voidness of unregistered charges—see below, and special provision is made for the late delivery of the particulars.

Section 400 allows such late delivery, without a court order as previously required, and in that case the charge will not in general be void as against any liquidator, administrator, chargee or purchaser for value who acquired his rights over the property after the date of the late delivery. In other words, delivery of the particulars after the 21 day period takes effect from that date. The exception to this is where at the time of late delivery the company is either unable to pay its debts or becomes so unable as a consequence of the transaction concerned.[38] In that case the charge is still void against a liquidator or administrator appointed under insolvency proceedings beginning within two years of the delivery in the case of a floating charge created in favour of a connected person,[39] one year in the case of any other floating charge and six months in any other case. Thus there can be a wait and see period of up to two years as to the validity of such a charge.

Effect of incomplete or inaccurate registration

Because the registrar no longer provides any statement as to the accuracy of the particulars filed for registration the new registration system makes provision for the possibility that they will either not be completely accurate at the time of presentation or may become inaccurate as the result of subsequent changes. Prior to the 1989 Act the registrar's certificate was conclusive for all purposes that the charge was validly registered. Under the new system, as we have seen, the certificate only relates to the timing of the furnishing of the particulars. For that reason the chargee must be careful to check the contents of the particulars and monitor changes to the charge. To assist him, section 401 allows for the delivery of further particulars, signed by both the chargor and chargee. These may either correct mistakes in the original particulars or

[38] As defined in s.123 I.A. 1986.
[39] See s.249 IA 1986, *ante*, p. 675.

reflect changes in the terms of the charge. There is no 21 day period so that delivery should take place as soon as possible.

Failure to correct such an error or to update the particulars may be costly. Under section 402 any charge is potentially void to the extent that the rights of the chargee are not completely and accurately[40] reflected in the registered particulars. Thus any increase in the powers of the chargee which is not registered may prove to be void. The charge is void to the extent of the inaccuracy against any liquidator or administrator appointed under insolvency proceedings[41] which begin whilst the inaccuracy persists unless the court orders otherwise on the basis that no harm has been done to any unsecured creditor since none arose during the inaccuracy or where no unsecured creditor has been misled. The charge is also void to the extent of the inaccuracy against a subsequent purchaser or chargee unless the court orders otherwise on the basis that he did not rely on the registered particulars.

If a charge becomes partially void as the result of an incorrect registration the whole of the sum secured becomes payable at once on demand: section 407.

Restrictions on voidness of unregistered or inaccurately registered charges

It would be clearly unfair if a charge which is totally or partially void for non-registration suffered as against a later charge which is itself not completely registered. Thus section 404 provides that a charge is not void against a later charge unless the particulars of the later charge, which contain rights inconsistent with the earlier charge, are delivered within 21 days of the creation of the later charge or before complete and accurate particulars are delivered of the earlier charge. It follows that the later chargee cannot rely on rights which it fails to register accurately as against an earlier unregistered charge.

Further under section 405(1) no charge is void for incomplete registration or non-registration as against a subsequent chargee

[40] This does not include any omission or inaccuracy as to the name of the chargee: s.402(6).

[41] Defined in s.419(5) as the commencement of any winding up or administration procedure. There does not appear to be any wait and see period as with late registration under section 400.

or purchaser of the same property where that acquisition is expressly subject to the earlier charge.[42] In addition under section 405(2) no charge is void as against the liquidator, administrator, later chargee or purchaser of the property charged where the latter's rights accrue after the date when the company which created the charge has disposed of the whole of its interest in the property. Thus if a company sells property subject to an unregistered charge the subsequent insolvency of the company will not affect the validity of the charge.

Finally under section 406 where property is sold by a chargee or receiver to a purchaser for value acting in good faith,[43] that purchaser takes free of any problem that the charge might be void for non or incomplete registration. Once the charge has been realised the invalidity disappears. The section expressly provides that the purchaser is not concerned to see or inquire as to whether the charge is or becomes void. Thus purchasers[44] are not concerned with any defect in the charge. Instead the chargee (or receiver) must hold the proceeds of sale upon a statutory trust. In essence this requires him to pay the money in the following order:

(i) to repay any sums owed on a prior encumbrance to which the sale was not made subject;
(ii) to pay the costs of the sale;
(iii) to repay the chargees' own security if effective and any effective charge ranking equally to it;
(iv) to repay any effective later charges; and
(v) to pay any residue to the company.

No charge is effective for this purpose if it would be void as against a liquidator or administrator.

Effect of registration on priority of charges

So far we have considered the effect of non-registration or incomplete registration of a charge. If a charge is completely

[42] This overrules the earlier position: see, *e.g. Re Monolithic Building Co. Ltd.* [1915] 1 Ch. 643.
[43] This term is not defined. See the definition in s.35A, *ante*, p. 116.
[44] The section protects purchasers for value in good faith who acquire title from a person who is not such a person who in time acquired it from the chargee or receiver: s.406(6).

and accurately registered, however, does this have any effect on the rules for priority of charges discussed above?[45] In general the answer is no but there is one significant feature which can affect the common law rules on priority. Under section 416(1) any person taking a charge over a company's property is deemed to have constructive notice of any matter which required registration and was disclosed on the register at the time of the charge's creation. It is important to note that there is no constructive notice of anything which is not required to be registered. This may therefore affect the priority of a later chargee who may take with constructive notice of an earlier charge as the result of this section.[46]

Under section 416(2), however, there is no constructive notice for any other person, *e.g.* a subsequent purchaser of the property, simply by virtue of registration. Nor is such a person to be fixed with notice of any matter as the result of a failure to search the register in the course of making such inquiries as he ought to have made. Thus a purchaser will not be fixed with notice of an equitable charge by virtue of its registration (and so be liable to it) unless he has actual notice of the charge.

Additional notification requirements

In addition to the provisions relating to a series of debentures,[47] section 409 requires notification to the registrar of the appointment or cessation of office of a receiver or manager within seven days of the order of appointment or cessation.[48] There are no civil consequences of failure to do so, but such failure may lead to a fine.

Section 410 allows the Secretary of State to provide by regulations for the registration of certain events affecting the nature of the security under a registered English floating charge, or the exercise of powers conferred by a registered fixed or floating charge or by a court order. In particular this may apply to automatic crystallisation clauses[49] and may specify that in the

[45] *Ante*, p. 668.
[46] In all other areas of company law such constructive notice has been abolished by s.711A.
[47] s.408.
[48] *Ante*, p. 664.
[49] *Ante*, p. 664.

absence of such notification any such crystallisation will be ineffective.

Release of registered charges

A memorandum of discharge signed by the company and the chargee may be delivered to the registrar who is required to file it and note the date of its delivery to him in the register. A copy of the memorandum and his note must be sent by the registrar to the company, the chargee and anyone who delivered the memorandum: section 403.

If the memorandum is inaccurate and the charge continues to affect the property of the company, the charge is effectively de-registered and accordingly becomes void as against any liquidator, administrator, chargee or purchaser who acquire their rights after the date of delivery of the memorandum.

Remedies of Debenture Holders

1. If a debenture confers no charge, a debenture holder is an ordinary unsecured creditor. Thus, if there is default in the payment of principal or interest he may (*a*) sue for the principal or interest and, after obtaining judgment, levy execution against the company,[50] or (*b*), as will be explained later,[51] petition either for an administration order or for the winding up of the company by the court on the ground that the company is unable to pay its debts.

2. When a charge is conferred on the company's assets by way of security, and default is made in the payment of principal or interest, a debenture holder, or the trustees where there is a trust deed, may:

(*a*) sue for the principal or interest; or
(*b*) present a petition for an administration order; or
(*c*) present a petition for the winding up of the company; or
(*d*) exercise any powers conferred by the debenture or the trust deed, *e.g.* of appointing a receiver or administrative receiver of the assets charged, of selling the assets

[50] The Scots equivalent is "do diligence on the decree obtained."
[51] *Post*, Chaps. 26 and 27.

charged or of taking possession of the assets and carrying on the business; or

(*e*) if the debenture or the trust deed does not contain powers in that behalf, apply to the court for:

(i) the appointment of a receiver or a receiver and manager; or

(ii) an order for sale or foreclosure.

A debenture or trust deed will normally contain an express power to appoint a receiver or administrative receiver of, or to sell, the company's assets charged by way of security. If there is no express power there will be an implied power under the Law of Property Act 1925, s.101,[52] if the debenture or trust deed is under seal. Failing an express or an implied power, an application may be made to the court for the appointment of a receiver or an order for sale. A company's inability to pay its debts for the purpose of appointing a receiver is to be assessed at the date of appointment. Further where the receiver is to be appointed by a deed, his appointment is not invalidated by an appointment in another manner—that operates as an agreement to perfect the power if necessary.[53]

Where the debenture is an "all moneys" debenture (*e.g.* one for all sums owed to a bank) the demand for payment need not specify the exact sum due and a receiver may be appointed once reasonable time to make payment has passed.[54] Similarly a demand for an amount less than the full amount due will be sufficient for the appointment of a receiver, although there is no authority if the demand is excessive, *i.e.* for more than the amount due.[55]

In England, where there are numerous debentures of the same class, a *debenture holders' action* is usually brought. This is brought by one debenture holder on behalf of himself and all other debenture holders of the same class as himself. In it a claim may be made for:

[52] Not applicable to Scotland.
[53] *Byblos Bank S.A.L.* v. *Al Khudhairy*, *Financial Times*, November 7, 1986.
[54] *Bank of Baroda* v. *Panessar*, [1987] Ch. 335.
[55] *N.R.G. Vision Ltd.* v. *Churchfield Leasing Ltd.* (1988) 4 BCC 56.

(1) a declaration that the debenture holders are entitled to a (first) charge on the property of the company;
(2) if there is a trust deed, the enforcement of the trusts;
(3) an account of what is due to the debenture holders;
(4) the enforcement of the charge by sale or foreclosure;
(5) the appointment of a receiver and manager.[56]

An order for foreclosure will only be made if all the debenture holders of the same class as the plaintiff are before the court. If the assets require immediate protection an application for the appointment of a receiver is made.[57]

In Scotland, prior to the Companies (Floating Charges and Receivers) (Scotland) Act 1972, there was no provision for the appointment of receivers, and this constituted a major difference between Scots and English law in the remedies available to the holder of a floating charge and in the procedure for enforcing the security. On the recommendation of the Scottish Law Commission[58] receiverships were introduced to Scotland by the Act of 1972. Though based in general on the English model, the Scottish provisions form a distinct self-contained code and are given separate consideration below.

The various remedies are discussed in the following chapters.

[56] Palmer's *Company Precedents* (16th ed.), Pt. III, p. 498.
[57] *Re Continental Oxygen Co.* [1897] 1 Ch. 511.
[58] *Report on the Companies* (*Floating Charges*) (*Scotland*) *Act 1961*, (1970) Cmnd. 4336, para. 38.

Chapter 24

CORPORATE INSOLVENCY

THE Insolvency Act 1985 enacted major changes to the legal regulation of both corporate and personal insolvencies. This process began in 1976 when the Department of Trade announced the setting up of a Review Committee on Insolvency Law and Practice, which was actually established in 1977, under the chairmanship of Sir Kenneth Cork, and thus became known as the Cork Committee. The Final Report of that Committee led first to a Government White Paper, *A Revised Framework for Insolvency Law*[1] in 1984 and then the Insolvency Act 1985, which adopted some but by no means all of the Cork Committee's recommendations. The Insolvency Act 1985 directly affected companies, not only by introducing new concepts and controls but also by amending (or repealing) several sections of the Companies Act 1985 concerned with corporate insolvency. The interraction of the two Acts led to the consolidation of Parts XIX, XX and XXI of the Companies Act 1985 and the Insolvency Act 1985 into the Insolvency Act 1986.

The Insolvency Act 1986 is thus the major Act which applies to this and the next five chapters. Chapter 25 deals with receivers and the concept, introduced by the Insolvency Act 1985, of an administrative receiver, usually appointed by a debenture holder as the most efficient way of protecting his security in the face of possible insolvency. Such appointments may or may not lead to the ultimate liquidation of the company. Chapter 26 deals with one alternative to the liquidation of an insolvent company—the making of an administration order. Such orders were also introduced by the Insolvency Act 1985. Chapters 27 to 29 are, on the other hand, concerned with liquidations, that is to say the effective demise of the company, which may in fact arise otherwise than on an insolvency. The

[1] 1984 Cmnd. 9174.

majority of liquidations, however, are caused by such an eventuality. We have already discussed, in Chapter 15, one other aspects of insolvency law introduced by the 1985 Insolvency Act, *i.e.* that in relation to the disqualification of directors of insolvent companies.[2]

The present chapter is concerned with three general matters. The new framework for corporate insolvency, the controls on insolvency practitioners involved in the various aspects of insolvency, *e.g.* as administrative receivers, liquidators, administrators etc, and a second alternative to the liquidation of an insolvent company—a voluntary arrangement, *i.e.* a composition with creditors.[3]

The New Framework for Insolvency

One of the two main themes of the Insolvency Act 1986 was to tighten up the controls on the abuses of the corporate insolvency system. These included less than scrupulous liquidators, dubious acts by directors of companies which they knew to be hopelessly insolvent, and the general updating of a system which in large dated from the Bankruptcy Act of 1914. The second aim of the legislation was to provide genuine alternatives to the drastic remedy of liquidation for an insolvent company, where such remedies would provide a better opportunity for the creditors to recover their debts and for the companies concerned to remain in existence. Measures designed to assist in the first aim include the regulation of insolvency practitioners,[4] the disqualification of directors' provisions (including the concept of wrongful trading[5]) and the many amendments to the laws relating to receiverships and liquidations, including the new statutory concept of an administrative receiver. To achieve the second aim the Act introduced the new administration procedure[6] and a simplified procedure for a composition with creditors.[7]

[2] *Ante*, p. 355. These were in fact the most controversial provisions of the Insolvency Act 1985 and also the first to come into force (in April 1986).
[3] For the other alternative see Chap. 26, *post*.
[4] *Post*, p. 693.
[5] *Ante*, pp. 355, 417.
[6] *Post*, Chap. 26.
[7] *Post*, p. 695.

These statutory provisions are supplemented by many rules and regulations. In particular, under section 411 of the Insolvency Act 1986, the Lord Chancellor, with the concurrence of the Secretary of State for Trade and Industry and in consultation with the Insolvency Rules Committee (I.A. 1986 s.413) is empowered to make rules and regulations for the purpose of giving effect to the Act; most of the rules are to be found in the Insolvency Rules 1986.[8] Also, by s.419 of the Act, the Secretary of State is enabled to make regulations relating to Qualified Insolvency Practitioners.[9]

The Insolvency Act 1986 also retained and redefined the role of official receivers for England and Wales in all types of corporate proceedings.[10] In effect, although they are civil servants under the control of the Secretary of State official receivers are also officers of the court and are attached to the High Court or to one or more County Court having insolvency jurisdiction. They assume the functions and responsibilities specified in the Act or the Rules in those cases falling within the jurisdiction of the court to which they are attached. Deputy Official Receivers can be appointed and have the same status and functions as an official receiver.

By virtue of section 426 of the Insolvency Act 1986 the courts in each part of the United Kingdom are required to recognise and enforce orders made by the courts of all other parts of the UK in relation to insolvency law. Thus where property exists *e.g.* in Scotland, but the insolvency proceedings are taking place in London, all such property can be protected and claimed for the benefit of creditors.[11]

INSOLVENCY PRACTITIONERS

Part XIII of the Insolvency Act 1986 subjects insolvency practitioners to proper regulation by ensuring that they are

[8] S.I. 1986 No. 1925 as amended in S.I. 1987 No. 1919, S.I. 1987 No. 1959, and S.I. 1988 No 1739. For regulations made under the Rules see S.I. 1986 No. 1994. For Scotland see the Insolvency (Scotland) Rules 1986 (S.I. 1986 No. 1915 (s.139) as amended.

[9] See Insolvency Practitioners Regulations 1986, S.I. 1986 No. 1995 as amended by S.I. 1986 No. 2247.

[10] I.A. 1986, ss.399–401.

[11] This replaced a much narrower and more difficult provision in the Bankrupty Act 1914.

"qualified" within the terms of section 390. To act as an insolvency practitioner in relation to a company when not qualified to do so is a criminal offence under section 389. For this purpose "acting as an insolvency practitioner" means acting either as a liquidator,[12] administrator,[13] administrative receiver[14] or as the supervisor of a composition with creditors[15]: section 388. This offence is one of strict liability—the knowledge of the person concerned is irrelevant. It does not, however, apply to the official receiver. The official receiver does not come within the terms of section 388 and therefore escapes the qualification requirements of section 390 and the criminal penalty in section 389; the control exercised over such public officials within the Department of Trade and Industry is deemed sufficient safeguard.

Section 390 sets out the requirements for qualification. Only an individual can be qualified to act as an insolvency practitioner.[16] He must be currently authorised to act as an insolvency practitioner either by virtue of membership of a professional body recognised under section 391[17] or by a direct authorisation granted by a competent authority set up by the Secretary of State,[18] and must have provided the requisite security for the proper performance of his functions.[19]

Even if a person is so qualified to act he may be disqualified if (a) he is an undischarged bankrupt,[20] or (b) he is subject to a disqualification order under the Company Directors Disqualification Act 1986[21] or (c) he is a patient under the Mental Health Act 1983 or the Mental Health (Scotland) Act 1984.[22]

12 *Post*, p. 766.
13 *Post*, Chap. 26.
14 *Post*, Chap. 25.
15 *Post*, p. 699.
16 I.A. 1986, s.390(1).
17 See Insolvency Practitioners (Recognised Professional Bodies) Order 1986, S.I. 1986 No. 1764.
18 *Ibid*, s.390(2)(*b*).
19 s.390(3); by means of a fidelity bond in the amount of £250,000 plus an additional sum varying with the value of the assets in relation to which he is to act in the particular case: Insolvency Practitioners Regulations 1986, r. 10.
20 See I.A. 1986, ss.278–282, and Bankruptcy (Scotland) Act 1985, ss.54–56.
21 These are the same provisions as apply to the disqualification of a person from acting as a director. They are set out *ante*, p. 352.
22 *i.e* someone who has been judicially assessed to be mentally incapable of managing and administering his affairs.

Most individuals will qualify by virtue of being members[23] of a recognised professional body who are permitted to act as such by the rules of that body. The bodies currently recognised by the Secretary of State include the established accountancy bodies, the Law Society and the Insolvency Practitioners Association. The intention is that the control exercised by such bodies over their members shall be equivalent to that exercised by the competent authority over those directly authorised by that body under sections 392 to 398 of the Insolvency Act 1986. For those who cannot qualify as a qualified insolvency practitioner by virtue of membership of a recognised professional body, those sections of the Act allow a direct application to the competent authority appointed to deal with such matters.[24] The Secretary of State is the competent authority for this purpose and he must grant the application if satisfied that the applicant is a fit and proper person to be an insolvency practitioner and satisfies prescribed educational and experience requirements: Section 393. Regulations set out the matters which he is to take into account and prescribe the educational and other requirements.[25] Such authorisation is for a maximum of 3 years and may be withdrawn earlier on his ceasing to comply with the s.393 requirements or where he was authorised by virtue of false, misleading or inaccurate information, There is a right to make representations before a refusal or withdrawal of authorisation and a right to appeal against an adverse decision to the Insolvency Practitioners Tribunal.[26]

VOLUNTARY ARRANGEMENTS—COMPOSITIONS WITH CREDITORS

Sections 1 to 7 of the Insolvency Act 1986 introduced a new procedure which enables an insolvent or potentially insolvent company to come to a legally binding arrangement with its creditors. If the procedure is complied with it will bind all the

[23] This includes those who, although not members, are subject to the rules of a recognised body in the practice of their profession: I.A., s.391.

[24] I.A. 1986, s.419. The fee is currently £200.

[25] Insolvency Practitioners Regulations 1986. (S.I. 1986 No. 1995), regs. 4–9.

[26] I.A. 1986, ss.395, 396. This Tribunal is governed by Schedule 7 to I.A. 1986, and by the Insolvency Practitioners Tribunal (Conduct of Investigations) Rules 1986. (S.I. 1986 No. 952).

creditors, even those who have not agreed to it (I.A. 1986, s.5(2)) and so perhaps will avoid a liquidation. There are alternative methods of effecting such a scheme under sections 425 to 427[27] of the Companies Act 1985 or section 110 of the Insolvency Act 1986[28] but these procedures were not designed expressly for the purpose of enabling an insolvent company to rationalise its affairs and proved to be cumbersome in practice for such a purpose. Schemes of arrangement under sections 425 to 427 require the court's involvement at every stage and the court's ultimate consent. Schemes of reconstruction under section 110 do not bind dissentient creditors. The essence of the Insolvency Act scheme is to simplify both the procedure and the court's involvement whilst maintaining the ability to bind all creditors to the scheme if the requisite procedure is complied with.

Implementing a voluntary arrangement

Section 1 of the Insolvency Act 1986 allows either a liquidator or administrator of a company (if it is in liquidation[29] or subject to an administration order[30]) or, if there is no liquidator or administrator, the directors, to make a proposal to the company and to its creditors for a composition in satisfaction of its debts or a scheme of arrangement of its affairs, to be known as a voluntary arrangement.[31] This proposal must provide for some person who is qualified to act as an insolvency practitioner in relation to the company[32] to act as the *nominee* of the scheme, *i.e.* as trustee or otherwise for the purpose of implementing the scheme. It is a criminal offence for an unqualified person to act as a nominee.[33]

Where the nominee is not the liquidator or administrator, he must observe the formalities in section 2 of the Insolvency Act

[27] See *post*, Chap. 30.
[28] *Ibid.* See also administration orders, *post*, Chap. 26.
[29] See *post*, Chap. 27.
[30] See *post*, Chap. 26.
[31] For a discussion of the meaning of "scheme of arrangement" see *post*, Chap. 30.
[32] This is someone qualified by virtue of s.390 of the I.A. 1986 and not connected with the company so as to be in breach of the professional or regulatory rules.
[33] I.A. 1986, ss.388, 389.

1986 which involve the scrutiny by him of the soundness of the proposed arrangement and the submission of a report to the court stating whether in his opinion meetings of the company and of its creditors should be summoned to consider the proposal, and, if so, the date, time and place he proposes the meetings should be held. In effect he is required to state that the scheme is worth pursuing.

No such report is needed where the nominee is the liquidator or administrator; proper scrutiny by such office holders is assumed. In such a case the liquidator or administrator may proceed directly by virtue of section 3(2) of the Insolvency Act 1986 to summon meetings of the company and its creditors to consider the proposal for such a time, date and place as he shall think fit. Following a positive report by a nominee other than a liquidator or administrator, under section 2 of the Insolvency Act, that nominee should call the meetings as stated in that report unless the court orders otherwise: I.A. 1986 section 3(1). Section 3(3) requires every creditor of the company of whose claim and address the nominee is aware to be given notice of the creditors' meeting. There is no requirement to hold separate meetings for separate classes of creditors[34] which is a feature of schemes of arrangement under section 425 to 427 of the Companies Act 1985.[35]

Consideration of a voluntary arrangement

It is for the two meetings convened by the nominee to decide whether to approve the proposed composition or scheme, with or without modifications. Any such modification is allowed, including a change in the nominee, subject to three limitations. First no modification is allowed if the proposal would thereby cease to comply with the terms of section 1 of the Insolvency Act, *i.e.* it would no longer be a voluntary arrangement as there defined. Second no modification can affect a secured creditor's rights to enforce his security without his consent,[36] and third no modification can interfere with the rights of a preferred creditor,

[34] See *post*, p. 841.
[35] See *post*, Chap. 30.
[36] See *ante*, p. 688.

either as against ordinary creditors or other preferred creditors[37] The Insolvency Rules 1986 regulate the conduct of the meetings and it is for the chairman to make a report of the result to the court and other prescribed persons: I.A. 1986, section 4.

If both the company and creditors' meetings approve the proposal in identical terms, the scheme or composition "takes effect as if made by the company at the creditor's meeting," and binds every person who in accordance with the rules had notice of, and was entitled to vote at, that meeting (whether or not he was present or represented at the meeting) as if he were a party to the voluntary arrangement": I.A. 1986, section 5(1), (2). There can be no such effect if only one meeting approves the scheme or the meetings approve different proposals (*e.g.* by inserting different modifications). Once the arrangement is duly approved a supplier of gas, electricity and other public utilities cannot make it a precondition of any further supply that outstanding charges in respect of earlier supplies are met.[38]

If a proposal is approved and the company is in liquidation or subject to an administration order the court may stay the winding up proceedings or discharge the administration order or do anything to facilitate the scheme. No such order can be made within 28 days from the date when the court received the reports of the meeting since that is the period allowed for the meetings' approval to be challenged in the courts,[39] or at any time when such a challenge is under consideration by the courts: I.A. 1986, section 5(3), (4).

Challenge to a voluntary arrangement

Within 28 days of the report of the meeting having been made to the court, anyone who was entitled to vote at either meeting, the nominee or his replacement or the liquidator or administrator (if any) can challenge the approval of the scheme by an application to the court. This challenge can, however, only be made on one of two grounds: either that the scheme will

[37] Preferred creditors are defined in the same way as for a liquidation except that they are calculated by reference to the date of the approval of the proposal if there is no liquidation or administration order in force: I.A. 1986, s. 387. See *post*, p. 822.

[38] S.233 I.A. 1986 and see *post*, p. 768.

[39] See below.

unfairly prejudice[40] the interests of a creditor, member or contributory[41] of the company, or there has been some material irregularity at or in relation to either of the meetings: I.A. 1986, section 6(1), (2), (3).

If the court is satisfied that the challenge is a valid one it can revoke or suspend the approval or approvals in question or order further meetings to be held to consider any revised proposal, or to reconsider the original proposal in a proper manner: I.A. 1986, section 6(4), (5), (6).

It is important to note that section 6(7) of the Insolvency Act 1985 provides that unless a challenge is made under that section within the 28 day period no irregularities at the meeting can be used to invalidate the proposal.

Supervising an approved voluntary arrangement

An approved scheme which is not subject to a challenge is then put into effect. At this stage the person carrying out the nominee's functions is known as the *supervisor* (who must also be a qualified insolvency practitioner). The supervisor is under the control of the court and any interested party may apply to the court if his conduct is unsatisfactory and the court may make an order to give him directions as it thinks fit. In return the supervisor himself may apply to the court for directions and can petition for a winding up or the making of an administration order. *In extremis* the court can replace the supervisor or appoint an additional one: I.A. 1986, section 7. Under the Insolvency Rules 1986, the supervisor must keep accounts and records and must report annually upon the progress of the arrangement.

[40] There is no definition of this but the words are used in section 459 of the Companies Act 1985 in relation to the protection of a minority shareholder generally: see *ante*, p. 458. And see *Re Primlaks (UK) Ltd. (No. 2)* [1990] BCLC 234.

[41] This is the term used for a member once the company has gone into liquidation.

Chapter 25

RECEIVERS AND ADMINISTRATIVE RECEIVERS

English and Scots law

The law relating to receivers has developed quite separately in England and Scotland and for that reason this chapter is divided into two parts, the first dealing with English law and the second with Scots law. The relevant statute law is also quite separate; sections 28 to 49 of the Insolvency Act 1986 apply only to English law and sections 50 to 71 of that Act apply only to Scotland. The two sets of provisions are mutually exclusive.[1] On the other hand section 72 of the Insolvency Act 1986 provides that a receiver appointed under a floating charge in one jurisdiction may exercise his powers in the other "so far as their exercise is not inconsistent with the law applicable there."

ENGLISH LAW

Receivers and administrative receivers

A receiver takes possession of the property of the company over which he is appointed and realises it for the benefit of the debenture holder(s). He should not be confused either with a liquidator or an administrator. A liquidator is appointed with the object of winding up the company and terminating its existence whereas a receiver may be paid out and the company will continue business as before. An administrator is appointed with the object of saving a company from a winding up and acts for the benefit of the company's creditors and shareholders generally,[2] whereas a receiver is usually appointed by a specific debenture holder to protect his security under a fixed or floating

[1] See I.A. 1986, ss.28 and 50.
[2] See *post*, Chap. 26.

charge. A receiver may take possession of only part of a company's property[3] (*e.g.* of a specific asset secured by a fixed charge) but if he takes possession of the whole (or substantially the whole) of the company's property and was appointed by the holders of a floating charge, he is known as an *administrative receiver.*[4] Most receivers will in fact be administrative receivers since the major creditors appointing them, *e.g.* the banks, usually take extensive fixed and floating charges as a security. Administrative receivers are subject to special rules and given special powers by the Insolvency Act 1986. An administrative receiver must be distinguished from an administrator—their aims and intentions are quite different although they enjoy many of the same powers.

As mentioned in Chapter 23, a receiver can be appointed: (1) under an express or implied power contained in the debenture or trust deed; or (2) by an order of the court where there is no such power.

Receiver appointed by the court

While the Insolvency Act refers to receivers appointed by the court, *e.g.* in section 32, and certain of its provisions, applicable to all receiverships, would seem to apply to them, it has little to say about them. It is accepted that the court may appoint a receiver when—

(1) the principal or interest is in arrear[5]; or
(2) the company is being wound up[6]; or
(3) the security is in jeopardy.

A creditor obtained judgment against the company and was in a position to issue execution. There was no default in payment of debenture principal or interest. *Held*, the debenture holders with a floating charge on the undertaking and property of the company were

[3] I.A. 1986, s.29(1)(*a*).
[4] *Ibid.* s.29(2)(*a*). So long as his security extends to the whole or substantially the whole of the company's property, the fact that some other person has previously been appointed receiver of part of the company's property under a charge having priority to the floating charge and that consequently he does not in fact have possession of the whole or substantially the whole of the company's property, does not prevent him from coming within the definition of an administrative receiver: s.29(2)(*b*).
[5] *Bissill* v. *Bradford Tramways* [1891] W.N. 51.
[6] *Wallace* v. *Universal Automatic Machines Co.* [1894] 2 Ch. 547 (C.A.).

entitled to the appointment of a receiver because the security was in jeopardy: *Re London Pressed Hinge Co. Ltd.* [1905] 1 Ch. 576.

The security is in jeopardy when there is a risk of its being seized and taken to pay claims which are really not prior to the debenture holders' claims. Accordingly a receiver was appointed where the company's works were closed and creditors were threatening actions,[7] where execution was actually levied by a judgment creditor,[8] where a creditor's winding up petition was pending and compulsory liquidation was imminent,[9] and where the company proposed to distribute its reserve fund, which was its only asset, among its members.[10] Mere insufficiency of security is not jeopardy where the company is a going concern, is not being pressed by its creditors and there is no risk of its assets being seized by its creditors.[11]

Appointments by the court are infrequent and usually occur because there is no adequate power of appointment in the instrument of charge. The appointment is made on the application of the debenture holders. A body corporate cannot be appointed: section 30 I.A. 1986. Where the company is being wound up by the court, the court can appoint the official receiver as receiver: section 32 I.A. 1986. A receiver appointed by the court is an officer of the court, not an agent of the company or of the debenture holders.[12] He is personally liable on contracts he enters into.

B was appointed receiver and manager by the court. He gave a signed order for goods, with the words "receiver and manager" appended to his signature. *Held*, he was personally liable to pay for the goods: *Burt, Boulton and Hayward* v. *Bull* [1895] 1 Q.B. (C.A.).

However, he is entitled to an indemnity, out of the assets in his hands, for liabilities properly incurred.[13] He "supersedes the company which becomes incapable of making contracts on its own behalf."[14]

His appointment causes floating charges to crystallise and thus prevents the company from dealing with assets without his

[7] *McMahon* v. *North Kent Ironworks* [1891] 2 Ch. 148.
[8] *Edwards* v. *Standard Rolling Stock Syndicate* [1893] 1 Ch. 574.
[9] *Re Victoria Steamboats Ltd.* [1897] 1 Ch. 158.
[10] *Re Tilt Cove Copper Co.* [1913] 2 Ch. 588.
[11] *Re New York Taxicab Co.* [1913] 1 Ch. 1.
[12] *Moss S.S. Co. Ltd.* v. *Whinney* [1912] A.C. 254.
[13] *Ibid.* Where he is appointed manager of the business pending its sale within a limited time, unless that time is extended, expenditure incurred outside that time will be disallowed: *Re Wood Green Steam Laundry* [1918] 1 Ch. 423.
[14] *Ibid.* n. 12, at p. 260.

consent. To enable him to carry on the business of the company or to preserve the property of the company, the court can authorise the receiver to borrow money ranking in priority to the debentures.[15] The company's servants are automatically dismissed (but they may be entitled to damages for breach of contract) although they may be employed by the receiver.[16] As an officer of the court he cannot sue or be sued without leave of the court[17] but such leave may be given to enable an action to be brought against him by a person at whose instance he was appointed.[18] His remuneration is fixed by the court.

Notice of his appointment must appear on invoices, business letters, orders for goods, etc.: section 39 I.A. 1986.

Receivers appointed out of court

A body corporate is disqualified for appointment as receiver[19]: I.A. 1986, section 30. Also, an undischarged bankrupt is disqualified from acting as receiver or manager, unless he is appointed by the court: I.A. 1986, section 31. Persons subject to the various disqualification orders under the Company Directors Disqualification Act 1986[20] cannot act as receivers.

Since an administrative receiver, but not an ordinary receiver, is acting as an insolvency practitioner within section 388 of the Insolvency Act 1986, only a qualified insolvency practitioner may be appointed as such[21] and it is a criminal offence for anyone else so to act.[22]

Appointment of manager

If the debentures give a charge over the company's "business" or "undertaking and property," a manager may be appointed.

15 *Greenwood* v. *Algesiras Rly. Co.* [1894] 2 Ch. 205 (C.A.).
16 *Reid* v. *Explosives Co. Ltd.* (1887) 19 Q.B. 264 (C.A.).
17 *Viola* v. *Anglo American Cold Storage Co.* [1912] 2 Ch. 305; *Searle* v. *Choat* [1884] 25 Ch. 723 (C.A.).
18 *L. P. Arthur Insurance Ltd.* v. *Sisson* [1966] 1 W.L.R. 1384.
19 An attempted appointment of a body corporate is a nullity, and the body corporate does not thereby become an agent for the purpose of the Law of Property Act 1925, s.109, and the Limitation Act 1980: *Portman Building Society* v. *Gallwey* [1955] 1 All E.R. 227.
20 *Ante*, p. 352.
21 *Ante*, p. 393.
22 I.A. 1986, s.389.

The same person is usually appointed receiver and manager. A manager is appointed to carry on the business with the object of selling it as a going concern.

Time of appointment and defects in appointment

A receiver or manager is appointed when the document of appointment is handed to him or his agent provided that he accepts such an appointment by the end of the next business day after such receipt[23]; I.A. 1986, section 33. The person delivering the document to the receiver or his agent must be a person having authority to appoint and the circumstances must be such that it could fairly be said that he was appointing the receiver.[24]

If the appointment of a receiver is discovered to be invalid (*e.g.* the document of appointment was defective[25] or the charge has been set aside for non-registration) the court can order the person appointing the receiver to indemnify him against any liability which arises solely by reason of that invalidity: I.A. 1986, section 34. This section will not protect a receiver from liability arising from other causes, *e.g.* his negligence in managing the company's affairs, simply because his appointment was also invalid. The court has a complete discretion in cases where the section applies and it may well seek to establish where the blame for the invalidity lies.

Effect of appointment of receiver

When a receiver is appointed:

(1) Floating charges crystallise and become fixed. This prevents the company from dealing with the assets charged, without the receiver's consent.[26]

(2) When a receiver of the undertaking of the company is appointed, the directors' power of controlling the company is suspended. However, this does not prevent a director from

[23] Administrative receivers must confirm in writing within 7 days: Insolvency Rules 1986, r. 3.

[24] *A. Cripps & Son Ltd.* v. *Wickenden* [1973] 1 W.L.R. 944, applying *Windsor Refrigerator Co. Ltd.* v. *Branch Nominees Ltd.* [1961] Ch. 375 (C.A.).

[25] But see *Byblos Bank S.A.L.* v. *Al Khudhairy*, *Financial Times*, November 7, 1986.

[26] *Ante*, p. 664.

pursuing an action on behalf of the company if the debenture holders' interests are not thereby threatened.[27] They cannot claim remuneration from the receiver unless he employs them, but they can still claim from the company any remuneration to which they are entitled.[28]

(3) On the appointment of a receiver by the court the company's employees are dismissed.[29] As to the position where a receiver is appointed by the debenture holders, in *Re Foster Clark Ltd.'s Indenture Trusts*,[30] Plowman J. obsered[31] that there appears to be no good reason in principle why an appointment out of court of a receiver who is the agent of the company should of itself determine contracts of employment made with the company, and this observation was applied in *Re Mack Trucks (Britain) Ltd.*[32] Further, in *Griffiths* v. *Secretary of State for Social Services*[33] it was held that the mere appointment out of court by debenture holders of a receiver and manager as agent of a company did not automatically terminate an employee's subsisting contract of employment with the company where the continuation of his employment was not inconsistent with the role and functions of the receiver and manager. This reasoning was approved by the Court of Appeal in *Nicoll* v. *Cutts*[34] where the distinction between the effect of an appointment by the court and that of an appointment out of court was explained on the basis that the former involved a change in the personality of the employer while in the latter the company remains the employer through the agency of the receiver. Where the appointment of a receiver is accompanied by a sale of the business to a subsidiary, this does operate as a dismissal.[35]

(4) Every invoice, order for goods or business letter which is issued by or on behalf of the company or the receiver and on

[27] *Newhart Developments* v. *Co-operative Commercial Bank* [1978] 2 All E.R. 896.
[28] *Re South Western of Venezuela etc. Rly.* [1902] 1 Ch. 701.
[29] *Ante*, p. 703.
[30] [1966] 1 W.L.R. 125.
[31] At p. 132.
[32] [1967] 1 W.L.R. 780.
[33] [1974] Q.B. 468.
[34] [1985] BCLC 322 (C.A.).
[35] *Re Foster Clark Ltd.'s Indenture Trusts*, *supra*. For the position of administrative receivers see *post*, p. 709.

which the company's name appears must contain a statement that a receiver has been appointed: I.A. 1986, section 39.

(5) Within seven days after the appointment, the person who made or obtained the appointment must give notice of the fact to the Registrar who must enter it in his register of charges: Companies Act 1985, section 405(1).

(6) When a receiver appointed under a power in an instrument ceases to act, he must give notice to the Registrar: Companies Act 1985, section 405(2).

(7) A receiver appointed under a power in a debenture has his remuneration fixed by agreement. The court may, however, on the application of the liquidator, fix the receiver's remuneration. Under this power the remuneration may be fixed retrospectively, and any excess paid before the making of the order must be accounted for: I.A. 1986, section 36. This power does not entitle the court to interfere with the receiver's right to be indemnified for disbursements which have been properly incurred.[36]

Position of receiver other than administrative receiver

In the case of a receiver appointed under a power in a debenture or a trust deed the debenture usually provides[37] that he is to be the agent of the company. Consequently the debenture holder(s) or the trustees are not liable for his acts, though the company is. Through this agency the company can claim documents brought into existence in the course of the receivership in discharge of the receiver's duties to the company but not otherwise.[38]

Contracts made by the company and current at the date of his appointment are not binding on the receiver personally, unless they become binding by a novation.[39] One exception to this is a contract of employment which is adopted by the receiver: I.A. 1986, section 37(1), (2).[40] The receiver must however carry out

[36] *Re Potters Oils* [1986] 1 W.L.R. 201.

[37] If it does not, he is agent of the debenture holders who are answerable for his faults and omissions: *Re Vimbos* [1900] 1 Ch. 470.

[38] *Gomba Holdings U.K. Ltd.* v. *Minories Finance Ltd.* [1989] BCLC (C.A.).

[39] *Parsons* v. *Sovereign Bank of Canada* [1913] A.C. 160 (P.C.).

[40] See below.

the company's current contracts if not to do so would injure the company's goodwill,[41] but if the contracts can only be carried out by borrowing money ranking in priority to the debenture holders and are unprofitable, he need not carry them out.[42] As agent of the company, he is immune from personal liability for breach of such contracts or for inducing a breach of contract so long as his decision not to carry out the contract is bona fide and within his authority.[43]

Under section 37(1), (3) of the Insolvency Act 1986, a receiver appointed under a power in any instrument (other than an administrative receiver) is, to the same extent as if he had been appointed by the court, personally liable on contracts made by him in the performance of his functions except so far as they otherwise provide and on any contract of employment adopted by him in the performance of his functions. Nothing he does or does not do within 14 days of his appointment can be regarded as his adopting such a contract of employment.[44] He has a right of indemnity out of the assets: section 37(1)(*b*). This is without prejudice to any contractual indemnity he can claim, against the debenture holders, under the terms of his appointment: I.A. 1986, section 37(3). Where the receiver has acted outside the performance of his functions, section 37 does not apply to impose personal liability upon him but he may nonetheless have accepted personal liability and in relation to such personal liability there is no statutory right of indemnity.

On the commencement of a winding up of the company the receiver ceases to be the company's agent and his authority to bind the company ceases[45] but his powers with regard to the property charged are unaffected[46] so that he may continue to use the company's name for that purpose.[47] On a liquidation the receiver may well become the agent of the debenture holder who will then be liable for his acts.[48] If a receiver carries on an

[41] *Re Newdigate Colliery Ltd.* [1912] 1 Ch. 468 (C.A.) and see *Airlines Airspares Ltd.* v. *Handley Page Ltd.* [1970] Ch. 193.
[42] *Re Thames Ironworks Co. Ltd.* (1912) 106 L.T. 674.
[43] *Lathia* v. *Dronsfield Bros. Ltd.* [1987] BCLC 321.
[44] This overrules *Nicoll* v. *Cutts* [1985] BCLC 322 (C.A.).
[45] *Gosling* v. *Gaskell* [1897] A.C. 575; *Thomas* v. *Todd* [1926] 2 K.B. 511.
[46] *Gough's Garages Ltd.* v. *Pugsley* [1930] 1 K.B. 615.
[47] *Sowman* v. *David Samuel Trust Ltd.* [1978] 1 W.L.R. 22.
[48] *American Express International Banking Corp.* v. *Hurley* [1985] 3 All E.R. 564.

action after the company has been wound up by the court he may be liable to pay the costs of that action provided that he can recover them from his debenture holders.[49] The Court of Appeal has held that a receiver appointed by a debenture holder, but not as the agent of the debenture holder, owed a duty of care both to the borrower and to a guarantor of the debt to take reasonable care to obtain the best price that the circumstances permitted, and he also had a duty to exercise reasonable care in choosing the time for the sale.[50] It further held that the debenture holder might be liable for the receiver's actions if it were shown that he interfered with the conduct of the receivership, even if the receiver was not his agent: *Standard Chartered Bank* v. *Walker*.[51] This decision was applied in *American Express International Banking Corp.* v. *Hurley*[52] where the company concerned went into liquidation and the debenture holder had by its actions constituted the receiver as its agent (until the liquidation he had been the agent of the company). He also owes a duty of care to the debenture holders who appointed him and other secured creditors[53] but not to the unsecured creditors[54] or to one with a beneficial interest in the charged property.[55]

Since the receiver is usually the agent of the company his appointment does not alter the occupation of the company for the purpose of local rates and so a demand cannot be served on him personally.[56]

A company in receivership cannot interfere with the receiver in the proper exercise of his powers but, in *Watts* v. *Midland Bank plc*,[57] Peter Gibson J. thought that it could maintain an action against him for the proper performance of his duties and so refused to allow a minority shareholder to bring a derivative action[58] against him.

[49] *Bacal Contracting Ltd.* v. *Modern Engineering (Bristol) Ltd.* [1980] 2 All E.R. 655.
[50] But compare in *Re Charnley Davies Ltd.*, The Times, June 26, 1990.
[51] [1982] 1 W.L.R. 1410 (C.A.).
[52] [1985] 3 All E.R. 564.
[53] *Midland Bank Ltd.* v. *Joliman Finance Ltd.* (1967) 203 E.G. 1039.
[54] *Lathia* v. *Dronsfield Bros. Ltd.* [1987] BCLC 321, 324.
[55] *Parker-Tweedle* v. *Dunbar Bank plc.* [1990] 2 All E.R. 577.
[56] *Ratford* v. *North Avon District Council*, [1986] 3 W.L.R. 771.
[57] [1986] BCLC 15.
[58] *Ante*, p. 438.

A receiver appointed out of court, or the person who appointed him, may apply to the court for directions in any matter concerning the performance of his functions: I.A. 1986, section 35. He must within one month of his first year of appointment, every subsequent period of six months and on ceasing to act, deliver to the registrar the requisite accounts of his receipts and payments: I.A. 1986, section 38. Since the receiver is usually the agent of the company he must produce full accounts to the company when required to do so.[59] The court may order the receiver to make any returns or give any notices which he is by law required to give or make: I.A. 1986, section 41.[60]

Administrative receivers

Section 44 of the Insolvency Act 1986 provides that an administrative receiver is deemed to be the agent of the company unless and until it goes into liquidation[61] so that the company remains liable as principal on all contracts made by him. The section also provides that an administrative receiver is personally liable on all contracts he makes in carrying out his functions including any contract of employment he adopts (*i.e.* allows to continue for more than 14 days after his appointment).[62] He is entitled in respect of that liability to an indemnity out of the assets of the company and this is without prejudice to any indemnity he can claim under any express clause in his appointment or in an order of the court under section 34 of that Act, but not in respect of any liability which arises because he acts outside his authority. Section 44 therefore applies similar provisions to administative receivers as section 37 does to other receivers.

An administrative receiver has the powers set out in Schedule 1 to the Insolvency Act 1986, subject to any contrary express terms in the relevant debenture: Insolvency Act 1986, section 42(1). Schedule 1 in fact states the powers given to an administrator appointed under an administration order and they are set out in the following chapter of this book. Section 42(2)

[59] *Smiths Ltd.* v. *Middleton* [1979] 3 All E.R. 843.
[60] This section also applies to administrative receivers.
[61] See *American Express Banking Corp.* v. *Hurley* [1985] 3 All E.R. 564.
[62] Reversing *Nicoll* v. *Cutts* [1985] BCLC 322.

of the Act adapts those powers to an administrative receiver by making it clear that they only apply to the property actually covered by the charge under which he was appointed and not over the whole property of the company and not to property subject to a prior charge under which a receiver has been appointed. Section 42(3) of the Insolvency Act 1986 provides that a person dealing with an administrative receiver in good faith and for value does not need to inquire whether the receiver is acting within his powers. This is comparable to section 35A of the Companies Act 1985[63] save that the third party, to avail himself of the latter section, does not have to show that he gave value and has the benefit of a presumption of good faith. Where an administrative receiver not only exceeds his powers under Schedule 1 of the Insolvency Act, as modified by the express terms of the debenture, but also acts *ultra vires* the company then, perhaps now, the third party is protected by the new section 35(1) of the Companies Act 1985. This provides that the validity of the company's act (in this instance via its agent, the administrative receiver) shall not be called in question on the ground of lack of capacity. Section 42(3) can be relied upon only by the third party; section 35(1) can be relied upon by the third party or the company.

By virtue of section 43(1) of the Insolvency Act an administrative receiver can sell property[64] which is subject to a security having priority over the security of his appointor[65] free of that security if the court is satisfied that such a sale is likely to promote a more advantageous realisation of the company's assets.[66] The secured creditor whose security is thus overturned is protected by section 43(3) so that the net proceeds of sale must be used to discharge his debt together with, if the court regards such proceeds as less than the open market value of the property, such additional sums as are necessary to make good the deficiency.[67] The receiver must send an office copy of any

[63] *Ante*, p. 115. It is inapplicable to the circumstances under discussion as it relates to the powers of directors.

[64] Being property in relation to which he is the receiver or would be the receiver but for the appointment of a receiver by a prior chargee: I.A. 1986, s. 43(7).

[65] I.A., s.43(2).

[66] Following a recommendation of the *Cork Report* paras. 1510–1513; *cf.* I.A., s.15, *post*, p. 735.

[67] If there is more than one charge on the property they are to be repaid in order of priority: I.A. 1986, s.43(4).

court order under this section to the registrar within 14 days, with a fine in default.

Duties of administrative receiver

On appointment an administrative receiver must forthwith inform the company of his appointment and publish that fact in the Gazette and a newspaper appropriate for ensuring that it comes to the notice of the companies creditors: Insolvency Rules 1986, r. 3.2(3). Within 28 days of his appointment he must send a notice of his appointment to all the creditors of the company[68] so far as he is aware of their addresses. There are fines in default: I.A. 1986, section 46.

He must also obtain "forthwith" a statement of the company's affairs from some or all of the officers of the company (past or present), its promoters (if they acted within the year prior to his appointment), its employees (if they are in his opinion capable of giving the information required and are either current employees or have been employed within the preceding year) and the officers of any company which is (or has been within the previous year) an officer of the company concerned. Such a statement must be made within 21 days of being asked for, with a fine in default. Such persons are entitled to be paid their reasonable expenses by the administrative receiver.[69] The receiver may excuse any person from this obligation or extend the time limits although the court may intervene and exercise the power on his behalf: I.A. 1986, section 47.

Statements submitted under section 47 must be verified by affidavit and contain particulars of the company's assets, debts and liabilities, the names and addresses of its creditors, any securities held by them and when they were given and such further information as may be prescribed. Similar statements are required to be given to an administrator.[70]

Within three months of his appointment, unless the court allows an extension, an administrative receiver must report to the registrar, the trustees for secured creditors and all secured

[68] Unless the court othwerise directs, not the shareholders.
[69] Insolvency Rules 1986, r. 3.7(1).
[70] *Post*, p. 736.

creditors of whose addresses he is aware; I.A. 1986 section 48(1). This report must include details of the events leading up to his appointment, any dealings of his with company property and his carrying on of the company's business, the amounts of principal and interest payable to those debenture holders who appointed him and the amounts payable to preferential creditors, and the amount (if any) likely to be available for the payment of other creditors. It must also include a summary of the statement of affairs submitted to him under section 47 together his comments: I.A. 1986, section 48(5). It need not include anything "which would seriously prejudice the carrying out by the administrative receiver of his functions": I.A. 1986, section 48(6).

In addition, within three months an administrative receiver must also either send a copy of his report to all the company's unsecured creditors (of whose addresses he is aware) or publish an address to which they may write for copies to be sent to them free of charge. In either case he must also summon a meeting of the unsecured creditors on not less than 14 days' notice, before which he must lay a copy of the report. The court may dispense with such a meeting if the report states that the receiver intends to apply for such an order and the other requirements as to publicity are complied with at least 14 days before the application: I.A. 1986, section 48(2), (3). Such a meeting may appoint a committee, which may summon the receiver to attend before it and to give it such information as is reasonable, provided it gives him 7 days' notice: I.A. 1986, section 49. If the receivership is overtaken by a winding up, the report must be sent to the liquidator within 7 days: I.A. 1986, section 48(4). The administrative receiver must provide annual and final accounts of his receipts and payments to the Registrar of Companies, the company, the person who appointed him and each member of the creditors' committee (where there is one).[71]

These provisions replaced more limited ones in the Companies Act 1985 and reflect the Cork Committee's intention that creditors should be more aware and receivers more accountable.

[71] *Gomba Holdings U.K. Ltd.* v. *Homan* [1986] 1 W.L.R. 1301; I.R. 1986. r. 3.32(1).

Preferential payments

A receiver appointed to enforce a charge which, as created, was a floating charge, must pay the preferential debts[72] in priority to any claims arising out of the charge under which he was appointed. This obligation applies even if the charge had crystallised prior to the appointment of a receiver, but it does not apply to a charge which as created was fixed. Creditors relying on a floating charge are thus deferred to the preferential debts but they are entitled to have the consequent depletion of assets made good out of assets available for the payment of general creditors: I.A. 1986, section 40.[73]

The receipt of monies by the debenture holder with notice of a statutory duty under which the monies should have been applied in settlement of a prior claim makes the debenture holder directly liable to the preferential creditors as a constructive trustee.[74]

Vacation of office by receiver

An administrative receiver may only be removed from office by an order of the court although he may resign on giving due notice. In addition he must vacate his office if he ceases to be a qualified insolvency practitioner. When he does give up office he must inform the registrar within 14 days and is subject to a fine in default: I.A. 1986, section 45. Any administrative receiver must also vacate his office if an administration order is made: I.A. 1986, section 11(1)(*b*).

When any receiver vacates office any remuneration, expenses or indemnity to which he is entitled at that time take priority over any security held by the person who appointed him: I.A. 1986, sections 11(4), 37(4), 45(3). Where the expenses of a receiver appointed by the court exceed the assets in his hands, he is not entitled to recover them off the person who appointed him or the company.[75]

[72] See section 386 and Sched. 6 I.A. 1986. *Post*, p. 822. In this case the periods mentioned in Schedule 6 run from the appointment of the receiver or the taking of possession.

[73] See also s.196 Companies Act 1985.

[74] *Re Christonette International Ltd.* [1982] 1 W.L.R. 1245.

[75] *Evans* v. *Clayhope Ltd.* [1988] BCLC 238 (C.A.).

Scots Law

The reasons for the introduction of the office of receiver to Scotland by the Companies (Floating Charges and Receivers) (Scotland) Act 1972[76] were:

(*a*) to enable the fortunes of a company to be revived and thus prevent unnecessary liquidation;
(*b*) to strengthen the rights of a holder of a floating charge by making it possible for him to take possession of and realise the security without liquidation; and
(*c*) to lessen the difficulties which could arise from the difference between Scots and English law where a group of companies included both Scottish and English companies.[77]

This Act was consolidated into the Companies Act 1985 and then, after amendments made by the Insolvency Act 1985 the general purpose of which was to standardise the English and Scottish provisions, into the Insolvency Act 1986. References are to sections of the 1986 Act, except when there is a statement to the contrary.

A receiver may be appointed by either the holder of a floating charge or the court on the application of the holder of a floating charge: section 51. The term "holder of the floating charge" is sufficiently widely defined as to include, in the case of a series of debentures, the trustees acting for the debenture holders under a trust deed, or, if there are no such trustees, specified majorities of the debenture holders: section 70.

[76] A petition for the appointment of a judicial factor *ad interim* on the affairs of a limited comany is competent at common law: *Fraser*, *Petitioner*, 1971 S.L.T. 146. (O.H.) (appointment made in a "position of chaos requiring urgently to be dealt with"). Where both a liquidator and a receiver were appointed, the receiver was held (*i*) to be entitled to take control of the property to satisfy the debt of the holder of the floating charge and (*ii*) to be primarily liable for the payment of the fixed securities and preferential debts of the company: *Manley*, *Petitioner*, 1985 S.L.T. 42 (O.H.). In *McGuinness, Petitioner; Black, Petitioner*, 1989 G.W.D. 37–1689 (O.H.), there were circumstances in which the appointment of a judicial factor was preferred to the appointment of a provisional liquidator.

[77] *Report on the Companies* (*Floating Charges*) (*Scotland*) *Act 1961*, (1970) Cmnd. 4336, paras. 37, 38.

Appointment by holder of floating charge

A receiver may be appointed by the holder of the floating charge on the occurrence of any event which, by the instrument creating the charge, entitles the holder to make that appointment, and, in so far as the instrument does not provide otherwise, on the occurrence of any of the following:

(*a*) expiry of 21 days after the making of a demand—which is unsatisfied—for payment of the whole or part of the principal sum secured;
(*b*) expiry of two months during which interest has been in arrears;
(*c*) making of an order or passing of a resolution to wind up the company;
(*d*) appointment of a receiver by virtue of any other floating charge created by the company: section 52(1).

The appointment is made by means of an "instrument of appointment," validly executed by the holder of the charge or by a person having his written authority. A certified copy of the instrument of appointment must be delivered by the person making the appointment to the Registrar within seven days of its execution, and the Registrar enters particulars of the appointment in the register of charges. The receiver is regarded as having been appointed on the date and at the time when the instrument of appointment is received by him provided he accepts the appointment by the end of the business day next after such receipt (either by him or on his behalf).[78] As from the date of the receiver's appointment the floating charge, subject to sections 410 to 414 of the Companies Act 1985 and section 245 of the 1986 Act, attaches to the property and takes effect as if it were a fixed security. Failure without reasonable excuse duly to register the certified copy of the instrument of appointment attracts a daily default fine but does not affect the validity of the appointment: section 53.

In the case of a floating charge which covers the whole of the property from time to time comprised in the company's undertaking (an "all-assets" floating charge), any property which comes into the company's hands after the receiver's

[78] The rules make special provision for joint receivers.

appointment will be attached and be available, if need be, for realisation by the receiver.

A receiver appointed to a company under an "all-assets" floating charge discovered that, before his appointment, the company had sold part of its stock-in-trade to a loan creditor and that the purchase price had been set off against the amount then due to that creditor. The receiver persuaded the creditor to return the stock to the company and allowed the debt to be correspondingly reinstated. The receiver then realised the assets of the company, including the restored stock. A liquidator was thereafter appointed, and he contended that the repurchased stock should not have been regarded as attached by the charge under what is now section 53. *Held*, it was not relevant to inquire whether particular assets were or were not comprised in the company's undertaking at the date of the receiver's appointment; the question was whether the instrument creating the floating charge covered the assets in question, and as the instrument in this case was expressed to cover assets whenever they came to be comprised in the company's undertaking, the reacquired stock was attached and available for realisation by the receiver: *Ross* v. *Taylor*, 1985 S.C. 156.

The interpretation of the phrase "as if the charge were a fixed security" in section 53 must take into account the definition of "fixed security" in section 70. The definition provides that "fixed security" means any security, other than a floating charge, which on the winding up of the company in Scotland would be treated as an effective security over the property.

Joint receivers were appointed by a bank over the whole of a company's property. The following day another creditor of the company purported to arrest in the hands of a third party a sum owing to the company. *Held*, because, by the appointment of the receivers, the floating charge had attached to, *inter alia*, the debt purported to be arrested, that debt had to be treated as if it had been attached as a fixed security, *i.e.* as if there had been an assignation of the debt in security in favour of the holders of the floating charge, followed by due intimation of the assignation to the third party; the liability of the third party to pay the debt to the company had therefore disappeared and the debt could not be effectively arrested: *Forth & Clyde Construction Co. Ltd.* v. *Trinity Timber & Plywood Co. Ltd.*, 1984 S.C. 1.

Appointment by court

The circumstances in which a receiver may be appointed by the court are the same as those for an appointment by the holder of the floating charge (*ante*, p. 715) except that for paragraph (*d*) there must be substituted:

(*d*) where the court is satisfied that the position of the holder of the charge is likely to be prejudiced if no appointment is made: section 52(2).

The application to the court for the appointment is by petition, which must be served on the company. A certified copy of the court's interlocutor making the appointment must be delivered by or on behalf of the petitioner to the Registrar within seven days of the date of the interlocutor or such longer period as the court may allow, and the Registrar enters particulars of the appointment in the register of charges. The receiver is regarded as having been appointed on the date of the interlocutor, and as from that date the floating charge attaches to the property and takes effect as if it were a fixed security. Failure without reasonable excuse duly to register the certified copy of the interlocutor attracts a fine of £5 for every day during which the default continues, but does not affect the validity of the appointment: section 54.

Who can be appointed receiver

The following are disqualified from being appointed as receiver:

(*a*) a body corporate;
(*b*) an undischarged bankrupt; and
(*c*) a Scottish firm: section 51(3).

It is permissible to have joint receivers: section 51(6).

Where there are two or more floating charges, the same person may be appointed receiver by virtue of both or all of them: section 56(7).

Powers of receiver

A receiver has the powers, if any, conferred on him by the instrument creating the floating charge, and in addition he has the extensive powers listed in Schedule 2 to the Act in so far as these are not inconsistent with any provision contained in the instrument creating the charge: section 55(1), (2). The statutory powers are such as to place the receiver in a position corresponding to that of an administrative receiver in England, and include the following powers:

(*a*) to take possession[79] and dispose of the company's property;
(*b*) to raise or borrow money and grant security over the property;
(*c*) to appoint agents and professional persons such as a solicitor and an accountant and to employ and dismiss employees;
(*d*) to bring or defend legal proceedings in the name and on behalf of the company[80];
(*e*) to refer questions to arbitration;
(*f*) to insure the company's business and property;
(*g*) to use the company's seal and execute documents, including bills of exchange and promissory notes, in the name and on behalf of the company;
(*h*) to carry on the company's business or any part of it;
(*i*) to grant or accept a surrender of a lease and to take on leases;
(*j*) to make any arrangement or compromise on behalf of the company;
(*k*) to call up any uncalled capital of the company;
(*l*) to establish subsidiaries of the company and to transfer to subsidiaries the business of the company or any part of it or any of the property;

[79] It is a matter of controversy whether this empowers a receiver to take proceedings in his own name against debtors to the company without having acquired an assignation of the debts from the company: *McPhail* v. *Lothian Regional Council*, 1981 S.C. 119 (O.H.), not followed in *Taylor*, *Petitioner*, 1982 S.L.T. 172 (O.H.). Funds consigned in court as a condition of recall of arrestment and inhibition on the dependence were held not to fall within the company's property in *Hawking* v. *Hafton House Ltd.*, 1990 G.W.D. 6–332 (O.H.).

[80] In *Imperial Hotel* (*Aberdeen*) *Ltd.* v. *Vaux Breweries Ltd.*, 1978 S.C. 86 (O.H.), it was held not competent for the directors to raise actions in connection with the property which was within the receivership, but in *Shanks* v. *Central Regional Council*, 1987 S.L.T. 410 (O.H.), it was observed that, while the *Imperial* case was applicable to *most* situations, it did not mean that an action brought by a company in receivership was inherently incompetent or necessarily a fundamental nullity: it could not be held that directors were not empowered in any circumstances to deal in any way, including the raising of proceedings, with assets which were the subject of the floating charge.

(*m*) to change the situation of the company's registered office;

(*n*) to present or defend a petition for the winding up of the company; and

(*o*) to do all other things incidental to the exercise of his other powers.

The receiver may require to exercise only some of these wide statutory powers of management. It is a matter for his discretion as to which powers he will exercise and when he will exercise them. The company, through its directors, cannot normally interfere with the exercise by the receiver of his discretion by, for instance, raising actions which the receiver considers should not be raised but, where a receiver in the exercise of his discretion does not pursue an asset such as a claim for damages, the directors are entitled, and may be bound by their duty to other creditors, to vindicate the asset.[81]

The exercise by the receiver of his powers is subject to the rights of persons who have effectually executed diligence[82] before his appointment and to the rights of persons who hold a fixed security or floating charge with prior or equal ranking: section 55(3).

A person dealing with a receiver in good faith and for value is not concerned to inquire whether the receiver is acting within his powers: section 55(4).

Precedence among receivers

Where there are two or more floating charges, a receiver may be appointed by virtue of each charge, but the receiver whose charge has priority of ranking is entitled to exercise the statutory powers to the exclusion of any other receiver. Where two or more floating charges rank equally and two or more

[81] *Imperial Hotel (Aberdeen) Ltd.* v. *Vaux Breweries Ltd.*, and *Shanks* v. *Central Regional Council, supra.*

[82] An arrestment which has not been followed by a decree of forthcoming is not an "effectually executed diligence" for this purpose: *Lord Advocate* v. *Royal Bank of Scotland Ltd.*, 1977 S.C. 155; nor is a landlord's hypothec for rent: *Cumbernauld Development Corporation* v. *Mustone*, 1983 S.L.T. (Sh. Ct.) 55. The *Royal Bank* case was distinguished in *Iona Hotels Ltd., Petitioners*, 1990 G.W.D. 18–986.

receivers have been appointed by virtue of these charges, the receivers are deemed to be joint receivers. The powers of a receiver whose charge has a ranking postponed to that of another charge by virtue of which a receiver has later been appointed are, from the date of the later appointment, suspended so far as is necessary to enable the second-mentioned receiver to exercise his statutory powers, and they revive when the prior floating charge ceases to attach to the property: section 56.

Agency and liability of receiver for contracts

A receiver is deemed[83] to be the agent of the company in relation to the property attached by the floating charge. He is personally liable on any contract entered into by him in the performance of his functions, except in so far as the contract otherwise provides, and on any contract of employment adopted by him in the carrying out of those functions, but he is entitled to be indemnified out of the property in respect of which he was appointed. As regards contracts of employment, nothing that is done or omitted within 14 days after his appointment is to be taken as an adoption of the contract by the receiver.

Contracts entered into by or on behalf of the company before the receiver's appointment continue in force, subject to the terms of the contract, after the appointment,[84] but the receiver does not, merely by his appointment, incur personal liability on such contracts. These provisions do not limit any right to indemnity which the receiver would have apart from them. Nor do they limit his liability on contracts made or adopted without authority.[85] Contracts entered into by a receiver whose powers

[83] This presumption was held to be rebuttable in *Inverness District Council* v. *Highland Universal Fabrications*, 1986 S.L.T. 556 (O.H.) (landlords seeking payment from receiver personally for occupation of premises after his appointment).

[84] See *Myles J. Callaghan Ltd.* v. *City of Glasgow District Council*, 1988 S.L.T. 227 (O.H.).

[85] In *Hill Samuel & Co. Ltd.* v. *Laing*, 1989 S.L.T. 760 (O.H.) (affirmed 1989 G.W.D. 24–1016), a receiver who had recommenced business was held not to be exempted from personal liability by a clause in the debenture, that being a contract between the chargeholder and the company to which the receiver was not a party.

are later suspended under section 56, *ante*, continue in force, subject to the terms of the contract, after that suspension: section 57.[86]

Remuneration of receiver

The remuneration to be paid to a receiver is fixed by agreement between the receiver and the holder of the floating charge, but where there has been no such agreement or the remuneration fixed is disputed by the receiver, the holder of any floating charge or fixed security, the company or the liquidator, it may be fixed instead by the Auditor of the Court of Session: section 58.

Preferential payments and distribution of monies

The Act provides that where a company is not at the time of the receiver's appointment in course of being wound up the debts which would be preferential payments in winding up[87] must be paid out of any assets coming into the receiver's hands in priority to claims of the holder of the floating charge. This applies only to debts which have been intimated to the receiver or have become known to him within six months after he has advertised for claims in the *Edinburgh Gazette* and in a local newspaper. Payments made in accordance with these provisions must be recouped as far as may be out of the assets available for ordinary creditors: section 59.

The monies received by the receiver are distributed in the following order:

(*a*) to the holder of any fixed security which ranks prior to or equally with the floating charge, persons who have effectually executed diligence on any part of the property, creditors to whom the receiver has incurred

[86] See *Macleod* v. *Alexander Sutherland Ltd.*, 1977 S.L.T. (Notes) 44 (O.H.). (Decree of implement refused). For judicial comment on the receiver's position in general and on the distinction between receivership and liquidation, see *Lord Advocate* v. *Royal Bank of Scotland Ltd.*, 1977 S.C. 155, and *Taylor, Petitioner*, 1982 S.L.T. 172 (O.H.).

[87] See note 72, above.

liability, the receiver himself in respect of his liabilities, expenses and remuneration, and preferential creditors entitled to payment under section 59, *ante*;

(*b*) to the holder of the floating charge in or towards satisfaction of the debt secured by the floating charge; and

(*c*) to any other receiver, to the holder of a fixed security over the property, and to the company or its liquidator, according to their respective rights and interests.

Where there is doubt as to the persons entitled to a payment, or where a receipt or discharge of a security cannot be obtained for a payment, the receiver must consign the amount in a bank of issue in Scotland in name of the Accountant of Court for behoof of the person entitled to it: section 60.

Cessation of appointment

A receiver may, on application to the court by the holder of the floating charge, be removed from office by the court on cause shown. He may resign his office on giving the prescribed notice. In addition he must vacate office if he ceases to be a qualified insolvency practitioner.

Where at any time a receiver vacates office, his remuneration, any expenses properly incurred by him and any indemnity to which he is entitled out of the company's property must be paid out of the property which is subject to the floating charge and has the priority provided for in section 60, above.

Except where the cessation of a receiver's appointment is due to his death or removal by the court, he must give notice of the cessation to the Registrar within 14 days. Where the receiver has been removed by the court, the duty to give such notice lies on the holder of the floating charge. The Registrar enters the notice in the register of charges. Default in complying with the requirement as to notice makes the receiver or the holder of the charge as the case may be liable to a fine.

If, on the expiry of one month after cessation of a receiver's appointment, no other receiver has been appointed, the charge then ceases to attach to the property and becomes again a floating charge: section 62.

Powers of court

Under the Act the court may exercise certain powers in relation to receiverships, whether the receiver has been appointed by the holder of the floating charge or by the court:

(*a*) The court may give directions in connection with the performance by the receiver of his functions. The application to the court may be made either by the receiver or by the holder of the floating charge: section 63(1).

(*b*) The court may, on the application of the holder of the floating charge, remove the receiver on cause shown: section 62, *ante*.

(*c*) Where the property which is subject to the floating charge is also subject to another security or burden or is affected by diligence, and the receiver wishes to sell or dispose of the property but is unable to obtain the necessary consent of the other parties, the court may, on the application of the receiver, authorise the sale or disposal of the property free of the security or burden or diligence.

However, where there is a fixed security over the property ranking prior to the floating charge, the court must not authorise the sale or disposal unless it is satisfied that this would be likely to provide a more advantageous realisation of the company's assets than would otherwise be effected. In such a case the court must impose the condition that the net proceeds of the disposal be applied to discharge the sums secured by the fixed security, together with, if the court regards such proceeds as less than the open market value of the property, such additional sums as are necessary to make good the deficiency.

Within 14 days of the granting of the authorisation the receiver must send a certified copy of the authorisation to the Registrar, and if without reasonable excuse he fails to comply with that provision he is liable to a default fine.

Where a sale or disposal has taken place under such court authorisation, the receiver must grant to the purchaser or disponee an appropriate document of transfer or conveyance, which, when recorded, intimated or registered as the case may be, has the effect of disencumbering the property of the security affecting it, and freeing the property from the diligence executed upon it.[88]

These provisions do not prejudice the right of any creditor of the company to rank for his debt in the winding up of the company: section 61.

(*d*) Where the appointment of a person as a receiver by the holder of a floating charge is discovered to be invalid (whether because of the invalidity of the instrument or otherwise), the court may order the holder to indemnify the person appointed against any liability which arises solely on account of the invalidity of the appointment: section 63(2).

(*e*) If the receiver makes default in delivering the documents or giving the notices which are required of him, *post*, the court may order him to make good the default within a specified time. Application to the court for this purpose may be made by any member or creditor of the company or by the Registrar. Similarly, if the receiver fails, on the liquidator's request, to render proper accounts of receipts and payments and to pay over the proper amount to the liquidator, the court may, on the liquidator's application, order the receiver to make good the default within a specified time: section 69.

Requirements as to notification and information

When a receiver is appointed:

(*a*) Every invoice, order for goods or business letter which is issued by or on behalf of the company or the receiver or the liquidator and on which the company's name appears must contain a statement that a receiver has been appointed: section 64.

[88] An example of a sale authorised by the court where inhibiting creditors had refused consent occurred, under the 1972 Act, in *Armour and Mycroft, Petitioners,* 1983 S.L.T. 43 (O.H.).

(*b*) The receiver must forthwith send to the company and publish notice of his appointment: section 65(1).

(*c*) The receiver must forthwith require a statement of the company's affairs to be submitted to him by some or all of the officers of the company (past or present), its promoters (if they acted within the year prior to his appointment), its employees (if they are in his opinion capable of giving the information required and are either present employees or have been employed within the preceding year) and the officers of any company which is (or has been within the previous year) an officer of or in the employment of the company concerned. Such a statement must be submitted within 21 days of its being asked for, with a fine in default. The receiver may excuse any person from this obligation or extend the time limits, and if the receiver has refused to exercise such powers, the court may do so.

A statement submitted under these provisions must be verified by affidavit and show particulars of the company's assets, debts and liabilities, the names and addresses of its creditors, the securities held by them and the date when they were given and such further information as may be prescribed: section 66.

(*d*) Within three months of his appointment, unless the court allows an extension, a receiver must send to the Registrar, the holder of the floating charge by virtue of which he was appointed and to any trustees for secured creditors of the company and (so far as he is aware of their addresses) to all secured creditors a report as to the events leading up to his appointment, his disposal of any property of the company and the carrying on by him of any business of the company, the amounts of principal and interest payable to the holder of the floating charge by virtue of which he was appointed and the amounts payable to preferential creditors, and the amount, if any, likely to be available for the payment of other creditors. The report also includes a summary of the statement of affairs submitted to the receiver under section 66 of his comments, if any, on it.

The receiver must also, within three months (or longer if the court allows) after his appointment either send a copy of the report to all unsecured creditors of whose addresses he is aware, or publish a notice stating an address to which unsecured creditors should write for copies of the report to be sent to them free of charge. In either case he must summon a meeting of the unsecured creditors on not less than 14 days's notice and must lay a copy of the report before that meeting. The court may dispense with such a meeting if the report states that the receiver intends to apply for such an order and the other requirements as to publicity are complied with at least 14 days before the application.

If the company has gone or goes into liquidation, the receiver must send a copy of the report to the liquidator, at latest within seven days after the liquidator's appointment: section 67.

(*e*) The meeting of creditors summoned under section 67 may establish a committee ("the creditors' committee"), and that committee may, on giving at least seven days' notice, require the receiver to attend before it and furnish it with such information as to the carrying out by him of his functions as it may reasonably require: section 68.

Penalties are imposed for failure to comply with the requirements of sections 64 to 67.

Chapter 26

ADMINISTRATION ORDERS

THE Insolvency Act 1985 introduced an entirely new concept into U.K. company law—the administration order.[1] It is intended to provide an alternative to a liquidation for companies unable to pay their debts, either by rehabilitating the company and continuing it as a going concern or by providing a better way of either realising its assets or affecting a scheme or compromise with its creditors. It is therefore a form of "company rescue." An administrator is appointed by the court to control all the company's assets in an attempt to achieve the purpose of the administration order and as such he has different aims from that of an administrative receiver[2] appointed under a floating charge. Nevertheless the administrator is modelled on such receivers and many of the provisions relating to the two concepts are similar. If an administration order is made the company has a breathing space from any winding up orders, appointment of receivers or other financial processes (*e.g.* enforcement of a hire purchase agreement). The procedure is, however, subject to the veto of any creditor who has validly appointed an administrative receiver prior to the consideration of the petition by the court—he must consent before the court can make such an order.

Power to make an administration order

The court may only make an administration order if it is satisfied that the company is or is likely to become unable to

[1] See the *Cork Report*, Chapter 9.
[2] *Ante*, p. 700.

pay its debts[3] and that such an order would be likely to achieve one or more of the following purposes:

(a) the survival of the company, and the whole or any part of its undertaking as a going concern;
(b) the approval of a voluntary arrangement with creditors[4];
(c) the sanctioning of a scheme of arrangement under section 425 of the Companies Act 1985[5], and
(d) a more advantageous realisation of the company's assets than would be effected on a winding up.

No such order can be made after a company has gone into liquidation or if it is an insurance[6] or banking company[7]: I.A. 1986, s.8. The court will only make an order if the purpose specified, or, if several are relied upon, one at least of them, has a real prospect of being achieved. Thus in *Re S.C.L. Building Services Ltd.*[8] the creditor sought an order relying upon purposes (a), (b) and (d) but the order granted was limited to (d)—the only purpose likely to be achieved. The court has jurisdiction to make an order where, though the company cannot meet its debts as they fall due, it has a surplus of illiquid assets over liabilities.[9] Any order must specify the purpose or purposes for which it was made and can subsequently be varied.[10] In *Re St. Ives Windings*[11] the purposes specified were (a) or (d). Purpose (d) had been achieved but the court held that the administrator had no power under the order, to distribute the proceeds. It therefore varied the order to add purpose (b).

[3] As defined in I.A. 1986, s.123 See *post*, p. 745.
[4] *Ante*, p. 695.
[5] *Post*, p. 838.
[6] As defined in the Insurance Companies Act 1982, ss.1, 96(1).
[7] Within the meaning of the Banking Act 1979, ss.16, 18, 48, 50.
[8] (1989) 5 B.C.C. 746; *Re Consumer Industrial Press Ltd.* [1988] BCLC 177 suggested that achievement of the purpose had to be "more likely than not" but this interpretation has been criticised in *Re Harris Simons Construction Ltd.* [1989] BCLC 202, *Re Primlaks* [1989] BCLC 734 and *Re Rowbotham Baxter Ltd.* [1990] BCLC 397.
[9] *Re Business Properties Ltd.* (1988) 4 BCC 684; though it will not exercise its jurisidiction if the creditor was adequately secured, see *Re Imperial Motors U.K. Ltd.* [1990] BCLC 29.
[10] I.A. 1986, s.18.
[11] (1987) 3 B.C.C. 643.

Application for an administration order

A petition for an administration order can be made by the company, the directors[12] or by a creditor, or any combination of those people. The Secretary of State cannot present a petition and the court cannot make an order of its own accord. Notice of the petition must be given to anyone entitled to appoint an administrative receiver[13] and other prescribed persons.[14] Once presented a petition cannot be withdrawn except with leave of the court: I.A. 1986, s.9(1)(2).

In the period between the presentation of the petition and the date when the court either makes the order or dismisses the petition, section 10(1)(*a*) of the Insolvency Act 1986 imposes a freeze on important aspects of the company's affairs so that the purpose of any order made can be achieved. In particular no resolutions for the voluntary winding up of the company nor any compulsory winding up order can be made; no steps may be taken to enforce any security against the company or to repossess any goods under a hire purchase agreement or similar arrangement[15] without the court's consent; and "no other proceedings" can be commenced or enforced against the company or its property without such consent. However, the presentation of a petition does not prevent a winding up petition being presented[16] nor the appointment and activities of an administrative receiver: I.A. section 10(2).

Effect of appointment of an administrative receiver

The role played by administrative receivers in the past was the model upon which the administration order procedure was based and therefore nothing in the new procedure is intended to

[12] Acting collectively as a board. *Re Equiticorp International* ((1989) 5 B.C.C. 599): petition by a single director authorised by a resolution at a board meeting at which he was not present, held, to be properly presented.

[13] *i.e.* the holder of a floating charge: *ante*, p. 700.

[14] I.R. 1986 r. 2.6(2).

[15] These are conditional sale agreements under s.189(1) of the Consumer Credit Act 1974, chattel leasing arrangement as defined in s.251 of the I.A. 1986, and retention of title agreement as defined in s.251: I.A. 1986, s.10(4).

[16] Though its advertisement may be restricted until the hearing of the petition for an administration order: Re A Company No. 001992 of 1988. [1989] B.C.L.C. 9.

undermine the position of an administrative receiver. Thus, although in general the administration order procedure gives companies a breathing space during which its creditors cannot enforce their rights, it does not prevent creditors under a charge which, as created, was a floating charge from appointing an administrative receiver. As we have seen, anyone presenting an administration petition must notify anyone who has the right to appoint an administrative receiver and such a person may appoint such a receiver at any time prior to the court's decision. If he has already done so at the date of the petition the freezing period between the petition and order does not start to run until the debenture holder has consented to an administration order being made: I.A. 1986, section 10(3). On the other hand if he has not already appointed a receiver but does so at any time before the making of an order the court must dismiss the petition unless either the debenture holder consents to an order being made or the debenture itself is invalid under the various controlling sections of the Insolvency Act [17]: I.A. 1986, section 9(3).

Thus the holder of a floating charge has an effective veto on the making of an administration order. To exercise it, he has to appoint an administrative receiver before the administration order is made.[18] If he fails to do so, the court is free to make the order without his consent and thereafter the administrator can dispose of the charged property without his consent.[19]

Court's discretion

Subject to the existence of an administrative receiver the court on hearing a petition for an administration order may dismiss it, adjourn the hearing conditionally or unconditionally, make the order or make any interim order it thinks fit, *e.g.* restricting the powers of the directors: I.A. 1986, section 9(4) (5). Where the company is in deadlock, the appropriate remedy is winding up and the court will not make an administration order.[20]

[17] I.A. 1986, ss.238–240, 242–243, 245. See Chap. 29, *post*.
[18] He is precluded from doing so afterwards by s.11(3)(*b*) I.A. 1986.
[19] See s.15(1) and (3) I.A. 1986.
[20] *Re Business Properties Ltd.* (1988) 4 B.C.C. 684.

The effect of an administration order

If the court makes an administration order, section 11 of the Insolvency Act 1986 provides for certain consequences since the administrator will need to assume control of all the company's affairs and be given time in which to operate the proposed scheme and achieve the purpose stated in the order. The following are the consequences of such as order being made:

(1) any winding up petition is dismissed;
(2) any administrative receiver shall vacate office[21];
(3) any other receiver must vacate office if the administrator requires him to do so[22];
(4) whilst the order is in force, no resolution may be passed to wind up the company voluntarily and no administrative receiver can be appointed[23];
(5) whilst the order is in force, no steps may be taken to enforce any security over the company's property or to repossess any goods in the possession of the company under a hire purchase agreement,[24] without the consent of the administrator or the court. Goods are in the possession of the company even if it has sublet them to an end user and thus consent to repossess is necessary in such circumstances: In *Re Atlantic Computer Systems plc*.[25] The exercise by an airport of a statutory right to detain an aeroplane requires consent but the airport is not in contempt in detaining prior to such consent so long as it is simultaneously making every effort to get the court's consent: *Bristol Airport plc.* v. *Powdrill*[26];

[21] Such a receiver is protected as to his fees, expenses and indemnity: I.A. 1986, s.11(4).
[22] On vacation of office an administrative or other receiver is excused from any obligation to preferential creditors: I.A. 1986, s.11(5).
[23] Thus a floating charge holder who consents to the order being made loses his right to appoint such a receiver.
[24] Including a conditional sale agreement, a chattel leasing agreement and a retention of title agreement. See Note 15, above.
[25] *The Times*, September 18, 1990. C.A. (leave granted).
[26] [1990] 2 All E.R. 493; and see *Re Paramount Airways Ltd.* [1990] BCC 130 C.A.

(6) whilst the order is in force, no proceedings can be commenced, continued or enforced against the company by its creditors[27] without the consent of the administrator or the court; and

(7) whilst the order is in force, all documents[28] issued by the company or the administrator must state that an administration order is in force together with the administrator's name and the fact that he is managing the company's affairs, business and property: I.A. 1986, section 12.[29]

(8) suppliers of utilities cannot make it a pre-condition of further supplies, that charges outstanding for supplies before the administration order was made, are paid.[30]

The court will appoint an administrator who must be a qualified insolvency practitioner and there are provisions for filling any vacancy which might occur: I.A. 1986, section 13.

The administrator has complete control of the company's affairs and is charged with carrying out the purpose or purposes specified in the order. In many respects he is similar to an administrative receiver and has similar powers and duties.

On the appointment of an administrator certain prior transactions may be challenged by him. These provisions also apply on a liquidation and are set out on Chapter 29, *post*.[31]

Powers of an administrator

By virtue of section 14(1) of the Insolvency Act 1986 an administrator has the power to do anything which is necessary for the management of the company's affairs, business or property. In particular he has the following powers specified in Schedule 1 to the Act.[32]

[27] The administration order does not prevent a competitor applying to the court to have the company's air transport licence revoked: *Air Ecosse* v. *Civil Aviation Authority* 1987 S.L.T. 751.

[28] Invoices, orders and business letters.

[29] There is a fine in default of this section.

[30] I.A. 1986 s.233; *post*, p. 768.

[31] p. 814.

[32] These are the powers which are also available to an administrative receiver.

i) To take possession of, collect and get in the property of the company and, for that purpose, to take such proceedings as may seem to him expedient.

ii) To sell or otherwise dispose of the property of the company by public auction or private contract or, in Scotland, to sell, feu, hire out or otherwise dispose of the property of the company by public roup or private bargain.

iii) To raise or borrow money and grant security therefore over the property of the company.

iv) To appoint a solicitor or accountant or other professionally qualified person to assist him in the performance of his functions.

v) To bring or defend any action or other legal proceedings in the name and on behalf of the company.

vi) To refer to arbitration any question affecting the company.

vii) To affect and maintain insurances in respect of the business and property of the company.

viii) To use the company's seal.

ix) To do all acts and to execute in the name and on behalf of the company any deed, receipt or other document.

x) To draw, accept, make and endorse any bill of exchange or promissory note in the name and on behalf of the company.

xi) To appoint any agent to do any business which he is unable to do himself or which can more conveniently be done by an agent and power to employ and dismiss employees.

xii) To do all such things (including the carrying out of works) as may be necessary for the realisation of the property of the company.

xiii) To make any payment which is necessary or incidental to the performance of his functions.[33]

[33] Where a company has sublet goods held by it on a hire purchase agreement to a third party, the owners of the goods are not entitled to receive the rental paid to the administrator by the third party while the administration order is in force, as an expense of administration: In *Re Atlantic Computers plc.*, *The Times*, September 18, 1990, C.A.

xiv) To carry on the business of the company.

xv) To establish subsidiaries of the company.

xvi) To transfer to subsidiaries of the company the whole or any part of the business and property of the company.

xvii) To grant or accept a surrender of a lease or tenancy of any of the property of the company, and to take a lease or tenancy of any property required or convenient for the business of the company.

xviii) To make any arrangement or compromise on behalf of the company.

xix) To call up any uncalled capital of the company.

xx) To rank and claim in the bankruptcy, insolvency, sequestration or liquidation of any person indebted to the company and to receive dividends, and to accede to trust deeds for the creditors of any such person.

xxi) To present or defend a petition for the winding up of the company.

xxii) To change the situation of the company's registered office.

xxiii) To do all other things incidental to the exercise of the fore-going powers.

In addition the administrator has the power to remove or appoint any director of the company, thus enabling him to provide the company with a new management, and to call any meeting of the members or creditors: I.A. 1986, section 14(2). He does not have power to make distributions to members.[34] When in doubt as to his powers he can apply to the court for directions: IA 1986 s.14(3).

In exercising his powers the administrator is the agent of the company[35] and his status overrides that of the directors: their constitutional powers cannot be exercised in such a way as to interfere with his powers without his consent, general or specific: I.A. 1986, section 14(4), (5). A person dealing with the

[34] *Re Business Properties Ltd.* (1988) 4 B.C.C. 684.

[35] This is also the position of an administrative receiver but note that there is no provision imposing personal liability on an administrator though such liability could arise independent of statute if such was intended: see *ante*, p. 707.

administrator in good faith and for value is not concerned to inquire whether he is acting within his powers: I.A. 1986, section 14(6). This is an identical provision to that relating to persons dealing with an administrative receiver[36] so that the burden of proof of good faith is on the third party, unlike section 35A of the Companies Act 1985 which deals with directors' powers.[37]

Section 15(1) of the Insolvency Act 1986 gives an administrator the power to sell any property subject to a floating charge free of that charge.[38] The debenture holder retains his priority in respect of the proceeds of the disposal.[39] In addition the administrator can apply to the court for permission to dispose of property free of any other existing security and of goods free of any hire purchase agreement[40] on the grounds that such a disposal would be likely to promote the purpose (or purposes) specified in the administrative order: I.A. 1986, section 15(2). The proceeds of the disposal (together with any sums necessary to make that up to open market value) must be used to redeem the security: I.A. 1986, section 15(5). Notice of such application should be given to the security holder.[41] The fact that he disputes the valuation put upon the property by the administrator will not prevent the court making the order: so long as the company has ample funds to make up any deficiency between the valuation and the market value, the existence and extent of such deficiency can be determined subsequently under section 15(5) I.A. 1986.[42] An office copy of the court's order must be sent to the registrar[43]: I.A. 1986, section 15(5), (7). In the application of section 15 to Scotland, the administrator must grant to the disponee an appropriate document of transfer or conveyance to enable the property to be effectively disencumbered or freed from the security: I.A. 1986, section 16.

36 I.A. 1986, s.42(3); *ante* p. 710.
37 *Ante*, p. 115.
38 An administrative receiver requires the court's consent for this.
39 I.A. 1986, s.15(4).
40 This includes conditional sale agreements, chattel leasing arrangements and retention of title agreements: I.A. 1986, s.15(9). See Note 15, above.
41 I.R. 1986, r. 2.51(2); but note r. 7.4(6) which applies in cases of urgency.
42 *Re A. R. V. Aviations Ltd.* (1988) 4 B.C.C. 708.
43 There is a fine in default: I.A. 1986, s.15(8).

Duties of an administrator

On appointment the administrator takes into his custody or control all the company's property. He owes a duty to take reasonable care to obtain a proper price for the company's property and in choosing the time to sell.[44] He replaces the directors in taking control of the company's affairs.[45] His first duty is to publish the fact that an administration order has been made to the registrar and other prescribed persons[46] within 14 days, and to all the creditors of whose addresses he is aware within 28 days. He must inform the company "forthwith." There are fines in default: I.A. 1986, section 21.

His other immediate task is to require a statement of affairs of the company by giving notice of that requirement to the company's officers and other relevant people. The statement must show the company's assets and liabilities, the names and addresses of its creditors, details of securities held by the persons making the statement and other information to be prescribed: I.A. 1986, section 22. The detailed rules relating to this statement of affairs are the same as those applicable to the statement of affairs to be submitted to an administrative receiver which are set out in the previous chapter.[47]

The central element in the administration procedure is the formulation of a plan, or proposals, by the administrator, for the purpose of achieving the purpose or purposes specified in the order. Section 23 of the Insolvency Act 1986 requires the administrator to send these proposals to the registrar and the company's creditors within three months of the order. He must also send a copy to each member of the company (or publish an address from which they may obtain a free copy) within that time span. Finally he must lay a copy of his proposals before a meeting of the company's creditors summoned on not less than 14 days' notice: I.A. 1986, section 23. They vote according to the amount of their debts at the date of the administration order and a resolution may be passed by a simple majority in value present and voting.[48] Secured creditors can only vote in respect

[44] In *Re Charnley Davies Ltd.* [1990] BCLC 729.
[45] I.A. 1986, s.17(1).
[46] See I.R. r. 2.10.
[47] *Ante*, p. 711.
[48] See I.R. r. 2.28(1) but see also r. 2.28(1A).

of the balance, if any, of their debt after deducting the estimated value of their security.[49]

If the administrator subsequently wishes to make substantial[50] revisions of his proposals he must publish them to the creditors and members and summon another creditors' meeting to approve the revisions in the same way as the original proposals were published and approved: I.A. 1986, section 25. Where the original purposes are incapable of achievement and time is of the essence, the court may dispense with the section 25 procedure upon application by the administrator for directions under section 14(3).[51]

In principle the implementation of the proposals should be postponed pending the outcome of the creditors' meeting. However the administrator enjoys his powers from the date of the order[52] and section 17(2)(*a*) merely provides that prior to the creditors' meeting he must act in accordance with any directions given by the court. In the absence of negative directions by the court he may, therefore, have power to take steps which would effectively pre-empt any decision at the creditors' meeting, *e.g.* sale of the undertaking. This could however expose him to proceedings under section 27[53] and jeopardise his subsequent release under section 20. Before taking such steps it would be advisable for the administrator to seek directions from the court under section 14(3) authorising the transaction. In Consumer Industrial Press Ltd.[54] Peter Gibbs J. opined that only in exceptional circumstances should the court make a direction which would render nugatory the requirement for a creditors' meeting. Where he is proposing, not a sale of the undertaking, but a sale of a single asset at a good price and time is short, no application for directions is required.[55] After the creditors have approved the proposals he must act in accordance with those proposals or any subsequent revisions: I.A. 1986, section 17(2). He must summon a meeting of the creditors if he is requested to do so by one tenth in value

[49] See I.R. r. 2.24 *et seq.*
[50] This is a matter for the administrator himself to decide.
[51] *Re Smallman* [1989] BCLC 420.
[52] I.A. 1986, s.14.
[53] See *infra.*
[54] (1988) B.C.C. 72.
[55] *Re N.S. Distribution Ltd.* [1990] BCLC 169.

of the company's creditors or the court: I.A. 1986, section 17(3).

The administrator and the creditors

If the meeting of creditors approves the administrator's proposals without modifications the administrator is simply required to carry out his duties in the light of those proposals. If modifications are suggested by the meeting they cannot be approved unless the administrator consents. The result of the meeting must be published to the court, the registrar and other prescribed persons. If the meeting rejects the proposals and no modifications can be agreed the court can discharge the administration order, adjourn the hearing or make any order or interim order it thinks fit: I.A. 1986, section 24. If the meeting approves the proposals (modified or otherwise) it may appoint a committee which may require the administrator to attend before it (on not less than seven days' notice) and to supply reasonable information as to his progress: I.A. 1986, section 26.

Any member or creditor of the company can petition the court under section 27 of the Insolvency Act 1986 if the administrator is acting in manner which is unfairly prejudicial[56] to the interests of the creditors or members generally or of some part of its creditors or members (including the petitioners) or if any actual or proposed act or omission of the administrator is or would be so prejudicial. The court is given wide powers on such a petition, including orders regulating the administrator's future conduct, or requiring him to do or not to do something, summoning a meeting or discharging the administration order. On the other hand no such order may interfere with the implementation of an approved voluntary arrangement[57] or a sanctioned scheme of arrangement.[58] It may only interfere with the implementation of proposals approved under sections 24 and 25 of the Insolvency Act 1986 if the petition was presented within 28 days of such approval: this prevents disruption of the administrator's work when it is substantially underway.

[56] *cf.* C.A. s.459, *ante*, p. 458.
[57] *Ante*, p. 695.
[58] *Post*, p. 838.

Where an administrator has acted fairly and impartially and with proper regard for the interests of all the creditors (and members where necesssary) conscientiously endeavouring to do his best, but through an oversight or inadvertence, has fallen below the standards of a reasonably competent insolvency practitioner in the carrying out of some particular transaction, it is a misuse of language to describe him as having managed the affairs of the company in a manner unfairly prejudicial to the creditors. A petition under section 27 is inappropriate therefore. The proper course is to discharge the administration order, put the company into liquidation and bring proceedings under section 212 of the Insolvency Act 1986: In *Re Charnley Davies Ltd.*[59]

Variation or discharge of an administration order

Section 18 of the Insolvency Act 1986 entitles the administrator to apply to the court for the administration order to be discharged or to be varied so as to specify an additional purpose. He may do this if either the original stated purposes have been achieved or cannot be achieved or he is requested to do so by a creditors' meeting. The court has wide powers on hearing such an application. If the order is discharged or varied the registrar must be informed within 14 days.

Vacation of office and release

An administrator may be removed by the court and he may also resign in the prescribed circumstances[60] by giving notice to the court. He vacates his office if the administration order is discharged or he ceases to be a qualified insolvency practitioner.[61] On vacation of his office his remuneration and proper expenses are charged upon any property of the company in his custody or under his control at that time, and such charge has priority ahead of any security which, as created, was a floating charge. It does not have priority over debts and liabilities incurred while he was an administrator under contracts entered

[59] [1990] BCLC 729.
[60] I.R. 1986, r. 2.53 (ill-health, retirement, conflict of interest).
[61] *Ante*, p. 693.

into or contracts of employment adopted by him, or a predecessor of his, in the carrying out of his or the predecessor's functions[62]: I.A. 1986, section 19. This provision provides some encouragement to third parties to deal with a company in administration.

A person who has ceased to be an administrator has his release, in case of death, when the prescribed notice is given[63] and in any other case at such time as the court may decide. A release may be withheld to enable the administrator's conduct to be investigated.[64] Once he has his release, the administrator is discharged from all liability in respect of his acts or omissions in the administration and otherwise in relation to his conduct as administrator, save in relation to proceedings under section 212 of the Insolvency Act 1986 (summary proceedings against delinquent office holders).[65]

Adjustment of prior transactions

On the making of an administration order certain charges and other transactions involving the company may be set aside under sections 238 to 246 of the Insolvency Act 1986. These sections also apply on a liquidation and are dealt with in Chapter 29 below.

[62] A contract of employment is not deemed to have been adopted by reason of anything done or omitted to be done within 14 days after appointment: I.A. 1986, s.19(5).

[63] See I.R., r. 2.54.

[64] *Re Sheridan Securities* [1988] 4 B.C.C. 200.

[65] *Ante*, p. 419.

Chapter 27

WINDING UP BY THE COURT

[*N.B. References in this chapter are to sections of the Insolvency Act 1986 unless otherwise specified.*]

THIS chapter and the following three chapters deal with the winding up of a company, which is governed by the Insolvency Act 1986. That Act is a consolidation of parts of the Companies Act 1985 (itself a consolidation) and the Insolvency Act 1985. A winding up may be—

(1) by the court; or
(2) voluntary; (s.73).[1]

and there are two kinds of voluntary winding up, namely—

(a) a members' voluntary winding up; and
(b) a creditors' voluntary winding up (s.90).

It will be recalled that winding up by the court on the "just and equitable ground" was explained in Chapter 18. Chapter 29 (Contributories and Creditors; Completion of the Winding Up) is partly concerned with winding up by the court, as well as the present chapter. Chapter 28 is concerned with voluntary winding up.

Section 652 of the Companies Act 1985, which is explained in Chapter 29,[2] provides a method of dissolving a defunct company

[1] A third form, winding up subject to the supervision of the court, was abolished by the Insolvency Act 1985. In practice that form was not used.
[2] *Post*, p. 831.

by striking it off the register without a winding up, and under section 427 of the Companies Act 1985, *post*,[3] the court may order dissolution without winding up where there is a compromise or an arrangement to facilitate a reconstruction or an amalgamation.

A company cannot in Scotland be sequestrated.[4]

In addition to the statutory provisions, section 411 of the 1986 Act provides for the making of rules governing the conduct of company liquidations and section 414 for fixing fees.[5] These rules, the Insolvency Rules 1986,[6] replaced the Companies Winding Up Rules 1949, as amended. The Rules are made by the Lord Chancellor with the concurrence of the Secretary of State. In relation to Scotland, rules can be made by the Secretary of State.[7]

JURISDICTION TO WIND UP COMPANIES

In England

To obtain a winding up by the court, a petition must be presented to the court having the necessary jurisdiction. Section 117 provides that the courts having jurisdiction are—

(1) the High Court, *i.e.* the Companies Court,[8] in the case of all companies registered in England;

(2) Where the paid-up share capital does not exceed £120,000,[9] the county court of the district in which the registered office is situate, provided that such county court has winding up jurisdiction.[10]

[3] p. 843.

[4] *Standard Property Investment Co. Ltd.* v. *Dunblane Hydropathic Co. Ltd.* (1884) 12 R. 328; Bankruptcy (Scotland) Act 1985, s.6(2). A Scottish company could, however, be made notour bankrupt for the purpose of the statutory provisions relating to equalisation of diligences: *Clark* v. *Hinde, Milne & Co.* (1884) 12 R. 347; see now section 185 of the Insolvency Act 1986, applying section 37(1) to (6) of the Bankruptcy (Scotland) Act 1985.

[5] Insolvency Fees Order 1986 (S.I. 1986, No. 2030).

[6] S.I. 1986 No. 1925.

[7] See S.I. 1986, No. 1915 (S.139).

[8] *Eastern Holdings* v. *Singer & Friedlander Ltd.* [1967] 1 W.L.R. 1017.

[9] This amount can be varied by order.

[10] See Civil Courts Order 1983 (S.I. 1983 No. 713) as amended; s.117(4).

In Scotland

The courts having jurisdiction are—

(1) the Court of Session, in the case of all companies registered in Scotland;
(2) where the paid-up share capital does not exceed £120,000,[11] the sheriff court of the sheriffdom in which the registered office is situated: section 120.

GROUNDS FOR WINDING UP BY THE COURT

Section 122 provides that a company[12] may be wound up by the court if—

(1) the company has by special resolution resolved to be wound up by the court[13]; or
(2) in the case of a public company first registered as such, no certificate of ability to commence business has been issued and the company has been registered for more than one year[14]; or
(3) the company does not commence business within a year after its incorporation, or suspends business for a whole year[15]; or
(4) the number of members is reduced below two; or
(5) the company is unable to pay its debts; or
(6) the court is of opinion that it is just and equitable that the company should be wound up. This part of the section was explained in connection with statutory protection of the minority.[16] It should be added that the power to wind up a company under this part is not confined to cases in which there are grounds analogous to those mentioned earlier in the section[17]; or
(7) in the case of a Scottish company, there is subsisting a floating charge over property comprised in the

[11] See note 9.
[12] *i.e.* one formed or registered under the Companies Act 1985 or a former Companies Act: C.A. 1985, s.735, I.A. 1986, s.73.
[13] *cf.* s.84, *post*, p. 790 which is more commonly resorted to, under which a company may pass a special resolution to be wound up voluntarily.
[14] *Ante*, p. 172.
[15] *cf.* C.A. 1985 s.652, *post*, p. 831, under which a defunct company may be struck off the register and so dissolved without being wound up.
[16] *Ante*, p. 449.
[17] *Loch* v. *John Blackwood Ltd.* [1924] A.C. 783 (P.C.); *Symington* v. *Symingtons' Quarries Ltd.* (1905) 8 F. 121; *Baird* v. *Lees*, 1924 S.C. 83; *Ebrahimi* v. *Westbourne Galleries Ltd.* [1973] A.C. 360.

company's property and undertaking and the court is satisfied that the security of the creditor entitled to the benefit of the floating charge is in jeopardy.[18]

There is another, transitional, ground, *viz* that the company is and old public company, *i.e.* a pre-1981 public company which does not comply with the criteria for such a company[19] and did not re-register as a private company in 1981.[20]

Ground (3): Company not carrying on business

The period of a year is fixed by section 122, *ante*, so as to give the company a reasonable time in which to commence or resume business, as the case may be.

A winding-up order will only be made on this ground if the company has no intention of carrying on business.[21]

A company was formed to build and use assembly rooms. Owing to a depression in trade in the neighbourhood, building was suspended for more than three years although the company intended to continue its operations when trade prospects improved. A shareholder presented a winding-up petition which was opposed by four-fifths of the shareholders. *Held*, the petition should be dismissed. Since the conduct of the majority was not unreasonable or something of which the minority had a right to complain, the wishes of the majority were not to be disregarded. It would have been different if business could not have been carried on or there was an intention to abandon the undertaking: *Re Middlesborough Assembly Rooms Co.* (1880) 14 Ch.D. 104 (C.A.).

If a company is formed to carry on business in England and abroad and has carried on business abroad, it will not be wound up merely on the ground that it has not started its business in England within the year if it intends to do so as soon as possible.[22] There is no need to wait a year if it is apparent within the year that the company cannot carry out the objects for which it was formed.[23]

Ground (5): Company unable to pay its debts

This is the ground on which a petition for a compulsory winding up is usually presented.

[18] s.122(2), for the meaning of "in jeopardy" see *ante*, p. 674.
[19] *Ante*, p. 46.
[20] See the Companies (Consequential Provisions) Act 1985, ss.1–9.
[21] *Re Metropolitan Rlwy. Warehousing Co.* (1867) 36 L.J. Ch. 827.
[22] *Re Capital Fire Insurance Association* (1882) 21 Ch.D. 209.
[23] *Re German Date Coffee Co.* (1882) 20 Ch.D. 169 (C.A.) (petition on the "just and equitable" ground).

A company is *deemed* to be unable to pay its debts if—

(*a*) a creditor by assignment or otherwise, to whom the company is indebted in a sum exceeding £750[24] then due has served on the company, by leaving it at the registered office,[24a] a demand in the prescribed form[25] requiring the company to pay the sum so due, and the company has for three weeks thereafter neglected to pay the sum due or to secure[26] or compound for it to the creditor's satisfaction; or

(*b*) in England and Wales, execution issued on a judgment in favour of a creditor is returned unsatisfied in whole or in part; or

(*c*) in Scotland, the induciae of a charge for payment on an extract decree have expired without payment being made; or

(*d*) It is proved to the satisfaction of the court that the company is unable to pay its debts as they fall due; or

(*e*) If it is proved to the satisfaction of the court that, taking the company's contingent and prospective liabilities into account, the value of its assets is less than the amount of its liabilities: section 123.

A company has not neglected to pay a debt within (*a*), *ante*, if it bona fide and upon substantial grounds disputes the debt,[27] or its amount.[28]

[24] This sum may be increased by order.

[24a] The demand need not be served by an officer of the court (*Lord Advocate* v. *Traprain*, 1989 S.L.T. (Sh. Ct.) 99, but, if it is not, the court must have evidence that the person who served the statutory demand was duly authorised by the creditor (*Lord Advocate* v. *Blairwest Investments Ltd.*, 1989 S.L.T. (Sh. Ct.) 97).

[25] See I.R. 1986, rr. 4.4–4.6; Form 4.1; a telex has been held to be an inappropriate form for such a demand: *Re A Company* (1985) BCLC 37.

[26] The security must be a marketable security covering the amount of the debt: *Commercial Bank of Scotland Ltd.* v. *Lanark Oil Co. Ltd.* (1886) 14 R. 147.

[27] *Re London and Paris Banking Corporation* (1874) L.R. 19 Eq. 444; *Cuninghame* v. *Walkinshaw Oil Co. Ltd.* (1866) 14 R. 87; *W. & J. C. Pollok* v. *Gaeta Pioneer Mining Co. Ltd.*, 1907 S.C. 182. Where it is doubtful whether there is a bona fide dispute, the Scots court may sist the petition in order that the petitioners may constitute their debt: *Landauer & Co.* v. *Alexander & Co. Ltd.*, 1919 S.C. 492. There were held to be substantial grounds for dispute in *Walter L. Jacob & Co.* v. *FIMBRA*, 1988 S.C.L.R. 184 (Sh. Ct.). In *Craig* v. *Iona Hotels*, 1988 S.C.L.R. 130 (Sh. Ct.) the sheriff held that (1) where a company was in bona fide doubt as to the identity of a creditor, liquidation proceedings were not a legitimate means of enforcing payment and (2) the statutory demand for payment was defective because it was sent by recorded delivery post to, and not left at, the company's registered office.

[28] *Re A Company* [1984] BCLC 322; compare *Re Tweed's Garages Ltd.* [1962] Ch. 406.

The period of three weeks' neglect required in (*a*) above, has been held to be a period of three clear weeks, excluding the day of service of the demand for payment and the day of presentation of the petition.[29] A creditor will not rely upon a statutory demand where there is a risk of dissipation of the assets in the three week interval. If available, he may use (*b*), (*c*) or (*e*) above; otherwise he can employ the more general ground in (*d*) — that the company is unable to pay its debts as they fall due. Thus in *Taylor's Industrial Flooring Ltd.* v. *M. H. Plant Hire Manchester Ltd.*[30] it was held that if a debt was due and unpaid and could not be disputed on some substantial ground, the presentation of a petition under ground (*d*), *supra*, was amply warranted even in the absence of a statutory demand. The Court of Appeal commented that the practice of prevaricating in the payment of due debts was to be discouraged. A company is also unable to pay its debts if its acceptances have been dishonoured[31] or it has informed a judgment creditor that it has no assets on which to levy execution,[32] or the petitioner has demanded the sum due to him without success.[33] A company is not unable to pay it debts just because it is carrying on a losing business, if its assets exceed its liabilities.[34] However, a company may be unable to pay its debts under (*d*) where its assets exceed its liabilities if its assets are not presently available to meet its current liabilities. Where a company persistently fails or neglects to pay its debts until forced to do so, the court may find that it is unable to pay its debts under (d): *Re A Company* [1986] BCLC 261.

While grounds (*b*)–(*d*) *supra*, do not require the petitioner's debt to be £750 or more, in practice, an order will not usually be made unless this condition is complied with, since there must be circumstances which justify an inference that the company is insolvent.[35] On the other hand, where a company refused to pay a debt of £35 on the ground that it was too small to be the

[29] See *Re Lympne Investments Ltd.* [1972] 1 W.L.R. 523.

[30] [1990] BCLC 216.

[31] *Re Globe, etc., Steel Co.* (1875) L.R. 20 Eq. 337; *Gandy, Petitioner*, 1912 2 S.L.T. 276.

[32] *Re Flagstaff etc., Co. of Utah* (1875) L.R. 20 Eq. 268; *Re Douglas Griggs Engineering Ltd.* [1963] Ch. 19.

[33] *Stephen, Petitioner* (1884) 21 S.L.R. 764.

[34] *Re Joint Stock Coal Company* (1869) L.R. 8 Eq. 146.

[35] *Re Industrial Assurance Association* [1910] W.N. 245.

foundation of a petition, an order was made.[36] The Scottish practice has been to apply the rule that "any creditor, whatever the amount of his debt, is entitled to a winding-up order, unless special circumstances exist for refusing it."[37]

Persons who may Petition for Winding Up by the Court

Subject as below, a winding-up petition may be presented on any of the grounds mentioned above, by any of the following parties—

1 the company or its directors[38];
2 a creditor or creditors (including contingent and prospective creditors);
3 a contributory: section 124(1);
4 in England, where the company is already being wound up voluntarily, the Official Receiver (s.124(5));
5 the Secretary of State for Trade and Industry (Insolvency Act 1986, s.124(4); Insurance Companies Act 1982, s.54; Companies Act 1985, s.440[39]); or
6 in England, in the case of a charitable company, the Attorney-General (Charities Act 1960, s.30.);
7 In England, in the case of a banking company, the Bank of England (Banking Act 1979, s.18).

A creditor

A compulsory liquidation is usually initiated by a creditor's petition. A secured creditor may petition but will normally rely on his security so that the petitioner is almost always an unsecured creditor. Where a petitioning creditor's debt is disputed on a substantial ground the court will usually restrain

[36] *Re World Industrial Bank* [1909] W.N. 148.
[37] *Per* Lord Johnston in *Speirs & Co.* v. *Central Building Co. Ltd.*, 1911 S.C. 330 at p. 333.
[38] All: see *Re Instrumentation Electrical Services* (1988) 4 BCLC 550—some or a majority will not do.
[39] *Ante*, p. 472.

the prosecution of the petition as an abuse of the process of the court, even if the company appears to be insolvent.[40] On the other hand, even if the company is solvent, a creditor whose debt is clearly established can present a petition if there is a persistent refusal to pay the debt.[41]

A creditor whose debt is presently due and who cannot obtain payment normally has a right as between himself and the company *ex debito justitiae* to a winding-up order,[42] even if the company is being wound up voluntarily[43] or is in receivership.[44] This is not displaced merely by showing that the company has appealed against the judgment giving rise to the debt,[45] or has a disputed claim against the petitioning judgment creditor which is the subject of litigation in other proceedings.[46] Where there is a cross-claim the matter is one for the discretion of the judge.[47] It is, however, an improper use of the court to present a petition on the basis of a debt which has never been demanded and for which no opportunity to repay has been given.[48]

The above rule applies only between the petitioning creditor and the company. As between the petitioning creditor and the other creditors he is invoking a class right and so it is improper for him to present a petition for some private purpose. On the other hand if the petition is genuinely for the benefit of the class of creditors, malice on his part will not make the petition improper.[49] As with all matters relating to winding up, the court may have regard to the wishes of the creditors or contributories of the company, as proved by sufficient evidence, and may, for the purpose of ascertaining those wishes, direct meetings to be called, and in the case of creditors regard must be had to the value of each creditor's debt: section 195. This gives the judge a

[40] *Mann* v. *Goldstein* [1968] 1 W.L.R. 1091. A creditor must show an interest in the winding-up; a petitioner who has been paid in full after the presentation of the petition no longer has such an interest: *Furmston, Petitioner*, 1987 S.L.T. (Sh. Ct.) 10.

[41] *Cornhill Insurance plc* v. *Improvement Services Ltd.* [1986] 1 W.L.R. 114.

[42] See *Re Chapel House Colliery Co.* (1883) 24 Ch.D. 259 (C.A.); *Gardner & Co.* v. *Link* (1894) 21 R. 967.

[43] *Re James Millward & Co. Ltd.* [1940] Ch. 333 (C.A.); *Smyth & Co.* v. *The Salem (Oregon) Capitol Flour Mills Co. Ltd.* (1887) 14 R. 441.

[44] *Foxhall & Gyle (Nurseries) Ltd., Petitioners*, 1978 S.L.T. (Notes) 29 (O.H.).

[45] *Re Amalgamated Properties of Rhodesia (1913) Ltd.* [1917] 2 Ch. 115 (C.A.

[46] *Re Douglas Griggs Engineering Ltd.* [1963] Ch. 19; *cf. Re Fitness Centre (South East) Ltd.* [1986] BCLC 518.

[47] *Re L. H. F. Wools Ltd.* [1969] 3 All E.R. 882 (C.A.).

[48] *Re A Company* [1983] BCLC 492.

[49] *Ibid.*

wide unfettered discretion to decide whether to make the order or not. Once an administration order has been made, however, no winding up order can be made and any such petition must be dismissed.[50]

Where the company is insolvent the views of the creditors alone, as the only persons interested, are considered. In other case the views of the contributories are considered.[51] Where there are different classes of creditors the wishes of those particularly interested will be given most weight and, in particular, where the company's assets are not entirely charged in favour of debenture holders the wishes of the unsecured creditors will be primarily considered. Where the assets are entirely charged in favour of debenture holders, if the petition of an unsecured creditor is opposed by the debenture holders the petitioner is entitled to a winding-up order unless the opposing creditors can show that there is no reasonable possibility of the unsecured creditors obtaining a benefit from a winding up.[52] The court must not refuse a winding-up order just because the assets of the company have been mortgaged to an amount in excess of those assets or there are no assets: section 125(1).

If the petition of an unsecured creditor is opposed by the majority in value of the unsecured creditors, although the court has a complete discretion under section 125(1), *ante*, to make or refuse an order and the fact of the majority opposition is not conclusive, if they oppose for good reason (*e.g.* because the assets exceed the liabilities and there are prospects of the company being able to continue business) their wishes will prevail in the absence of special circumstances making winding up desirable.[53] Similarly if the petition is opposed by a minority of creditors this will normally not prevent the order being made although the wishes of the minority may prevail in special cases.[54]

If a company is being wound up voluntarily a compulsory order will not usually be made if the majority of the creditors

[50] *Ante*, p. 731.

[51] If only a contributory opposes a petition it will usually be granted: *Re Camburn Petroleum Products Ltd.* [1979] 1 W.L.R. 86.

[52] *Re Crigglestone Coal Co. Ltd.* [1906] 2 Ch. 327 (C.A.); *Gardner's* case, *ante*.

[53] *Re Vuma Ltd.* [1960] 1 W.L.R. 1283 (C.A.); *Re P. & J. Macrae Ltd.* [1961] 1 W.L.R. 229 (C.A.). See also *Re A. B. C. Coupler Co.* [1961] 1 W.L.R. 243, *Re Fitness Centre (South East) Ltd.* [1986] BCLC 518.

[54] *Re Southard & Co. Ltd.* [1979] 1 W.L.R. 1198 (C.A.).

want the voluntary liquidation to continue.[55] Where there are special circumstances the court may give effect to the wishes of the minority.[56]

Any assignee of a debt or a definite part of a debt can petition,[57] even if a petition was presented in respect of the debt before the assignment.[58] A secured creditor can petition, and his security will not be prejudiced; the holder of bearer debentures can also petition.[59] It has been held that the holder of debenture stock secured by a normal trust deed cannot present a petition as he is not a creditor of the company,[60] the trustees being the proper persons to present the petition in such case.[61]

It has been held in England that a garnishor of a debt due from the company cannot petition, because he is not a creditor, a garnishee order only giving him a lien on the debt and not operating as a transfer of the debt,[62] and that a petition cannot be presented by a person with a claim against the company for unliquidated damages.[63] However, it may be that such persons can petition as "contingent or prospective creditors."[64]

A contributory

The term "contributory" means every person liable to contribute to the assets of the company in the event of its being wound up. As we shall see, it includes the present members and

[55] *Re Home Remedies Ltd.* [1943] Ch. 1; *Re B. Karsberg Ltd.* [1956] 1 W.L.R. 57 (C.A.); *Re J. D. Swain Ltd.* [1965] 1 W.L.R. 909 (C.A.); *cf. Pattisons Ltd.* v. *Kinnear* (1899) 1 F. 551 and *Elsmie & Son* v. *The Tomatin etc. Distillery Ltd.* (1906) 8 F. 434, *Re Fitness Centre (South East) Ltd.* [1986] BCLC 518.

[56] *Bell's Trustees* v. *The Holmes Oil Co. Ltd.* (1900) 3 F. 23; *Bouboulis* v. *Mann, Macneal & Co. Ltd.*, 1926 S.C. 637; *Re Southard & Co. Ltd.* [1979] 1 W.L.R. 1198 (C.A.); *Re H.J. Tomkins & Son* [1990] BCLC 76 and see *post*, p. 804.

[57] See *Re Steel Wing Co.* [1921] 1 Ch. 349.

[58] *Perak Pioneer Ltd.* v. *Petroleum National Bhd* [1986] 3 W.L.R. 105 (P.C.); *cf. Re Paris Skating Rink* (1877) 5 Ch.D. 959.

[59] *Re Olathe Silver Mining Co.* (1884) 27 Ch.D. 278.

[60] *Re Dunderland Iron Ore Co. Ltd.* [1909] 1 Ch. 446.

[61] But see Palmer's *Company Law*, Vol. 1, para. 47.07, n. 45.

[62] *Re Combined Weighing Machine Co.* (1889) 43 Ch.D. 99 (C.A.).

[63] *Re Pen-y-Van Colliery Co.* (1877) 6 Ch.D. 477.

[64] In *Re A Company* [1973] 1 W.L.R. 1566 it was pointed out by Megarry J. at p. 1571 that the *Pen-y-Van* case was decided on section 82 of the 1862 Act which, unlike the present section, says nothing about contingent or prospective creditors and it is very doubtful whether it is an authority for the proposition that a claim for unliquidated damages will not support a petition.

certain past members of the company: section 79.[65] A holder of fully paid-up shares in a limited company is a contributory.[66]

By Section 124(2) the right of a contributory to present a petition is limited to cases where—

(1) the number of members is reduced below two; or
(2) his shares, or some of them, were originally allotted to him or have been held by him, and registered in his name, for at least six months[67] during the 18 months before the commencement of the winding up, or have devolved on him through the death of a former holder: section 124.

The object of the latter provision is to prevent a person acquiring shares to qualify himself to present a petition to wreck the company.

A shareholder whose calls are in arrear can petition, but he must first pay the amount of the call into court.[68] A person to whom shares have been allotted can petition even though the shares have not been registered in his name, unless there is a bona fide dispute as to the allotment.[69] A person who is not an original allottee cannot petition unless he has been registered as a shareholder.[70] A registered shareholder has *locus standi* to petition not withstanding that he is disputing the beneficial ownership of other shares. However, the court may order that the petition should not be advertised until the dispute has been settled.[71]

In the case of the holder of a share warrant the shares are not "registered in his name," so that unless, *e.g.* he is an original allottee, he cannot petition.[72]

[65] *Post*, p. 806.
[66] *Re National Savings Bank Association* (1866) L.R. 1 Ch.App. 547; *Walker and Others, Petitioners* (1894) 2 S.L.T. 230 and 397 (O.H.).
[67] See *Re Gattopardo Ltd.* [1969] 1 W.L.R. 619 (C.A.), where an order was made that a name be entered on the register of members but the company was not a party to the proceedings and therefore was not bound to register the individual as a shareholder, and so the six months' period did not commence when the order was made.
[68] *Re Diamond Fuel Co.* (1879) 13 Ch.D. 499 (C.A.).
[69] *Re* J.N. 2 [1978] 1 W.L.R. 183.
[70] *Re Quickdrome* (1988) BCLC 370 (mere agreement to acquire shares).
[71] *Re Garage Door Associates Ltd.* [1984] 1 W.L.R. 35.
[72] *Re* Chitty J. in *Re Wales Wynaad India Gold Mining Co.* (1882) 21 Ch.D. 849, at p. 853.

The trustee in bankruptcy of a bankrupt shareholder, where the trustee is not on the register of members, is not a contributory and cannot petition.[73] It seems that the personal representative of a deceased shareholder is a contributory.[74]

A person who may be required to repay an amount to an insolvent private company following a payment out of capital by that company for the purchase or redemption of its own shares under section 76,[75] may petition to wind up the company on either the just and equitable or insolvency grounds, but no others: section 124(3).

The court will not, as a rule, make an order on a contributory's petition unless the contributory alleges and proves a financial interest in the winding-up. A member's liability to contribute to the assets of the company on a winding up will suffice for this purposes. A holder of fully paid shares however will have to show, at least to the extent of a prima facie case, that there will be assets for distribution among the shareholders,[76] or that the affairs of the company require investigation in respects which are likely to produce a surplus of assets available for such distribution.[77] However, where a contributory's petition is based on the just and equitable ground[78] and alleges a failure by the company to supply accounts and information about its affairs, so that he cannot tell whether

[73] *Re H. L. Bolton Engineering Co. Ltd.* [1956] Ch. 577. (s.82(2)), by which the trustee represents the bankrupt shareholder, does not come into effect until a winding-up order is made.) In the Scottish case *Ker, Petitioner* (1897) 5 S.L.T. 126 (O.H.), a trustee in bankruptcy was held entitled as a contributory to petition for the removal of a liquidator and for a supervision order.

[74] See *Re Norwich Yarn Co.* (1850) 12 Beav. 366; *Re Cuthbert Cooper & Sons Ltd.* [1937] Ch. 392, at p. 399, where Simonds J. assumed, without deciding, that such a personal representative is a contributory, *per* Wynn-Parry J. in *Re H. L. Bolton Engineering Co. Ltd.* [1956] Ch. 577, at p. 582; and *Re Meyer Douglas Pty. Ltd.* [1965] V.R. 638, where Gowans J. pointed out at p. 655 that in Re Norwich Yarn Co. the statutory definition of "contributory" included not only every member, but also every other person liable to contribute, whether as heir, devisee, executor or administrator of a deceased member. See also *Re Bayswater Trading Co. Ltd.* [1970] 1 W.L.R. 343, and *Howling's Trustees* v. *Smith* (1905) 7 F. 390.

[75] *Ante*, p. 214; *post*, p. 807.

[76] *Re Rica Gold Washing Co.* (1879) 11 Ch.D. 36 (C.A.); followed in *Re Expanded Plugs Ltd.* [1966] 1 W.L.R. 514; *Black* v. *United Collieries Ltd.* (1904) 7 F. 18, *per* Lord Trayner at p. 20.

[77] *Re Othery Construction Ltd.* [1966] 1 W.L.R. 69, considering *Re Haycraft Gold etc., Co.* [1900] 2 Ch. 230 and *Re Newman and Howard, post.*

[78] *Ante*, p. 449.

there will be a surplus for contributories,[79] a surplus need not be shown. The jurisdiction of the court to order the winding up of a company on the just and equitable ground on a contributory's petition is very wide and depends upon a full investigation of the facts at the hearing. A contributory may rely on a report by Department of Trade and Industry inspectors to support his petition.[80]

A petition by a contributory is uncommon. Such a petition which is opposed by the majority of the contributories will not be granted except where the conduct of the majority is something of which the minority have a right to complain.[81]

The right of a contributory to petition cannot be excluded or limited by the articles.

The articles provided that no winding-up petition could be presented without the consent of two directors, or unless a resolution to wind up was passed at a general meeting, or unless the petitioner held one-fifth of the share capital. None of these conditions was fulfilled. *Held*, the restrictions were invalid and a petition could be presented: *Re Peveril Gold Mines Ltd.* [1898] 1 Ch. 122 (C.A.).

The Official Receiver

The Official Receiver can petition for a winding up by the court when a company is already in voluntary liquidation in England. An order will only be made if the court is satisfied on a balance of probabilities,[82] that the existing liquidation cannot be continued with due regard to the interests of the creditors or contributories: section 124(5). The fact that a liquidator must now be a qualified insolvency practitioner and, in a creditors voluntary winding up, his powers are restricted prior to the creditors' meeting, may reduce the occasions upon which this can be shown.

[79] *Re Newman and Howard Ltd.* [1962] Ch. 257.
[80] *Re St. Piran Ltd.* [1981] 3 All E.R. 270.
[81] *Re Middlesbrough Assembly Rooms Co.* (1880) 14 Ch.D. 104 (C.A.), *ante*, p. 704; *Galbraith* v. *Merito Shpg. Co. Ltd.*, 1947 S.C. 446; *Re Tivoli Freeholds Ltd.* [1972] V.R. 445; *Re St. Piran Ltd.* [1981] 3 All E.R. 270.
[82] *Re J. Russell Electronics Ltd.* [1968] 1 W.L.R. 1252.

The Secretary of State for Trade and Industry

Where a petition for compulsory winding up is presented by the Secretary of State after he has reached the conclusion, as a result of investigations, that it is expedient in the public interest to wind up the company compulsorily,[83] his conclusion, without being decisive, ought to be given appropriate weight by the court; where there are circumstances of suspicion it is highly desirable that the winding up be by the court; and the passing of a resolution for voluntary winding up shortly before the petition is presented ought not to be allowed to put the voluntary winding up in an entrenched position which can only be demolished if the Secretary of State can show that voluntary winding up would be markedly inferior to compulsory winding up.[84]

A report of inspectors appointed by him is prima facie evidence on which the court may act in deciding to make a winding up order on a petition by the Secretary of State.[85] The Secretary of State's petition is in his own capacity and not that of a notional creditor.[86]

PETITION FOR WINDING UP BY THE COURT

In England the winding-up petition must be in one of the forms specified in the Insolvency Rules 1986.[87]

In England it has been held (in a case where the Secretary of State presented the petition on the ground that winding up was expedient by reason of matters referred to in a report of inspectors appointed to investigate the affairs of the company) that when grave charges are leveled against individuals in a petition, the court will not be satisfied with merely prima facie evidence. The petitioner must, if practicable, prove facts by the evidence of witnesses who have first-hand knowledge of the matters on which they give evidence.[88] However, in a later case

[83] See I.A. 1986, s.124A and p. 472, ante.

[84] *Re Lubin, Rosen and Associates* [1975] 1 W.L.R. 122.

[85] *Re Armvent Ltd.* [1975] 3 All E.R. 441.

[86] *Re Highfield Commodities Ltd.* [1985] 1 W.L.R. 149.

[87] S.I. 1986 No. 1925, r. 12.7(1); forms 4.2 & 4.3. For Scotland see S.I. 1986 No. 2298 (S. 170) and 1986 No. 2297 (S. 169).

[88] *Re A. B. C. Coupier Co. (No. 2)* [1962] 1 W.L.R. 1236; not followed in *Re Travel & Holiday Clubs Ltd., post.*

it was held that the report of inspectors stands in a wholly different position from the ordinary affidavit evidence and represents the conclusions of a statutory fact-finding body, after hearing oral evidence and examination of books. The court is entitled to look at the report and accept it not as hearsay evidence but as material of a different character. At least where the report is not challenged by the company, the court does not have to be satisfied anew by evidence of the ordinary nature as to the facts found in the report.[89]

After the presentation of a petition (which has not been struck out or dismissed[90]) an application may be made to the court for the appointment of a *provisional liquidator*: I.A. 1986, s.135. The applicant must provide a deposit or security for the appointee's remuneration.[91] In England the appointment may be made at any time before the making of a winding-up order, and the person usually appointed is the Official Receiver. In Scotland the appointment may be made at any time before the first appointment of liquidators: section 135. An appointment is made if the assets are in jeopardy,[92] or to avoid possible prejudice.[93]

The provisional liquidator takes all the company's property into his custody or under his control (s.144), and after his appointment no legal proceedings can be commenced or continued against the company without leave of the court: section 130(2). An inter pleader summons to which the company is made respondent is a proceeding against the company[94]; so also is distress levied on the company's property by the Commissioners of Customs and Excise for non-payment of VAT.[95] In one case the court gave leave to proceed to a person

[89] *Re Travel & Holiday Clubs Ltd.* [1967] 1 W.L.R. 711, where it was said (at p. 716c) that it is undesirable that inspectors who have conducted an enquiry should have to give evidence of their findings upon which they would be liable to be cross-examined. This case was followed in *Re S.B.A. Properties Ltd.* [1967] 1 W.L.R. 799. And see *Re Allied Produce* [1967] 1 W.L.R. 1469.

[90] *Re A Company* [1973] 1 W.L.R. 1566.

[91] I.R. 1986, rr. 4.27 & 4.28.

[92] *e.g. Levy* v. *Napier*, 1962 S.C. 468, in which a deferred shareholder whose petition was opposed by the controlling ordinary shareholders averred that he was apprehensive that the proceeds of the sale of the company's business and assets were being depleted to his prejudice.

[93] *e.g. McCabe* v. *Andrew Middleton (Enterprises) Ltd.* 1969 S.L.T. (Sh.Ct.) 29.

[94] *Eastern Holdings* v. *Singer & Friedlander Ltd.* [1967] 1 W.L.R. 1017.

[95] *Re Memco Engineering Ltd.* [1986] Ch. 86.

who had an unimpugnable right to a claim for specific performance of an agreement to sell property belonging to the company.[96] The appointment of a provisional liquidator has the same result as the making of a winding-up order in that the board of directors of the company becomes *functus officio* and its powers are assumed by the liquidator,[97] but notwithstanding the appointment the board has some residuary powers, *e.g.* it can instruct solicitors and counsel to oppose the petition and, if a winding-up order is made, to appeal against it.[98] The board can also act in interlocutory proceedings, including a motion to discharge the provisional liquidator.

The court may also, after the presentation of a petition (which is still subsisting[99]) and before a winding-up order has been made, on the application of the company or of any creditor or contributory, stay or restrain any pending legal proceedings against the company: section 126. Section 126 is an exception to the rule[1] that proceedings pending in the Supreme Court cannot be restrained by injunction. The object of sections 126 and 130(2) is "to put all unsecured creditors upon an equality, and to pay them *pari passu.*"[2]

Withdrawal of petition

A petitioner can apply to the court for leave to withdraw his petition so long as he does so at least five days prior to the hearing and satisfies the court that the petition has not been advertised, that no notices (whether in support or in opposition) have been received by him with reference to the petition, and that the company consents to an order being made.[3]

Hearing of petition

The company and any creditor or contributory may attend the hearing of the petition. For this purpose a person is a creditor if

[96] *Re Coregrange Ltd.* [1984] BCLC 453.
[97] *Post*, p. 763.
[98] *Re Union Accident Insce. Co. Ltd.* [1972] 1 W.L.R. 640.
[99] See note 90, above.
[1] In the Supreme Court of Judicature (Consolidation) Act 1925, s.41.
[2] *Per* Lindley L.J. in *Re Oak Pits Colliery Co.* (1882) Ch.D. 322 (C.A.) at p. 329.
[3] I.R. 1986, r. 4.15 and see Practice Direction [1987] 1 All E.R. 107.

he is a creditor for a present debt. a prospective debt or a contingent debt. Whether a person is a contingent creditor depends on circumstances existing at the date of the hearing.[4]

On the hearing of a petition the court may dismiss it, or adjourn the hearing conditionally or unconditionally, or make any interim order, or any other order that it thinks fit: section 125(1).[5]

The court may have regard to the wishes of the creditors or contributories: section 195.[6]

When a judgment creditor[7] is deprived of the right *ex debito justitiae* to a winding-up order because his petition is opposed by the majority of the creditors, the fair practice is to make no order as to costs.[8] The same is true where the petitioning creditor is not a judgment creditor but his debt is undisputed.[9] *Aliter* if the petitioning creditor acted unreasonably in presenting or prosecuting his petition,[10] or the company is being wound up voluntarily and no evidence is filed on behalf of the petitioner beyond an affidavit verifying the petition.[11] In special circumstances costs may be awarded against one party, *e.g.* where the company failed to defend an action so that the plaintiff petitioned to wind up the company, on the petition being dismissed and the action set aside, the company was held liable for the costs of the petition.[12] Although, where a petitioner was paid in full by the company, apart from his costs, the petitioner was unable to recover his costs because he had not complied with the rules as to advertisement of the petition.[13]

When a winding-up order is made, it is usual to order the costs of (1) the petitioner, (2) the company, and (3) one set of

[4] *Re S.B.A. Properties Ltd.* [1967] 1 W.L.R. 799.
[5] *Ante.*
[6] *See also Re Middlesbrough Assembly Rooms Co.* (1880) 14 Ch.D. 104 (C.A.), and *Galbraith* v. *Merito Shpg. Co. Ltd.*, 1947 S.C. 446.
[7] Scots equivalent, a creditor who has obtained a decree.
[8] *Re R. W. Sharman Ltd.* [1957] 1 W.L.R. 774; *Re A. B. C. Coupler Co.* [1961] 1 W.L.R. 243.
[9] *Re Sklan Ltd.* [1961] 1 W.L.R. 1013.
[10] *Re A. E. Hayter & Sons (Porchester) Ltd.* [1961] 1 W.L.R. 1008.
[11] *Re Riviera Pearls Ltd.* [1962] 1 W.L.R. 722.
[12] *Re Lanaghan Bros. Ltd.* [1977] 1 All E.R. 265. See also *Re M. McCarthy & Co. (Builders) Ltd. (No. 2)* [1976] 2 All E.R. 339 and *Re Arrow Leeds Ltd.* [1986] BCLC. 538.
[13] *The Shushella Ltd.* (1982) 126 S.J. 577.

creditors and one set of contributories, to be paid out of the assets. Any other creditor who wishes to appear does so at his own expense. As a general rule no order for costs will be made in favour of one creditor against another.[14]

A copy of the order must be sent by the company to the Registrar of Companies: section 130(1).

Section 711 of the Companies Act 1985 provides that the Registrar must cause notice of the receipt by him of the copy of the order to be published in the *Gazette*. The notice must state the company's name, a description of the document received and the date of receipt.

The court has power to stay a winding-up order either altogether or for a limited time,[15] on such terms and conditions as it thinks fit, if an application is made to it by the liquidator or (in England) the Official Receiver or any creditor or contributory. In England the court may require the Official Receiver to furnish a report on matters relevant to the application. A copy of any order made by the court under this provision must be sent to the Registrar: section 147. Such an order is not usually made unless all the creditors are paid or satisfied, but the court will have regard to commercial morality and not just to the interests of the creditors.[16] As a matter of practice a stay is never granted, and there are good reasons for the practice.[17]

An appeal from the making of a winding-up order in England may be brought within 4 weeks: R.S.C., Ord. 59, r. 4.[18] An order made by a Lord Ordinary in Scotland may be reviewed by the Inner House if a reclaiming motion is enrolled within 14 days: section 162.[19]

Where an order winding up a solvent company was made on a contributory's petition opposed by the company and another contributory, and the company appealed against the order, the company

[14] *Re Esal (Commodities) Ltd.* [1985] BCLC 450. This case also provides guidance for costs where an alternative scheme of arrangement under section 425 of the Companies Act 1985, *post*, p. 838, is under consideration.

[15] See *Re Boston Timber Fabrications Ltd.* [1984] BCLC 328.

[16] *Re Telescriptor Ltd.* [1903] 2 Ch. 174.

[17] See, *per* Plowman J. in *Re A. & B.C. Chewing Gum Ltd.* [1975] 1 W.L.R. 579, at p. 592.

[18] See I.R. 1986, r. 7.47.

[19] *e.g. Levy, Petitioner*, 1963 S.C. 46.

had to provide security for the costs of the appeal otherwise than from the company's assets. It would have been wrong, if the appeal failed, for the petitioner to be liable to bear any proportion of the costs of the appeal or of a liquidation. An order was made that security be provided by the directors or shareholders promoting the appeal: *Re E. K. Wilson & Sons Ltd.* [1972] 1 W.L.R. 791 (C.A.).

CONSEQUENCES OF A WINDING-UP ORDER

The consequences of the making of a winding-up order date back to an earlier date than that on which the order was actually made. This date is called the *commencement of the winding up* and is:

(1) the time of the presentation of the petition; or
(2) where, before the presentation of the petition, the company was in voluntary liquidation, the time of the passing of the resolution for voluntary winding up (s.129).

The consequences of a winding-up order are:

(1) Any disposition of the property of the company, and any transfer of shares or alteration in the status of the members, after the commencement of the winding up, is void unless the court otherwise orders: section 127.

The effect of a winding-up order is to divest the company of beneficial ownership of its assets despite its continuance as legal owner.[20]

The object of section 127 is to prevent, during the period which must elapse before a petition can be heard, the improper alienation and dissipation of the property of a company *in extremis*. However, where a company is trading, the court can sanction transactions in the ordinary course of business—otherwise the presentation of a petition, whether well- or ill-founded, would paralyse the company's trade.[21] Thus the court may sanction the continued operation of the company's bank account in the ordinary course of business, so long as there is no serious doubt as to the company's solvency.[22] Further in the

[20] *Ayerst* v. *C. & K. (Construction) Ltd.* [1976] A.C. 167.
[21] *Per* Lord Cairns in *Re Wiltshire Iron Co.* (1868) L.R. 3 Ch.App. 443, at p. 447; see also *United Dominions Trust Ltd., Noters*, 1977 S.L.T. (Notes) 56 (O.H.) (warrant to sell security subjects valid).
[22] *Re A Company (No. 007532 of 1986)* [1987] BCLC 200.

case of a solvent company the court will normally sanction a disposition which the directors consider to be necessary or expedient in the interests of the company for reasons which an intelligent and honest man could reasonably hold.[23]

Between the date of the presentation of the petition and the making of a winding-up order X advanced £1,200 to the company to enable it to pay wages due to the staff and took a debenture as security. X knew, at the time of the issue of the debenture, of the presentation of the petition. *Held*, the debenture was valid: *Re Park, Ward & Co. Ltd.* [1926] Ch. 828.

The court may order that a debenture taken after the commencement of the winding up is not void if the money is advanced, not for the payment of wages, but for the company's benefit to enable it to carry out its contracts and the lender has acted in good faith and with the honest intention of benefiting the company.[24] If however the disposition was made with a view to assisting the company's creditors, it will not be validated.[25]

Where the company has an overdraft on its bank account the court will freeze that account as at the date of the presentation of the petition by discontinuing all further dealings on the existing account and will require all subsequent dealings to be on a new and separate account.[26]

After the presentation of a petition property may safely be transferred or payment made *to* the company,[27] but payments made *by* the company in respect of debts previously incurred must be refunded by the recipient,[28] and property transferred is held by the recipient on trust for the company, unless an order under section 21 is obtained.[29]

The word "disposition" in section 127 includes dispositions of a company's property whether made by the company or by a

[23] *Re Burton & Deakin Ltd.* [1977] 1 W.L.R. 390.
[24] *Re Steane's (Bournemouth) Ltd.* [1950] 1 All E.R. 21, applied in *Re Clifton Place Garage Ltd.* [1970] 1 All E.R. 352 (C.A.).
[25] *Re Webb's Electrical* [1988] BCLC 332.
[26] *Re Gray's Inn Construction Co. Ltd.* [1980] 1 W.L.R. 711 (C.A.).
[27] *Mersey Steel Co.* v. *Naylor, Benzon & Co.* (1882) 9 Q.B.D. 648 (C.A.); (1884) 9 App.Cas. 434; *Millar* v. *The National Bank of Scotland Ltd.* (1891) 28 S.L.R. 884 (O.H.).
[28] *Re Civil Service and General Store Ltd.* (1888) 57 L.J.Ch. 119; *M'Lintock* v. *Lithauer*, 1924 S.L.T. 755 (O.H.).
[29] *Re French's Wine Bar* [1987] BCLC 499.

third party, or whether made directly or indirectly.[30] However where prior to the petition, the company has entered into an unconditional contract capable of specific performance to sell its property the completion of the contract after the presentation of the petition is not a disposition of its property within section 127 because whatever interest the company has at that time gives it no control over the property. Leave is therefore not required: *Re French's Wine Bar.*[31]

The court may, under the section, authorise a disposition of a company's property after presentation of the petition notwithstanding that a winding-up order has not yet been made and will do so if the disposition will benefit creditors of the company if an order is made.[32]

Section 127 contains no express provision as to who can apply for the validation of dispositions. However, an applicant must have some discernible interest in the matter. The company can apply under the section. A shareholder has a sufficient *locus standi* to apply. A director may have a sufficient *locus standi.*[33]

The rule which makes transfers of shares and alterations in the status of members void operates for the benefit of the company and its creditors, not for the benefit of third parties, and so, in Scotland, an assignation of shares, if duly intimated to the company, cuts out a subsequent arrestment of the shares.[34]

(2) As regards English companies and such property of Scottish companies as is situated in England, any attachment, sequestration, distress or execution put in force against the estate or effects of the company after the commencement of the winding up is void: section 128.[35] As regards Scottish companies and such

[30] *Re Leslie Engineers Co. Ltd.* [1976] 1 W.L.R. 292. But see *Re Mal Bower's Macquarie Electrical Centre Pty. Ltd. (in Liqdn.) etc.* [1974] 1 N.S.W.L.R. 254 to the effect that the section does not affect agencies such as a bank interposing between a company, as disponor, and the recipient of the property, as disponee.

[31] *Ibid.* In *Site Preparations* v. *Buchan Development Co.*, 1983 S.L.T. 317 (O.H.), a floating charge created after the presentation of a petition was held to be a disposition.

[32] *Re A. I. Levy (Holdings) Ltd.* [1964] Ch. 19.

[33] *Re Argentum Reductions (U.K.) Ltd.* [1975] 1 W.L.R. 186.

[34] *Jackson* v. *Elphick* (1902) 10 S.L.T. 146 (O.H.).

[35] A prior charging order nisi will not be confirmed after a liquidation: *Roberts Petroleum Ltd.* v. *Bernard Kenny Ltd.* [1983] A.C. 192.

property of English companies as is situated in Scotland, any winding up is, as at the date of its commencement, equivalent to an arrestment in execution and decree of furthcoming, and to a completed poinding, and also to a decree of adjudication of the heritable property of the company for payment of the whole of its debts: section 185.

In spite of its plain words, section 128 is subject to the provisions of section 126, *ante*, and section 130(2), *post* the combined effect of which is that a creditor who wishes validly to proceed to execution can apply to the court for leave.[36]

The effect of section 185 is to equalise diligence in Scotland by depriving any creditor who does diligence after the commencement of winding up (or within 60 days before that date) of the benefit which his diligence would otherwise have given him. The section is not restricted by the provisions of section 130(2), *post.* Accordingly the court could not under section 130(2) sanction diligence contrary to section 185.[37] Section 185 has been held not to render ineffectual an arrestment executed within 60 days before the commencement of winding up but superseded, owing to payment of the debt, before that date.[38]

(3) After a winding-up order has been made or a provisional liquidator has been appointed, no action can be proceeded with or commenced against the company except by leave of the court: section 130(2).

The purpose of section 130(2) is to ensure that when a company goes into liquidation the assets are administered for the benefit of all the creditors.[39]

Notwithstanding the section, if a company in liquidation brings an action the defendant may, without leave of the court, set up a cross-demand for liquidated or unliquidated damages,

[36] *Re Lancashire Cotton Spinning Co.* (1887) 35 Ch.D. 656 (C.A.); *The Constellation* [1966] 1 W.L.R. 272.

[37] *Allan* v. *Cowan* (1892) 20 R. 36; see also opinion of Lord Trayner in *Radford & Bright Ltd.* v. *D. M. Stevenson & Co.* (1904) 6 F. 429, at p. 431.

[38] *Johnston* v. *Cluny Trustees*, 1957 S.C. 184.

[39] *Per* Widgery L.J. in *Langley Constructions* (*Brixham*) *Ltd.* v. *Wells* [1969] 1 W.L.R. 503 (C.A.), at p. 508; *cf.* the effects of an administration order, *ante*, p. 732.

but only as a set-off to reduce or extinguish the plaintiff's claim.[40]

Since "the court" is defined as "the court having jurisdiction to wind up the company" (Companies Act 1985, s.744), an action brought in a Scottish court against a company registered in England requires to be sisted until leave of the English court has been obtained.[41]

(4) On a winding-up order being made in England, the Official Receiver becomes the liquidator, and he continues to act until another person becomes liquidator. He also acts as liquidator during any vacancy: section 136(2), (3).

(5) On a winding-up order being made, the powers of the directors cease,[42] and are assumed by the liquidator. Some of the duties of the directors cease, too, *e.g.* as to the mode of keeping the company's accounting records under what is now section 221 to 223 of the Companies Act 1985.[43] One of the duties which remains after the making of a winding-up order is the duty not to disclose confidential information.[44]

(6) On a winding-up order being made, the employees of the company are *ipso facto*, dismissed,[45] and may be able to sue for damages for breach of contract, but an employee who continues to discharge the same duties and receive the same wages as before may be held to have entered by tacit relocation into a contract of service with the liquidator.[46] Where a liquidator re-engaged employees in order to complete certain contracts and thereafter dismissed them on the ground of redundancy, the employees were held, for the purposes of the Redundancy Payments Act 1965, to have been continuously employed by one employer (*i.e*

[40] *Langley Constructions (Brixham) Ltd.* v. *Wells*, *supra*.
[41] *Martin* v. *Port of Manchester Insce. Co. Ltd.*, 1934 S.C. 143. And see *Coclas* v. *Bruce Peebles & Co. Ltd.* (1908) 16 S.L.T. 7 (O.H.).
[42] *Fowler* v. *Broad's Patent Night Light Co.* [1893] 1 Ch. 724.
[43] *Ante*, Chap. 20.
[44] *Re Country Traders Distributors Ltd. etc.* [1974] 2 N.S.W.L.R. 135.
[45] *Chapman's Case* (1866) L.R. 1 Eq. 346; *Laing* v. *Gowans* (1902) 10 S.L.T. 461 (O.H.).
[46] *Day* v. *Tait* (1900) 8 S.L.T. 40 (O.H.).

the company) from the dates of their initial engagement by the company down to the dates of their dismissal by the liquidator.[47]

Every invoice, order for goods or business letter issued by or on behalf of the company or the liquidator, on which the company's name appears, must contain a statement that the company is being wound up: section 188.

Appointment of special manager

Where either a company has gone into liquidation or a provisional liquidator has been appointed, the liquidator or provisional liquidator, as appropriate, may apply to the court for the appointment of a special manager of the company's business or property if the nature of that business or property or the interests of the creditors, members or contributories require it. The court may give the special manager such powers as it thinks fit. Such a person need not, however, be a qualified insolvency practitioner but must give such security (or in Scotland, caution) as is prescribed[48]: section 177. This power applies to all kinds of liquidation.

PROCEEDINGS AFTER A WINDING UP

Statement of company's affairs and investigation by the official receiver

Where the court has made a winding up order or appointed a provisional liquidator the official receiver[49] may require a statement of affairs to be produced. The persons who may be required to make such a statement, its contents and the procedural aspects are the same as those on the appointment of an administrative receiver[50] or administrator[51]: section 131.

In England it is the duty of the official receiver after a winding up order has been made to carry out two investigations: (1) if the company has failed, into the causes of the failure, and

[47] *Smith* v. *Lord Advocate*, 1978 S.C. 259.
[48] I.R. 1986, rr. 4.206–4.210.
[49] In Scotland, the liquidator, or provisional liquidator as appropriate.
[50] *Ante*, Chap. 25.
[51] *Ante*, Chap. 26.

(2), in any case, into the promotion, formation, business dealings and affairs of the company. Consequently, he may make a report to the court, which is prima facie evidence of the facts stated in it in any proceedings: section 132. The official receiver is therefore bound under (2) to investigate all compulsory liquidations and not just those concerned with insolvency, but he need only make a report to the court if he thinks fit.

If the company has insufficient assets to cover the expenses of the liquidation and the official receiver is satisfied that no further investigation is required he may apply for an early dissolution, in which case his responsibilities cease. This procedure is dealt with in Chapter 29, *post.*[52]

Public examination of officers

The Cork Committee recommended the revival of the use of public examinations in cases of corporate insolvency.[53] Accordingly section 133(1) provides that the official receiver[54] may at any time before the dissolution of the company apply to the court for the public examination of (a) anyone who is or has been an officer of the company; (b) has acted as liquidator, administrator, receiver, or manager of its property; or (c) anyone else who has been concerned or has taken part in the promotion, formation or management of the company.

The official receiver must apply for a public examination if he is requested to do so by either one half of the creditors or three quarters of the contributories: section 133(2).

The court will appoint a day for the examination and failure to attend is a contempt of court. Failure to attend without a reasonable excuse may even lead to the issue of a warrant for a person's arrest and the seizure of any relevant papers etc. in his possessions: section 134.

At the public examination, questions as to the company's formation, promotion, management or as to the person's conduct of its affairs or dealings with that company may be put by the official receiver, liquidator, special manager,[55] any

[52] p. 826.
[53] Paras. 653–657.
[54] In Scotland, the liquidator.
[55] *Ante*, p. 764.

creditor who has tendered a claim or any contributory: section 133(3), (4).

Appointment of a liquidator

In England the official receiver becomes the first liquidator until another person is appointed. There are two ways in which such a successor may be appointed:

(1) Within 12 weeks of the winding up order the official receiver must decide whether or not to summon separate meetings of the company's creditors and contributories so that they might choose a liquidator in his place. If he decides not to do so he must notify the court, creditors and contributories to that effect but he must summon the meetings if requested by one quarter in value of the creditors, and any notice to the creditors of his refusal to summon the meetings must refer to that obligation: section 136.

If such meetings are held, each meeting may nominate a liquidator and, in the event of a disagrement, the creditors' nominee is to be the liquidator of the company subject to an application by any creditor or contributory to the court for the appointment of the contributories' nominee or some other person: section 139. This is similar to the appointment of a liquidator in a creditors' voluntary winding up except that the directors as such cannot apply to the court.[56] If no person is chosen as liquidator by the meetings, the official receiver must decide whether to refer the question of the appointment to the Secretary of State: section 137(2).

(2) The official receiver always has the alternative of applying to the Secretary of State for the appointment of a liquidator rather than summoning the meetings of creditors and contributories. The Secretary of State has complete discretion whether to appoint a liquidator but if he does so, the liquidator must give notice of his appointment to the creditors or advertise his appointment as directed by the court: section 137(3), (4).

Where a winding-up order either follows the discharge of an administration order[57] or is made at the time of a voluntary

[56] *Post*, p. 796.
[57] *Ante*, p. 739.

arrangement,[58] the court may appoint the administrator or supervisor, as appropriate, as liquidator. In such cases the official receiver does not become the liquidator at all: section 140.

The liquidator is to be known by the style of "the liquidator" of the particular company unless he is also the official receiver, where he is to be known as "the official receiver and liquidator" of the company: section 163.

In Scotland a liquidator, referred to as the "interim liquidator" is appointed by the court at the time when the winding-up order is made. He must, within 28 days of the winding-up order, summon separate meetings of creditors and contributories to choose another person or himself to be liquidator, except that, if the ground for winding-up is inability to pay debts, the interim liquidator need summon only a meeting of creditors. If at the meeting or meetings no person is appointed liquidator, the interim liquidator reports that fact to the court which makes the appointment: section 138.

The provisions of sections 139 and 140 apply to Scotland as in England.

Liquidation committees

If meetings of creditors and contributories are summoned to choose a liquidator, they may also, in England, appoint a committee (of creditors and contributories) to be known as the liquidation committee. This committee then fulfils several functions in the liquidation procedure the main one being to sanction certain actions of the liquidator.[59] Their exact composition and functions are governed by the Rules.[60] Such a committee may alternatively be appointed by general meetings of creditors and contributories summoned by the liquidator (not the official receiver). The liquidator must summon such meetings if requested to do so by one tenth in value of the creditors. If there is no liquidation committee or the liquidator is the official receiver the functions of the committee are vested in the Secretary of State: section 141.

[58] *Ante*, p. 695.
[59] See, *e.g.* s.167, I.A. 1986.
[60] I.R. 1986, rr. 4.151–4.172.

In Scotland a liquidation committee may be established by the meetings of creditors and contributories (or of creditors only) summoned under section 138: section 142. The provisions of section 142 are the same as those of section 141 applicable to England except that where there is no liquidation committee, the functions of the committee are vested in the court, and that a liquidation committee may have conferred on it the powers and duties of commissioners in a sequestration.

The Liquidator as Office Holder

Office holders

The Insolvency Act applies certain basic rules and gives certain common powers to office holders. These are an administrator appointed under an administration order,[61] an administrative receiver,[62] a liquidator and a provisional liquidator (in any form of winding up). All such persons must be qualified insolvency practitioners[63]: section 230. If any joint appointment is made the terms of the appointment must specify whether they are required to act together or may operate individually: section 231. The acts of an office holder are valid despite any defect in his appointment, nomination or qualifications[64]: section 232.

Administrative receivers and administrators have been the subject of Chapters 25 and 26 but it is convenient to deal with the provisions applicable to all office holders in one place. The following provisions apply therefore to both those earlier Chapters, this Chapter and Chapter 28 on voluntary winding up.

Supplies by public utilities

Although the utilities, such as gas, water and electricity are unsecured creditors, they could exercise considerable power against an office holder by refusing to continue supplies unless their debts from the company were paid in full. If the

[61] *Ante*, Chap. 26.
[62] *Ante*, p. 700.
[63] *Ante*, p. 693.
[64] *cf.* C.A. 1985, s.285; *ante*, p. 127.

company's business was continuing this would be a potent threat. The Cork Committee therefore recommended[65] that an office holder must be treated as a new customer with a statutory right to receive supplies independently of the company whose account is in arrears. This recommendation was accepted and is contained in section 233.

The utilities affected are the British Gas Corporation, all public electricity suppliers,[66] water undertakers and telecommunications operators.[67] Although they may not require outstanding bills of the company to be paid[68] before supplying the office holder, they may require a personal guarantee from him for any subsequent supplies.

This section also applies to the supervisor of a voluntary arrangement who is not an office holder for any other purpose.[69]

Getting in the company's property

The court may order any person who possesses any property, books, papers or records apparently belonging to the company to transfer them to the office holder. If the office holder[70] seizes or disposes of property which does not belong to the company but which he reasonably believes he is entitled to take or deal with, he is not liable for any loss or damage except that caused by his own negligence and is entitled to a lien on the property to recover any expenses: section 234.

Co-operation with the office holder—private examination

Any person who may be asked to furnish a statement of affairs[71] to an office holder (including the official receiver) must on request give such information concerning the company's affairs as the office holder may reasonably require and must attend on him when required to do so: section 235. Such private

[65] Paras. 1451–1462.
[66] As defined in the Electricity Act 1989.
[67] See the Telecommunications Act 1984 and s.233(5)(*c*).
[68] Directly or indirectly, *e.g.* by insisting on a coin-operated meter supply so calibrated as to recoup the previous unpaid amounts.
[69] *Ante*, p. 699.
[70] This includes the official receiver.
[71] *Ante*.

examinations are designed to assist the office holder to carry out his task quickly and effectively.

Inquiry into company's dealings

The office holder[72] is given powers to apply to the court if there is insufficient co-operation under the provisions detailed above. On such an application the court may summon any officer of the company, any person known or suspected of possessing company property or to be indebted to the company, or any person it thinks capable of giving information about the company's affairs, to appear before it and to submit an affidavit to produce any relevant documents: section 236.

The court may examine such a person on oath (in any part of the U.K. or abroad) and he may be ordered to hand over property to the office holder or to pay to him any amount due to the company; section 237.

THE PROPERTY OF THE COMPANY IN A WINDING UP BY THE COURT

Custody of company's property

When a winding-up order has been made, or a provisional liquidator appointed, the liquidator must take into his custody or under his control all the property to which the company is or appears to be entitled. In Scotland, if and so long as there is no liquidator, all the company's property is deemed to be in the custody of the court: section 144.

Winding up does not, as does bankruptcy or sequestration, operate as a *cessio bonorum* or transfer of property: the company's property remains vested in it as before[73] unless, under section 145, the court makes an order vesting it in him in his official name. Section 234[74] and section 160[75] also contain

[72] Including at any time, the official receiver.

[73] *Per* Warrington L.J. in *Re H. J. Webb & Co.* (*Smithfield*, *London*) *Ltd.* [1922] 2 Ch. 369 (C.A.), at p. 388; *Per* Lord President Inglis in *Queensland Mercantile etc. Co. Ltd.* v. *Australasian Investment Co. Ltd.* (1888) 15 R. 935 at p. 939; *per* Lord Hailsham in *Alexander Ward & Co. Ltd.* v. *Samyang Navigation Co. Ltd.*, 1975 S.C. (H.L.) 26 at p. 47.

[74] *Ante.*

[75] *Applies to England only.*

wide powers to enable the liquidator to get the company's property into his custody.

Restriction of rights of creditor as to execution or attachment where company being wound up in England

In the case of a company being wound up in England, section 183 provides that where a creditor has issued execution against the goods or lands of a company or has attached any debt due to it, and the company is subsequently wound up, he is not entitled to retain the benefit of the execution or attachment against the liquidator unless he completed the execution or attachment before the commencement of the winding up[76] or, if he had notice of a meeting at which a resolution for voluntary winding up was to be proposed, before such notice. A purchaser in good faith, under a sale by the sheriff, of goods on which execution has been levied acquires a good title to them against the liquidator. The section does not apply to a distress for rent by a landlord.[77]

An execution against goods is taken to be completed either by seizure and sale or by the making of a charging order,[78] and an attachment of a debt by receipt of the debt, and an execution against land by seizure, the appointment of a receiver or by the making of a charging order[78]: section 183(3).

Where a judgment creditor issued a writ of *fi. fa.* in respect of the judgment and the sheriff seized the company's goods and, after a petition for a compulsory winding up had been presented (although this was unknown to the sheriff), sold them, when an order for winding up was made the sheriff had to hand over the proceeds to the liquidator.[79]

The phrase "the benefit of the execution" does not refer to "the fruits of the execution" but to the charge conferred on the creditor by the issue of execution.

Where a creditor has issued a writ of *fi. fa.* against a company, money paid to the sheriff or his officers in order to avoid a sale and which remains in their hands at the commencement of the winding up is outside "the benefit of the execution" so that the liquidator is not entitled to such money as against the creditor.[80]

[76] *Ante*, p. 759.
[77] *Re Bellaglade Ltd.* [1977] 1 All E.R. 319.
[78] Under section 1 of the Charging Orders Act 1979.
[79] *Bluston & Bramley Ltd.* v. *Leigh* [1950] 2 K.B. 548.
[80] *Re Walkden Sheet Metal Co. Ltd.* [1960] Ch. 170.

"The benefit of the attachment" means the right to take the necessary steps to complete it.

If a judgment creditor who has obtained a garnishee order obtains payment after receipt by him of notice of a meeting called for the winding up of the company, he must, subject to the court's discretion under section 183(2)(*c*), *post*, account to the liquidator for the money.[81]

By section 183(2)(*c*), the rights conferred by section 183(1), *ante*, on the liquidator may be set aside by the court in favour of the creditor. The basic scheme of the Insolvency Act is that in a winding up unsecured creditors rank *pari passu* and an execution creditor who has not completed his execution at the commencement of the winding up is for this purpose in the same position as any other unsecured creditor. Section 183(2)(*c*) gives the court a free hand to do what is right and fair according to the circumstances of the case,[82] but weighty reasons are necessary to justify the court in exercising its discretion.[83]

Where a judgment creditor of a company refrained from levying immediate execution because of a promise of payment by a director, there being no dishonesty by the director, and the execution was not completed before the commencement of the winding up, the court refused to set the liquidator's rights aside. To allow the creditor to retain the benefit of the execution would have been contrary to the basic scheme of the Acts and unfair to the other creditors. During the year before the winding up the company was keeping its general body of trade creditors at bay and there was no reason why one execution creditor who had not completed execution should be preferred to the other creditors whether or not they had obtained judgment or commenced execution.[84]

On the other hand, where before the action the company stalled the creditors' claims by promises and defended the action by disputing a debt already admitted, the liquidator's rights were set aside.[85]

Duties of sheriff as to goods taken in execution

Section 184 provides that where goods are taken in execution in England and Wales and, before their sale or the completion

[81] *Re Caribbean Products* (*Yam Importers*) *Ltd.* [1966] Ch. 331 (C.A.); overruling *Re Rainbow Tours Ltd.* [1964] Ch. 66.
[82] *Re Redman* (*Builders*) *Ltd.* [1964] 1 W.L.R. 541.
[83] *Re Caribbean Products* (*Yam Importers*) *Ltd.*, *ante.*
[84] See note 82, above.
[85] *Re Suidair International Airways Ltd.* [1951] Ch. 165.

of the execution, notice of the appointment of a provisional liquidator, of a winding up order or resolution for voluntary winding up, is served upon the sheriff, he must, if required, deliver up the goods to the liquidator. The costs of execution are however a first charge upon them. Where goods are seized in respect of a judgment exceeding £500 the sheriff must deduct the costs of execution and retain the balance for 14 days and pay it to the liquidator if so required. The rights of the liquidator may be set aside in favour of the creditor as the court thinks fit.

Scottish companies, and property of English companies in Scotland

As regards Scottish companies and such property of English companies as is situated in Scotland, section 185 applies section 37(1) to (6) of the Bankruptcy (Scotland) Act 1985 with the following effect[85a]:

(*a*) The winding up is, as at the date of commencement, equivalent to an arrestment in execution and decree of furthcoming, and to a completed poinding, and no arrestment or poinding of the funds or effects of the company executed on or after the sixtieth day before that date is effectual as against the liquidator except to the limited extent that an arrester or poinder who is thus deprived of the benefit of his diligence is entitled to a preference for the expense bona fide incurred by him in his diligence.

C. brought an action of payment against a company and arrested the sum sued for in the hands of S., a debtor of the company. On the instructions of the company, S. paid the sum arrested to C. with the result that the arrestment was superseded. Later, but less than 60 days after the execution of the arrestment, an order was made for the winding up of the company, and the liquidator brought an action to recover the amount paid to C. *Held*, the only arrestments made ineffectual by section 185 were those which, but for it, would have been effectual at the commencement of winding up, and therefore the

[85a] The phrase "date of commencement" in the following provisions in (*a*), (*b*) and (*c*) means the day on which the winding-up order *was made*. (In other contexts it is the date of presentation of the petition). See *Morrison* v. *Integer Systems Control Ltd.*, 1989 G.W.D. 24–1017 (Sh. Ct.) (refusal of recall of arrestments because out with the 60-day period before the winding-up order).

section did not apply to arrestments which had been withdrawn or superseded by payment of the debt before that date: *Johnston* v. *Cluny Trustees*, 1957 S.C. 184.

In *Commercial Aluminium Windows Ltd.* v. *Cumbernauld Development Corporation*, 1987 S.L.T. (Sh. Ct.) 91, where an arrestment had been executed more than 60 days before the winding up, the liquidator defended an action of forthcoming made during the winding up. *Held*, that the arrestment was effectual, because the liquidator had by this statutory provision the equivalent of an arrestment *and decree of forthcoming*. Contrast *Lord Advocate* v. *Royal Bank of Scotland Ltd.*, 1977 S.C. 155 (*ante*, p. 719): in receivership, an arrestment by itself was not "effectually executed diligence."

(*b*) The winding up is, as at the date of its commencement, also equivalent to a decree of adjudication of the heritable estates of the company for payment of the whole debts of the company, subject to any preferable heritable rights and securities which are valid and unchallengeable and subject to the limited right to poind the ground provided for in (*c*).[86]

(*c*) A poinding of the ground which has not been carried into execution by sale of the effects 60 days before the commencement of winding up is of no effect in a question with the liquidator unless the poinder holds a heritable security which is preferable to the right of the liquidator, in which case the poinding is available for the interest for the current half-year and for the arrears of interest for the preceding year, but for no more.

Attendance of officers at meetings in Scotland

While the public examination which may be required in sequestration[87] has no place in the liquidation of a company, the court in the compulsory winding up of a Scottish company has power to require any officer of the company to attend any meeting of creditors or of contributories or of a liquidation committee for the purpose of giving information as to the trade, dealings, affairs or property of the company: section 157.

[86] For an instance of the application of provision (*b*), see *Turnbull* v. *Liquidator of Scottish County Investment Co. Ltd.* 1939 S.C. 5; on the interrelation of this provision and the Conveyancing and Feudal Reform (Scotland) Act 1970, s.24 (application to court for warrant to sell), see *United Dominions Trust Ltd.*, *Noters*, 1977 S.L.T. (Notes) 56 (O.H.).

[87] Bankruptcy (Scotland) Act 1985, s.45.

Fraudulent trading

Section 213 provides that if in the winding up of a company it appears that business has been carried on with intent to defraud creditors or for any fraudulent purpose, the court, on the application of the liquidator, may declare that any persons who were knowingly parties to the fraudulent trading shall make such contributions to the company's assets as the court thinks proper.

Fraudulent trading (so defined) is also a criminal offence under section 458 of the Companies Act 1985.[88] The criminal offence, unlike the civil penalties in the Insolvency Act, however, is not linked to a winding up.

In general it may be properly inferred that there is an intent to defraud creditors if a company carries on business and incurs debts when, to the knowledge of the directors, there is no reasonable prospect of the company being able to pay them.[89] It is not necessary to show that there was no prospect of the creditors *ever* being paid. It is enough that there is no reason for thinking that they will be paid as the debts fall due or shortly thereafter.[90]

The expression "parties to" the fraudulent trading in section 213(2) indicates no more than "take part in" or "concur in" and involves some positive steps. Mere omission by the secretary to give certain advice (that the company is insolvent and should cease to trade) is not being a party to carrying on the business in a fraudulent manner.[91] However, a creditor who, knowing of the circumstances, accepts money fraudulently obtained by the company may be liable to repay it even if he took no part in the fraudulent trading itself.[92]

It is not fraudulent trading for a parent company to give promises of support to a subsidiary which are not implemented. The fraud of the parent company cannot be linked to the subsidiary, since to establish liability the fraudulent trading must be committed by someone carrying on the business, *i.e.* the subsidiary. In any event such general statements would not be sufficient to prove fraud.[93]

[88] There must be a finding of dishonesty for the criminal offence to be committed: *R.* v. *Cox* [1983] BCLC 169.
[89] *Re William C. Leitch Bros. Ltd.* [1932] 2 Ch. 71.
[90] *R.* v. *Grantham* [1984] Q.B. 675.
[91] *Re Maidstone Buildings Provisions Ltd.* [1971] 1 W.L.R. 1085.
[92] *Re Gerald Cooper Chemicals Ltd.* [1978] Ch. 262.
[93] *Re Augustus Barnett & Son Ltd.* [1986] BCLC 170.

It is not fraudulent trading to intend to prefer one creditor to another even if all could not be paid in full,[94] nor to sell goods which prove to be defective knowing that liability for such defects might not be met.[95]

The court may charge the liability of a person declared liable under section 213 on any debt due to him from the company, or on any charge on any assets of the company held by him, or any company or person on his behalf, or certain assignees from him or such a company or person: section 215.

Wrongful trading

The difficulties of establishing the "fraudulent" element of fraudulent trading led to many directors who had carried on the business recklessly being exempt. The Insolvency Act introduced another concept, that of wrongful trading which is designed to apply to such cases. Wrongful trading, which applies only to directors and to insolvent liquidations, has been dealt with in Chapter 15, *ante*.[96] As far as directors are concerned wrongful trading will largely replace fraudulent trading. Fraudulent trading, however, remains for other persons and as a criminal offence for serious cases (wrongful trading is not a criminal offence).

Summary remedy against delinquent directors etc.

This was explained in the chapter on directors.[97]

Disclaimer in case of company wound up in England

Where any part of the property of a company which is being wound up is onerous property, the liquidator may on giving notice disclaim that property. Onerous property for this purpose is (a) any unprofitable contract; or (b) any other property of the company which is unsaleable or not readily saleable or is such

[94] *Re Sarflax Ltd.* [1979] Ch. 592.

[95] *Norcross Ltd.* v. *Amos* (1981) 131 N.L.J. 1213. See also *Rossleigh Ltd.* v. *Carlaw* 1986 S.L.T. 204 in Scotland as to the knowledge required of the intent to defraud.

[96] *Ante*, p. 417.

[97] *Ante*, p. 419.

that may give rise to a liability to pay money or perform any other onerous act: section 178(1)–(3).

A disclaimer operates to determine the rights and liabilities of the company in respect of the property disclaimed but does not, except for the purpose of releasing the company from liability, affect the rights or liabilities of any other person: section 178(4). The liquidator cannot disclaim any property if notice in writing is served on him by a person interested in the property, requiring him to decide whether he will disclaim or not, and he does not, within 28 days, or any longer period allowed by the court, give notice of disclaimer: section 178(5).

Any person injured by a disclaimer is deemed a creditor of the company to the extent of his loss or damage and may prove for that amount in the winding up: section 178(6).

Where the property is a leasehold, no disclaimer can take effect unless the liquidator has served a notice on every person claiming under the company as underlessee or mortgagee and either no application for a vesting order (see below) has been made by such a person within 14 days or, if such application has been made, the court nevertheless directs that the disclaimer shall take effect: section 179.

The court may, on the application of any person interested in the property, or who is under an undischarged liability in respect of the disclaimer,[98] make an order for the vesting or delivery of the property to that person or his trustee, but only if it would be just compensation in the case of a person subject to the liability. The effect of any such order must be taken into account in assessing any loss subsequently provable in the winding up: section 181. Where the property is a leasehold, such a vesting order cannot be made in favour of an underlessee or mortgagee, unless it is either (a) subject to the same liabilities and obligations as those to which the company was subject under the lease at the commencement of the winding up, or (b), if the court thinks fit, subject only to the same liabilities and obligations as if the lease had been assigned to that person at that date: section 182.

Any person who is, or is against the liquidator, entitled to the benefit or subject to the burden of a contract with the company

[98] *e.g.* the tenant-company's surety, see *Re A.E. Realisations* (1985) [1987] BCLC 486.

may apply to the court for an order rescinding the contract. The court may grant rescission on such terms as it thinks fit, including the payment of damages for breach of contract. Any damages payable to such a person under the order may be proved for in the liquidation: section 186.

The Insolvency Act widened the former disclaimer provisions in two major respects. First the consent of the court is no longer required and second the definition of onerous property has been widened to include unsaleable property.[99]

Repudiation in case of company wound up in Scotland

By the common law of Scotland the liquidator may either adopt or repudiate current contracts, and if he repudiates them the company is liable in damages for breach of contract. If the liquidator does not within a reasonable time declare his intention to adopt a contract, he will be held to have abandoned it and to be liable in damages.[1]

Where the company is bound under two separate contracts with the same party, the liquidator is entitled to adopt one and repudiate the other, and the other party to the contracts is not entitled to retain a sum due to the company under the contract adopted, either in security for the proper fulfilment of that contract by the company or in security for a claim for damages in respect of the contract repudiated.[2]

The main criticism of the common law in this connection was the possible uncertainty of the other contracting party as to his position. Following a recommendation of the Scottish Law Commission,[3] the Bankruptcy (Scotland) Act 1985, section 42, enables the other contracting party to require the permanent trustee to reach a decision within 28 days of receiving written notice. By section 169 of the Insolvency Act 1986 the liquidator has the same powers, subject to the Rules, as a trustee on a bankrupt estate.

[99] *cf. Re Potters Oils Ltd.* [1986] 1 W.L.R. 201 decided on the old law.

[1] *Crown Estate Commissioners* v. *Liquidators of Highland Engineering Ltd.*, 1975 S.L.T. 58 (O.H.).

[2] *Asphaltic Limestone Concrete Co. Ltd.* v. *Glasgow Corpn.*, 1907 S.C. 463; see also *Gray's Trustees* v. *Benhar Coal Co. Ltd.* (1881) 9 R. 225.

[3] *Report on Bankruptcy and Related Aspects of Insolvency and Liquidation*, 1982 Scot. Law Com. No. 68, para. 10.26.

THE LIQUIDATOR IN A WINDING UP BY THE COURT

The liquidator in a winding up by the court is an officer of the court.[4]

Appointment

The liquidator is appointed in the manner already discussed.[5] He is an office holder[6] and as such must be a qualified insolvency practitioner.[7]

The court has appointed as liquidator a person resident beyond the jurisdiction of the court but such an appointment was only made where there was an adequate reason.[8]

It was held under the previous rules that it was no objection to the appointment of a person as liquidator that he has been a director,[9] the secretary[10] or the auditor[11] of the company, but where there were to be joint liquidators it was not thought desirable, at least where creditors objected, that both should be connected with the company.

Any person who gives, or agrees or offers to give, any member or creditor of the company any valuable consideration with a view to securing his own appointment or nomination, or to securing or preventing the appointment or nomination of someone else, as the liquidator, is liable to a fine: section 164.

Resignation and removal

A liquidator may resign by giving notice to the court before the completion of the liquidation: section 172(6).

In Scotland leave to resign was granted to an official liquidator where it was stated that there was nothing to recover

[4] *Per* Megarry J. in *Re Rolls Razor Ltd.* (*No.* 2) [1970] Ch. 576, 586.
[5] p. 766.
[6] *Ante*, p. 768.
[7] *Ante*, p. 693.
[8] *Brightwen & Co.* v. *City of Glasgow Bank* (1878) 6 R. 244 (appointment as joint liquidator of accountant resident in London refused); see also *Barberton Development etc. Ltd., Petitioners* (1898) 25 R. 654, and contrast *Liquidators of Bruce Peebles & Co. Ltd.* v. *Shiells*, 1908 S.C. 692.
[9] *Liquidators of Bruce Peebles* case, *ante*; *Sanderson & Muirhead and ors., Petitioners* (1884) 21 S.L.R. 766.
[10] *Gilmour's Trustees* v. *Kilmarnock etc. Investment Co. Ltd.* (1883) 10 R. 1221.
[11] *Argylls Ltd.* v. *Ritchie & Whiteman*, 1914 S.C. 915.

from the estate, and the liquidator's application was concurred in by substantially all the creditors and was unopposed.[12]

A liquidator must vacate his office on ceasing to be a qualified insolvency practitioner[13] and on the holding of the final meeting of creditors[14]: section 172(5), (8).

A liquidator may be removed either by the court or by a meeting of the creditors: section 172(2). Grounds on which a liquidator has been removed by the court include personal unfitness (due to, *e.g.*, his character, his residence,[15] or his personal interest or involvement[16]), insanity,[17] prosecuting a claim against the wishes of a majority of the creditors where the company is insolvent,[18] or failing to carry out his duties with sufficient vigour and displaying a relaxed and complacent attitude towards wrongdoing by the directors.[19]

On the other hand the court has refused to remove a liquidator merely because he is a shareholder and former director,[20] or because the majority of the creditors or of the contributories desire it.[21]

The meeting of the creditors to replace a liquidator may be called by the liquidator himself, the court or one quarter in value of the creditors. If the liquidator was appointed by the Secretary of State only the Secretary of State may remove him.

A vacancy in the office of the liquidator appointed by the court is filled in England by the official receiver: section 136(3).

Duties

The functions of a liquidator are to secure that the assets of the company are got in, realised and distributed to the

[12] *Jamieson, Petitioner* (1877) 14 S.L.R. 667.
[13] *Ante*, p. 693.
[14] *Post*, p. 826.
[15] *Skinner, Petitioner* (1899) 6 S.L.T. 388 (O.H.) (residence in England of sole liquidator).
[16] *Lysons* v. *Liquidator of the Miraflores Gold Syndicate Ltd.* (1895) 22 R. 605; *Re Corbenstoke* (*No.* 2) [1990] BCLC 60 (liquidator was the company's debtor).
[17] *Re The North Molton Mining Co. Ltd.* (1886) 54 L.T. 602.
[18] *Re Tavistock Ironworks Co.* (1871) 24 L.T. 605.
[19] *Re Keypak Homecare* [1987] BCLC 409.
[20] *M'Knight & Co. Ltd.* v. *Montgomerie* (1892) 19 R. 501; but see *Re Corbenstoke*, *ibid.*, where Harman J. considered it unlikely that a director would ever be a suitable person to act as liquidator.
[21] *Ker, Petitioner* (1897) 5 S.L.T. 126 (O.H.).

company's creditors and, if there is a surplus, to the persons entitled to it: section 143(1).

A liquidator must:

(1) in England, give all information, assistance and documents to the official receiver as he may reasonably require: section 143(2);
(2) take all the property of the company into his custody as soon as possible: section 144;
(3) in England, as soon as may be, settle a list of contributories,[22] collect the company's assets, apply them in discharge of its liabilities and distribute any surplus among the members according to their rights and interests in the company: sections 148, 154, 160.

In Scotland, he must perform such duties as will enable the court to exercise the functions mentioned: sections 148, 154.

The word "liabilities" excludes claims which are not legally enforceable. Thus it does not include arrears of tax claimed by a foreign state, even one which adheres to the Commonwealth.[23]

If the liquidator distributes the assets without making provision for the liabilities he is liable to pay damages to the unpaid creditors.

The company had a lease of premises expiring in 1938 at a yearly rent of £1,217 10s. The lease was assigned to M., and in 1933 the company went into voluntary liquidation. M. was insolvent and unable to pay the rent. The liquidator distributed the assets without making any provision for the company's liabilities under the lease. *Held*, the liquidator had committed a breach of his duty and was liable in damages to the lessor: *James Smith & Sons (Norwood) Ltd.* v. *Goodman* [1936] Ch. 216. (C.A.).

(4) In England, summon meetings of the creditors or contributories when directed by resolution of the creditors or contributories or requested in writing by one-tenth in value of the creditors or contributories: section 168(2). He may summon meetings on his own initiative whenever he wants to ascertain the wishes of the creditors or contributories: section 168(2).

[22] But see *post*, p. 807.
[23] *Government of India* v. *Taylor* [1955] A.C. 491; *cf. Clyde Marine Insurance Co. Ltd.* v. *Renwick & Co.*, 1924 S.C. 113.

In Scotland the committee or any member of it may apply to the court for an order on the liquidator to summon a meeting of creditors or contributories or both: R.C. 218M (Court of Session) and Sheriff Court Company Insolvency Rules 1986, Rule 30.

(5) Summon a final meeting in accordance with section 146.[24]

Powers of the liquidator

Section 167 provides that:

(1) The liquidator (including a provisional liquidator[25]) in a winding up by the court has power, *with the sanction of the court or of the liquidation committee*:

(*a*) To bring or defend actions and legal proceedings in the name and on behalf of the company.

It is a matter for his discretion whether he should litigate or not and so the court will not give guidance as to whether he should appeal to a higher court.[26] If the liquidator brings an unsuccessful action he is personally liable as to costs and these are not limited to the assets of the company.[27]

(*b*) To carry on the business of the company so far as may be necessary for beneficial winding up.

When a liquidator carries on the business of the company he does so as the company's agent[28] and is not personally liable on contracts which he enters into as liquidator.

S. had a contract with the company to deliver cotton in monthly instalments from November, 1929, to August, 1930. The company went into liquidation and C. was appointed liquidator by the court in May, 1930. C. did not disclaim the contract, and arranged with S. that payment should be made after and not before delivery. The goods were delivered but not accepted by C. *Held*, C. was not personally liable for damages for non-acceptance: *Stead*, *Hazel & Co.* v. *Cooper* [1933] 1 K.B. 840.

In *Liquidator of Burntisland Oil Co. Ltd.* v. *Dawson* (1892) 20 R. 180, the court refused the liquidator's application to carry on the

[24] *Post*, p. 826.
[25] *Wilsons* (*Glasgow and Trinidad*) *Ltd.*, *Petitioners*, 1912, 2 S.L.T. 330.
[26] *Note for Liquidator in Liquidation of S.S. "Camelot" Ltd.* (1893) 1 S.L.T. 358 (O.H.).
[27] *Re Wilson Lovatt & Sons Ltd.* [1977] 1 All E.R. 274.
[28] See *Smith* v. *Lord Advocate*, 1978 S.C. 259.

business for an indefinite period on the ground that the company's property could not then be sold except on ruinous terms but granted power to carry on for six weeks while the property was advertised for sale. However, in *M'Intyre, Petitioner*, (1893) 30 S.L.R. 386 (O.H.) power was granted to carry on business until the time of the year when the company's property, which consisted of a hall let for public entertainments, could be sold to best advantage.

(*c*) To pay any classes of creditors in full.
(*d*) To make any compromise or arrangement with creditors.
(*e*) To compromise all calls and liabilities to calls and other debts and liabilities.

If a liquidator does any of the acts listed without the necessary sanction of the court or the liquidation committee he is personally liable although the court may retrospectively sanction such an act.[29]

(2) On his own responsibility and *without obtaining any sanction*, the liquidator can:

(*a*) Sell the property of the company.
(*b*) Do all acts and execute, in the name and on behalf of the company, all deeds and documents, and use the company's seal therefor.
(*c*) Prove, rank and claim in the bankruptcy, insolvency or sequestration of any contributory.
(*d*) Draw, accept, make and indorse any bill of exchange or promissory note in the name and on behalf of the company.
(*e*) Raise money on the security of the company's assets.
(*f*) Take out letters of administration to any deceased contributory and do any other act necessary for obtaining payment of money due from a contributory or his estate.
(*g*) Appoint an agent to do business which he cannot do himself.
(*h*) Do all such other things as are necessary for winding up the affairs of the company and distributing its assets.

The exercise of these powers is subject to the control of the court and any creditor or contributory may apply to the court

[29] *Re Associated Travel Leisure and Services Ltd.* (*in Liquidation*) [1978] 1 W.L.R. 547.

with respect to such exercise: section 167(3). If, in England, any person is aggrieved by any act or decision of the liquidator, that person may apply to the court, which may make such order as it thinks just: section 168(5).

In England the liquidator may apply to the court for directions in relation to any particular matter arising under the winding up: section 168(3). The right should be exercised in every case of serious doubt or difficulty in relation to the performance by the liquidator of his statutory duties. The omission to exercise it may lead the liquidator into serious liabilities.[30]

Subject to the various statutory provisions the liquidator may use his own discretion as to the management and distribution of the company's assets: section 168(4).

In Scotland, the liquidator has (subject to the Rules) the same powers as a trustee on a bankrupt estate: section 169(2).

Liability

A liquidator is not strictly speaking a trustee for the individual creditors or contributories, his position being that of agent of the company.

During a liquidation a claim was made by a contributory for damages for delay in handing over to the contributory his proportion of the surplus assets of the company. *Held*, in the absence of fraud, bad faith or personal misconduct, an action for damages would not lie against the liquidator at the suit of a creditor or contributory, the proper remedy being an application to the court to control the liquidator in the exercise of his powers: *Knowles* v. *Scott* [1891] 1 Ch. 717.[31]

On the other hand, for breach of any of his statutory duties the liquidator will be liable in damages to a creditor or contributory for injury caused to them.

[30] See *Re Windsor Steam Coal Co. (1901) Ltd.* [1929] 1 Ch. 151, and *Re Home and Colonial Insurance Co. Ltd.* [1930] 1 Ch. 102, *post.* The opinion was expressed in *Ross* v. *Smith*, 1986 S.L.T. (Sh. Ct.) 59, that the liquidator in Scotland was entitled to seek directions from the court in appropriate circumstances. The test to be applied was the same as that which applied to applications to the court by a liquidator in a voluntary winding up, *i.e.* the court had to be satisfied that the determination of the question would be "just and beneficial."

[31] *cf. Liquidator and Upper Clyde Shipbuilders Ltd.*, 1975 S.L.T. 39 (O.H.), *per* Lord Grieve (Ordinary), p. 40.

A liquidator distributed the assets of the company without paying X, a creditor, who had no notice of the liquidation. The books of the company showed X to be a creditor but the liquidator made no attempt to communicate with X beyond issuing an insufficient advertisement for creditors. The company was dissolved. *Held*, the liquidator was liable in damages to X. The duty of the liquidator was not merely to advertise for creditors but to write to those of whom he knew and who did not send in claims: *Pulsford* v. *Devenish* [1903] 2 Ch. 625.

A liquidator should make provision for contingent claims of which he has notice, *e.g.* where the company, having assigned a lease, is under a contingent liability for the rent,[32] or where he knows of possible claims by workmen for injuries not covered by insurance.[33]

If a liquidator applies the company's assets in paying a doubtful claim, which turns out to be unfounded, without taking proper legal advice or applying to the court for directions, he will be liable to refund the amount paid on a misfeasance summons taken out by a creditor or contributory.[34]

A liquidator, however, is not liable for admitting a proof of debt which is ill-founded, provided he exercises all due care beforehand. But a "high standard of care and diligence is required from a liquidator in a . . . winding up. He is of course paid for his services; he is able to obtain wherever it is expedient the assistance of solicitors and counsel; and, which is a most important consideration, he is entitled, in every serious case of doubt or difficulty . . . to submit the matter to the Court and to obtain its guidance."[35]

H. Co. made a reinsurance agreement with L. Co. which was invalid. On H. going into liquidation, L. tendered a proof which the liquidator ultimately accepted for £89,100, on which £38,000 was paid to L. in dividends. On learning that he should have disallowed the claim, the liquidator sued L. but the claim was dismissed, as no mistake of fact on the part of the liquidator was made. A creditor took out a misfeasance

[32] *James Smith & Sons (Norwood) Ltd.* v. *Goodman* [1936] Ch. 216 (C.A.); *cf. Lord Elphinstone* v. *Monkland Iron etc. Co. Ltd.* (1886) 13 R. (H.L.) 98.

[33] *Re Armstrong Whitworth Securities Co. Ltd.* [1947] Ch. 673.

[34] *Re Windsor Steam Coal Co. (1901) Ltd.* [1929] 1 Ch. 151 (C.A.); where the court refused to grant him relief under s.61 Trustee Act 1925 (s.32 Trusts (Scotland) Act 1921).

[35] *Per* Maugham J. in *Re Home and Colonial Insurance Co. Ltd.* [1930] 1 Ch. 102 at p. 125. In *Macrae* v. *Henderson*, 1989 S.L.T. 523 (O.H.), the question was whether the liquidator owed a duty to guarantors or cautioners to take reasonable care in realising assets to maximum advantage. *Held*, the liquidator did owe the duty, but on evidence the offer which the liquidator had refused was not a reasonable one, and the liquidator was assoilizied.

summons. *Held*, the liquidator was negligent in admitting so large a proof without taking legal advice or applying for directions, and was liable to pay compensation to the company: *Re Home and Colonial Insurance Co. Ltd.* [1930] 1 Ch. 102, *ante.*[36]

Where a liquidator has paid money to shareholders under an error in law, caused, *e.g.* by an underestimation of tax liability, he is not entitled to recover it under the *condictio indebiti*, there being no special relationship between the liquidator and the shareholders such as to take the situation outside the general rule.[37]

Release (England)

When a liquidator ceases to hold office, the question is whether and when he can be released from his obligations. If the liquidator is the official receiver he can be released either by notifying the Secretary of State that the winding up is for all practical purposes complete or, if he is replaced by another liquidator, on giving notice to the court that he has been so replaced. If he is replaced by a liquidator appointed by the court, it is for the court to determine his release: section 174(2)(3).

If the liquidator is someone other than the official receiver his release takes effect as follows:

(a) if he was removed by the creditors' meeting which did not resolve against his release, or if he has died, at the time when notice of removal or death is given to the court;
(b) if the creditors' meeting voted against his release but removed him from office, or he ceases to be a qualified insolvency practitioner he must apply to the Secretary of State for his release;
(c) on resignation his release is governed by the Rules[38];
(d) if he has vacated office having called the final meeting of creditors he is released at that time unless the meeting votes to the contrary, in which case (b) applies: section 174(4).

[36] p. 421.
[37] *Taylor* v. *Wilson's Trustees*, 1975 S.C. 146.
[38] I.R. 1986, r. 4.121.

The effect of a release is to discharge the liquidator from all liability in respect of his acts or omissions as such: section 174(6).

Release (Scotland)

Section 174 applies to Scotland with the following modifications:

(a) the provisions relating to the official receiver have no application;
(b) for references to the Secretary of State substitute references to the Accountant of Court: section 174(7).

WINDING UP OF UNREGISTERED COMPANIES

Section 221(5) provides that an unregistered company may be wound up by the court[39] if—

(i) it is dissolved, or has ceased business, or is carrying on business only for the purpose of winding up its affairs; or
(ii) it is unable to pay its debts; or
(iii) the court is of opinion that it is just and equitable that the company should be wound up.

The expression "unregistered company" includes any association or company with the exception of, *e.g.*—

(i) a company registered under the Companies Acts or Joint Stock Companies Act; or
(ii) a railway company incorporated by Act of Parliament: section 220.

For the purpose of determining the court having jurisdiction in the winding up, an unregistered company is deemed to be registered in England or Scotland according to whether its principal place of business is situated in England or Scotland: section 221(2).

[39] Such a company cannot be wound up voluntarily: I.A. 1986, s.221(4). For a petition by a member of an incorporated association for the appointment of a judicial factor, see *Munro* v. *Edinburgh and District Trades Council Social Club*, 1989 G.W.D. 6–240 (O.H.).

An unregistered company is deemed unable to pay its debts if—

(i) a creditor, by assignment or otherwise, for at least £750 has served on the company a written demand for payment and the company has neglected to pay the same or to secure or compound it for three weeks: section 222.

(ii) an action has been instituted against a member for any debt due from the company, or from him in his character of member, and written notice of the institution of the action has been served on the company and the company has not within three weeks paid, secured or compounded for the debt, or procured the action to be stayed, or indemnified the defendant against the action and against all costs damages and expenses to be incurred by him by reason of the same: section 223.

(iii) in England, execution issued on a judgment in favour of a creditor against the company or any member thereof is returned unsatisfied;

(iv) in Scotland, the induciae of a charge for payment of an extract decree, registered bond or registered protest have expired without payment being made;

(v) it is otherwise proved to the satisfaction of the court that the company is unable to pay its debts: section 224.

Section 227 extends section 126[40] (stay of proceedings against company) to proceedings against a contributory where the application to stay is by a creditor, and section 228 provides that where an order has been made for winding up an unregistered company, no action or proceeding shall be proceeded with or commenced against any contributory of the company in respect of any debt of the company, except by leave of the court.

The provisions of Part V of the Act (sections 220 to 229) with respect to unregistered companies are in addition to and not in restriction of the provisions with respect to the winding up of companies by the court, and the court or liquidator has the same powers in the case of unregistered companies as in the

[40] *Ante.*

case of the winding up of companies formed and registered under the Act: section 229.

Chapter 28

VOLUNTARY WINDING UP

FROM the point of view of the company itself, a voluntary winding up has many advantages over a compulsory winding up, the chief being that there are not so many formalities to be complied with. In consequence the great majority of liquidations are voluntary liquidations. The Cork Committee, however, made several recommendations to prevent abuses in the system of voluntary liquidation and some of these were adopted by the Insolvency Act 1985, since consolidated into the Insolvency Act 1986.

[*N.B. All references in this chapter are to the Insolvency Act 1986 unless otherwise stated*].

Initiation of voluntary winding up

Section 84 provides that a company may be wound up voluntarily:

(1) When the period, if any, fixed for its duration by the articles expires, or the event, if any, occurs, on the occurrence of which the articles provide that it is to be dissolved, and the company in general meeting passes a resolution (*i.e.* an *ordinary resolution*) to be wound up voluntarily.

(2) If it resolves by *special resolution*[1] to be wound up voluntarily.

A company can be wound up by special resolution without any reason being assigned.

(3) If the company resolves by *extraordinary resolution* that it cannot by reason of its liabilities continue its business and that it is advisable to wind up.

[1] *Ante*, p. 338.

An extraordinary resolution is allowed here because time is of the essence since the company is insolvent and a special resolution would normally require a longer period of notice.[2]

A resolution for voluntary winding up must be advertised in the *Gazette* within 14 days after it is passed: section 85. In Scotland, where failure to make timeous advertisement was due to inadvertence and no prejudice had been suffered as a result of the failure, the Court of Session, in the exercise of its *nobile officium*, authorised the liquidator to make a belated advertisement, the expenses of the proceedings to be borne by the liquidator personally.[3]

A voluntary winding up commences at the time of the passing of the resolution: section 86.

Kinds of voluntary winding up

A voluntary winding up may be either (1) a members' voluntary winding up; or (2) a creditors' voluntary winding up: section 90.

MEMBERS' VOLUNTARY WINDING UP

A members' voluntary winding up takes place only when the company is solvent. It is entirely managed by the members, and the liquidator is appointed by them. No meeting of creditors is held and no liquidation committee is appointed. To obtain the benefit of this form of winding up, a declaration of solvency must be filed: section 89.

Declaration of solvency

This is a statutory declaration made by the directors or, if there are more than two of them, by the majority, at a board meeting, that they have made a full inquiry into the company's affairs and, having done so, they have formed the opinion that the company will be able to pay its debts in full together with

[2] *Ante*, p. 338.
[3] *Liquidator of Nairn Public Hall Co. Ltd., Petitioner*, 1946 S.C. 395.

interest at the official rate[4] within a specified period not exceeding 12 months from the commencement of the winding up.[5] The declaration has no effect unless it is made within the five weeks immediately preceding the date of the passing of the winding-up resolution. It may even be made on that date providing that it precedes the resolution.

The declaration must be filed with the Registrar within 15 days of the passing of the resolution. Further, the declaration has no effect unless it embodies a statement of the company's assets and liabilities as at the latest practicable date before it is made: section 89. If there is something which can reasonably be described as "a statement of the company's assets and liabilities," then, even if it subsequently appears that there were errors and omissions, these will not prevent it from being a statement within section 89.[6]

A director making a declaration of solvency without reasonable grounds is liable to imprisonment for six months, or a fine or both. If the debts plus interest are not paid or provided for within the period stated, he is presumed not to have had reasonable grounds: section 89(5).

If a declaration is made in accordance with the section the winding up is a members' voluntary winding up: section 90.

The liquidator

Unlike the liquidator in a winding up by the court, a liquidator in a voluntary winding up is not an officer of the court.[7] He is the agent of the company, but not of the individual members.[8] He is appointed, by the company in general meeting (s.91), and within 14 days he must give notice of his appointment to the Registrar of Companies and publish it in the *Gazette*: section 109.[9] He may be appointed at the meeting at which the resolution for voluntary winding up is passed. If there is no liquidator acting, the court may appoint one. The court may also, on cause shown, remove a liquidator

[4] See s.251.
[5] See above.
[6] *De Courcy* v. *Clement* [1971] Ch. 693.
[7] *Per* Megarry J. in *Re Rolls Razor Ltd.* (*No. 2*) [1970] Ch. 576, 586.
[8] See *Taylor* v. *Wilson's Trustees*, 1975 S.C. 146.
[9] This provision applies to all voluntary liquidations.

and appoint another: section 108.[10] Where a person had been appointed liquidator without his knowledge and he declined to act, it was held that the appointment was invalid and there was therefore no need to remove him.[11] Anyone subject to a disqualification order under the Company Directors Disqualification Act 1986 cannot act as a liquidator.[12] The liquidator is also an office holder under the Insolvency Act.[13] He must be a qualified insolvency practitioner[14] and has the powers and duties of an office holder.

If a vacancy occurs in the office of liquidator, whether by death, resignation or otherwise, the company at a general meeting, summoned by any contributory or by a continuing liquidator, may fill it: section 92.

Until a liquidator is appointed the directors cannot exercise their powers without the sanction of the court, except those which relate to the disposal of perishable goods or goods which are likely to fall in value if not disposed of immediately, and to the necessary preservation of the company's assets: section 114. This provision was introduced following a recommendation of the Cork Committee to prevent dissipation of the company's assets prior to the appointment of a liquidator.

A special manager may also be appointed under section 177.[15]

Vacation of office by or removal of a liquidator

Being an office holder, a liquidator must vacate office if he ceases to be a qualified insolvency practitioner.[16] He may resign by giving notice to the registrar. He vacates office on giving notice to the Registrar of the final meetings held under section 94.[17]

He may be removed at any time by a general meeting of the company summoned for that purpose or by the court. If the liquidator has been appointed by the court (*e.g.* to fill a

[10] *Ibid.*
[11] *Liquidator of Highland etc. Dairy Farms Ltd. and Another, Petitioners*, 1964 S.C. 1.
[12] *Ante*, p. 352.
[13] *Ante*, p. 768.
[14] *Ante*, p. 693.
[15] *Ante*, p. 764.
[16] *Ante*, p. 693.
[17] *Post*, p. 794.

vacancy) he may be removed and replaced by a meeting of members holding not less than one half of the total voting rights, or by a general meeting of the company summoned by the liquidator or the court: section 171.

Release of a liquidator

The liquidator is released at the time of the final meeting. If he has been removed from office his release operates from the date at which notice was given to the registrar in accordance with the Rules,[18] unless the meeting resolves against his release in which case he must apply to the Secretary of State for his release. If the liquidator has resigned he is released in accordance with the Rules. Such a release absolves him from all liability in relation to the winding up except for proceedings against him under section 212.[19]

Conduct of liquidation

Subject to section 96,[20] within three months after the end of the first and every succeeding year of the liquidation, the liquidator must summon a general meeting of the company and lay before it an account of his acts and dealings and of the conduct of the winding up during the preceding year: section 93.

As soon as the affairs of the company are fully wound up the liquidator must call a general meeting of the company. This is done by advertisement in the *Gazette* at least one month before the meeting. At the meeting the liquidator must present an account of the winding up, showing how the winding up has been conducted and how the company's property has been disposed of. A copy of this account, together with a return of the holding of the meeting, must be sent to the Registrar within a week after the meeting: section 94. It is not necessary for the affairs of the company to be fully wound up before the liquidator can validly make his return, only that they should be fully wound up so far as the liquidator is aware.[21]

[18] I.R. 1986, r. 4.144.
[19] *Ante*, p. 419.
[20] *Post*, p. 795.
[21] *Re Cornish Manures Ltd.* [1967] 1 W.L.R. 807.

If a quorum is not present at the final meeting, the liquidator must make a return that the meeting was summoned but no quorum was present, and this has the same effect as a return of the holding of the meeting: section 94(5).

The Registrar must publish in the *Gazette* notice of the receipt of the return (Companies Act 1985, s.711).

Effect of insolvency on a members' voluntary winding up

If the liquidator is of the opinion that the company will in fact be unable to pay its debts in full (including interest) within the time specified by the directors in their declaration of solvency he must call a creditors' meeting within 28 days, giving them at least seven days' notice by post and advertising it in the *Gazette* and two local newspapers.[22] He must also supply the creditors with any information they might reasonably require in that period: section 95(1), (2).

The liquidator must lay before the meeting a statement of affairs set out in accordance with the Rules,[23] showing, in particular, the company's assets, debts and liabilities, its creditors and their securities, together with the dates on which they were created: section 95(3), (4).

The effect of holding such a meeting is that the winding up proceeds as if the declaration of solvency had never been made; *i.e.* as a creditors' voluntary winding up: section 96.

CREDITORS' VOLUNTARY WINDING UP

If no declaration of solvency is filed with the Registrar, a voluntary winding up is a creditors' voluntary winding up: section 90.

In such a case the company must summon a meeting of creditors[24] for a date not later than 14 days after the passing of

[22] *i.e.* within the location of its principal place of business during the preceding six months.

[23] I.R. 1986, r. 4.34—CVL.

[24] If the winding up has been converted to a creditors' winding up the creditors' meeting making such a decision under s.95, *supra*, is the creditors' meeting for this purpose: section 102.

the resolution to wind up the company. Notices of the meeting must be sent to the creditors at least seven days before the meeting. Notice of the meeting must also be advertised in the *Gazette* and two local newspapers.[25] The notice must also state either the name and address of a person qualified to act as an insolvency practitioner in relation to the company who will provide such information as the creditors may reasonably request prior to the meeting or a place in the locality where on two business days prior to the meeting a list of the creditor's name and addresses will be available free of charge: section 98.

Management of such a winding up is shared by the members and creditors but in all cases the creditors have the ultimate control by virtue of the following provisions.

Meeting of creditors

The meeting of creditors is presided over by one of the directors nominated for that purpose by the directors: section 99. The business of the meeting is:

(1) To receive a full statement by the directors as to the company's affairs, together with a list of the creditors, and details of any securities and other information required by the Rules[26]: section 99.
(2) To appoint a liquidator: section 100, *post*.
(3) To appoint a liquidation committee: section 101, *post*.

The liquidator

The creditors and the company at their respective meetings may nominate a liquidator and, if different persons are nominated, the person nominated by the creditors is the liquidator, subject to any order made by the court. If the creditors make no nomination the company's nominee is the liquidator. If different persons are nominated, any director, member or creditor of the company may, within seven days after the creditors' nomination, apply to the court for an order that the company's nominee be liquidator instead of or jointly

[25] See note 22, above.
[26] I.R. 1986, r. 4.34—CVL.

with the creditors' nominee, or that some other person be liquidator: section 100.

Under this system of appointing a liquidator it is still possible for the company to appoint a liquidator elect for the 14 days before a creditors' meeting is required to be held. Prior to the Insolvency Act it was possible to delay the creditors' meeting for several weeks because of the decision in *Re Centrebind Ltd.*[27] to the effect that failing to call such a meeting did not invalidate the acts of the company's nominated liquidator. This abuse, known as "centre-binding" whereby the company's assets were in fact unprotected and beyond the creditors' control has been countered by many provisions, following recommendations of the Cork Committee.[28] These include the requirement that any liquidator be a qualified insolvency practitioner,[29] that until any liquidator is appointed the directors' powers are subject to the court's control[30] and the 14 day time limit within which the creditors' meeting must now be held.[31]

In addition where the company nominates a liquidator prior to the creditors' meeting his powers can only be exercised with the court's consent. He may, however, assume custody of the company's property, dispose of perishable goods and those likely to diminish in value unless disposed of, and protect the company's assets. He must attend the creditors' meeting and report to that meeting on the exercise of any of his powers in the meantime. He is also charged with the duty to apply to the court if the company or the directors fail to comply with the requirement *vis-à-vis* the creditors' meeting: section 166. This effectively prevents "centre-binding" since any liquidator acting in default can be fined and will be liable under section 212.[32]

Any vacancy, by reason of death, resignation or otherwise, in the office of a liquidator, other than a liquidator appointed by the court may be filled by the creditors: section 104.

A liquidator may vacate office by removal and be released from liability in the same way as a liquidator in a members' voluntary winding up, except that the function of the members'

[27] [1967] 1 W.L.R. 377.
[28] Paras. 667–673.
[29] *Ante*, p. 693.
[30] *Post.*
[31] *Post.*
[32] *Ante*, p. 419.

meetings are carried out by a meeting of creditors: sections 171, 173, *ante.*[33]

Liquidation Committee

The creditors, at their first or any subsequent meeting, may appoint a liquidation committee of not more than five persons to act with the liquidator.[34] If they do so, the company in general meeting may appoint not more than five persons to act as members of the committee, but the creditors may resolve that these persons ought not to be members of the committee, and thereupon, unless the court otherwise directs, they cannot act on the committee: section 101.

Conduct of liquidation

Within three months after the end of the first and every succeeding year of the liquidation the liquidator must summon a general meeting of the company and a meeting of creditors, and lay before the meetings an account of his acts and dealings and of the conduct of the winding up during the preceding year: section 105.

When the liquidation is complete, the liquidator must, by at least one month's notice in the *Gazette*, call final meetings of the company and the creditors, and present his account. Within a week after these meetings, a copy of the account and a return of the holding of the meetings or a return that no quorum was present thereat must be filed with the Registrar, who must publish it in the *Gazette* (Companies Act 1985, s.711).

Consequences of any Voluntary Winding Up

The commencement of a voluntary winding up is the date of the passing of the resolution for voluntary winding up: section 86. Even if the company is subsequently wound up by the court, the commencement of the winding up is the date of the passing of the resolution: section 129.

The consequences of a voluntary winding up are:

[33] p. 794.
[34] *Post*, p. 802.

(1) As from the commencement of the winding up the company must cease to carry on business except so far as is required for its beneficial winding up, although the corporate state and powers continue until the company is dissolved: section 87. Notification that the company is in liquidation must be given on the company's documents on which its name appears: section 188.[35]

(2) No transfer of shares can be made without the sanction of the liquidator and any alteration in the status of the members is void: section 88. A transfer of debentures can, however, be made.[36]

(3) On the appointment of a liquidator the powers of the directors cease except so far as the company in general meeting or the liquidator (in a members' voluntary winding up), or the liquidation committee or, if there is no such committee, the creditors (in a creditors' voluntary winding up), sanction their continuance: sections 91(2) and 103.

A voluntary winding up does not automatically operate as a discharge of the company's employees[37]; it has been suggested that it will do so if it takes place because the company is insolvent.[38] In any event, the liquidator has power to terminate contracts of employment and may do so by his conduct.[39] Premature termination of a written fixed term agreement may entitle the employee to damages.[40] When the terms of the contract of employment are to be found in the articles, no damages for breach of contract are recoverable.[41]

After the commencement of the winding up the liquidator may continue the employment of the company's employees if required to ensure a more beneficial winding up of the company.[42]

[35] *Ante*, p. 764.
[36] *Re Goy & Co. Ltd.* [1900] 2 Ch. 149.
[37] Compare a winding up by the court; *ante*, p. 763.
[38] *Fowler* v. *Commercial Timber Co. Ltd.* [1930] 2 K.B. 1 (C.A.), *per* Greer L.J.; compare amalgamation, see *Midlands Counties District Bank Ltd.* v. *Attwood* [1905] 1 Ch. 357.
[39] *Fowler* v. *Commercial Timber Co. Ltd.*, *ibid.*
[40] *Ibid.*
[41] *Re T. N. Farrer Ltd.* [1937] Ch. 352.
[42] *cf. Day* v. *Tait* (1900) 8 S.L.T. 40 (O.H.).

In England there is no statutory provision for the stay of actions and other proceedings against the company in the case of a voluntary winding up (*cf.* sections 126, 128, 130, *ante*),[43] but on an application under section 112, *post*,[44] the court has a discretion to stay proceedings.[45] Executions will usually be stayed when it is necessary to ensure the distribution of assets among the creditors *pari passu*,[46] but actions will not be stayed when there is a dispute as to liability, or when no advantage will be gained, *e.g.* no expense will be saved, by a stay.[47]

In Scotland, the provision now in section 112 has been interpreted as not giving the court power to stay proceedings against the company,[48] and section 113 provides that, on the application of the liquidator of a Scottish company, the court may direct that no action or proceeding shall be proceeded with against the company except by leave of the court. Section 185 (relating to diligence in Scotland)[49] applies to voluntary, as well as to compulsory, winding up.

Distribution of the Property of the Company in a Voluntary Winding Up

The costs, charges and expenses properly incurred in a voluntary winding up, including the remuneration of the liquidator, are payable in priority to all other claims: section 115. The pre-liquidation expenses of a person who expected to be liquidator but was not, in the event, appointed, can be paid but only in so far as they were incurred to enable the company to pass the winding up resolution. Expense incurred in collecting the assets was not recoverable: *Re Sandwell Copiers*.[50] The liquidator must then apply the property[51] of the company first in paying the preferential debts[52] and then in discharging the

[43] Chap. 27, pp. 761, 762.
[44] p. 802.
[45] *Currie* v. *Consolidated Kent Collieries Corpn. Ltd.* [1906] 1 K.B. 134 (C.A.).
[46] *Anglo-Baltic Bank* v. *Barber & Co.* [1924] 2 K.B. 410 (C.A.).
[47] *Cook* v. *"X" Chair Patents Co. Ltd.* [1960] 1 W.L.R. 60.
[48] *Sdeuard* v. *Gardner* (1876) 3 R. 577.
[49] *Ante*, p. 762.
[50] [1988] BCLC 209.
[51] *Post*, Chap. 29.
[52] See s. 175, *post*, p. 822.

liabilities of the company *pari passu*. The liquidator has a duty to inquire into all claims against the company.[53] Even where the company is solvent, statute-barred debts cannot be paid unless the contributories consent.[54] Any surplus must then be distributed amongst the members according to their rights and interests in the company: I.A. 1986, section 107.

Provision may be made for employees on the cessation of business if it is approved by the members or otherwise in accordance with the articles either before or during the liquidation. Such payment must be made out of the assets available to the members: Companies Act 1985, section 719. Any exercise of this power is not subject to section 107: section 187.

A contracting out of the provisions of section 107 is contrary to public policy.[55] Section 107 does not, however, affect contracts which bona fide deprive the company of ownership prior to the winding up, *e.g.* the creation of a trust fund.[56] Such contracts may, however, be invalid under alternative provi-sions.[57]

Powers and Duties of the Liquidator in a Voluntary Winding Up

In every voluntary winding up it is the duty of the liquidator to pay the debts of the company and adjust the rights of the contributories among themselves.[57a]

To enable him to do this, section 165[58] and Schedule 4 provide that he may *without sanction*:

[53] *Austin Securities Ltd.* v. *Northgate and English Stores Ltd.* [1969] 1 W.L.R. 529 (C.A.) applying *Pulsford* v. *Devenish* and *Re Armstrong Whitworth Securities Co. Ltd.*, *ante*, p. 785.

[54] *Re Art Reproduction Co. Ltd.* [1952] Ch. 89. The Scottish equivalent of "statute-barred" is "prescribed."

[55] *British Eagle International Air Lines Ltd.* v. *Compagnie Nationale Air France* [1975] 1 W.L.R. 758 (H.L.), where the rules of the general liquidation prevailed over the International Air Transport Association clearing house arrangements and, despite such arrangements, the plaintiff company was entitled to recover the sums payable to it by other airlines for services rendered by it and not cleared through the I.A.T.A. system and vice versa.

[56] *Carreras Rothmans Ltd.* v. *Freeman Matthews Treasure Ltd.* [1985] Ch. 207.

[57] *Post*, Chap. 29.

[57a] The duty to pay the company's debts is a fiduciary one and the liquidator of a Scottish company, no matter where he resides, can be called to account before the Court of Session; his duty continues despite the dissolution of the company, and the jurisdiction of the court is not brought to an end by dissolution: *Lamey* v. *Winram*, 1987 S.L.T. 635 (O.H.).

[58] Subject to s.166.

(1) commence or defend legal proceedings on behalf of the company;
(2) carry on the company's business so far as it is beneficial for the winding up;

He may carry on the business of the company, if he reasonably thinks it is necessary for the beneficial winding up of the company. If he does so, those to whom he incurs obligations are entitled to be paid in priority to the creditors at the commencement of the winding up: *Re Great Eastern Electric Co. Ltd.* [1941] Ch. 241.[59]

(3) exercise all the general powers of a liquidator listed in Part II of Schedule 4, I.A. 1986.

In a members' voluntary winding up, *with the sanction* of an extraordinary resolution of the company, and in a creditors' voluntary winding up, *with the sanction* of the court or the liquidation committee or (if there is no such committee) a meeting of the creditors, the liquidator may:

(1) pay any classes of creditors in full;
(2) make any compromise or arrangement with creditors;
(3) compromise all calls and liabilities to calls and other debts and liabilities: section 165, Schedule 4.

Power to apply to court

In a voluntary winding up the liquidator, or any contributory or creditor, may apply to the court to determine any question arising in the winding up or to exercise any of the powers which the court could exercise if the company were being wound up by the court: section 112.[60] This gives the liquidator in a voluntary winding up the same right to the guidance of the court as in a compulsory liquidation. For example, in England, if he is of opinion that fraud has been committed in the formation or promotion of the company or in relation to the company since

[59] *cf. Day* v. *Tait* (1900) 8 S.L.T. 40 (O.H.).
[60] For examples of applications under s.112, see *Liquidators of North British Locomotive Co. Ltd.* v. *Lord Advocate*, 1963 S.C. 272 (O.H.); *Smith and Another, Petitioners*, 1969 S.L.T. (Notes) 94 (O.H.) (as to exercise of directors' discretionary powers under a pension scheme) and *Liquidators of Highland Engineering Ltd.* v. *Thomson*, 1972 S.C. 87 (O.H.) (as to provisional liquidator's right to retain funds to pay his remuneration and expenses).

its formation, he can obtain an order of the court for the public examination[61] of any promoter, director or other officer of the company concerned. Again, he can apply for an order for private examination.[62]

In 1971 a company went into voluntary liquidation. In 1976 it became apparent that it might be liable for claims in tort for negligence during its operations. In 1979, after the liquidators had started preparing the final accounts, solicitors warned the liquidators of the possible claims. The liquidators applied for an order that they should distribute the final dividend to the members without regard to the claims on the basis of delay. Alternatively they sought an order that the claimants should bear the costs of the delay in distribution. Megarry V.-C. held that the test was whether in all the circumstances it was just to make either of the orders sought. Default or lack of diligence by either party was relevant and the court was less likely to facilitate a distribution among the members than among the creditors. In the circumstances, both orders would be refused: *Re R-R Realisations Ltd.* [1980] 1 All E.R. 1019.

Duty to report criminal offences

If the liquidator thinks that any past or present officer, or any member, of the company has committed a criminal offence in relation to the company, he must report the matter, in an English winding up, to the Director of Public Prosecutions, and in a Scottish winding up, to the Lord Advocate. The matter may then be referred to the Department of Trade and Industry, who have the same powers of investigating the company's affairs as in an investigation into the affairs of a company under sections 431 or 432 of the Companies Act 1985: section 218.

Compulsory Liquidation after Commencement of Voluntary Liquidation

A voluntary liquidation does not bar the right of any creditor or contributory to have the company wound up by the court: section 116. A creditor of a company in voluntary liquidation is not entitled *ex debito justitiae* as between himself and the company to a compulsory winding-up order and the views of the

[61] *Re Campbell Coverings Ltd.* (*No.* 2) [1954] Ch. 225.
[62] As in *Re Rolls Razor Ltd.* (*No.* 2) [1970] Ch. 576.

contributories must be taken into consideration,[63] unless the company is insolvent.[64] Even in such a case it has been said that the court will require reasons as to why the voluntary winding up is inappropriate since the creditors are not being completely deprived of a class remedy.[65] However, more recently it has been stated that a compulsory order should be made wherever the creditors would otherwise be left with a justifiable feeling of grievance that they had been prevented from having the company's affairs investigated by a liquidator who was not appointed by the directors.[66] There is no rule that the probity or competence of the liquidator must be attacked[67] but he must not only be independent but must be seen to be independent.[68] Further, the court is bound to have regard to the wishes of all the creditors,[69] and if the majority favour the continuance of the voluntary liquidation an order will not be made unless the petitioner can show special circumstances.[70] The court can, however, examine the motives of the creditors,[71] and, in particular, of those creditors who are also members.[72] Considerations of fairness and commercial morality should also be taken into account.[73] A contributory must satisfy the court that the rights of the contributories will be prejudiced by a voluntary winding up: section 116. What the Secretary of State must show when he is the petitioner has been dealt with already.

When a voluntary winding up is superseded by a compulsory winding up, all proceedings in the voluntary winding up are deemed to have been validly taken unless the court, on proof of

[63] *Re Surplus Properties (Huddersfield) Ltd.* [1984] BCLC 89.

[64] *Ibid.*; *Re James Millward & Co. Ltd.* [1940] Ch. 333 (C.A.).

[65] *Re Medisco Equipment Ltd.* [1983] BCLC 305, *per* Harman J.

[66] *Re M.C.H. Services* [1987] BCLC 535, Vinelott J.

[67] *Re Palmer Marine Services Ltd.* [1986] 1 W.L.R. 573.

[68] *Re Lowestoft Traffic Services Ltd.* [1986] BCLC 81: and see *Re H.J. Tomkins & Son* [1990] BCLC 76.

[69] *Re Home Remedies Ltd.* [1943] Ch. 1; *Re Lowestoft Traffic Services Ltd.* [1986] BCLC 81; *cf. Pattisons Ltd.* v. *Kinnear* (1899) 1 F. 551 and *Elsmie & Son* v. *The Tomatin etc. Distillery Ltd.* (1906) 8 F. 434.

[70] *Re B. Karsberg Ltd.* [1956] 1 W.L.R. 47 (C.A.); *Re J. D. Swain Ltd.* [1965] 1 W.L.R. 909 (C.A.); for special circumstances, see *Bouboulis* v. *Mann, Macneal & Co. Ltd.*, 1926 S.C. 637: and see *Re H.J. Tomkins, ibid.*, where the court followed the wishes of creditors representing a majority in value, though not in number.

[71] *Re Falcon (R.J.) Developments* [1987] BCLC 437.

[72] *Re Palmer Marine Surveys Ltd.* [1986] 1 W.L.R. 573.

[73] *Ibid.*

fraud or mistake, thinks fit to direct otherwise: section 129, *ante*.

Chapter 29

CONTRIBUTORIES AND CREDITORS: COMPLETION OF THE WINDING UP

[*N.B. References in this chapter are to sections of the Insolvency Act 1986 unless otherwise stated*].

AS soon as may be after a winding-up order is made, it is the duty of the liquidator in England to—

(1) settle a list of contributories;
(2) collect the company's assets and apply them in discharge of its liabilities: sections 148, 160.

In Scotland it is for the court to settle a list of contributories and to cause the assets of the company to be collected and applied in discharge of the company's liabilities: section 148. Section 160, which provides for delegation of the court's power to the liquidator, does not apply to Scotland.

CONTRIBUTORIES

A contributory is a person liable to contribute to the assets of a company in the event of its being wound up: section 79. A fully paid-up shareholder in a company limited by shares falls within this definition.[1] Section 74 provides that on a winding up every present and past member is liable to contribute to the assets of the company to an amount sufficient for payment of its debts and liabilities, and the expenses of the winding up, and for the

[1] *Re Anglesea Colliery Co.* (1866) L.R. 1 Ch.App. 555, followed, *e.g.*, in *Paterson* v. *M'Farlane* (1875) 2 R. 490.

adjustment of the rights of the contributories among themselves. This is subject to certain qualifications, *post*, *e.g.* a past member is not liable to contribute if he ceased to be a member one year or more before the commencement of the winding up[2]: section 74(2)(*a*).

Where a private company which has purchased or redeemed its own shares out of capital under section 170 of the Companies Act 1985 goes into liquidation within one year of such payment, and is found to be insolvent, the directors and the recipient are liable to contribute the amount of the payment to cover any insolvency. Such persons are not, however, governed by sections 76 or 79 and are not true contributories: section 76.[3]

The list of contributories

The list of contributories is in two parts, the A list and the B list. The A list consists of the members of the company at the commencement of the winding up, *i.e.* present members. The B list consists of persons who were members within a year before the commencement of the winding up. The B list is often not settled at all, and is never settled unless it appears that the A contributories are unable to satisfy their contributions.[4] The list must distinguish between contributories who are liable in their own right and those liable as representatives of others[5]: section 148(3).

The court may dispense with the settlement of a list of contributories where it appears that it will not be necessary to make calls on or adjust the rights of contributories: section 148(2). The distribution of surplus assets among the contributories does not of itself involve an adjustment of the rights of the contributories among themselves and therefore no list need be settled.[6] The court should not exercise its discretion to dispense with a list of contributories if the company has a large number of shares held by a large number of shareholders.[7]

[2] *Ante*, p. 43; this qualification does not apply to the winding-up of an unlimited company which has re-registered as limited under s.51 Companies Act 1985, see s.77.
[3] *Ante*, p. 217.
[4] See s.74(2)(*c*) IA 1986.
[5] See *post*.
[6] *Re Phoenix Oil, etc., Co.* [1958] Ch. 560.
[7] *Re Paragon Holdings Ltd.* [1961] Ch. 346.

Liability of contributories

The liability of a contributory in a company limited by shares[8] is qualified as follows—

(1) The liability of a contributory, whether on the A list or the B list, is limited to the amount unpaid on his shares: section 74(2)(*d*). Where shares are partly paid, a past member only has to contribute if the existing member has not paid up in full. Where there are several past members in the year before the winding up, all will appear on the B list but the primary liability will be on the latest transferor.[9] The fact that all debts have been paid does not necessarily absolve the holder of partly paid shares from his liability: a contribution may still be required to adjust the rights of the contributories amongst themselves.[10]

(2) B contributories are not liable to contribute in respect of any debt or liability of the company contracted *after* he ceased to be a member: section 74(2)(*b*).

The assets of the company, including the amount received from A contributories, are first applied *pari passu* in payment of the debts of the company, irrespective of the time when they were contracted.[11] The liability of the B contributories is therefore further restricted, because they are liable only for such of the company's debts contracted before they ceased to be members as have not been satisfied by the distribution of the company's other assets among the creditors generally. The B contributories may therefore not be fully called upon although the creditors are not paid in full.

The liquidator made calls on the B contributories of 5p a share in 1925, and 7½p a share in 1927. The amount so realised exceeded by about £10,000 the debts of the company contracted while the B contributories were members but the total of all the calls did not suffice to pay the creditors in full. The liquidator asked to retain the full amount of the calls on the B contributories as assets available for the creditors. *Held*, he could not retain the full amount, but must return

[8] See s.74(3) for companies limited by guarantee.
[9] *Humby's Case* (1872) 26 L.T. 936.
[10] *Re Anglesea Colliery Co.* (1866) L.R. 1 Ch. 555.
[11] *Morris' Case* (1871) L.R. 7 Ch.App. 200.

the £10,000 to the B contributories: *Re City of London Insce. Co. Ltd.* [1932] 1 Ch. 226.

B contributions are part of the general assets of the company, and are not to be applied, preferentially or exclusively, to the payment of debts incurred before the B shareholders ceased to be members.[12]

(3) B contributories are not liable to contribute unless it appears to the court that the existing members are unable to satisfy their contributions: section 74(2)(*c*).

Example: C and D are holders of £1 shares, 37½p. paid. C transfers his shares to X and D transfers to Y. Within a year the company is wound up, and is insolvent. X pays up his shares in full, but Y pays nothing. No contribution will be required from C. A contribution will be required from D.

A member cannot claim any dividend in competition with any other creditor not a member of the company: section 74(2)(*f*). For the purposes of this section the word "member" includes a past member.[13] This provision has been held in Scotland not to apply to dividends which have been carried to an account current between the company and a member.[14] In England the section has been applied to dividends due to a holding company but retained by the subsidiary for use in its business. The judge decided that the onus of proving that such sums were not due as dividends to a member was on the holding company. This could be done by an express or implied agreement which created a loan by the holding company of the money involved or recognition of that fact with the passage of time, but there was no such evidence in that case.[15]

The liability of a contributory creates a debt (in England of the nature of a specialty) accruing at the time when his liability commenced, but payable when a call is made: section 80.

If a contributory dies either before or after he has been placed on the list of contributories, his personal representatives

[12] *Webb* v. *Whiffin* (1872) L.R. 5 H.L. 711.
[13] *Re Consolidated Goldfields of New Zealand Ltd.* [1953] Ch. 689.
[14] *Liquidator of Wilsons (Glasgow and Trinidad) Ltd.* v. *Wilson's Trustees*, 1915, 1 S.L.T. 424 (O.H.).
[15] *Re L. B. Holliday & Co. Ltd.* [1986] 2 All E.R. 367.

are liable. They are not personally liable; they are liable in their representative character. In England, if they make a default in payment, proceedings may be taken for administering the estate of the deceased: section 81.

If a contributory becomes bankrupt, his trustee in bankruptcy represents him for all the purposes of the winding up and is a contributory accordingly. Calls already made and the estimated value of the bankrupt's liability to future calls may be proved against the estate.[16]

There are special provisions as to the liability of B contributories where a company has re-registered under section 49 or 51 of the Companies Act[17]: sections 77, 78.

Calls on contributories

In England calls on contributories are made by the liquidator with the leave of the court or the sanction of the liquidation committee: section 160. In Scotland calls are made by the court: section 150.

Calls may be made either before or after the insufficiency of the assets has been ascertained. They are made for an amount necessary to satisfy the debts and liabilities of the company, and the costs of winding up, and for adjustment of the rights of the contributories among themselves. In fixing the amount regard is had to the probability that some contributories may fail to pay the call: section 150.

A debt due from the company to a contributory cannot be set off against calls, whether made before or after the winding up,[18] except—

(1) where all the creditors have been paid in full (s.149); or

(2) in the case of an unlimited company, where the debt is due to him on an independent dealing with the company and not due to him as a member in respect of dividend or profit (s.149); or

[16] s.82.

[17] *Ante*, Chap. 2.

[18] *Grissell's Case* (1866) L.R. 1 Ch.App. 528; *Cowan* v. *Gowans* (1878) 5 R. 581; this has been held to be so where a shareholder deposited money with the company against calls: *Millar* v. *Aikman* (1891) 28 S.L.R. 955 (O.H.).

(3) where the contributory is bankrupt.[19]

A contributory on the list may be ordered by the court, at any time after the making of a winding-up order, to pay any money due from him to the company: section 149.[20] The court can also order the arrest of, and seizure of the movable personal property of, a contributory believed to be about to abscond or to remove his property with the object of evading payment of calls: section 158.

CREDITORS

The Rules apply with regard to (1) the respective rights of secured and unsecured creditors, (2) debts provable, and (3) the valuation of annuities and future and contingent liabilities.

Secured creditors

A secured creditor is one who holds some security for a debt due to him from the company, such as a mortgage, charge or lien. He must give credit for the realised or estimated value of his security unless he surrenders it. Thus he may—

(1) realise his security and prove,[21] as an unsecured creditor, for any balance due to him after deducting the amount realised; or
(2) value his security and prove, as an unsecured creditor, for any balance due after deducting the value of the security; or
(3) surrender his security and prove, as an unsecured creditor, for the whole debt; or
(4) where he is fully secured, rely on his security and not prove at all.

A secured creditor who has realised his security for less than the total amount of his debt, part of which is preferential,[22] can

[19] *Re Duckworth* (1867) L.R. 2 Ch.App. 578.
[20] The effect of s.149 dies with the company when it is dissolved: *Butler* v. *Broadhead* [1975] Ch.D. 97.
[21] The term used in Scotland is "claim."
[22] *Post*, pp. 822 *et seq*.

appropriate the proceeds of sale to that part of his debt which is not preferential, so that he can prove for the preferential part.[23]

If the creditor has made a mistake in the valuation of his security, he may amend it by application to the court. If he subsequently realises his security, the amount realised must be substituted for the amount in the proof.

Proof of debts

The debts which are provable on a winding up, and the manner of proof, are governed by the Insolvency Rules 1986.[24] The liability must exist at the commencement of the winding up but, subject to that, it may be present or future, certain or contingent, ascertained or sounding only in damages. The liquidator can estimate the value of any debt of uncertain amount[25] or, in difficult cases, he can apply to the court for directions: section 168(3).[26] It is no longer the case that in an insolvent winding up unliquidated claims in tort are excluded. Some claims can only be proved when those of all other creditors have been paid in full, with interest, *e.g.* those arising by virtue of restitution orders under section 6 and 61 of the Financial Services Act 1986.[27] Statute-barred debts cannot be proved.[28]

If a debt is owed in foreign currency it must be paid at the rate of exchange prevailing at the commencement of the liquidation and not at the date of payment.[29]

Where there have been mutual credits, mutual debts or other mutual dealings between the company and one of its creditors, an account is taken of what is due from one to the other, and the balance of that account and no more can be claimed or paid.[30]

[23] *Re William Hall (Contractors) Ltd.* [1967] 1 W.L.R. 948.
[24] r.2.3 and r.r. 4.72–4.99.
[25] r. 4.86.
[26] Any person aggrieved can also apply: s.168(5).
[27] See S.I. 1987, No. 1919, Sch. 1 Pt. I, para. 143.
[28] *Re Art Reproduction Co. Ltd.* [1952] Ch. 89; *Re Overmark Smith Warden Ltd.*, *The Times*, March 22, 1982.
[29] *Re Lines Brothers Ltd.* [1983] Ch. 1 (C.A.).
[30] I.R. 1986, r. 4.90; on mutuality see I. F. Fletcher, *The Law of Insolvency* (1990), p. 253. Note also *Re Norman Holdings Co. Ltd.* [1990] 3 All E.R. 757.

A Co. borrowed money from B Co. on the security of bills of sale charging some machinery and providing for its insurance against fire. The policies were in the name of B, and A paid the premiums. The machinery was destroyed by fire and the insurance amounting to £1,600 paid to B. A then went into liquidation. £744 was owing to B on the bills of sale at the date of the fire, so that B had £856 in hand, but A owed B £2,099 unsecured book debts. *Held*, B could set off the £856 against the £2,099: *Re H. E. Thorne & Son Ltd.* [1914] 2 Ch. 438.

The holder of a life policy in an assurance company mortgaged the policy to the issuing company. On the company's going into liquidation the policy holder claimed to set off the value of the policy against his mortgage debt. *Held*, he was entitled to do so: *Re City Life Assurance Co. Ltd.* [1926] Ch. 191.

This statutory set-off cannot be excluded by agreement between the parties.[31] It applies automatically, irrespective of the wishes of the parties, wherever there are mutual debts (or provable claims) between the company and a creditor, so that the liquidator cannot deal with the subject of such mutual cross-claims free of the right of set-off.[32] Where the company is entitled to set-off a claim against a preferential creditor[33] who is also a non-preferential creditor, the company's claim must be set-off rateably in proportion to the amounts of the preferential and non-preferential claims.[34]

Interest is payable on all debts provable in the winding up, including interest which has accrued under the contract rate prior to the winding up. Post-winding-up interest is only payable, however, if there is a surplus after paying all debts (including pre-winding-up interest), and is paid before any surplus is returned to the contributories. The rate of post-winding-up interest is that specified by order made under section 17 of the Judgments Act 1838[35] on the commencement of the winding up, unless the contract itself provided for a higher rate of interest[36]: section 189. If interest is payable on a foreign currency debt it should be calculated with respect to the exchange rate at the date of winding up and not when it is paid.[37]

[31] *Rolls Razor Ltd.* v. *Cox* [1967] 1 Q.B. 552 (C.A.).
[32] *Farley* v. *Housing and Commercial Development Ltd.* [1984] BCLC 442.
[33] *Post*, p. 822.
[34] *Re Unit 2 Windows Ltd.* [1986] BCLC 31.
[35] In Scotland see the Insolvency (Scotland) Rules 1986 (S.I. 1986 No. 1915).
[36] Such a rate may be challenged by the liquidator under s.244, *post*, p. 820.
[37] *Re Lines Brothers Ltd.* (*No. 2*) [1984] Ch. 438.

Adjustment of prior transactions

The Insolvency Act contains provisions which enable the liquidator to apply to the court to set aside certain prior transactions which are disadvantageous to the general body of creditors. These provisions also apply where an administration order has been made.[38]

Transactions at an undervalue and preferences in England

A transaction at an undervalue entered into by a company is a transaction whereby a company makes a gift to another person or enters into a transaction on terms which provide that the company either receives no consideration or significantly less consideration than the value of the consideration it provides, measured in money or money's worth: section 238(4). However, this does not include transactions entered into by the company in good faith for the purpose of carrying on its business and at the time there was reasonable grounds for believing that the transaction would benefit the company: section 238(5). Further such a transaction must have taken place at a time when the company was unable to pay its debts[39] (or became unable to pay them as a result of the transaction) and also within two years prior to the commencement of the winding up.[40] If the transaction is with a person connected with the company the company is assumed to have been insolvent at the time unless the contrary is shown: section 240.

A company gives a preference to a creditor[41] if it does anything or suffers anything to be done which has the effect of putting the creditor into a position which, in the event of the company going into insolvent liquidation, would be better than the position he would have been in if that thing had not been done, and the company in doing that was influenced by a desire to produce that effect. Such a motive is presumed if the creditor is connected with the company: section 239. The preference must have been given at a time when the company was unable to pay its debts[42] (or became unable to do so as a result of the preference) and also within six months of the commencement of

[38] *Ante*, p. 740.
[39] As defined in s.123, *ante*, p. 745.
[40] Or presentation of the petition for an administration order.
[41] Including a surety or guarantor for any of its debts or liabilities.
[42] See n. 39.

the winding up. The time limit is extended to two years if the creditor is connected with the company: section 240.

Both transactions at an undervalue and preferences may be challenged by the liquidator who can apply for a court order to return the position to what it would have been if the company had not entered into the transaction or given the preference: sections 238, 239. The court can make any order it thinks fit and section 241 gives it wide powers relating to the transfer of property, return of benefits received and release of any security. A charge may therefore be set aside under these provisions.[43] The court cannot, however, prejudice any purchaser of property for value who purchased without notice and in good faith from a person other than the company, or require any person who received a benefit from the transaction or preferences in good faith for value and without notice, to repay that benefit unless he was a party to the transaction itself[44]: section 241.

These sections replaced sections of the Companies Act 1985 which required proof of a "fraudulent" preference. The major difference is that under the old law the liquidator had to prove not only an intention to prefer one creditor over another but also that it was a voluntary act of the company, *i.e.* not a payment under pressure.[45] The Cork Committee[46] recommended that a similar concept be introduced and section 239(5) provides that the company must be *influenced by a desire* to create the preference. If such a desire is operative, it does not matter that other intentions predominated.[47] However if the preference is given under pressure (*e.g.* to avoid the bank appointing a receiver or calling in an overdraft) it may successfully be argued that it was solely the company's desire to continue trading, not any desire to prefer, which motivated the transaction, particularly if the creditor is not connected with the company, and therefore the transaction cannot be set aside. Where there is no pressure, the result may be otherwise.[48]

M. and his wife were the sole directors and shareholders of a company. The company's overdraft was guaranteed by them. The

[43] A floating charge may also be attacked under s.245, *ante*, p. 675.
[44] The liability is still wider than that under the doctrine of constructive trusts.
[45] *Re M. Kushler Ltd.* [1943] Ch. 248 (C.A.).
[46] Chap. 28.
[47] *Re Clasper Group Services* [1989] BCLC 143 (intention to channel money through the creditor to another company).
[48] *Re M.C. Bacon Ltd.* [1990] 6 BCC 78.

company's overdraft was cleared without pressure from the bank. The company went into liquidation. M. believed at the time of payment that all the debts would be paid in due course even though they could not be paid as they became due. The Court of Appeal held that this was not sufficient to prevent the payment to the bank being a fraudulent preference: *Re F. P. & C. H. Matthews* [1982] 1 All E.R. 338.

"Where the debtor company is unable to pay its debts as they arise, that circumstance seems to us to fall clearly within the words a preference over the other creditors'. The receiving creditor gets its money in full and the rest of the creditors are left with the risk that they may not be paid in full." *per* Lawton L.J. at p. 342.

Where a creditor making an advance takes from the debtor a promise to execute a charge on request the court has, in the absence of other circumstances, inferred that the purpose of the parties is to give the creditor the right to be preferred on request. Such an arrangement although for value was therefore unenforceable, and when the debtor creates the charge the court, in the absence of other circumstances has inferred that the debtor's intention is to prefer the creditor. Where the creation of the charge is part of a wider arrangement, the debtor's intention as a whole has been determined by reference to the arrangement as a whole.[49] The fact that the amount paid by the company vastly exceeds the amount due to the creditor, and is a misapplication of funds, does not prevent it from being a preference of the creditor and the whole can be recovered from him.[50]

Gratuitous alienations and unfair preferences (Scots law)

In Scotland sections 242 and 243 relate, respectively, to the challenge of gratuitous alienations and unfair preferences.[51]

By section 242, once a winding up has commenced an alienation to which the section applies may be challenged by:

(*a*) any creditor the debt to whom was incurred on or before the date of the commencement of the winding up; or

[49] *Re Eric Holmes (Property) Ltd.* [1965] Ch. 1052.

[50] *Re Clasper Group Services*, *ibid.*

[51] Formerly governed by the Bankruptcy Acts of 1621 and 1696, respectively. *Bank of Scotland, Petitioners*, 1988 S.L.T. 690, made it clear that gratuitous alienations by companies can be challenged at common law; the common law right had not been taken away but had been extended by sections 242 and 243. In this case there was held to be a prima facie case for an interim interdict. In *Bob Gray (Access)* v. *T.M. Standard Scaffolding*, 1987 S.C.L.R. 720 (Sh. Ct.) the liquidator was entitled to recover £6,000 paid by the debtor to a particular creditor under the 1696 Act.

(*b*) the liquidator.

The section covers any alienation by which any part of the company's property has been transferred or by which any claim or right of the company has been discharged or renounced, provided the alienation has become completely effectual:

(*a*) if it favours an "associate," on a day not earlier than five years before the commencement of the winding up; or
(*b*) if it favours any other person, on a day not earlier than two years before such commencement.

The definition of "associate" is incorporated from section 74 of the Bankruptcy (Scotland) Act 1985, a section which may be altered by regulations. By that section the term "associate" extends to husband, wife, relative (*i.e* brother, sister, uncle, aunt, nephew, niece, lineal ancestor or lineal descendant), partner, employer, employee (any director or other officer of a company being treated as an employee of the company for this purpose), and the section has been amended by the Bankruptcy (Scotland) Regulations 1985 (S.I. 1985 No. 1925, para. 11) to provide for circumstances in which a company is an "associate" of another company.

On a challenge being brought within these provisions, the court must grant decree of reduction or for such restoration of property to the company's assets or other redress as may be appropriate, unless the person seeking to uphold the alienation establishes:

(*a*) that immediately, or at any other time, after the alienation the company's assets were greater than its liabilities; or
(*b*) that the alienation was made for adequate consideration; or
(*c*) that the alienation was a reasonable alienation by way of a birthday, Christmas or other conventional gift or by way of a gift for a charitable purpose to a person other than an associate of the company.

A challenge does not prejudice any right or interest acquired in good faith and for value from or through the transferee in the alienation.

Further, a liquidator has the same right to challenge a gratuitous alienation as a creditor has at common law. For a successful challenge at common law the challenger would require to prove that the company was absolutely insolvent at the date of the transaction (or was made so by the transaction) and continued to be absolutely insolvent at the date of the challenge, as well as that the transaction was gratuitous and to the prejudice of lawful creditors. While proof of these points would make a common law challenge more difficult, such a challenge is not restricted to alienations made to associates nor is it restricted to alienations made within two years prior to the commencement of winding-up.

Section 243 applies to transactions entered into by a company which have the effect of creating a preference in favour of a creditor to the prejudice of the general body of creditors, provided the preference has become completely effectual not earlier than six months before the commencement of the winding up.

There are the following exceptions to the right of challenge under section 243:

(*a*) transactions in the ordinary course of trade or business;

(*b*) payments in cash of debts due, unless the transaction was collusive with the purpose of prejudicing the general body of creditors;

(*c*) transactions by which both parties undertook obligations, unless the transaction was collusive as under (*b*), above;

(*d*) any mandate granted by the company authorising an arrestee to pay over arrested funds to an arrester, where:

 (i) there has been a decree for payment or a warrant for summary diligence; and

 (ii) the decree or warrant has been preceded by an arrestment on the dependence of the action or followed by an arrestment in execution.

The challenge may be brought by:

(*a*) any creditor the debt to whom was incurred on or before the date of commencement of the winding up; or
(*b*) the liquidator.

On a challenge being brought, the court, if satisfied that the transaction challenged is one to which section 243 applies, must grant decree of reduction or for such restoration of property to the company's assets or other redress as may be appropriate.

A challenge does not prejudice any right or interest acquired in good faith and for value from or through the creditor in whose favour the preference was created.

As with gratuitous alienations, the liquidator has the same right to challenge a preference created by the debtor company as a creditor has at common law.

At common law the challenger must prove that—

(*a*) the debtor was insolvent at the date of the transaction and continuously thereafter down to the date of the challenge;
(*b*) the debtor was aware at the date of the transaction that he was insolvent;
(*c*) the transaction was voluntary and in satisfaction or further security of a prior debt; and
(*d*) the transaction was to the prejudice of the debtor's other creditors.[52]

At common law the following are recognised as exceptions and are not reducible unless there is proof of fraudulent contrivance between debtor and creditor[53]—(i) cash payments of debts actually due, (ii) transactions in the ordinary course of trade[54] and (iii) *nova debita*, namely, new debts arising out of new transactions.

A transaction is not "voluntary" if the debtor is doing "the very thing which he is bound to do,[55] such as implementing a

[52] For a comprehensive review of the authorities see *Nordic Travel Ltd.* v. *Scotprint Ltd.*, 1980 S.C. 1.
[53] Mere knowledge on the creditor's part of the debtor's absolute and irretrievable insolvency at the time of payment is not enough: *Nordic Travel Ltd.* v. *Scotprint Ltd.*, *ante.*
[54] See *Nordic Travel Ltd.* v. *Scotprint Ltd.*, *ante.*
[55] *Taylor* v. *Farrie* (1855) 17 D. 639 at p. 649 (joint opinion).

prior obligation to grant a specific security provided that obligation is part of the original contract.[56]

The preference is equally challengeable whether conferred directly (*e.g.* where security is given to a creditor previously unsecured) or indirectly.[57]

An isolated and unprecedented assignation by an insolvent company cannot claim the protection afforded to transactions "in the ordinary course of trade," and is therefore reducible.[58]

Avoidance of certain floating charges

As we have seen section 245 provides that certain floating charges created within 12 months prior to the liquidation are voidable unless new consideration was supplied by the creditor.[59] This provision operates in addition to sections 238 to 244 detailed above.

Extortionate credit transactions

A transaction is an extortionate credit transaction if credit has been supplied to a company on terms which are extortionate (grossly extortionate) having regard to the risk involved or it otherwise grossly contravenes the ordinary principles of fair dealing.[60] All credit transactions are presumed to a be extortionate until the contrary is proved. The transaction must have been entered into within three years prior to the commencement of the winding up.

In such cases the liquidator may apply to the court for an order setting aside the transaction, varying its terms, for repayment of money or property held as security to the company or for the taking of accounts. This power may be used concurrently with the power to avoid transaction at an undervalue: section 244.

[56] *T.* v. *L.*, 1970 S.L.T. 243 (O.H.).

[57] *Walkraft Paint Co.* v. *Lovelock*, 1964 S.L.T. 103 (O.H.) (mandates given by the company to certain of its debtors to pay the favoured creditor); *Walkraft Paint Co. Ltd.* v. *James H. Kinsey Ltd.*, 1964 S.L.T. 104 (O.H.) (cheque from company's debtor endorsed by company to the favoured creditor).

[58] *Walkraft Paint Co. Ltd.* v. *James H. Kinsey Ltd.*, *ante.*

[59] *Ante*, p. 675.

[60] *cf.* Consumer Credit Act 1974, ss.137–139.

Unenforceability of liens in England

Under section 246 a liquidator can override any lien or other right to retain possession of any books, papers or records of the company in order to gain possession of them. The only exception is a lien on documents which give a title to property and are held as such.

Order of application of assets

The effect of sections 175, 176 and the Rules is that in a winding up the assets of the company are applicable in the following order:

(1) costs, charges and expenses properly incurred in the winding up, including the remuneration of the liquidator;
(2) the preferential debts;
(3) debts secured by a charge which as created was a floating charge[61];
(4) the ordinary unsecured debts;
(5) post insolvency interest on debts;
(6) deferred debts;
(7) the balance (if any) to be returned to the contributories.

All liabilities belonging to a higher category must be paid for or provided for in full before any payment can be made in respect of liabilities of a lower category. None of this will affect creditors with a fixed charge (so long as it is valid and properly registered): they may simply pay themselves out of their security. In relation to any balance remaining unpaid, they rank as ordinary or preferential unsecured creditors.[62]

In the event of the assets being insufficient to satisfy the costs, charges and expenses incurred in the winding up, there is an internal order of priority: section 156 and Insolvency Rules

[61] s.175(2)(*b*) and s.251; where necessary the property subject to the charge can be used to pay liabilities in categories (1) and (2).

[62] See, *e.g. Re Mesco Properties* [1980] 1 W.L.R. 96.

1986, rule 4.218.[62a] Unless the court orders otherwise, the order of priority is:

(*a*) Fees and expenses properly incurred in preserving, realising or getting in the assets. The costs of an unsuccessful action to set aside a security under s. 239 cannot be regarded as incurred in realising or getting in the company's assets.[63]

(*b*) Costs of the *petition*[64] including costs of those appearing on the petition whose costs are allowed by the court.[65]

(*c*) Remuneration of the special manager (if any).

(*d*) Costs and expenses of any person who makes the company's statement of affairs.

(*e*) Charges of a shorthand writer appointed to take an examination.

(*f*) Disbursements of the liquidator.

(*g*) Costs of any person properly employed by the liquidator.

(*h*) Remuneration of the liquidator.

(*i*) Expenses of the liquidation committee.

Where the company is a lessee rent accrued due after the winding-up order is an expense of the liquidation if the liquidator retained the lease solely for the benefit of the liquidation, and not for the joint benefit of himself and the lessors.[66]

The *preferential debts* rank equally among themselves and must be paid in full, after the expenses of winding-up, unless the assets are insufficient to meet them, in which case the preferential debts abate in equal proportions: section 175(2)(*a*).

By section 386 and Schedule 6 the preferential debts include:

[62a] For Scotland, see Insolvency (Scotland) Rules 1986, Chapter 9.

[63] *Re M.C. Bacon Ltd.* [1990] 3 WLR 646, 652.

[64] See *Re Bostels* [1968] Ch. 346.

[65] In *Re Bathampton Properties Ltd.* [1976] 1 W.L.R. 168 the company's costs were increased by its unsuccessful and unjustifiable opposition to the petition, and only its costs down to and including the first hearing, when it could have consented, were paid out of the assets.

[66] *Re A.B.C. Coupler & Engineering Co. Ltd.* (*No. 3*) [1970] 1 W.L.R. 702; and see *Re Owner Enterprises Ltd.* [1974] 1 W.L.R. 1460, where an intermediate lessee paid the arrears of rent and was held entitled to the lessor's rights by way of subrogation; such rent does not however fall within para. (a) but para. (f), see *Re Linda Marie* [1898] BCLC 46.

(*a*) Value added tax which is referable to the period of six months next before the relevant date.[67] Car tax, general betting and other gaming duties which have become due within 12 months next before the relevant date.

The expression "the relevant date" means, when the company is being wound up compulsorily, the date of the appointment of a provisional liquidator or, if no such appointment was made, the date of the winding-up order; if the company is or was being wound up voluntarily, it means the date of the passing of the resolution for winding up: section 387. If the winding up follows the discharge of an administration order the "relevant date" is the date of the making of that order. There are equivalent rules for voluntary arrangements, administration orders and receiverships: section 387.

(*b*) Sums due from the company to the Inland Revenue as deduction from the employees' salaries under PAYE for the period of 12 months next before the relevant date. The former preference given to arrears of corporation tax was repealed by the Insolvency Act.

Apart from these provisions as to taxes, Crown debts have no priority.[68]

(*c*) Remuneration owed to an employee in respect of services rendered to the company within four months next before the relevant date, not exceeding £800 per claimant.[69]

In England a full-time company secretary is probably an employee,[70] but in Scotland there may be more doubt.[71] A

[67] See *Re Liverpool Commercial Vehicles Ltd.* [1984] BCLC 587. Formerly the period was 12 months and also included rates.

[68] *Food Controller* v. *Cork* [1923] A.C. 647.

[69] These include other sums payable to employees by virtue of s.121 of the Employment Protection (Consolidation) Act 1978 and various other statutory benefits: see Sched. 6, para. 13.

[70] *Cairney* v. *Back* [1906] 2 K.G. 746. The former wording was "clerk or servant."

[71] *Scottish Poultry Journal Co.* (1896) 4 S.L.T. 167 (O.H.) (secretary and manager); *Clyde Football etc. Co. Ltd.* (1900) 8 S.L.T. 328 (O.H.); *Laing* v. *Gowans* (1902) 10 S.L.T. 461 (O.H.). *Quaere* whether these still apply to the changed wording.

managing director[72] is not an employee nor is a director as such. However, a director may, under power in the articles, be employed in a salaried position with the company and so be an employee. Thus, where a director could be, and was, employed as editor of a periodical, he was a preferential creditor.[73]

A chemist engaged two days a week at a salary to work on formulae for perfumiers is an employee.[74] A contributor, even a regular contributor, to a newspaper, although paid by a fixed salary, is not.[75]

(*d*) National Insurance contributions due from the company as class 1 or 2 payments under the Social Security Act 1975, for 12 months next before the "relevant date," and certain class 4 contributions due to the Inland Revenue for the preceding tax year.

(*e*) Accrued holiday remuneration in respect of any period of employment before the relevant date payable to an employee whose employment has been terminated before, on, or after that date.

(*f*) Debts due under Schedule 3 of the Social Security Pensions Act 1975.

(*g*) Debts in respect of levies on the production of coal and Steel, or any surcharge for delay, as imposed under the European Coal and Steel Treaty.[76]

In England if a landlord or other person has distrained on the company's goods within three months next before a winding-up order, the preferential debts are a first charge on the goods or the proceeds of the distress. The landlord or other person, however, has the same priority as the persons paid out of the proceeds: section 176. This section applies to anyone who has seized goods and is holding them for the purpose of sale at the time of the winding up order.[77]

The ordinary debts rank and abate equally *inter se*.[78]

[72] *Re Newspaper Proprietary Syndicate Ltd.* [1900] 2 Ch. 349.

[73] *Re Beeton & Co. Ltd.* [1913] 2 Ch. 279.

[74] *Re G. H. Morison & Co. Ltd.* (1912) 106 L.T. 731.

[75] See note 71, above.

[76] See S.I. 1987, No. 2093.

[77] *Re Memco Engineering Ltd.* [1986] Ch. 86. The position is different in a voluntary winding up: *Re Herbert Berry Associates Ltd.* [1977] 1 W.L.R. 1437 (C.A.).

[78] *Per* Lord Selbourne in *Black & Co.'s case* (1872) L.R. 8 Ch. 254 at p. 262.

It may be mentioned here that a sum of money paid into a company's bank account for behoof of the company's employees and which is at the date of the liquidation "clearly distinguishable and capable of being disentangled from the company's own funds" does not form part of the company's assets but must be paid to the employees.[79]

Where a company fails to implement an agreement to purchase its shares under section 162 of the Companies Act 1985[80] or to redeem its shares under section 159 of that Act,[81] and the company subsequently goes into liquidation the vendor/shareholder may enforce the agreement as a creditor. This will not apply if at any time between the date for purchase or redemption and the commencement of the winding up the company could not have fulfilled its obligation out of distributable profits: Companies Act 1985, section 178.[82]

Completion of Winding up by the Court

When the liquidator has collected the assets and received the proofs of the creditors, he proceeds to divide the assets among the creditors.

If there is any surplus after the costs of the liquidation and the company's debts have been paid, the court must adjust the rights of the contributories among themselves and distribute any surplus among the persons entitled thereto: section 154. The section requires a court order before the liquidator can distribute surplus assets, whether or not an adjustment has to be made among the contributories.[83] It will be remembered that under normal articles preference shareholders are entitled to priority over ordinary shareholders in the return of capital.[84]

For tax purposes a distribution on a winding up does not count as income of the shareholder who receives it, whether it consists of a return of capital or a share in surplus assets.[85]

[79] *Smith* v. *Liquidator of James Birrell Ltd.*, 1968 S.L.T. 174 (O.H.).

[80] *Ante*, Chap. 10.

[81] *Ibid.*

[82] *Ante*, Chap. 10.

[83] *Re Phoenix Oil, etc., Co. Ltd.* (*No.* 2) [1958] Ch. 565, where a list of contributories was dispensed with and the register of members was seven years out of date.

[84] *Ante*, Chap. 12.

[85] See *Davies*, *op. cit.*, pp. 269 *et seq.*

If the liquidation is not completed within a year after its commencement, the liquidator must send to the Registrar of Companies, at such intervals as may be prescribed, a statement in the prescribed form and giving prescribed particulars as to the position of the liquidation: section 192.

Final meetings and release of the liquidator

The holding of final meetings of the company or its creditors as appropriate in the case of a voluntary winding up has been dealt with already,[86] together with the release of the liquidator consequential upon such a meeting.[87]

In a compulsory winding up the liquidator, other than the official receiver, if he is satisfied that the liquidation is for practical purposes complete, must call a final general meeting of the creditors. The liquidator will then make his report to that meeting which must then decide whether to release him. He may also give notice of any final distribution of the company's property at the same time. If he cannot do so the meeting must be adjourned until he can do so. The costs of the final meeting must be covered by the company's assets and so the liquidator must retain sufficient for this purpose; section 146. The release of a liquidator consequential on this meeting has been dealt with above.[88]

Early dissolution of company in England

If the company is in compulsory liquidation and the official receiver, who is automatically the first liquidator,[89] discovers that the realisable assets of the company will be insufficient to cover even the expenses of the winding up he may apply to the registrar of companies for an early dissolution of the company. Before he can do this, however, he must be satisfied that the company's affairs do not require any further investigation and he must give 28 days' notice of his intention to the creditors, contributors and any administrative receiver. Once such a notice

[86] *Ante*, p. 794.
[87] *Ibid.*
[88] *Ante*, p. 786.
[89] p. 763.

is given the official receiver's duties are at an end, although any creditor, contributory, administrative receiver or even the official receiver himself, may apply to the Secretary of State for directions within three months on the grounds either that the assets are sufficient to cover the expenses, the company's affairs do merit further investigation or that an early dissolution would be inappropriate: sections 202, 203.

If no such application is made the company is automatically dissolved three months after the registrar receives the application. If the Secretary of State does give directions, those would be that the winding up should proceed as if no notice of early dissolution had been given and he may defer the date of dissolution as he thinks fit. Notice of such directions must be given to the registrar of companies by the applicant within seven days. There is an appeal from the Secretary of State's decision to the court: sections 202, 203.

This procedure was adopted on the recommendation of the Cork Committee.[90] Up to one third of companies in compulsory liquidation are likely to be subject to these provisions.

Early dissolution of company in Scotland

If after a meeting or meetings under section 138 (which deals with appointment of a liquidator in a compulsory winding up in Scotland) it appears to the liquidator that the realisable assets of the company are insufficient to cover the expenses of the winding up, he may apply to the court for an order that the company be dissolved, and the court then makes an order for early dissolution under section 204 if it appears to the court appropriate to do so.

Within 14 days from the date of the order, the liquidator must forward a copy of the order to the registrar of companies, who immediately registers it, and, at the end of the period of three months from the day of that registration, the company is dissolved.

The court may, however, on an application made to it by any person who appears to the court to have an interest, order that the date of dissolution be deferred for such period as the court thinks fit. If such an order for deferment is made, the person

[90] Paras. 649–651.

who applied for it must, within seven days of the making of the order, deliver a copy of it to the registrar of companies.

Dissolution of company

In the case of a compulsory winding up where either the liquidator gives notice to the registrar that the final meeting has been held and that he has vacated office,[91] or the official receiver gives notice that the winding up is complete, the registration of that notice begins a period of three months at the end of which the company will be automatically dissolved unless on the application of an interested party the Secretary of State defers that date.[92] There is an appeal to the court from any such decision: section 205.

In a voluntary winding up the three month period ending with the automatic dissolution of the company begins with the registration of the liquidator's final account and return under either section 94 or 106.[93] Otherwise the procedure is the same as on a compulsory winding up: section 201.

Subject to any order which may at any time be made by the court under sections 651 or 652 of the Companies Act 1985, any property vested in or held on trust for a company immediately before its dissolution (excluding property held by the company on trust for any other person) vests in the Crown as *bona vacantia*: section 654 of the Companies Act 1985. The Crown may disclaim such property by a notice signed in the case of property in England by the Treasury Solicitor (and in the case of property in Scotland by the Queen's and Lord Treasurer's Remembrancer). The effect of such disclaimer is much the same as if the property had been disclaimed under section 178, *ante*.[94] The notice of disclaimer must be executed within 12 months after the vesting of the property came to the notice of the Crown representative or, where any person interested in the property applies in writing to the Crown representative requiring him to decide whether he will disclaim, usually within

[91] *Ante*, Chap. 27.

[92] In Scotland there can be no application to the Secretary of State to defer the date of dissolution if the winding-up order was made by the court, but the court can itself defer the date.

[93] *Ante*, Chap. 28.

[94] Chap. 27.

three months after the application. The notice of disclaimer must be delivered to the registrar of companies and registered by him, and copies must be published in the *Gazette* and sent to persons who have given the Crown representative notice of their interest in the property: sections 656, 657 of the Companies Act 1985.

Where a company has been dissolved the court may, make an order declaring the dissolution void. Such an order may be made on the application of the liquidator or of any other person who appears to the court to be interested: section 651 of the Companies Act 1985.[95] A solicitor acting on behalf of a client with a claim against the dissolved company, and having neither a financial nor a proprietary interest, is not a "person . . . interested" within section 651.[96] A liquidator de son tort, *i.e.* a person who has never been a duly appointed liquidator of the company but who has, without lawful authority, been carrying on the liquidation of the company, is.[97] So is a contributory in the liquidation.[98] The Inland Revenue may apply where an assessment for taxes has been made but the assessments were under appeal when the company was struck off the register under section 652 of the Companies Act 1985, *post.*[99]

As a general rule, the application cannot be made more than two years after the date of the dissolution. This has caused some hardship, *e.g.* to employees who contract an industrial disease which becomes apparent in later years, and special provision has now been made for such cases. An application for the purpose of bringing proceedings against the company for damages for death, personal injuries or funeral expenses can now be made at any time. No order will be made if the limitation period for such action under the Limitation Act 1980 has already expired but the court has power to extend such limitation period by the period between the dissolution and the order declaring the dissolution void: section 651(5) and (6). Application can be

[95] As amended by Companies Act 1989, s.141 and Sched. 24.

[96] *Roehampton Swimming Pool Ltd.* [1968] 1 W.L.R. 1693.

[97] *Re Wood and Martin (Bricklaying Contractors) Ltd.* [1971] 1 W.L.R. 293.

[98] *Re Thompson and Riches Ltd.* [1981] 2 All E.R. 477.

[99] *Re Belmont and Co. Ltd.* [1952] Ch. 10; followed in *Re Test Holdings (Clifton) Ltd.* [1970] Ch. 285. The Inland Revenue can also apply under s.652 of the C.A. 1985, *post*: *Re Avondale Hotel Southport Ltd.* (1951) (unreported).

made in relation to dissolutions occurring before the enactment, *i.e.* before November 16, 1989, so long as the dissolution was not more than two years (or, in the case of subsection (5) applications, 20 years) before that date.

When a dissolution is declared void, any property of the company which vested in the Crown under section 654 of the Companies Act 1985 remains the Crown's property. Instead the company will receive a cash payment equivalent to those assets. This payment will be either the sum the Crown received or the value of any property which has since been disposed of by the Crown. This provision allows the Crown to dispose of such property without fear of a revival of the company: section 655. An office copy of the order declaring the dissolution void must be delivered to the Registrar of Companies within seven days: section 651. Such an order does not validate proceedings taken on behalf of the company between the dissolution and its avoidance.[1] Thus it does not revive a misfeasance summons issued, but not served, before dissolution.[2]

It is incompetent for the court to declare the dissolution void for a limited purpose only.[3]

Grounds for declaring a dissolution void are that there are unsatisfied claims by creditors,[4] or the discovery of undistributed assets such as a sum wrongly paid to the Inland Revenue,[5] or to enable the liquidator to grant a title to property of the company sold since the dissolution.[6]

A testatrix by her will gave a share of her residuary estate to a company but the company was dissolved before she died. An order under section 352 was refused because the share of residue did not belong to the company before dissolution. The next of kin therefore took the lapsed share as on a partial intestacy: *Re Servers of the Blind League* [1960] 1 W.L.R. 564.

Relief will not automatically be granted whenever a petitioner comes within section 651. The court has an absolute discretion

[1] *Morris* v. *Harris* [1927] A.C. 252.
[2] *Re Lewis and Smart Ltd.* [1954] 1 W.L.R. 755.
[3] *Champdany Jute Co. Ltd., Petitioners*, 1924 S.C. 209 (for the purpose of receiving a repayment from the Inland Revenue).
[4] *Re Spottiswoode, Dixon and Hunting Ltd.* [1912] 1 Ch. 410.
[5] *Champdany* case, *ante*.
[6] *M'Call and Stephen Ltd., Petitioners* (1920) 57 S.L.R. 480.

and the petition may be opposed, *e.g.* by the Official Receiver or the Treasury Solicitor. The delay between the dissolution and the petition is another factor in the court's exercise of its discretion.[7]

In very special circumstances the Court of Session in the exercise of its *nobile officium* may declare a dissolution void, although the application has not been made within the two years.[8]

Defunct Companies

By sections 652 of the Companies Act 1985, if the Registrar of Companies has reasonable cause to believe that a company is not carrying on business or is not in operation, he may, after carrying out a specified procedure, strike the company's name off the register, after which it is dissolved and sections 654 to 657, *ante*, apply.

The procedure under section 652 is:

(1) The Registrar sends to the company by post a letter asking whether the company is carrying on business.
(2) If no answer is received within one month, he sends within the next 14 days a registered letter, stating that if no reply is received within one month a notice will be published in the *Gazette* with a view to striking the company's name off the register.
(3) If no satisfactory reply is received he sends to the company by post and publishes in the *Gazette* a notice, stating that unless cause is shown to the contrary the company will be struck off after three months.
(4) If cause is not shown to the contrary, he strikes the company off and publishes notice thereof in the *Gazette*, whereupon the company is dissolved.

Striking the company's name off the register does not affect the liability of any director or member of the company, and the

[7] *Per* Slade J. in *Re Thompson and Riches Ltd.* [1981] 2 All E.R. 477, 483.
[8] *Collins Brothers and Co. Ltd., Petitioners*, 1916 S.C. 620. Contrast *Kerr* (*Lord Macdonald's Curator Bonis*) *and Another, Petitioners*, 1924 S.C. 163, and *Forth Shipbreaking Co. Ltd., Petitioners*, 1924 S.C. 489.

company may still be wound up by the court. If the company is to be wound up, it should first be restored to the register under section 653 of the Companies Act 1985.[9]

Section 653 provides that if the company, or any member or creditor thereof, feels aggrieved by the striking off the register, it or he may within 20 years, apply[10] to the court which, if satisfied that it is just that the company be revived, may order that the name of the company be restored to the register. A petition for restoration under the section should contain an outline explanation of why the company was struck off.[11] Upon an office copy of the order being delivered to the Registrar the company is deemed to have continued in existence as if its name had not been struck off. The court may, by the order, give directions for placing the company and all other persons in the same position as nearly as may be as if the company had not been struck off. This provision should be compared with section 651, *ante*, as to the persons who may apply for a court order. A contributory may apply under either section although the time limits are different; 20 years under section 653 and two years under section 651.[12] The word "creditor" in section 653 extends to a plaintiff claiming damages under the Fatal Accidents Acts 1846 to 1959 and having therefore an unquantified claim against the company.[13]

To qualify as a "member or creditor" within section 653 an applicant for restoration must have been a member or creditor of the company at the date when it was struck off the register.[14] However, the personal representative of a deceased sharehold has been held entitled to apply for restoration of a company's name to the register, and then for its winding up, even though he is not registered as a shareholder.[15]

On an application for restoration to the register, the court may only restore or refuse to restore and cannot, *e.g.* impose a

[9] *Re Cambridge Coffee Room Association Ltd.* [1952] 1 All E.R. 112. *Alliance Heritable Security Co. Ltd., Petitioners* (1886) 14 R. 34; *Beith Unionist Association Trustees, Petitioners*, 1950 S.C. 1.

[10] By petition: R.S.C. O. 102, r. 5; R.C. 189.

[11] Practice Note (Companies Court) [1974] 1 W.L.R. 1459.

[12] *Re Thompson and Riches Ltd.* [1981] 2 All E.R. 477.

[13] *Re Harvest Lane Motor Bodies Ltd.* [1969] 1 Ch. 457.

[14] *Re New Timbiqui Gold Mines Ltd.* [1961] Ch. 319; *Re Aga Estate Agencies* [1986] BCLC 346.

[15] *Re Bayswater Trading Co. Ltd.* [1970] 1 W.L.R. 343.

penalty (beyond costs) as a condition of restoration.[16] It may, however, make the restoration conditional on the company's filing such statutory returns with the Registrar as are necessary to bring the company' file up to date.[17]

The restoration of the company to the register under section 653 validates retrospectively all acts done on behalf of the company between its dissolution and its restoration.[18] In one English case, where the petition was that of a contributory and there were assets available for the shareholders or creditors, as the case might be, the court directed that, as regards creditors whose debts were not statute-barred at the date of dissolution, the period between dissolution and restoration to the register was not to be counted for the purposes of any Statute of Limitations.[19] Where, *e.g.* a creditor petitions and there is no indication that other creditors might be unfairly affected by an order not containing a special provision as to the limitation of actions, no such provision will be inserted in the order.[20] In so far as the property of the company has passed to the Crown under section 651, *ante*, the provisions of section 655 apply and the Crown may validly dispose of those assets paying a cash sum in lieu on the company's revival, *ante*.

Where the company is in breach of its statutory obligations and at least one applicant is guilty of some default, the normal order for taxation of costs under R.S.C. Order 62, rule 28, should be on a common fund basis (instead of the usual order on a party and party basis).[21]

[16] *Re Brown Bayley's Steel Works Ltd.* (1905) 21 T.L.R. 374; *Re Moses and Cohen Ltd.* [1957] 1 W.L.R. 1007.

[17] *Healy, Petitioner* (1903) 5 F. 644, followed in *Charles Dale Ltd., Petitioners*, 1927 S.C. 130.

[18] *Tymans Ltd.* v. *Craven* [1952] 2 Q.B. 100 (C.A.), applied in *Re Boxco Ltd.*. [1970] Ch. 442 (Legal charge created by company after being struck off. Order for restoration made. Company put in same position retrospectively as if charge duly created and registered).

[19] *Re Donald Kenyon Ltd.* [1956] 1 W.L.R. 1397. *Aliter* where the company is already in liquidation: *Re Vickers and Bott Ltd.* [1968] 2 All E.R. 264n.

[20] *Re Huntingdon Poultry Ltd.* [1969] 1 W.L.R. 204, distinguishing *Re Donald Kenyon*, *ante*, and *Re Rugby Auto Electric Services Ltd.*, *ante*.

[21] *Re Court Lodge Development Co. Ltd.* [1973] 1 W.L.R. 1097.

Chapter 30

RECONSTRUCTION AND AMALGAMATION

NEITHER of the words "reconstruction" and "amalgamation" has any definite legal meaning. A reconstruction is where a company transfers its assets to one or more new companies with substantially the same shareholders. The latter case is commonly referred to as a de-merger or division. An amalgamation is the merger of two or more companies into one. This occurs, *e.g.* where a company acquires the assets of or the shares in two or more companies whose shareholders are issued with the appropriate number of shares in the new company. In this chapter the procedures applicable to reconstructions and agreed amalgamations; *i.e.* where all the companies concerned are in agreement, are set out. The alternative, an often contested form of amalgamation, is usually referred to as a "take-over," *i.e.* the acquisition of shares in one company by another company. Such take-overs are the subject of Chapter 31, *post.*[1]

Both a reconstruction and an amalgamation in the sense used in this chapter may be effected (1) under section 110 of the Insolvency Act 1986, or (2) under sections 425 to 427A of the Companies Act 1985.[2] The latter procedure becomes more complex in certain mergers and divisions involving public companies, as a result of the implementation of the third and sixth EEC directives[3] by Schedule 15B.

A scheme of arrangement under section 425 can also be used for purposes other than reconstructions and amalgamations, *e.g.*

[1] p. 849.

[2] For examples of amalgamation see *Head (Henry) & Co. Ltd.* v. *Ropner Holdings Ltd.* [1952] Ch. 124. *Governments Stock etc. Investment Co. Ltd.* v. *Christopher* [1956] 1 W.L.R. 237; *Rights and Issues Investment Trust Ltd.* v. *Stylo Shoes Ltd.* [1965] Ch. 250; and *Clydesdale Bank Ltd., Petitioners*, 1950 S.C. 30.

[3] Adopted on October 9, 1978, O.J. 1978 L295/36, and December 17, 1982, O.J. 1982 L378/47, respectively. See p. 845 *post.*

to effect a composition with creditors or a variation of class rights.

RECONSTRUCTION OR AMALGAMATION UNDER SECTION 110 OF THE INSOLVENCY ACT 1986

Under section 110 a company (1) which is in voluntary winding up; (2) may transfer or sell the whole or part of its business or property to another company, whether a company within the meaning of the Act or not; and (3) may, in the case of a members' voluntary winding up, pass a special resolution authorising the liquidator to receive as consideration cash or shares, policies or other like interests in the transferee company for distribution among the members of the transferor company according to their rights and interests in that company. The sanction of the court is unnecessary in a members' voluntary winding up. In the case of a creditors' winding up the liquidator's authority for (3) must come either from the court, or the liquidation committee.

The sale may be to a foreign company.[4] However, it must be to a company and not to a speculator who hopes to form a company to take over the assets.[5]

The following procedure might be adopted under section 110 if a members' voluntary winding up is involved. A meeting of the transferor company is summoned in order to pass resolutions for reconstruction or amalgamation. At the meeting, resolutions are passed for the voluntary winding up of the company, the appointment of a liquidator, and giving authority to the liquidator to enter into an agreement with the transferee company on the terms of a draft submitted to the meeting. The agreement provides that the transferee company shall purchase the assets of the transferor company, except a sum retained by the liquidator to discharge its liabilities, that the consideration shall be the allotment by the transferee company to the liquidator or his nominees of shares, fully or partly paid up, in the transferee company, that the liquidator shall give notice to the shareholders of the transferor company of the number of shares to which they are entitled, and the time within which

[4] *Re Irrigation Co. of France* (1871) L.R. 6 Ch.App. 176.
[5] *Bird* v. *Bird's Patent, etc., Sewage Co.* (1874) L.R. 9 Ch.App. 358.

they must apply, and that failure to apply for shares within that time shall preclude their rights to any shares.

A reconstruction scheme provided that shareholders in the old company should apply for shares in the new company within 10 days after being given notice requiring them to apply, and that the liquidator should dispose of all shares not applied for. On June 12 the liquidator sent out notices requiring application for shares in the new company to be made before June 25. P., a shareholder in the old company, applied on August 24. *Held*, P. was not entitled to an allotment of shares in the new company, or to any other relief: *Postlethwaite* v. *Port Philip, etc., Gold Mining Co.* (1889) 43 Ch.D. 452.

In the case of a creditors' winding up the necessary authority would come from the liquidation committee.[6]

Instead of the liquidator being authorised to dispose of all shares not applied for by the members of the transferor company, an underwriting agreement may be made in respect of such shares.[7] If the agreement is silent as to the disposal of the proceeds of sale of the shares not applied for, the proceeds must be distributed among the members of the transferor company who have not applied for shares in the transferee company.[8]

Shares may be given directly to the members of the transferor company instead of being applied for in the manner explained above.

Protection of dissentient members

A sale or arrangement under section 110 of the Insolvency Act 1986 is binding on all members of the transferor company, whether they agree to it or not: section 110(5). However, a member who (1) did not vote in favour of the special resolution, and (2) expressed his dissent from it in writing addressed to the liquidator and left at the registered office within seven days after the passing of the resolution, may require the liquidator either to abstain from carrying the resolution into effect or to purchase his interest at a price to be determined by agreement or arbitration: section 111 of the Insolvency Act 1986. Subsection 111(3) below shows that the election is that of the liquidator.

[6] *Ante*, p. 798.
[7] *Barrow* v. *Paringa Mines* (1909) *Ltd.* (1909)2 Ch. 658.
[8] *Re Lake View Extended Gold Mine Co.* [1900] W.N. 44.

The Jenkins Report[9] recommended that members who vote in favour of the resolution should be able to express dissent.

A transferee of shares whose transfer was not registered when the special resolution was passed may be entitled to have the register of members rectified and to dissent from the resolution.[10]

If the liquidator elects to purchase the member's interest, the purchase money must be paid before the transferor company is dissolved, and be raised by the liquidator as is determined by special resolution: section 111(3). The agreement usually provides for the retention by the liquidator out of the assets of the transferor company of a sum to cover the interests of the dissentient shareholders.

The articles cannot deprive a member of his statutory right to the value of his shareholding if he dissents.[11]

Protection of dissentient creditors

The liquidator must pay the creditors of the transferor company in the usual way in a winding up. If, however, the creditors conceive that they will be prejudiced by the transfer of all the company's assets to the transferee company, they may petition for a compulsory winding up order. Section 110(6) of the Insolvency Act 1986 provides that the special resolution for reconstruction shall not be valid if, within a year, an order is made for winding up the company by the court, unless the court sanctions the resolution.

Sale under power in memorandum

The memorandum of association may give power to a company to sell its undertaking for shares in another company. If, however, the whole of the undertaking is to be sold and the proceeds are to be distributed among the shareholders, the procedure laid down in section 110 of the Insolvency Act 1986, including the provisions for the protection of dissentient shareholders and creditors, cannot be excluded.[12]

[9] Para. 503.
[10] *Re Sussex Brick Co.* [1904] 1 Ch. 598 (C.A.).
[11] *Payne* v. *The Cork Co. Ltd.* [1900] 1 Ch. 308.
[12] *Bisgood* v. *Henderson's Transvaal Estates Ltd.* [1908] 1 Ch. 743 (C.A.); *cf. Waverley Hydropathic Co. Ltd., Petitioners*, 1948 S.C. 59.

Scheme of Arrangement under Section 425 of the Companies Act 1985

Compromise or arrangement

Under section 167 of the Insolvency Act an arrangement with a company's creditors can be made by a liquidator when it is about to be or is in course of being wound up but in that case a liquidation is already in progress.[13]

Under sections 1 to 7 of the Insolvency Act the directors, and administrator or liquidator of a company may propose a voluntary arrangement with the company's creditors.[14] Under section 425 of the Companies Act 1985 a company can also enter into a compromise or arrangement with its creditors, and also its members, or any class thereof, without going into liquidation. Schemes of arrangement under section 425 have a wider potential than voluntary arrangements under the Insolvency Act and can be used for an agreed merger of two companies subject to the requirements of the section as to consent of the members and the court. Voluntary arrangements were introduced to provide a cheaper and quicker way of making a composition with creditors.

The proper way to distribute the assets of a company otherwise than strictly in accordance with creditors' rights has been held to be by a scheme of arrangement under section 425 which binds all creditors, and not by an agreement of compromise under section 167 of the Insolvency Act which would deprive non-assenting creditors of the court's protection and prevent them from expressing their views.[15] However voluntary arrangements are equally permissible.

Section 425 provides that a compromise or arrangement will be binding on the company and the creditors or class of creditors or the members or class of members, as the case may be, if:

(1) The court, on the application in a summary way of the company or of any creditor or member of the company (or, if the company is being wound up, of the

[13] *Ante*, p. 782.
[14] *Ante*, p. 695.
[15] *Re Trix Ltd.* [1970] 1 W.L.R. 1421.

liquidator), orders a meeting of the creditors or class of creditors, or of the members or class of members, to be summoned.

The application for the meeting or meetings in England is by originating summons (R.S.C., Ord. 102, r. 2) and in Scotland by petition to the Outer House (R.C. 189).

(2) The compromise or arrangement is agreed to by a majority in number representing three-fourths in value[16] of those present and voting either in person or by proxy at the meeting.
(3) It is sanctioned by the court.

The application for sanction is by petition: R.S.C., Ord. 102, r.5; R.C. 189.

If the scheme involves the merger or division of one or more public companies additional requirements are imposed.[17]

The word "company" in sections 425 and 426[18] means any company liable to be wound up under the Act: section 425(6). Thus it includes a company formed and registered under the 1985 Act, an existing company (in effect, a company formed and registered under a previous Companies Act), or an unregistered company.[19]

The word "arrangement" has a very wide meaning, and is wider than the word "compromise."[20] An arrangement may involve debenture holders giving an extension of time for payment, accepting a cash payment less than the face value of their debentures,[21] giving up their security in whole or in part, exchanging their debentures for shares in the company[22] or in a new company[23] or having the rights attached to their debentures varied in some other respect[24]; creditors may take cash in part

[16] In the case of creditors the value of their debts is the relevant criterion; see, *e.g. Re Exchange Securities and Commodities Ltd.* (1987) 3 BCC 48.
[17] See p. 845, *post*.
[18] *Post*.
[19] s.220, I.A. 1986, *ante*, p. 787.
[20] *Re Guardian Assce. Co.* [1917] 1 Ch. 431 (C.A.).
[21] *e.g. The Philadelphia Securities Co.* v. *The Realisation etc. Corpn. of Scotland Ltd.* (1903) 11 S.L.T. 217 (O.H.).
[22] *e.g. Gillies* v. *Dawson* (1893) 20 R. 1119 (O.H.).
[23] *Re Empire Mining Co.* (1890) 44 Ch.D. 402.
[24] *e.g. Wright & Greig Ltd., Petitioners*, 1911 1 S.L.T. 353.

payment of their claims and the balance in shares or debentures in the company; preference shareholders may give up their rights to arrears of dividends,[25] agree to accept a reduced rate of dividend in the future, or have their class rights otherwise varied[26] (the use of section 425 to vary class rights has already been dealt with[27]). Or the members of a company in liquidation may agree with the company to seek or not to oppose a stay of the winding up, whereunder the members will give up their existing right to have all the proceeds of the company's assets distributed among them and instead be remitted to their contractual rights under the articles.[28] It even includes a scheme whereby the shareholders transfer their shares to another company, since that affects the contractual arrangements between the shareholders and their company so that there is an arrangement between them.[29]

Section 425 itself provides that the expression "arrangement" includes a reorganisation of the share capital of the company by the consolidation of shares of different classes or by the division of shares into shares of different classes. The word "compromise" implies some element of accommodation on each side. It is not apt to describe a total surrender. Similarly, the word "arrangement" implies some element of give and take.[30]

Where an arrangement under section 425 is essentially a scheme for the purchase by an outsider of all the issued shares of a company the scheme will not be sanctioned unless that company consents. Such consent may be expressed by the members in general meeting or by the board of directors.[31] It cannot be used therefore for a contested take-over or merger. Even if the take-over or merger is an agreed one the court will not allow the provisions of sections 428 to 430F,[32] which require the outside purchaser to acquire 90 per cent. of the shares

[25] *e.g. Balmenach-Glenlivet Distillery Ltd., Petitioners*, 1916 S.C. 639.
[26] *City etc., Trust Corporation Ltd., Petitioners*, 1951 S.C. 570.
[27] *Ante*, p. 266.
[28] *Per* Megarry J. in *Re Calgary and Edmonton Land Co. Ltd.*, [1975] 1 W.L.R. 355 at p. 363.
[29] *Re. N.F.U. Development Trust* [1972] 1 W.L.R. 1548.
[30] *Re Savoy Hotel Ltd.* [1981] 3 All E.R. 646.
[31] But not all such schemes will fail, see *Re National Bank Ltd.* [1966] 1 W.L.R. 819; *The Singer Manufacturing Co. Ltd.* v. *Robinow*, 1971 S.C. 11 (scheme to enable parent company to acquire remaining 7·3 per cent. shareholding in subsidiary held competent).
[32] As substituted by the Financial Services Act 1986; *post*, p. 867.

before he may compulsorily acquire the remainder,[33] to be circumvented by the use of section 425 where the necessary resolution under section 425 can only be passed with the assistance of votes of the wholly-owned subsidiary of the taking-over company.[34]

The meaning of the term "class" has been considered already.[35] The interests of a wholly-owned subsidiary of a company which is taking shares in another company under a scheme of arrangement, when the subsidiary holds shares in that other company, are different from those of the other ordinary shareholders in the other company and therefore the subsidiary is in a different class from the other ordinary shareholders and separate meetings must be held to approve the scheme.[36] Separate class meetings are required whenever the parties are not all on an equal footing, *e.g.* where some creditors are secured and others unsecured.[37]

It is the responsibility of the petitioners to see that the class meetings are properly constituted, and if they fail the court has no jurisdiction to sanction the arrangement.[38]

As to (1) *ante*, where a meeting of creditors or members is summoned under section 425, with every notice of the meeting there must be sent a statement explaining the effect of the compromise or arrangement and, in particular, stating any material interests of the directors in any capacity and the effect thereon of the compromise or arrangement in so far as it is different from the effect on the like interests of other persons. If the meeting is summoned by advertisement, a similar statement, or a notification of the place where such a statement may be obtained, must be included. Where the compromise or arrangement affects the rights of debenture holders the statement must give the like explanation as respects the trustees of a deed for securing the issue of debentures as it is required to give as respects the directors: section 426.

Section 426 must be faithfully complied with; the court "has no discretionary power to dispense with the procedural

[33] *Re Savoy Hotel Ltd.*, *supra*.
[34] *Re Hellenic & General Trust Ltd.* [1976] 1 W.L.R. 123.
[35] p. 259.
[36] See note 34, above.
[37] *La Lainière de Roubaix* v. *Glen Glove etc. Co. Ltd.*, 1926 S.C. 91.
[38] See note 34, above.

requirements of section [426]."[39] Thus a scheme will not be sanctioned if the explanatory statement, while stating that the company's assets have been revalued, does not give the amount of the revaluation,[40] or if a copy of the petition[41] or a copy of the scheme[42] has been sent without any further explanation. Material interests of directors must always be stated, even although those interests are in no way differently affected by the scheme from the interests of other persons.[43]

Where there is a change in the material interests of the directors or of any other material circumstances between the issue of the statement and the meetings to consider the scheme the court will nevertheless sanction the scheme, even though the meetings are not informed of the change, if it is satisfied that no reasonable shareholder would have altered his decision as to the scheme had he known of the changes.[44] The test is whether all material changes of circumstances which have come to the attention of the board between the issuing of the circular and the meeting have been disclosed to those entitled to vote at the meeting. A material change for this purpose is one which would be likely to affect a reasonable shareholder's voting intentions.[45]

As to (2) *ante*, "three-fourths in value of the members or class of members" in section 425 refers to the size of the stake which each member has in the company. "The purpose is to prevent a numerical majority with a small stake outvoting a minority with a large stake, *e.g.* to prevent 51 members with one share each outvoting 49 members with 10 shares each."[46]

Any proper form of proxy may be used and it is not necessary to its validity that it should be sent to the company's offices before the meeting.[47] Directors who, pursuant to the court's

[39] *Per* Lord Guthrie in *The Scottish Eastern etc. Trust Ltd., Petitioners*, 1966 S.L.T. 285 at p. 288.

[40] *Re Dorman, Long & Co. Ltd.* [1934] Ch. 635.

[41] *Rankin & Blackmore Ltd., Petitioners*, 1950 S.C. 218.

[42] *Peter Scott & Co. Ltd., Petitioners*, 1950 S.C. 507.

[43] *Coltness Iron Co. Ltd., Petitioners*, 1951 S.C. 476; contrast *Second Scottish Investment Trust etc., Petitioners*, 1962 S.L.T. 392.

[44] *Re Jessel Trust Ltd.* [1985] BCLC 119; *Re Minister Assets plc* [1985] BCLC 200.

[45] *Re MB Group plc* (1989) 5 BCC 584.

[46] *Per* Brightman J. in *Re N.F.U. Development Trust Ltd.* [1972] 1 W.L.R. 1548 at p. 1553.

[47] *Re Dorman, Long & Co. Ltd.* [1934] Ch. 635; *La Lanière de Roubaix* v. *Glen Glove etc. Co. Ltd.*, 1926 S.C. 91.

order, receive proxies must use them whether they are for or against the scheme.[48]

As to (3) *ante*, before giving its sanction to a scheme of arrangement the court will see "First, that the provisions of the statute have been complied with. Secondly, that the class was fairly represented by those who attended the meeting and that the statutory majority are acting bona fide and are not coercing the minority in order to promote interests adverse to those of the class whom they purport to represent; and, thirdly, that the arrangement is such as a man of business would reasonably approve."[49]

An order sanctioning a compromise or arrangement under section 425 has no effect until an office copy has been delivered to the Registrar of Companies. A copy of the order must also be annexed to every copy of the memorandum issued after the making of the order: section 425(3).

The costs of the scheme may be borne by the company and there may be one set of costs for opposing creditors but not for any supporting creditors. In general, costs should be kept to a minimum and one set of creditors should not be ordered to pay the costs of another set of creditors.[50]

Facilitating a reconstruction or an amalgamation

Section 425, *ante*, can be used not only to effect arrangements with creditors and members, but also to carry out a scheme of reconstruction or amalgamation. One advantage of using section 425 to carry out such a scheme is that dissentient creditors are bound if the scheme is approved by the requisite majority. When the section is so used there is no statutory provision for the protection of dissentient members, and such members are bound by the arrangement if it is approved by the requisite majority. However, the court may, and usually will, as a

[48] See note 43, above.

[49] *Per* Astbury J. in *Re Anglo-Continental Supply Co. Ltd.* [1922] 2 Ch. 723 at p. 736. See to the same effect *per* Lindley L.J. in *Re Alabama, etc. Rlwy. Co.* [1891] 1 Ch. 213 (C.A.) at p. 238. For adoption in Scotland, see *per* Lord President Dunedin in *Shandon Hydropathic Co. Ltd., Petitioners*, 1911 S.C. 1153 at p. 1155.

[50] *Re Esal (Commodities) Ltd.* [1985] BCLC 450.

condition of sanctioning the scheme, if it thinks it reasonable to do so, require dissentient members to be given the same rights as they would have had under section 110 of the Insolvency Act 1986, *ante*.

In order to facilitate schemes of reconstruction and amalgamation, section 427 provides that when an application is made to the court under section 425 for the sanctioning of a compromise or arrangement, where the compromise or arrangement is for the purposes of a scheme for the reconstruction of a company or the amalgamation of two or more companies and the scheme involves the transfer of the whole or part of the undertaking or property of a company (called "a transferor company") to another company (called "the transferee company"), the court may make an order providing for the following matters:

(1) The transfer to the transferee company of the whole or part of the undertaking and of the property or liabilities of a transferor company. An order so made cannot operate to transfer to the transferee company the benefit of a personal contract such as a contract of service between the transferor company and a person employed by it.[51] Further, a scheme under section 425, or an order under section 427 for giving effect to such a scheme, cannot transfer the office of executor from one bank to another; such an office of personal trust is incapable of assignment.[52]

(2) The allotting by the transferee company of any shares, debentures, policies or other similar interests in such company to the appropriate persons.

(3) The continuation by or against the transferee company of any legal proceedings pending by or against a transferor company.

(4) The dissolution, without winding up, of a transferor company.

(5) The provision to be made for persons who dissent from the scheme.

This has been dealt with already.

[51] *Nokes* v. *Doncaster Amalgamated Collieries Ltd.* [1940] A.C. 1014.

[52] *In the Estate of Skinner* (*decd.*) [1958] 1 W.L.R. 1043.

(6) Any incidental matters.

An office copy of an order made under section 427 must be registered with the Registrar of Companies within seven days.

The word "company" in section 427 means a company within the meaning of the Act. Thus it means a company formed and registered under the Act or an existing company, in effect a company formed and registered under a previous Companies Act: section 735.[53]

Mergers and divisions of public companies—additional requirements

Following the implementation of the Third and Sixth EC directives on company law[54] by the Companies (Mergers and Divisions) Regulations 1987,[55] additional requirements to those already required by sections 425 to 427 are imposed where the scheme of arrangement falls within one of the following three categories as defined in section 427A.

Case 1—Mergers by acquisition

Where a public company proposes to transfer all of its undertaking, property and liabilities to another public company (which has not been formed for that purpose) in return for shares in the transferee company to be held by the transferor shareholders.

Case 2—Mergers by formation of a new company

Where two or more public companies propose to transfer all their undertakings, etc. to any type of company formed for that purpose, members of the transferor company receiving shares in the new company by way of total or part consideration.

Note that case 1 does not apply where the transferee company is specially formed to receive the assets, etc. of the transferor and that case 2 applies where the transferee company is a private company provided it was set up for the purpose of the merger.

[53] *Cf.* s.425(6), *ante.*
[54] Dir. 78/885 EEC, O.J. 1978 L295/36 and Dir. 82/891, O.J. 1982 L378/47.
[55] S.I. 1987 No. 1991.

Case 3—Divisions

Where a public company proposes to divide all its undertaking, etc. between two or more companies which are either public companies or companies formed for the purpose of the division, members of the transferor company receiving shares in the transferee companies by way of total or part consideration.

In all these cases there is therefore an agreed arrangement involving a share exchange by the transferee company's shareholders. It is envisaged that the transferor company or companies will be dissolved after the scheme has gone through.[56]

Where section 427A applies the court cannot sanction a scheme unless the additional requirements specified in Schedule 15B have been complied with. These are somewhat complex since there are eight additional requirements for specified mergers and divisions with a further two for divisions alone, whilst at the same time there are seven different exemptions from some or all of these additional requirements. As a final complication, in three of these exemptions additional exemptions from parts of sections 425 and 426 are also included.

The following is a summary of the additional requirements and exemptions:

The additional requirements

(i) In a case 1 or case 3 scheme there must be a meeting of each class of members of any transferee company not formed for the purpose of the merger or division. Section 425 already requires a meeting of the transferor company.

(ii) The directors of all transferor and transferee companies[57] must draw up draft terms of the merger or division. These must include details of the companies

[56] The new requirements do not apply if the transferor company is already in liquidation and so do not apply to reconstructions under section 110 of the Insolvency Act 1986, *ante*.

[57] Except those formed specifically for the purpose of the scheme.

involved, the share exchange ratio, the allotment of the new shares, the directors' benefits, and, in a division, the allocation of the shares.

(iii) The draft terms must be delivered to the registrar who will publish a notice of receipt in the Gazette. This gives official notification of that receipt.[58]

(iv) There must be at least one month's gap between such publication and the holding of any meeting[59] to consider the scheme.

(v) The directors[60] must draw up a report consisting of the explanatory statement already required by section 426[61] together with the legal and economic grounds for the draft terms including the share exchange ratio, and in a division, the allocation arrangements.

(vi) An expert's report must be drawn up for each transferor and transferee[62] company involved, dealing in particular with the share exchange ratio and any valuation problems. A statement as to the reasonableness of these must be included.

(vii) The draft terms, directors' report, experts' report and the previous three years' accounts must be available for inspection for at least one month prior to any meeting required under section 425 or (i) above.

(viii) The memorandum and articles of any transferee company set up for the purpose of the scheme must be approved by an ordinary resolution of each transferor company involved.

(ix) In a division the directors of the transferor company must report any material changes between the time when draft terms were adopted and any meeting, to that meeting and to the directors of the transferee company.

(x) Following receipt of a report under (ix) the transferee directors must notify the change to any meetings of the transferee companies or send a notice to every member entitled to attend such meetings.

[58] *Ante*, p. 67.
[59] Including one under s.425.
[60] Of all the companies.
[61] *Ante*, p. 841.
[62] Except those formed specifically for the purpose of the scheme.

Exceptions to the additional requirements

(a) The requirement to hold a meeting of the transferee company may be dispensed with if five per cent. of the transferee members could have required such a meeting and no such meeting has been requested, provided requirement (vii) has been complied with.

(b) There need be no directors' or experts' reports in a case 3 scheme if all the relevant shareholders agree.

(c) The court may decide that no meetings at all need be held (including ones held under section 425) in a case 3 scheme.

(d) In a case 1 scheme where the transferor is wholly owned by the transferee company, the draft terms of the merger can omit all references to share exchange ratios etc., the directors' and experts' reports can be omitted and no explanatory circular under section 426 need be given.

(e) Where exemption (d) applies the court may order that no meetings of either company be held, even under section 425.

(f) In a division, where the transferor is wholly-owned by the transferee companies the court may dispense with the need for a meeting of the transferor company under section 425.

(g) In a case 1 scheme, where the transferor is an 80 per cent. or more but not wholly owned subsidiary of the transferee company the court may dispense with a meeting of the transferee company.

Chapter 31

TAKE-OVERS AND SUBSTANTIAL ACQUISITIONS OF SHARES

MOST amalgamations take place without a scheme of arrangement under section 425 or a reconstruction under section 110 of the Insolvency Act 1986, but by the simple method of one company acquiring a majority or the whole of the shares of another company from its shareholders. In such a case it is usual for the acquiring company (the offeror company) to make an offer (called a take-over bid) to the shareholders in the other company (the target or offeree company) to purchase their shares at a stated price and to fix a time within which the offer is to be accepted, with a condition that if a named percentage of the shareholders do not accept the offer, the offer is to be void. The offer is usually at a higher price than the current market price of the shares as quoted on the Stock Exchange and it may be in cash (*e.g.* £2 per share) or in kind (*e.g.* 2 of the offeror company's shares for each of the target company's shares). There are many economic reasons why such an offer is made. Sometimes more than one take-over bid is made for the same company so that there are rival bidders. As has already been seen[1] this form of amalgamation is the only practical form where the two companies do not agree to the merger.

There is little in the Companies Act of specific relevance to such take-overs. Sections 428–430F allow an offeror who has a 90 per cent. acceptance to purchase compulsorily the remaining 10 per cent. Those sections are considered below. Other areas of the law are clearly relevant. These include questions as to the fiduciary duties of the directors of both companies involved,[2] the law of contract and of tort,[3] aspects of the Financial Services

[1] *Ante*, p. 840.
[2] See, *e.g.* *Dawson International plc* v. *Coats Patons plc* (1989) 5 BCC 405; *John Crowther Group plc* v. *Carpets International plc* [1990] BCLC 460.
[3] See, *e.g.* *Lonrho plc* v. *Fayed* (1989) 5 BCC 411.

Act 1986[4] and the public control of mergers by the Monopolies and Mergers Commission and the European Commission. However it is fair to say that the most important controls on the conduct of take-overs are those set out in the City Code on Take-overs and Mergers and administered by the City Panel, a "voluntary" self-regulatory code to which all who deal in shares on the Stock Exchange are subject. The City Code is not, however, part of the general self-regulatory system applicable to the investment industry generally, which was dealt with in Chapter 19, although its provisions are incorporated by reference in the relevant rule-books.

City Code on Take-overs and Mergers

The eighth edition of the City Code was published in October 1990.[5] Unlike the early editions, this edition is in loose leaf form and can be regularly amended.[6] It is administered by the City Panel which was instituted by the Bank of England and contains representatives of all the major City institutions, so that anyone in breach of its provisions is liable to fall foul of his own professional organisation and may suffer penalties in consequence. In particular the Stock Exchange is represented, and withdrawal of a licence to deal on the Exchange is a potent threat against those dealing in shares on a take-over. The City Panel is an autonomous body which also administers the Rules governing Substantial Acquisitions of Shares. Those Rules, dealt with below,[7] relate to pre-bid acquisitions of shares. The Panel also has a full-time executive, under a full time Director General, which is available for advice at any time during the course of the bid, not as to the merits of the offer but as to procedure and conduct.

Administration of the Code

The Panel and the executive have the joint responsibility for the administration of the Code. In *R.* v. *Panel on Take-overs*

[4] Chap. 19, *ante*.
[5] Copies may be obtained from the Secretary, Issuing Houses Association, Granite House, 101 Cannon Street, London EC4N 5BA.
[6] There were four subsequent updates to the previous edition of 1988.
[7] p. 867.

and Mergers, *ex parte Guinness plc* Watkins L.J. expressed the function of the executive as follows[8]:

> "It is the executive which takes the lead in examining the circumstances of take-over bids and, if thought necessary, referring them to the Panel for consideration and adjudication according to the rules. Almost daily it is called upon to give advice and rulings, which mostly are accepted . . . . It acts as a sort of fire brigade to extinguish quickly the flames of unacceptable and unfair practice."

If either the executive or either of the parties considers that the matter is serious enough it will be referred to the Panel for a full hearing. This is a quasi-judicial affair and at the end the Panel may give a definitive ruling imposing either disciplinary sanctions or a course of action which the parties must adhere to.

There is only an automatic right of appeal if disciplinary action is taken[9] or the dispute is as to the Panel's jurisdiction. In other cases there is only a right of appeal with the Panel's consent. Any appeal lies to the Appeals Committee with a former judge as chairman. That Committee will only interfere if it concludes that the Panel was wrong or, where the Panel's exercise of a discretion is being challenged, if either that power has been wrongly exercised or the Panel has misdirected itself.[10]

The City Panel and the Law

In 1987 a Canadian-based company, Datafin, became the first party to challenge a Panel decision in the courts by way of an application for judicial review. In the Court of Appeal it was established that the Panel was subject to the process of judicial review.[11] Lord Donaldson M.R., however, stressed that an application for judicial review should not be used as a ploy to hinder a bid and that in general the Panel's decisions would remain binding until otherwise directed. He considered that a challenge could be made against the Panel acting as legislator if

[8] (1988) 4 BCC 325 (D.C.).
[9] Including a ruling as to exempt market status, *post*, p. 864.
[10] Appeal Statement on *BAT Industries plc* [1990] J.B.L. 67.
[11] *R.* v. *Panel on Take-overs and Mergers, ex parte Datafin* [1987] Q.B. 815 (C.A.).

it made a rule contrary to its own terms of reference; as interpreter of the Code; and as a disciplinary body, but in that case the internal appeals procedure should be used first.

The dispute in *Datafin* was as to the Panel's interpretation of a particular rule. The Court of Appeal rejected the application on the basis that a challenge would have to show that the Panel's view was so far removed from the natural and ordinary meaning of the words that no ordinary user of the market could reasonably be misled. In the case of an exercise of the Panel's discretion the Court would only interfere in a totally inequitable case.

A second challenge to the Panel by way of judicial review was mounted by Guinness plc on the basis of a breach of natural justice in the Panel's proceedings. This too failed, the Court finding that although the Panel had been inconsiderate and harsh there was no procedural impropriety and no breach of the rules of natural justice.[12] The Court of Appeal accepted again, however, that judicial review could apply and Lord Donaldson M.R. suggested the test as being whether something had gone wrong of a nature and degree which required the intervention of the court.

Occasionally the Code has been involved in other legal proceedings. In *Dunford & Elliott Ltd.* v. *Johnson & Firth Brown Ltd.*[13] one party to a bid sought an injunction to prevent the abuse of alleged confidential information in a take-over situation. Both Lord Denning M.R. and Roskill L.J. quoted the Code and used it as a guide to good commercial practice in an area where the court had a discretion. Again in *Re St. Piran Ltd.*[14] the Court said that when considering whether to wind-up a company on the just and equitable ground[15] the fact that the directors of a public company chose to flout the City Code or to ignore, without good reason, the consequent directions of the City Panel so that the minority shareholders were hurt by a withdrawal of the company's Stock Exchange quotation,[16] would be strong evidence in favour of granting the petition.

[12] *R.* v. *Panel on Take-overs and Mergers, ex parte Guinness plc* [1990] Q.B. 147 (C.A.).
[13] [1977] 1 Lloyd's Rep. 505 (C.A.).
[14] [1981] 3 All E.R. 270.
[15] *Ante*, p. 449.
[16] This effectively prevents the shares being sold.

On the other hand the Court has awarded injunctions preventing the Panel from issuing statements,[17] and the Panel has, on one occasion, had a battle of words with the Department of Trade and Industry following an inspectors' report under section 432.[18]

The code is applicable to all mergers and take-over transactions involving public companies and applies to all those involved whether as directors, advisers, offerors, offerees or in any other capacity. However, it only applies where a merger or take-over bid is concerned.[19] The panel does not see itself as being concerned with the merits of a bid but as an instrument of investor protection.

The Code itself is divided into General Principles and Rules. The following is a summary of some of the more important parts of the Code. The references in this chapter to Panel decisions and statements are to *The Journal of Business Law* which monitors the Panel on a regular basis.

General principles

There are 10 general principles concerned with the provision of adequate and timely information to the shareholders so that all are to be treated equally, and with the general responsibilities of the boards of directors of both the offeror and the offeree companies. The introduction to the general principles emphasises that the spirit as well as the precise wording of the Code must be observed. This enables the Panel to find that there has been a breach of the Code even though no specific provision was involved.[20]

The boards of both companies are required to act in the best interests of their respective shareholders. The offeree board should seek competent independent advice on receiving an offer and must not do anything to frustrate the offer without the general meeting's approval. In particular, rights of control must

[17] Panel statement on *Sandstar Ltd.* v. *Graff Diamonds Ltd.* [1979] J.B.L. 274.
[18] Panel statement of May 14, 1979 [1979] J.B.L. 364.
[19] Panel statement on *N.F.U. Development Trust* [1976] J.B.L. 162; *cf.* Panel statement on *Chaddesley Investments Ltd.* [1979] J.B.L. 271. The Code does not apply to offers for non-voting non-equity capital.
[20] Panel statement on *Mount Charlotte Investments* v. *Gale Lister & Co. Ltd.* [1974] J.B.L. 310.

be exercised in good faith—minority oppression is "wholly unacceptable" (G.P.s 1, 7 and 8).[21]

General Principle 4 requires that the shareholders be put in possession of all the facts necessary for an informed judgment as to the merits of an offer and must have sufficient time to make an assessment and decision. No relevant information is to be withheld from them. No false market in shares is to be created—this can cause problems in relation to the disclosure of information about preliminary negotiations.[22] Rumour and speculation can drastically affect the quoted share price of a company (G.P. 6). The Panel have indicated that a false market usually involves an element of contrivance but it may also be caused by any step which results in a market price which is manifestly unrealistic.[23]

General Principal 9 relates to the responsibilities of the directors of the companies involved, in effect reminding them of their fiduciary duties to their company and warning them against entering into binding commitments which could restrict their freedom to advise shareholders.[24]

The Rules

There are 38 rules currently in the Code. However, many of these are subdivided and are further amplified by notes.

(1) *The approach, announcements and independent advice* (*Rules 1–3*)

An offer should be made first to the board of the offeree company or its advisers. The identity of the offeror if it is not the person making the bid should be disclosed at the outset and the offeree board is entitled to be satisfied that the offeror company will be in a position to implement its offer (either in cash or by shares) in full. The offeree board must circulate the

[21] Thus the offeree must not take any action to frustrate a bid or to prevent their shareholders considering it on its merits without shareholder consent. This includes taking legal action. See, *e.g.* Appeal Committee Statement on *BAT Industries plc* [1990] J.B.L. 67.
[22] Panel statement on *Rockwell International Corporation* v. *Wilmot Breedon* (*Holdings*) *Ltd.* [1979] J.B.L. 387.
[23] Panel statement on *Gateway plc* [1990] J.B.L. 72.
[24] See, *e.g. John Crowther Group plc* v. *Carpets International plc* [1990] BCLC 460.

independent advice it receives, usually from a Merchant Bank, to its shareholders. This independent advice must come from outside any financial conglomerate involved in the bid.

When a firm intention to make an offer is notified from a serious source a press notice must be issued immediately followed by a circular to the shareholders. More difficult is the announcement of approaches which may or may not lead to an offer. Too early an announcement may kill the offer, too late and the market will have reacted in advance with all the possibilities of insider dealing by those with insider information.[25] Accordingly, an announcement, together with a temporary halt in dealings on the Stock Exchange, is normally expected either when negotiations have reached a point at which a company is reasonably confident that an offer will be made for its shares or when negotiations are about to be extended to embrace more than a small group of people. The responsibility is on the offeree company to make the announcement.[26] However, the Code requires a statement from the potential offeror company where, prior to an approach, the offeree company is the subject of rumours and speculations or an untoward price movement, and there are reasonable grounds for concluding that it is the potential offeror's actions which have led to the situation.[27] An announcement that a block of shares carrying over 30 per cent. of the voting rights or that the board is seeking offers for the company will be treated as an announcement of a possible offer for the purposes of the Code. Offerers will usually be bound by so-called denial statements, *i.e.* that no bid is intended. Such statements must be clear and unambiguous.[28]

The formal announcement of an intention to make an offer must include any conditions to which the offer is subject including the conditions as to acceptance levels, the ability to achieve a quotation for the new shares and the authority to issue those new shares[29] if a share for share offer is being made.

[25] See *ante*, Chap. 19.

[26] See Panel statement on *Dickinson Robinson Group Ltd.* v. *Royal Sovereign Group Ltd.* [1978] J.B.L. 66; *Teachers (Distillers) Ltd.* v. *Allied Breweries Ltd.* [1978] J.B.L. 67; and *Balfour Ltd.* v. *Aurora Holdings Ltd.* [1979] J.B.L. 366.

[27] Panel statement on *Argyll Group plc/Distillers Group plc* [1986] J.B.L. 233.

[28] Panel statement on *Storehouse plc* [1989] J.B.L. 518.

[29] See *ante*, p. 164.

Thus where a requirement as to the giving of a proxy vote was included in the offer documents but not in the original announcement the former were held to be void.[30] If a formal offer is not forthcoming within 28 days after the announcement the offeror must be prepared to justify this to the Panel.[31] If necessary the Panel will take steps to enforce completion of the offer, *e.g.* by freezing the voting rights of shares already obtained.[32]

(2) *Dealings and restrictions on the acquisition of shares and rights over shares* (*Rules 4–8*)

Rule 4 provides that no person, other than the offeror, may deal in the offeree company's shares if he is privy to confidential price-sensitive information[33] relating to the offer, between the time when there is reason to suppose that an approach or offer is contemplated and the public announcement. Nor should such persons make any recommendations to any other person as to dealing in the relevant securities. Together with Rule 2 relating to the announcement of a prospective offer, this provision is an attempt to inhibit insider trading by preventing both the leakage of information and dealings by the "informed." Nevertheless, a pattern has been established. There is a substantial price movement in the market price of shares in a company the reason for which becomes apparent when a take-over bid involving the company is subsequently announced. Subsequent investigations rarely bring to light any dealings by actual "insiders."[34]

[30] Panel statement on *Bassishaw Investment Ltd.* v. *UDS Group plc* [1982] J.B.L. 329.

[31] Panel statement on *Combined English Stores Ltd.* v. *David Greig Ltd.* [1974] J.B.L. 312.

[32] Panel statements on *St. Martins Property Ltd.* v. *Hays Wharf Ltd.* [1974] J.B.L. 312; *B.S.Q. Securities Ltd.* v. *Court Hotels* (*London*) *Ltd.* [1976] J.B.L. 162.

[33] As defined by the Code. See also the Panel statement on *Johnson & Firth Brown Ltd./Dunford & Elliott Ltd.* [1977] J.B.L. 161.

[34] See the Panel statements on *United Drapery Stores Ltd./William Timpson Ltd.* [1973] J.B.L. 37; Panel statement on *G.K.N. Ltd.* and *Miles Drew & Co. Ltd.* [1974] J.B.L. 309; Panel statement on *Boots Co. Ltd.* and *House of Fraser Ltd.* [1975] J.B.L. 43; *cf.* the Panel decision on *P. R. Grimshawe & Co. Ltd. Grimshawe-Windsor Merger* [1973] J.B.L. 46 and *D. R. Lyons & Co. Ltd.* [1973] J.B.L. 451.

If the offeror, potential offeror, or anyone acting in concert[35] with him purchases shares at above the offer price, then that price must be increased to the highest price, excluding stamp duty and commission, so paid. If 15 per cent. or more of the shares of a class are acquired for cash, the offer must include a cash alternative, being the highest price paid for such shares. A cash alternative may also be required if the offeror cannot fulfil the paper offer.[36] When a revised offer is announced it should "whenever practicable" disclose the number of securities purchased and the price paid. Purchases by a financial adviser for discretionary clients must be cleared by the Panel unless he is an exempt fund manager (see below).

Voting rights are defined in the City Code as all voting rights attributable to the share capital of a company currently exercisable at a general meeting. This will include preference shareholders whose shares have acquired temporary voting rights through their dividends being in arrears during the entire course of an offer. It is not clear how this will operate if the preference shareholders lose their votes during the course of a bid.

Rule 8 requires dealings by parties to the offer and their associates either for themselves or for discretionary or non-discretionary clients, to be disclosed daily. This applies to dealings whereby an associate indemnifies a third party who has acquired relevant shares against any loss on the resale of those shares.[37] Such disclosure must now reveal the true identity of the person dealing, and in the case of an associate why such disclosure was necessary. Disclosure of dealings must also be made by a holder of one per cent. of the shares in either company. Further, any type of inducement to deal or refrain from dealing or for any connected person to bear any investment risk[38] must be disclosed if a party to the bid is involved. Disclosure is also required by intermediaries and they must warn their clients if dealings exceed £25,000 in any one account period.

[35] As defined in the Code. See Panel statement on *United Newspapers plc/Fleet Holidays plc* [1986] J.B.L. 230.

[36] To avoid the problems such as those raised in the Panel statement on *St. Martin's Property Ltd./Hays Wharf Ltd.* [1974] J.B.L. 312.

[37] Panel statement on *Turner and Newall plc/AE plc* [1987] J.B.L. 140.

[38] Following the Guinness plc revelations. See [1989] J.B.L. 520.

In 1981 Rules governing Substantial Acquisitions of Shares were published.[39] These were originally framed for "dawn raids" of the type experienced in 1980 and apply to acquisitions giving a holding of between 15 and 30 per cent. The Rules, which are dealt with below, basically provide a seven day freeze on all offers to acquire more than a 15 per cent. but less than a 30 per cent. holding.

At the same time the City Code was amended by what is now Rule 5. Anyone who owns less than 30 per cent. of the voting rights of a company may not increase his holding above 30 per cent. prior to the first closing day[40] of an offer. Anyone who owns 30 per cent. already, but less than 50 per cent., may not acquire more than two per cent. prior to that time. There are four exceptions: acquisitions which immediately precede and are conditional on the announcement of an agreed bid, acquisitions from a single shareholder; where the offer has been recommended by the offeree board or declared unconditional; and where it is by way of acceptance of an offer. In one case the Panel has excused a breach of Rule 5 where the breach was due to inaccurate professional advice.[41]

Following the ending of single capacity on the Stock Exchange a new Rule 38 has been added to deal with the problems of multi-service financial organisations: see below.[42]

(3) *The mandatory offer and its terms* (*Rule 9*)

Since January 1972 the Code has contained rules which require a compulsory bid to be made by a purchaser of shares who has amassed a significant holding of the shares without making a formal offer. This has presented problems of enforcement, particularly in times of economic depression, and the present position, set out in Rule 9, is that anyone who,

[39] These were revised in 1985 and 1988. See *post*, p. 867.

[40] The time limits in these Rules relate to midnight on the day in question and not to 3.00 p.m. as had been previously thought. Panel statement on *Arthur Bell & Sons plc/Gleneagles Hotel plc* [1984] J.B.L. 421.

[41] Panel statements on *Glanfield Lawrence plc/Gregory Securities Ltd.* [1985] J.B.L. 47.

[42] p. 864.

together with persons acting in concert,[43] has acquired 30 per cent. or more of the voting rights by a series of transactions or who, owning between 30 and 50 per cent. of such rights within a period of a year shall make an offer. The rule is activated by a relevant purchase by any one member of a group who have previously "come together" to obtain control of a company. The obligation extends to each of the principal members of a consortium if the facts so warrant. The Panel has drawn a distinction between a group acting to obtain control of a company (a "wide concert party") and those dealing with a community of interest in the purchase of a dealing profit. The latter, known as a "fan club," do not fall within this Rule but it may well be difficult to distinguish between them.[44]

If the implementation of such an offer would require a resolution, then no purchases which would give rise to the offer shall be made.[45] The offers must be in cash or have a cash alternative. The offer must be conditional on acceptances carrying 50 per cent. of the voting rights and, if it does not become conditional, then no further shares may be purchased.[46]

(4) *The voluntary offer and its terms* (*Rules 10–13*)

No offer which, if accepted in full, would result in the offeror having voting control can be declared unconditional unless acceptances are received or promised amounting to a total of 50 per cent. of the voting rights of the equity share capital.[47] If 15 per cent. or more of the shares of any class under offer are purchased by the offeror during the offer period or within 12

[43] See, *e.g.* Panel statement on *St. Martin's Property Ltd./Hays Wharf Ltd.* [1974] J.B.L. 312; *Ashbourne Investments Ltd.* [1975] J.B.L. 44; *St. Piran Ltd.* (*No.* 1) [1980] J.B.L. 270; *St. Piran Ltd.* (*No.* 2) [1980] J.B.L. 358 and the preceding section of this chapter; *cf.* Panel statement on *Inoco plc/Petranol plc* [1986] J.B.L. 409.

[44] Panel statement on *Glanfield Lawrence plc/Bajou Ltd.* [1985] J.B.L. 47.

[45] Panel statement on *Manx & Overseas Investments Ltd.* [1978] J.B.L. 184. See also Panel statement on *Rothmans International Ltd.* [1981 J.B.L. 373.

[46] See [1980] J.B.L. 270; [1980] J.B.L. 358; Panel statement on *Westminster Property Group plc* [1983] J.B.L. 358; Panel statements on *Westminster Property Group plc* [1983] J.B.L. 491, and [1983] J.B.L. 492; and Panel statement on *Gilgate Holdings Ltd.* [1980] J.B.L. 269.

[47] As to what can be counted as acceptances see [1986] J.B.L. 317 and [1990] J.B.L. 71. For difficulties in the counting process see Panel statement on *Blue Circle Industries plc/Britoil Qualcast plc* [1988] J.B.L. 323, and [1989] J.B.L. 69.

months prior to its commencement a cash alternative must be included in the offer of at least the highest price paid for those shares during that period, excluding stamp duty and commission, unless the Panel agrees to the contrary.[48] Failure to make such a cash alternative will make the offeror liable to compensate those who have suffered as a result.[49] Further if there is a possibility of a reference to the monopoly and Mergers Commission then the offer must be subject to withdrawal on such a reference.

(5) *Provisions applicable to all offers* (*Rules 14–18*)

Rule 14 applies where there is more than one class of share capital involved[50] and Rule 15 states the appropriate offer for convertible securities etc. Rule 16 prohibits an offeror from entering into arrangements to make purchases of shares in the offeree company if such arrangements have attached thereto favourable conditions which are not extended to all shareholders. The Panel does, however, allow an exception if the payments can be justified commercially.[51]

Rule 17 is concerned with the announcement or failure to announce acceptance levels at critical times during the offer period.[52]

(6) *Conduct during the offer* (*Rules 19–22*)

Rule 19 relates to the quality of and responsibility for information issued during the course of an offer, together with its distribution. In addition to the imposing of a standard of care equivalent to that required in preparing a prospectus (see Chap. 7, *ante*), it prohibits statements which whilst not factually inaccurate may mislead shareholders and the market or may create uncertainty. In particular, an offeror should not make a statement to the effect that it may improve its offer without

[48] See, *e.g.* Panel statement on *Hillsdown Holdings plc/S & W Beresford plc* [1986] J.B.L. 407.

[49] Panel statement on *Guinness plc/Distillers Company plc* [1989] J.B.L. 520.

[50] See Panel statement on their usual practice in *Stead & Simpson plc* [1990] J.B.L. 72.

[51] Panel statement on *Mooloya Investments Ltd.* v. *Customagic Manufacturing Co. Ltd.* [1979] J.B.L. 49.

[52] For an interesting example of the crucial importance of such announcements see the Panel statements on *Burton Group plc/Debenhams plc* [1985] J.B.L. 231.

commiting itself to doing so and specifying the improvement.[53] Following an increase in newspaper advertisements made in connection with take-overs and the nature of the material used, Rule 19 restricts such advertisements to nine specific types, seven of which require Panel clearance in advance.[54] Special attention is paid to organised telephone campaigns[55] and media interviews and debates.

Copies of all documents must be sent at the time of release to the press to the Panel and the advisers to all the other parties involved in the offer, even outside office hours. Statements made whilst an offer is being referred to the Monopolies and Mergers Commission or the European Commission must be capable of being substantiated if the offer is subsequently revived.

Rule 20 applies to the equality of the supply of the information subject to Rule 19. In particular all competing offerors are entitled to receive information given to one, favoured offeror, at least where there has been a public announcement of that offeror's existence. A less welcome offeror is required to specify the questions to which it requires answers.

Rule 21 provides that in the case of an actual or imminent offer, the offeree board must not, without approval of the members, issue shares or grant options or sell or otherwise dispose of material assets except under a pre-existing obligation.[56]

(7) *Documents from the offeror and the offeree board* (*Rules 23–27*)

The rules elaborate General Principle 5 that all documents, etc. falling within these headings must be treated with the same standard of care as if they were prospectuses.[57] Amongst the

[53] See [1984] J.B.L. 422.

[54] See Panel statements on *Imperial Group Ltd.* [1986] J.B.L. 315 and on advertisements [1986] J.B.L. 318. See also Panel statement on graphs and diagrams [1985] J.B.L. 476.

[55] Following the Panel statement on *B.P.C.C. plc/John Waddington plc* [1983] J.B.L. 491.

[56] Rule 21. See, *e.g.* Panel statements on *W. Henshall & Sons (Addlestone) Ltd./Bovbourne Ltd.* [1979] J.B.L. 46; *Burton Group plc/Debenhams plc* [1985] J.B.L. 231.

[57] Panel statement on *York Trust Ltd./Greenword and Batley Ltd.* [1978] J.B.L. 68.

minimum content of the information to be disclosed must be the social and employment consequences of the projected take-over, including the offeror's intention with regard to the continuance of the business.

Rule 25 requires that documents sent to shareholders of the offeree company recommending acceptance or rejection of offers must contain particulars of all service contracts over 12 months of any director or proposed director with the offeree company or any of its subsidiaries. Further, any amendment to such contract within six months of the date of the document must be stated; if there are no such amendments that should be stated.

(8) *Profit forecasts* (*Rule 28*)

This rule, together with its note occupies seven pages of the Code, which reflects the many problems encountered by the Panel in the area. Despite the hazard of forecasting, profit forecasts must be compiled with "care and objectivity" by the directors and checked on that basis by their financial advisors. It is now mandatory to include in a forecast: taxation, extraordinary items and minority interests where these are expected to be significant. The rule also defines a profit forecast for its own purpose.[58]

In one statement the Panel condemned the publication by an offeror of a profit forecast produced by the offeree company and sent to the offeror in confidence. This was based on the facts that the Panel did not feel it right to require the offeree to publish the forecast, that publication here was in breach of confidence and that what was made public was the profit forecast of another company on which the offeror was not in a position to obtain the reports acquired by the Code.[59]

(9) *Asset valuations* (*Rule 29*)

This rule requires valuations to be supported by a named independent valuer (as defined) and lays down criteria for the valuer. It applies wherever a valuation is given "in connection

[58] See Panel statement on *Guinness Peat/The Distillers Company* [1986] J.B.L. 316.

[59] Panel statement on *Yule Catto & Co. plc/Donald Macpherson Group plc* [1984] J.B.L. 425.

with an offer" although this will not normally include the usual estimates for accounting purposes. The basis of valuation must be stated; in general this is to be open market value and there are special rules for land with development value.

(10) *Timing and revision* (*Rules 30–34*)

Rule 30 relates to the timing of the offer document and the offeree circular, 28 days from an announcement in the first case and 14 days from the offer document in the second. Rule 31 is concerned with the timing of the offer, specification of further closing dates and the well established rule that an offer must remain open for 14 days after being declared unconditional as to acceptances. No offer may be declared so unconditional after midnight on the 60th day after the posting of the offer based on acceptance up to 1.00 p.m. on that day.[60] The effect of this is to limit any changes in an offer to the first 46 days since all revised offers must be kept open for 14 days. This includes the making of a "no increase" statement by the offeror.[61] Since no offer may be open for more than 60 days all such amendments are restricted to the first 46 days. This has caused many problems, in particular where there are competing offers still extant at the end of the 46 day period and an auction situation has in effect arisen.[62] The Panel may vary these time limits in exceptional cases.[63] Rule 34 gives the acceptor of an offer the right to withdraw his acceptance within 21 days of the first closing date of the offer unless it has then become unconditional.

(11) *Restrictions following offers* (*Rule 35*)

Rule 35 provides that where an offer has not become unconditional in all respects the offeror (and persons acting in concert) may not within 12 months from the offer's withdrawal or lapse make a further offer or purchase shares so as to either fall within the mandatory bid rules or, if it holds 48 per cent. but less than 50 per cent. of the offeree shares. There are

[60] See the Panel statement on *Burton Group plc/Debenhams plc* [1986] J.B.L. 231.

[61] Panel statement on *Siebe Gorman/Telecamit* [1984] J.B.L. 159.

[62] Panel statement on *Allianz Versicherungs A.G./Bat Industries plc/Eagle Star Holdings plc* [1984] J.B.L. 158.

[63] Panel statements on *Woolworth Holdings plc/Dixons plc and Emess Lighting plc/Rotaflex plc* [1986] J.B.L. 410.

exceptions to this rule, *e.g.* where the subsequent offer is an agreed offer, or the original offer was referred to the Monopolies and Mergers Commission or the European Commission.[64] The rule will be applied, however, even if there has been no formal offer but the target company has been subjected to a state of siege by a threatened offer.[65] If the offeror holds over 50 per cent. of the offeree shares it cannot purchase shares at above the offer price for six months. Nor may it conclude special deals with favourable conditions during that period.

(12) *Partial offers* (*Rule 36*)

The Panel's consent is required for a partial offer. There are complex provisions governing these offers, *e.g.* an offer for 30 per cent. or more requires 50 per cent. approval.

(13) *Redemption or purchase by a company of its own voting shares* (*Rule 37*)

Following the provisions of the Companies Act allowing companies to purchase their own shares the Code is concerned with the position whereby a shareholder will, as a result of such a purchase or redemption, come to hold shares which carry more than 30 per cent. or more of the voting rights of that company, or to have increased the percentage of his holding by more than two per cent. in the relevant 12 months period if he already holds 30 per cent. or more. Rule 37 states that such a shareholder will not be obliged to make a mandatory bid if he only votes in favour of a resolution authorising the board to exercise the powers of purchase or redemption. However, when the board actually exercises the power, the Panel will examine the relationship between the board and the shareholder concerned.

(14) *Dealings by connected exempt market makers* (*Rule 38*)

Multi-service financial organisations—acting in concert. With the repeal of the existing single capacity on the Stock Exchange, *i.e.* the separation of jobbers, brokers and corporate advisers, etc., it is now perfectly allowable for one financial organisation

[64] Panel statement on *GC & C Brands/Irish Distillers Group plc* [1989] J.B.L. 150.

[65] Panel statement on *Storehouse plc* [1989] J.B.L. 518.

to perform all those functions, *i.e.* it can act as a market-maker, broker, investment adviser and corporate finance adviser. This has clear implications for the City Code since the same organisation may be acting as adviser to the offeror (or offeree), making investment decisions for its discretionary clients, providing information as brokers to other clients and making a market in the offeree company's shares. Opportunities to influence an offer clearly abound—for example an adviser to an offeror may acquire offeree shares as a market maker, deal in those shares for its discretionary clients and influence others to deal.

The City Panel therefore amended the City Code in two ways. First, as to the circumstances in which a market maker can be regarded as acting in concert with an offeror who is being advised by the corporate finance arm of the same organisation, and the restrictions on dealings by or with such a market maker. Second, as to restrictions on dealings by the investment arm for its discretionary clients when the corporate finance arm is so involved in a bid. These amendments were published by the Panel in its statement on Multi-service Financial Organisations and the Take-over Code on October 10, 1986.

Market-making and other dealings as a principal. The basic rule is that where one arm of a multi-service financial organisation is advising an offeror, any dealings by that organisation as principal (*i.e.* not as agent for its clients) in the offeree's securities will be presumed to be acting in concert with the offeror. This will affect the price to be paid, the mandatory bid rule and the possible obligation to make a cash offer, etc.

However, there is an exception to this presumption in the case of market-making only (and not for other dealings as principal) if the market maker arm of the organisation achieves the status of an *exempt market maker*, *i.e.* one which is recognised as such by the Panel. Exemption will be by application to the Panel who must be satisfied that an effective "Chinese Wall" system operates within the whole organisation, in particular separating the market making division from the corporate finance division.

Exempt market makers will, however, be subject to Rule 38 of the Code. Rule 38.1 provides that if they are connected with an offeror or offeree company they must not carry out any dealings with the purpose of assisting the offeror or offeree, as appropriate. An exempt market maker will be so connected if it is controlled by, controls or is under the same control as the offeror, offeree, or any bank, broker, financial or other professional adviser to the offeree or offeror company. The sanction for a breach of this rule will be loss or exempt status—which may amount to exclusion from the market in practical terms.[66]

Rules 38.2 to 4 provide three restrictions on dealings with an exempt market-maker where it is connected with the offeror or offeree.[67] These are: (i) a ban on dealings by the connected offeror (or concert parties) with the market-maker during the offer period; (ii) a ban on assents of shares owned by the market-maker to the offeror until the offer has become or been declared unconditional as to acceptances; and (iii) the exempt market-maker must not vote with shares in the connected offeror or offeree in the context of a take-over or possible take-over. Liability under (i) is on the offeror, under (ii) and (iii) on the market-maker.

Finally rule 38.5 requires disclosure by the exempt market-maker of dealings in relevant shares where there is a connected offeree or offeror company by noon on the next business day. This must include details as to amount, price, the nature of the connection and, if appropriate, the relevant overseas location.

Discretionary fund management. Under the previous provisions of the code the management of investment accounts on a discretionary basis by one arm of a financial conglomerate were governed by rule 7.2 which applied when the corporate finance arm's involvement became public. In such cases fund managers were required to consult with the Panel if dealings could affect the consideration or mandatory bid rules had they been effected by the offeror itself.

Following the amendments there will still be no presumption of acting in concert between fund managers and connected offerors before the involvement of the corporate finance arm has become public (although that situation may of course exist in fact). However, such fund managers may now apply for

[66] See Panel statement on *Raine Industries plc/Tarmac plc/Ruberoid plc* [1989] J.B.L. 67.

[67] See Panel statement on *Peachey Property Corporation plc/Estates Property Investment Co. plc* [1988] J.B.L. 325.

exemption from certain Code consequences which would otherwise follow once the connection with the offeror/offeree is public knowlege. Exemption is to be achieved by application to the Panel, the criteria being the existence of a "Chinese Wall" as with exempt market-makers. Rule 7.2 was substantially restructured to reflect the new regime. The presumption is that a fund manager will be acting in concert with a connected offeror or offeree unless he is an exempt fund manager, thus bringing into play the consideration, mandatory bid and partial offer rules (the notes to which are also amended accordingly). No such presumption will apply to an exempt fund manager.

Where the exempt fund manager is associated with a party to a take-over it will not have to disclose its dealings in the relevant securities except privately to the Panel. One exception to this will arise where the associate status arises because the fund manager holds five per cent. or more of the issued equity capital of an offeror or offeree company (*i.e.* under paragraph (6) of the definition of an associate in the Code).

Rules Governing Substantial Acquisitions of Shares

The City Code on Take-overs only operates in a take-over situation and this effectively commences either on an offer being made or a 30 per cent. holding of shares being amassed by one person or consortium.[68] In 1980, however, there were a series of "dawn raids" on the Stock Exchange where one person would acquire, in a matter of minutes, less than 30 per cent. of the shares of a public company but nevertheless a significant amount. Such practices were considered undesirable for two reasons. First, the identity of the acquirer would often be disguised, *e.g.* by several linked companies each acquiring five per cent. of the shares on behalf of an unnamed person, and, second, it was obvious that only a few shareholders benefited from being able to dispose of their shares on a "dawn raid" at above market value. This opportunity was not available to the other shareholders.

The first problem was countered by pressure on the Government which led to the rules on share disclosures by shareholders or groups owning originally five per cent., now

[68] Rule 9, *ante*.

three per cent., or more of the shares of a public company introduced by the 1981 Act.[69] The second problem, that of equal opportunity, was to be the subject of another self-regulatory code, the Rules Governing the Substantial Acquisition of Shares.[70] The City Panel[71] is responsible for administering this Code.

The Rules apply to acquisitions of quoted shares in United Kingdom companies[72] within seven days amounting to 10 per cent. or more of the voting rights in any one company and which take the purchaser's holding to 15 per cent. or more of that company's voting rights but less than 30 per cent., at which stage the City Code will come into operation.[73] Purchase by two or more connected or "concert" parties are regarded as purchases buy a single purchaser, including those held on a discretionary basis by a non-exempt fund manager (for the purposes of the City Code).

Any acquisition caught by the Rules must now either follow the strict rules for partial bids set out in the City Code on Take-overs[74] or be acquired by means of a tender offer.[75] Under this procedure the buyer makes a firm offer to buy a specified number of shares for cash only either at a fixed price or up to a maximum price. Shareholders then offer their shares by tender, in the latter case at any price up to the maximum specified. Shareholders are bound by their tenders and the purchaser and his asociates must not deal in the shares during the tender period of at least seven days. Tenders are to be advertised in two national newspapers and sent to the company and the Stock Exchange. Top up arrangements are no longer allowed, *e.g.* a share offer with a promise to make good to the vendor any difference between the tender price and any subsequent successful offer.

The effect of these rules is to check advances in shareholdings between 10 per cent. and 30 per cent.

[69] *Ante*, p. 246.
[70] Introduced on December 11, 1980, and revised on April 7, 1982. The Rules were again revised in April 1985 and January 1988 and are contained in the back of the City Code.
[71] *Ante*, p. 850.
[72] As defined in the City Code.
[73] Rule 9, *ante*.
[74] Rule 36.
[75] See Panel statement on *Norton Opax plc* [1989] J.B.L. 148.

Power to Acquire Shares of Shareholders Not Accepting Take-over Offer Accepted by Majority

Sections 428 to 430F of the Companies Act 1985 were substituted by section 172 and Schedule 12 to the Financial Services Act 1986. That Act repealed the original sections 428 to 430 which had consolidated the 1948 Act provisions. All these sections have had the effect of tidying up after a successful take-over offer, so that if an offeror has achieved a 90 per cent. acceptance he may compulsorily acquire the remaining shares, or, alternatively, the minority may require such an offeror to buy them out. The new sections do not alter that basic framework but the wording of the original provisions was inadequate and difficult to apply to modern take-overs. The Jenkins Committee made several recommendations in 1962,[76] some of which were eventually adopted by the 1986 provisions.

Scope of sections 428 to 430F

Before the powers conferred by these sections can be used there must be a take-over offer made by an offeror to acquire all the shares (or for all of a class of shares) of a company on the same terms,[77] except for those shares already owned by the offeror[78] at the date of the offer: section 428(1). The offer must be for all the shares (or class of shares) allotted on the date of the offer but it may also include shares allotted subsequently to the offer before a date specified by or determined in accordance with the offer: section 428(2).

Any revised offer is not a new offer for the purpose of the timetable laid down in the sections: section 428(6).

The sections apply not only to an offeror but also to his associates, *i.e.* his nominees, members of the same group of companies or a company which is de facto controlled by the offeror or part of a consortium: section 430E(4)–(8). Thus in

[76] 1962 Cmnd. 1949, para. 294.

[77] A variation is allowed if it is necessary to comply with any foreign laws as to what consideration must be provided under the offer to shareholders resident abroad (*e.g.* in the USA): s.428(3), (4).

[78] These include shares he has contracted to buy but not those which he has contracted to buy in consideration of making the offer: s.428(5).

deciding whether an offer has been made for *all* the shares (or class of shares) the following are to be discounted:

(i) shares already owned by the offeror (s.428(1));
(ii) shares which the offeror has contracted to buy at the date of the offer except for acquisitions without consideration and, in England, by deed or only by virtue of having promised to make the offer (s.428(5)); and
(iii) shares already owned or contracted to an associate of the offeror at the date of the offer (s.430E(1)).

The remaining shares (or class) form the target against which the 90 per cent. thresholds are to be judged.

Joint offers

Section 430D allows joint offerors to take advantage (or be subject to) the sections, provided they acquire the shares jointly and accept joint or several liability for other purposes. In general their rights under the section are joint rights whereas their obligations are joint and several (*i.e.* each is liable for whole). Offeror is so construed unless the particular provision expressly states to the contrary. This section reverses the Privy Council decision in *Blue Metal Industries Ltd.* v. *Dilley*.[79]

Convertible securities

Problems arose with the original sections over convertible securities, *e.g.* debentures which can be converted into shares on a take-over offer being made. In *Re Simo Securities Trust Ltd.*[80] some such debentures were converted into shares in the name of the offeror, others were converted into shares and then transferred to the offeror, and others were not converted at all. The Judge decided that those debentures which were converted could be counted towards the 90 per cent. acceptance—those not converted were ignored. Now section 430F provides that all securities which are convertible into shares or entitle the holder to subscribe for shares are shares for the purposes of the

[79] [1970] A.C. 827 (P.C.).
[80] [1971] 1 W.L.R. 1455.

sections but they are to be treated as a separate class of shares separate from other shares. The effect of this is that such securities have a 90 per cent. threshold of their own since each class of shares is treated separately by the new sections.[81]

Compulsory purchases by the offeror

If the offeror achieves a 90 per cent. (in value) acceptance figure[82] he can serve a notice on those who have not accepted the offer that he desires to acquire their shares. The 90 per cent. threshold applies to each class of shares separately so that each class is the subject of a separate offer for this purpose: section 429(1), (2).

The 90 per cent. threshold does not include shares to which the offer does not relate (*i.e.* shares already held or contracted to an offeror or his associates at the date of the offer). However, the offeror can count shares acquired by the offeror or his associates during the course of the offer otherwise than by acceptance of the offer (*e.g.* by market purchase) provided either that they have been so acquired for less than the offer price or the offer price is revised upwards to the price paid[83]: sections 429(8), 430E(2).

To take advantage of the compulsory purchase power the 90 per cent. threshold must be acquired within four months of the date of the offer and the notice served in the prescribed manner within two months of achieving the threshold: section 429.

Provided that the notice has been validly served, the offeror "shall be entitled and bound to acquire" the non-acceptor's shares "on the terms of the offer": section 430(2). If the offer provided for alternative consideration, *e.g.* cash or shares in the offeror company, the offeror must give the non-acceptors the same choice with six weeks in which to choose. Any notice must specify this choice, the time limit and which will be paid if no choice is initiated: section 430(3). If the non-cash consideration is no longer available[84] the cash equivalent must be paid[85]: section 430(4).

[81] See the next paragraph.
[82] *i.e.* acquired or contracted to acquire by offeror (plus associates).
[83] This adopts the principle of rule 4 of the City Code.
[84] From any of joint offerors.
[85] This confirms the decision in *Re Carlton Holdings Ltd.* [1971] 1 W.L.R. 918.

The mechanics of the acquisitions are that six weeks after the notice has been issued,[86] the offeror sends a copy to the offeree company and pays it the consideration due (or allots the shares, as appropriate) together with an instrument of transfer executed by a person nominated by the offeror. The offeree company must then register the offeror as owner of the shares. The offeree company must keep the consideration so received in a separate bank account on trust for the former shareholders. If they cannot be traced within 12 years after reasonable enquiries have been made at reasonable intervals, the money, etc. is to be paid into court: section 430(5)–(15).

If the offeror fails to achieve the necessary number of acceptances the court, on his application, may nevertheless allow him to acquire the remaining shares if the reason is that some shareholders have proved to be untraceable. The court can only do this, however, if the total of acceptances plus the untraceable shareholders amount to the 90 per cent. figure and the consideration is fair and reasonable. In making its decision the court must decide that it is just and equitable to allow such an acquisition having regard to the number of known shareholders who have rejected the offer: section 430C(5).

Minority right to apply to the court to prevent acquisition

The offeror's right to acquire the non-acceptors' shares under section 429 is subject to their right to apply to the court under section 430C. Within six weeks of receiving a notice of intent to acquire, any non-acceptor can apply to the court for an order (a) preventing the compulsory acquisition or (b) specifying different acquisition terms: section 430C(1). The effect of such an application is to freeze the compulsory acquisition process until the application has been disposed of: section 430C(2). No order for costs or expenses may be made against an applicant unless the application was improper or vexatious, or there has been unreasonable delay or conduct on his part: section 430C(4).

In *Re Britoil plc*,[87] the Court of Appeal ruled that an application will not be vexatious (and so will not incur a penalty

[86] Unless there is an application to the court by the dissentients—see *post*.
[87] [1990] BCC 70 (C.A.).

in costs) if there is evidence justifying the court's looking at the offer to make sure it was fair. The fact that, of necessity, only a small minority of shareholders have not accepted the offer will not preclude the operation of section 430C(4).

The minority had a similar right to petition under the former sections although only to prevent an acquisition. The cases decided on the former sections are therefore of relevance.

Under the former sections the court has decided that it would only make such an order if it was satisfied that the scheme was unfair to the general body of shareholders in the transferor company. There was normally a heavy burden of proof on the dissentients[88]—since the scheme has been approved by nine-tenths of the shareholders, prima facie it must be taken to be a fair one.[89] The test was one of fairness to the body of shareholders as a whole and not to individual shareholders, and it was not enough merely to prove that the scheme was open to criticism or capable of improvement.[90] It was not enough that the materials put before the shareholders were inadequate to enable them to form a just conclusion as to the acceptance or refusal of the offer.[91] Where there was a Stock Exchange quotation for the shares, prima facie that could be taken as the value of the shares.[92] The element of control of the transferor company, which would accrue to the transferee company from the acquisition of all the shares in the transferor company, was not taken into account in determining the value of the shares of a minority shareholder.[93] It was also held that dissentient shareholders, who were not satisfied with the price offered, could not obtain an order for discovery so as to enable them to carry out an investigation into the value of the shares, unless there were special circumstances[94] but a more recent decision has established that discovery will apply unless the court is satisfied that it is unnecessary.[95]

[88] *Re Sussex Brick Co. Ltd.* [1961] Ch. 289n: *Nidditch* v. *The Calico Printers' Association Ltd.*, 1961 S.L.T. 282.

[89] The onus is the other way round under s.425, *ante*: *per* Templeman J. in *Re Hellenic & General Trust Ltd.* [1976] 1 W.L.R. 123, at pp. 130, 131.

[90] *Re Grierson, Oldham & Adams Ltd.* [1968] Ch. 17.

[91] *Re Evertite Locknuts Ltd.* [1945] Ch. 220.

[92] See *Re Press Caps Ltd.* [1949] Ch. 434 (C.A.).

[93] See note 89, above.

[94] *Re Press Caps Ltd.* [1948] 2 All E.R. 638.

[95] *Re Lifecare International plc* [1990] BCLC 222.

However, if the dissentient shareholders showed that in substance the transferee company was the same as the majority holding in the transferor company the onus was on the majority to satisfy the court that the scheme was one which the minority ought reasonably to be compelled to fall in with.

A and B were the two shareholders, each holding 50 shares, in the transferee company which offered to purchase the shares in the transferor company in which there were three shareholders, A and B, who each held 4,500 shares and who accepted the offer, and C, who held 1,000 shares and who dissented. *Held*, that C, by showing that the transferee company was, for practical purposes, equivalent to the holders of nine-tenths of the shares in the transferor company who accepted the offer, had, prima facie, shown that the case was one in which the circumstances were special and that the court ought to "order otherwise" within the meaning of section [430C], and the majority had not shown that there was some good reason in the interests of the company (*e.g.* that the minority shareholder was acting in a manner highly damaging to the interests of the company) for allowing the section to be invoked for the purpose of enabling the majority to expropriate the minority: *Re Bugle Press Ltd.* [1961] Ch. 270 (C.A.).

The directors of an offeree company (*i.e.* a transferor company) have a duty towards their shareholders to be honest and not to mislead them. A shareholder in such a company may be prejudiced if his co-shareholders are misled into accepting the offer. A minority can therefore complain if it is being wrongfully subjected to the power of compulsory purchase as a result of a breach of duty by such directors.[96]

Non-acceptor's right to be bought out by the offeror

If the offeror has acquired 90 per cent. in value of all the shares in a company (or all the shares of a class) any non-acceptor can require the offeror to acquire his shares: section 430A(1), (2). Note that this is not 90 per cent. of the shares subject to the offer but of all the shares, so that shares held by the offeror etc. at the date of the offer or contracted to him are included both in the total and the 90 per cent. threshold.[97] This

[96] *Gething* v. *Kilner* [1972] 1 W.L.R. 337, particularly at pp. 341, 342.
[97] Associates are counted in for this purpose: section 430E(3).

is different from the threshold which enables the offeror to acquire the shares under section 429.

If the offer is still open for acceptances the shareholder can apply to be bought out by a written communication to the offeror.[98] Otherwise within one month of gaining his 90 per cent. threshold (and not necessarily that for a compulsory purchase) the offeror must inform the non-acceptors of their rights to be bought out—unless he has already served a compulsory purchase notice: section 430A(3), (5). The offeror must give non-acceptors at least three months from the end of the offer period in which to apply to be bought out: section 430A(4).

If a non-acceptor sends such a written communication the offeror is then "entitled and bound" to acquire the shares on the terms of the offer or such other terms as may be agreed: section 430B(1), (2). The provisions relating to alternative consideration under the offer are the same as for a compulsory purchase: section 430B(3), (4).[99]

In the case of any dispute any non-acceptor who has applied to be bought out can apply to the court to set the terms for the acquisition: section 430C(3). Again such an applicant is protected as to costs: section 430C(4).

[98] To one of two or more joint offerors will suffice.

[99] *Ante*, p. 871.

INDEX